THE OXFORD HANDBOOK OF

RELIGIOUS DIVERSITY

OXFORD
UNIVERSITY PRESS

Oxford University Press, Inc., publishes works that further
Oxford University's objective of excellence
in research, scholarship, and education.

Oxford   New York
Auckland   Cape Town   Dar es Salaam   Hong Kong   Karachi
Kuala Lumpur   Madrid   Melbourne   Mexico City   Nairobi
New Delhi   Shanghai   Taipei   Toronto

With offices in
Argentina   Austria   Brazil   Chile   Czech Republic   France   Greece
Guatemala   Hungary   Italy   Japan   Poland   Portugal   Singapore
South Korea   Switzerland   Thailand   Turkey   Ukraine   Vietnam

Published by Oxford University Press, Inc.
198 Madison Avenue, New York, New York 10016

www.oup.com

Oxford is a registered trademark of Oxford University Press

Library of Congress Cataloging-in-Publication Data
The Oxford handbook of religious diversity / edited by Chad Meister.
p.   cm.
Includes index.
ISBN 978-0-19-534013-6
1. Religious pluralism. 2. Religion. 3. Religions. I. Meister, Chad V., 1965–
BL85.O94   2010
201'.5—dc22   2009050128

1 3 5 7 9 8 6 4 2

Printed in the United States of America
on acid-free paper

ACKNOWLEDGMENTS

I wish to express my appreciation to a number of individuals who have been instrumental in the development of this book. First and foremost, the contributors have done a superb job of presenting state-of-the-art, original, and authoritative contributions, and they have done so in clear and accessible language—something not easy to achieve. These colleagues rank at the top of their respective areas of research, and their contributions are outstanding. Second, a number of colleagues (and two blind reviewers) provided insights into the general structure, appropriate themes, and selection of contributors for this book; to them I am most grateful. Third, I am indebted to David Cramer and Kristin Swartz for their editorial assistance with a number of the chapters. Fourth, my wife, Tammi, and sons, Justin and Joshua, have been very gracious in granting me additional time to finalize this project; I owe them an extended vacation. Finally, I wish to thank Theo Calderara for his wholehearted support of this project and the entire editorial staff at Oxford University Press for their collaboration and encouragement.

CONTENTS

PART III DIFFERING PERSPECTIVES ON RELIGIOUS DIVERSITY

A. Multifaith Perspectives

B. Gender and World Perspectives

Contributors

PAMELA SUE ANDERSON is Reader in Philosophy of Religion at the University of Oxford and Fellow of Regent's Park College.

DAVID BASINGER is Professor of Philosophy and Ethics and Chair of the Division of Religion and Humanities at Roberts Wesleyan College.

BRUCE ELLIS BENSON is Professor and Chair of Philosophy at Wheaton College.

PETER BEYER is Professor in the Department of Classics and Religious Studies at the University of Ottawa.

DAVID BURTON is Senior Lecturer in Religious Studies at Canterbury Christ Church University.

PETER BYRNE is Professor of Ethics and the Philosophy of Religion at King's College, London.

CHUNG-YING CHENG is Professor of Philosophy at the University of Hawaii at Manoa.

PETER B. CLARKE is Professor Emeritus of the History and Sociology of Religion at King's College, London, and professorial member of the Faculty of Theology at the University of Oxford.

GAVIN D'COSTA is Professor in Christian Theology at the University of Bristol.

MICHELE DILLON is Professor of Sociology at the University of New Hampshire.

MAJID FAKHRY is Adjunct Professor at Georgetown University and Professor Emeritus of Philosophy at the American University of Beirut.

ROGER S. GOTTLIEB is Professor of Philosophy at Worcester Polytechnic Institute.

PAUL J. GRIFFITHS is Warren Professor of Catholic Theology at Duke Divinity School.

SALLIE B. KING is Professor of Religion at James Madison University.

IAN S. MARKHAM is Dean and President of Virginia Theological Seminary.

MARTIN E. MARTY is Fairfax M. Cone Distinguished Service Professor Emeritus at the University of Chicago Divinity School.

CHAD MEISTER is Professor of Philosophy at Bethel College.

DALIA MOGAHED is Senior Analyst and Executive Director at the Gallup Center for Muslim Studies.

PAUL K. MOSER is Professor and Chairperson of Philosophy at Loyola University of Chicago.

FREDERICK W. NORRIS is Professor Emeritus of World Christianity at Emmanuel School of Religion.

MICHAEL L. PETERSON is Professor and Chair of Philosophy at Asbury College.

TOM PYSZCZYNSKI is Professor of Psychology and Director of the Department of Psychology Honors Program at the University of Colorado.

JOSEPH RUNZO is Professor of Philosophy and Religious Studies at Chapman University.

MICHAEL RUSE is Lucyle T. Werkmeister Professor and Director of the History and Philosophy of Science Program at Florida State University.

ARVIND SHARMA is Birks Professor of Comparative Religion at McGill University.

DAVID SHATZ is Professor of Philosophy at Yeshiva University.

CHRISTIAN SMITH is William R. Kenan Professor of Sociology at the Center for the Study of Religion and Society at the University of Notre Dame.

JOHN G. STACKHOUSE, JR. is Sangwoo Youtong Chee Professor of Theology and Culture at Regent College.

JESSICA STERN is Lecturer on Counterterrorism at Harvard University and a member of the Task Force on National Security and Law at Stanford University's Hoover Institution.

LEONARD J. SWIDLER is Professor of Catholic Thought and Interreligious Dialogue at Temple University.

CHARLES TALIAFERRO is Professor of Philosophy at St. Olaf College.

BRANDON VAIDYANATHAN is a doctoral candidate at the Center for the Study of Religion and Society at the University of Notre Dame.

KEITH WARD is Professorial Research Fellow at Heythrop College, University of London, Regius Professor of Divinity Emeritus at the University of Oxford, and a Fellow of the British Academy.

KWASI WIREDU is Distinguished University Professor of Philosophy at the University of South Florida.

GEORGE YANCEY is Associate Professor of Sociology at the University of North Texas.

KEITH E. YANDELL is Julius R. Weinberg Professor of Philosophy and South Asian Studies at the University of Wisconsin.

THE OXFORD HANDBOOK OF

RELIGIOUS DIVERSITY

political matters, as well as differences of religious practice. *Religious pluralism*, on the other hand, is often used to denote the acceptance and even encouragement of diversity or (and perhaps because of) the view that salvation/liberation is to be found in all of the great world religions (with the proper qualifications, of course, such as sincerity), that belonging to a particular religion is not essential for the attainment of salvation/liberation, although belonging to one or another might be.[3] These terms are used in other ways as well, but this is how they are generally appropriated in this book.

Much of the recent work on religious diversity has been done in isolation from that in other fields. Given the pervasive nature of religious diversity, those in the various fields could benefit by learning from others outside their particular disciplines and areas of expertise in order to build respect, empathy, and perhaps even trust.[4] *The Oxford Handbook of Religious Diversity* attempts to bring together leading voices from different fields and disciplines and from a variety of perspectives and traditions, with the aims of raising awareness of some of the central challenges of religious diversity, creating mutual recognition of religious differences, and fostering authentic, ecumenical dialogue.

The *Handbook* includes essays addressing both conceptual and practical issues raised by the presence of religious diversity. It is divided into three parts: (I) Contours of Religious Diversity, (II) Key Issues Relevant to Religious Diversity, and (III) Differing Perspectives on Religious Diversity.

Chapters in Part I trace the general features of religious diversity discussions from four different fields: history, religious studies, philosophy, and sociology. Chapter 1 provides a historical overview of religious diversity and offers insightful reflections from history to set the stage for the following interdisciplinary discussion. Chapter 2 describes the religious studies approach as one that begins outside the particular traditions and seeks to understand the traditions on their own terms. Chapter 3 covers four main areas of the philosophical study of religious diversity: the epistemology of religious belief, the production of theories of religion, reflections on the concept of God and Uultimate Rreality, and the relationship between religion and the human good. Chapter 4 outlines a sociological approach to religious diversity, focusing on diversity in the United States and Europe.

Part II—which makes up the bulk of the book—explores key issues relevant to religious diversity and is divided into two sections. The nine chapters of the first section (A) focus on theological and philosophical issues. It seems that philosophical reflection on religious diversity is on the rise. This is not surprising, for as technology has advanced exponentially in recent decades, so have familiarity and contact with religious others. This, coupled with the escalation in the number of religions coexisting in such pluralistic democracies as the United States and the United Kingdom, has ushered in an unprecedented awareness of religious diversity and an attending desire for deeper reflection on what it means for one's own religious (or irreligious) beliefs. Thus, for religious adherents, one of the greatest challenges today might well be how to understand and live out one's own faith in relation to the diversity of other faiths.

All of the major world religions make claims—for example, claims about the nature of ultimate reality, about the self, about the need for salvation, restoration, or liberation and how to achieve it. Some of these claims contradict one another, so a central theme that runs through many of the chapters in this section has to do with what to make of the various claims in religion (indeed, the issue of truth in religion comes up time and again in every part of this book). Religious exclusivism, pluralism, and relativism are three approaches to understanding such issues, and Chapters 5, 6, and 7 discuss them. Furthermore, how we engage in dialogue with religious others with whom we disagree, how we treat the religious "alien," and how we might promote a universal ethic among the religions are also important issues that arise in a global milieu of religious diversity, and they are discussed in Chapters 8, 9, and 10. Chapters 11, 12, and 13 address three major theological topics relevant to diversity: general challenges for theology amid diversity, theodicy and the problem of evil, and the role of revelation in religion.

Section B of Part II presents sociological and public-policy issues. As the world continues to become more unified and globalized, are its different dimensions, including its religious dimensions, becoming more alike? Or is globalization accentuating the differences? Furthermore, is the world becoming more or less religious? Is religion evolving? And how do race and ethnicity affect religious belief, and vice versa? Chapters 14 through 17 tackle these issues of globalization, changing demographics, new religious movements, and race and religion. Chapters 18 and 19 focus on secularization, multiculturalism, postmodernism, and multiple modernities—major themes in the social sciences with respect to religious diversity. Chapters 20, 21, and 22 address the issues of religious violence, public education, and the role of religion with respect to environmental concerns—all important public-policy issues in these early decades of the twenty-first century.

Part III of this book provides differing perspectives on religious diversity and is also divided into two sections. Section A addresses multifaith perspectives and includes seven chapters, 23 through 29, each presented from a different religious viewpoint: Hinduism, Buddhism, African religions, Chinese religions, Judaism, Christianity, and Islam. These chapters are not intended to provide "*the* word" from the various traditions on religious diversity; indeed, there is no such word. Rather, each presents one prominent voice from a recognized authority.

Section B examines gender and world perspectives. Chapter 30 focuses on a feminist perspective of religious diversity and examines gender bias in religions and relevant epistemic issues. Chapter 31 details a Continental perspective on religious diversity and looks at how several quite diverse Continental thinkers—including Emmanuel Levinas, Jean-Luc Marion, Jacques Derrida, and Slavoj Žižek—have uniquely appropriated certain religious themes. Chapter 32 provides a naturalistic perspective on religious diversity and explores some of the ways such diversity has evolved from more primitive forms, noting particular insights from David Hume and Charles Darwin.

Each of the thirty-two chapters in this book is written by a leading scholar in his or her respective field. Each makes an original contribution by surveying essential issues and questions regarding the theme of the chapter, offering a critical analysis of the issues, and guiding the course of future discussions. It is my hope that these pioneering and perspicacious essays will provide readers with a unique and useful reference work on religious diversity that will be beneficial for decades to come.

NOTES

1. For fuller articulation of the recent welcoming of religious diversity in the West (and particularly in the United States), see William R. Hutchison, *Religious Pluralism in America: The Contentious History of a Founding Ideal* (New Haven, Conn.: Yale University Press, 2003).

2. In *The Origin and Goal of History*, Michael Bullock, trans. (London: Routledge and Kegan Paul, 1953), Karl Jaspers argues that during this period, new "axes" were created that influenced philosophical and religious thought for the next two millennia.

3. John Hick and Paul Knitter are lucid and ardent defenders of religious pluralism. See, for example, John Hick, *An Interpretation of Religion: Human Responses to the Transcendent*, 2nd ed. (New Haven, Conn.: Yale University Press, 2004); and Paul Knitter, *One Earth Many Religions: Multifaith Dialogue and Global Responsibility* (Maryknoll, N.Y.: Orbis, 1995).

4. For more on interreligious harmony and the value of understanding religious others, see Rebecca Kratz Mays, ed., *Interfaith Dialogue at the Grass Roots* (Philadelphia: Ecumenical Press, 2008); see also Tenzin Gyatso, the Dalai Lama, *Ethics for the New Millennium* (New York: Riverhead, 1999), 219–231.

PART I

CONTOURS OF
RELIGIOUS DIVERSITY

CHAPTER 1

....

HISTORICAL REFLECTIONS
ON RELIGIOUS DIVERSITY

....

MARTIN E. MARTY

HISTORIANS and other scholars, who have enough difficulty defining the *religious* or *religion* about which they write, also have to wrestle over the meanings of *religious diversity* when that combination of two words is their subject. *Diversity* as such represents no more of a problem to historians than it does to dictionary writers: "the condition or quality of being diverse, different, or varied." That English word has been in print since at least 1340 CE.

Complication arises because *religious diversity* has acquired a kin, *religious pluralism*. The latter has been in use for less than a century and often gets used as a virtual synonym for *diversity*. Encyclopedia, dictionary, and handbook writers, including some in this book, use the words interchangeably. However, the concept of pluralism introduces many themes that are not, or do not have to be, treated when mere diversity is the subject. The historian of diversity can complete the writing of the agenda for his or her longer work merely by noticing that there are very many religions and religious groupings "out there" and letting it go at that. The historian of pluralism will find that his or her subject matter has come to refer to what people *do* with diversity. This doing could deal with civil, political, or theological concepts. These are themselves so "diverse, different, or varied" that treating them would carry us far afield. We will be clear and efficient by separating diversity and pluralism and turning the latter over to other historians and scholars.

HISTORIANS NEED GROUPS TO WRITE ABOUT

The term *religious diversity* does not usually refer to the fact that an isolated individual holds religious ideas and beliefs that are, at least in part, independent of what the community to which he or she belongs would hold. Thus, a modern Roman Catholic might devote more energy to New Age religion than to Catholic creeds, and a Jew might be swayed by Buddhism and might choose to engage in some of Buddhism's practices. But as long as such a Catholic individual remains on the rolls of Catholicism and can be counted as a member of the church or unless the Jew pointedly dissents, neither has added to the complex of religious diversity.

The honest priest, rabbi, or minister who surveys and truly knows the adherents in even the most strict and separatist bodies recognizes that under the shelter of the chapel and the confining definitions of dogma and creed, wildly diverse opinions thrive and different practices go on. As sociologist Peter Berger put it, when the officials of a faith are too precise and narrow about beliefs, ordinary members will "smuggle in their gods in plain brown wrappers." Right under the noses of inquisitors, dogmatists, enforcers, and crusaders, whatever the symbols on the banners might imply, each adherent does some tailor-made fashioning and comes up with something that does not match the beliefs of the person with whom he or she shares a pew, a Sabbath, or a bed.

The human brain, with its billions of neurons and possibilities for synapses, has trillions of impressions and choices available, and it would be mathematically impossible and the product of a dulled imagination to picture that no differences among members of mosque, church, or synagogue exist. The varied hearings and interpretations of even the most precisely defined and stipulated doctrines show up everywhere, and alert social scientists and reporters will grasp them, even where those clergy who have not listened to adherents fail to hear them or choose to cover them up. Such internal diversity, often the result of accidental and idiosyncratic free enterprise in response to a variety of pitches and proclamations, is interesting, colorful, even beguiling, but it makes little contribution to what is usually meant by religious diversity. For confronting differences in these categories, one deals with groups, whether they are small or large. And when they talk and act, they leave stories that attract historians, who now have something about which to write.

HISTORIANS NEED TIMES AND PLACES
FOR THEIR STORIES

To write credibly and for useful purpose, historians have to locate their stories in times and places, something that sounds banal but is important for describing what to expect in a book like this. To open an encyclopedia that lists hundreds of religious groups throughout history in neat alphabetical order is not to encounter written history. Thus, to point to a religious practice implied in archaeological research at digs that reveal life in 30,000 BCE and in Aum Shinrikyo in today's Japan is not of interest to the historian, although an encyclopedist of comparative religion might draw on both to illustrate a theme. Similarly, religious diversity obviously exists in a paragraph that mentions a religious phenomenon in Tibetan Buddhism along with one issuing from the Church of Scientology in New York City, but such listings and mentions are not the kind out of which historians make stories.

Religious diversity is of interest when inhabitants of a distinct place, as large as a continent or as small as a precinct, can be identified with it. Think of Buddhism, Hinduism, Jainism, and Daoism in sixteenth-century Asia, and you have a subject for historians, since there are common observations and experiences among them to be compared. The Jesuit explorers and missionaries sent to Japan or Portuguese Goa in that century came back with stories of bewildering religious diversity and thus provided material for research-hungry historians. Then think of Bowne Street in today's Flushing, New York, where immigrants from many places share space, meet one another on the way to their different worship places, fight over parking spaces, express prejudices about strangers—those "other people"—or engage in interreligious dialogue. Religious diversity comes very close to home and might even be represented at home, under roof, where there has been religiously exogamous marriage or where exiles and refugees are fostered by host families that do not share their faith and community.

The Dream of Homogeneity and the Nightmare for the Dreamers

Most, though of course not all, religious communities tend to be or become exclusive in their claims, advertisements, and policies. While some are religiously syncretistic, making efforts to embrace and encourage varieties of religions in a particular time and place, and allowing for differences-within-unity or seeking unity-among-differences, most historians have found that the majority experience their own faith and practice as superior to all others, while all others must be kept at a distance. When they are at a distance, they do not represent the challenge of religious diversity to what majorities consider to be host cultures, inhospitable though they would usually be. Scholars note that monotheistic religions especially attract believers who are exclusive. They might engage in exiling or even killing those who offend them, although in other cases, they might find it advisable to pretend away their differences.

For an illustration, historians have found that the Dutch colonists in New Amsterdam wanted only the Dutch Reformed church to be established, privileged, and supported, recognizing that to do business or to minimize lethal potentials, they had to allow for Anglicans and Catholics among them. They made no bones about their choice of policy; they would wink or blink, turning only a covered eye in their direction. There, religious diversity was being pretended away, providing grist for historians even if it represented a kind of hypocrisy in the eyes of minorities who were pressing for acknowledged diversity and thus the beginnings of religious liberty.

Historians have to make distinctions between diversity-at-a-distance and diversity-close-up, distinctions made vivid in times of modern communication. American visitors to Europe are often impressed to see how long cultural practices can exist in isolation. Two peoples have lived on two sides of a narrow river for centuries but still are ignorant of each other's language and so remote from each other psychically that they do not well know each other's culture. So they hardly experience the religious diversity that is at once visible to the historian who takes up, for example, "religions in central Europe." A provincial area with a Muslim majority or monopoly in one part of India experiences the Hindu at a distance as enemy, stranger, or merely "other," and the story ends there. A province in which a variety of Hindu "sects" share space with Muslim varieties, where temple and mosque all but adjoin each other, on the other hand, is an example of experienced religious diversity. When modern communications, especially visual versions such as movies and television, exist, images of "the other" come into homes of all sorts, and religious diversity becomes the frame for historians' stories.

Since religious diversity can be nettling, even where it does not rouse hostilities that end in warfare, most societies strive for homogeneity. Leaders are concerned lest the different religions might be alluring and could win conversions or gain privilege. We can speak of a "dream of homogeneity." In the Federalist Papers, written by James Madison, John Jay, and Alexander Hamilton to sell the new United States Constitution to the colonies, now states, in a Federal Union, Madison welcomed diversity and saw that multiplicity could promote freedom. His colleague Jay, however, used the terms *one* and *same* repeatedly to contrive a history that he could use to overlook or demean the diverse others. That dream has lived on in the modern United States or wherever significant numbers of citizens try to amend constitutions, pass laws, create privileges, and limit dissenters or mere religious strangers. The assumption is that religious homogeneity makes the promotion of shared values easier, while recognizing and validating that religiously diverse communities can lead to relativism at best, subversion at second-best, and takeover by the other at worst.

The dream of homogeneity can turn into a nightmare for all participants in a place where religious diversity becomes a subject of controversy. This is so because most dominant groups claim privilege because they were on the scene longest, had fought for common values most sacrificially, or argued the case for their superiority best, so they have regularly turned to law for props and for prosecution of their claim. This nonrecognition or discouragement of religious diversity and favoring one religion is called in Western legal terms "establishment of religion." Throughout history, regimes have found it profitable to link governments with religions, but ordinarily in each case, they mean *religion* in the singular. They link "religion and regime," "throne and altar," "church and state," and use custom, law, prison, persecution, and execution as instruments to enforce the privileges and favors shown the single religion that has been created by their agents that has put these civil authorities in place. Religious diversity seems not to be present to historians who do not visit and do research in prisons or on islands of exile or at gravesites where nightmares of the favored majority are supposedly done away with and buried.

Religious Diversity Is Hard to Suppress Even by Totalitarians

Medieval Europe provides one case study. Religious diversity was not supposed to be experienced within a polity. For the Holy Roman Empire, the papacy, and the monarchs who were related to such entities, all were supposed to be one. Muslims were present along with Jews on the Iberian Peninsula before 1492, but in the interest of imperial and papal unification, Muslims were defeated and pushed back to Africa, and Jews were expelled to any place that would take them or to where they simply took up residence and suffered in a variety of presences. Muslims had threatened Europe after they took Constantinople in 1453 and were on the move into central Europe for a century more. In the space between, Christendom held sway. Theologies supporting homogeneity and enforced sameness favored governmental policies that made legal room for only one religion.

Even there, however, some forms of religious diversity prevailed. Christendom was not one thing after 1054 but at least two: East and West, Orthodox and Roman Catholic. Whoever would look more closely to the areas of the East would find that throughout these centuries, varied expressions grew up within Orthodoxy; religious diversity, never permitted, had its place. So it was also in the West. Break the West into its innumerable local fragments, and diversity might well not be seen or recognized. Some medieval historians hypothesize or generalize, on the basis of good warrant in the archives, that many people in the Middle Ages went through life never having laid eyes on more than about one hundred fifty other people. I wonder whether my own ancestors in Canton Bern back then ever met anyone who was not Catholic before the sixteenth century or who was not what we would call Swiss Reformed after that. The landscape was broken by mountains and valleys into innumerable independent and isolated segments. My great-grandfather, who arrived in the diverse United States in 1859, might well have been among those who had never met someone other than the Reformed until the trek to the boat or the transatlantic ship brought a vision of other kinds of people. Religious diversity became part of family lore and experience when, upon arrival in Nebraska, these "evangelical" *(Evangelisch)* Protestants were surrounded by non-Reformed *Evangelische* Protestants called Lutheran.

It would be bad manners to turn autobiographical as I just did were it not for a pedagogical point or device I choose to introduce. Assemble a company of twenty-first-century North Americans, and have them do research about their ancestors. Most of those whom census makers would call Caucasian, heirs of Christendom, would find that not too many generations earlier, the people who have gone before them and given them a name never met anyone who was not from, say, another Jewish shtetl in the Pale or Europe or another all-Catholic village in Ireland or Italy. The story of Africans in America is harder to trace because of the forced uprooting of Africans for slavery, but the bits of documentation and historical records that we do have suggest that these also came from different isolated "tribes" in diverse, separated, and remote religious communities.

Retracing steps back to Europe, we left late-medieval citizens living in enforced homogeneities, putatively beyond the range of religious diversity or not recognizing that such diversity did exist. Two generations of social historians—that is, scholars who observe and report on societies "from below," among the common people and not the princes and bishops—have shown that while there might have been some overarching official system or symbols, diverse expressions in abundance plagued the homogenizers and monopolists who favored religious uniformity. The antireligious diversity had everything going for it among those who sought hegemony or monopoly. They recognized a hierarchy pinnacled by a chief bishop who was Vicar of Christ and who, in papal doctrine, bore one of the two swords Christ had handed over. They all had to use Latin in worship and teaching, aware that religious diversity often sprouted and prospered in the midst of, or because of, linguistic choices and traditions. Behind them were laws and towers or dungeonlike prisons, plus nooses, to suppress diversity. They had the assent and loyalty of great numbers of people who, not only out of fear of God and hell and punishment but also because they liked to belong, welcomed the comforts of worship and needed leadership, which pope and emperor, bishop and prince, could provide.

If they had all that, what choice did the ordinary lay person or the rebel-minded cleric have if he—in the latter case, always "he"—chose or was called to be diverse, different, or varying? None on formal and official levels. Yet these social historians who track pilgrimages, count relics, observe shrines, and find scraps of documents written by those who had been involved make a judgment that the real religion of most of Europe remained what the historians used to call pagan or superstitious. True, some of these pagan—in observers' eyes—practices endure, such as adoration of relics. In effect, they "trickled up" and made their way into the official church, which benefited from the dual loyalty of the partly wayward. Yet these deviants and experimenters were sufficiently visible to be true representatives of religious diversity.

There was another option alongside but apart from these expressions. Medieval critics of the forced monopolists could have fresh revelations, make new studies of old scriptures, or just decide to form what the historians called sects or cults. Their diversity was not always visible and felt by comfortable majorities, which had the dissenters described to them. They were not visible because they had to be in hiding, to take refuge in remote mountain areas, or pass their signals quietly and subversively. The reference here is to groups such as the Albigensian, Cathari, Lollard, Wycliffite, and Hussite varieties. Some of them were persecuted into oblivion; others changed cover and color often enough and long enough that they could later contribute to permanent variations of Christian faith. A familiar illustration of these were the "Brethren" in Bohemia, called Hussite, after reformer Jan Hus. He offered differences, such as restoring the sacred cup at communion and promoting the use of the Bible. After being offered safe conduct by the officials at the Council of Constance in 1415, Hus was seized, convicted, and burned for holding to his differences.

Authority could not put down all of the Lollards in England or the Hussites and Brethren in central Europe. Many of them made original contributions to the varieties of Protestantism that erupted in central Europe in the middle of the sixteenth century, and some live on into our time.

We could extend this story into England, where religious diversity also flourished in the sixteenth century. Various sects—Levelers, Diggers, Fifth Monarchy Men, and Puritan varieties—contended and could not be put down by either Anglican or Catholic monarchs. Somewhat later, varieties under the blanket of Eastern Orthodoxy, especially in Russia, regionally separated in a number of geographical jurisdictions, also transformed into or were succeeded by sects of various descriptions. They represented religious diversity in the Church of the East. Mention of them can serve as transitional comment on our larger theme, that authority and repression cannot always and permanently reduce or suppress religious diversity.

Here we are referring to one of the most dramatic case studies in modern times: the Soviet Union. After the revolution of 1917, the Leninists and later the Stalinists developed as large, powerful, efficient, and ruthless a system of repression and suppression as the world had known. Ecumenical in its persecuting efficiency, its politburo and armed police used all of the instruments available—gulags, spies, radios, and more—to track down deviant religious voices or any voices displeasing to the regime at all. Russian Orthodox, Russian sects, Roman Catholics, Lutherans, and Baptists alike suffered. Only a tightly observed subservient and restricted version of Russian Orthodoxy was more or less allowed. Rivers of ink were spilled to define and defend the ideology that opposed religious diversity; barbed wire that could have stretched to the moon and back imprisoned representatives of such variety.

Then, in 1989, when the Iron Curtain was torn, it was immediately apparent that all of the old varieties had survived. They could not flourish, and they had lost many adherents to prison camps and firing squads, but the believers were still there, in their own way militant and sometimes somehow exuberant in their freedom. And they were joined by new varieties, successors and partners to the Jehovah's Witnesses and Baptist sects; this now includes many kinds of evangelicals and some of the new religious movements of the century. Something similar is occurring in China, which opposes and suppresses the varieties of Buddhism found in Tibet, many kinds of Muslims, and all but the officially licit but still hampered and limited Catholic and Protestant churches. If they number perhaps eleven million known or knowable members, estimates of those in "underground" varieties are believed to include more than fifty million Chinese. It is hard to number them, underground and housed instead of churched as most of them must be, but that the public and officialdom are aware of religious diversity in all its irrepressibleness is obvious.

THE MAIN STORY: RELIGIOUS DIVERSITY
THROUGH THE AGES

Scan a table of contents in any atlas of religions, and you will find categories that often point to and include or sometimes throw one off the trail of persistent and pervasive religious diversity. The people known to us only through architectural digs might not have known that they were religious and could not have envisioned that their remains might someday be subject to inquiry and speculation about their rites and practices, which later came to be called religious. But even before there was "organized religion," diversity was present, as relics of vessels associated with burial, rites for stages of life or seasons, cave paintings, and a variety of artifacts reveal abundantly. Their heirs, whom scholars, they hope without condescension, call "primal religions," formerly "primitive religions," are nothing if not diverse. One could say "as many religions as there are 'tribes'"—although *tribe* also is an imposed term, resented by some. Call them, with the best of intentions, *primal,* and you will find almost limitless variations, all of which help spell *diversity.* Most of the expressions appear as challenges to homogeneous or majority faiths, and as they pick and choose in adaptations to "modernity," they are part of the religious-diversity mix. The famed cargo cults in Melanesia are an example, as they fused their timeless myths with their experience of ships and airplanes from the larger world.

If the earliest known religions now called organized flourished and left some remains in Mesopotamia, their traces indicate religious diversity long before there might have been terms in "Mesopotamian" languages for them. Sacred kings and Egyptian pharaohs were in position to enforce their rites on their populations, but any listings of the "-ites" and "-ians" about which we know from that time— Hittites, Semites, Assyrians, Babylonians, and more—represent these diversities. They may, as we noted up front, enjoy a monopoly within a kingdom, but records such as those in the Hebrew scriptures show how physically close to one another they were. Israel's prophetic religious texts offer virtual catalogs of religious varieties that were close to one another, having overlapping spheres of influence and being competitors to one another's lures for converts everywhere. The rise of monotheism in these lands did not mean the end of religious diversity. It did mean the development of strategies by purifiers, reformers, and prophets in service of the rulers to the one God.

The Greek sages invented philosophical ways to conceive of a single God, which ought to have meant that under efficient rulers, there should have been ideological uniformity. Yet every schoolchild learns about "the Greek gods" in the plural and the diverse cults devoted to them. A period called the Axial Age, in which most of the "high" world religions took form, might have been characterized by the absence of diversity in the separate realms and under different regimes. Yet there were so many interactions as a result of military actions, migration, and trade that diversity was open to observation and lure to great numbers of people. One hears accounts of thousands of gods in the Roman Empire, where examples of many expressions of religious diversity were visible and partly free, as long as some respect was shown or obeisance paid to the religion of *Romanitas*, under the emperor. Even something as unsettling to monopolists as Judaism was permitted in the Roman pattern, and only when a Jewish sect such as the Christians withheld even that nominal obeisance were its members persecuted. Paul the apostle said that "gods there be many and lords there be many," but for the followers of Jesus Christ, there was only one. This first ambitious missionary faced religious diversity on Mars Hill in Athens, according to the Book of Acts. There, altars to many gods were attracting devotees.

Meanwhile, in the East, numerous forms of Buddhism—Theravada, Mahayana, and the like—were creating religious diversity, although people who lived in an area where one predominated often might not have heard stories of or experienced other versions. In other words, the Buddhisms represent challenges to and opportunities for historians, who delight in researching them and telling their stories. However, we cannot assume that ordinary folk kept a mental file of them, were attracted to them, or were on borderlands where they would greet "the other" with suspicion and even warfare.

Islam would seem to represent a special case, because as a textual religion based on the Qur'an as a direct utterance of Allah and under quasi-military religious forces, its brand of monotheism spread rapidly and was imposed efficiently. Yet Islam also demonstrated variety from early on, as Shiite vied with Sunni, and Sufi sects went partly their own way. What is more, Islam often coexisted with Christian Orthodoxy or shared a life in late-medieval Spain, where diversity was visible. And the Ottoman Empire, using a system called *rum millet*, made room for conquered people to have limited freedom to govern themselves and worship as they chose. Thus, they contributed to a distinctive brand of religious diversity.

Islamic literature in the Middle Ages has given historians rich fare as they study diversity. Muslim architecture, science, medicine, and mathematics often set paces to which Christian Europe related and adapted. Atlas makers can and do use single colors to shade maps of separate regions in which a religion dominated, whether it is a version of Buddhism, Islam, or Christianity, for examples. Yet closer to the ground, this solid coloring of regions and places confuses the real issue: there were mutual religious awarenesses, aggressions, attempts at conversion, and cultural overlap no matter what custom, taste, or the police dictated.

NORTH AMERICA AS A CASE STUDY,
NOT AS CLIMAX

Historians in North America and especially in the United States, myself among them, sometimes in exhaustion and at other times in exuberance, tend to point to our local environs, the northern part of the hemisphere called Western, as being as notable an example of religious diversity as humans have known. It is easy to make that case based on observation and using devices of measurement cherished by moderns, yet one cannot know much about this for sure, because we lack data to match that which is gathered efficiently in the era of modern censuses, recording devices, and computers. Rather than claim the rights to brag or complain, historians devote themselves, along with other social scientists, to trying to account for their exemplary case study.

Some of these come easily to mind. When Europeans were the only chroniclers as Africans, bound for slavery, joined Europeans and arrived to stay in the Americas after 1492, they came upon the scene of impossibly complex diversity. Students of the rites of each of the peoples—Mayan, Incan, Iroquois, Pawnee, and the like—differ from one another as one would expect the rites of peoples who are not literate to do. While the Europeans who came did not want to call these rites "religion," by most known definitions of religion in the past five centuries, they were explicitly, formally, and we might say flagrantly religions. They had beliefs, often about a Great Spirit, along with patterns of sacrifice, mythic justifications for war, and interpretations of childbearing, love, and death. All over the Americas, even where and while the native peoples were being pushed to reservations, being killed in warfare, or dying out from diseases to which they had not been immune, they represented challenges of religious diversity to the whites just as the newcoming invaders represented diversity to them.

In North America, when Catholic settlers in Florida were seeking monopoly early in the sixteenth century, they were challenged by French Protestants who would settle in northern Florida. The Catholic settlers and their military guards were not accurate accountants for the new settlers, calling them Lutheran, which they were not. Never mind; they represented colonial challenges and religious alternatives and had to be done in. In the Northeast, French Canadians became aware of Native American religion, often close at hand, as when some priests were martyred, but they were also alert to the intrusions of Protestants from the South. Most of those who came to what became the thirteen colonies were resisting religious diversity back home in Europe. In the Southern colonies, all would establish singly the Anglican (here called the Episcopal) church and would even repress the one non-Anglican settlement, Catholic Maryland. In New England, members of Puritan offshoots of the Anglican church who embodied religious diversity in old England were extremely efficient at excluding non-Puritans in most colonies.

They were not able to continue the pattern they sought. One colony, Rhode Island, welcomed diversity from the first, since it was led by Baptists, who had been so irritating to Anglican establishment in the old country. They were too close for comfort to Massachusetts and Connecticut, two uniformity-seeking colonies that banished Quakers and dissenters such as Anne Hutchinson. They also made their places utterly unwelcoming sites for their feared Catholic counterparts. Catholics, after the first few years in Maryland, never had a place legally their own, were a minority almost everywhere for a couple of centuries, and in the Protestant-dominated United States remained a vivid symbol of the threat of religious diversity for a long time. Native Americans and Jews were also often "the other," and if anti-Semitism was never the official policy that Jews had suffered under elsewhere often before, they did feel the stigma and suffer from some societal restrictions.

When in 1924 the U.S. Congress passed legislation restricting the number of annual immigrants, especially newcomers of the wrong kinds, it did not employ the language of religious monopoly, threat, and stigma any longer—it was too late and impossible to do so. Yet it would be hard to disguise the efforts or see them as other than attempts to include religious differences, along with race and ethnicity, in their scope. In 1965, changes in immigration law made possible a rush of immigrants who rendered religious diversity more visibly and socially palpable than ever before. Protestant majorities in the upper Midwest found themselves sharing communities with Southeast Asian people. Muslim growth was frightening to nativists who, for presumably "security" reasons, scrutinized Muslims and invented new names (e.g., "Islamofascist") to stigmatize them and so took words associated with small minorities and applied them to the whole of the billion-member Muslim "community."

Religious diversity is not going to wane or disappear in free societies that foster advocacy of free markets and live with the ethos of globalization. Such diversity assumes ever new forms and helps generate ever fresh stories. As these unfold and become available to researchers and narrators, the record of history suggests that historians are not going to run out of subjects or stories. How each religious group and the people who live apart from them will regard one another and interact in the decades ahead will be fateful to the public and fruitful to historians.

FOR FURTHER READING

Barrett, David, ed. 1982. *World Christian Encyclopedia: A Comparative Study of Christianity and Religions in the Modern World, AD 1900–2000.* New York: Oxford University Press.

Casanova, José. 1994. *Public Religions in the Modern World.* Chicago: University of Chicago Press.

Eliade, Mircea. 1978–1983. *A History of Religious Ideas*. Chicago: University of Chicago Press.

Seager, Richard Hughes, ed. 1993. *The Dawn of Religious Pluralism: Voices from the World's Parliament of Religions, 1893*. LaSalle, Ill.: Open Court.

Smart, Ninian, ed. 1999. *Atlas of the World's Religions*. New York: Oxford University Press.

Wiggins, James B. 1996. *In Praise of Religious Diversity*. New York: Routledge.

CHAPTER 2

A RELIGIOUS STUDIES APPROACH TO QUESTIONS ABOUT RELIGIOUS DIVERSITY

IAN S. MARKHAM

A central goal of religious studies is to make sure that we are completely fair to the different religious traditions in the world. This is difficult. We all come to the challenge of religious diversity from a certain vantage point; this is inescapable and unavoidable. The emergence of religious studies as a discipline was part of a quest to approach religious diversity in a way that ensures that we approach the exploration of "the other" in a way that does not misrepresent the other.

In this chapter, we start by looking at the traditional approach to the study of religion. Then we touch briefly on the key persons who were instrumental in developing the religious studies approach. Finally, we look at some of the contemporary questions and debates in this area.

THE TRADITIONAL APPROACH TO RELIGIOUS DIVERSITY

Religious diversity has always been with us. The Bible was clearly written in a pluralist setting. The New Testament authors constantly struggled with the relationship of Christianity to Judaism and to the many competitor gods and temples.

Pluralism is not simply a reality that shapes the scriptures, but it also pervades much of the Christian tradition. There are moments when the Christian conversation with pluralism is constructive. So, for example, Augustine of Hippo makes imaginative use of Neoplatonic thought in much of his work. And later, Thomas Aquinas in the thirteenth century is in conversation with both Muslim and Jewish thinkers to shape his theology. David Burrell sees this medieval period as a golden age of constructive engagement with religious diversity:

> [B]y the twelfth century a Jewish thinker of Mosaic stature, Moses Maimonides, immersed in the culture of the Islamicate, adapted the stringent criticisms his Muslim predecessor, al-Ghazālī, had made of Islamic "philosophers," to defend the free creation of the universe by one God, in the face of alternatives inspired by Plotinus. Thomas Aquinas adopted the signal philosophical work of the one whom he called "Rabbi Moses," The Guide of the Perplexed, to advance his project of expounding Christian revelation by using the philosophies of Aristotle and Plato which he encountered through the writings of Ibn Sina (Avicenna). Thus, the task of articulating the free creation of the universe, and thereby showing how human inquiry begun in wonder can peak there as well, became the fruit of an unwitting but immensely fruitful collaboration among Jewish, Christian, and Muslim scholars, on the strength of initiatives taken by Islamic thinkers.[1]

Aquinas, to his credit, was a conscious interfaith theologian; as Burrell notes, his sources explicitly include Rabbi Moses and Ibn Sina, and his enormous debt to that other "pagan," Aristotle, is well established.

So it is important not to caricature the traditional approach. There is much that is commendable here. However, the generosity of Aquinas runs parallel with a damning assessment of, for example, Muhammad the prophet. Aquinas writes:

> He (Mohammed) seduced the people by promises of carnal pleasure to which the concupiscence of the flesh urges us. His teaching also contained precepts that were in conformity with his promises, and he gave free rein to carnal pleasure. In all this, as is not unexpected, he was obeyed by carnal men. As for proofs of the truth of his doctrine, he brought forward only such as could be grasped by the natural ability of anyone with a very modest wisdom. Indeed, the truths that he taught he mingled with many fables and with doctrines of the greatest falsity.
>
> He did not bring forth any signs produced in a supernatural way, which alone fittingly gives witness to divine inspiration; for a visible action that can be only divine reveals an invisibly inspired teacher of truth. On the contrary, Mohammed said that he was sent in the power of his arms—which are signs not lacking even to robbers and tyrants. What is more, no wise men, men trained in things divine and human, believed in him from the beginning.
>
> Those who believed in him were brutal men and desert wanderers, utterly ignorant of all divine teaching, through whose numbers Mohammed forced others to become his followers by the violence of his arms. Nor do divine pronouncements on the part of preceding prophets offer him any witness. On the contrary, he perverts almost all the testimony of the Old and the New Testaments by making them into a fabrication of his own, as can be seen by anyone who examines his law. It was, therefore, a shrewd decision on his part to forbid his

followers to read the Old and New Testaments, lest these books convict him of falsity. It is thus clear that those who place faith in his words believe foolishly.[2]

This is exceptionally ugly; it captures certain classic attitudes that are embedded deep within Western Islamaphobia. So, although Aquinas can admire Islam, his achievement is marred by this propensity to read Islam in an entirely confessional way—that is, in a way that sees the tradition entirely through Christian eyes.

Confessionalism and conversion have been two important dynamics in the traditional approach to religious diversity, which the religious studies approach sought to amend. For Christians approaching the other, the Christian truth claims dominate the conversation, which is what is meant by confessionalism. And of course, for members of other faith traditions, their approach to the other is dominated by the confession they are in. Linked to confessionalism, we often have a conversion motivation at work. The goal is to understand the other so that certain conversion techniques can be discovered.

The entire discipline of missiology continues this approach today. There is a lively debate within the discipline about the nature of missiology. For some, it is a branch of theology. The theological claims about God require witness, which in turn requires mission. For others, it is an interdisciplinary subject in its own right. Missiology brings together sociological, cultural critique with the recognition that God has obligated a tradition to witness and evangelize.

While conversion, confessionalism, and missiology all start within a discourse of a particular tradition, the religious studies approach starts from outside the particular traditions. It is shaped by one primary value: to be fair to the other. In short, the religious studies approach seeks to understand other faith traditions *on their own terms*.

KEY PEOPLE IN THE EMERGENCE OF THE RELIGIOUS STUDIES APPROACH

Many of the key people in the development of this tradition emerge from the European Enlightenment. Part of the hope was a "scientific" approach to the study of religion—an approach that "studies" rather than "follows" religion. The German Friedrich Max Müller captured the essence of this approach, which he outlined to the Royal Institution in London in 1870:

> A Science of Religion, based on an impartial and truly scientific comparison of all, or at all events, of the most important, religions of mankind, is now only a question of time. It is demanded by those whose voice cannot be disregarded. Its title, though implying as yet a promise rather than a fulfillment, has become more or less familiar in Germany, France and America; its great problems have attracted the eyes of many inquirers, and its results have been anticipated either

with fear or with delight. It becomes therefore the duty of those who have devoted their life to the study of the principal religions of the world in their original documents, and who value religion and reverence it in whatever form it may present itself, to take possession of this new territory in the name of true science.[3]

Max Müller was a philologist; he was particularly sensitive to language and culture. He was undoubtedly under the spell of the Enlightenment. The Enlightenment is important because it birthed a historical sensitivity that recognized that the Bible (and all religious books) emerged in a certain setting. Certain questions came to prominence. Instead of simply assuming divine inspiration, questions about authorship and community were taken much more seriously. While the focus was initially on the Christian scriptures, this approach extended to other faith traditions.

A good illustration was William Robertson Smith (1846–1894). Smith lived in Scotland and served as a Presbyterian minister. He was a leading advocate of applying rational, scientific methods to the Bible. Questions about authorship (for example, he thought that there were at least two authors of the book of Isaiah) and social context came to prominence. Toward the end of his life, he started to write about other religious traditions in the same way. For example, in *The Religion of the Semites* (1889), Smith looked at the ways in which Israelites intersected with their neighbors—the Babylonians, Assyrians, Phoenicians, and Syrians. A religious studies approach was being taken to the history of theological ideas.

Others started taking a comparable religious studies approach to religious history. Edward Burnett Tylor (1832–1917) was an anthropologist who thought it important to read the past while taking other religious traditions seriously in their own right. He also anticipated a problem that would haunt religious studies, for he provided an evolutionary account of religion: it starts with animism, moves to polytheism, and then slowly evolves into monotheism. In other words, in his attempt to ensure that the narrative of the religious past was not written through overt Christian spectacles, he imposed a "secular" and "modernist" narrative on the data. We will return to this point below.

Whereas Tylor was an anthropologist interested in religion, others started looking at the world from the vantage points of other disciplines. The father of modern sociology, Emile Durkheim (1858–1917), began to explore the issues of religion from the perspective of the social. He stressed the ways in which religion was an important glue for the sense of identity within a community. And Sigmund Freud, from the perspective of psychology, insisted that various dynamics related to the development of the mind are important in understanding religion. An undoubted classic, which owes a great debt to the discipline of psychology, is William James's *The Varieties of Religious Experience: A Study in Human Nature* (1902).

The basic ingredients of a religious studies approach were emerging. The approach did not insist that a person should look at the texts of other faith traditions through the spectacles of one's own religion but attempted to be more neutral. And this willingness to be neutral ran parallel with a sense that the insights of anthropology, sociology, and psychology can help us understand the phenomena of religion more accurately.

There were countless scholars in the twentieth century who contributed to this growing trajectory and approach. Mention should be made of Mircea Eliade (1907–1986), who provided two of the great classics in religious studies. In *Patterns in Comparative Religion* (1958) and *The Sacred and the Profane* (1959), Eliade pioneered a distinctive methodology for the study of religion, namely, the phenomenological approach. This approach has its roots in Hegel and will be described in further detail below.

For the English-speaking world, the work of Ninian Smart (1927–2001) is perhaps most influential. This is partly because Smart held prominent academic positions both in the United States (at the University of California) and in the United Kingdom (at the University of Lancaster). Smart thought it helpful to talk of "worldviews," thereby enabling the religious aspects within Marxism to be recognized. He suggested that worldviews possess six dimensions. The first is the *ritual dimension*. Smart explains that religion "tends . . . to express itself through such rituals: through worship prayers, offerings, and the like," some experience of the divine or supernatural.[4] The second is the *mythological dimension*. This, Smart explains, means not "false" but "story." These are the narratives that extend beyond "stories about God (for instance the story of the creation in Genesis), about the gods (for instance in Homer's *Iliad*), etc., but also the historical events of religious significance in a tradition."[5] This dimension captures the narrative (the stories) that underpins the worldview. The third is the *doctrinal dimension*, certain truth claims that are captured in teachings about the nature of the world and its relationship with the transcendent. Smart writes: "Doctrines are an attempt to give system, clarity, and the intellectual power to what is revealed through the mythological and symbolic language of religious faith and ritual."[6] The fourth is the *ethical dimension*, the actions that are encouraged or required. Smart writes: "Ethics concern the behavior of the individual and, to some extent, the code of ethics of the dominant religion controls the community."[7] This community aspect of ethics flows into the fifth dimension, which is the *social dimension*. "Religions," Smart writes, "are not just systems of *belief*, they are also organizations, or parts of organizations. They have a communal and social significance."[8] The sixth is the *experiential dimension*. Smart writes: "Although men may hope to have contact with, and participate in, the invisible world through ritual, personal religion normally involves the hope of, or realization of, experience of that world."[9] Smart goes on to explain that this sense of experience is why Marxism should not be characterized as a religion.

Smart aspired to create a system that was fair to religious diversity. He stressed the similarities between traditions by creating these six categories that seem to apply to almost all worldviews. In addition, he was clearly building on the insights suggested by the other modern disciplines of anthropology, sociology, and psychology.

APPROACHES WITHIN RELIGIOUS STUDIES

By the 1960s, a distinctive religious studies approach to diversity had emerged. As the discipline started reflecting on the appropriate approach, it was clear that advocates within religious studies tended to be more sympathetic to either the historical-comparative method or the phenomenological method.[10]

The historical-comparative method suggests that the study of religion should involve a comparison of the historical formulations of each tradition. It seeks to demonstrate historical connections and differences, thereby identifying independent occurrences of similar phenomena.

The phenomenological method defies easy description. Douglas Allen points out correctly: "The term has become very popular and has been utilized by numerous scholars, who seem to share little if anything in common."[11] The word *phenomenological* comes from *phenomenon*, which literally means "appearance." Most phenomenologists try to systematize and classify the phenomena of religion—the things that "appear" to us. Among the numerous schools using this method, the following features seem to be important. The study of religion should be *empirical*, in that one studies religion free from any a priori assumptions; it should be *descriptive* and *historical*, in that one is trying to understand these traditions objectively; and finally, it will be *antireductionist*, opposed to any attempt to turn religion into a branch of psychology or sociology. It accepts religion as a distinctive phenomenon in its own right.

The phenomenological approach shares with the historical-comparative approach a stress on the need for objectivity when studying religion. Although it is true that some phenomenologists have suggested that the concept of *epoché* (a "means of bracketing beliefs and preconceptions we normally impose on phenomena"[12]) provides a way of empathizing with and understanding the object of study that removes the "coldness" that might seem to be a drawback of the traditional detachment of the scholar, most phenomenologists have wanted to stress fairness and the objectivity that entails.

CHALLENGES AND ISSUES

There is no doubt that a religious studies approach to religious diversity is helpful in many ways. It takes "the other" seriously on its own terms. It seeks to understand precisely what is meant within a tradition. So, instead of reading the entire Hebrew scriptures as the Old Testament (which primarily is anticipating the coming of Jesus Christ), the text is read as part of a distinguished religious tradition in its own right—as the text belonging to the Jewish people. It also has the advantage of applying some of the useful tools of modernity to the religious traditions. It takes the social seriously and is not afraid to use sociological insights to illuminate a tradition.

However, the religious studies approach is entering a period of analysis and revision. One factor is the emergence of the "postmodern," which insists that the approaches of modernity (of which religious studies is one) are not really "neutral." Tylor, for example, was really imposing a secular worldview on religious traditions. Part of the postmodern insight is that all people come to questions with a perspective. There is no vantage point transcending traditions. The religious studies approach tends to live within the tradition of modernity (or perhaps the "confession of modernity").

This reality does lead to bias. Returning to Tylor, to insist that animism is primitive and monotheism is advanced ignores the rich religious dynamics at work in indigenous religious traditions. In fact, these indigenous traditions are undergoing a revival precisely because they turn the mountain and the river into sacred entities. To impose an evolutionary model on the development of religions ignored the complexity of traditions.

However, the accusation of imposing modernity on religion goes further than Tylor. Are the stories in Hinduism about Lord Krishna true? Did the virgin birth of Jesus really happen? Did Muhammad make the night flight to Jerusalem? Because the religious studies approach is so deeply infected by the bias of the reductionism of modernity, there is a tendency for this approach to be skeptical of such language. In other words, many exponents of a religious studies approach give such a high value to the scientific worldview that these stories are so contrasting that any historicity is denied a priori.

There is another related danger here. In the attempt to provide an "outsider's" perspective on religion, the result is that all religions look strange. In fact, the outsider perspective is the only one that looks sensible. The net result is that it looks as if the secular is the default setting—the place to be. It ignores the "secular" as a worldview in its own right and privileges the vantage point in conversation with other religious traditions. The standard religious studies textbook takes us through the different beliefs, practices, and history of each tradition. One learns about Muslims praying five times a day, but one does not learn that the intent is to live as if God really is and to stay connected with God throughout the day.

CONCLUSION

The religious studies approach to diversity is an important tool. And for many public universities, it is viewed as the only legitimate approach. For those institutions that oppose any form of confessional religious identity, the religious studies approach seems to provide the best way to study religious traditions. It seems to suggest neutrality and appropriate scholarly detachment.

Although it is true that the religious studies approach avoids some of the drawbacks of a strongly confessional approach, which is often directly opposed to other faith traditions, we now recognize that there is hidden bias and perspective embedded in the much-prized neutrality. In terms of education, this approach can be distorting. It, too, can mislead. The secular and scientific worldview is being privileged. Students are often left with a relativist impression. For many students, religion appears to be the realm of many metaphysical options, where truth is impossible to discern. The concept that there are better and worse accounts of religion can easily be obscured.

The religious studies approach, then, should be seen as one tool among many. It makes use of the major disciplines that have shaped modernity in the task of understanding the various religions of the world. However, it should not be treated as the only legitimate approach to religious diversity. The assumptions underpinning this approach can be contested. It is not neutral, and in many ways, it is not better than the alternative approaches.

NOTES

1. David Burrell, *Faith and Freedom: An Interfaith Perspective* (Oxford: Blackwell, 2004), xiii–xiv.
2. Thomas Aquinas, *Summa Contra Gentiles*, Book 1, Chapter 16, Article 4, footnote 1.
3. Friedrich Max Müller, *Introduction to the Science of Religion*, 1873, 34. London: Longmans, Green, and Company. 26. Reprint 1899.
4. Ninian Smart, *The Religious Experience of Mankind*, 3rd ed. (New York: Charles Scribner's, 1984), 7.
5. Ibid., 8.
6. Ibid.
7. Ibid., 9.
8. Ibid.
9. Ibid., 10.
10. Some of the material that follows is taken from Ian S. Markham with Christy Lohr, *A World Religions Reader*, 3rd ed. (Oxford: Wiley-Blackwell, 2009).
11. Douglas Allen, "Phenomenology of Religion," in Mircea Eliade, ed., *The Encyclopedia of Religion*, vol. 11 (New York: Macmillan, 1987), 273.
12. Ibid., 281.

FOR FURTHER READING

Chryssides, George D., and Ron Geaves. 2007. *The Study of Religion: An Introduction to Key Ideas and Methods*. London and New York: Continuum.
Connolly, Peter, ed. 1999. *Approaches to the Study of Religion*. London and New York: Cassell.
Markham, Ian, with Christy Lohr. 2009. *A World Religions Reader*, 3rd ed. Oxford: Wiley-Blackwell.
Sharpe, Eric. 1986. *Comparative Religion: A History*, 2nd ed. London: Duckworth.
Smart, Ninian. 1984. *The Religious Experience of Mankind*, 3rd ed. New York: Charles Scribner's.

CHAPTER 3

A PHILOSOPHICAL APPROACH TO QUESTIONS ABOUT RELIGIOUS DIVERSITY

PETER BYRNE

THE fact of religious diversity provides problems for a variety of approaches to the study of religion. In the philosophical study of religion, there are at least four main areas in which issues are raised by the fact of religious diversity: the epistemology of religious belief, the production of theories of religion, reflection on concepts of God and the Ultimate, and discussion of the relationship between religion and the human good.

THE EPISTEMOLOGY OF RELIGIOUS BELIEF

For the purposes of this chapter, I follow J. L. Schellenberg's definition of religion in terms of "ultimism." A religion is a set of symbols, beliefs, and practices centered on the affirmation "that there is a reality metaphysically and axiologically ultimate (representing the deepest fact about the nature of things and also unsurpassably great), in relation to which an ultimate good can be attained. Otherwise put, religious claims are those entailing that there is an ultimate and salvific reality" (Schellenberg 2007, 3; see also Byrne 1999).

The fact of religious diversity means that different religions contain competing accounts of the nature of the metaphysically and axiologically ultimate reality and competing accounts of the character of the ultimate good human beings can attain through relation to this reality. Religions are not wholly, or perhaps even primarily, theories, but each contains or implies a theory about the character of the ultimate reality and about the nature of the ultimate good for humans. Even where there is considerable overlap in the accounts of the transcendent, sacred reality and of salvation offered by more than one religion (as with, for example, Christianity and Islam), there will be deep incompatibilities among the theories embedded in them. Moreover, within what we conventionally label as unitary religions, there are similar incompatibilities between one sect's detailed account of the transcendent, sacred reality and salvation and another's. Diversity thus throws up "epistemic peer conflict" (Basinger 2002, 1). Religious epistemic peer conflict consists in the fact that different people, by virtue of adhering to different religions or to different forms of the same religion, hold conflicting opinions on important religious questions while being equally sincere and equally knowledgeable about nonreligious matters.

Religious epistemic peer conflict (hereafter "peer conflict" for short) goes deeper than disagreements over questions of truth. Peer conflict over the truth of religious propositions implies, although it does not entail, that there will be conflict about which religious believers have genuine religious experience and which believers are on a genuine path to salvation. These implications—of competition for genuine religious experience and genuine salvific effectiveness—can be avoided only if we can detach success in these two dimensions of religion from the truth of doctrines.

Peer conflict could be denied if it were plausible to assert that we cannot find equally sincere and knowledgeable people in different religions, but this seems a hopeless strategy (but note that reformed epistemology, discussed below, in the end denies the fact of peer conflict). Given peer conflict, then, we have a serious problem about judging which, if any, religion possesses true theories about the Ultimate and which, if any, religious believers have warrant for their beliefs about the Ultimate. By warrant I mean substantive truth-indicative grounds for religious beliefs. Warrant is important because the fact of peer conflict seems too easy to reconcile with the concession that epistemic peers across different religions are all *entitled* to their religious convictions, where entitlement is a matter of having broken no epistemic obligations in the forming and maintaining of one's beliefs. In this minimal sense, atheists might indeed concede that many religious believers are entitled to their beliefs even though they are false—just as pre-Copernican astronomers in Europe were entitled to believe that the earth was the stationary center of a concentric universe. But warrant, as defined, is a different matter. If "substantive truth-indicative grounds" means "grounds that make a belief more probable than not," then it is flatly impossible for two incompatible beliefs to be both warranted.

There are at least four responses to the epistemological problems arising out of religious diversity that are worth discussing: apologetic investment, atheism, agnosticism, and antievidentialism.

Apologetic Investment

Writers such as Griffiths (1991) and Swinburne contend that the appropriate response to peer conflict consists in the search for and presentation of, arguments that will pick out one religion as true over and against the rest. Across seven books, Swinburne presents such a strategy in favor of the truth of Christian theism, that is, for a form of theism that is more than the assertion of the existence of a creator God but includes the fundamental items in the creeds common to Orthodoxy, Roman Catholicism, and the main Protestant denominations. Swinburne takes the implicit demands of peer conflict seriously. Starting from facts and moral intuitions common to educated people in the contemporary world, he moves to a demonstration of the coherence of a core belief in a personal creator (Swinburne 1993). Next, by reference to such facts and to agreed, accepted standards of inductive arguments (vouched for in the natural sciences), a cumulative, inductive case for the truth of that theism is developed (Swinburne 2004). This cumulative case shows that it is more probable than not that such a God exists. Faith and trust in this God is then shown to be reasonable (Swinburne 2007a). From this minimal theism, four books (Swinburne 1989, 2007b, 1994, 1998) extend the apologetic case to distinctly Christian beliefs. These seven works are backed up by a separate study of the probability of the resurrection of Jesus (Swinburne 2003). By reference to further facts and moral intuitions, these books provide warrant for the account of God, atonement, and providence contained in agreed Christian creeds.

Note what the strategy of apologetic investment implies about peer conflict. Peer conflict exists, but it can be overcome by fuller investigation and reflection. Peers in "other religions" are not stupid or ignorant in general. Once religious peers confront the fact of diversity—and included in that is the fact that some epistemic peers reject religion altogether—they have a duty to engage in the processes of critical rationality that, when conducted correctly, lead to the discovery of apologetic arguments that settle the incompatibilities among religious beliefs in favor of one existing religion.

Atheism

Atheism in this context means more than denial of the existence of a theistic God—in that sense, Buddhists are atheists. I use the term to mean rejection of the indeterminate claim about sacred, transcendent reality within Schellenberg's definition of religion. Atheists agree with apologetic investors on one main point: diversity entails that religious individuals are under an obligation to reflect critically on their beliefs and come up with substantive, truth-indicative grounds for those beliefs. (Let us call this the apologetic obligation.) If such grounds cannot be produced, upon reflection, then the appropriate conclusion is that there are no such grounds. That means that at best, religious peers are entitled to their religious beliefs, but if they have undergone the reflection and examination demanded by the fact of peer conflict, then they are no longer entitled to them. Atheism affirms that the reasonable conclusion from the failure of apologetic investment is that no religion is true. There is no sacred, transcendent reality.

Atheists affirm that there is no successful apologetic showing one religion to be true and the others false. Leaving aside critiques of particular apologetic strategies, there are general grounds for lack of confidence in apologetic investment. These include the persistence and extent of religious disagreements. If there is an apologetic tiebreaker, why has it not been produced before? The profundity of religious disagreements suggests that there will be problems in appealing to agreed moral intuitions to break the tie: the moral universe of one religious believer might not be that of another. Religious disagreements also involve matters of metaphysics and of ancient history that are notably difficult to resolve intersubjectively.

Agnosticism

One obvious response to persistent peer conflict is that after balancing what can be said for the truth of each religion, there seem to be no strong, truth-indicative grounds for any religious beliefs. The appropriate stance is to remain agnostic about all of them. We can reach this conclusion by going down the same route that took us toward atheism. Agnostics affirm the apologetic obligation. They conclude with atheists that it has not been met and is not likely to be so. Agnostics will deny that this must take us to atheism. They will contend that atheism is bound up in peer conflict as much as any substantive religious position. It, too, must meet the apologetic obligation. According to agnostics, atheists must provide positive, neutrally based proofs of claims of the form "The empirical universe is all there is; no sacred, transcendent reality exists." Agnostics will claim that proofs of atheism are as hard to come by as proofs of the truth of Buddhism or Judaism. They will thus deny that we can, in the religious case, apply the inference schema "In the absence of cogent evidence for X, it is safe to conclude that there is no X." In sum, agnostics will deny that there should be a presumption of atheism (contra Flew 2005). An agnostic stance of this kind is worked out in great detail in Schellenberg (2007). It draws on the fact of diversity at a number of points.

Antievidentialism

The key to the response to peer conflict that I call antievidentialism is the denial of the apologetic obligation. According to this approach, religious individuals who are faced with peer conflict arising from religious diversity are under no obligation, after reflecting on their beliefs, to come up with substantive, truth-indicative grounds for those beliefs. *Antievidentialism* is an appropriate label for this stance insofar as it denies an important implication of the apologetic obligation: that we should search for evidence (of a neutral kind) for religious beliefs. Religious individuals can be aware of peer conflict but remain assured of their particular beliefs in the absence of any attempt, let alone any successful attempt, to secure apologetic evidence for them and against those of their peers.

Antievidentialism is typical of the stance toward religious epistemology and toward the epistemology of religious diversity found in reformed epistemology. A developed example can be found in Plantinga (2000). Central to the Plantinga approach to the epistemic problems created by religious diversity is a denial of two elements bound up with the apologetic imperative urged on us by the likes of Griffiths and Swinburne. These elements are evidentialism and internalism. As applied to religion, evidentialism is the doctrine that the truth-indicative grounds for religious beliefs must include other beliefs that imply them. Religious beliefs cannot be wholly truth-indicatively grounded in the way my belief that there is a goldfinch in my garden is grounded when I just see the goldfinch before me. I need propositional evidence for religious beliefs. Internalism is the doctrine that truth-indicative reasons for beliefs cannot make them truly warranted unless the subject is aware, or could readily be aware, of them. Thus, religious individuals faced with peer conflict have a duty to resort to apologetics. Plantinga denies the application of evidentialism to religious beliefs by claiming that they are, or might be, such that they are grounded nonevidentially, as is my belief regarding the goldfinch. They are, or might be, properly basic, that is, rightly affirmed with confidence even though they are not inferred from other warranted beliefs. In general, he favors an externalist epistemology. According to externalism, beliefs can be warrantedly held if they are the product of cognitive mechanisms that function to produce true beliefs for the most part. Then they are based on truth-indicative grounds, but the subject need not know what these grounds are to hold the beliefs properly.

Plantinga postulates that it is plausible to suppose that Christian beliefs (he is a Christian exclusivist; see below) are the products of cognitive mechanisms of a distinctive sort: a *sensus divinitatis* and the Internal Instigation of the Holy Spirit (IIHS). The former allows for the proper formation of core theistic beliefs once this "sense of the divine" is appropriately stimulated by, say, awareness of beauty in nature. The latter allows for the proper formation of distinctively Christian beliefs once, say, the words of Christian scripture are read and understood.

Armed with this externalist account of warranted belief, Plantinga contends that religious believers who are aware of the fact of peer conflict can justifiably sit tight and not let diversity produce any diminution of confidence in their beliefs. Plantinga's externalism entails that the de jure question of the right of believers to hold their beliefs cannot be separated from the de facto question of whether those beliefs might be true (see Plantinga 2000, vi–ix). If standard Christian claims are true, then de facto Christian believers are in a different epistemic position from their apparent epistemic peers in other religions. Even if Christians do not have an evidential case to hand that is superior to that of non-Christian believers, they might well have a functioning *sensus divinitatis* and IIHS. Thus, if Christian beliefs are true, they might be warranted. This means that Plantinga has the means to hand for turning the force of the fact of peer conflict. It can no longer be shown that believers have no right to be certain of beliefs that are denied by their epistemic peers. A version of one of Plantinga's own examples shows how this result can be accomplished (see Plantinga 2000, 450–451). I am hauled before the police. They accuse me of committing a crime. All manner of witnesses are produced who saw me at the scene. But I know that at the time of my alleged offense, I was elsewhere. I have a distinct memory of being fifty miles away. Here the fact of peer conflict is very strange, but I could not be wrong over a deliverance of my memory of this clarity. I stick to my belief that I did not commit the crime, not because I have evidence for it or because I can produce evidence that rebuts those who say I did it. I am just confident through memory that I am not the one who committed the crime and that, in some way, these witnesses have it wrong. My simple memory belief means that they are not my epistemic peers after all.

In denying the apologetic obligation, reformed epistemology denies a premise shared by apologetic investment, atheism, and agnosticism. Those three approaches accept that peer conflict means that the surety of religious claims must diminish unless the apologetic obligation can be met. Much depends, then, on the adequacy of the externalist account of warrant that Plantinga brings to bear on the epistemological problems raised by religious diversity.

Theories of Religion

Philosophers, and others, produce theories of religion. Such theories endeavor to plot the place of religion in human life and culture, providing answers to such questions as "What is the meaning of human religiousness?" or "Is religion an enterprise that can be explained in wholly human terms, or is it something that is only comprehensible as the outcome of human interaction with some ultimate reality?" Religious diversity is a very important factor in the formulation and appraisal of theories of religion. This is in large measure because of the interaction between the epistemological issues discussed above and questions about the interpretation and explanation of religion.

How do the epistemology and the interpretation of religion interact? At first glance, it might seem as if they are wholly separate concerns. We might think that the question of whether religious beliefs are true and capable of being warranted is quite distinct from the question of what moves people to embrace them. Questions about the origin and maintenance of religion are different from questions about its truth. Thus, even if it were the case, as many skeptical interpreters of religion contend, that religion is everywhere the product of wish fulfillment and other nonrational factors, it might still be the case that the beliefs of one or more religion were true. A second look, however, will show that epistemological questions and explanatory questions cannot be sharply divorced. While a belief might be true and yet be the outcome of nonrational factors in the minds of those who hold it, further questions must be considered. An important epistemological question concerning religion is "Do/can any religious beliefs amount to knowledge?" It is not sufficient that a belief happens to be true for it to count as knowledge. It must be warranted as well. And that implies something about the belief's causation. It is so caused that it is no accident that it is true. If a subject's belief that p amounts to knowledge that p, then this implies something about how the belief that p is generated. Awareness of the fact that p must be a causally necessary condition of the knowing subject's coming to hold that p. If the dogmas of a particular religion just happened to be true of a sacred, transcendent reality, then those beliefs would not arise from cognitive contact with that reality. That reality's existence and character could have been quite other than they are, and yet the dogmas would still have the content that they have. But then those dogmas could not count as knowledge. In religions, there is the tacit claim that their beliefs, moral systems, and traditions of spirituality arise out of contact with the Ultimate. This means that they are not wholly human products, for all that they are rooted in human history and culture.

The epistemological reflections on religious diversity are thus vital to the interpretation of religion. There are three main types of theory of religion that arise from or bear upon the fact of religious diversity: naturalism, confessionalism, and pluralism.[1]

Naturalism

Naturalism is linked to atheism in the epistemology of religious diversity. Atheism is the denial that any sacred, transcendent reality exists. *Naturalism* in the theory of religion is the name for theories of religion that explain it in wholly human, natural terms. We get from atheism to naturalism in the following way. If atheism is the best bet given diversity, then we must assume that there is no ultimate reality. Causal, cognitive contact with such a reality has not, then, been a moving force in the development of religions. No religious experiences are veridical. Religion is then best seen as wholly naturally caused. Reductive, nonrealist explanations of religion now look plausible. So, diversity gives rise to atheism (as defined earlier in this chapter), and atheism gives rise to naturalism. Moreover, diversity might seem to be best explained by a typical offshoot of atheism: the assertion that religion is everywhere the product of the human imagination fed by desires and needs in the context of different strands of human culture. In contrast, if we supposed that religion, in at least some of its forms, put us in touch with a human-transcending truth, then we would expect that it is not simply the product of the human imagination.

According to the naturalist, a nonrealist interpretation of religion looks likely in the light of diversity. Religions come and go. There is a seemingly endless birth and death of sects in the history of religion. There is no accumulation of reliable belief and no convergence in religion. The overwhelmingly plausible explanation of the manifold forms of human religiousness is the naturalist's appeal to the imagination and its historical and cultural setting. Religion is not truth-oriented, does not track the truth, and is a fiction.[2]

Confessionalism

Within each of the main, long-established religions of the world, dogmatic structures have developed to take account of and explain "other religions." It is possible to interpret religious diversity from the standpoint provided by one of the extant religious confessions. There are thus (varieties of) Christian, Buddhist, Islamic, and other interpretations of the fact that the world contains diverse forms of belief and practice. It is of the essence of a confessionalist interpretation of religion that it is nonegalitarian. For naturalism, in contrast, all religions are works of fiction. The confessionalist is nonegalitarian about the cognitive successes claimed by religions, such as truth, warrant, soteriological effectiveness, veridical religious experiences, and perhaps sound morality. In these things, the confessionalist's favored religion is superior to "other religions." The superiority can be a matter of black and white, or it can manifest in shades of gray. For the confessional exclusivist, the successes of the favored religion exclude success in other religions. If the favored religion is true, the others are false. If it offers a means of salvation, the others do not. There is no route to the Ultimate but via the one, true faith.[3]

However, for the inclusivist, success of the favored religion in some or other of these important dimensions does not altogether exclude success in other religions. Thus, the inclusivist might claim that although the favored religion has the definitive account of truth about the Ultimate and about the human condition, people in other religions have some apprehension of the sacred. This apprehension is not free from error, but it might be enough to allow, for example, adherents of the other religions to act rightly and thus gain salvation. For example, it is common in Orthodox Judaism to contend that while Judaism has the truth about the Almighty, people in other faiths can still be saved. They can be if they know of and adhere to the seven Noachide laws (a set of fundamental socioethical norms). Other religions might be of use and value if they preach the Noachide laws, even though the truth about God is in Judaism.[4]

In committing themselves to these nonegalitarian perspectives on religion, it is essential for confessionalists to take a particular stand on the epistemological issues raised by religious diversity discussed earlier in this chapter. They must assume that peer conflict does not significantly dent their well-grounded confidence in the truth of their confession's beliefs. Either the apologetic obligation can be met by, and on behalf of, their confession, or it can be successfully sidestepped (as, for example, per Plantinga).

Pluralism

Pluralism is a return to an egalitarian view of the cognitive successes and failures of human religions. Pluralism can flow from a form of agnosticism. Suppose we accept the validity of the apologetic obligation, judge it not to be met, but conclude that there is enough to be said in favor of the generic belief in a sacred, transcendent reality to avoid atheism.[5]

Pluralism views all, or at least the major, religions as partial successes or as mitigated failures. It can be summed up in three propositions: (1) All major forms of religion are equal in respect of making common reference to a single, transcendent sacred reality; (2) they are likewise equal in respect of offering some means or other to human salvation; And (3) all religious traditions are to be seen as containing revisable, limited accounts of the nature of the Ultimate; none is certain enough in its specific dogmatic formulations to provide the means of interpreting the others.

Pluralism is a kind of quasi-realist interpretation of religion. Yes, religions are in large measure the product of the human imagination set in unique cultures, but they are not wholly so. There is some accumulation and overlap among them. By far the most widely discussed version of a pluralist theory of religion is that of Hick (2004).

Concepts of Ultimate Reality

Philosophers reflect on and develop conceptions of God, or the Ultimate. The fact of religious diversity provides a particular input to such reflection and development. It does so more especially for those who respond to diversity in a pluralist or inclusivist spirit. Thinkers in both of these camps will maintain that believers in many different faiths succeed in establishing cognitive contact with the sacred, transcendent reality postulated by religion. The contact will be in one or more of these dimensions: experience of the divine; descriptions of the divine that have some verisimilitude; ethical and religious practices that provide right orientation toward the divine; worship, contemplation, or prayer that contains a successful reference to the divine. The general problem that this claim to panreligious success raises can be stated thus: How can such success be possible given that there are deep incompatibilities among (and within) religions on the matter of what the Ultimate is like? Crudely, we can ask, how can incompatible accounts of the Ultimate all have some measure of truth when they contradict one another?

Hick's version of pluralism produces a radical, and much debated, solution to the above nest of problems. He distinguishes between the Ultimate (which he calls "the Real") as it is in itself and as it appears to human beings through the lens of the particular religious traditions to which human beings belong. The distinction recalls Kant's distinction between the world as it is in itself and as it appears to human beings. Hick's distinction is based on the Kantian thought that human modes of cognition (in this instance, the conceptual structure supplied by a religious tradition) shape our awareness of reality. Since we cannot but cognize the Ultimate via the concepts furnished by a given human tradition, we cannot have an unmediated apprehension of it. Hick calls this postulate of a distinction between the Ultimate in itself and as it appears to us "the Pluralist Hypothesis" (see Hick

2004, chaps. 14–15). With it there goes a reinterpretation of truth in religion. At one level, different religions have pictures of the divine that are true of different manifestations of the Real, for there are many ways in which the Real appears to human beings in history, and the different religions contain true accounts of those different phenomenal manifestations. At another level, different religions contain metaphorically true accounts of the Ultimate as it is in itself, and for that metaphorical truth, incompatibilities among their accounts literally interpreted do not matter. This is because metaphorical truth in this context is, for Hick, a form of pragmatic truth. A religion is true of the Real in itself insofar as its concepts and practices provide a successful way of orienting its followers in behavior; that is, it puts believers on a path toward genuine moral and spiritual transformation. Hick calls this theory of religious language and truth a "mythological" reading of them (Hick 2004, chap. 19).

There are other paths that pluralists who are not impressed by Hick's mythological theory can tread. A less radical move than Hick's "appearance versus reality in itself" distinction consists in viewing the divine as similar to a natural kind. A natural kind, such as water, has a real essence (its molecular structure) that is invariant, but it manifests different, and incompatible, sensible qualities in different environments. In one set of circumstances, it is a solid (ice); in another, it is a liquid (normal water); and in a third, it is a gas (water vapor). In a corresponding fashion, the Ultimate might be one while manifesting itself to human beings now as personal God or now as an impersonal absolute. This is the notion that the one transcendent, sacred reality is one but has many aspects. Different religions provide pictures of different aspects. This multiaspectual view of the Ultimate is explored by Byrne (1995), McKim (1988), and Ward (1987).

The reflections on the nature of the Ultimate summarized thus far best fit pluralist responses to diversity, for they entail that the accounts of the Ultimate in existing religions are quite radically incomplete or limited. Confessional inclusivists need not go so far. One way of securing the aims of inclusivism in the face of the fact that the other religions contain accounts of the divine that seriously conflict with that found in the favored confession consists in separating reference from truth. What matters to the inclusivist may be that the faithful in other religions use concepts and symbols that refer to the divine. By this means, they can be said to worship it and pray to it and perhaps experience it (although the experiences are not wholly veridical). It is possible to argue that in many nonreligious cases, successful reference can be made to an entity through false descriptions. Reference can be established through contextual factors in the absence of descriptive adequacy. This point can then be applied to the religious case. Thus, it is possible for the Christian inclusivist to conclude that the faithful Muslim refers to the one true God in his or her prayers and worship, although his or her account of that being's nature contains many errors, judged from the Christian standpoint.[6] This is another method whereby descriptive adequacy and truth in the theologies of the different religions can be downplayed in order to maintain some convergence among faiths despite theoretical conflicts among them.

Religion and the Human Good

In the pursuit of affirming convergence among faiths despite theoretical conflicts among them, both inclusivists and pluralists will typically maintain that people in different religions can be on a path to salvation/liberation. Once this last commitment is made, it almost inevitably brings with it another one: the claim that there is a wide measure of agreement on matters of moral good and right across the major religions. This alleged moral consensus is something that allows for the affirmation of a degree of convergence among the religions despite the many things that divide them. Hick affirms the moral convergence of the faiths as part of his pluralism, telling us that there is a range of moral values that all of the major religions agree on (Hick 2004, chap. 18). They agree that a life of generous goodwill, love, and compassion is the constitutive means of attaining both the human good and a life lived in authentic relation to the Ultimate.[7]

Although this commitment to moral convergence beneath doctrinal differences is widespread among pluralist and inclusivist interpreters of religion, it is not without its critics. D'Costa is one who has argued that the commitment is based on a superficial reading of the moral teachings of the great world religions (see D'Costa 1993). The commitment fails to appreciate that it is only when viewed at a misleading level of generality that the moral values of the different religions can be seen as the same. To illustrate, while we might say that both Christianity and Theravada Buddhism are committed to a life of self-renunciation as the best and the most liberating, on close examination, we find divergence. For the Christian, the life of self-renunciation is one of loving God through loving the other self that is one's neighbor, while for the Buddhist, self-renunciation is a matter of seeing through the illusion behind the "fact" of enduring, separate selves (see D'Costa 1993, 94).

The difference of opinion noted above is part and parcel of a larger debate in ethical theory between what might be called universalists and particularists. The former affirm that there are substantive moral values (rules and principles) that transcend different moral traditions; there is a common moral sense among humankind. The latter insist that moral values are constituted in their definite meaning only against the backdrop of tradition-bound forms of awareness and thought. The writings of Alasdair McIntyre have been influential in shaping such particularism.[8]

However we judge the truth between universalists and particularists, it is evident that moral universalism is an important component of a typical pluralist and inclusivist outlook. Without it, it is very hard to see convergence within the diversity of faiths.

NOTES

1. For a fuller and more detailed list, see Byrne 1995, 2–16.
2. For a contemporary defense of these assertions, see Zamulinski 2003.

3. See Craig 1989 for a contemporary Christian form of exclusivism.

4. See Solomon 1993.

5. What might be said in favor of this generic belief is John Hick's argument that moral transformation in the major world faiths is evidence of human interaction with ultimate reality; for Hick's epistemic strategy, see the overview in Twiss 1990.

6. See Alston 1989 and Miller 1986 for versions of this theory.

7. Compare Solomon's Jewish inclusivism, described above.

8. See McIntyre 1988; surveys of aspects of the debate can be found in Kent 1994 and Byrne 1995, 103–105.

REFERENCES

Alston, William. 1989. "Referring to God." In *Divine Nature and Human Language*. Ithaca, N.Y.: Cornell University Press, 103–117.

Basinger, David. 2002. *Religious Diversity: A Philosophical Assessment*. Aldershot, U.K.: Ashgate.

Byrne, Peter. 1995. *Prolegomena to Religious Pluralism*. Basingstoke, U.K.: Macmillan.

———. 1999. "The Definition of Religion: Squaring the Circle." In J. Platvoet and A. Molendijk, eds., *The Pragmatics of Defining Religion*. Leiden, Neth.: Brill, 379–396.

Craig, William. 1989. "'No Other Name': A Middle Knowledge Perspective on the Exclusivity of Salvation through Christ." *Faith and Philosophy* 6: 172–188.

D'Costa, Gavin. 1993. "Whose Objectivity? Which Neutrality? The Doomed Quest for a Neutral Vantage Point from Which to Judge Religions." *Religious Studies* 29: 79–95.

Flew, Anthony. 2005. *God and Philosophy*. New York: Prometheus.

Griffiths, Paul. 1991. *An Apology for Apologetics*. Maryknoll, N.Y.: Orbis.

Hick, John. 2004. *An Interpretation of Religion*, 2nd ed. Basingstoke, U.K.: Palgrave.

Kent, Bonnie. 1994. "Moral Provincialism." *Religious Studies* 30: 269–285.

MacIntyre, Alasdair. 1988. *Whose Justice? Which Rationality?* Notre Dame, Ind.: University of Notre Dame Press.

McKim, Robert. 1988. "Could God Have More than One Nature?" *Faith and Philosophy* 5: 378–398.

Miller, Richard 1986. "The Reference of 'God.'" *Faith and Philosophy* 3: 3–15.

Plantinga, Alvin. 2000. *Warranted Christian Belief*. New York: Oxford University Press.

Schellenberg, John. 2007. *The Wisdom to Doubt*. Ithaca, N.Y.: Cornell University Press.

Solomon, Norman. 1993. "Is the Plurality of Faiths Problematic?" In A. Sharma, ed., *God, Truth and Reality*. Basingstoke, U.K.: Macmillan, 189–199.

Swinburne, Richard. 1989. *Responsibility and Atonement*. Oxford: Clarendon.

———. 1993. *The Coherence of Theism*, 2nd ed. Oxford: Clarendon.

———. 1994. *The Christian God*. Oxford: Clarendon.

———. 1998. *Providence and the Problem of Evil*. Oxford: Clarendon.

———. 2003. *The Resurrection of God Incarnate*. Oxford: Clarendon.

———. 2004. *The Existence of God*, 2nd ed. Oxford: Clarendon.

———. 2007a. *Faith and Reason*, 2nd ed. Oxford: Clarendon.

———. 2007b. *Revelation*, 2nd ed. Oxford: Clarendon.

Twiss, Sumner. 1990. "The Philosophy of Religious Pluralism: A Critical Appraisal of John Hick and His Critics." *Journal of Religion* 70: 533–568.

Ward, Keith. 1987. *Images of Eternity*. London: Darton, Longman and Todd.

Zamulinski, Brian. 2003. "Religion and the Pursuit of Truth." *Religious Studies* 39: 43–60.

FOR FURTHER READING

DiNoia, Joseph. 1992. *The Diversity of Religions*. Washington, D.C.: Catholic University Press of America.

Gellman, Jerome. 2000. "In Defence of a Contented Religious Exclusivism." *Religious Studies* 36: 401–417.

Kraft, James. 2007. "Religious Disagreement, Externalism and the Epistemology of Disagreement: Listening to Our Grandmothers." *Religious Studies* 43: 417–432.

McKim, Robert. 2001. *Religious Ambiguity and Religious Diversity*. New York: Oxford University Press.

Netland, Harold. 1991. *Dissonant Voices*. Grand Rapids, Mich.: Eerdmans.

Quinn, Phillip. 1995. "Toward Thinner Theologies: Hick and Alston on Religious Diversity." *International Journal for the Philosophy of Religion* 38: 145–164.

Quinn, Phillip, and Kevin Meeker, eds. 2000. *The Philosophical Challenge of Religious Diversity*. New York: Oxford University Press.

Runzo, Joseph. 1993. *World Views and Perceiving God*. Basingstoke, U.K.: Macmillan.

CHAPTER 4

A SOCIOLOGICAL APPROACH TO QUESTIONS ABOUT RELIGIOUS DIVERSITY

MICHELE DILLON

RELIGIOUS DIVERSITY IN THE UNITED STATES AND EUROPE

RELIGIOUS diversity has many faces. In the United States, from as early as the late eighteenth century, a broad array of Protestant denominations highlighted the religious pluralism of American society, a dynamic fostered by the populist ideas of individualism and freedom associated with the American Revolution. With a cultural emphasis on the fact that religion was "the people's choice" (Hatch 1989, 6), Americans have long been religious shoppers, moving from one church to another and innovatively starting new churches—Christian Science, Mormonism—to express their own particular sense of theology. This ethos took many new directions in the 1960s: a loosening of immigration restrictions opened up new patterns of Eastern immigration into the United States, Vatican II opened up a new emphasis for Catholics on religious freedom, and the cultural mood of the 1960s accentuated individual freedom in everyday choices and lifestyle, including new self-oriented understandings of religious authority and spiritual fulfillment. The impact of these converging and transformative changes has been immense, such that today, at the beginning of the twenty-first century, the diversity of American religion is again in the headlines. Report after report (e.g., Pew Forum 2008a, 2008b) documents some new twist on the American narrative of religious vitality, a vitality first observed by the French nobleman and philosopher Alexis de Tocqueville during his travels through the eastern part of the country in the 1840s. De Tocqueville was particularly impressed with the way in which religious institutions and individual freedom intertwined in American society. Unlike in France, where Enlightenment ideas of modern democracy translated into freedom *from* the controlling power of religion, in America, de Tocqueville found, "the spirit of religion and the spirit of freedom . . . were intimately united and . . . reigned in common" (1848/1951, 308). This spirit appears to endure; the United States is the most religious country in the Western world, with the exception of Ireland and Poland, whose very different histories account, in part, for the continuing though notably declining relevance of religion in those societies.

What is new about contemporary trends in the United States, however, is that unlike the case in the nineteenth and early twentieth centuries, religious diversity has stretched beyond the denominationalism and the church-based beliefs and practices largely contained historically within the walls of Christianity. We catch a glimmer of the new and changing character of religious diversity when we look at patterns of religious affiliation. Protestants (of varying denominations) still dominate in the United States, making up 51 percent of the population, but for the first time in American history, they are on the verge of becoming a minority (Pew Forum 2008a); in the 1970s, for example, Protestants accounted for close to 70 percent of the population (Lyons 2005). Catholics account for 24 percent of the American population.

Beyond the secure foothold of these Christian traditions, other religions, though a small minority (5 percent), are also present. And, reflecting the emerging public recognition of a new religious diversity, they are beginning to be numerically counted by polling organizations (e.g., Pew) in a more comprehensive way than in the past, when Jews and others were relegated to the category of "other," their numbers too small for the sampling and statistical techniques used by many sociologists. The latest count confirms their small numbers but nonetheless important presence: Jews at 1.7 percent, Buddhists at 0.7 percent, Muslims at 0.6 percent, and Hindus at 0.4 percent (Pew Forum 2008a, 5).

Amid this mosaic of belief, the most striking fact is the substantial proportion of Americans who are religiously unaffiliated. For many decades, about 7 percent described themselves as religiously unaffiliated, but this figure has more than doubled since the 1990s; it is now true of 16 percent. Among the religiously unaffiliated, however, there is a lot of religious and spiritual activity. Large proportions of unaffiliated and of non-churchgoing Americans express belief in God or a universal spirit (70 percent), life after death (48 percent), and miracles or the supernatural (55 percent); many engage in regular prayer (44 percent) or meditation (39 percent) (Pew Forum 2008b, 26–48). Furthermore, many Americans, some churchgoing and some not, are also committed to spiritual practices that blend ideas and rituals adapted from a mix of religious and spiritual traditions (see Roof 1999; Dillon and

Wink 2007). Further complicating American religious diversity are substantial numbers among the religiously affiliated whose doctrinal beliefs and political attitudes deviate from the official theological views articulated by church leaders (see D'Antonio et al. 2007; Greeley and Hout 2006). In sum, as a large body of sociological research indicates, even the most homogenized religious/spiritual group is likely to be characterized by a certain amount of diversity in religious beliefs and practices, whether driven by gender, generation, region, race, cohort, or issue-specific variation.

EUROPEAN DIVERSITY: RETURN OF RELIGION

The situation in Europe, though very different historically and culturally from that in the United States, is no less complex. At the end of the twentieth century, it was deceptively easy to contrast Europe and the United States with a statement to the effect that whereas the United States was a highly religious society, Europe was largely secular—a contrast rooted in the different historical relations between church and state and in the institutionalization of religion more generally. Crossing the Atlantic from east to west is to move between two remarkably different societal and religious environments. But just as historical and sociological analyses of American religion are accused of having a Protestant bias (e.g., Carroll 2007), the received view of the decline of religion in Europe betrays, perhaps not surprisingly, a Eurocentric bias. This is one that construes Europe as settled, white, predominantly Christian—passively Christian now—and divided by national boundaries, to be sure, but immune to the vagaries of cultural otherness within its own territories. Empirically, this, of course, is not true. Muslims account for approximately 5 percent of the European Union's population (Pew Forum 2005, 3), a small minority overall but more pronounced in some member states, notably France (8 percent) and the Netherlands (6 percent). Despite decades of postcolonial immigration into several European countries (e.g., France, the Netherlands, the United Kingdom, Spain), for many Europeans, it took the events of September 11, 2001, to force an awareness that European culture and identity must increasingly reckon with a societal reality that includes not only racial otherness but also, even more strikingly, religious otherness in the guise of Islam.

For the French and the Dutch, in particular, their respective histories as colonizing powers—as the creators of colonized others (Said 1978)—have come back to undermine their preferred, highly secular understanding that civilized society means the privatization, if not the suppression, of religious identity. Thus, recent years have seen a steady increase in scholarly interest in understanding the varieties of European Islam and its interface in everyday practices with "native" (i.e., civilized) European cultural and political traditions. The puzzle presented by this new European religious-societal reality has salience beyond the academy; it also preoccupies European policy makers and political leaders. Recent controversies in France over the accommodation of religious symbols (e.g., Muslim scarves/veils) in public institutions and public spaces point to the poverty of an overaccentuated Enlightenment heritage that is unable to accommodate a modern reality in which religion not only has not disappeared but also presents itself in ever more diverse forms. It is historically and culturally ironic that in France today, many French Muslims find a haven in Catholic secondary schools, which are ranked among the country's best (Bennhold 2008a).

Notably, France's highest administrative court has ruled that the wearing of an Islamic veil (the hijab) is a legitimate barrier to French citizenship (Bennhold 2008b). It would seem that France's long-established project of secular rationalism cannot avoid undermining in practice the very freedoms that secular democratic societies are supposed to guarantee: freedom of expression, including religious expression. Given the long tradition of anti-clericalism in France, perhaps it is not surprising that the Catholic Church in France has emerged as a supporter of Muslim women's right to wear full-face veils. French bishops have argued that the rights of all believers to practice their faith must be protected, and that France must protect the rights of its Muslims if it wants Muslim countries to do the same for their Christian minorities. The complexity entailed in crafting a civil society which successfully balances secular principles and the freedom of religious expression is further highlighted by the fact that in Turkey, a long-established Muslim secular democracy, educated elites vigorously protested the government's recent elimination of the ban on women wearing head scarves at university (Tavernise 2008).

Taken as a whole, these various trends caution against any brief summation regarding the sociological character and significance of religious diversity in contemporary society. But we can explore sociological frameworks that help illuminate why religious diversity can lead to cultural conflict as well as to institutional accommodation—core questions of interest more generally to sociologists.

THE SOCIAL CONTEXT AND POWER OF SACRED SYMBOLS

As the controversies over Muslim veils illustrate, the public face and much of the public's awareness of religious diversity are filtered through the mosaic of symbols that demarcate religious differences. Symbols are powerful precisely because they are collective representations; their significance derives, as George Herbert Mead underscored, from the fact that their meanings are socially shared by a particular collectivity: "A symbol is nothing but the stimulus whose [interpreted] response is given in advance" (1934, 181). It is through symbols that societies, groups, and communities demarcate the sacred from the profane. Emile Durkheim expansively construed religion as including all of those things that a society deems sacred, that is, all of those things demanding reverential awe, "What makes a thing holy is . . . the collective feeling attached to it" (1912/2001, 308). What is deemed sacred, therefore, does not inhere in the thing itself but is so defined by the particular society: "Since neither man nor nature is inherently sacred, this quality of sacredness must come from another source" (76). Because that source is society, Durkheim argues, "it is the unity and the diversity of social life that creates both the unity and the diversity of sacred beings and things" (309).

Amid this diversity, symbols produce group identity and cohesion among those who "share a common conception of the sacred world and its relation to the profane world. . . . Religious beliefs proper are always held by a defined collectivity that professes them and practices the rites that go with them. These beliefs are not only embraced by all the members of this collectivity as individuals, they belong to the group and unite it. The individuals who make up this group are bound to one another by their common beliefs" (42–43).

Accordingly, in everyday life, shared symbols can exert a unifying force, integrating individuals in solidarity with others of similar identity. For example, one recent study (Haddad 2007) finds that certain young American Muslims, the daughters of immigrant Muslims, use the hijab to project a public Islamic identity that both affirms an American Islamic identity—including trust in the American protection of freedom of religious expression—and expresses an anticolonial solidarity with other Muslims against hegemonic efforts in the West to demonize Islam. Symbols rarely have only one use, however. Given that, as Durkheim underscores, it is the social setting that determines what is deemed sacred and how the sacred is represented and demarcated from the profane, we expect any given symbol to be deployed differently depending on its social-generational-cultural context. Williams and Vashi (2007) point to the multiple uses of the hijab among young American Muslim women. In using the veil to negotiate a Muslim-American identity, these young women are simultaneously demarcating a generational identity that differentiates them from their parents and a cultural identity that distinguishes them from their non-Muslim age peers.

Religious Diversity and Cultural Boundaries

The distinction Durkheim draws between the sacred and the profane also anticipates the specter of religious intolerance. If shared adherence to the sacred reflects, produces, and affirms the unity of the collectivity, by the same token, what is defined as profane by a particular collectivity can produce resilient religious boundaries in contexts in which one collectivity or society categorizes another's religion as profane. The awe toward the in group's sacred things can translate into disdain toward the profane, the out group. It is not surprising, then, that in an increasingly diverse environment, many religious-cultural conflicts are energized by the contestation of religious symbols. The sacred symbols of one religious group are, or become, profane symbols for those who are not members of that group. Thus, from the perspective of French secularists, Muslims' public wearing of the veil in France is seen as a profane rather than a sacred act; religious diversity translates into cultural divisiveness. The proposed building of an Islamic mosque and cultural center close to the site of the World Trade Center in New York City which was destroyed by terrorist attacks on September 11, 2001, is also controversial. While some observers see it as evidence of American religious pluralism and tolerance, others see it as a profane symbolic assault on American culture and values.

It is noteworthy too that in England, a highly secular society—notwithstanding the peculiar anomaly of having the queen as the head of both church and state— ethnic and religious conflicts converge in disputes over building permits for mosques. With a dramatic rise in the number of mosques in England—from 613 in 1997 to close to 1,000 in 2003 (Pew Forum 2005, 9)—sites designated for new mosques literally become contested sites. Their symbolism threatens English notions of authentic English culture; locals express "unease at minarets competing in the urban landscape with the spires and stones of centuries-old cathedrals" (Perlez 2007, 13).

Despite the many postcolonial cultural hybrids that characterize contemporary British society and the new normalcy of the idea that, for example, being black *and* British is an actual lived identity (see Hall 1990), Paul Gilroy's caution that "There is no black in the Union Jack" (1987) reminds us that cultural identities, though negotiable, are contested and resisted. Today's new racism, based on cultural rather than biological distinctions, is no less exclusionary than past definitions (Gilroy 2000). Any analysis of contemporary forms of racism must necessarily include an examination of what might be called religious racism, the institutional and symbolic exclusion of religious individuals and groups from full participatory citizenship in society based on a rationale of cultural difference. The argument, sometimes more implicit than explicit, that the cultural values and practices of the religious other (e.g., religiously active Muslim women in France) make them so at odds with the dominant culture that they should be excluded from mainstream society seems to carry more of the legacy of racist than of secular thinking. Secularism, after all, in its democratic republican frame, seeks to accommodate rather than exclude religion.

It should also be acknowledged, moreover, that religious prejudice exists across many different societies. My examples thus far have concentrated on Western countries' dilemmas in accommodating Islam. Yet it is, of course, also the case that Arabic societies have great difficulty in acknowledging religious pluralism, not to mention institutionalizing minimalist accommodations toward the freedom of religious expression. Non-Muslims, for example, are not allowed to visit the holy mosques of Mecca and Medina in Saudi Arabia, and "it is illegal to build a church, a synagogue or a Hindu or Buddhist temple in Saudi Arabia, or to practice any of these religions publicly" (Friedman 2007, 12). In defending these prohibitions, "the Saudi authorities cite a tradition of the prophet Muhammad that only Islam can be practiced in the Arabian peninsula" (Friedman 2007, 12). Clearly, despite the impact of globalizing economic processes in contributing to the diminishment of economic and cultural borders (especially evident in Dubai, e.g.), several cultural boundaries remain intact; these lines of cultural difference are often most readily seen when we gaze toward religion.

Political Culture and the Practical Challenges Posed by Religious Diversity

For many decades in the United States and in Europe, it was relatively easy to accommodate religious denominational and ethnic divisions around common symbols such as those embodied by a nation's flag. In a highly influential and controversial article, Robert Bellah (1967) used the term "civil religion" to refer to the relatively nonsectarian civic-political ceremonies and rituals (e.g., presidential inaugurations, State of the Union addresses) that characterize the public life of American society. Influenced by Durkheim and by Talcott Parsons's (1967) emphasis on the functional significance of generalized value commitments in integrating modern societies, Bellah saw these events as symbolically powerful ways through which to affirm the overarching unity of the nation (indivisible, under God), notwithstanding partisan political conflict (itself a value affirmed by the nation's founding ideals).

In current times, the invocation of phrases such as "God bless America" and the convening of the leaders of church and state at formal civil religious ceremonies—as occurs, for example, once a year at a Red Mass celebrated by the Catholic archbishop of Washington, D.C., to mark the opening of the judicial calendar in October and attended by members of the judiciary and the executive branch—have become more complicated. If the power of civil religion is its effectiveness in unifying across political differences and institutional divisions, how can the long-established civil religion that appears so culturally natural to most Americans be modified to be inclusive of the new religious diversity that is the growing social reality? The answers to this question are not at all obvious.

The findings from recent studies of attitudes toward religious diversity offer mixed evidence toward the possibility of bridging religious differences in either civil society or everyday life. On the one hand, Americans are notoriously tolerant of a wide range of religious beliefs. Large majorities of religiously affiliated individuals say that many religions can lead to eternal life (70%), and that there is more than one true way to interpret the teachings of their particular religion (Pew Forum 2008b, 4). On the other hand, however, as Robert Wuthnow (2005) shows, a large proportion of Americans whom he calls "Christian exclusivists" (34 percent), demonstrate a tribal religiosity characterized by strongly drawn, in-group/out-group boundaries. Exclusive Christians, many of whom are college graduates, recognize other people's freedom to worship, but they are nonetheless guided by the compelling truth to "firmly defend what they regard as an old-fashioned, exclusivist version of the gospel truth" (Wuthnow 2005, 159). This includes the belief that "Christianity is the only way to have a true personal relationship with God," a view endorsed by 78 percent of Christian exclusivists (197). Similarly, approximately two-thirds of Christian exclusivists agree with the statement that "The United States was founded on Christian principles" (200). When even a small minority of individuals hold such exclusionary beliefs, it becomes difficult to establish public rituals and institutional practices that embody an inclusive pluralistic ethos.

Moreover, notwithstanding the symbolic value that many political and religious leaders attach to religious tolerance, there is a remarkable paucity of efforts among church leaders to initiate interreligious interaction. Wuthnow, using in-depth interviews with Christian pastors and leaders and members of Jewish, Muslim, Hindu, and Buddhist worship centers and organizations from various neighborhoods across the country, finds "insularity and largely ceremonialized contacts" in churches' responses to religious diversity (256). He argues that pastors and congregations "could do a lot better than they currently are in providing interfaith opportunities capable of attracting a significant share of their members" (233)

It remains to be seen how churches in the United States and Europe will respond to the challenges posed by a de facto religious diversity. For some time now, the sociology of religion has been dominated by a theoretical approach that emphasizes a market paradigm of church behavior. This framework, elaborated most notably by Finke and Stark (1992), argues that religious diversity nurtures religious competition. They use a supply-side model to argue that in religiously diverse and competitive religious marketplaces, such as the (Christian) United States in the nineteenth and twentieth centuries, the churches that thrived—that is, those that won a larger market share of religious adherents—were those that actively sought to win and maintain new members. In this view, competition, or diversity, fosters entrepreneurial activity on the part of religious organizations.

With a monopoly religious situation dominating historically in most European societies or regions (e.g., Catholic Ireland, Catholic France, Lutheran Germany), European churches did not have much motivation to compete for new members or to retain the ones they had. Hence the notable decline of religion in Europe and its contrast with the United States. The changing and more visible religious pluralism in Europe today might provide an incentive for all religious traditions—Christian, Muslim, Jewish, and so on—to seek actively to increase their share of religiously affiliated individuals. One effect of this might be to increase the vibrancy of European religion—at least, based on the relatively superficial indicator of church membership—and make it more comparable to the United States in levels of belief and practice. Yet, while a competitive market might well foster increased religious participation, the paradigm of competition might also suppress the motivation toward increasing interreligious dialogue and respect. Cooperation and collaboration, not competition per se, are what is required if a spirit of cultural inclusion is to be created amid religious diversity.

The impetus toward the practical accommodation of religious diversity might find an ally in current globalization processes. The unprecedented global flows in population, culture, and ideas that are accompanying economic globalization are already making their mark in societies that heretofore were relatively homogeneous. Part of the disruptive effect of globalization is that it pushes the implosion of old habits and attitudes as local communities and national governments necessarily adjust to the changes wrought in a globalizing society. While cultural defensiveness against new immigrants and their beliefs and habits is one response, another is cultural accommodation.

This is, in fact, what we currently glimpse in Ireland. The increased presence of African immigrants working and living in Ireland has caused some tensions, but it has also given rise to an emergent de facto religious pluralism that one might not have expected in a society in which for many decades the special position of the Catholic Church was upheld in the Constitution and reflected in state laws (on divorce, etc.). Yet today, the Irish government has endorsed the view, held by a (slim) majority of the Irish people, that Muslim students should be free to wear the hijab in state schools (O'Brien 2008). This is a small but highly significant symbolic step on the path toward institutional and cultural accommodation to religious diversity. Perhaps it can become a model for other societies for which ethnic and religious diversity is more normative historically but nonetheless threatening.

Some scholars argue that the nation-state is losing its authority as a result of globalization processes and the attendant rise of transnational and supranational organizations (e.g., Bauman 2000). Yet the creation of a civil religious environment that affirms religious diversity in practice is one critical task that the state, acting both within its own territory and in alliance with other states (e.g., through the EU), can vigorously tackle. Its task lies, as Habermas notes, in ensuring a postsecular space in which tolerance is "practiced in everyday life. Tolerance means that believers of one faith, of a different faith and non-believers must mutually concede to one another the right to those convictions, practices, and ways of living that they themselves reject" (Habermas 2008, 7). There are limits, however, to what the state or other institutions can accomplish in nurturing a political culture of religious tolerance (see Dillon 2010). Religious differences give rise to and embed differences in worldviews, institutional practices, and everyday habits. These differences matter, as I discuss below.

RELIGIOUS WORLDVIEWS AND PRACTICAL ACTION

It is important to recognize that the origins and sociohistorical development of the different world religions have given rise to each institutionalizing different worldviews - different ways of seeing the world and the nature and place of action in the world. This is a topic that Max Weber wrote about extensively based on his detailed comparative-historical analyses of the five world religions (Christianity, Judaism, Islam, Buddhism, Hinduism). Weber differentiated between theocentric or personal-God-centered religions (e.g., Christianity, Judaism, Islam) and cosmocentric, impersonal orientations (e.g., Buddhism). Theocentric religions construe human beings as God's instruments who engage in practical rational action in this world as a way of glorifying God. By contrast, cosmocentric religions, according to Weber, nurture a world-rejecting ethic, seeing this-worldly material action as an impediment to the illumination necessary to "escape from the wheel of karma-causality . . . a search that is, and can only be, the highly individualized task of a particular person" (Weber 1909–1920/1978, 627). The distinction drawn between theocentric and cosmocentric religions accounts for major cultural differences in how one approaches the world. Additionally, among the theocentric world-oriented religions, there is also variation. The different historical and geographical contexts in which, for example, Christianity and Islam emerged gave rise to their different ways of rationalizing action in this world, and these respective differences in motivations for social action produce different practical consequences (a point to which we return below).

How are we to account for the diversity of religiously driven social action and to make sense of it, especially when so many practices might appear as nonrational and lacking intelligibility—such as veiling, polygamy, celibacy? For Weber, if we are to understand social action, we must immerse ourselves in knowing what motivates it; we need to understand the subjectively meaningful frames that drive action. If we do this, Weber advises, then we will appreciate the complexity and meaningfulness of behavior that otherwise might appear to us as unfathomable. We will also come to recognize that differences in worldviews can constitute divides that are not always easily, if at all, bridgeable.

Weber himself modeled his interpretive methodology in his studies of world religions. In *The Protestant Ethic and the Spirit of Capitalism* (1904–1905/1958) Weber explored what appeared to be intertwined puzzling facts: the preponderance of Protestants over Catholics in business and industrial occupations and the extent to which the character of modern capitalism (approximately from the seventeenth through the mid-nineteenth centuries) was marked by a frugal asceticism regarding the wealth accumulated through hard work; this contrasted with material acquisition in preindustrial eras which was driven by individuals' basic survival needs and also differed from the greed of adventurers and pirates.

What might initially appear to us as nonrational behavior—working hard but not enjoying the fruits of one's labor—becomes intelligible and appears, in fact, as rational behavior once Weber unearths the motivations underlying the Calvinists' habits. He shows how the early Calvinists' beliefs, specifically their beliefs in glorifying God, predestination, and their attendant concerns about salvation, led them to rationalize their everyday conduct in this world as proof to themselves and others of their salvation in the next world. Their religious beliefs led them to construe this-worldly work as a calling, a rational, purposive vocation to be followed methodically in glorifying God, and anything that interfered with work was to be suppressed (e.g., leisure, spontaneous enjoyment). Thus, a rational commitment to frugality and hard work became a meaningful way for Calvinists to act on their commitment to God (and to deal with their uncertainty about salvation), a rational process that, in turn, indirectly contributed to the expansion of capitalism. The Calvinists thus acted rationally on and in this world not to acquire this-worldly success for the sake of success but as proof of their otherworldly salvation.

Like Protestantism, Islam also is a theocentric, this-world-oriented religion. But, Weber argues, the this-worldliness of the Calvinist contrasts with the this-worldliness that came to characterize Islam. Weber accentuated the differences among religions in order to draw out and analytically contrast their practical implications. He thus proposed ideal typical characterizations which he used as heuristic constructs rather than as empirically validated types (Weber 1903-1917/1949). Accordingly, in this framing, Weber argued that if the ideal typical Protestant is the industrialist, the ideal typical Muslim is the warrior. Discussing the Islamic worldview, Weber states:

> In the evolution of the early Islamic communities, the religion was transformed . . .
> into a national Arabic warrior religion. . . . The religious commandments of the
> holy war were not directed in the first instance to the purpose of conversion.
> Rather the primary purpose was war 'until they (the followers of alien religions of
> the book) will humbly pay the tribute (*jizyah*),' i.e., until Islam should rise to the
> top of this world's social scale, by exacting tribute from other religions. . . . The
> ideal personality type in the religion of Islam was not the scholarly scribe (*Literat*,
> [in Judaism]), but the warrior. (1909–1920/1978, 624–626)

It is unfortunate in the contemporary moment that Weber's accentuation of the Muslim warrior, taken out of its analytical context, feeds into the anti-Islamic biases that have come to the fore since September 11, 2001. Weber's larger and more useful point, however, is that religions—and groups, institutions, societies, and so on—have different histories and different cultural rationales that give rise to different worldviews and institutional structures and that it is impossible to understand or explain social and institutional practices without appreciating the cultural engines that drive those practices. Thus, for example, we can achieve a better understanding of current public controversies in France over veiling once we reframe the controversies as clashes of worldviews and make an attempt to trace where those worldviews originate and migrate. If we were to embark on this task, we might come to see that it is rational for France's urban affairs minister, herself a Muslim of Algerian descent, to argue: "The veil is not a religious insignia but the insignia of a totalitarian political project that promotes inequality between the sexes and is totally lacking in democracy." By the same token, we might come to see that it is equally rational for the veil-wearing Moroccan-French Muslim woman who is seeking citizenship to argue: "I wear the niqab because . . . it is my choice. I take care of my children. I leave the house when I please. I have my own car. Yes, I am a practicing Muslim, I am Orthodox. But is that not my right?" (Bennhold 2008b).

In this instance, both protagonists are speaking a language of rights and equality, but they differ in how they construe, interpret, and apply those rights. This difference likely comes from the different social and institutional contexts in which these two Muslim women move and, as Weber would also highlight, from the different authority structures that legitimate worldviews in any given social context (e.g., the state versus the family). Different worldviews, and the contexts of meaning and power in which those worldviews get expressed, make some interpretations more intelligible and practical than others. When there is a clash of worldviews (as also seen in the ongoing abortion debate in the United States), it is very difficult for the state and other institutions (the courts, schools, etc.) fully to accommodate competing perspectives. The hegemonic worldview—whether cultural Protestantism in the United States (e.g., Parsons 1967), secularism in France, or opposition to Christianity in Saudi Arabia—is the one more likely to win out. The recent political uproar in the United Kingdom in response to the Anglican archbishop of Canterbury's pluralistic suggestion that Britain should think about adopting aspects of Islamic sharia law in its courts' dealings with religious Muslims (Burns 2008) is a case in point.

Conflicts in worldviews such as those concerning veiling or other religious-social practices also point to the importance of recognizing the concrete social intersectionality of all lived experiences. Patricia Hill Collins (1990), a leading feminist sociological theorist, emphasizes how experiences are shaped and interpreted based on the interlocking gender, race, social class, and other social forces situating individuals. Different intersectional contexts give rise to different experiences and different contradictions and how these contradictions are and can be negotiated. Ethnic Muslim professional women whose job it is to uphold the secular values of the French state as lawyers and political officials will most likely experience inequality differently from Muslim immigrant working-class women. Recognizing that an individual is never simply a Muslim but a Muslim woman, a Muslim unemployed immigrant woman, and so on, thus cautions us against assuming a priori the existence of worldviews that are intellectually pure. Worldviews, rather, are always complicated by the intersecting social locations (of age, gender, race, social class, sexuality, religion, etc.) that shape an individual's reality and from which it is experienced.

The sociological approach, then, is to identify the particular historical and sociocultural contexts that make some worldviews and institutional responses to those worldviews more culturally meaningful and more practical than others. Hence the need for many diverse case-by-case and comparative case studies of how religion orients social and political action. In Iran, for example, religious individuals are more likely than their less religious fellow citizens to have a religious-political worldview that favors clerical rule and state enforcement of Islamic rules (Tezcur and Azadarmaki 2008, 220). The religiously committed, nonetheless, are not acquiescent toward the Iranian government; as Tezcur and Azadarmaki's research shows, "pious Tehranis are not necessarily the ones who attend state-sponsored Friday prayers." Moreover, they argue, "there are no a priori reasons to expect that religious Iranians are less likely to support reformers than less or nonreligious citizens" (221). In sum, as Weber demonstrated, religious worldviews shape social and political action, but the course and consequences of that action are highly contingent on the sociohistorical and political circumstances contextualizing beliefs and action.

CONCLUSIONS

Religious diversity is likely to increase in the United States and Europe over the next several decades. Several social forces will shape its contours and character. Sociologists will necessarily be attentive to how changing demographic patterns (e.g., fertility, migration); globalizing economic, political, and cultural processes; and shifts in the institutional fortunes of religious groups and organizations affect what is already a highly differentiated religious and spiritual landscape. Undoubtedly, diverse religious symbols will enrich public culture even as their apprehension, negotiation, and contestation will variously fuel local, national, and transnational debates. It remains unknown whether we can eke out sufficient common ground across, and tolerance of, different religious worldviews in our attempt to refashion institutional and cultural practices that can forge community out of diversity.

I am grateful to Chad Meister for his helpful comments on an earlier draft of this chapter.

REFERENCES

Bauman, Zygmunt. 2000. *Liquid Modernity*. Cambridge, U.K.: Polity.

Bellah, Robert. 1967. "Civil Religion in America." *Daedalus* 96: 1–21.

Bennhold, Katrin. 2008a. "Spurning Secularism, Many French Muslims Find Haven in Catholic Schools." *New York Times*, September 30.

———. 2008b. "A Veil Closes France's Door to Citizenship." *New York Times*, July 19.

Burns, John. 2008. "Top Anglican Seeks a Role for Islamic Law in Britain." *New York Times*, February 8.

Carroll, Michael. 2007. *American Catholics in the Protestant Imagination*. Baltimore: Johns Hopkins University Press.

Collins, Patricia Hill. 1990. *Black Feminist Thought: Knowledge, Consciousness, and the Politics of Empowerment*. New York: Routledge.

D'Antonio, William, James Davidson, Dean Hoge, and Mary Gautier. 2007. *American Catholics Today: New Realities of Their Faith and Their Church*. Walnut Creek, Calif.: AltaMira.

De Tocqueville, Alexis. 1848/1951. *Democracy in America*, vol. 1. New York: Knopf.

Dillon, Michele. 2010. "Can Post-Secular Society Tolerate Religious Differences?" *Sociology of Religion* 71: 139–156.

Dillon, Michele, and Paul Wink. 2007. *In the Course of a Lifetime: Tracing Religious Belief, Practice, and Change*. Berkeley: University of California Press.

Durkheim, Emile. 1912/2001. *The Elementary Forms of Religious Life*, Carol Cosman, trans. Oxford: Oxford University Press.

Finke, Roger, and Rodney Stark. 1992. *The Churching of America: Winners and Losers in the Religious Economy*. New Brunswick, N.J.: Rutgers University Press.

Friedman, Thomas. 2007. "Democracy's Root: Diversity." *New York Times*, November 11.

Gilroy, Paul. 1987. "There Ain't No Black in the Union Jack." In *The Cultural Politics of Race and Nation*. London: Hutchinson.

———. 2000. *Against Race: Imagining Political Culture beyond the Color Line*. Cambridge, Mass.: Harvard University Press.

Greeley, Andrew, and Michael Hout. 2006. *The Truth about Conservative Christians*. Chicago: University of Chicago Press.

Habermas, Jürgen. 2008. "Notes on Post-Secular Society." *New Perspectives Quarterly* (Fall): 1–12.

Haddad, Yvonne Yazbeck. 2007. "The Post-9/11 Hijab as Icon." *Sociology of Religion* 68: 253–267.

Hall, Stuart. 1990. "Cultural Identity and Diaspora." In Jonathan Rutherford, ed., *Identity: Community, Culture, Difference*. London: Lawrence and Wishart, 222–237.

Hatch, Nathan. 1989. *The Democratization of American Christianity*. New Haven, Conn.: Yale University Press.

Lyons, Linda. 2005. "Tracking U.S. Religious Preferences over the Decades." TheGallup Poll Tuesday Briefing (May 24). Washington, D.C.: Gallup Organization.

Mead, George Herbert. 1934. *Mind, Self, and Society*. Chicago: University of Chicago Press.

O'Brien, Carl. 2008. "Pupils' Right to Wear Hijab Is Backed by Almost Half Surveyed." *Irish Times*, June 9.

Parsons, Talcott. 1967. "Christianity and Modern Industrial Society." In Talcott Parsons. *Sociological Theory and Modern Society*. New York: Free Press, 385–421.

Perlez, Jane. 2007. "A Battle Rages in London over a Mega-Mosque Plan." *New York Times*, November 4.

Pew Forum on Religion and Public Life. 2005. *An Uncertain Road: Muslims and the Future of Europe*. Washington, D.C.: Pew Research Center.

———. 2008a. *The U.S. Religious Landscape Survey*. Washington, D.C.: Pew Research Center.

———. 2008b. *The U.S. Religious Landscape Survey: Religious Beliefs*. Washington, D.C.: Pew Research Center.

Roof, Wade Clark. 1999. *Spiritual Marketplace: Baby Boomers and the Remaking of American Religion*. Princeton, N.J.: Princeton University Press.

Said, Edward. 1978. *Orientalism*. New York: Random House.

Tavernise, Sabrina. 2008. "Move to lift ban on head scarves gains in Turkey." *New York Times*, February 10.

Tezcur, Gunes Murat, and Taghi Azadarmaki. 2008. "Religiosity and Islamic Rule in Iran." *Journal for the Scientific Study of Religion* 47: 211–224.

Weber, Max. 1903–1917/1949. *The Methodology of the Social Sciences*. Edward A. Shils and Henry A. Finch, trans. and eds. New York: Free Press.

———. 1904–1905/1958. *The Protestant Ethic and the Spirit of Capitalism*, Talcott Parsons, trans. New York: Scribner's.

———. 1909–1920/1978. *Economy and Society*, vol. 1, Guenther Roth and Claus Wittich, eds. Berkeley: University of California Press.

Williams, Rhys, and Gita Vashi. 2007. "Hijab and American Muslim Women: Creating the Space for Autonomous Selves." *Sociology of Religion* 68: 269–287.

Wuthnow, Robert. 2005. *America and the Challenges of Religious Diversity*. Princeton, N.J.: Princeton University Press.

FOR FURTHER READING

Habermas, Jürgen. 2008. "Notes on Post-Secular Society." *New Perspectives Quarterly* (Fall): 1–12.
University of London. "Re-emergence of Religion as a Social Force in Europe." www.
    relemerge.org.
Weber, Max. 1946. *The Social Psychology of the World Religions*. In H. H. Gerth and C.
    Wright Mills, trans. and eds., *From Max Weber: Essays on Sociology*. New York: Oxford
    University Press, 267–301.
Wuthnow, Robert. 2005. *America and the Challenges of Religious Diversity*. Princeton, N.J.:
    Princeton University Press.

PART II

KEY ISSUES RELEVANT TO RELIGIOUS DIVERSITY

A

THEOLOGICAL AND PHILOSOPHICAL ISSUES

CHAPTER 5

··

PLURALISM AND RELATIVISM

··

JOSEPH RUNZO

AN ever-increasing awareness of religious diversity inevitably raises religious and philosophical issues about pluralism and relativism in religion. Those already in a religious tradition can no longer ignore the religions of others, much less the variant strands of religious belief and practice within their own tradition. Sunnis are not Shiites, Pure Land Buddhists are not Rinzai Zen Buddhists, Advaita Vedantists are not Bhakti Hindus, and not all Christians believe in the literal transubstantiation of the Eucharist. Likewise, the antireligious (including Schleiermacher's "cultured despisers") can no longer facilely dismiss religious belief under one lump rubric. But then, how should we go about comparing, contrasting, and evaluating the claims of the diverse traditions, strands, offshoots, geographic variations, and cultural variants of the world's religions?

One's religious beliefs seem largely an accident of birth. If you are born in Japan, you are likely to be a Buddhist; if you are born in Indonesia, you are likely to be a Muslim; and if you are born in Brazil, you are likely to be a Christian. About one-third of the world's population are nominal Christians (one out of every six humans is Roman Catholic), one-fifth are Muslim, one-sixth are Hindu, and one out of every eighteen humans is Buddhist. There are millions of Sikhs, Jains, Mormons, and Baha'i and about 14 million Jews. In addition, there are large indigenous traditions, such as Shinto in Japan and Yoruba in western Africa, the latter group with a large diaspora in the Americas giving it almost as many adherents as all of Buddhism. Yet none of these traditions has an even distribution around the globe. Christianity has never made significant inroads into the large populations of Japan, China, and India or into the heartland of Islam across northern Africa and central Asia. Likewise, Islam has not been particularly successful in the Americas or Russia or East Asia. Hinduism is only dominant in India, and the Chinese traditions of Confucianism and Daoism are primarily influential in the areas of the world directly affected by Chinese culture, including Korea, Japan, Vietnam, Cambodia, and Malaysia.

The world's religious traditions hold conflicting views about the nature of both the transcendent and human destiny. These mutually conflicting systems of truth claims all appear rationally justified, and each tradition has produced moral exemplars and religious saints. But since the religious tradition that one follows is largely determined by such factors as where and when one was born, one's ethnic background, and past colonial influences on one's culture, this raises doubts about the veracity of any religious claims to the sole truth. What is referred to as the problem of religious relativism is this: Is only one system of religious truth claims correct, or is more than one system correct as religious pluralists and relativists claim, or are all religious systems mistaken?

History of Pluralism/Relativism

Relativism holds that truth or value or methods of inquiry must be evaluated relative to a society or culture or worldview and that some or all truth or value or methodologies cannot be evaluated by "objective" standards apart from a specific social or cultural or worldview context. In the West, this theory was first developed in the ancient Greek world (Jains developed this idea even earlier). Heraclites famously said, "You can never step in the same river twice"; Protagoras said, "Man is the measure of all things"; and variations of human behavior and thought led the Skeptics to deny that general standards apply to all people.

Relativistic attitudes of ancient Greece became marginalized in the Roman Empire by a wide acceptance of Platonic and Neoplatonic absolutism and of Judeo-Christian dogmatic views of revelation but reemerged during the Renaissance in more pluralist ways of thinking. Both the Reformation and the fascination with the "Oriental" ways of the Ottoman Empire further undermined the sense of one monolithic truth or right practice. Hume's *Natural History of Religion* (1757) generated interest in viewing religion as a human activity that is relative to culture, an approach developed further by J. G. Herder, who influenced Hegel, Schleiermacher, and Nietzsche. But the most important influence on modern pluralist philosophical perspective can be traced to Immanuel Kant's distinction between *phenomena* and *noumena* and his emphasis on the mind's ineluctable conceptual contribution to experience.

This pluralist revolution would become more relativistic in the American pragmatism of figures such as William James, who declared in *The Varieties of Religious Experience* (1902): "why in the name of common sense need we assume that only one . . . system of ideas can be true? The obvious outcome of our total experience is that the world can be handled according to many systems of ideas." Ludwig Witt-genstein's later emphasis on the variety of coherent language games influenced British and American philosophical thinking throughout the latter half of the twen-tieth century, while American philosophers such as Nelson Goodman, W. V. O. Quine, Nicholas Rescher, and Richard Rorty continued the pragmatist influence.

Parallel relativistic ideas developed in anthropology, sociology, psychology, and historical critical methodology in the work of, for example, Fuerbauch and the History of Religions school, whose exponent Ernst Troeltsch concluded: "a study of the non-Christian religions convinced me more and more that their naive claims to absolute validity are also genuinely such. I found Buddhism and Brahminism espe-cially to be really humane and spiritual religions, capable of appealing in precisely the same way to the inner certitude and devotion of their followers as Christianity" (1957, 52). This was joined by pluralistic approaches in linguistic theory (e.g., the Wharf hypothesis), literary criticism (which influenced Rorty), and relativistic work in the philosophy of science by Paul Feyerabend, Paul Hansen, and, most notably, Thomas Kuhn, who argued in *The Structure of Scientific Revolutions* (1996) that the incrementally changing "normal science" can undergo revolutions or "par-adigm shifts," leaving scientists working in different paradigms.

These pluralist trends in Western thought brought it closer to the long-standing Asian traditions of philosophical pluralism. Hinduism, the oldest extant world religion, has the inclusive idea of *istadevata* ("the god of one's choice"). As one Rig Vedic hymn says, "Truth is One, though the sages know it variously" (*Ēkam sat vipra bahudā vadanti*). Even though Buddhism explicitly rejected the Hindu ideas of *atman* ("soul") and Brahman, Hinduism treats Sakyamuni Buddha as one of the ten avatars of Vishnu. Buddhism itself prescribes *upaya* ("skillful means") to explain Buddhist principles to non-Buddhists using terms Buddhists would not ordinarily accept. The Edicts of King Ashoka, the famous Hindu convert to Buddhism, state: "All religions should reside everywhere, for all of them desire self-control and purity of heart" (Rock Edict 7). Jainism, the other major "Axial Age" offshoot of Hinduism, espouses the doctrine of *anekantavada* ("non-onesidedness"), which holds that all views are subject to revision. In the Chinese traditions, Daoism has always been inclusively flexible, and there is a pluralistic openness in Neo-Confucian religiosity.

One of the most significant modern events in the movement toward religious pluralism and relativism was the First Parliament of the World's Religions in Chi-cago in 1893. While the archbishop of Canterbury refused to attend because of his view that Christianity was the only true religion, the Zen master Soyen Shaku and the Hindu Swami Vivekananda, among others, dispelled the negative caricatures that Western practitioners had constructed of Asian practitioners. However, from the late nineteenth century until the 1960s, the Roman Catholic tradition went through the "Modernist Crisis," a term first used in Pope Pius X's 1907 Encyclical *Pascendi Dominici Gregis*, in which scientific methods of archaeology, literary and historical criticism, and other modern critical methodologies were prohibited, and critical engagement with other religious traditions was discouraged. Still, by 1965, the Vatican II Dogmatic Constitution *Nostra Aetate* declared: "The Catholic Church rejects nothing which is true and holy in [the other world religions]. She looks with sincere respect upon those ways of conduct and of life, those rules and teachings which ... often reflect a ray of that Truth which enlightens all men."

Roman Catholicism has taken an official inclusivist position, illustrated as we will see below by the ideas of Karl Rahner and Gavin D'Costa. However, Paul Knitter and the most influential exponent of religious pluralism, Protestant philosopher of religion John Hick, have come under severe criticism from Pope Benedict XVI. And among Protestants, there is a divide between more conservative exclusivists, such as Richard Swinburne and the reformed epistemologist Alvin Plantinga, and the relativists and pluralists such as Hick and Knitter. Even more than Christianity, Islam has experienced deep resistance to "modernist" thinking, although Abdolkarim Soroush introduced pluralism to Islamic philosophy by using the work of the Sufi poet Rumi.

Finally, a number of more recent world religions, such as the Sikh and Bahai'i traditions, have been pluralistic from their foundation. Sri Guru Granth Sahib says, "One who recognizes that all spiritual paths lead to the One shall be emancipated," and "Do not say that the Vedas, the Bible and the Qur'an are false. Those who do not contemplate them are false." Bahai'ís believe that God's will is revealed progressively to humankind through messengers such as Abraham, Moses, Krishna, Buddha, Jesus, Muhammad, and Baha'u'llah, the founder of the faith, who himself urged religious tolerance.

Responses to the Problem of Religious Pluralism

A religion or religious tradition is a set of symbols and rituals, myths and stories, concepts and truth claims, which a community believes give ultimate meaning to life, via its connection to an ultimate reality or transcendent such as God or Nirvana. World religions are traditions that are concerned with the relation of all humans to a transcendent, they have persisted over time and spread worldwide, and they accept converts. Every religion involves beliefs at two levels: (1) the meta-belief that the religion in question provides access to a transcendent reality, which gives meaning to life, and (2) specific beliefs about the nature of that ultimate reality and the way in which it gives meaning to life. The first level is shared by the world religions, while the second is a point of conflict among them.

Even though all world religions have borrowed from other traditions, the vital core beliefs of one world religion are often prima facie incompatible with the vital core beliefs of other world religions. This raises a number of possible basic responses to the problem of religious pluralism. At the opposite extremes are:

1. *Religious antipathy*: All world religions are mistaken, and their vital core beliefs are false.
2. *Religious exclusivism*: Only one world religion is correct, and any conflicting vital core beliefs of all others are false.

Then there are the pluralist responses:

3. *Religious pluralism*: Ultimately, all world religions are correct, each offering a different path to salvation/liberation and each offering a partial perspective on the one ultimate reality.
4. *Religious inclusivism*: Only one world religion is fully correct, but other world religions participate in or partially reveal some of the truth of the one correct religion.

Then there are the relativist responses:

5. *Religious subjectivism*: Every individual perspective within each world religion is correct, and every individual perspective is correct and incontrovertible insofar as it is good for the individual who adheres to it.
6. *Religious relativism*: At least one world religion is correct, and the truth of any religion's truth claims is relative to the worldview(s) of its community of adherents.

And then there is the nonexclusivist fideist response:

7. *Religious henofideism*: One has a faith commitment that one's own world religion is efficacious for accessing the transcendent, while acknowledging that other world religions might also be efficacious.

RELIGIOUS EXCLUSIVISM VERSUS RELIGIOUS PLURALISM

Confronted with the conflicting truth claims among the world religions, religious traditions can take on a strong religious exclusivism that holds that salvation (or liberation) can only be found inside a particular institutional structure, exemplified by the traditional Roman Catholic dogma *Extra ecclesiam nulla salus*, or can only be found within a particular religious tradition, exemplified by Karl Barth's Protestant declaration that "the Christian religion is true, because it has pleased God, who alone can be the judge in this matter, to affirm it to be the true religion" (1956, I/2, 350).

Alvin Plantinga defends a strong version of Christian exclusivism on the basis of a reformed epistemology that argues that Christian truth claims are warranted because Christians acquire beliefs that are properly basic and do not need further justification, just as we acquire true perceptual beliefs that are properly basic. Even if this view of the proper basicality of Christian beliefs is correct, it does not seem to warrant Christian exclusivist claims, since the adherents of other religious traditions can also claim that their fundamental religious beliefs are properly basic and can be epistemically properly held without any justifying reasons. David Tien has argued that on Plantinga's model of warrant, the Neo-Confucianist Wang Yangming's very different religious beliefs are equally warranted (2004). Moreover, religious beliefs are not like basic perceptual beliefs insofar as there is far more disagreement over the former.

Plantinga attempts to shore up his account of Christian belief warrant by appealing to Calvin's notion of a *sensus divinitatis*. Stephen Hales explains this notion and responds:

> Calvin's argument for the universality of the sensus divinitatis is the widespread
> acceptance of some sort of religion in all cultures and locations. Even the fact of
> pagans, heretics, and animists Calvin took as a sign of a crude use of the groping
> toward the truth of the Christian god. . . . The apparent fact that there is a
> universal tendency to form religious beliefs does not show that there is a truth-
> conducive human faculty that allows us to apprehend the divine, any more than
> our propensity to accept the gambler's fallacy shows that there is a reliable
> human faculty to estimate probabilities. (2006, 51)

Plantings also defends his view by saying:

> I will use the term *exclusivism* in such a way that you don't count as an exclusivist
> unless you are rather fully aware of other faiths, have had their existence and their
> claims called to your attention with some force and perhaps fairly frequently, and
> have to some degree reflected on the problem of pluralism, asking yourself such
> questions as whether it is or could be really true that the Lord has revealed
> Himself and His programs to us Christians, say, in a way in which He hasn't
> revealed Himself to those of other faiths. (1995, 195)

But once again, it would seem that the adherent of another religion could use the same reasoning, mutatis mutandis, and arrive at the same warrant for his or her views. Also, what would it mean to be "fully aware" of other faiths? Merely knowing about the alternative metaphysics or knowing about the rituals of other traditions would not be sufficient, since being religious is not simply a cognitive affair. And while Western traditions tend to adhere to orthodoxy, Asian traditions tend to be orthopraxic. Would one need to live among those of other faiths, or even immerse oneself in another religion, to be fully aware of other faiths?

PLURALISM AND RELIGION

Nicholas Rescher defines pluralism as the doctrine that any substantial question admits of a variety of plausible but mutually conflicting responses. In particular, on Rescher's account, epistemic pluralism "raises the question of whether the truth is something that admits not only of different *visions* but of different *versions*, whether there are different and incompatible truths or simply different and incompatible opinions regarding the monolithic truth" (1993, 79). Epistemic pluralists hold that we have no direct access to "the Truth" and that our conceptions of truth are dependent on the conceptual scheme or worldview that we bring to experience.

Modern pluralist approaches to religion are usually grounded in epistemic pluralism. But even apart from this epistemic thesis, certain historical factors lend support to a religious pluralist perspective that there are a variety of plausible but mutually conflicting responses to fundamental religious questions and also call into question the plausibility of religious exclusivism. Not only, as Plantinga acknowledges, is the religious tradition a person follows usually a product of where and when he or she was born, but religious traditions themselves emerge out of other traditions. Thus, Hinduism arose out of Indo-Aryan religious traditions interacting with the indigenous traditions of India around 1500 BCE, contemporary Confucianism has Daoist and Buddhist influences, Christianity arose in the first century CE from Hebrew religious traditions in the context of both Greek philosophy and Zoroastrian ideas (e.g., hell and a last judgment), and Islam draws on both Hebrew and Christian scriptures. Additionally, individual lives contain religious transitions. Some people convert to another tradition, many people change sectarian commitments within a tradition, and many modify their religious outlooks by borrowing concepts, rituals, myths, and even scriptural sources from other traditions. Finally, there is the diversity of religion within each tradition. There are Mahayana and Theravada Buddhists, Sunni and Shiite Muslims, Advaita Vedantist and Bhakti Hindus, Roman Catholics and Calvinists and Coptic Christians.

RELIGIOUS PLURALISM AS INCLUSIVISM

One pluralist response to the problem of religious pluralism is religious inclusivism, which can be divided into "closed" and "open" versions. Representing the former, Gavin D'Costa illustrates his idea of how the Christian inclusivist should encounter other religious traditions with the following lines from T. S. Eliot:

> We shall not cease from exploration
> And the end of all our exploring
> Will be to arrive where we started
> And know the place for the first time. (D'Costa 1986, 137)

This is a "closed inclusivism," because there is a closed circle that precludes extensive transformation of one's own tradition through contact with other world religions, treating interaction with other traditions as a way to enhance one's already held views.

A more accepting view of the value of other traditions and of what they might add to one's own religious understanding is found in "open inclusivism," which is held, for example, by Karl Rahner in his proposal that adherents of religious traditions other than Roman Catholicism can be "anonymous Christians." For Rahner and other Christian open inclusivists, a Buddhist might be progressing toward the salvation that Roman Catholicism articulates (just as for a Buddhist open inclusivist, a Christian could be an "anonymous Buddhist" who is progressing toward liberation). Rahner says that the Christian has, "other things being equal, a still greater chance of salvation than someone who is merely an anonymous Christian" (1966, 132). The open inclusivist is not proposing a syncretic religion. As the Dalai Lama has said of Christianity and Buddhism, "If [the] view of integration envisions all of society following some sort of composite religion which is neither pure Buddhism nor pure Christianity, then I would have to consider this form of integration impossible" (Gyatso 2001). But still, as Brian Hebblethwaite says, speaking from the side of Christian open inclusivism, "The Christian has no monopoly of the ways of God with humankind. There may well be forms of the religious life that encapsulate and manifest values understressed in the Christian traditions. Christianity's historically dynamic and eschatologically oriented moral faith needs to be complemented by Eastern cosmic wisdom" (1992, 13).

RELIGIOUS PLURALISM

Wilfred Cantwell Smith proposed a pure form of religious pluralism that greatly influenced the modern discussion. Smith argued that the notion of "religion," particularly the notion of "a religion," is obsolete (1978). He held that, in fact, the only global universals or "givens" are God and humanity. Consequently, in his view, the emphasis we place on religion as a central conception is misguided, and, more especially, the conception we do have of a religion as a belief system is mistaken. Smith reached the pluralist conclusion that there is one truth about the religious life of humankind and that it is conveyed in the various forms of religious traditions—such as Buddhism, Christianity, and Islam—which are not fundamentally belief systems but expressions of apprehension of the divine and our humanity (1981, 3–20). This assumes that there is a universal, innate experience or conception of the divine. However, Smith himself argues against Christian exclusivism by asking how one could possibly know that only the Christian faith is correct. But this same reasoning could be applied to Smith's own position. How could one be sure that there is a global, innate apprehension of God and humanity, especially given nontheistic traditions such as Buddhism (which also has the notion of *anatman* or "no-self")?

The most impressive religious pluralism has been developed by John Hick, who, citing Jalalu'l-Din Rumi's statement that "the lamps are different, but the light is the same," argues that the post-Axial religious traditions constitute different ways of experiencing, understanding, and relating to ultimate reality, "which transcends all our varied visions of it" (1989, 235–236). Hick follows Smith's rejection of the idea that a religion is fundamentally a set of beliefs, proposing instead that religion definitively concerns "the transformation of human existence from self-centredness to Reality-centredness" (1989, 164). He argues that the conflicting truth claims of the world's religions are ultimately irrelevant and that the world religions can be reconciled through this more fundamental shared goal of moving from self- to reality-centeredness. Hick employs the Kantian thesis that all experience is structured by the mind and suggests that differences in religious awareness of ultimate reality result from differences in the religious concepts of the different traditions. Hick also suggests that religious truths should be understood as mythological truths, which, while not literally true, do evoke appropriate dispositional attitudes toward ultimate reality. In this way, the various world religions can all be conveying equally salvific or liberating mythological truth.

In Rescher's terms, Hick attempts to avoid the apparent conflict among the truth claims of the world religions by accepting different *visions* of ultimate reality while deemphasizing them as different *versions*. Now, some religions view ultimate reality as personal, while others hold the seemingly contradictory view that it is nonpersonal. Hick tries to reduce the cognitive significance of such apparently conflicting religious truth claims by arguing that "To the extent that [the religious notions of] a *persona* or *impersona* is in soteriological alignment with the Real, an appropriate response to that deity or absolute is an appropriate response to the Real" (1989, 248). As Peter Byrne notes, this religious pluralist outlook has three minimal elements: belief in the existence of a Transcendent, belief in "a basic cognitive equality" among traditions as a "vehicle of salvation," and agnosticism about "the specifics of any confessional stance toward religion" (1995, 11).

Hick's position has received considerable attention, and several kinds of objections have been raised. One objection is that most religious people intend their religious professions of belief to be making claims about reality. Consider the Christian faith. In general, it is part of the fundamental meta-belief (1) of religion that the ultimate reality or transcendent about which humans speak is real and not a metaphysical illusion or psychological delusion. And the conception of an essentially personal God or that Jesus Christ is the unique incarnation of the triune God is typically central to both corporate and individual Christian faith. Now, a personal reality might have nonpersonal aspects, but it could not be identical to something that is nonpersonal. Hence, Hick's pluralist account entails that the Christian's experience of a personal divine reality cannot correctly represent the nature of the real in itself. Moreover, unless some core religious truths are taken as literally true, Christians would not know what an appropriate response to the real would be. If the transcendent is not personal, then it is inappropriate to act as if the transcendent were personal (an implication with which Zen Buddhists would readily agree).

Another sort of objection has been raised by Gavin D'Costa, who suggests that Hick's "transcendental agnosticism" is actually a form of exclusivism (1996, 229). D'Costa argues that since religious people often make claims that the real has revealed itself, yet in Hick's view the real cannot be known in itself, this putatively tolerant religious pluralism is actually intolerant toward orthodox religious belief. In short, the argument is that the cognitive content of religious faith should not be deemphasized, for it is essential for providing a coherent view of reality as a basis for a purposive religious life and an effective guide to salvation/liberation. Thus, the notion of the imitation of Christ or of striving for Buddahood requires conceptual understanding (or in Buddhist terms, knowledge plus wisdom).

A different pluralist approach is suggested by Paul Knitter in his liberation theology of religions. Knitter is concerned with the efficacy of interreligious dialogue, since in his view, one cannot understand one's own religion without "conversations with others." In Knitter's liberation theology of religions, only where socioeconomic and spiritual liberation actually occur is the Divine present. For Knitter, the "truth" of religions consists in the degree to which they promote the life-transforming process of liberation.

In his *Theologies of Religions* (2002), Knitter addresses several models for interreligious understanding. The goal in the "Replacement Model" is to replace the differences in other traditions so as to bring the followers of these religions into the "unity of the Christian family." In the "Fulfillment Model," one affirms the "truth and beauty" of other religions but assesses that truth and beauty in one's own terms and hopes to bring greater value (fulfillment) to those other traditions by inviting them to be fulfilled in one's own tradition. In the "Mutuality Model," when features of another tradition are identified as insightful, that is because those same features are in one's tradition. Finally, in the "Acceptance Model," everyone is an unconscious inclusivist, always understanding other religious perspectives from one's own perspective, yet the other religious traditions of the world are to be accepted as "*really* different."

Unlike the other models, the Acceptance Model does not treat differences as something to get beyond but rather as something to be valued and learned from, so that differences are as valuable as similarities. Here the goal of interreligious dialogue is not to achieve a greater unity among religions but to respect their diversity and learn from it. Thus, Knitter would be opposed to D'Costa's choice of T. S. Eliot's poem to explain that we should approach other religious traditions in such a way that "the end of all our exploring will be to arrive where we started and know the place for the first time."

In general, pluralists most naturally approach the apparently conflicting truth claims of world religions from the perspective of a "global theology" that looks at religious traditions from an external or all-embracing point of view. (This is explicit in Hick 1982.) We can see this in Knitter's use of "theology"—which, arguably, does not properly apply to either Buddhism or Advaita Vedanta—to describe all religious traditions. But pluralism also accepts the historicity and the inherent enculturation of our thought, and this would appear to undermine the very possibility of being able to assume this global perspective and see each religion from an objective standpoint.

RELATIVISM AND RELIGIOUS RELATIVISM

There are descriptive, methodological, and normative forms of relativism. Descriptive relativism is the empirical thesis that different cultural groups have different modes of thought. Anthropological relativism is a methodology that attempts to understand other cultures within their local contexts and thereby avoid ethnocentrism. Normative relativism holds that evaluative claims about beliefs, standards of reasoning, or values are only right or wrong relative to a framework or worldview. For example, in defense of normative relativism, Stephen Hales argues, "It is no more incoherent to relativize the truth of propositions to perspectives given a perspectivist semantics than it is to relativize the truth of propositions to possible worlds given a possible worlds semantics or to relativize truth to languages given an array of languages" (2006, 106).

Subjectivism is the extreme relativist epistemological position that truth is relative to each individual's idiosyncratic worldview. In a subjectivist view, religion is a radically private affair, often understood as purely a matter of the individual's own relation to ultimate reality. However, it is usually argued that subjectivism is conceptually incoherent. Truth bearers are statements or propositions, and statements or propositions are made up of concepts. As Wittgenstein's "private-language" argument demonstrates, concepts are social constructions and cannot be purely private, individual understandings. Thus, since statements and propositions are made up of concepts and concepts are social constructs, truth cannot be idiosyncratically individualistic.

Religious relativism both accepts the ineluctable sociohistorical conditioning of one's perspective and tries to avoid the religious absolutism of exclusivism and closed inclusivism. For the religious relativist, meta-criteria such as the internal coherence of a worldview, its comprehensiveness and thoroughness of explanation, the efficaciousness of the worldview in producing its intended end, and its degree of parsimony can be applied across worldviews to assess the acceptability of each. Like open religious inclusivism, religious relativism recognizes that salvation or liberation *could* come to others in other traditions yet supports strong commitment to one's own tradition. While the pluralist attempts to solve the problem of religious pluralism by setting aside conflicting truth claims and emphasizing a universality and unity of all religions, the religious relativist attempts to resolve the problem of religious pluralism by accepting these conflicting truth claims as an appropriate manifestation of transcendent/human interaction. Modern religious relativism recaptures the relativist sentiments of the ancient Greek world in the face of religious diversity, follows the Kantian revolution in philosophy, and builds on, for example, the History of Religions perspective, and the pragmatist, Wittgensteinian, and Kuhnian currents in modern thought.

Two sources of resistance to religious relativism are the natural law tradition in the West and the Indic notion of dharma (to this might be added the notion of the Dao in the Chinese traditions). Regarding the former, Leo XIII was the first pope to use the word *relativism*, in the encyclical *Humanum Genus* condemning Freemasonry, while a century later, John Paul II emphasized the law of God in *Veritatis Splendor* and warned that man "giving himself over to relativism and skepticism, goes off in search of an illusory freedom apart from truth itself." Joseph Cardinal Ratzinger warned that the world was "moving towards a dictatorship of relativism," and as Pope Benedict XVI, he told educators that "today, a particularly insidious obstacle to the task of education is the massive presence in our society and culture of that relativism which, recognizing nothing as definitive, leaves as the ultimate criterion only the self with its desires" (2005). Turning to the dharmic notion of the eternally structuring laws (including moral laws) of the cosmos, this also tends to produce inclusivist rather than pluralist/relativist outlooks. Hindusm has the inclusive view that all *istadevata* are under the one dharma, and even the religiously tolerant Dalai Lama speaks about how fortunate a person is to be born in a Buddhist country (it is worth noting again that the Jain tradition of *anekantavada*, which is as old as Buddhism, is relativistic).

Religious pluralism and religious relativism share two underlying Kantian theses: the metaphysical division between noumena and phenomena, distinguishing, for example, between the transcendent in itself and the transcendent as humanly experienced; and the epistemic notion that all experience, and so all religious experience, is structured by the (culturally and historically conditioned) worldview of the percipient. Thus, religious pluralism and religious relativism hold that differences of religious perception cannot just be treated as a matter of some people simply being wrong about the nature of the divine reality but rather that such differences of perception are inherent to religious perception and conception.

However, religious relativism reasserts the central role of cognition in a religious life. In this view, the path to salvation or liberation is itself part of the salvific process, and one's cognitive religious worldview, as a guide for attitudes and actions, is inseparable from that path. To borrow a metaphor that Hick employs, pluralism holds that just as the historian does not have direct access to figures of history, and consequently different historians develop different perspectives on historical figures because they have different methods of inquiry, cultural backgrounds, and so on, so, too, different religious traditions, not having direct access to ultimate reality, offer different enculturated "images" of the one ultimate reality. Religious relativism not only allows with pluralism that the world's great religions could have the same telos, but it also allows for the likelihood that more than one of the conflicting sets of truth claims, which adherents of the differing world religions themselves regard as vital to their faith, is correct.

The religious relativist would admit that we cannot know with certainty that our ideas do properly refer to the transcendent, but it does not follow that the religious person is unjustified in his or her beliefs, nor does it follow that religious beliefs do not, in fact, properly refer to the transcendent. But perhaps the most common objection to normative relativism, which includes religious relativism, is that it is self-defeating because it is subject to the paradox of relativism: if all truth is relative, this "truth" of relativism cannot itself be absolutely true. However, Hales presents a "new-and-improved relativism," which holds that some propositions are absolutely true and that perspectival truth is also "real" truth. "Indeed, 'real' truth is just truth in this perspective, just as actual truth is truth in this world. Absolute truth turns out to be truth in all perspectives" (2006, 102). I offer a similar analysis of religious relativism in *Reason, Relativism, and God* (Runzo 1986). In these views, relativism and religious relativism are forms of pluralism in Rescher's sense.

A second sort of objection to religious relativism was raised by then-Cardinal Ratzinger. In his view, because normative relativism emphasizes the need to take into account the sociohistorical conditioning of human perspectives, it will lead to a less corporate, more egoistic manner of thinking and acting. Normative relativism might lead to a less corporate, more egocentric perspective. However, it might be difficult to show that it is pluralist or relativist religious thinking that is the problem in a narcissistic world and not, for example, a great increase in readily available, affordable material comforts. Pluralists and relativists seem to have no corner on narcissism, and even an anti-pluralist exclusivist could just as easily be a model of narcissism.

HENOFIDEISM

One type of henofideism is found in Jainism with its principle of *anekantavada* ("non-onesidedness"). In this view, claims to absolute truth will always be a form of *adhgajanyāyah*, the story of the blind men and the elephant, in which each blind man touches one part of the elephant yet thinks with his limited perspective (onesidedness) that he knows the appearance of the whole elephant. Unlike the open inclusivist, the henofideist does not emphasize the preeminence of his or her own tradition over others. Rather, the henofideist emphasizes his or her personal faith and commitment to his or her chosen tradition. Keith Ward expresses what might be characterized as a henofideistic Christian appraisal of other world religions. After rejecting Hick's religious pluralist assessment that all world religions are "equally authentic manifestations of ultimate truth," Ward suggests, "The rational course is to commit oneself to a tradition of revelation, which delivers one from the pretense that one can work out the truth entirely for oneself. Such commitment should, however, involve an acceptance that the Supreme Reality has not been silent in the other religions of the world, which delivers one from a myopia which confines God to one small sector of human history" (1994, 324).

Here, a strong faith commitment to a specific "tradition of revelation" is retained. Ward then employs an *anekantavada*-like perspective to explain his idea of a possible "convergent spirituality," a convergence of common core beliefs, which involves "an acceptance of the partiality and inadequacy of all human concepts to capture the object of [the quest for unity with supreme perfection] definitively" (1994, 339). Since the henofideist takes other world religions to be possible versions of the truth, the henofideist can engage in an open interaction with other traditions and be willing to synergistically shape his or her present religious understanding with understandings in other traditions.

INTERRELIGIOUS DIALOGUE AND MORAL MATTERS

One area where the specific response one has to the problem of religious pluralism makes a practical difference is in interreligious dialogue regarding ethical issues. Generally, pluralist perspectives are more conducive than antipluralist perspectives for open human dialogue about religion and ethics. Indeed, as shared problems of violence, tyranny, natural disasters, and pandemics have been more frequently addressed across religious and cultural divides, human-rights dialogue has, in turn, become a focal point for encouraging a pluralistic approach to ethical issues (Grelle 2005, 133). Exclusivist (and closed inclusivist) religious views might hinder interreligious moral dialogue if exclusivist religious communities are only open to other religious communities when there is consensus with their own traditional interpretations of morality. For example, Islamic exclusivists such as the "puritans" (e.g., Wahhabists) and the "apologists" (e.g., Sayyid Qutb) demand consensus about morality but find it only within the close confines of sharia and so reject dialogue with Western human-rights advocates.

In moral matters, sometimes the best consensus one can reach is to agree to disagree about the sources for ethics in order to act together morally to aid the poor, the vulnerable, and the oppressed. Arguing about whether God or dharma or self-cultivation is the reason to prevent genocide or aid the destitute, instead of working to prevent genocide or aid the destitute, would seem to be itself immoral. Similarly, religious groups that tightly tie desperately needed medical aid or education to proselytizing in developing countries devalue human-rights concerns in their desire for ideological truth consensus. The good news is that while there are many disagreements among the world religions about the kind of religious *reasons* that should be given to support moral judgments, from a shared disapprobation for stealing and murder to the general moral principle of the "golden rule," there is much moral consensus among the world religions. Further, a key point of moral agreement among the world religions is the emphasis on benevolence, or taking others into account in one's actions, not just out of self-interest but because one respects them as persons. And benevolent respect for others is itself a motive for open interreligious dialogue in the face of religious diversity.

REFERENCES

Barth, Karl. 1956. *Church Dogmatics*. Edinburgh: T. and T. Clark.
Benedict XVI. Address to the Ecclesial Diocesan Convention of Rome, June 6.
Byrne, Peter. 1995. *Prolegomena to Religious Pluralism: Reference and Realism in Religion*. New York: St. Martin's.

Copan, Paul, and Chad Meister. 2008. *Philosophy of Religion: Classic and Contemporary Issues*. Oxford: Blackwell.

D'Costa, Gavin. 1986. *Theology and Religious Pluralism: The Challenge of Other Religions*. Oxford: Blackwell.

———. 1996. "The Impossibility of a Pluralist View of Religions." *Religious Studies* (June): 223–232.

———. 2000. *The Meeting of Religions and the Trinity*. Maryknoll, N.Y.: Orbis.

Grelle, Bruce. 2005. "Culture and Moral Pluralism." In W. Schweiker, ed., *The Blackwell Companion to Religious Ethics*. Oxford: Blackwell.

Gyatso, Tenzin (His Holiness XIV Dalai Lama). 2001. "Buddhism and Other Religions." In M. Peterson, W. Hasker, B. Reichenbach, and D. Basinger, eds., *Philosophy of Religion*. New York: Oxford University Press.

Hales, Steven D. 2006. *Relativism and the Foundations of Philosophy*. Cambridge: MIT Press.

Hebblethwaite, Brian. 1992. "The Varieties of Goodness." In Joseph Runzo, ed., *Ethics, Religion and the Good Society: New Directions in a Pluralistic World*. Louisville, Ky.: Westminster.

Hick, John. 1982. "On Grading Religions." *Religious Studies* 17.

———. 1989. *An Interpretation of Religion: Human Responses to the Transcendent*. London: Macmillan.

———. 1993. *God and the Universe of Faiths*. Oxford: Oneworld.

———. 1999. *The Fifth Dimension*. Oxford: Oneworld.

Hick, John, and Paul F. Knitter. 1987. *The Myth of Christian Uniqueness: Toward a Pluralistic Theology of Religions*. Maryknoll, N.Y.: Orbis.

Hume, David. *The Natural History of Religion* (1757) in: *Dialogues and Natural History of Religion*, ed. by J.A.C. Gaskin (Oxford & New York: Oxford University Press, 1993).

James, William. 1902. *The Varieties of Religious Experience: A Study of Human Nature*. London: Longmans.

———. 1909. *A Pluralistic Universe*. New York: Longmans.

Knitter, Paul F. 1985. *No Other Name? A Critical Survey of Christian Attitudes toward the World Religions*. London: SCM.

———. 1995. *One Earth Many Religions: Multifaith Dialogue and Global Responsibility*. Maryknoll, N.Y.: Orbis.

———. 2002. *Theologies of Religions*. Maryknoll, N.Y.: Orbis.

Kuhn, Thomas. 1996. The Structure of Scientific Revolutions. 3rd edition. Chicago: University of Chicago Press.

Lewis, Charles M., ed. 1995. *Relativism and Religion*. New York: St. Martin's.

Plantinga, Alvin. 1995. "Pluralism: A Defense of Religious Exclusivism." In Thomas D. Senor, ed., *The Rationality of Belief and the Plurality of Faith: Essays in Honor of William P. Alston*. Ithaca, N.Y.: Cornell University Press, 191–215.

Race, Alan. 1983. *Christians and Religious Pluralism: Patterns in the Christian Theology of Religions*. London: SCM.

Rahner, Karl. 1966. *Theological Investigations*, vol. 5. Graham Harrison, trans. New York: Crossroads.

Ram-Prasad, C. 2001. "Multiplism: A Jaina Ethics or Toleration for a Complex World." In Joseph Runzo and Nancy M. Martin, eds., *Ethics in the World Religions*. Oxford: Oneworld, 347–369.

Rescher, Nicholas. 1993. *Pluralism: Against the Demand for Consensus*. Oxford: Oxford University Press.

Rorty, Richard. 1981. *Philosophy and the Mirror of Nature*. Princeton, N.J.: Princeton University Press.

Runzo, Joseph. 1986. *Reason, Relativism, and God*. London: Macmillan.

———. 2001. *Global Philosophy of Religion: A Short Introduction*. Oxford: Oneworld.

Smith, Wilfred Cantwell. 1978. *The Meaning and End of Religion*. New York: Harper and Row.

———. 1981. "A History of Religion in the Singular." In *Towards a World Theology*. Philadelphia: Westminster, 3–20.

———. 1982. *Religious Diversity*. New York: Crossroad.

Tien, David W. "Warranted Neo-Confucian Belief: Religious Pluralism and the Affections in the Epistemologies of Wang Yangming (1472–1529) and Alvin Plantinga." *International Journal for Philosophy of Religion* 55: 31–55.

Troeltsch, Ernst. 1957. "The Place of Christianity among the World Religions." In Baron R. Hugel, ed., *Christian Thought: Its History and Applications*. New York: Meridian.

Ward, Keith. 1994. *Religion and Revelation*. New York: Oxford University Press.

Wei-Ming, T. 1985. *Confucian Thought*. Albany: State University of New York Press.

Wittgenstein, Ludwig. 1958. *Philosophical Investigations*, G. E. M. Anscombe, trans. Oxford: Blackwell.

FOR FURTHER READING

Byrne, Peter. 1995. *Prolegomena to Religious Pluralism: Reference and Realism in Religion*. New York: St. Martin's.

Hales, Steven D. 2006. *Relativism and the Foundations of Philosophy*. Cambridge: MIT Press.

Hick, John. 1989. *An Interpretation of Religion: Human Responses to the Transcendent*. London: Macmillan.

Knitter, Paul F. 2002. *Theologies of Religions*. Maryknoll, N.Y.: Orbis.

Smith, Wilfred Cantwell. 1978. *The Meaning and End of Religion*. New York: Harper and Row.

Ward, Keith. 1994. *Religion and Revelation*. New York: Oxford University Press.

CHAPTER 6

......

RELIGIOUS EXCLUSIVISM

......

PAUL K. MOSER

It is no small task to specify clearly when something is a religion (and when something is not) and when we have one religion rather than two or more religions. Familiar candidates for a religion include, of course, Judaism, Christianity, Islam, Buddhism, Hinduism, Confucianism, Sikhism, Daoism, Shinto, and Baha'ism. Sometimes we call a system of claims of a particular kind a religion, and sometimes we call a human commitment of a particular kind a religious commitment.

In general, we might say that a commitment is religious for a person if and only if the commitment is intrinsic (that is, not merely instrumental toward something else) and is intended to be life-defining (that is, intended to be constitutive of living) for that person. This is a broad, latitudinarian approach to something being a religious commitment; it might even allow some intrinsic commitments of sports fans to their favorite sports to count as religious. This is no defect for current purposes, specifically for our asking: Can't all religions get along? This question is intolerably vague until we specify what getting along consists of. Perhaps advocates of various religions can get along even if religions cannot. We need to examine both (1) the sense in which religions can be exclusive and excluded and (2) the sense in which advocates of religions can also be exclusive and excluded. We shall see that some versions of religious exclusivism are undeniably true and that at least one version is undeniably false.

Exclusivism Clarified

......

Whatever else religions have, they obviously have diversity and even logical conflict in their religious statements, at least in comparisons across religions. Some religions affirm that God exists; others don't. Some religions affirm that just one God exists, others affirm that many gods exist, and still others claim that no God exists. Even among versions of monotheism, diversity and conflict in positions flourish. For instance, some versions of monotheism teach that God has and promotes love for all people, including even God's enemies; others deny this. In addition, some versions of monotheism hold that we humans must earn our approval before God; others deny this and affirm instead that God approves of people by way of a gracious divine gift. Of course, this is just a small sample of the extensive diversity and conflict in positions among religions. The history and the sociology of religions uncover such diversity and conflict in remarkable detail.

We can easily see that no complete thematic unity across religions is to be had, however much some people might allege otherwise. Taken together, the claims of the various religions are logically inconsistent; they can't all be true. (It is astonishing that anyone would suggest otherwise after even a cursory review of the religions in question.) Any available unity of religions will thus be at best partial, that is, incomplete. Even if, for example, Judaism and Hinduism in their most prominent forms can agree on some religious views, they disagree on monotheism. The monotheism of classical Judaism is denied, at least by implication, by the prominent versions of Hinduism. So, we should not expect both Judaism and Hinduism to be true; they are logically contrary religious positions, at least regarding some key religious claims. The same holds among many, if not all, other mainline religious positions. It follows that some mainline religious positions logically exclude some other mainline religious positions. This view might be called *logical religious exclusivism*, regarding logically contrary religious positions, and its truth cannot be denied with any plausibility. We will consider whether any other kind of religious exclusivism merits acceptance.

For the sake of manageable focus, we limit our talk of religion to theistic religions, that is, religions that acknowledge the existence of a divine agent. Let's also use the terms *divine agent* and *God* as maximally honorific titles that signify a being worthy of worship. The title *God*, given this use, connotes an authoritatively and morally perfect agent who is inherently worthy of worship as wholehearted adoration, love, and trust. This connoting holds, in keeping with titles generally, even if a titleholder does not actually exist; that is, the title *God* is intelligible even if it lacks an actual titleholder. Let's use *authoritative* to signify worthiness of an executive decision-making status in some area and *perfectly authoritative* to connote such inherent worthiness regarding every relevant area. So, one does not become authoritative just by acquiring power to control one's surroundings. One must be worthy if one is to have the status in question.

Some proponents of the traditional monotheism of Judaism, Christianity, and Islam use the term *God* as a title connoting a unique agent worthy of worship. Other proponents of such monotheism claim that their use of the title *God* connotes a unique agent worthy of worship, but they set the standard for worthiness of worship too low for actual moral perfection. For instance, some proponents of monotheism acknowledge a God who arguably lacks moral perfection, at least by the most compelling standard of such perfection, in virtue of their God's hating evil people. The writer (or writers) of Psalms 5:5 and 11:5, for example, claims that God "hates" wicked people and not just wicked thoughts, desires, intentions, or actions. The psalmist's view of a God who hates some people conflicts irredeemably with the portrait of God offered by Jesus's Sermon on the Mount, in Matthew 5:43–48 (Luke 6:27–36; John 3:16–17); in fact, Jesus appears to be correcting a misguided view of God offered by some of the Hebrew scriptures. (See Matthew 5:43–45: "You have heard that it was said . . . 'hate your enemy,' but I say to you, 'love your enemies . . . in order that you may be children of your Father in Heaven.'")

Jesus identifies God's love of even enemies of God as central to divine moral perfection, and this approach to moral perfection is preeminently commendable in virtue of excluding divine hate of people. Such hate would be destructive and condemning of people in a way incompatible with perfect moral goodness and thus with worthiness of worship. We may plausibly hold, then, that there is significant religious diversity and even conflict within the teachings of the Jewish and Christian scriptures and that a God who hates some people lacks moral perfection and therefore is not worthy of worship. Jewish and Christian monotheism, accordingly, comes in sharply conflicting varieties relative to the moral characters those varieties ascribe to God. Given the preeminent standard of worthiness of worship, we are well advised to rank the competing varieties by means of the required standard of moral perfection. By that standard, the perfectly loving God acknowledged by Jesus would, if real, trump the psalmist's God who hates some people. The God of Jesus, in any case, is a viable candidate for the title *God* that signifies worthiness of worship, but the psalmist's God is definitely not. The psalmist's God is morally too much like us wayward humans to be worthy of worship.

Monotheism seems more credible than polytheism, at least initially, because it is hard to find even one case of an agent who is morally perfect and worthy of worship. The various gods of the polytheist pantheon turn out to be too much like us morally imperfect beings, at least regarding their moral failings. In particular, these gods are similar to the hateful God of Psalms 5:5 and 11:5 in falling short of moral perfection and thus of worthiness of worship. Polytheists might find it convenient, or at least self-supporting, to relax the standard for being divine, but we then would divorce being divine from worthiness of worship, and the category of being divine would thereby lose its moral preeminence. This is a serious problem for the prominent versions of polytheism in circulation, and, as just suggested, some variations on monotheism also fall prey to it.

Logical religious exclusivism is altogether compelling, given the actual logically contrary claims made by various religions. It leaves us with the platitude that the claims of some religions logically exclude some claims of some other religions; that is, necessarily, if the claims of the former religions are true, then some claims of the latter religions are false. If this were the only species of religious exclusivism in circulation, our present topic would be easy; we then should all be avid religious exclusivists. Dissenters would be guilty of demonstrable logical confusions, and could be offered some straightforward logical corrections. Matters are, however, more complicated.

Some people propose what we might call *redemptive religious exclusivism*: the view that some religions are redemptively exclusive, that is, exclusive regarding the redemption, or salvation, of humans by God. Redemptive religious exclusivism offers two main variations: programmatic redemptive exclusivism and personal redemptive exclusivism. We need to clarify this distinction.

Programmatic redemptive exclusivism states that some *programs* for religious redemption exclude some other such programs. Consider a Jewish-Christian program that characterizes redemption as originating solely from divine grace (as a free-gift) through human faith. Such a program excludes any program that characterizes redemption as originating from the human earning of salvation from God via a righteousness of one's own, say, from one's obeying a law. Redemption originating solely from divine grace, at least in the Pauline Christian program (see Romans 4:4–5), logically excludes redemption originating from human earning in terms of one's own righteousness (see Philippians 3:9 and Romans 9:32 for Paul's suggestion that as a zealous Pharisee, he had promoted the latter kind of redemption originating from human earning). Necessarily, in other words, if the divine redemption offered to humans originates solely in a humanly unearned gift from God, then it does not originate in any human's own righteousness, including one's righteousness from obeying a law. The redemptive program offered by the Christian religion of the apostle Paul thus excludes the earlier redemptive program offered by the religion of Saul of Tarsus. (This does not suggest, of course, that all versions of Judaism agree with the Pharisaism of Saul of Tarsus; clearly, the Judaism of Jesus, for instance, did not agree.)

Programmatic redemptive exclusivism is a specification of logical religious exclusivism, regarding, of course, programs for religious redemption. Such redemptive exclusivism is undeniably true, given at least the logical conflict between the redemptive program of Saul of Tarsus and the later redemptive program of the apostle Paul. We could illustrate this kind of logical conflict across the redemptive programs of various religions, but we need not digress. Any sustainable philosophy or sociology of religion will embrace programmatic redemptive exclusivism.

Personal redemptive exclusivism states that given certain religions, some people are excluded from divine redemption or salvation. We need to distinguish between two positions:

1. *Hypothetical personal exclusivism*: If certain religions are correct in what they explicitly state or at least imply, then some people are excluded from divine redemption.
2. *Actual personal exclusivism:* Religion X is correct in explicitly stating or at least implying that some people are excluded from divine redemption.

Hypothetical personal exclusivism is undeniably true, because it is obvious that some religions deny universalism about salvation; that is, they deny that all people will be redeemed by God.

Consider, for instance, the Reformed Protestant predestinarian view of either John Calvin's 1536 *Institutes of the Christian Religion* or the 1647 Westminster Confession of Faith (while bracketing any theological differences between the two). Following the later Augustine, Calvin offered an influential predestinarian exclusivist position as follows: "By predestination we mean the eternal decree of God, by which he determined with himself whatever he wished to happen with regard to every man. All are not created on equal terms, but some are preordained to eternal life, others to eternal damnation; and, accordingly, as each has been created for one or other of these ends, we say that he has been predestinated to life or to death." (Calvin 1536/1989, Book 3, chap. 21, sec. 5)

Here's how the Westminster Confession of Faith, under the influence of Calvin's theology, puts an equivalent predestinarian exclusivist view, at least regarding humans:

> By the decree of God, for the manifestation of his glory, some men and angels are predestinated unto everlasting life, and others foreordained to everlasting death. These angels and men, thus predestinated and foreordained, are particularly and unchangeably designed; and their number is so certain and definite that it cannot be either increased or diminished. . . . The rest of mankind [beyond those foreordained to everlasting life], God was pleased, according to the unsearchable counsel of his own will, whereby he extendeth or withholdeth mercy as he pleaseth, for the glory of his sovereign power over his creatures, to pass by, and to ordain them to dishonor and wrath for their sin, to the praise of his glorious justice. (Schaff 1919b, chap. 3)

The clear implication (particularly of the second sentence just quoted) is that God's foreordaining activity makes some people "particularly and unchangeably designed" for "everlasting death." Calvin's corresponding idea is that God "determined with himself whatever he [that is, God] wished to happen" to each person, including each person excluded from salvation.

The Reformed exclusivist view implies that God in divine sovereignty foreordains, or predestines, some people to everlasting damnation rather than salvation and that this divine decision to exclude some people is ultimately *God's* own will and is thus *un*determined by human wills. In Calvin's way of putting the matter, what God wishes to happen to people who are not redeemed does, in fact, happen to them; that is, they are excluded by God from redemption, and this is by divine intent. Regardless of the questionable moral character of a God who would proceed in this way, we cannot plausibly deny that hypothetical personal exclusivism follows from some influential religious views. Such exclusivism, we shall see, also follows from some religious views that oppose predestinarian Calvinism and attribute the cause of redemptive exclusion to humans themselves who resist salvation.

Excluding God

Regarding any proposed version of actual personal exclusivism (as characterized above), the critical initial question is: On what basis, or in virtue of what, are some people (allegedly) excluded from divine redemption? One exclusivist Christian view, in keeping with the aforementioned Reformed predestinarian view, implies that some people are excluded from divine redemption in virtue of God's own decisively condemning sovereign will and that God's will in this connection is not determined by human wills. So, in this view, God is causally responsible for the exclusion of some humans, given that God intentionally wills their exclusion. Another exclusivist Christian view avoids a predestinarian view but implies that if an adult person of normal intelligence fails to believe a redemptive Christian message about what God has accomplished via Jesus Christ, then that person is thereby excluded from salvation. This view has been embraced by many Christians who hold that a person's lacking a specific belief about salvation excludes that person from salvation. We will see that both of these exclusivist views, the predestinarian and doxastic views, are actually implausible, because they exclude a God worthy of worship.

As noted above, we are using the term *God* as a preeminent title with definite semantic content, requiring worthiness of worship and thus moral perfection in its holder. We thus should ask how our corresponding notion of God bears on any proposed version of actual personal exclusivism. Let's consider the predestinarian variation first. It implies that God chooses to exclude some people from redemption on the basis of God's own sovereign condemning will and that this divine choice is not determined by any human will, such as a human will to oppose redemption. God, according to this predestinarian view, foreordains some people to be condemned and not to be redeemed by God, and this sovereign divine action causes the actual exclusion of these people from redemption. Some predestinarians invoke a dubious reading of chapter 9 of Paul's Epistle to the Romans for support, even though chapter 11 of Romans explicitly states that the unredeemed people in question are excluded on the basis of their own distrust, or unbelief, toward God (see Romans 11:20). Paul does not teach, in any case, that a sovereign divine choice itself causes some people to be excluded from salvation. On the contrary, Paul writes concerning God: "But of Israel he says, 'All day long I [God] have held out my hands to a disobedient and contrary people'" (Romans 10:21, citing Isaiah 65:1–2).[1]

A God worthy of worship, as suggested above, must be morally perfect; that is, worthiness of worship excludes moral deficiency of any sort. One who is morally defective in some way lacks the moral character needed for worthiness of adoration and complete trust. As a result, such a being lacks worthiness of worship. One who fails to be perfectly loving toward all people (when one could be so) is morally deficient, at least regarding one's failure to love others perfectly. In addition, if one condemns another person, even *one* other person, to destruction as *the* (intended constitutive) result of one's own will, then one fails to be perfectly loving toward the person condemned. Accordingly, one fails to be worthy of worship. One's perfect love toward a person excludes, by definition, one's condemning that person to destruction as *the* (intended constitutive) result of one's own will. So, if one excludes a person from redemption as the result of one's own will, then one fails to be perfectly loving and thus fails likewise to be worthy of worship. If, therefore, one excludes a person from redemption as the result of one's own will, one fails to be

God. The God of the aforementioned predestinarian position is thus not the true God; that position actually excludes the true God in excluding divine perfect love toward all human persons.

An influential representative of the aforementioned doxastic exclusivist view is the Christian trinitarian Athanasian Creed (ca. 500, according to many historians). The relevant affirmations of the Athanasian Creed are as follows:

1. Whosoever will be saved, before all things it is necessary that he hold the catholic faith;
2. Which faith, except every one do keep whole and undefiled, without doubt he shall perish everlastingly.
3. And the catholic faith is this: that we worship one God in trinity, and trinity in unity; ...
4. This is the catholic faith which, except a man believe faithfully, he cannot be saved. (Schaff 1919a)

The doxastic redemptive exclusivism of the Athanasian Creed is straightforward: if a person does not actually believe the Christian trinitarian faith in question, then that person "cannot be saved." Specifically, the required belief in question is irreducibly propositional: it is belief "that we worship one God in trinity, and trinity in unity." By implication, Jewish and Muslim monotheists (including perhaps even Abraham, Isaac, Jacob, Moses, and David)—and, for that matter, all others who are not Christian trinitarians—are excluded from salvation, owing to their lacking trinitarian belief regarding God. Augustine and Thomas Aquinas, among many other Christians, seem committed to such exclusivism, at least regarding people who have lived since the time of the inception of the trinitarian faith.

The exclusivism of the Athanasian Creed conflicts with the character of a perfectly loving God. Consider a simple case in which an adolescent child, call her Vanna, from an isolated island in, say, Vanuatu (in the South Pacific) has not heard of the trinitarian "catholic faith" and furthermore will not hear of it during her life on earth. Is Vanna's mere failure to believe sufficient for morally acceptable exclusion by a perfectly loving God? Clearly not. Suppose that Vanna fails to believe the "catholic faith" only because she has not heard of it at all and that she would believe it if she heard of it, although (as it happens) she will not be presented with it in her life on earth. So, Vanna is disposed to believe it (because she would believe it if she heard of it), but she does not actually believe it and will not actually believe it during her earthly life. Suppose, in addition, that Vanna has a will (that is, a motivational set) open to God's will and that therefore she is willing to receive, and even to obey, any well-grounded redemptive message from God. It is arguable that God is not obligated to redeem Vanna (or any other morally defective person) on the basis of what she (or any other mere human) has earned, but God's morally perfect character must nonetheless uphold the highest moral standards, including in connection with human redemption. So, if God condemned Vanna to everlasting death solely as a result of her failing to believe the "catholic faith," we could rightly question the moral perfection of God's character.

Divine moral perfection entails morally perfect love, and such divine love seeks what is morally best for a morally imperfect person, including a received offer of forgiveness for the sake of reconciling wayward people to God. Of course, an offer of forgiveness and reconciliation might or might not actually be received by a person, and divine coercion of a person would undermine genuine divine-human reconciliation. More specifically, God's condemning Vanna to everlasting death would not include seeking what is morally best for her, because God would have a morally better alternative at hand: namely, at some point to remove Vanna's doxastic deficiency (with suitable evidence for belief) and thereby to enable her to enter into explicit fellowship with God. The latter alternative would obviously be morally better for Vanna than for her to undergo condemnation to everlasting death solely for a doxastic deficiency. A God of perfect love would not allow such a morally insignificant deficiency to preclude Vanna's ultimately entering into explicit fellowship with God. The doxastic version of personal exclusivism fails to accommodate this point about God's perfectly loving character and thus offers a morally deficient God. In short, that version excludes the God worthy of worship.

Reformed exclusivists will reply that God is "sovereign" and therefore has a right to exclude whomever he wishes. That might sound remarkably pious and even orthodox to some, but it neglects divine worthiness of worship as central to God's character. Specifically, God's will is not permitted to violate the moral perfection inherent in worthiness of worship. An agent's violating such moral perfection would exclude that agent automatically from the category of divinity. Accordingly, given a perfectly loving God, one's being excluded from salvation is not the result of one's failure to pass a mere informational test, because a perfectly loving God would always seek what is best for one, including the provision of needed information at the opportune time. Conversely, salvation is not anchored in one's passing a mere informational test. Various gnostic and intellectualist approaches to redemption imply otherwise, but they neglect the inherent morally perfect character and concerns, including redemptive concerns, of a God worthy of worship.

Morally perfect divine concerns would approach redemption (or salvation) relative to a person's will and moral character and thus steer clear of any mere informational test. A mere informational test is both too hard and too easy from the standpoint of divine moral perfection. It is too hard given the consideration just mentioned: one can fail an informational test owing just to an easily correctable cognitive inadequacy, even while one's will is genuinely open to conformity to God's will and moral character. In such a case, one would not be a lost cause at all relative to divine redemption; on the contrary, one would be an excellent candidate, that is, "good soil" for redemption, in the language of Mark 4:20. A mere informational test is also too weak, given that one can pass the test by having the correct belief (say, belief that the "catholic faith" in the aforementioned Athanasian sense is true) but hold this belief solely out of selfishness and hate, even with one's will largely and resolutely opposed to God's will and moral character. Doxastic versions of exclusivism run afoul of these considerations.

INCLUSIVE EXCLUSIVISM

We should not confuse doxastic Christian exclusivism with a more inclusive Christian version of exclusivism regarding the unique redemptive role of Jesus as God's atoning son. The relevant inclusive Christian version of exclusivism affirms that Jesus is God's unique mediator for redemption and that therefore the divine redemption of humans depends uniquely on Jesus. The big question concerns what the language "depends uniquely on" means. We have seen that it would be a mistake, given divine moral perfection, to affirm that a person must believe, or trust, in Jesus in this earthly life to be a candidate for redemption by God. The aforementioned discussion of the isolated Vanna illustrates this point. So, the relevant sense of "depends uniquely on Jesus" must not require that one "believe in Jesus" in this earthly life. Of course, one could consistently hold nonetheless that a candidate for divine redemption must *ultimately* believe in Jesus as Lord, even if after death.[2]

According to the inclusive Christian exclusivism under consideration, divine salvation of humans is inherently christological, being mediated uniquely by Jesus Christ, but such salvation can be christological *de re* without being *de dicto* in a human's earthly life. That is, given this inclusive exclusivism, the ultimate offer of divine-human reconciliation includes Jesus as atoning mediator, in reality, but it does not follow that ultimate recipients of the offer must assent to or even conceive of such christological mediation in this earthly life. So, we should contrast the inclusive Christian exclusivism under consideration with the aforementioned doxastic exclusivism as represented in the Athanasian Creed. Like traditional Christian orthodoxy, this inclusive exclusivism excludes as false any account or doctrine of redemption that omits Jesus as the unique divinely appointed mediator for human redemption. Unlike doxastic Christian exclusivism, however, it allows for (i.e., in principle includes) human candidates for redemption who do not and will not acknowledge Jesus as Lord in their earthly lives. We should briefly consider both of these features, the exclusive and the inclusive.

The exclusive side of the present view fits with the traditional Christian view, suggested by various writers of the New Testament documents, that Jesus is God's unique revealer and mediator for redemption. For instance, Matthew's gospel states:

> At that time Jesus said, "I praise you, Father, Lord of heaven and earth, because you have hidden these things from the wise and learned, and revealed them to little children. Yes, Father, for this was your good pleasure. All things have been committed to me by my Father. No one knows the Son except the Father, and no one knows the Father except the Son and those to whom the Son chooses to reveal him." (Matthew 11:25–27; compare Luke 10:21–22; John 5:22–23, 17:25–26)

Jesus thus refers to himself as "the Son" of God and identifies himself as the only one who can reveal God to humans. Going beyond talk of knowledge of God, some later writings in the New Testament characterize Jesus as the unique atoning mediator between God and humans. For instance: "there is one God and one mediator between God and men, the man Christ Jesus, who gave himself as a ransom for all men" (1 Timothy 2:5–6). In addition: "It is by the name of Jesus Christ of Nazareth, whom you crucified but whom God raised from the dead, that this man stands before you healed. . . . Salvation is found in no one else, for there is no other name under heaven given to men by which we must be saved" (Acts 4:10, 12). The New Testament thus includes claims implying that Jesus is *exclusively* the revealer and mediator for God. A single brief chapter such as this cannot, of course, establish this demanding exclusivist position, but it can identify how it can be inclusive in an important manner.

The inclusive side of the Christian exclusivism under consideration finds support in the following story of judgment told by Jesus in Matthew's gospel:

> When the Son of Man comes in his glory, and all the angels with him, he will sit on his throne in heavenly glory. All the nations will be gathered before him, and he will separate the people one from another as a shepherd separates the sheep from the goats. He will put the sheep on his right and the goats on his left. Then the King will say to those on his right, "Come, you who are blessed by my Father; take your inheritance, the kingdom prepared for you since the creation of the world. For I was hungry and you gave me something to eat, I was thirsty and you gave me something to drink, I was a stranger and you invited me in, I needed clothes and you clothed me, I was sick and you looked after me, I was in prison and you came to visit me." Then the righteous will answer him, "Lord, when did we see you hungry and feed you, or thirsty and give you something to drink? When did we see you a stranger and invite you in, or needing clothes and clothe you? When did we see you sick or in prison and go to visit you?" The King will reply, "I tell you the truth, whatever you did for one of the least of these brothers of mine, you did for me." Then he will say to those on his left, "Depart from me, you who are cursed, into the eternal fire prepared for the devil and his angels. For I was hungry and you gave me nothing to eat, I was thirsty and you gave me nothing to drink, I was a stranger and you did not invite me in, I needed clothes and you did not clothe me, I was sick and in prison and you did not look after me." They also will answer, "Lord, when did we see you hungry or thirsty or a stranger or needing clothes or sick or in prison, and did not help you?" He will reply, "I tell you the truth, whatever you did not do for one of the least of these, you did not do for me." Then they will go away to eternal punishment, but the righteous to eternal life. (Matthew 25:31–46)

The surprise experienced by "the righteous," coupled with the King's focus on their caring behavior toward others, suggests something other than a doxastic standard for approval by God. This fits with the remark of Jesus in Matthew 7:21: "Not everyone who says to me, 'Lord, Lord,' will enter the kingdom of heaven, but only the one who does the will of my Father who is in heaven." One can do the will of God, as Jesus illustrated, without explicit doxastic commitment to God. This consideration speaks against excluding Vanna in the aforementioned case.

Still, there is an exclusivist nondoxastic criterion at work in Matthew's judgment story from Jesus: the human manifestation of divine unselfish love toward others. Such a manifestation, it is arguable, requires one's yielding, and being conformed, to the divine unselfish love manifested in one's own life, but it does not follow that one must have an explicit doxastic commitment to God. One could yield volitionally to God's unselfish love and thereby to God *de re*, without corre-sponding acknowledgment *de dicto* and thus without one's knowing that one is yielding to God or even knowing that God exists. This consideration accounts for the element of surprise in Matthew's judgment story from Jesus.

We should acknowledge a corresponding *de re* approach to rejection of God, in keeping with the judgment story from Jesus. One can resist, or otherwise neglect, conformity to the unselfish love presented to one and thereby resist, or otherwise neglect, *de re* the purported redemptive activity of God in one's life. That would amount to resisting or neglecting *God*, especially on the Christian view that "love [*agape*] is from God" (1 John 4:7) or that "God is love" (1 John 4:16). In fact, one's resisting or neglecting unselfish love could have dire cognitive results regarding one's knowing divine reality. As one New Testament writer states, "The one who does not love does not know God, because God is love" (1 John 4:8).[3] If hell is just exclusion from a life of fellowship with God, then hell should be understood as ultimately *self-exclusion* from such a life with God.[4] Such self-exclusion can be *de re* in the sense indicated and need not be *de dicto* in terms of an explicit corresponding belief that one is rejecting God or even belief that God exists (or does not exist). As a result, one can be living in hell or moving toward hell without even knowing this *de dicto*.

CONCLUSIONS

Variation in beliefs among humans regarding divine redemptive activity raise numerous difficult questions, including questions about evidence and knowledge of divine reality. For instance, why do some people (avowedly) have evidence regarding God's redemptive activity and believe (or trust) in God on that basis, whereas others (avowedly) lack the needed evidence and thus refrain from trust in God? Perhaps some people are not ready to receive the needed evidence correctly, on God's terms of unselfish love. If anything is clear, however, it is clear that we have no simple answer to the question.

It is arguable (in keeping with Moser 2008) that divine redemptive purposes account for divine evidence given and not given among humans, but it does not follow that we can always specify the exact divine purposes at work among humans. Just as we have no comprehensive exact theodicy regarding evil (and, for that matter, should not expect to have one in our cognitively limited situation), so also we have no comprehensive exact account of divine elusiveness regarding divine self-revelation. Even so, our lacking any such comprehensive account does not undermine one's having conclusive evidence of divine reality. The lesson of this chapter is that even in the absence of explicit *de dicto* human acknowledgment of divine intervention and evidence, God can properly advance human redemption and judgment. As a result, in connection with redemption and judgment, we are well advised to consider human attitudes deeper than mere belief and then to understand redemptively relevant "faith" toward God accordingly. This would be in keeping with the divine redemptive purposes of a God truly worthy of worship.

NOTES

1. See Meadors 2006, chaps. 8–10, on divine judgment in Paul's Epistle to the Romans.

2. The apostle Paul might have had the latter view in mind in Philippians 2:9–11.

3. For an attempt to make good cognitive sense of this distinctive position, in keeping with divine elusiveness, see Moser 2008.

4. Compare Kvanvig 1993.

REFERENCES

Calvin, John. 1536/1989. *Institutes of the Christian Religion*, Henry Beveridge, trans. Grand Rapids, Mich.: Eerdmans.

Kvanvig, Jonathan L. 1993. *The Problem of Hell*. New York: Oxford University Press.

Meadors, Edward P. 2006. *Idolatry and the Hardening of the Heart*. New York: T. and T. Clark.

Moser, Paul K. 2008. *The Elusive God: Reorienting Religious Epistemology*. New York: Cambridge University Press.

Schaff, Philip, ed. 1919a. *The Creeds of Christendom, Vol. 2: The Greek and Latin Creeds*. New York: Harper and Row.

———. 1919b. *The Creeds of Christendom, Vol. 3: Evangelical Protestant Creeds*. New York: Harper and Row.

FOR FURTHER READING

Farmer, H. H. 1954. *Revelation and Religion*. London: Nisbet.

Forsyth, P. T. 1913. *The Principle of Authority*. London: Independent.

Meadors, Edward P. 2006. *Idolatry and the Hardening of the Heart*. New York: T&T Clark.

Meister, Chad, and Paul Copan, eds. 2007. *The Routledge Companion to Philosophy of Religion*. London: Routledge.

Moser, Paul K. 2008. *The Elusive God: Reorienting Religious Epistemology*. New York: Cambridge University Press.

Perry, Edmund. 1958. *The Gospel in Dispute: The Relation of Christian Faith to Other Missionary Religions*. Garden City, N.Y.: Doubleday.

Quinn, Philip, and Kevin Meeker, eds. 2000. *The Philosophical Challenge of Religious Diversity*. New York: Oxford University Press.

CHAPTER 7

THE DIVERSITY OF RELIGIOUS EXPERIENCE

KEITH E. YANDELL

THERE is agreement about neither religion nor religious experience. To await agreement is to write about neither. I take a religion to be a conceptual system, embedded in persons and texts (verbal or written), rites and rituals, and institutions and practices, that diagnoses a universal deep nonmedical disease and prescribes its cure. An individual experience (our concern here) occurs when a person is in a conscious state. Religious experiences are conscious states whose content is religiously positively significant according to some religion.

SAMPLES

A few descriptions partially indicate the variety of religious experiences. I take these to be reports or descriptions based on religious experiences. If not these, many others could replace them.

Group One

Judaism: 1. [God] said [to Moses] "Do not come near . . . I am the God of your Father, the God of Abraham, the God of Isaac, the God of Jacob." And Moses hid his face, for he was afraid to look at God (Exodus 3:5–6); 2. In the year that King Uzziah died, I saw the Lord, high and holy . . . [Seraphim] said: "Holy, holy, holy is the Lord of Hosts." . . . And the foundations of the thresholds shook at the voice of him who called. . . . I said: "Woe is me! For I am lost; for I am a man of unclean lips and I dwell in the midst of a people of unclean lips; for my eyes have seen the king, the Lord of hosts!" Then flew one of the seraphim to me . . . and said . . . "your guilt is taken away, and your sin forgiven" (Isaiah 6:1–9). *Christianity:* 3. I [John] was in the Spirit on the Lord's day, and I heard behind me a loud voice. . . . I turned to see the voice that was speaking to me, and . . . saw . . . one like a son of man clothed with a long robe. . . . When I saw him, I fell at his feet as though dead. But he laid his right hand upon me, saying "Fear not, I am the first and the last, and the living one; I died, and behold I am alive forevermore, and I have the keys of Death and Hades" (Revelation 1:10–18). *Islam:* 4. I love Thee with two loves: a love of passion and a love prompted by Thy worthiness as an object of love. As for the love of passion, it is indeed the repetition of Thy name, to the exclusion of anything else. As to the love of worthiness, it is the love in which Thou removest the veil, so that I can see Thee (Rabiah al-Adawiyah, d. 80; Smith 1995, 223). *Vsistadvaita and Dvaita Vedanta Hinduism:* 5. Father of all, Master supreme, Power supreme in all the worlds, Who is like thee? Who is beyond thee? I bow before thee. I prostrate before thee, and I beg thy grace, O glorious Lord. As a father to his son, as a friend to his friend, as a lover to his lover, be gracious unto me, O God. In a vision I have seen what no man has seen before; I rejoice in exultation, and yet my heart trembles with fear (*Bhagavagita* [Song of the Blessed Lord], chap. 11, paragraphs 43–44).

Group Two

Buddhism: 1. [W]hen I comprehended, as it really is, the satisfaction of the world as satisfaction, the misery as misery, and the escape as escape, then I understood fully and accepted full Buddha status, and the knowledge and the vision arose in me: sure is the release of my mind: this is my last birth (*Anguttara Nikaya* I, 259); 2. [W]hen we come to examine the elements of being one by one, we discover in the absolute sense that there is no living entity there to form a basis for such figments as "I am" or "I"; in other words, that in the absolute sense there is only name and form. The insight of him who perceives this is called the knowledge of the truth (*Visuddhimagga* XVIII 3, 13; Koller and Koller 1991, 284–285); 3. There is no establishment of self which is other than the aggregates; therefore the object of observation is only the aggregates (*Madhyamakavatarra* 24b.6). *Jainism:* 4. [I]n deep meditation, he [Mahavira] reached Nirvana, the complete and full, the unobstructed, unimpeded, infinite and supreme, best knowledge and intuition, called Kevala . . . he was a Kevalin, omniscient and comprehending all objects, he knew all conditions of the world he saw and knew all conditions in the whole world of all living beings (*Jaina Sutras* I, 201, 202); 5. Liberation is the freedom from all karmic matter, owing to the nonexistence of the cause of bondage and to the shedding of all the karmas. After the soul is released, there remain perfect right-belief, perfect right-knowledge, and the state of having accomplished all (Koller and Koller 1991, 260); 6. [M]odifications cannot exist without an abiding or eternal something—a permanent substance. (Koller and Koller 1991, 269).

Group Three

Advaita Vedanta Hinduism: 1. When a seer sees the brilliant Maker, Lord, Person, the Brahman-source, then, being a knower, shaking off good and evil, stainless, he attains supreme identity with Him. . . . Not by sight is it grasped, not even by speech, not by any other sense-organs, austerity, or work, by the peace of knowledge, one's nature purified—in that way, however, by meditating, one does behold him who is without parts (*Mundaka Upanishad* III, i, 3, 8); 2. That which is the finest essence— the whole world has that as its self. That is Reality. That is Atman. That art thou (*Chandogya Upanishad* VI, ix, 4); 3. If the soul . . . is not considered to possess fundamental unity with Brahman—an identity to be realized by knowledge—there is not any chance of its obtaining final release (Thibaut 1896/1962, vol. 2, 399); *Buddhism:* 4. There is, monks, a domain where there is no earth, no water, no fire, no wind, no sphere of infinite space, no sphere of nothingness, no sphere of infinite consciousness, no sphere of neither awareness nor non-awareness; there is not this world, there is not another world, there is no sun or moon. I do not call this coming or going, nor standing nor dying, nor being reborn; it is without support, without occurrence, without object. Just this is the end of suffering (Gethin 1998; 5. Whatever comes about conditioned by something else is quiescent from the point of view of inherent existence. Therefore both the process of origination and the act of production itself are quiescent. . . . Like an illusion, a dream, or a castle in the air are production, duration, and cessation declared to be (*Madhyamaka-kararika* 7:16/34); 6. He is not to be called a Bodhi-being [enlightened one] in whom the notion of a self or of a being should take place, or the notion of a living soul, or a person (Koller and Koller 1991, 258).

Two comments nicely state the deep contrast between theistic Hinduism (and theism generally) and much of Buddhist tradition. First, the latter:

> The moment an individual realizes that he is the Reality, that Samsara is identical to Nirvana, he becomes perfect, i.e. a Buddha. One must eradicate from his mind not only its own individuality but also the substantiality of anything whatever perceived or cognized by him. When a being attains a state of mind, in which he cannot distinguish himself from any other thing of the world, or from the Absolute, he is said to attain Nirvana in the Mahayanic sense. (Dutt 1976, 264)

Then the former:

> Consciousness is not unowned, . . . as appears from ordinary judgments such as . . . "I understand this matter, I am conscious of this piece of cloth" [Sri-bhasya 1.1.1]. To maintain that the consciousness of the "I" does not persist in the state of final release is again altogether inappropriate. It, in fact, amounts to the doctrine—only expressed in somewhat different words—that final release is the annihilation of the self . . . moreover, a man who, suffering pain, mental or of other kind . . . puts himself in relation to pain—"I am suffering pain"—naturally begins to reflect how he may once and for all free himself from all these manifold afflictions and enjoy a state of untroubled ease; the desire of final release thus having arisen in him, he at once sets to work to accomplish it. If, on the other

hand, he were to realize that the effect of such activity would be the loss of personal existence, he surely would turn away as soon as somebody began to tell him about "release." . . . Nor must you maintain against this that even in the state of release there exists pure consciousness; for this by no means improves your case. No sensible person exerts himself under the influence of the idea that after he himself has perished there will remain some entity called "pure light." (Thibaut 1962, 56)

Structural Difference: Subject/ Consciousness/Object, Subject/Aspect, and Introspective-like Experiences

Experiences in Group One above are subject/consciousness/object (s/c/o) in structure. The subject at least seems to experience something such that if it exists, it exists distinct from and independent of the subject and his experience. Phenomenologically, there is no sense of the subject experiencing himself or herself or some feature, ordinary or extraordinary, of himself or herself. Apparent experience of God—numinous experience—is of s/c/o structure and has affective content (e.g., awe toward, a sense of one's dependence on, being impure before, or loved by God). Such feelings, like the experience as a whole, are outer-directed as well as being aspects of the subject.

Subject/aspect (s/a), or introspective, experiences are matters of a subject being aware of himself or herself as having some feature (e.g., having a headache or feeling dizzy). The s/a experience is inner-directed (e.g., being aware of generalized bliss, peace, or detachment). Such affective content is typically ascribed to enlightenment experience.

Experiences in Group Two, in religious context, are said to involve recognizing "oneself" as having a certain metaphysical structure. What is evident to one sort of Buddhist enlightenment is that what lies behind talk of persons is merely a collection of conscious states (strictly, aggregates that fall under the rubrics body, feeling, perception, consciousness, mental formations) and nothing over and above these states. What is evident to Jain enlightenment experience is that persons are *in* mental states. The states are not collections but features of a subject of experience. Knowing which view is true is viewed as essential to even the possibility of gaining freedom from transmigration and karma, ignorance and attachment, in both Buddhism and Jainism. What is required is that the metaphysical structure of (what lies behind talk of) persons be accessible in experience. Such experience is not introspective in the sense of involving awareness of psychological states. It is like introspective experience in that it is inner-directed, and what is said to be experienced is oneself or what lies behind talk of oneself. Since in both traditions, enlightenment experiences are said to involve bliss, peace, and detachment—introspectible properties—both sorts of experience are commonsensically said to be, in part, s/a. Strictly, one is aware of oneself (say) being in pain or feeling elated. The Jain has no quarrel with the final accuracy of this description, but the typical Buddhist will want to revise it in accord with a no-self doctrine. These introspection-like experiences can be veridical only if the structure allegedly recognized is both possibly experientially accessible and actually present. Both Buddhist and Jain traditions hold, regarding its own type of experience, that it occurs and is veridical.

There is an interesting dissimilarity. One can hold that the Buddhist is correct that only conscious states are observed and infer that, since conscious states must be some subject's states, the Jain doctrine is correct. One cannot hold that conscious states are actually observed as states of a subject, but really there is no subject. The descriptions of everyday experiences as owned are rejected by typical Buddhist tradition, but the Jain can accept the Buddhist enlightenment description and make the indicated inference. A relevant Jain claim is that necessarily, experiences must be had by subjects, and the subjects can be aware that they are having them, and a relevant Buddhist claim is that necessarily (?), all that lies behind talk of persons is states that are manifest in enlightenment experience.

Experiences in Group Three illustrate another sort of experience that does not fit nicely into s/c/o or s/a classification. Serious questions have been raised about whether there can be experiences that satisfy such descriptions. Advaita Vedanta and (arguably) Mahayana Madhyamika enlightenment experience is viewed as a matter of recognition that all that exists is a quality-less state or an ineffable being. Within both Hindu and Buddhist traditions, it is replied that if all relations and distinctions are illusions, then there is no subject of experience, no experience, and no experiential content, and were the "recognition" accurate, there would be nothing that could have a disease or receive a cure. Why, then, religion? Further, there are s/c/o and s/a experiences, and this is incompatible with the claim that there are no qualities or relations. A typical response is to claim that what is confirmed in enlightenment experience is ineffable, thus denying the claim that an experience is evidence only under some description and raising the question "What, exactly, is it for there to be experience or experiential evidence if there is nothing of which these concepts are true?" The proponent of the Advaita or Madhyamika view can appeal to a doctrine of content-less "direct" experience of an unconditioned (but then not altogether ineffable) state or being, while his or her opponent will assert that property-less existence is necessarily impossible in the case of persons, states, and everything else.

FURTHER ISSUES

For much of the Buddhist tradition, there is no s/c/o or s/a experience, although in everyday commonsense experience, there seems to be. If there is no self, this entails that conscious states are unowned; they have no subject, and no subject has them. Sometimes it is added that reflexive experiences are impossible. If there is no self, then self-awareness is impossible. But things are complex here. Much of the tradition also holds that in enlightenment experience, "we" are aware of our own structure—"we" are directly aware of currently being composed only of momentary conscious states (and, the reasoning goes, if currently, then always). This requires something like a second-order state, the objects of which are first-order states. If there is no self, and "we" are aware of our being only conscious states, there being second-order states that are aware of first-order states seems to be the only possibility for there being this awareness. Some states in a causally connected bundle join another that is (directly) aware of its colleagues so that it observes that all there is to the bundle is conscious states that nothing has. This must include an observational awareness that nothing has *it*. Second-order states have reflexive awareness, although strictly, it isn't *self*-awareness, since that would require a self.

This entailment of the doctrine concerning the nature of enlightenment is not emphasized. Second-order states will resemble substances in that they are aware of conscious states and have properties and will be unlike them in that they are momentary and depend for their existence on exactly their first-order states. Typical Buddhist doctrine entails that they do not endure, although this goes beyond observation; still, introduction of second-order states is one step toward admitting a self. In any case, regarding the Buddhist tradition and enlightenment experience, it seems that we are dealing with an at least implicit claim that there is quasi-introspective experience where the "inspector" is a state, not a self or substance. Its affective content is not peace at, bliss about, or detachment from something but just peace, bliss, and detachment. These are not matters of sensing the world, or some part of it, that is distinct from oneself. They do not even seem to be outer-directed.

A basic question is whether the properties ascribed to the conscious states, or in the Jain case to the subject of such states, are observable properties, features that are accessible to an inner-directed, quasi-introspective experience. Is the metaphysical structure of persons open to inner-directed inspection? Both "sides" answer in the affirmative and differ about what is inspected. For the Jain, one is aware of oneself as having a headache, whereas for the Buddhist, one is aware of an unowned conscious state that has "headachy" content. One could hold that some of the things we call people have one metaphysical structure and others have another, but then the universalism of the claims of both Jainism and Buddhism would be compromised.

An experience of something that exists distinct from and independent of the subject and her experience goes beyond anything contained in the purely affective content of the conscious state in question. To report that there is an eternal blissful state into which you have "entered" or of which you have "become a part," setting aside the question of whether any such thing is so much as possible, would be to claim something that went far beyond anything simply contained in the phenomenology of the experience.

AFFECTIVE CONTENT

The religious experiences we have discussed have structure. They are said to have propositional content, content that is true or false—that God exists, that there are subjects of experiences, that subjects are only causally connected unowned states, that one is identical to a quality-less being or state, even by those traditions that also deny this. They also have affective content. In a numinous experience in which the subject is awestruck by the power and holiness of the putative object of the experience, the sense of being awed blends with a belief that God is present. A person who experiences God does not feel godlike but fragile and humbled, just as a person who is moved by a magnificent night sky does not feel his or her own universal significance but feels small and insignificant. Reverence, worship, and repentance are outer-directed. The affective content of numinous experience is central to the identification of the putative object of the experience—to the experience seeming to be an experience of God. Generalized bliss, peace, and detachment are inner-directed.

What is religiously central to one sort of enlightenment experience is that there is in it what the tradition in which it occurs will insist is recognition that one is identical to quality-less being (Brahman) or state (Nirvana). No state lacking the relevant affective content would be counted as an enlightenment experience. What is religiously central to another sort of enlightenment experience is what is said to be the recognition that instead of a self, there is merely a bundle of unowned conscious states. Central to still another is that there is a self, namely, an inherently immortal enduring mind that has experience but is not identical to the experiences it has. The claim, in each case, is that the relevant recognition, accompanied by the proper affective content, brings enlightenment. Being able to recognize affective content requires a reflexive transcendence of that content, and we are back to subjects or second-order states.

EXPERIENTIAL EVIDENCE

A central philosophical question is whether religious experience provides evidence for religious beliefs. Does it, and how can one tell? Various arguments are offered for a negative answer. First, it is argued that religious experiences are literally ineffable (no concepts apply to them). Since experiences can provide evidence only under some description, they cannot provide evidence for religious belief. But we have already applied various concepts to such experiences, among them being ineffable and being evidence only under some description. These are concepts that the argument itself applies to the experiences in question, which makes the argument that these experiences are ineffable self-defeating. Further, an experience to which no concepts applied cannot be an experience to which conscious states the achievement of which constitutes enlightenment or having received God's forgiveness and grace apply.

Second, it is claimed that a religious tradition provides a filter that allows in only those experiences that support, or at least conform to, the beliefs that partly constitute the tradition. The facts that people who are not members of a religious tradition have religious experiences and that members of one tradition sometimes have experiences that fit a different tradition tell against this view. Further, it is hard to see a principled point at which to stop reasoning along these lines: Are all traditions self-protective in this manner, including those from within which the filter doctrine itself arises?

People have had experiences that they have taken to be experiences of God. We need not take every possible such claim seriously. Someone who observed an ant make its way over a sidewalk and reach the other side or who munched on crackers and cheese could not correctly claim thereby to have (directly) experienced God. The concept of God, as it is used in monotheistic traditions, guarantees that God is not an ant or crackers and cheese, and only confusion results from denying it. The monotheistic traditions don't mean by "God" something like "everything there is" or "an essence that pervades all things" or "that to which everything is identical." They hold that there isn't anything to which everything is identical other than all of the different things that exist, each of which is necessarily self-identical and necessarily not anything that it is not, which is everything else.

Putative experiences of God are s/c/o in structure. They irrevocably at least seem to be of a being quite other than the person who has the experience. They do not seem simply to be experiences of something deep in the subject of experience, and if they are simply that, then they are not veridical; things are not as the experience represents them as being. The s/c/o experiences have a relevant inherent feature. Formally put, it is this: If Tom's having an experience E that is a matter of his at least seeming to experience an X, then this is evidence that there is an X that Tom experiences. The evidence can obviously be overturned. Tom need not take it as evidence in order for it to be evidence—it is *being taken to be evidence* that is person-dependent, not *being evidence*.

INTERPRETATIONS

Sensory experience does not seem to be cut up into Humean perceptions or Buddhist transitory states. Having sensory experience seems to be a matter of seeing a wall as long as one's eyes are open, hearing a siren for some time, tasting a hard candy for a while, and the like. Further, not every sense operates between something like eye blinks. Some of the very data by which a Humean explains our coming to believe in material objects—we have repetitive, perceptually unbroken sequences of experience and the occurrence and memory of these elicit propensities to think in terms of enduring, mind-independent things—belie the Humean's own claim concerning the transitoriness of experience. A sense of the presence of God need not be interrupted, broken into intervals, nor need an enlightenment experience.

One challenge to the idea that religious experience provides evidence for religious claims begins by proposing a relevant set of interpretive frameworks. If someone has an intentional experience that seems to be an awareness of God, then there are these alternatives:

1. *Realist:* This is reason to think that God exists.
2. *Kantian:* This would be reason to think that God exists, were it not the case that (most of our) concepts do not apply to anything but experiential content.
3. *Antirealist:* What exists is simply affective content, which reveals something only about the subject, whatever the intentional content of the experience might be.
4. *Subjectivist:* The content of this experience can be translated into, or replaced by, descriptions of how the subject feels.

One problem is that alternatives 3 and 4 are mistaken. At least, seeming to experience God is not purely affective—seeming to see God is not a matter of having a godly feeling (whatever that might be), and any even vaguely adequate description of how the subject feels will include reference to what it is about which the subject feels the way he or she does. Alternative 2 can grant the intentionality of (some of) religious experience but denies its veridicality in the light (or darkness) of a highly controversial, and unproven, view concerning the limitations of conceptual applicability. The fact is that, typically at least, religious experiences are not like pliable clay, able to be formed into whatever shape you like. Like any experience, a religious experience can be interpreted however you like. Seeing that three succeeds two can be interpreted as watching the moon disintegrate. But it cannot reasonably be so interpreted, since its content lends no support to the interpretation, nor is there anything even slightly plausible connecting the propositional content and the interpretation. Suspicion about the idea of "the given" notwithstanding, what I at least seem to see now is a computer screen, and what I feel now is a dull headache. What some subjects of religious experience, based on the content of their experience, seem to be aware of is God's presence. Not all experiential content is open to every interpretation. Not every interpretation is possibly correct. Major factors in determining whether an interpretation is correct are the structure and content of the experience being interpreted.

ABSTRACT AND CONCRETE DESCRIPTIONS

Highly abstract descriptions of experiences contain less specific information regarding their content. It does not follow that they are more probably true, since their content might be inconsistent, incoherent, or incompatible with content more clearly, or as clearly, true. There is also the possibility of vacuity or something close. The more abstract descriptions have logical contraries as well as contradictories.

Further, a more abstract description is true in virtue of a less abstract description being true. That the rose has a property, and a color property, follows from its being red. The conditions that make a more abstract definition true exist because conditions that make less abstract descriptions true exist, down to the conditions in virtue of which fully concrete—fully determinate—descriptions are true. The idea that experiences provide evidence for more abstract claims without providing evidence for less abstract claims cannot be correct.

One assumption behind the notion that this is possible is that there are experienceable items of which only more abstract descriptions are true—that below a certain level of abstraction, no description is true; and this is not even possibly true. By one account, there is no such property as being a property or being a color property. There are the descriptions "having a property" and "having a color property," but these descriptions are true of something only in virtue, say, of its being navy blue, which is a concrete property. On this view, so to speak, actual properties correspond only to fully determinate descriptions. By another account, for any level LD of descriptive abstraction, there is a corresponding property, but for every property of level LP, it belongs to something if and only if that thing also has properties at level LP1 on down to properties at the "bottom level." (This account can be sophisticated by regarding properties as abstract objects of which concrete properties are exemplifications and replacing "property" in the description of the previous view with "property exemplification.") The fundamental point is that to exist is to have concrete properties, whatever else it might be—and this rules out ineffability. It is also negatively relevant to the idea that the more ramifications a description has, the more interpretive the description is, and the more concrete a description is, the more ramifications it has. "I am aware of my identity with quality-less Brahman" is highly abstract and entails—presumably, ramifications are entailments—that for any determinate thing you think exists, it does not, and for every relation you think holds, it doesn't, either. "I am aware of the presence of a holy God" is more concrete and lacks the entailments of the more abstract identity claim.

PRINCIPLE OF EXPERIENTIAL EVIDENCE

A principle of experiential evidence will answer three questions: (1) Under what conditions does an experience provide evidence for a proposition? (2) Under what conditions does a subject of experience properly take an experience as evidence for a proposition? (3) Under what conditions is the evidence provided also in some way counterbalanced? Our concern here is with direct evidence—evidence not mediated by a theory. Answering question 1 requires an account of when there is the right sort of "fit" between experience and proposition.

Relative to question 1, a plausible principle of experiential evidence is: (P1) An s/c/o experience E provides evidence for proposition P of the form "O exists" or "O has Q," where O is such that, if it exists, it does so independently of E and E's subject S, if and only if S's having E is a matter of its experientially seeming to S that O exists or that O has Q; an s/c or s/a experience E provides evidence for proposition P of the form "S has property Q" or "S is in state X" if and only if S's having E is a matter of its experientially seeming to S that S has Q or that S is in X.

Relative to question 2, something like this seems true as a sufficient condition: (P2) S takes experience E to be evidence for proposition P if E is evidence for P, according to (P1), and in the light of knowing this, S accepts E as evidence for P.

This leaves question 3. No doubt, there are many ways in which evidence is countered or outweighed. It is hard to have justified confidence that any list of ways in which this can occur is complete. The way to proceed seems to be to list all of the possibilities one can think of. This leads to something in the broad neighborhood of: (P3) If things will (or are as likely as or more likely to) appear to S as they do whether they are that way or not, there is a sound and valid argument that shows that things are not the way they seem or are, at least as likely as not, not to be the way they seem, as they are to be the way they seem; there are natural laws that entail that if S is in the circumstances in which S has the experience, then S is (or as probably as not is) not experiencing things as they are; there is a deceiving factor (e.g., a hologram or façade) relative to S's experience that causes things to seem to S as they are not; S himself or herself is in a condition in which S's experiences will (or as likely as not will) be unreliable; then S's experiential evidence is counterbalanced or outweighed; if S nonculpably has no reason to suppose that any of these things (or things relevantly like them) are the case, then S properly does not suppose that S's experiential evidence is counterbalanced or outweighed. Of course, this only scratches the surface of a complex matter.

REFERENCES

Dutt, Nalinaksha. 1976. *Mahayana Buddhism*. Calcutta: Firma KLM.

Gethin, R. 1998. *The Foundations of Buddhism*. Oxford: Oxford University Press.

Koller, John M., and Patricia Koller. 1991. *A Sourcebook in Asian Philosophy*. New York: Macmillan.

Smith, Margaret. 1995. *Studies in Early Mysticism in the Near and Middle East*. Oxford: Oneworld.

Thibaut, George, trans. 1896/1962. *The Vedanta Sutras of Badarayanna with the Commentary of Sankara*. New York: Dover.

FOR FURTHER READING

Alston, William. 1991. *Perceiving God*. Ithaca, N.Y.: Cornell University Press.

Bowker, John. 1971. *The Sense of God*. New York: Oxford University Press.

Gellman, Jerome. 1987. *Experience of God and the Rationality osf Religious Belief.* Ithaca, N.Y.: Cornell University Press.

Hardy, Alister. 1979. *The Spiritual Nature of Man.* New York: Oxford University Press.

Martin, C. B. 1959. *Religious Belief.* Ithaca, N.Y.: Cornell University Press.

Mavrodes, George I. 1970. *Belief in God: A Study in the Epistemology of Religion.* New York: Random House.

Mueller, Max, ed. 1895–1910, *Sacred Books of the East,* 50 vols. Delhi: Motilal Banarsidass.

Pike, Nelson. 1992. *Mystic Union.* Ithaca, N.Y.: Cornell University Press.

Wainwright, William. 1981. *Mysticism: A Study of Its Nature, Cognitive Value, and Moral Implications.* Madison: University of Wisconsin.

Yandell, Keith E. 1994. *The Epistemology of Religious Experience.* Cambridge, U.K.: Cambridge University Press.

CHAPTER 8

INTERRELIGIOUS DIALOGUE

SALLIE B. KING

DEFINITION AND TYPES

ONE might assume that interreligious dialogue could be defined quite simply as discussion or conversation among members of different religions. Most interreligious dialogue is indeed captured by such a definition; however, some events that are considered part of interreligious dialogue do not fit this definition. Intermonastic visitation, in which, for example, Buddhist monastics live in a Christian monastery, living the same life and doing the same practices as the Christian monks, is given as an example of interreligious dialogue, as is a group of Christian laypeople attending a Jewish religious service in a local synagogue. A city's Jews, Christians, Muslims, Hindus, Buddhists, and Sikhs jointly serving a Thanksgiving dinner to the homeless might be considered interreligious dialogue, and indeed would-be dialogue groups in a community are often encouraged to begin their interactions with a joint service project. In the face of this, it is best to define interreligious dialogue as intentional encounter and interaction among members of different religions *as* members of different religions.

There is quite a variety of types of interreligious dialogue, with no overall agreement about what these types are—that is, how the many phenomena that fit into the category of interreligious dialogue should be divided and ordered—but the following list will give an idea of the variety of phenomena included and some of the factors that are important in conceptualizing these types.[1]

1. *Official or institutional dialogue between or among elites chosen by their religions as official representatives.* This kind of dialogue has many of the features of diplomacy and is often intended to resolve points of friction among religions in order to avoid or assuage practical conflicts.

2. *Parliamentary-style dialogue in which religious leaders speak in an open forum with the main objective of making their views widely known.* This kind of dialogue can seem more like a series of monologues, at least within the official program, but the individual presentations spur a great deal of true dialogical exchange during question-and-answer sessions and offstage. Dialogue of this type promotes mutual understanding and better interreligious and intercommunity relations.

3. *Verbal dialogue, in which the objective is to come to a better understanding of another religion through a focus on a religion's doctrines, philosophy, theology, or worldview.* Verbal dialogue is the prototypical form of dialogue in most people's minds. Verbal dialogue might initially be fairly shallow, involving merely making the intellectual acquaintance of the other. However, if it progresses to the point at which one learns something startling that forces a shift in one's own worldview, such dialogue can take on a profound spiritual dimension.

4. *Intervisitation, in which members of one religious community visit with another religious community.* Sometimes such visits involve members of one or several religious communities being present at a religious service of another religious community. Sometimes a religious leader is invited to visit a religious community in its place of worship, practice, or learning and to address them. Again, members of a monastic community might live with another monastic community for short or long periods. This kind of dialogue might have intellectual, affective, and spiritual dimensions.

5. *Spiritual dialogue, in which one learns and engages in the spiritual practices of another religion, such as the other religion's form of prayer, meditation, or worship, or participates in a ritual together with members of another religion.*

6. *Practical dialogue, in which the objective is to carry out a concrete project in the community or in the world.* In the community, one works side-by-side with members of another religious community. Here, the primary goal is to promote community harmony through people from different communities getting to know one another in a nonthreatening way.

7. *Internal dialogue, in which a single individual has an internal conversation going on between two religions to which he or she has been exposed, ordinarily at some depth and over some time.* It might be questioned whether this is truly dialogue, and yet it is an important aspect of the process of interreligious encounter and needs to be recognized as such.

Some of the factors involved in this typology are (a) whether a type of dialogue is, or must be, practiced by an official or elite group or is open to all; (b) whether its goals are primarily on the personal level (understanding, spiritual growth) or on the community or social level (to resolve intercommunity conflicts, to avert violence); (c) whether it works with the human intellect, human spirituality, human emotions, practical action, or some combination of these. These factors can combine in all manner of ways, and as a consequence, there can be no standard list of types of dialogue. Later in this chapter, we will take the distinction between dialogue on the personal level and intercommunity dialogue as particularly important.

HISTORY

The 1893 World's Parliament of Religions is generally recognized as the beginning of organized interreligious dialogue. Held in Chicago in conjunction with the World Columbian Exhibition, it was the first time religious leaders were invited to speak for themselves and their religions on a footing of equal respect and dignity. It was also the first effort to produce an inclusive, global gathering of religions. Although it was dominated numerically by Christian presentations, the Parliament was a major globalizing moment. Indeed, it was an unprecedented occasion for the West to meet the East, not as a colony or as part of an empire but as an equal, in fact, an attractive and impressive equal, as represented by such luminaries as the Hindu leader Swami Vivekananda and the Buddhist Anagarika Dharmapala.

Interreligious dialogue expanded very rapidly after World War II. There are compelling reasons that made this inevitable. Before the war, particularly within the British Empire, Christian missionaries were sheltered by the might of the empire and its soldiers. Missionaries could be aggressive and insult the local religions without fear of reprisal. Good relations with Christian leaders, or even conversion, were helpful in many colonies in currying favor with the foreign rulers and perhaps earning their patronage; attending Christian schools was often the road to power. With the end of World War II, empires disbanded, and colonies became independent. Christianity was transformed very rapidly from a favored and protected arm of the empire to a minority presence with unsavory recent associations. Throughout Asia, Africa, and the Middle East, former colonies were interested in establishing a national identity in which the former imperial master's religion could have no part. Christianity, though still the most powerful religion in the world and aligned with the most powerful political-military bloc in the world, was in an awkward position. Christian leaders had to reconceive their place and posture in the world.

At about the same time, attitudes in the West toward other countries and cultures underwent a fundamental shift. Whereas formerly in the West there was an attitude of assured superiority vis-à-vis other cultures, after World War II, and particularly beginning in the 1960s, there developed a growing awareness of other cultures as interesting and worthy in their own right. This new attitude was both expressed and furthered through the development of the academic disciplines of anthropology and religious studies in Western universities. The development of academic religious studies since the 1960s deserves special note. In many ways, it prepared the field for interreligious dialogue by presenting the world's religions on an equal basis, without preferential treatment.

Another major development of the 1960s was Vatican II. This was also a watershed event in the development of interreligious dialogue. Convened by Pope John XXIII and held in Rome from 1962 to 1965, the council was called to rethink Catholic teachings, structures, and actions in response to developments in the modern world.

One focus of attention in Vatican II was the relation of the Catholic church to non-Christian religions. The outcome of the council's deliberations on this subject was a document called *Nostra Aetate* ("In Our Time"), which announced a radically changed posture in the Catholic church toward other religions. Gone in this document is the former exclusivist position (i.e., the position stating that only one's own teachings are true and others are false); gone is language of "no salvation outside the Church." In *Nostra Aetate*, the church speaks with admiration of Hindu philosophy, Buddhist spiritual aspirations, and Muslim submission to God and speaks of the Jews as remaining "very dear to God." In short, with *Nostra Aetate*, the Catholic church officially took up an inclusivist position with respect to other religions, a position maintaining that while one's own religion expresses the supreme truth, other religions also contain teachings of truth and value. As a corollary to this inclusivist stance, the church urged its members to participate in interreligious dialogue.[2]

Following the publication of this document, the Vatican established a standing office for dialogue, the Pontifical Council for Interreligious Dialogue. This office promotes good relations with other religions by means of visitation, communications, and formal dialogue and issues guidelines for Catholics on dialogue and on relations with particular religions. The World Council of Churches (WCC) issued its own policy statement and guidelines on "dialogue with people of living faiths and ideologies" in 1971, revised in 1979. It also has an office dedicated to dialogue, the Subunit on Dialogue with People of Living Faiths. Given the wide variety of churches in the WCC, it is not surprising that dialogue is a contentious issue in that body.

Christians have been by far the world's leaders in promoting interreligious dialogue, largely for the reasons cited above, although this is also partially a matter of the ways in which the religions are organized. Because of this leadership role, interreligious dialogue has been conceived and structured according to Western norms and ways of thinking. While this is recognized as a problem and greater non-Western leadership would be welcomed, the latter has not been forthcoming.

CONTEMPORARY IMPORTANCE AND DYNAMICS

Interreligious dialogue is an inevitability in the world today as a result of globalization, the process of drawing together all parts of the world into a single system. As a result of this process, people today in many countries live their daily lives in community with people of other religions as neighbors, schoolmates, coworkers, and friends. Religious intermarriage is becoming more common. Many people are simply curious about other religions or wonder whether there is something they can learn from them. They might look to their own religion to give them guidance in how to think about other religions, or they might do their own exploring with the help of the Internet or by simply talking with the people of other religions who are all around them.

Interreligious dialogue is also important today because of the hope that it might contribute to the resolution, or prevention, of some global conflicts. Many people wrongly believe that interreligious hostility is the cause of most contemporary wars. Religion can be a cause of violence, as in Christian-Muslim riots over Muslim sharia law. More commonly, religion plays a secondary role in justifying conflict, in elevating the level of conflict, and in inciting people to participate in it. In particular, since ethnicity, language, physical location, and religion often overlap, religion can be an integral part of individual and communal identity and in this way is often very quickly brought into conflicts that are fundamentally conflicts among peoples.

Probably the greatest contribution that interreligious dialogue makes to the elimination of violence is in prevention. Since religious institutions are in many countries the most important nongovernmental institutions, ongoing, established interfaith groups on the local level can play an essential role in preventing conflict by keeping the major divisions of the community in communication with one another, continually making an effort to build goodwill and mutual understanding, intervening quickly in the early stages of conflict, and working cooperatively on civic projects.

Interreligious dialogue among peoples with a mutually hostile relationship is particularly important, but it is also particularly difficult. Dialogue requires give and take, hearing the other out, and an openness to seeing where one, or one's group, might be in the wrong. Such a stance might seem like disloyalty when two groups are in a situation of acute conflict. This is not to say that, for example, dialogue between Jews and Muslims cannot occur today. It can and does occur, but it requires an extra degree of stamina and courage on the part of its participants. People might be received with hostility or even violence when they return from a dialogue if they were perceived as being too giving or saying the wrong thing. Some people might be willing to speak freely in dialogue behind closed doors but will not sign any statements or allow the contents of the dialogue to be publicized for fear of retribution. This, while entirely understandable, robs dialogue of much of its public benefit. Again, sometimes dialogue among mutually hostile peoples is attempted but degenerates into useless shouting matches.

We live in an age in which the vast forces of global politics and ordinary, daily life interact in a profound way. Since September 11, 2001, Muslims in the West have greatly stepped up their efforts to be available for interfaith dialogue, have opened their mosques to visitors, and vigorously participate in civic interfaith projects, all in an effort to be better known, to be less "other," to fit into the larger community. Another response can be seen in *The Faith Club* (Idliby, Oliver, and Warner 2007). This book is the product of three New York City women—a Christian, a Muslim, and a Jew—who were deeply disturbed by the events of September 11, 2001, and wanted to do something constructive in response. They found that their first need was to understand one another. Thus began a multiyear dialogue, a model of its kind, in which no questions or challenges were forbidden, each woman let her vulnerabilities be known, and each grew in understanding of the others, in her own personal and spiritual development, and as a contributing citizen of a globalized world. Many similar dialogues have been going on quietly all over the United States.

Principles and Theory of Dialogue

The following principles for the conduct of verbal dialogue have reached close to a consensus among elites active in dialogue circles.

Principles of Dialogue

1. The first requirement of dialogue is to listen, to hear the words of the other. Here, dialogue points in a direction very different from that of the dominant approach to interreligious relations in the past, which was the will to have the other hear oneself. True dialogue cannot occur unless one actively wants to hear what the other has to say and does one's best to take it in and allow it to make whatever impact it will.

2. The second principle is to speak and speak well. This requires the participant to have a particular position within a faith tradition, to be knowledgeable about that position, and to be able to articulate it. Here, we can see why so much dialogue is done by scholars and theologians who are also members of particular religious traditions. The information conveyed about a religious tradition needs to be as well informed, accurate, and insightful as possible.

3. One should have as much knowledge of the religion of one's dialogue partner as possible. While one is participating in dialogue in order to learn about the other, one should not enter the dialogue in a state of complete ignorance about the other but should learn as much as possible about the other before face-to-face meetings. In-depth understanding starts from a wealth of information. The dialogue process itself will nuance, complexify, challenge, or perhaps negate the information with which one starts, but one needs to have the raw material of initial information in order to enter into that process in a more effective way.

4. It is forbidden to enter dialogue with the intention or desire of converting one's dialogue partner. People participating in dialogue don't want to be converted; they want to belong to the religion they already belong to. If people discover that their dialogue partner's purpose is to convert them, they will stop attending. Dialogue is fundamentally incompatible with mission, when mission is understood as proselytizing, planting churches/mosques/temples, or seeking conversion. Would-be dialogue participants are often suspicious that dialogue is just a new word and/or a cover for missionizing. If it is, they want nothing to do with it. On the other hand, dialogue is fully compatible with witnessing to one's religion; in fact, it requires witness, understood as expressing one's own perspective, experience, and commitment to one's religion. Dialogue is also compatible with mission understood as the expression of love through service.

5. One should enter the dialogue without preconceptions of where the dialogue will lead. Dialogue is a process of discovery. One does not know where it will lead, partly because until one hears the words spoken, one does not know what one's dialogue partner will say.

6. Each party to the dialogue must be recognized as occupying a place of respect equal to the others.

7. Each party to the dialogue must speak for himself or herself and define himself or herself. No one can tell another what the other believes and thinks, how another sees things.

8. When comparing features of two (or more) religions, one should always compare one religion's ideals with the ideals of the other religion and one religion's realities with the realities of the other.

9. One should be prepared and able to engage in appropriate self-criticism of one's tradition. All religious traditions are embodied in human institutions, which are limited and fallible. Defensiveness is contrary to the process of growth, which is inherent in dialogue.

Theory of Dialogue

The above principles are largely rooted in the philosophy of hermeneutics (the study of interpretation), especially as formulated by German philosopher Hans-Georg Gadamer (1975). Dialogue and hermeneutics are at base about a very mysterious thing: the process of coming to understand the other. By definition, the other is not I. He or she is different, other than me. In interreligious dialogue, we might be concerned only with our partner's religion as a kind of external thing—for example, as a community that has had a painful historical relationship with my religious community. Or we might be interested in our partner's religion as something more internal, something interdependent with, even interchangeable with, a worldview, a way of thinking and being, and a whole orientation toward life. The former scenario largely calls for the rules and skills of a diplomat. The latter scenario is the one to which Gadamer's thought is relevant. The mystery that Gadamer seeks to understand is: How can I understand the other—here, another worldview and way of thinking—when by definition it is other than my own worldview and way of thinking? How would such a thing even be possible, and if it is possible, how would it best be achieved? By means of a sophisticated analysis of language, culture, and the dynamics of understanding, Gadamer's hermeneutics sheds a great deal of light on this abstruse subject.

We begin by recognizing that we all see, think, and cognize from a particular perspective. That is, we never see from a God's-eye point of view, we never think from a neutral place or tabula rasa, but always from a particular point of view rooted in our culture, our language, our worldview and/or religion, and our own individual life experiences. There is no escaping being rooted in the particular in this way. The particular conceptual/linguistic/cultural/experiential "place" from which we perceive shapes not only how we perceive but also what we perceive. It is like when we stand at a particular place—from that place, we can see up to the horizon that it is possible to see from that place; we can see the things that are within the scope of that horizon. If we were not standing in a particular place, we would not see at all. Just so, our particular conceptual/linguistic/cultural/experiential place determines what is within our ken, our range of knowledge. It determines our "horizon," the limit of our understanding. We literally cannot conceive what is outside our horizon.

However, while we cannot avoid remaining always grounded in a particular conceptual place (principle 2 above is based on this realization), we *can* expand our horizon. In interreligious dialogue, it is the encounter with the other and the gradual and difficult process of taking in that otherness and making it conceptually one's own, part of one's ken, that expands our horizon (principle 1 above is based on this). It is this incorporation of the conceptual/cultural/experiential world of the other that makes interreligious dialogue so intellectually fascinating and gives it such potential for stimulating personal and spiritual growth. Gadamer points out that there is and can be no "method" by which this is achieved; it is a process of discovery of what one does not know, what is outside one's horizon, what is conceptually other. By definition, there can be no method constructed by the self using its own conceptual framework with which the known can control the process of knowing the unknown, the other (principle 5). Rather, one learns everything one can about the other (principle 3), and then one listens with great care to the words of the other (principle 1 again) in order to discover wherein the other brings to light what one does not know—the other is the agent here, not the self. One will hear things that don't sound quite right or confuse or jar or provoke questions. It is a given that the other is representing his or her own view (principle 7). Therefore, this point of confusion, not knowing, or incommensurability is a critical signal that here, at this point, there is something one does not yet understand; it is an invitation to expand one's horizon, by continuing to ask and listen until something the other says manages to get through, prompting a eureka experience. At this point, one has taken in or incorporated what formerly was not one's own, what was other, so that it is now within one's own horizon. This is not to say that one needs to agree with or like everything one hears, just that one is now capable of hearing it and accurately understanding it.

Thus, while the purpose of dialogue is to understand the other, it often has personal growth as a consequence. Participants commonly report that dialogue somehow refreshes their spirituality such that they become better members of their own religion. People often report that they go back to their own religion and, seeing things with fresh eyes, find something there that they had never before noticed and that becomes very important to them. What is probably responsible for these phenomena is the process of expanding one's horizon.

Gadamer's principles, moreover, make clear why interreligious dialogue is not an effort to forge a single, syncretized world religion. At every step of dialogue, one retains the particularity of one's perspective; even when one's horizon has expanded such that one now comprehends another religion more deeply, one still remains rooted in a particular conceptual/linguistic/cultural/experiential place.

PARTICULAR DIALOGUES

We will use the Jewish-Christian dialogue to exemplify intercommunity dialogue and the Buddhist-Christian dialogue to exemplify dialogue for personal growth.

Intercommunity Dialogue: Jewish-Christian Dialogue

The Jewish-Christian dialogue has had by far the most important and concrete results of any of the interreligious dialogues. The primary motivation behind this dialogue for Christians has been the great shock of the Holocaust, Christians' need to examine what responsibility they bore for that horror, and their determination to make whatever changes are necessary to ensure that such a thing could never happen again. The primary Jewish interest in dialogue has been to protect Judaism and the Jewish people, motivated by a sense of finally, after two thousand years of domination and extensive mistreatment, having caught the sympathetic attention of the Christian world. While the starting motivations have been entirely practical, the outcome has been not only practical change but also quite profound theological learning and rethinking on the Christian side.

Some of these changes are reflected, quite dramatically, in the text of *Nostra Aetate*, which focuses largely on the Catholic church's reappraisal of its relationship with Judaism. The emphasis of the text is on the ways in which Christianity is forever tied to Judaism and is unthinkable without it. It recognizes that the roots of the church are to be found in God's covenant with the Jews and in the biblical (Jewish) patriarchs and prophets. Thus, the church "takes her nourishment from the root of the cultivated olive tree onto which the wild-olive branches of the Gentiles have been grafted." In short, the text brings out not only the Jewish foundations of the church but indeed also the *ongoing* Jewishness of the church, which is, in effect, grafted onto the primary body, represented as Jewish roots. Finally, *Nostra Aetate* makes plain something that, notwithstanding its obviousness, the church had successfully buried in its teachings over the years: the Jewishness of Jesus, "according to the flesh."

In a way probably unforeseeable at the time, the acknowledgment of the Jewishness of Jesus and the Jewishness of the church has had a substantial and positive theological impact on Christianity, both Catholic and Protestant. Since Vatican II, the Jewishness of Jesus has come to be embraced with great enthusiasm in the church, not only by liberals but very much by conservatives as well. The church, both liberal and conservative, is full of seder meals at Passover. It is full of Sunday school classes and adult religious education programs studying the Jewish roots of such Christian practices as communion and atonement. Many Christians have found that a better understanding of the Jewishness of Jesus and the Jewish roots of Christianity gives their faith a greater richness and fullness. At the same time, it is fair to say that a full searching of the Christological implications of Jesus's Jewishness remains to be done.

Nostra Aetate also takes up issues directly related to the Christian persecution of Jews. It explicitly negates one of the historical Christian justifications for the persecution of the Jews, the charge that they are "Christ killers," arguing that even though, according to scripture, the Jewish authorities and their followers urged the death of Christ, his death "cannot be blamed on all Jews living at that time ... or on the Jews of today." It forbids the church teaching that the Jews are rejected by God or accursed, which in previous centuries was common language from the pulpit. It explicitly condemns all persecutions of the Jews (or any persons). All of these changes and condemnations of past teachings and practices are absolute necessities from a Jewish perspective.

Another matter of concern for Jews that Christians have taken up as a result of the Jewish-Christian dialogue is traditional Christian teachings that state or imply that Christianity supersedes Judaism. This is the previously common traditional Christian teaching that Judaism merely served to prepare the way for Christianity; now that Christianity exists, there is no longer any need for Judaism to continue to exist. In this understanding, the New Testament replaces the Old, and all Jews should become Christians. To a people and a religion nearly wiped out (Judaism), it is a matter of great importance that the powerful Christian religion not wipe Judaism out by considering it merely anticipatory and no longer necessary, as if Jews who "cling" to Judaism are somehow a purposeless relic. Judaism, Jews point out, is a living religion with its own inherent necessity for continuing to exist. A major accomplishment of the Jewish-Christian dialogue is that these points have, in fact, been embraced by mainstream Christianity, which has changed its teaching accordingly. For example, *Nostra Aetate* states that the Jews remain "very dear to God" and that God does not repent of the gifts he makes (i.e., the covenant with the Jews). The World Council of Churches emphasizes that it is in dialogue with people of "living" faiths, including Judaism. Of course, some very conservative Christian churches see no need for such changes—an example of how interreligious dialogue often makes necessary intrareligious dialogue.

Another matter of concern among Jews remains at present unresolved: the frequent negative statements made about Jews in the Christian gospels and the Book of Acts (Cook 1991). These hostile statements sometimes come from the mouth of Jesus himself. Jewish leaders and "the Jews" as a group are variously called blind guides, hypocrites, whitewashed tombs, a brood of vipers, and deserving of hell; in John's gospel, Jesus tells the Jews that they are the children of the devil, not of God, and have never known God (John 8:39–55). They are shown as villains plotting and urging the death of Jesus. There is so much hostility and negativity expressed toward Jews in the New Testament that many Jews consider it to be an anti-Judaic text.

It comes as a dismaying shock to many Christians to learn that Jews perceive the New Testament in this way—as a message of hate—when Christians see it as preaching a message of love. Because of this, and because of the past use of these texts to inspire anti-Judaic hatred, it is an imperative for many Christian scholars to find ways to understand these passages that will void them of anti-Judaic meaning. Many ways to do this are under discussion. These include, for example, the arguments that the worst language applied to individuals or groups *among* the Jews, not the Jews as such; Jesus's chastising words are like those of the Hebrew prophets, a rebuke made out of love; and the negative language reflected early Christians' concern to separate themselves from the Jews. The jury is still out among both Christians and Jews, however, regarding whether any of these approaches actually resolves the problem.

The Jewish-Christian dialogue has resulted in some very significant and highly publicized apologies, two of which might be mentioned. The Evangelical Lutheran Church in America issued a statement in 1994, acknowledging "with pain" the violent anti-Jewish diatribes and the violent recommendations of their founder, Martin Luther, in his later writings. The church publicly rejected this language and deplored its use by modern anti-Semites. "Grieving" Lutheran "complicity" with this history of hatred, the Lutherans pledged themselves to oppose such bigotry both within the church and in the larger society.[3]

The Catholic apology to the Jews has thus far been less explicit than the Lutheran. In 2000, Pope John Paul II asked God's forgiveness for the sins of Roman Catholics over the ages, including "sins against the Jews," though without naming the Holocaust or any particular sins. Shortly thereafter, during a weeklong pilgrimage to the Holy Land, the pope visited Yad Vashem, the main Holocaust memorial in Israel, and paid tribute to the dead in deeply emotional language. The entire event was broadcast live on Israeli television. While it was recognized that both of these events were major historic steps, many Jews were disappointed that in neither event did the pope explicitly and verbally apologize for the silence of the Catholic church during the Holocaust. This leaves a sense of unfinished business from the Jewish perspective.

Jewish resentment of the Christian drive to convert them to Christianity is a long-standing and bitter complaint that continues to this day. It is based not only on the wish to be left alone but also on a long history of forced conversions, convert-or-die ultimatums, and baptism of children against parental will. They see it as another attempt to eliminate Jews from the world (if all Jews converted to Christianity, there would be no more Jews). Jews are unhappy with all attempts to convert them and with the incessant, hounding nature of that effort. A particularly egregious offense to many Jews was the Southern Baptist decision to step up the conversion effort with special prayers for the conversion of Jews during the Jewish high holy days of Rosh Hashanah and Yom Kippur. Some Christians, however, have decided that efforts to convert Jews are ruled out by the biblical passage stating that the Jews remain beloved by God and that their covenant with God continues (Romans 11:28–29).

A final important issue in the Jewish-Christian dialogue concerns intermarriage and the children of intermarriages. While intermarriage is an issue in other dialogues, it is of particular importance in the Jewish-Christian dialogue. Since approximately 6 million Jews were killed in the Holocaust, the sheer number of Jews existing today and in the future is inevitably of foremost importance to Jews. In America, about half of Jews intermarry, mostly with Christians or nominal Christians. Only about one-third of the children born to these intermarriages remain Jewish. At this rate of attrition and with no malevolent intent on anyone's part—just the opposite, in fact—the survival of Judaism, in America at least, cannot continue for many generations.

The issues of conversion and of the children of intermarriage are good examples of how interreligious dialogue can at times be an exercise in incommensurability.

For some Jews, these are matters of the survival of the Jewish people than which there is nothing more important. For some Christians, however, the potential loss of personal identity as a Jew and the continuity of the Jewish religion simply can't compare in importance to personal faith decisions and the gaining of eternal life.

Dialogue for Personal Growth: Buddhist-Christian Dialogue

Compared with the Jewish-Christian dialogue (and many other dialogues), the Buddhist-Christian dialogue is relatively unburdened by history. There are certainly wounds stemming from the period of colonialism, but they are far less extensive than those in many other dialogues. There is also the occasional contemporary tiff, such as when Pope John Paul II wrote in a negative and inaccurate way about Buddhism in his 1994 book, *Crossing the Threshold of Hope*, and cautioned his readers against trying Buddhist meditation. The book prompted an outcry and was followed by a boycott of the pope's visit to Sri Lanka by the Buddhist leadership of that country. (Leaders from both religions subsequently met in dialogue and reaffirmed their friendly relationship.)

In the main, the Buddhist-Christian dialogue is flourishing as a dialogue among individuals searching for deeper mutual understanding and their own personal spiritual growth; official dialogue is relatively insignificant in this encounter. This is an excellent example of a dialogue that can get the full benefit of the process that Gadamer wrote about.

In this dialogue, two religions encounter each other that would seem at first to have very little in common. Doctrinally, God (in Christianity) meets no God (in Buddhism), soul meets no soul, one life meets many lifetimes. How can these two religions have anything to talk about? However, if one focuses on the dynamics of the lived religious life, rather than on doctrine, one comes to see that these two religions do have a great deal in common. For example, at the center of their respective value systems Christianity puts love and Buddhism puts compassion and loving kindness. To what extent are they talking about the same thing? Is compassion the same as love? To explore this requires using something like the procedure Gadamer described. Not that one wants them to come out "the same." To the contrary; while it is clear that both religions are exploring the territory of benevolence—and therefore are able to have a deep conversation—the differences in how they describe this territory are the most instructive part of the encounter.

Again, in their respective engagements with problems in society, both religions espouse an exalted nonviolence in their ideals. On closer examination, one discovers that Christianity holds the nonviolent ideal in the context of an imperative to achieve justice—a concept that Buddhism lacks—and allows the use of a certain amount of "righteous anger." Buddhists commonly challenge such a notion in dialogue with Christians, and Christians find themselves hard put to defend it. On the other hand, Buddhists in dialogue with Christians are frequently moved to self-criticism when they put their own meager record of engagement with problems in society alongside the Christian record and tend to come away feeling that they need to do much more.

A frequent topic of dialogue between Christians and Buddhists is the practice of contemplative prayer (Christianity) and meditation (Buddhism) and its role in spiritual development or personal transformation. Since this area has to do with nonverbal experience, it is difficult to speak about it; nevertheless, a great deal of speaking on the subject is attempted. Some issues examined include: Do the two religions agree that egocentricity is the root cause of what is wrong with human-kind? Do Buddhist and Christian contemplative/meditative methods share the same fundamental values and principles? Is it right when Christians use Buddhist meditative techniques? Is the loss of self in something greater that is described by some Christian mystics like the no-self (*anatman*) of Buddhism? Is the "something greater" of Christian mysticism—the God beyond all names and concepts—the same as Buddhist Nirvana? Questions like these, and many more, are explored at dialogue conferences and also in depth when monastics from the two religions visit in their monasteries, sharing the same life and practices for months at a time.

There is even a way in which evangelical Protestantism is brought into this dialogue. A very large Buddhist sect, Pure Land Buddhism, and especially one of its Japanese forms, Jodo Shinshu, teach that one must face one's own ignorance and intractable faults and admit that one is unable to overcome them by one's own efforts. Ultimately, one must turn one's life entirely around by accepting the liber-ation from all of this that Amida Buddha is constantly and gratuitously offering us. Once one does that, one's life is a life of thanksgiving, and one looks forward to being with the Buddha in the Pure Land after death. Putting aside major theological differences between the two religions (Amida Buddha, for example, is not said to have created the universe), the dynamics of the spirituality in this form of Bud-dhism are startlingly similar to those of evangelical Christianity. Conservative Christian theologian Karl Barth famously acknowledged this similarity but wrote that nevertheless, the only way to salvation is through Jesus Christ (Barth 1956). Others, struck by the similarity between the two, have found it difficult to find any nonarbitrary justification for such a statement.

It is widely observed that the gains in the Buddhist-Christian dialogue have gone to both sides. Christians generally feel that they have taken from the dialogue an enhanced understanding of the dynamics of spirituality and a deepened way of conceiving the divine, while Buddhists feel that they have benefited by the example and prodding of Christian spiritually based social action. The main practical ten-sion between Buddhists and Christians is some Christian leaders' anxiety about the rapidly growing interest in Buddhism among people in the West today (a worry shared by some Jewish leaders).

Conclusions

Interreligious dialogue represents a major paradigm change in the norms of inter-religious behavior. It is a change from the intentionality of wanting to change or control others to an intentionality that accepts others as they are. In the minds of many, it represents the only alternative to a future of interreligious hostility and violence. Yet its implications have scarcely been plumbed. It deeply challenges any religion's claim to exclusive truth, suggesting that each religion has its own unique value and contribution to make. It proposes that the religions should not see one another as competitors in a zero-sum game but instead should embrace the existence of other religions as good. It insists that there can be harmony amid diversity.

NOTES

1. I have drawn heavily on Diana Eck's discussion (Eck 1986). Our types do differ somewhat, however.
2. The official English translation of *Nostra Aetate* is available on the Internet at www.vatican.va/archive/hist_councils/ii_vatican_council/documents/vat-ii_decl_19651028_nostra-aetate_en.html.
3. Available online at www.jewishvirtuallibrary.org/jsource/anti-semitism/lutheran1.html.

REFERENCES

Barth, Karl. 1956. *Church Dogmatics*, vol. 1, part 2, G. W. Bromiley and T. F. Torrance, eds. Edinburgh: T. and T. Clark, 340–344.
Eck, Diana. 1986. "What Do We Mean by 'Dialogue'?" *Current Dialogue* (December): 5–15.
Cook, Michael. 1991. "The New Testament: Confronting Its Impact on Jewish-Christian Relations." In Michael Shermis and Arthur E. Zannoni, eds., *Introduction to Jewish-Christian Relations*. Mahwah, N.J.: Paulist, 34–62.
Gadamer, Hans-Georg. 1975. *Truth and Method*. London: Continuum.
Idliby, Ranya, Suzanne Oliver, and Priscilla Warner. 2007. *The Faith Club: A Muslim, a Christian, a Jew—Three Women Search for Understanding*. New York: Free Press.

FOR FURTHER READING AND VIEWING

Auteur Productions. 2001 *Jews and Christians: A Journey of Faith* (DVD).
Beversluis, Joel, ed. 2000. *Sourcebook of the World's Religions: An Interfaith Guide to Religion and Spirituality*, 3rd ed. Novato, Calif.: New World Library.
Braybrooke, Marcus. 1992. *Pilgrimage of Hope: One Hundred Years of Global Interfaith Dialogue*. New York: Crossroad.
———. 1998. *Faith and Interfaith in a Global Age*. Grand Rapids, Mich.: Co-Nexus.
Kasimow, Harold, John P. Keenan, and Linda Klepinger Keenan, eds. 2003. *Beside Still Waters: Jews, Christians, and the Way of the Buddha*. Boston: Wisdom.
Mitchell, Donald W., and James Wiseman, eds. 1997. *The Gethsemani Encounter: A Dialogue on the Spiritual Life by Buddhist and Christian Monastics*. New York: Continuum.
Shermis, Michael, and Arthur E. Zannoni, eds. 1991. *Introduction to Jewish-Christian Relations*. Mahwah, N.J.: Paulist.

CHAPTER 9

....

THE RELIGIOUS ALIEN

....

PAUL J. GRIFFITHS

WHO are one's religious aliens, and what is to be done about them? These are among the more important questions raised by the facts of religious diversity. They can be asked and answered by those who think of themselves as religious, as well as by those who do not, and they can be asked and answered by the institutions of governance (legislatures, judiciaries), by particular churches, and by individuals, among others. The questions are unavoidable once the categories that constitute them ("religion," "religious," "alien") are allowed, and for citizens of late-capitalist democracies, as most readers of this book are likely to be, the categories are so thoroughly at home in local speech and thought that they cannot be easily ignored or evaded. This means, in turn, that the questions are avoidable for us at neither the theoretical nor the practical level: our political and social habits prescribe them for us. Engaging the questions might certainly take the form of objecting to the terms in which they are put, perhaps by revealing the dubious genealogy of those terms, but this will not exempt us from the engagement.

How, then, to understand the terms of the questions?

To call someone *alien* sounds neither welcoming nor affirming, connoting as it does both otherness and danger. In contemporary English, the word is most commonly used as a label for extraterrestrial visitors, those extreme others whose imagined characteristics permit us to clarify what we think about our own. Close behind this is the legal usage, according to which aliens are noncitizens, strangers from elsewhere whose legal and moral status is ambiguous exactly because they are aliens. In both usages, there is a fundamental structural opposition between them and us, whether the "us" is as broad as the entire human race or as narrow as those who live in our neighborhood.

This opposition gives the fundamental syntax of thought about the alien. Thinking and acting within it requires attention to boundaries (is it always—or ever—clear who is inside and who is outside?), identity tests (the shibboleth), the scope of permissible relations (may we reproduce with the aliens, eat with them, touch them, sing with them, study with them?), and much else. Such thought and action are not avoidable; every culture uses a syntax of kinship, every state attends to its boundaries and to what constitutes citizenship, every corporation uses regulations to determine who is and who is not among its employees, and every sports team cultivates a division between supporters and foes. Whether to think and act within this syntax is not in question; we all do because we all must, even when we try to overturn it or leave it behind. The question is only how. What will our understanding and treatment of our aliens be? Here, there are many and rich possibilities: we might think the aliens, whoever they are, capable of overrunning us, erasing us, forcing themselves on us sexually, enriching us, becoming like us, transforming us into their likeness, living alongside us in harmonious difference, being our friends, and so on.

We might combine these inventions (they are all inventions) about aliens with an equally wide range of kinds of engagement: we might attempt their domestication, violently or otherwise, or, failing that, their erasure, for which violence is almost always necessary; we might shun them, hoping that they will do likewise; we might tolerate them, enduring their otherness within limits and hoping for the same from them; we might acknowledge their superiority and do all we can to become like them; we might cooperate with them in some agreed particular campaign; we might seek to learn from them; we might fight them in an attempt to get them to acknowledge our superiority and to assume a subject position before us; or, most difficult, we might love them exactly in their otherness, offering ourselves to them as servants. In most cases, our engagements with our aliens will exhibit aspects of several of these attitudes at once. Among those who administered the British Raj, for instance, were some who thought of their Indian subjects as aliens whose labor and goods should be expropriated to ornament the British crown; there were some who thought of themselves as gift bringers who would move the aliens in the direction of domestication; there were some eager to learn from local literary and philosophical traditions; there were some who abandoned their Englishness for an imagined Indianness; and some combined aspects of all of these in their engagements with the locals.

To add the modifier *religious* to *alien* might intensify the difficulties already noted. This is certainly true if, as I assume in what follows, to be religious is (at least) to inhabit a form of life that seems to one comprehensive (it takes account of everything), of central importance to the ordering of one's life (all other aspects of one's life are subsumed into it or circle it, satellite-like), and unsurpassable (it cannot be exceeded by any other, being *id quo nihil maius cogitari possit* among forms of life, as Anselm wrote of God, and for closely associated reasons). This is certainly not the only possible understanding of *religion* and its derivatives; but the complex and disputed history of the term and its understandings is explored elsewhere in this book, so I shall here leave this understanding as simply stipulated.

If some such understanding of religion is in play, then to think someone a religious alien might intensify the otherness and danger of the aliens so categorized by locating them in a form of life with a very high opinion of itself. Thinking of someone as an alien of that kind might encourage the more extreme among the inventions already mentioned, whether or not those making the judgment are themselves religious according to the understanding given. Such extreme imaginations are especially likely for those who do not themselves inhabit a religious form of life or who take themselves not to; they are more likely than those who are themselves religious to imagine that all of the religious are violently disposed toward erasure of their aliens. But in fact, the variety of religious forms of life, with the understanding of religion given, is very great, which means that the variety of ways in which the religious think of and respond to their aliens will be equally great. Ways of thinking about the alien and more general ways of thinking about the world and the human are intimate with one another, and since these latter are quite varied both among religions and between the religious and the nonreligious, so, correspondingly, are judgments about and attitudes toward aliens. There are no easy generalizations, therefore, about how the religious are likely to think about their aliens. It is also a matter of observable fact that the nonreligious are not notably less violent in their responses to their aliens than the religious are to theirs. Nevertheless, it is true that the questions provoked by aliens can be especially and intensely pressing for the religious just because they inhabit what seems to them an unsurpassable and comprehensive form of life.

To think of someone or some group as religiously alien according to the understandings in play here is to make an indexical judgment: the religious alien is anyone who seems to inhabit a religious form of life that one does not take oneself to inhabit. One might make this judgment as a nonreligious person; in this case, all those who do seem to inhabit a religious form of life are one's religious aliens. Or one might make it as a religious person, in which case, all and only those who seem to inhabit a religious form of life other than one's own are one's religious aliens. Understanding *religious alien* in this way permits avoidance of difficulties about boundaries and identity markers by leaving those difficulties to those making the judgments. If a Baptist chooses to consider a Catholic a religious alien (or vice versa), this suffices to make the Catholic one, without further discussion of difficulties about the relations among sortals such as *Christianity* and *Baptist* and *Catholic*. And if a Gelug Buddhist chooses not to consider a Catholic Christian a religious alien, this suffices for the Catholic Christian not to be one, without further discussion of sortals such as *Christianity* and *Buddhism*.

The questions with which I began—who are one's religious aliens, and what should be done about them—should now be clearer. What kinds of answers are possible?

DOMESTICATION

There is, first, the hope for domestication, typically, but not necessarily, coupled with actions aimed at bringing that result about. Domestication, thus, is evident in a set of attitudes and actions, belonging to those who take themselves to be religious and aimed at removing whatever is taken to separate the alien from the home community and providing whatever is thought necessary for making the alien a member of it. So, for example, Christian missionaries might take faith in the triune God and baptism in the triune name to be severally requisite for membership in the church and conjointly sufficient to bring it about; they might also take the practice of making offerings to members of the Sangha, the Buddhist monastic community, as an insuperable barrier to the possession of such faith and the reception of such baptism. They will, then, to the extent that they think domestication desirable and themselves effective agents in bringing it about, attempt to bring the offerings to an end and to preach the gospel with one hand while offering baptism with the other. Once the barriers have been removed and the offerings received, the alien will have been domesticated, which is just to say that the alien will now be thought of by the missionary and those who share the missionary's understandings to be one of themselves. In similar ways (though usually lacking the missionary emphasis), those who have undergone the ritual and legal aspects of naturalization as citizens of the United States will, as a result, be understood by native-born citizens—or at least by those who know and care about such things—no longer to be alien in respect of citizenship but rather to have been domesticated.

These examples show that an interest in domestication does not require erasure of every mark of alien identity. That would be impossible in any case; but even where a particular religious community uses the rhetoric of death and rebirth to describe the passage from being alien to being kin (as many do; such tropes are essential to the practice of Christian baptism, for instance), the idea is not complete replacement but rather partial remaking and reordering of what is already present. The old Adam (or Eve), though drowned in the baptismal bath and refigured as a new creation, does not vanish; he (or she) rises to the surface of the chaos waters along with the newly made Christian. This is a typical pattern of thought among those who seek to domesticate the alien.

Many religious forms of life shape those who live within them as missionaries, which is to say as advocates for domesticating the religious alien and performers of whatever seems necessary to bring this about. It is easy enough to see why. To claim comprehensiveness, unsurpassability, and centrality for one's form of life bears a strong affinity to thinking it good to share it with others, to persuading those alien to it of the goodness of their domestication, and to doing what one can to bring that transition about. The strength of this affinity is linked to the extent to which a particular religion understands itself to offer a gift of universal significance, as many, but by no means all, religions do. There is no strong missionary impulse among Orthodox Jews, for example, as there is also not among Brahmanical Hindus, and for much the same reasons: these are religious forms of life whose adherents are likely to think of it as being appropriate for only a small subset of human beings, even if it might have other kinds of relevance (as beacon, as warning, as lure) for that majority for whom domestication is inappropriate or impossible. But for religions such as Buddhism, Christianity, or Islam, self-conscious in their universalism, missionary activity of one kind or another is close to unavoidable.

Seeking to domesticate the alien can, but need not, coexist with a high evaluation of the benefits brought to the home community by newly domesticated aliens. When it does, emphasis will be placed by the home community on the importance of the newly domesticated alien placing what he or she knows and can do at the service of his or her new home community. When it does not—when, as Augustine wrote of scripture, the domesticating religion thinks that whatever is good among aliens is already found in the home community, and whatever is bad is already condemned there—then it is more likely that what the aliens bring will be treated at best as something indifferent. The three world-historical missionary religions (Buddhism, Christianity, Islam) have varied considerably within themselves along this spectrum, sometimes eager to embrace the alien gift (as Muslims once were with respect to Aristotle) and sometimes equally eager to reject the need for any such gifts (as Jerome was in his occasional repudiation of the idea that Christians might benefit from reading pagan literature). In this range of attitudes to alien gifts, they are like nonreligious missionaries—those who evangelize, for instance, in the service of the free market or of democracy.

Religious aliens faced by attempted domestication might find themselves under threat of compulsion by violence or seduction by the loving embrace. It is fair to say that those religions with deep and intense missionary inclinations are more likely than those without to find it attractive—or defensible—to strong-arm aliens into domestication. But there is no necessary connection even here; it is just that those communities for which domestication is of marginal interest are less likely to find it important enough to attempt compulsion. There might be a similar range of responses on the part of the religious alien: everything from happy acquiescence to the offer (or demand) of domestication to the violent rejection of that offer. Everything will depend on the particulars of the religious form of life to which the alien belongs.

SHUNNING

The impulse to domesticate seeks to make the alien kin, and it is a very common, probably the most common, religious response to the religious alien. But it is by no means the only one. Another set of attitudes and responses to the religious alien, whether by those who are themselves religious or by those who are not, seeks not domestication but separation. This response comes in kinds, but its fundamental grammar is most apparent in shunning. To shun the alien is to refuse contact of any kind: no touch, no sharing of food, no exchange of gaze, no reciprocal speech, no shared space. To shun is to seek to remove the shunned from one's presence and thought, to make the shunned as if he or she were not.

In its most extreme form, shunning requires killing followed by the removal of all evidence that those killed have ever inhabited the world. When the Romans erased Carthage or, much later, attempted the same with Jerusalem, they wanted not only to kill its inhabitants but also to destroy any evidence that they had ever been and to make impossible the future habitation of the places in which they had lived. Carthage's buildings were leveled, its land plowed over, its ground salted. In still more extreme form, the Nazi "final solution" had the same goal: Europe's Jews were not only to be slaughtered, but the memory of their presence was to be erased as well, which required the destruction of books and buildings and all other carriers of memory. Final and irreversible erasure is shunning's ideal goal, and it has been attempted often, sometimes by the religious but more often by the irreligious, sometimes directed at those who were religiously alien and sometimes directed at those whose alienness took other forms.

Shunning need not be as radical as this, and most often is not. Its most common less radical forms are separation by removal (exile), separation by enclosure (ghettoization), and prevention of an impending alien incursion by erecting a barrier against it (exclusion); none of these requires erasure, even though that always beckons as a possible end.

To separate oneself from one's aliens by removing them means that their bodies and possessions must be shipped out, taken from the homeland to somewhere else, a place of exile where they can safely be forgotten. The architects of the Nazi "final solution" considered this possibility for Europe's Jews and might perhaps have preferred it had it not proved impractical because of war's exigencies and other practical difficulties. In the 1930s, the idea of removing all of Europe's Jews to Madagascar was seriously considered by Nazi theorists. Somewhat less dramatically, shunning by removal was one of the main strategies used by the federal government of the United States during the nineteenth and early twentieth centuries in its handling of Native Americans. Evidence of this strategy remains in the reservation system, and it is clear that Native Americans were regarded by the lawmakers and policy makers who developed and applied these strategies as alien religiously, as well as in many other ways.

Closely similar to exiling one's aliens is the strategy of enclosing them. This is to keep close the aliens who are already here but erect barriers that prevent their interaction with one. They are ideally to be kept invisible though sometimes used. The late-medieval and Renaissance Christian practice of ghettoizing Jews was like this: they were not sent away, but their movements were restricted, as were the places where they could legally live or work. In that case, the separation was usually given legal sanction, but often it is not, being enforced instead by powerful local habits, backed by the imagination—and sometimes the reality—of violence. Contemporary urban ghettos usually work in this way, and when the locals throw up physical barriers intended to keep their undesirable aliens—ethnically, economically, and sometimes also religiously alien—enclosed in their places, as they did on the South Side of Chicago and in many other American cities in the 1960s, they are giving physical form to an already present local habit of enclosure.

Exclusion is like enclosure, except that the aliens at whom it is directed are not yet here. Their continued absence must be ensured by a physical barrier, a wall. The purpose of the wall is not to enclose them but to keep them out and thereby to maintain a separation already in place. Hadrian's Wall, built in the second century CE across the neck of land separating (roughly) what is now England from what is now Scotland, was of this sort. The aliens to be kept out in that case were the Pictish tribes. Contemporary instances include the walls now under construction along the U.S.-Mexican border and along the boundary between Israel and (inter alia) the West Bank. The aliens in the U.S. case are Spanish-speaking Catholics, understood by the wall builders to be an economic, religious, and cultural threat to the United States; those in the Israel case are mostly Arabic-speaking Muslims, understood by the wall builders to be an economic, religious, and cultural threat to the State of Israel. Walls can be intended to keep the locals in rather than the aliens out (the Berlin Wall was of that sort); but the kind of walling I have in mind here is an act of exclusion aimed at those outside and therefore a kind of shunning.

The examples given of each of these methods for shunning the alien show them in use by those with power to enforce them whether or not those at whom they are directed wish to accept them. This is the usual thing. But exile and enclosure, at least, might also be used voluntarily by groups without power. If one thinks contact with local religious aliens is undesirable for one reason or another but one lacks the power to do anything to or about the aliens one would like to shun, then one might exile oneself by leaving, or one might stay where one is but, to the extent possible, ghettoize oneself. Both strategies are widely evident among religious groups. Some Christian groups (Puritans, Mennonites, and many others) whose members found inhospitable or otherwise problematic the religious settlements of various European states in the seventeenth and eighteenth centuries left for the new promised land of the Americas. This is a form of shunning by self-exile.

Self-enclosure is also possible. This is likely to happen when those who inhabit a minority form of religious life consider their local aliens—usually a powerful majority—dangerous, threatening, or impure. The minority might have no choice but to stay where they are, and when that is the case, they are likely to try self-enclosure, though with varying degrees of intensity and consistency. To do this, they might adopt or preserve locally distinctive marks of identity (of dress, diet, language, education, reproduction, economic exchange), whose effect (and sometimes also purpose) is to show their difference; and they might refuse many or most forms of exchange with their aliens, the local majority, thus in effect ghettoizing themselves. Violence is less likely in cases like these than in those where shunning is enforced by a powerful majority; local minorities of these kinds usually lack the power to be effectively violent. But the syntax of the response might nonetheless be implicitly violent, suggesting, as it often does, that the world would be better were these aliens not in it.

These varieties of shunning are variously motivated. Fear and hatred of the alien might often be in play, which is why violence is typically near the surface when aliens are shunned. But shunning might also be motivated by a judgment that the world as presently constituted is deeply and apparently irreversibly hostile to what is held most dear and that shunning is essential to self-preservation. There is nothing peculiarly religious about these motives or about the varieties of shunning that they prompt or about the violence that often accompanies them. It is at least arguably the case that secular groups, perhaps most especially nation-states, are more likely than the religious to shun their aliens and to seek their erasure, exile, enclosure, or exclusion. For example, the German Nazis tried between 1933 and 1945 first to exile and then to kill all Jews within their territories. A less extreme case is the largely successful effort by the U.S. government between 1850 and 1910 to remake, by a combination of legal sanction and military threat, the marriage customs of the members of the Church of Jesus Christ of Latter-Day Saints so that they would accord with U.S. civil law rather than the doctrine of that church. But it is also the case that shunning will be an attractive response to the alien, religious or not, especially to those who inhabit a religious form of life that combines a strong sense of difference with a correspondingly weak sense of the importance of conversion. If one believes that one is definitively and fundamentally unlike the aliens, and one has no interest in domesticating them (perhaps they are so different that domestication seems hopeless), then shunning them will be attractive. How one does that will depend on what power one has, as well as on one's reasons for wanting to do it in the first place.

TOLERATION

The powers that be in contemporary late-capitalist democracies do not ordinarily attempt the domestication of their religious aliens; neither do they usually shun them or otherwise seek physical separation from them. Those responses are likely to be more attractive to totalitarian states; the recent persecutions of practitioners of Falun Gong by the authorities of the People's Republic of China provide a good example. In late-capitalist democracies, however, the religious alien is likely to be tolerated, and toleration is likely to be advocated as a civic virtue. Toleration is a set of responses to the religious alien distinct in some important ways from both domestication and separation. What is its syntax?

To advocate that an alien, whether religious or not, be tolerated is first to imply that there is something at least idiosyncratic about the alien, more likely something unpleasant or threatening. There is no need to tolerate something one likes or is fascinated by; toleration is, rather, a habit that requires the effort of putting up with something one does not like. Those who practice it grant those at whom it is directed space to do (or to think) something they would rather not have done (or thought); toleration is therefore ordinarily a gesture by the powerful toward the powerless, granting them space they cannot take for themselves. The gesture ordinarily rules out the thought that the tolerant might have something to learn from the alien or that they might think of those they tolerate as possible recipients of love or service or admiration. In all of these ways, those who practice toleration are likely to be less receptive to the importance of the alien's particular otherness than are those who seek the alien's domestication. The tolerant differ from those who seek separation from their aliens but perhaps not as much as is ordinarily thought. To tolerate some alien person or group locates them in a conceptual space in essential ways like the physical space of the ghetto; so, while toleration rules out exiling or excluding the aliens, and certainly bars seeking their erasure, it remains, in this attenuated fashion, a kind of separation.

For example, Christians and Jews have at various times been tolerated by Islamic states, most often by being given the status of *dhimmi* ("protected one"), which meant (usually) that they were recognized as subjects in a Muslim state and given a specific set of legal protections regarded as proper for non-Muslims. Those with this status could own property, marry, and do most of the other things ordinarily open to citizens. They could also, within limits (which could be severe), practice their religion without prompting state-sponsored efforts to domesticate them by making Muslims of them. They were, in short, tolerated by Muslim states in very much the same way that a deep-rooted tree tolerates drought. Drought is neither natural to it nor good for it, but it can be put up with for a while and even adapted to as a long-term condition. So, mutatis mutandis, for the presence of Jews and Christians in a Muslim polity and for the presence of any religious community in a secular one.

The toleration of religious aliens advocated and practiced in the United States is of essentially this sort. They are given legal (constitutional) guarantees of freedom to practice their religions, and the state also gives them some privileges not granted to the nonreligious—for example, exemption from some kinds of taxation and from some kinds of otherwise universally applicable public law (the Amish need not send their children to school beyond the age of fourteen; Jehovah's Witnesses need not repeat the Pledge of Allegiance in school; Quakers need not bear arms in the service of the state; Catholics need not abide by laws banning the provision of alcohol to minors; and so on). But at the same time, public space and state-owned property (a distinction now almost without purchase) are required by law to be free of some signs of religious observance, and the public profession of some religious identities has often, de facto if not de jure, barred those who make it from holding certain kinds of public office. Continuing judicial debate about the nature of the relation between the two religion clauses of the First Amendment to the U.S. Constitution ("Congress shall make no law respecting an establishment of religion, nor prohibiting the free exercise thereof") provides the principal engine for the construal of what tolerance for religious aliens means in the United States, and this is still very much a work in progress, as well as a work whose incoherence is becoming gradually more apparent. Refusing to establish requires, for instance, prohibition of free exercise for those religious aliens whose self-understanding requires their establishment. The logic of toleration remains the same, however: the body politic endures these more or less alien guests with the hope that eventually, their otherness will be diluted to the point where it no longer calls for toleration because it is scarcely any longer recognizable as alien. And in this respect, toleration as a response to the religious alien approaches domestication in its outcome.

Love's Embrace

A fourth family of responses to the religious alien differs from the other three—domestication, separation, toleration—in a fundamental way. Unlike them, it understands religious aliens as a gift and responds to them by embracing them as such, which is to say, as an unmerited and in-principle delightful gratuity, to be enjoyed exactly because of their otherness. Each of the other three families of response assumes that the alien's presence is in one way or another a difficulty, something to be changed, erased, removed, or—at best—put up with until a better state of affairs can be brought about. There are religious and nonreligious versions of these three families of response. The fourth family, however, is much more likely itself to be religious than not, and in my brief exposition of it here, I give it an explicitly Christian flavor. This is not to say that only Christians can or do advocate responses to the alien of this kind. There are certainly approximate Buddhist analogues and no doubt others not known to me; and there might also be secular versions, although these, I suspect (but will not here argue), have come into being as more or less degenerate offspring of Christianity.

To welcome others as a gift exactly in their otherness and to make aliens' alienness precisely what is to be loved about them seem difficult not only to do but also to understand. This is most fundamentally because it seems obvious that sometimes my aliens, religious or not, seek my woe rather than my weal, to damage rather than to heal me, and when that is the case, how can I regard their very otherness as a gift to be celebrated? The difficulty in understanding what is at stake here extends farther than this, however. What makes my aliens alien might often appear not in their desire to damage me or mine but rather in their apparent desire to damage themselves, whether by refusing to acknowledge or receive the good things I bring them or by actively seeking and performing, because of their own false and harmful understanding of the world and their place in it, what diminishes themselves. Love's embrace of the religious alien requires that these difficulties be met or at least that a trajectory be established toward meeting them.

The first move in the Christian form of love's embrace of the alien is to acknowledge the deep damage—the Christian word is *sin*—already present in oneself, the embracer. This is known with a depth and directness not available in the case of what seems to be the other's damage. Love's embrace requires, therefore, deep epistemic modesty about one's capacity accurately to judge the extent or nature of what is wrong with the other.

The second move is to distinguish good from evil as fullness is distinguished from lack. Even if, in this view, the alien is damaged, malevolent, and about to cause damage, these will be understood as lacks in the alien, not positive attributes. In judging these lacks for what they are, then, no judgment is offered about what the alien is in his or her otherness; the only judgment made—and tentatively, at that—is that the alien lacks some goods that he or she might have had. It is not the case that the alien's otherness, as a whole or in part, is itself to be resisted, erased, shunned, or domesticated.

The third move is to accept martyrdom if it is offered. If, as will sometimes be the case (as has sometimes been the case), religious aliens offer one violence just because one seems alien to them—if, that is, they take the path of erasure—those who offer love's embrace cannot respond in kind. They should instead respond by accepting the erasure offered. That is the syntax of the position, its deep structure. If they are Christians, they will know that erasure is not the outcome of being killed; they will know, too, that God's providence can bring good out of even this agonizingly dreadful situation.

The fourth move is to distinguish between offering the gift of oneself and what one knows from the aspiration to domesticate. The gifts one bears and offers might include, as is the case for Christians, knowledge of the triune God and his incarnation, crucifixion, and resurrection; they might include, as well, the hope that the blessing of this gift will finally be accepted by all. But bearing and offering these gifts neither requires nor even suggests that the point of offering them is conversion. The point is simply to offer them; love's embrace of the religious alien requires that. What follows from the offer is quite another question, and a standard Christian mode of putting that point is to say that God is the agent of conversion, not the evangelist or the church, except insofar as they serve as God's agents. I wrote above that Christians have been disposed to respond to their religious aliens with efforts aimed at domestication, and that is true. But the specifically Christian mode of that response, sketched here, undercuts its logic.

Conclusions

This sketch of the modes of deciding who one's religious aliens are and what to do about them is meant only to identify the most common among them. Others are possible, and even among those identified, many more sub-kinds could be discriminated. Some thought about even the few modes of decision about the religious alien discussed here should strongly suggest that this is perhaps the most intractable among the questions prompted by religious diversity. No stable solution seems possible at the level of the state: the tolerance advocated by democracies is certainly not one. And while some of the other families of response to the question are likely to prove attractive to one or another religious form of life—the last discussed to Christians, for instance—there is little hope that any among them will appeal to most, or even many, among the religions. The most that can be hoped for is that those inhabiting particular forms of life, whether religious or not, will come to see with increasing clarity the particularity of their own preferred modes of identifying and responding to their religious aliens. The deepest and most systematic violence in such responses comes from those blind to their own particularity.

FOR FURTHER READING

American Society for Political and Legal Philosophy. 2008. *Toleration and Its Limits*. New York: New York University Press.

Asad, Talal. 1993. *Genealogies of Religion: Discipline and Reasons of Power in Christianity and Islam*. Baltimore: Johns Hopkins University Press, especially chaps. 1–2, 7–8.

———. 2003. *Formations of the Secular: Christianity, Islam, Modernity*. Stanford, Calif.: Stanford University Press.

Barnes, Michael. 2002. *Theology and the Dialogue of Religions*. Cambridge, U.K.: Cambridge University Press, especially chap. 3.

Cavanaugh, William T. 2004. "Sins of Omission: What 'Religion and Violence' Arguments Ignore." *Hedgehog Review* 6/1: 34–50.

De Certeau, Michel. 1986. *Heterologies: Discourse on the Other*. Manchester, U.K.: Manchester University Press.

Dubuisson, Daniel. 2003. *The Western Construction of Religion: Myths, Knowledge, and Ideology*. Baltimore: Johns Hopkins University Press.

Fish, Stanley. 1997. "Mission Impossible: Settling the Just Bounds between Church and State." *Columbia Law Review* 97/8: 2255–2333.

Fitzgerald, Timothy, ed. 2007. *Religion and the Secular: Historical and Colonial Formations*. London: Equinox.

Griffiths, Paul J. 2001. *Problems of Religious Diversity*. Oxford: Blackwell, especially chap. 4.

Lindbeck, George. 1984. *The Nature of Doctrine: Religion and Theology in a Postliberal Age*. Philadelphia: Westminster, especially chap. 3.

Razavi, Mehdi Amin, and David Ambuel, eds. 1997. *Philosophy, Religion, and the Question of Intolerance*. Albany: State University of New York Press.

Ricoeur, Paul. 1992. *Oneself as Another*. Chicago: University of Chicago Press.

Sullivan, Winnifred. 2005. *The Impossibility of Religious Freedom*. Princeton, N.J.: Princeton: University Press.

Ward, Graham. 2003. *True Religion*. Oxford: Blackwell.

Zagorin, Perez. 2003. *How the Idea of Religious Toleration Came to the West*. Princeton, N.J.: Princeton University Press.

....

CHAPTER 10

RELIGIOUS DIVERSITY AND A GLOBAL ETHIC

....

LEONARD J. SWIDLER

I. From the Age of Monologue to the Age of Global Dialogue

THE world has always been religiously diverse. Moreover, for very many centuries, we humans have been aware that there were many different religious views abroad. So why is this always-present and long-known-about religious diversity suddenly a subject of human interest? I suggest that the reason is that humanity has reached a tipping point in a change of consciousness that is analogous to the beginning of a chain reaction in nuclear fusion.

Change has always taken place in human society, although most of the time, it seemed to most that things never changed because the change was mostly so slow and gradual. That is not the case today. Change is so rapid—and acceleratingly so—that everyone is suddenly very aware of it. So, too, we are suddenly aware that there are other religions in the world very different from our own, and they are as seriously articulated and espoused as ours.

In the past, we tended to think that those others were simply mistaken and not a little weird (which, of course, we were not). Now, however, all of those "weird" religions come into our living rooms through television and, even more, through the Internet. They are walking our streets, and we are walking theirs. We watch Buddhist monks in their orange robes march in protest—and cringe for them as they are beaten and killed—in the streets of that faraway land Myanmar. We watch the stunning display of contemporary technology and ancient culture/religion (always two sides of the coin of humanity) of Shamanism, Confucianism, and Daoism in the Chinese hosting of the Olympic Games (named for the mountain where the ancient Greek gods dwelled).

As humans spread out from their origin in central Africa, the forces of *divergence* necessarily dominated. New frontiers were like magnets, drawing humanity to ever new lands. However, since the world is a globe, we eventually and inevitably began to encounter one another more frequently, which often led to clashes, including Samuel Huntington's "Clash of Civilizations."[1] Thus, the forces of *convergence* have become dominant.

Something very special happened, however, in western Europe in modern times. Many thousands of years earlier, as humans grew in population and skills, they began to gather in large groups in what we call cities; their contiguity provided the possibility of a division of labor, which, in turn, drove the constant advancement of skills. As these cities grew and skills developed in them, "city-izations"—or, using the Latin for "city," *civis*, civilizations—were formed. There grew up four ancient major civilizations: Yellow River civilization, Indus River civilization, Mesopotamian/Egyptian Fertile Crescent civilization, and Greek civilization, basically independently and more or less simultaneously.

Along the way of human advances in these four ancient areas, there occurred an advance that was vastly more than simply a quantitative improvement, as had been going on for centuries in each civilization: a shift in human consciousness occurred that was of the magnitude of the prior shift from nomadic and tribal living to city-ization, with its qualitative leap forward. This qualitative shift in consciousness took place in all four of the civilizations between 800 and 200 BCE and was named the Axial Period by German philosopher Karl Jaspers.[2] Axial consciousness was focused on the *individual* and *internal* rather than the *collective* and *external*, as had been the case in "Primal" consciousness. The Hebrew prophets insisted that God was interested not in external sacrifices but in personal morality; Socrates claimed that only the personally "examined life" was worth living; Zoroaster and Confucius in the sixth and fifth centuries BCE expressed individual morality in the Golden Rule; Siddhartha the Buddha plotted the "Middle Path" not for the tribe but for each individual, to follow to bliss; and so on. This is also when the major religions of the world were launched, independent of one another but all within Axial consciousness.

The great world historian Arnold J. Toynbee listed some twenty-six civilizations throughout human history. Many of these—Egyptian, Chinese, Islamic, and so on—accomplished extraordinary things and more or less matched one another in attainments, although some were more advanced in one or another area than the others. Something unique, however, began to happen in Christendom as it was transformed into what is called Western civilization and is now morphing into global civilization. There took place a paradigm shift in consciousness, not only at the level that occurred every so often, such as the huge shift in astronomy from geocentrism to heliocentrism, or even of the magnitude of the shift of the Axial Period, which led Ewert Cousins to write of "the Second Axial Period."[3] Rather, there began to occur (what we are beginning to realize only now) a radical reordering of humanity on a global scale, which signals the end of the Age of Monologue and the dawn of the Age of Global Dialogue.

As Christendom through the Renaissance moved into what we retrospectively call modernity, it was transformed by the end of the eighteenth century into a quasi-secularized Western civilization, with its strong focus on freedom and reason. Throughout the nineteenth and twentieth centuries, as freedom and reason deepened and expanded (e.g., the "hermeneutics of suspicion"—Feuerbach, Marx, Durkheim, Freud, etc.), there was added the sense of history, dynamism, and evolution. By the latter part of the twentieth century, the fourth characteristic of modernity emerged: the awareness of pluralism and the consequent need for dialogue—understood as "talking with those who think differently from us so *we* can learn." This set the stage for the dawning of the Age of Global Dialogue—and the need for a global ethic.

Why did the need for dialogue arise in Western civilization, and why did it occur when it did? One can point to many external reasons, such as the spread of Christendom-Become-Western-Civilization from the Age of Exploration in the sixteenth century forward; the expansion of modernity, with its emphasis on reason, freedom, and democracy, from the eighteenth century forward; the rush of capitalism and the Industrial Revolution from the nineteenth century forward; and the dark side of modernity with two world wars in the twentieth century. All of these are important causes, but the underlying critical cause was the shift in how we humans understand how we understand, that is, our epistemology. At first blush, this might seem abstract and abstruse, but in fact, it is fundamental. All through the Age of Monologue, we humans have always spoken only with ourselves; we have spoken only either with those who agreed with us or those who should, for we had the truth (of course, we held a particular position because it was *the* truth).

However, the creation of "scientific" history by scholars such as Johann Georg Hamman, Johann Gottfried von Herder, and Leopold von Ranke in the late eighteenth and nineteenth centuries led us to realize that truth, that is, "statements about reality," was never absolute, unlimited, but was limited at least in the sense that any statement, any text, could be properly understood only in its context and hence is limited by it. Then came the various "Hermeneutics of Suspicion" mentioned above, followed by insights of scholars such as Karl Mannheim, who discerned that one's place in the world affects one's perception of reality (sociology of knowledge), and Max Scheler, who saw that we seek truth so that we may live by it (intentionality)—all of which naturally showed yet further limits on any statement about reality, about truth. More recently, Hans-Georg Gadamer and Paul Ricoeur more fully developed the science of hermeneutics, showing that all knowledge is interpreted knowledge. Knowledge itself was a necessarily relational process, for there is the *known* object, the *knower*, and the relation between the two, the *knowing*; the knower is essentially involved in the knowing process and hence limits the known, the truth.

Finally, the experience of and reflection on dialogue shows us that all of reality is fundamentally dialogic.

II. The Universe Is a Cosmic Dance of Dialogue

I would like to set this radically new way of understanding reality, dialogue, in its broadest context. Dialogue—understood most broadly as the mutually beneficial interaction of differing components—is at the very heart of the universe, of which we humans are the highest expression. From the basic interaction of matter and energy (in Einstein's formula $E = mc^2$ —energy equals mass times the square of the speed of light), to the creative interaction of protons and electrons in every atom, to the vital symbiosis of body and spirit in every human, through the creative dialogue between woman and man, to the dynamic relationship between individual and society. The very essence of our humanity is dialogical, and a fulfilled human life is the highest expression of the cosmic dance of dialogue.

In the past, during the Age of Divergence, we could live in isolation from one another; we could ignore one another. Now, in the Age of Convergence, we are forced to live in one world. We increasingly live in a global village. We cannot ignore the other, the different. Too often in the past, we have tried to make over the other into a likeness of ourselves, often by violence. But this is the very opposite of dialogue. This egocentric arrogance is in fundamental opposition to the Cosmic Dance of Dialogue. It is not creative; it is destructive. We humans today have a stark choice: dialogue or death.

There are four main dimensions to dialogue, four H's corresponding to the structure of our humanness: dialogue of the Head, dialogue of the Hands, dialogue of the Heart, and dialogue of Holiness.

1. *The Cognitive or Intellectual: Seeking the Truth*

In the dialogue of the Head, we mentally reach out to the other to learn from those who think differently from us. We try to understand how they see the world and why they act as they do. The world is far too complicated for any of us to understand alone; we can increasingly understand reality only with the help of the other, in dialogue. This is very important, because how we understand the world determines how we act in the world.

2. *The Illative or Ethical: Seeking the Good*

In the dialogue of the Hands, we join with others to work to make the world a better place in which we all must live together. Since we can no longer live separately in this one world, we must work jointly to make it not just a house but a home for all of us to live in. Stated differently, we join hands with the other to heal the world (*Tikkun ha Olam*). The world within us and all around us is always in need of healing, and our deepest wounds can be healed only together with the other, only in dialogue.

3. *The Affective or Aesthetic: Seeking the Beautiful*

In the dialogue of the Heart, we open ourselves to receive the beauty of the other. Because humans are body and spirit or, rather, body-spirit, we give bodily-spiritual expression in all of the arts to our multifarious responses to life: joy, sorrow, gratitude, anger, and, most of all, love. We try to express our inner feelings, which grasp reality in far deeper and higher ways than we are able to put into rational concepts and words; we create poetry, music, dance, painting, architecture, the expressions of the heart. All the world delights in beauty, and it is here that we find the easiest encounter with the other, the simplest door to dialogue; through the beauty of the other, we most easily enter the other.

4. *Holiness: Seeking the One*

Humans cannot long live a divided life. If we are even to survive, let alone flourish, we must "get it all together." We must not only dance the dialogues of the Head, Hands, and Heart, but also bring our various parts together in Harmony (a fourth H) to live a Holistic (a fifth H) life, which is what religions mean when they say that we should be Holy (a sixth H). Hence, we are authentically Human (a seventh H) only when our manifold elements are in Dialogue within each other and we are in Dialogue with the Others around us. We must dance together the *Cosmic Dance of Dialogue* of the Head, Hands, Heart, Holistically in Harmony within the Holy Human.

Those who know Western medieval philosophy will recognize that these are the Metaphysicals, the four aspects of Being Itself perceived from different perspectives: the One, the True, the Good, the Beautiful.

III. A Global Age Needs a Global Ethic

In the past, every civilization always had at its heart a religion, "an explanation of the ultimate meaning of life, and how to live accordingly, based on some notion of the transcendent."[4] The religion both shaped and reflected the values of the civilization: Islam for the Islamic civilization, Christianity for Christendom, Hinduism for Indian civilization, Marxism (ideology, as the functional equivalent of religion) for the Soviet civilization, and so on. However, in the now emerging global civilization, the question asks itself: What will be the religion at its heart? It cannot be any of the already existing religions/ideologies, for they all were tied to particular civilizations, even when they claimed to be universal. Despite their claims, when Christian missionaries went out, they preached European Christianity; it is only very recently that they have been making a serious effort at indiginization, which can happen only in dialogue. The same is true for Islam, Buddhism, Hinduism, and other religions. The answer to the question, then, can only be that religion (ideology)-in-dialogue will be the religion at the heart of the emerging global civilization.

If we unpack my brief definition of religion (ideology), we find that it has five elements: the four C's of creed, code, cult, and community structure and some notion of the transcendent.

> *Creed* refers to the cognitive aspect of a religion; it is everything that goes into the "explanation" of the ultimate meaning of life.
> *Code* of behavior or ethics includes all of the rules and customs of action that somehow follow from one aspect or another of the creed.

Cult means all of the ritual activities that relate the follower to one aspect or
another of the transcendent, either directly or indirectly, prayer being an
example of the former and certain formal behavior toward representatives
of the transcendent, such as priest§, being an example of the latter.

Community structure refers to the relationships among the followers; this can
vary widely, from a very egalitarian relationship as among Quakers,
through a "republican" structure such as Presbyterians have, to a monar-
chical one as with some Hasidic Jews vis-à-vis their *rebbe*.

Transcendent, as the roots of the word indicate, means "that which goes
beyond" the everyday, the ordinary, the surface experience of reality. It can
refer to spirits, gods, a personal God, an impersonal God, emptiness, and
so on.

If humanity is indeed moving into the Age of Global Dialogue with an emerging
global civilization (which produces not a gray uniformity but a richly colored diversity uniting the existing civilizations and cultures in dialogic fashion—unity and
integrity without uniformity), it will then need a global ethic, the second C, the
code of behavior, the "how to live accordingly."

The Movement for a Global Ethic, which Hans Küng and I launched in 1991,[5]
speaks of an "ethic" in the singular rather than "ethics" in the plural, because what
is needed is not a full-blown global ethics in great detail—indeed, such would not
even be possible—but a global consensus on the fundamental attitude toward good
and evil and the basic and middle principles to put it into action. Clearly, this ethic
must also be global. It will not be sufficient to have a common ethic for Westerners
or Africans or Asians, and so on. The destruction, for example, of the ozone layer or
the loosing of a destructive gene mutation by any one group will be disastrous for all.

Küng and I also thought that a Universal Declaration of a Global Ethic would
be a helpful instrument to bring the need for a global ethic to the consciousness of
a vast number of people. However, this declaration cannot be imposed from above
but must be arrived at by consensus through dialogue.

The following are the basic principles that I suggest are needed in such a declaration:

1. The declaration should use language and images that are acceptable to all
   major religions and ethical groups; hence, its language ought to be
   "humanity-based," rather than from authoritative religious books; it
   should be from "below," not from "above."

2. Therefore, it should be anthropocentric; indeed, more, it must be
   anthropocosmocentric, for we cannot be fully human except within the
   context of the whole of reality.

3. The affirmations should be dynamic in form in the sense that they will be
   susceptible to being sublated; that is, they might properly be reinterpreted
   by being taken up into a larger framework.

4. The declaration needs to set inviolable minimums but also open-ended
   maximums to strive for; but maximums might not be required, for they
   might violate the freedom minimums of some persons.

5. It could well start with—though not limit itself to—elements of the so-called Golden Rule: Treat others as we would be treated.

6. As humans ineluctably seek ever more knowledge and truth, so, too, do they seek to draw what they perceive as the good to their self (that is, they love). Usually, this self is expanded to include family and then friends. It needs to continue its natural expansion to the community, nation, world, and cosmos and the source and goal of all reality.

7. This human love, however, necessarily must start with self-love, for one can love one's neighbor only as one loves oneself; but since one becomes human only by interhuman mutuality, loving others fulfills one's own humanity and hence is also the greatest act of authentic self-love.

8. Another aspect of the Golden Rule is that humans are always to be treated as ends, never as mere means, that is, as subjects, never as mere objects.

9. Yet another implication of the Golden Rule is that those who cannot protect themselves ought to be protected by those who can.

10. A further ring of the expanding circles of the Golden Rule is that nonhuman beings are also to be reverenced and treated with respect because of their being.

11. It is important that not only basic but also middle ethical principles be spelled out in this declaration. Although most of the middle ethical principles that need to be articulated are already embedded in juridical form in the United Nations Universal Declaration of Human Rights of 1948, it is vital that the religions and ethical traditions expressly state and approve them. Then the world, including both adherents and outsiders of the various religions and ethical traditions, will know what ethical standards all are committing themselves to.

12. If a Universal Declaration of a Global Ethic is to be meaningful and effective, however, its framers must resist the temptation to pack too many details and special interests into it. It can function best as a kind of "constitutional" set of basic and middle ethical principles from which more detailed applications can be constantly drawn.

These, of course, are very general principles that I believe ought to guide the drafting of a Universal Declaration of a Global Ethic. They need to be reflected on, discussed, implemented, modified, added to, rejected, and so on. In fact, Küng and I have individually done that and, with broad consultation, have produced two separate versions, which can be found on our two Web sites; it is not at all sufficient to have two or more versions of a declaration available for reading, or indeed to have them read or even signed on to. Rather, the principles articulated in such a declaration must be first understood, then embraced, and finally lived.

That is not going to happen, however, simply by reading and signing a Universal Declaration of a Global Ethic. What is needed, in my judgment, is that various religious, ethical, and, indeed, all kinds of communities and groups, large and small, discuss and draft their own versions of a "universal declaration," that is, what they consider their own basic ethical principles, which they believe people of all other religious and ethical traditions could also affirm. The various groups could then share their versions and send them to the two Web sites (globalethic.org and weltethos.org), where they would be gathered and eventually synthesized into an integrated declaration.

The already existing drafts should certainly be used in this process, but all communities and regions need to make their own contributions to the final declaration. In the process of wrestling with the issues and forging the wording, they will make the concern for a global ethic their own and will thus be better able to mediate it with their constituents and enhance the likelihood of the declaration being adhered to in practice.

Such a project cannot be carried out only by the scholars and leaders of the world's religious and ethical communities, although obviously, the vigorous participation of these elements is vital. The ideas and sensitivities must also come from the grass roots. Moreover, it is also at the grass roots, as well at the levels of scholars and leaders, that, first, consciousnesses must be raised on the desperate need for the conscious development of a global ethic and, then, once drafted and accepted, the conviction of its validity must be gained. The most carefully thought-out and sensitively crafted declaration will be of no use if those who are to adhere to it do not believe in it. A global ethic must work on all three levels: scholars, leaders, grass roots. Otherwise, it will not work at all.

I offer below the version of the declaration that I put together after very wide consultation. It is meant as a declaration that religious and ethical institutions can sign and thereby publicly declare that they profess to live by these ethical principles and should be publicly held accountable to them—as are the signatories of the United Nations Declaration of Human Rights. It is hoped that this proposed declaration, along with the other material available, will stimulate every reader to gather his or her group(s) and create his or her own version of a Universal Declaration of a Global Ethic.

Universal Declaration of a Global Ethic

I. Rationale

We women and men from various ethical and religious traditions commit ourselves to the following Universal Declaration of a Global Ethic. We speak here not of *ethics* in the plural, which implies rather great detail, but of *ethic* in the singular, that is, the fundamental attitude toward good and evil and the basic and middle principles needed to put it into action.

We make this commitment not despite our differences but arising out of our distinct perspectives, recognizing nevertheless in our diverse ethical and religious traditions common convictions that lead us to speak out *against* all forms of inhumanity and *for* humaneness in our treatment of ourselves, one another, and the world around us. We find in each of our traditions:

(a) grounds in support of universal human rights,
(b) a call to work for justice and peace, and
(c) concern for conservation of the earth.

We confirm and applaud the positive human values that are, at times painfully slowly but nevertheless increasingly, being accepted and advocated in our world: freedom, equality, democracy, recognition of interdependence, commitment to justice, and human rights. We also believe that conditions in our world encourage—indeed, require—us to look beyond what divides us and to speak as one on matters that are crucial for the survival of and respect for the earth. Therefore, we advocate movement toward a global order that reflects the best values found in our myriad traditions.

We are convinced that a just global order can be built only upon a global ethic that clearly states universally recognized norms and principles and that such an ethic presumes a readiness and intention on the part of people to act justly—that is, a movement of the heart. A global ethic also requires a thoughtful presentation of principles that are held up to open investigation and critique—a movement of the head.

Each of our traditions holds commitments beyond what is expressed here, but we find that within our ethical and religious traditions, the world community is in the process of discovering elements of a fundamental minimal consensus on ethics that is convincing to all women and men of good will, religious and nonreligious alike, and that will provide us with a moral framework within which we can relate to ourselves, one another, and the world in a just and respectful manner.

In order to build a humanity-wide consensus, we find it is essential to develop and use a language that is humanity-based, although each religious and ethical tradition also has its own language for what is expressed in this declaration.

Furthermore, none of our traditions, ethical or religious, is satisfied with minimums, vital as they are; rather, because humans are endlessly self-transcending, our traditions also provide maximums to strive for. Consequently, this declaration does the same. The maximums, however, clearly are ideals to strive for and therefore cannot be required, lest the essential freedoms and rights of some thereby be violated.

II. Presuppositions

As a Universal Declaration of a Global Ethic, which we believe must undergird any affirmation of human rights and respect for the earth, this document affirms and supports the rights and corresponding responsibilities enumerated in the 1948 Universal Declaration of Human Rights of the United Nations. In conjunction with that first United Nations declaration, we believe there are five general presuppositions that are indispensable for a global ethic:

(a) Every human possesses inalienable and inviolable dignity; individuals, states, and other social entities are obliged to respect and protect the dignity of each person.

(b) No person or social entity exists beyond the scope of morality; everyone—
     individuals and social organizations—is obliged to do good and avoid evil.

(c) Humans are endowed with reason and conscience—the great challenge of
     being human is to act conscientiously; communities, states, and other
     social organizations are obliged to protect and foster these capabilities.

(d) Communities, states, and other social organizations that contribute to the
     good of humans and the world have a right to exist and flourish; this
     right should be respected by all.

(e) Humans are a part of nature, not apart from nature; ethical concerns
     extend beyond humanity to the rest of the earth, and indeed the cosmos.
     In brief, this declaration, in reflection of reality, is not just
     anthropocentric but also anthropocosmocentric.

III. A Fundamental Rule

We propose the Golden Rule, which for thousands of years has been affirmed in many
religious and ethical traditions, as a fundamental principle upon which to base a global
ethic: "What you do not wish done to yourself, do not do to others," or, in positive
terms, "What you wish done to yourself, do to others." This rule should be valid not
only for one's own family, friends, community, and nation but also for all other individuals, families, communities, and nations, the entire world, and the cosmos.

IV. Basic Principles

1. Because freedom is of the essence of being human, every person is free to exercise
and develop every capacity, as long as it does not infringe on the rights of other
persons or express a lack of due respect for things living or nonliving. In addition,
human freedom should be exercised in such a way as to enhance both the freedom
of all humans and due respect for all things, living and nonliving.

2. Because of their inherent equal dignity, all humans should always be treated
as ends, never as mere means. In addition, all humans in every encounter with
others should strive to enhance to the fullest the intrinsic dignity of all involved.

3. Although humans have greater intrinsic value than nonhumans, all such
things, living and nonliving, do possess intrinsic value simply because of their existence and, as such, are to be treated with due respect. In addition, all humans in
every encounter with nonhumans, living and nonliving, should strive to respect
them to the fullest of their intrinsic value.

4. As humans necessarily seek ever more truth, so, too, do they seek to unite
themselves, that is, their "selves," with what they perceive as the good; in brief, they
love. Usually, these "selves" are expanded/transcended to include family and
friends, seeking the good for them. In addition, as with the Golden Rule, the loving/
loved self needs to continue its natural expansion/transcendence to embrace the
community, the nation, the world, and the cosmos.

5. Thus, true human love is authentic self-love and other-love correlatively linked in such a way that ultimately it is drawn to become all-inclusive. This expansive and inclusive nature of love should be recognized as an active principle in personal and global interaction.

6. Those who hold responsibility for others are obliged to help those for whom they hold responsibility. In addition, the Golden Rule implies that if we were in serious difficulty wherein we could not help ourselves, we would want those who could help us to do so, even if they held no responsibility for us; therefore, we should help others in serious difficulty who cannot help themselves, even though we hold no responsibility for them.

7. Because all humans are equally entitled to hold their religion or belief—that is, their explanation of the ultimate meaning of life and how to live accordingly—as true, every human's religion or belief should be granted its due freedom and respect.

8. In addition, dialogue—that is, conversation whose primary aim is to learn from the other—is a necessary means whereby women and men learn to respect the other, ceaselessly to expand and deepen their own explanation of the meaning of life, and to develop an ever-broadening consensus whereby men and women can live together on this globe in an authentically human manner.

V. Middle Principles

The following "middle ethical principles" are, in fact, those that underlie the 1948 United Nations Universal Declaration of Human Rights, formally approved by almost every nation in the world.

1. *Legal Rights/Responsibilities*

Because all humans have an inherent equal dignity, all should be treated equally before the law and provided with its equal protection.

At the same time, all individuals and communities should follow all just laws, obeying not only the letter but most especially the spirit.

2. *Rights/Responsibilities concerning Conscience and Religion or Belief*

Because humans are thinking and therefore essentially free-deciding beings, all have the right to freedom of thought, speech, conscience, and religion or belief.

At the same time, all humans should exercise their rights of freedom of thought, speech, conscience, and religion or belief in ways that will respect themselves and all others and strive to produce maximum benefit, broadly understood, for both themselves and their fellow humans.

3. *Rights/Responsibilities concerning Speech and Information*

Because humans are thinking beings with the ability to perceive reality and express it, all individuals and communities have both the right and the responsibility, as far as possible, to learn the truth and express it honestly.

At the same time, everyone should avoid cover-ups, distortions, manipulations of others, and inappropriate intrusions into personal privacy; this freedom and responsibility are especially true of the mass media, artists, scientists, politicians, and religious leaders.

4. Rights/Responsibilities concerning Participation in All Decision Making Affecting Oneself or Those for Whom One Is Responsible

Because humans are free-deciding beings, all adults have the right to a voice, direct or indirect, in all decisions that affect them, including a meaningful participation in choosing their leaders and holding them accountable, as well as the right of equal access to all leadership positions for which their talents qualify them.

At the same time, all humans should strive to exercise their right, and obligation, to participate in self-governance so as to produce maximum benefit, widely understood, for both themselves and their fellow humans.

5. Rights/Responsibilities concerning the Relationship between Women and Men

Because women and men are inherently equal and all men and women have an equal right to the full development of all of their talents, as well as the freedom to marry, with equal rights for all women and men in living out or dissolving marriage.

At the same time, all men and women should act toward each other outside and within marriage in ways that will respect the intrinsic dignity, equality, freedom, and responsibilities of themselves and others.

6. Rights/Responsibilities concerning Property

Because humans are free bodily and social in nature, all individual humans and communities have the right to own property of various sorts.

At the same time, society should be so organized that property will be dealt with respectfully, striving to produce maximum benefit not only for the owners but also for their fellow humans, as well as for the world at large.

7. Rights/Responsibilities concerning Work and Leisure

Because to lead an authentic human life, all humans should normally have both meaningful work and recreative leisure, individuals and communities should strive to organize society so as to provide these two dimensions of an authentic human life for both themselves and all members of their communities.

At the same time, all individuals have an obligation to work appropriately for their recompense and, with all communities, to strive for ever more creative work and recreative leisure for themselves, their communities, and other individuals and communities.

8. *Rights/Responsibilities concerning Children and Education*

Children are, first of all, not responsible for their coming into existence or for their social-ization and education; their parents are. Where, for whatever reason, they fail, the wider community, relatives, and civil community have an obligation to provide the most humane care possible—physical, mental, moral/spiritual, and social—for children.

Because humans can become authentically human only through education in the broad sense and today increasingly can flourish only with extensive education in the formal sense, all individuals and communities should strive to provide an education for all children and adult women and men that is directed to the full development of the human person, respect for human rights and fundamental freedoms, the promo-tion of understanding, dialogue, and friendship among all humans—regardless of racial, ethnic, religious, belief, sexual, or other differences—and respect for the earth.

At the same time, all individuals and communities have the obligation to contrib-ute appropriately to providing the means necessary for this education for themselves and their communities and beyond that to strive to provide the same for all humans.

9. *Rights/Responsibilities concerning Peace*

Because peace, as both the absence of violence and the presence of justice for all humans, is the necessary condition for the complete development of the full humanity of all humans, individually and communally, all individuals and commu-nities should strive constantly to further the growth of peace on all levels—personal, interpersonal, local, regional, national, and international—granting that:

  (a) the necessary basis of peace is justice for all concerned;
  (b) violence is to be vigorously avoided, being resorted to only when its absence would cause a greater evil; and
  (c) when peace is ruptured, all efforts should be bent to its rapid restoration—on the necessary basis of justice for all.

At the same time, it should be recognized that peace, like liberty, is a positive value that should be constantly cultivated, and therefore all individuals and com-munities should make the necessary prior efforts not only to avoid its breakdown but also to strengthen its steady development and growth.

10. *Rights/Responsibilities concerning the Preservation of the Environment*

Because things, living and nonliving, have an intrinsic value simply because of their existence, and also because humans cannot develop fully as humans, or even survive, if the environment is severely damaged, all individuals and communities should respect the ecosphere within which "we all live, move, and have our being" and act so that:

  (a) nothing, living or nonliving, will be destroyed in its natural form except when used for some greater good, as, for example, the use of plants or animals for food; and

(b) if at all possible, only replaceable material will be destroyed in its natural form.

At the same time, all individuals and communities should constantly be vigilant to protect our fragile universe, particularly from the exploding human population and increasing technological possibilities that threaten it in an ever-expanding fashion.

NOTES

1. Samuel Huntington, "Clash of Civilizations," *Foreign Affairs* (July 1993): 22–49. See also his *The Clash of Civilizations and the Remaking of World Order* (New York: Simon & Schuster, 1996). Huntington saw the disappearance of the clash of the Cold War being replaced by a clash of several major world "civilizations," such as Western, Asian, Muslim.

2. *The Origin and Goal of History*, Michael Bullock, trans. (New Haven, Conn.: Yale University Press, 1953); *Vom Ursprung und Ziel der Geschichte* (Zurich: Artemis, 1949). For a further academic discussion of Jaspers's position on the Axial Period, see "Wisdom, Revelation, and Doubt: Perspectives on the First Millennium B.C.," *Daedalus* (Spring 1975); and S. N. Eisenstadt, ed., *The Origins and Diversity of Axial Age Civilizations*, (Albany: State University of New York Press, 1989).

3. "Judaism-Christianity-Islam: Facing Modernity Together," *Journal of Ecumenical Studies* 30/3–4 (Summer-Fall, 1993): 417–425.

4. Leonard Swidler and Paul Mojzes, *The Study of Religion in the Age of Global Dialogue* (Philadelphia: Temple University Press, 1999), 7.

5. "Toward a 'Universal Declaration of a Global Ethos,'" *Journal of Ecumenical Studies* 28/1 (Winter 1991): 123–125; and *Süddeutsche Zeitung* (November 16/17, 1991). See also Hans Küng and Karl-Josef Kuschel, *A Global Ethic: The declaration of the Parliament of the World's Religions* (New York: Continuum, 1993), 47. See Hans Küng, *Projekt Weltethos* (Munich: Piper Verlag, 1990); *Global Responsibility: In Search of a New World Ethic* (New York: Crossroad, 1991). The latter marks the beginning of the Global Ethic movement. See Leonard Swidler, ed., *For All Life: Toward Universal Declaration of a Global Ethic, An Interreligious Dialogue* (Ashland, Ore.: White Cloud, 1998). This volume contains the rationale for a global ethic and a serious interreligious dialogue on the project. Developing information on the Movement for a Global Ethic is available online at http://globalethic.org and www.weltethos.org.

FOR FURTHER READING

Dialogue Institute. n.d. www.institute.jesdialogue.org/resources/course. Additional resources on global business ethics.

"Envisioning a Global Ethic." n.d. www.astro.temple.edu/~dialogue/geth.htm. Includes several codes of global business ethics. There is also an online course in "Deep

Dialogue/Critical Thinking" related to a global ethic at www.astro.temple.
edu/~dialogue/course.

Küng, Hans. 1991. *Global Responsibility: In Search of a New World Ethic*. New York:
Crossroad.

———, ed. 1996. *Yes to a Global Ethic*. London: SCM. In this volume, more than thirty
world leaders endorse and comment on the Global Ethic movement, including
Ecumenical Patriarch Bartholomew I, Cardinal Joseph Bernardin, Archbishop George
Carey, Prince Hassan of Jordan, former Mayor of Jerusalem Teddy Kollek, President
of Ireland Mary Robinson, former German Chancellor Helmut Schmidt, Bishop
Desmond Tutu, and Elie Wiesel.

———. 1998. *A Global Ethic for Global Politics and Economics*. New York: Oxford University Press.

Swidler, Leonard, ed., 1998. *For All Life: Toward Universal Declaration of a Global Ethic, An
Interreligious Dialogue*. Ashland, Ore.: White Cloud.

———, ed. 2007. *A Global Ethic. Journal of Ecumenical Studies* 42/3 (Summer). Advancing
the dialogue further about the Global Ethic movement with the participation of a set
of American scholars.

CHAPTER 11

THEOLOGY AMID RELIGIOUS DIVERSITY

GAVIN D'COSTA

THE EARLY CHURCH

FROM the first days of the early church, Christians were confronted with religious pluralism. The Roman Empire was teeming with different religious cults. Three interesting attitudes to this religiously pluralist reality are discernible within the first few centuries that continue to shape the experience of most contemporary Christians. First, there was a clear emphasis on the necessity of faith in Christ for salvation, echoing John 14:6: "I am the way, and the truth, and the life; no one comes to the Father except through me." This faith had an ecclesial dimension, including the necessity of baptism into Christ's body, so that membership of the church (always assuming active faith and love in the person's heart) was required for salvation. This first emphasis meant that Christianity was a vigorous missionary religion with an explicit desire to convert all peoples. This was formulated in the *extra ecclesiam nulla salus* teaching ("no salvation outside the church"), which was formally proclaimed at the Council of Florence in the fifteenth century but originated as early as the fourth century. This missionary drive excluded no religion or culture, although large-scale Jewish rejection of the gospel was always an embarrassment in the early days and eventually led to a strong anti-Jewish polemic within Christianity.

Second, some early Christian intellectuals had learned greatly from Greek philosophy and could not help but wonder at the wisdom they had found there: truths that were consonant with revelation, moral exhortation of a high order, and, indeed, philosophical frameworks that allowed for the sophisticated explication of Christian revelation and for its defense against philosophical attacks. They developed three crucial theories to explain pagan wisdom: the *prisca theologia* ("ancient theology"), the *preparatio evangelica* ("preparation for the gospel"), and the *semina verbi* ("seeds of the word"). The first held that all pagan wisdom was actually an unacknowledged borrowing from the Old Testament—a theory of plagiarism held by some divines until the seventeenth century. The latter two theories, by contrast, argued that God provided knowledge in nature and in cultures that led people to the truth of the gospel, such that it was possible to know God and find truth, goodness, and beauty outside the Christian revelation. These truths found their fulfillment and culmination in Christian revelation, although some of the fathers posited a deep gulf between Athens and Jerusalem. The former position is more characteristic of most Catholic and Orthodox approaches, while many Reform and Protestant Christians emphasize the latter. For example, some Reform theologians have tended to emphasize the damage of original sin to qualify the *preparatio* and *semina* traditions or even use them to emphasize why non-Christians who have never heard the gospel might be damned: they have known truth yet rejected it. These generalizations should be treated judiciously, and in recent times, these Christian traditions have exemplified deep internal diversity.

Third, the early Christians were faced with the question of the righteous of Israel. Were they lost because they were born before the time of Christ? This was unthinkable to most of them. The saints of Israel had valid faith in God, for they partook of the very covenant that is the root upon which the church was grafted (Romans 11:11–24). Ideas of the justice of God (in tandem with passages such as Acts 2:7, Romans 10:6–7, Ephesians 4:8–9; 1 Peter 3:18–20) led to the notion that these righteous awaited the coming of Christ, who, as the creed has it, "descended into hell," where he preached salvation to those who deserved it so that they might be saved. This scenario led to the idea of the *limbus partum* ("limbo of the fathers") as a kind of holding tank for the righteous who died before Christ. Clement of Alexandria (ca. 150–ca. 215) and others included righteous pagans in the *limbus partum*, which suggested the possibility of salvation for all persons, not just Israelites. Augustine likewise insisted on an invisible church from the time of Abel composed of the righteous.

Together, these three attitudes run throughout Christian history, leading to three widely adopted theologoumena in the modern period: the necessity of Christ and his church for salvation; the justice of God toward the righteous before the coming of Christ; the possibility of goodness, truth, and beauty being present in pagan traditions but never in a manner equal to Christianity in kind or degree. In evaluating this background, however, it is important to recognize that well until the age of discovery in the fifteenth century, it was assumed by most theologians that after the time of Christ, everyone knew the gospel. Therefore, if a person was not a Christian, this was seen to imply that he or she had explicitly rejected the truth of God. This meant that both Judaism and eventually Islam (from the seventh century on) were seen as heretical and/or schismatic movements, rather than genuinely "other." Fueled greatly by European Christianity's territorial struggles with Islam, an anti-Islamic polemic arose, which has permeated into the modern period in what has been called Islamaphobia. At the same time, there were also important instances of dialogue between Christianity and Islam, including mutual hospitality and respect (in medieval Spain, for example), and between Christianity and Judaism, although the latter lacked the political power to be taken seriously by a powerful Christian state-related religion.

MEDIEVAL AND REFORMED CHRISTIANITY

It is thus possible to see how these dogmatic topics were well in place by the Middle Ages, which continued the teachings of no salvation outside Christ and his church. Of course, further subareas in theology are also related to this question. Missiology, inculturation, and apologetics are the three most important, but the latter two developed in the modern period (formally speaking). Missiology was internal to the gospel message, and throughout Christian history, Christians have conducted missionary enterprises but in very different contexts and situations. After the fourth century, with Christianity's growing allegiance with the emperor, mission became closely related to the Christianization of Europe. By the medieval period, this process had almost come to its climax, but it was spurred on through the discovery of the New World and a new phase of mission. Inculturation had implicitly taken place in many respects (liturgical, doctrinal, artistically, etc.) but became newly focused as Christian mission moved out of Europe. In Asia especially, missionaries had to grapple with the unintelligibility of the gospel given the alien categories and semantic fields of non-Christians. Apologetics, too, was injected with new blood as the missionary territories created new challenges, new opportunities both for defending the Christian faith against counterarguments and for proposing new arguments against alien faiths. As always, social and political power were important shaping factors.

This period of mission is complex and difficult to assess. Some of the *conquistadores* exemplify an imperial brutality and economic greed that are often associated with missionaries, sometimes quite justly. But there are also stories of costly sacrifice by missionaries, as in Japan, and a love of the new peoples and cultures they encountered. There was also careful transformation of cultures and lives so that both converts and non-Christians enjoyed better health, education, and civic developments catalyzed by the new missionary presence, as in parts of South America and India. Sometimes these social benefits and social status were the incentives to convert, rather than a conversion of heart to Christ. Some missionaries, such as the Jesuits Francis Xavier (1506–1552) and Robert de Nobili (1577–1656), found much to admire from the non-Christian cultures they encountered and saw clear evidence of the operation of natural law and grace, amid superstition and error. Both of these towering figures began a move toward inculturation, often inspired by a desire to make converts rather than critiquing the European inculturation in the formation of Christianity. Nevertheless, this laid seeds that were picked up by later missionaries. The Protestant missionaries also excelled in social work, biblical trans-lation, and planting and forming new indigenous Christian communities outside Europe. The Orthodox churches did not develop a theology regarding these matters until the modern period and were not involved in mission in the same way.

The Age of Discovery also brought on a development in doctrinal theology with the relentless discovery of millions who had never heard of the gospel through no fault of their own. In this context, it was no longer feasible to rely on Thomas Aquinas's speculation that if a young boy were brought up by wolves (and thus had never heard the gospel), God's justice would require that an angel visit him or that he have interior revelation. The evidence was that angels had not visited non-Christian peoples en masse and that if God had granted interior revelation, the many religions had not understood it correctly. New thinking was required.

The sixteenth-century Dominicans of Salamanca, Francisco de Vitoria (ca. 1480–1546) and Domingo de Soto (1494–1560), laid the seeds for later Catholic theology on this topic in two interesting ways. De Vitoria was outraged by the behavior of the Christian *conquistadores* and argued that unless the gospel was presented properly, without violence, threat, or coercion both before and after its preaching, the hearers were under no obligation to accept it and must not become enslaved. This sociopolitical sensitivity would mark modern theology's response to these matters. De Soto argued that implicit faith in Christ would suffice for those who had never heard the gospel but who followed the natural law evident in creation and through the use of reason. This meant that the necessity of the church for salvation was contextualized while nevertheless still being viewed as binding. This position, with various qualifications, remains the official Catholic position today. Not all Catholics at the time shared these opinions.

An alternative solution to this new problem arose from the emerging Reformed traditions. For instance, John Calvin, drawing on aspects of Augustine that had been neglected in his opinion, argued for predestination. Correspondingly, he rejected medieval Catholic arguments for the possibility of salvation for pagans as undermining both the necessity of faith in Christ for salvation and the fact that these pagans were justly condemned as they had been predestined to damnation. According to Calvin, because God had predestined those who did not know the gospel to damnation, there was no question to be answered about how they might be saved or how God's justice might be compromised. Some modern Calvinists have refined this argument, while others have modified it.

THE MODERN PERIOD

The modern period exhibits the development of the theological traditions we have already underlined above. In that sense, there is a deep continuity with the early tradition, but the modern period also marks deep cultural discontinuities that would seriously change the map of Christian theology. There are at least five important factors that mark the modern.

First is the end of Christendom (if indeed it ever existed). The point is that Europe slowly became secularized, first through the alleged war of religions whereby denominational allegiances were central to Christian identity and second through the nation-state's overcoming of these differences through a unitary identity found in belonging to the state rather than a particular religion.

The second factor that marks the modern is the profound crisis of two world wars fought in the heart of Christian Europe. Christians slaughtered one another savagely, and many Europeans had no confidence in the cultural resources of their ancient religion. Perhaps strangely, many found solace in modern science (strangely because without modern science, the horrors of the two wars would not have been possible or so widely known). Others turned to ethics without religion, and some intellectuals turned to the "East," which had been idealized by German Romanticism into traditions that seemed to offer something different from war and destruction.

A third factor was the Holocaust. The slaughter of nearly 6 million Jews at the heart of a Christian culture raised deep questions about Christianity's attitude to the religious other, as well as its own complicity in European anti-Semitism.

A fourth factor was the critique of missions from the viewpoint of secular modernity. Many liberal Europeans saw Christian mission as culturally arrogant, failing to learn from the deep wisdom of the East, being responsible for the destruction of primitive and ancient cultures, and falsely valuing Christianity over other faiths.

Fifth and finally, many of the foremost intellectual voices within Christianity, both Protestant and Catholic, saw the future as marked by an assimilation to modernity. This issue is still unresolved in many European Christian circles, but it certainly marked a new attitude toward religious diversity, through the emergence of pluralism, the view that sees all religions as more or less of equal positive status.

Pluralism goes radically beyond the previous "classical" Christian attitudes toward non-Christian religions identified above and breaks with the "no salvation outside Christ and/or his church" teaching. With growing knowledge of other religions and a strong historical approach to truth, the nineteenth century saw the emergence of a Christian theological view that held all of the great religions to be both salvific and equally marred with human error and superstition. Given the dark aspects of missionary history, the shame of empire, the Holocaust, and the wars of religion that ravaged Europe in the early modern period, the emergence of pluralism is not altogether surprising.

Pluralism's philosophical roots go back to the deists and rationalists of the seventeenth century, but it finds its major philosophical expression in the eighteenth-century figure of Immanuel Kant, the father of the German Enlightenment. Kant argued that God could not be just or wise to entrust his message to the contingencies of history, for this could never be a universal communication of the truths thereby revealed. Further, the arguments for the existence of God were also judged defective. Given that history and rationality were no longer paths to God, how could one find God? Kant's answer was: through the universal sense of obligation in ethics; the categorical imperative presupposed God. Christ's Sermon on the Mount was exemplary of this universal ethical requirement. This emphasis on the ethical over the intellectual/rational and historical became central for many theological pluralists who argued that a good and loving God could not simply communicate with a tiny sector of humanity and damn the rest. Of course, this was never the actual argument of mainstream Christianity, but for many, the plausibility of Christianity rested with this new approach.

Variants of all of these arguments are found in the work of contemporary theological pluralists, and pluralism is found across denominational lines. Schleiermacher began to march down that road with his emphasis on the universal feeling of dependency contained in all religions, but he never really took the decisive step and still emphasized the uniqueness (but also the continuity) of Christ with other religions. One of today's foremost pluralists is the United Reform philosopher-theologian John Hick. He adopts Kant's distinction between the noumenal, *an sich* ("in itself"), and the phenomenal, as it is known to us. Hick uses this distinction to argue that the divine reality is beyond all knowing and characterization (Kant's noumenal), and the different religions, like Kant's phenomenal, are varying representations of this divine reality. The variations of phenomena are a factor of culture, and what is central to Hick in judging the effectiveness of these divine images is whether they promote good ethical behavior. Taken to its logical end, this might be interpreted as neo-Pelagianism. Hick also vigorously argues against atheism and naturalism and wants to defend the language of religions in asserting a transcendent reality. Nevertheless, he deconstructs the Chalcedonian teaching about the incarnation and with it any claim for the uniqueness of Christ (other than that he is unique, as are the Buddha and Muhammad).

In Catholic theology, Paul Knitter has been at the forefront of pluralism, but he has drunk deeply from liberation theology and shifts the pluralist emphasis to social ethics. He argues that the criterion for true religion is its liberatory value. He, like Hick, has to dismantle the uniqueness of Christ and, as a Catholic, also has to argue against the role of the church in the process of salvation. This type of position can be found in a growing number of non-Western Catholic authors from what used to be "missionary territories" in Asia, such as the Jesuit Aloysius Pieris in Sri Lanka and the priest-academic Felix Wilfred in Madras. Pluralism is found in every major denomination except among Reformed Calvinists.

Pluralism's impact on key doctrines is significant and has heralded a profound theological revisionism, but because of its dependence on models of truth derived from the Enlightenment, pluralism raises many questions regarding its grounding in specifically Christian theological principles. This debate still rages today, and over the last twenty years, the Catholic church's doctrinal watchdog, the Congregation for the Doctrine of the Faith, has constantly challenged Catholic pluralist theologians for moving into what has been regarded as relativism and indifferentism (the condemned teaching that one religion is as good as another). Likewise, many Protestant church communities have been split over this question. I have perhaps given this movement inordinate space in comparison with its ecclesial influence, but it is a very important development in theology amid religious diversity.

Other developments in modern theology have also replicated pluralist patterns, sometimes with very different emphases and starting points. For example, feminist theology has made a challenging contribution in asking whether the fixation on the salvation of others is not part of the necrophilia latent within Christian theology (Grace Jantzen), whether theology has failed to recognize its material contexts and interdisciplinary nature (Catholic Jeanine Hill Fletcher), and whether all religions are to be interrogated regarding their stultifying patriarchy, so that no single one stands on a perch judging others (Catholic Rosemary Radford Ruether). I am not arguing that feminist theology leads to pluralism, far from it, but rather that most new methodological developments in theology have a pluralist wing. This can be found even in the turn to the postmodern, which has generally been critical of modernity's leveling out of difference, and in the hands of Catholic theologian Henrique Pinto, his Foucaultian theomethodology generates something very like Hick's pluralism.

Mainstream Christian theologians in the modern period have been very responsive to the challenges of modernity without giving up on the uniqueness of Christ, the necessity of Christ (and/or the church) for salvation, or the importance of mission. Rather, they have sought to develop these themes while taking seriously the many challenges noted above. I will chart such moves by looking at the history of the largest Christian denomination, the Roman Catholic Church. I will first look at the way the Catholic church has responded to the world religions in its 1965 *Nostra Aetate* ("Declaration on the Relationship of the Church to Non-Christian Religions"), promulgated at Vatican II, as this nicely exemplifies both the continuities and the discontinuities found in mainstream Christian tradition. I will then focus on a debate between two key Catholic theologians of the twentieth century. I am choosing a single tradition to allow some depth, which would otherwise be sacrificed in too wide a coverage.

Nostra Aetate contains the first formal statement of the Catholic church on other religions (understood in their own terms but theologically evaluated). It is worth noting that this Vatican council was primarily pastoral, not dogmatic. In its dogmatic teaching, there is continuity with the early tradition, as well as a new positive pastoral and historical appreciation of the major world religions. Let us briefly take the latter positive pastoral appreciation first, noting both its contents and its context.

Nostra Aetate relates the world religions to Catholicism historically and theologically in concentric circles of closeness. It is concerned to emphasize what "human beings have in common" (paragraph 1). Closest to the church is Judaism, sharing the covenant, scriptures, and many spiritual traditions. It is the only tradition of which the word *revelation* is used, and *Revelationem* refers solely to the Old Testament. Mutual understanding and respect are called for, as well as dialogues focusing especially on theological and biblical studies. "Anti-Semitism" is deplored "at any time and from any source" (paragraph 4). Then, in the next circle, comes Islam, with its devotional theism, strong ethics, Abrahamic roots, and reverence for Mary. All of these are held in high "esteem." The past "quarrels and hostilities" must give way to "mutual understanding" and cooperation on "common cause" in "fostering social justice, moral values, peace, and freedom." (paragraph 4). As with Judaism, it is important to note that many forms of cooperation, both practical and theological, are encouraged without any doctrinal change in the traditional teaching that salvation comes only through Christ and his church. Then come Hinduism and Buddhism, rather thinly characterized but nevertheless very positively, in terms of their meditation techniques, lofty philosophies, and devotional and ascetic elements (paragraph 3). Finally, "other religions to be found everywhere" are also acknowledged, referring to natural religions. Hence the overall positive appreciation of non-Christian religions is geared toward "dialogue and collaboration" and toward the "common good" in "society and culture" (paragraph 2). Interreligious dialogue on the practical level has been given strong endorsement inasmuch as it serves the aim of the "common good" and enshrines respect for the dignity of each person.

Alongside this positive appreciation and its practical context, it must be noted that nowhere in the council documents is there an affirmation of other religions per se as vehicles of salvation or allowing that they contain the truths of salvation. Indeed, in *Nostra Aetate*, it is expressly said at the outset that the church is called to "ever proclaim Christ, 'the way, the truth, and the life' [John 14:6], in whom men find the fullness of religious life, and in whom God has reconciled all things to Himself [2 Corinthians 5:18–19]" (paragraph 2). This contains the basic teaching regarding the necessity of Christ for salvation and baptism as a mark of this acceptance. This is expressly stated in the 1964 *Lumen Gentium* ("Dogmatic Constitution on the Church"): "that the Church, now so journeying on earth as an exile, is necessary for salvation" (14). This must be kept in mind through all of the positive evaluations of the religions. Hence, in *Lumen Gentium* 16, the council is unequivocal with the tradition that salvation can be attained by anyone, religious or nonreligious, on three conditions: (1) that they do not know the gospel through no fault of their own, (2) that the inculpably ignorant who have "not yet arrived at an explicit knowledge of God, but who strive to live a good life, thanks to His grace" are not lost, and (3) that the good life can be lived by following the dictates of conscience and the natural law within the created order. How this relates to the visible church is left to the theologians to explicate. Finally in *Ad Gentes* ("Decree on the Mission Activity of the Church"), it is said that missionary activity to the nations takes what is good and true and "frees" it "from all taint of evil and restores to Christ its maker, who overthrows the devil's domain and wards off the manifold malice of vice" (9).

In looking at these documents, we see the development and application of the three early theologoumena: the necessity of Christ and his church for salvation, the justice of God (who leaves no just person without the opportunity for salvation), and the possibility for goodness, truth, and beauty to be found throughout human cultures and religions. The reading I have offered is contested by some Catholic theologians, such as Paul Knitter.

We turn now to two of the giants of twentieth-century Catholic theology, Karl Rahner (1904–1984) and Hans Urs von Balthasar (1905–1984), and their debate over Rahner's notion of the "anonymous Christian" to explore further some of the methodological and theological issues. Rahner did not claim that Vatican II was in support of his position, nor did Balthasar, but both believed that their approaches were in keeping with the council. Balthasar's position in many respects echoes the concerns of Karl Barth's Protestant critique of Rahner and George Lindbeck's Lutheran critique, nicely developed by Bruce Marshall in *Christology in Conflict*.

Rahner's theory of the "anonymous Christian" is based on two possible types of argument. The first stems from his philosophy of the "supernatural existential," in which he argued that all people have an implicit revelation of God that is adequate for salvation, even though it is only fulfilled in the historically particular revelation of Jesus Christ and partially thematized and expressed in other religious texts and practices. This meant that while Christianity was the absolute truth and Christ the source of all salvation, other religions could act as provisional mediators of this saving grace because of the "supernatural existential." This position kept intact the stance of salvation coming only through Christ and only through the church—although both now take on an implicit and explicit dimension. Rahner explicated this in the notion of the "anonymous Christian" (Christ's grace working implicitly) and "anonymous Christianity" (through the provisional saving structures called religion). This argument is philosophically derived.

Rahner's second type of argument is theologically founded. He argued that since God desires the salvation of all people, many people do not know the gospel, and God is loving and good, there must be a means of salvation offered to all such people. Using the analogy of Israel, valid until confronted by the truth of Christ, Rahner suggested that other religions might be deemed, analogically to Israel, provisionally "lawful religions." It is through acts of faith, hope, and unconditional love that those in other religions say yes to God. Here again, he refers to the "anonymous Christian" and "anonymous Christianity."

Rahner's "anonymous Christianity" was bitterly attacked by Balthasar on two counts. The first, which was decisive against Rahner's first type of argument, was that Rahner's argument was dependent on German Idealism, and inasmuch as his theology was shaped by philosophy (rather than critically engaging with it), Rahner exemplified theology's capitulation to modernity. Here we see a formal problem affecting the material outcome of theology. In this sense, for Balthasar, Rahner was dangerously moving toward pluralism in his drawing from modernity rather than the scandal of the gospel. Hence, for Balthasar, there was very little difference between the anonymous and the explicit Christian—and that spelled the end of Christianity. The good Hindu, Buddhist, and atheist were already living Christ-filled lives, and nothing particular was added to their becoming Christians. The explicit form of the church was minimized. Second, and relatedly, Rahner's theology had no place for martyrdom, for the scandal of the cross, whereby the entire world was turned upside down and called into question by Jesus Christ. This was a material difference and would endure even if Balthasar's first criticism were deflected. The world for Rahner, according to Balthasar, was full of well-meaning people, hardly touched by the depths of sin, well able to survive within their human-made systems of religiosity. Mission was undervalued, even dissolved, for Rahner failed to understand the radical novelty of the Christian phenomenon. In this, Balthasar was supported by Henri de Lubac. In a word, Rahner had sold the Christian tradition into the hands of modernity. Later, Balthasar conceded some ground, agreeing with de Lubac that an "anonymous Christian" was possible (although the term was not felicitous), in that Christ's grace is operative outside the visible church, a position held clearly by the Catholic tradition and in Vatican II. But there could be no such thing as "anonymous Christianity," for this actually affirmed other religions as salvific structures, even if only provisionally.

In my opinion, Balthasar's first criticism is decisive against Rahner's first form of the argument (from philosophy) but not against his second (from theology). This exchange alerts us to the questions of methodology in theology. Oversimplifying, do we begin theology from the crucified Christ and then understand and practice "liberation," or do we begin from the philosophies or ideologies of the modern world? The latter might be expressed in German Idealism (Rahner's transcendental freedom) or via Marxism with its problematic notion of praxis preceding theory (found in Knitter and other liberationists), or in some forms of feminism that define what liberation is prior to the gospel (as found in Ruether). Please note that I am not saying that all forms of German Idealism, Marxism, feminism, and post-modernism (and other ideological influence) are negative. Rather, it is problematic only in the manner in which some theologians use these philosophies in determining theology.

Formally speaking, Balthasar's first criticism does not affect Rahner's second type of argument, and here I make the contentious assumption that the second type is independent of the first (supported by modern interpreters of Rahner such as Karen Kilby). Nevertheless, Balthasar's second criticism does affect even Rahner's second type of argument. Balthasar surely rightly criticizes the possibility of "anonymous Christianity," for it fails (without the huge number of qualifications provided by Rahner but infrequently employed by many neo-Rahnerians developing his position) to bring out the distortions, sinfulness, and even evil also present along with the good, truthful, and beautiful elements in other religions. It is not that Balthasar is unaware of the riches and depths present in the world religions or that he is against all types of practical cooperation between Christianity and others, but he simply sees that the Christian tradition is better articulated and practiced in terms of the explicit historical form and shape that Christ generates through his church.

In many respects, there are moments when the differences between these two theological giants are slim, for Balthasar strongly argues for universalism—that all people will be saved, regardless of whether they are Christian—and so does Rahner, although, ironically, he is more cautious than Balthasar. This is why labels such as *liberal* and *conservative* begin to dissolve. But these similarities should not mask the profound differences in theological method and emphasis present in these two theologians.

A more recent development in theology has been the attempt to view non-Christian religions in their own terms, as proposing different ends and means, which should be respected, so that these religions are not simply viewed as varyingly deficient forms of Christianity. The discipline of comparative theology has emerged with Catholic writers in the United States such as David Burrell, Francis Clooney, and Jim Fredericks. Here, the focus is on learning and patient conversation. Questions of personal salvation in particular and the salvific efficacy of religions in general are not central. Some, such as Fredericks, argue that a generalized theology of religions is a bogus discipline and that what matters are the specific engagements that happen when Christianity meets a particular religion. Each encounter will generate its own unique agenda to be addressed (including problems that require solution), as Christians theologize on the particular.

As religions become more engaged in the public square, as they are in the United States and other non-European countries, I believe that theology amid religious diversity will have to attend to the sociopolitical dimensions of Christian existence. This sociopolitical dimension was a normal part of Christian culture, even with distinctions between church and state, as Christianity (like the major religions of the world) is about transforming space and time and culture. It was only through European secularization that many have viewed religion as an inner event, a private choice, that should not be engaged in the public square. John Rawls and Jürgen Habermas classically taught the latter about the public square. At the same time, as this recovery of Christian social vocation is happening, Islam has also made its mark on the world as a "political" religion, although this has been perceived negatively by many because of the Western focus on "terrorism." Samuel Huntington predicted a clash of civilizations, but religious plurality need not lead in this direction. As we have seen in looking at the Catholic church, religions can be a great motor for harmonious cooperation and respect for difference, even safeguarding religious difference, which modernity has so successfully eradicated. The future holds great challenges for theology amid religious diversity.

CONCLUSIONS

Much of the modern debate is affected by the extent to which modernity has shaped theology. It is, of course, impossible simply to resort to premodern thinking, but the pervasive influence of pluralism is indicative of this methodological issue. There is room for both a theology of religions (which attends to general dogmatic questions and determines the parameters within which inquiry can continue) and a theology with and for specific religions (Buddhism is very different from Islam, and each is internally diverse). In this latter area, there is also a profound requirement for historians of religions, phenomenologists, and sociologists to work with theologians in an interdisciplinary fashion. Through these investigations, Christians might also learn how most effectively to present the gospel of Jesus Christ, who is good news to Jews and Gentiles, religious and nonreligious people.

FOR FURTHER READING

Balthasar, Hans Urs von. 1969. *The Moment of Christian Witness*. New York: Newman.

Clooney, Francis X. 2010. *Comparative Theology: Deep Learning Across Religious Borders*. Oxford: Wiley-Blackwell.

D'Costa, Gavin. 2000. *The Meeting of Religions and the Trinity*. Edinburgh: T. and T. Clark.

———. 2008. *Disputed Questions in the Theology of Religions*. Oxford: Blackwell.

Dupuis, Jacques. 1997. *Towards a Christian Theology of Religious Pluralism*. Maryknoll, N.Y.: Orbis.

Fredericks, James L. 1999. *Faith among Faiths. Christian Theology and Non-Christian Religions*. New York: Paulist.

Hick, John. 1988. *An Interpretation of Religion*. London: Macmillan.

Knitter. Paul F. *One Earth Many Religions: Multifaith Dialogue and Global Responsibility*. New York: Orbis Books.

Marshall, Bruce. 1987 *Christology in Conflict: The Identity of a Saviour in Rahner and Barth*. Oxford: Basil Blackwell.

Rahner, Karl. 1966. "Christianity and the Non-Christian Religions." In *Theological Investigations*, vol. 5. London: Darton, Longman and Todd, 115–134.

———. 1968. *Spirit in the World*, 2nd ed. London: Sheed and Ward.

Ruether, Rosemary R. 1993. *Sexism and God-Talk: Toward a Feminist Theology*. Boston, Mass: Beacon Press.

Strange, Daniel. 2002. *The Possibility of Salvation among the Unevangelised: An Analysis of Inclusivism in Recent Evangelical Theology*. Carlisle, U.K.: Paternoster.

Sullivan, Francis. 1992. *Salvation outside the Church? Tracing the History of the Catholic Response*. New York: Paulist.

Tanner, Norman, ed. 1990. *Decrees of the Ecumenical Councils, Vol. 2: Trent to Vatican II*. Washington, D.C.: Georgetown University Press.

CHAPTER 12

···

RELIGIOUS DIVERSITY, EVIL, AND A VARIETY OF THEODICIES

···

MICHAEL L. PETERSON

SUFFERING, injustice, tragedy, and death are basic to human experience. Peter Berger observes that each religion bears the burden of relating these negative phenomena—commonly called "evils"—to its understanding of ultimate reality (Berger 1967). The problem, then, is the challenge of coherently accounting for evil while preserving and developing essential commitments about the divine, the cosmos, and the human venture. But this means that there is no single problem of evil across all religions; instead, the exact formulation of the problem is specific to the commitments of each particular tradition. Likewise, there is no one formula for response that is common to religions. For present purposes, we employ Max Weber's broad definition of *theodicy* as a religious explanation for evil.

Interestingly, most of the famous critiques of religion somehow revolve around evil and suffering while failing to appreciate the central importance that developed religions give to accounting for these phenomena. The Freudian critique—that the guarantee of protection and well-being for the faithful is falsified by the countless evils of life that do not differentiate between believers and unbelievers—merely identifies the point at which most religions start, not where they end. The Marxist critique—that supernatural compensations in an afterlife are offered for the alienation and injustice of a capitalist system in order to support the status quo—does not recognize the substantial efforts of religions both to explain evil and to admonish believers to work against it. The truth is that religions deal with great integrity with evil as the point at which their intellectual and spiritual resources are put to the hardest test. Thus, what a religion says about evil and suffering reveals, probably more than anything else, what it believes the nature and purpose of existence to be.

This survey focuses on four major religions—Judaism, Christianity, Islam, and Hinduism—and explores key themes out of which their theodicies are typically constructed. Since it is simply not possible to inspect all religions here, this approach still allows the reader to get a measure of the depth and texture of how certain religions deal with evil. Predictably, the first three religions, all monotheistic, involve some similarities of theme in their theodicies but with differences in emphasis or proportion. Equally predictably, Hinduism, often classified as a version of panentheism, involves quite different concepts and provides instructive contrast to the other three. Of course, theodicy can address all evils generically or address some types of evils more specifically. While exploring various views of evil, this chapter particularly examines theories of human suffering as a phenomenon that calls forth the most profound responses. Since suffering is not simply an academic matter but is a pressing existential reality, I include here recommendations in each religion for how to face suffering in real life.

Judaism: Development of the Problem

The distinctive genius of ancient Israel was its realization that God might disclose himself in the events of history. This God, Yahweh, revealed himself also as creator of all of nature and as entering into covenant relationship with his people, the Hebrews. Belief in God so characterized actually creates the problems associated with evil and suffering. If God has participated in historical events, why does he not participate more often? As creator of the world, why does God not alter the course of nature to minimize or eliminate catastrophe, sickness, and death? As covenantal, why does God not vindicate the faithful in times of hardship or captivity? Such questions put the responsibility directly on God, since no second principle or creator is responsible for evil: "I form light and create darkness, I make weal and create woe; I the Lord do all these things" (Isaiah 45:11). To be sure, persons have been granted free choice, which they have abused, and nature is allowed to run its course. But the religion of Israel reflects unshakable confidence in God's purposeful control behind everything that happens; the difficulty lies in working out why this control is not always apparent.

The faith of Israel does not seek an explanation for suffering so much as it wrestles with the puzzlement arising from its distribution. Why do the wicked prosper while the faithful suffer? The acuteness of this problem, as well as the need to find authentic response, is readily seen in reading through the psalter (e.g., Psalm 73). The most common response was also the simplest, and it is written deeply into the Hebrew scriptures: suffering is punishment for wrongdoing, a just retribution for sin. However, when covenant conditions were broken, Yahweh's tendency was to show mercy instead of enact the strict justice that was deserved. Yet the Deutero-nomic theory, which posits a moral cause-and-effect operating in the universe and applies it to corporate as well as individual cases, is worked out in the final editing of the documents of Israel's history: "The fear of the Lord adds length to life, but the years of the wicked are cut short" (Proverbs 10:27). Unfortunately, the theory is vul-nerable to a decisive objection: it is demonstrably untrue. The more firmly Israel believed that God ensured a just universe, the stronger the problem of distribution of life's benefits and burdens became. In anguished terms, the prophet Jeremiah raised the problem and reflected on it in apocalyptic hope for a new creation and a new covenant (Jeremiah 12:1). In short, Jeremiah's answer was that proper retribu-tion is delayed and will occur in the future. Although the writer of Ecclesiastes (Ecclesiastes 8:10–14) finds the problem of distribution insoluble, some Hebrew scriptures search for more a positive view of suffering that is not preoccupied with the prosperity of the wicked. For example, suffering as a test of faith emerges in the story of Abraham's willingness to sacrifice Isaac (Genesis 22:1–19). The Hebrew scriptures voice a variety of opinions on evil and suffering, allowing us to envision their representatives as seated at a round table and engaging in one of the most important discussions imaginable.

JUDAISM: THE CASE OF JOB

At the round table is the writer of the Book of Job, who provides the most sustained and subtle treatment of the problem of distribution in the Hebrew scriptures. Job, that dignified ancient patriarch who becomes the prototypical case of the innocent sufferer, provides the ultimate rebuttal of the Deuteronomic understanding and offers glimpses of new approaches. Job's three friends represent ways of arguing for the Deuteronomic view, summed up in the rhetorical question "Whoever suffered being righteous?" The prologue of the book suggests the theme that Job's suffering is to test his faithfulness, while the epilogue suggests that Job's cooperation with God made his suffering redemptive. Yet it is in the cycle of speeches in the middle of the book that the great philosophical debate is waged.

The underlying logic of the dispute is critically important. The principle of just retribution (JR) states that God ensures that a person's character and deeds have appropriate consequences. Righteous deeds bring prosperity, symbolized in the Jewish mind as health, wealth, and progeny; wickedness, on the other hand, brings suffering, epitomized in Job's loss of his threefold prosperity. The logic of the friends—miserable comforters—is as follows: If God is just and Job is righteous, then Job should be prospering. But Job is not prospering. Since divine justice is stipulated, it follows that Job is not righteous. Although Job himself had always accepted this principle until suffering came his way, his new reasoning constitutes a significant religious breakthrough:

1. If God is just and a person is righteous, then the person prospers [assumption of JR for reductio].
2. I, Job, am not prospering [fact of experience].
3. It is not the case both that God is just and that I, Job, am righteous [implication of 1 and 2].
4. Either God is not just, or I, Job, am not righteous [equivalent of 3 for clarification].
5. God is just [truth of traditional theology].
6. I am righteous [truth of introspection].
7. God is just, and I, Job, am righteous [conjunction of 5 and 6, contradicts 3].
8. Therefore, JR is false [reductio ad absurdum of 1].

Unwavering trust in God's justice, coupled with the testimony of a clean conscience, allowed Job to achieve an understanding that God's justice is not adequately captured in the Deuteronomic view. Sometimes important progress is made by discovering what is false.

Job's later protests, which arise after persistent emotional pressure from the comforters and lead to the denouement of the story, suggest that God might not be just. Then God in the whirlwind confronts Job with a cascade of overwhelming questions that put his suffering in the larger context of creation. Rather than a power play to force submission, this is a poetically compelling—albeit philosophically incomplete—way of lifting Job's vision to the complexities of the divine ways. God even says to the comforters, "You have not spoken of me what is right" (Job 42:8). No interpretation of this literary masterpiece should miss the fact that God actually honored Job by coming to him and, in effect, validating the point that there is innocent suffering in the world that God superintends.

Such themes as suffering as a test of faith, as resulting from the operation of the world order without respect to desert, and as requiring larger perspective are identifiable in early Jewish sources. But even as the Book of Job closes, we can see an even more profound theme emerging in Jewish thought: that suffering purges and leads to life. According to Rabbi Simeon b. Yohai, "The Holy One, blessed be He, gave Israel three precious gifts, and all of them were given only through sufferings. These are: the Torah, the Land of Israel and the world to come"(Babylonian Talmud, Berakoth, 5a). One important theme in the Talmud and the Midrash is what the rabbis called *yissurin*, variously translated as "suffering," "chastisement," or "affliction" but probably better interpreted as "toil purposefully and redemptively accepted." There is an earthy realism in discussing *yissurin*, with less emphasis on the theoretical problem of how to explain God's justice and greater emphasis on how we respond in our freedom to actual suffering in order to learn the lesson that is offered and develop greater righteousness (Schwartz 1983). In the absence of a theologically complete theodicy, "practical theodicy" is still required to help us live usefully and meaningfully. *Why Bad Things Happen to Good People* is Rabbi Harold Kushner's exploration of this line of thinking made available to popular culture

(Kushner 1981). Of course, the eschatological reference above to "the world to come" reflects still another theme—poignantly developed from the fall of Jerusalem in 70 CE to the Holocaust in modern times—that one day God will act decisively to rectify all things and bring his people to full flourishing.

CHRISTIANITY: JESUS AND SUFFERING

As with Judaism, Christianity's approach to evil and suffering has had two dimensions: theoretical explanation and practical response. Themes of practical response originate in the teachings and actions of Jesus, which were inevitably related to the ways in which suffering was understood by Jews in his time. Yet Jesus's interpretation of what Judaism ought to be was distinctive and became the foundation of a new religion. His confidence in his relation to God as father gave him an all-important outlook on his life and ministry and eventual death. The focal point of the Christian understanding of suffering, of course, is the crucifixion, an event that epitomizes all of the fearful agonies that are distributed across the human race. The gospels report that Jesus met the realities of suffering in his own person and defeated them by his resurrection. The New Testament documents and subsequent theological writings speak of this ultimate victory over death being played out in the ways in which Jesus, actively and positively, dealt with the facts of suffering as he found them. In the company of Jesus, then, all suffering is potentially destroyed because of the all-embracing nature of his victory over death. So, the Christian's practical response to suffering is to trust in God as father, living out the pattern of Christ.

The theme that the cause of suffering is traceable to the direct activity of the devil or devils is detectable in Christian as well as Jewish documents. But the relative frequency of such references in the New Testament has more to do with the influence of dualistic Persian Zoroastrianism in Palestine during the intertestamental period than it does with suggesting a practically appropriate response. Clearly, the authority of Jesus over everything, including death, dispels any dualistic interpretation of the cause of evil. Far more important is Jesus's development of critical insights regarding the human relation to God. When eighteen people were killed by the falling of the tower at Siloam, Jesus asked if they were more guilty than other people living in Jerusalem (Luke 13:4). He was intent on helping his followers break through to the higher insight that there is no simple cause-and-effect understanding of suffering, that much of it is simply gratuitous, and yet that it can be an occasion for God to make his character known. Consider another telling instance in the ministry of Jesus: "As he walked along, he saw a man blind from birth. His disciples asked him, 'Rabbi, who sinned, this man or his parents, that he was born blind?' Jesus answered, 'Neither this man nor his parents sinned; he was born blind so that God's works might be revealed in him'" (John 9:1–3). As he heals the man's sight, Jesus sides immediately with the minority report of the Old Testament: Job's testimony that there is innocent suffering. Reference to purpose in the blindness is best interpreted not as God causing suffering but rather as God working redemptively in it. The practical Christian response to suffering, then, is to live on the basis of the risen life of Christ.

The apostle Paul eloquently reflected this theme:

> For I reckon that the sufferings we now endure bear no comparison with the splendour, as yet unrevealed, which is in store for us. For the created universe waits with eager expectation for God's sons to be revealed. . . . If God is on our side, who is against us? He did not spare his own Son, but surrendered him up for us all; and with this gift how can he fail to lavish upon us all he has to give? . . . Then what can separate us from the love of Christ? Can affliction or hardship? Can persecution, hunger, nakedness, peril, or the sword? "We are being done to death for thy sake all day long," as Scripture says; "we have been treated like sheep for slaughter"—and yet, in spite of all, overwhelming victory is ours through him who loved us. For I am convinced that there is nothing in death or life, in the realm of spirits or superhuman powers, in the world as it is or the world as it shall be, in the forces of the universe, in heights or depth—nothing in all creation that can separate us from the love of God in Christ Jesus our Lord. (Romans 8:18–25, 31–39)

Obviously, the work of Christ is somehow related to the justice of God, a connection Paul developed to the point of seeing it as combined with mercy.

CHRISTIANITY: PHILOSOPHICAL DISCUSSIONS

While practical response to suffering is important in the lives of the faithful, Christian thinkers have offered explanatory responses as well, since the conceptual coherence and plausibility of Christian ideas about God are at stake. Early Christian thinkers made substantial contributions to the question of why God allows suffering. In Augustine's theodicy, several themes are woven together in a total approach to the problem. From the doctrine of creation, he drew the implications that God brought about an originally good creation, that he endowed rational creatures with free choice, and that they fell into sin. Since God alone bestows being, and he is supremely good, his creation is good; this means that evil, metaphysically speaking, is the privation of good, the warping or damaging of what God originally intended. The great mystery of free will is the conundrum over why creatures would reject God's ways, but there is nothing else to blame but wrong free choice, from which, according to Augustine, all evils and sufferings flow. There is also an aesthetic theme in Augustine that the evils we experience are parts of a greater whole that must still be seen as good, even as beautiful, under God's sovereignty. Of course, God foreknew that the creature would fall into sin, but "God judged it better to bring good out of evil than to suffer no evil to exist" (Augustine 1887). The clear message of this theodicy, which has echoed down through the centuries in many Western Christian explanations of evil and suffering, is that the creature is completely culpable and that God is innocent.

In the early Eastern Church, Bishop Irenaeus developed a different theodicy. Rather than focusing on the causal genesis of evil, he emphasized the ways in which God is dealing with it and moving the world toward eschatological fulfillment. In the later half of the twentieth century, John Hick became a champion of this approach, which became known as "soul-making" theodicy and exhibited its own distinctive themes (Hick 1978). God's unswerving purpose is to bring creatures from self-centeredness into moral and spiritual maturity, a process that requires that persons face opportunities for displaying virtue or vice, grappling with temp-tation, and even participating in evil. Of course, it is impossible to create by fiat creatures who are perfectly morally mature, since moral maturity entails having made many choices over time. A soul-making environment, then, must be a com-munity of moral agents interacting in a variety of special ways, deciding on the kinds of relationships they will have, what projects they will pursue, and how they will live together. The possibility of moral evil is inherent in such a world. This environment will also be a physical order that includes impersonal objects that operate independently of the desires of personal agents, providing an arena of their choice and action but also making possible natural evils. Hick further argues that there must be "epistemic distance" between creator and creature—the presence of God cannot be impressed too forcefully upon human consciousness so that gen-uine faith in God is possible. Rather than blame humanity for the fall, Irenaean theodicy considers it virtually inevitable that the spiritually immature creature would organize its life apart from God. God's infinite resourcefulness entails that he will continue to work with all persons to draw them to himself—a theme that Hick follows to the point of universalism.

Since the 1970s, Christian philosopher Alvin Plantinga has been extremely influ-ential in discussions of the problem of evil. In his early career, Plantinga constructed the "free will defense" to show that atheistic critics (most notably, J. L. Mackie and Antony Flew) could not prove that God and evil are logically incompatible, but his more recent contribution to the discussion revolves around what he calls "*felix culpa* theodicy," which aims to express a positive reason for a good God to allow evil (Plantinga 2004, 1–25). The *Exultet* of the Antiochian Western Easter Vigil contains the line: "O truly necessary fault of Adam, which the death of Christ has blotted out! O happy fault, that merited such and so great a Redeemer!" Plantinga focuses on the idea that sin is necessary to achieving God's intended greater purposes and is there-fore a "happy fault" or a "fortunate flaw"—*felix culpa*. He compares the values of possible worlds, building on familiar lines of argument: first, that the finite goods of free will and all of the moral goods it makes possible outweigh finite evils (as in his free will defense); second, that God's necessary existence (i.e., existence in all pos-sible worlds vis-à-vis a modal ontological argument) means that in all possible worlds, God's infinite value outweighs all finite evils, making those worlds good on the whole. But Plantinga argues further that there is a contingent good-making feature that makes all worlds that include it far better than any worlds that do not: the incomparable good of incarnation and atonement. The beauty and love displayed in God's condescension to us, culminating in the suffering and crucifixion of Christ, is, according to Plantinga, a towering good with no equal. So, worlds containing incarnation and atonement are unsurpassably good worlds. But then all unsurpassably good worlds also contain sin and evil. For Plantinga, then, sin and evil are "fortunate" because they are necessary conditions for incarnation and atonement. It should be observed that other Christian thinkers maintain that it is a mistake to hold that if humanity had not fallen, then we would not have the greatest good of supremely valuable intimacy with God himself. Reflecting a traditional Anglo-Catholic perspective, C. S. Lewis argues that the classical Christian vision of the human *telos* as meant for intimate participation in the divine life entails that God would bring our *telos* to fulfillment even without the fall. Indeed, without the contingent fact of human sin, incarnation would still be possible, and indeed likely, to reveal the self-giving, self-sacrificing love of God to humanity.[1]

Marilyn Adams criticizes theodicies such as Plantinga's that are "global and generic," resulting in cost/benefit analyses that fail to explain how God is good to individual persons who experience evil and suffering. In fact, she poses the toughest challenge as the task of accounting for "horrendous evils," defined as "evils the participation in which (that is, the doing or suffering of which) constitutes prima facie reason to doubt whether the participant's life could (given their inclusion in it) be a great good to him/her on the whole" (Adams 1999, 26). Such evils—the rape and brutal murder of a woman, psychological torture that destroys personalities, extreme child abuse and murder, the explosion of nuclear bombs over populated areas—have the power to degrade the individual by devouring the possibility of positive personal meaning. But Adams believes that God must guarantee to each person a life he or she sees as having positive meaning and value. Since finite and temporal goods cannot defeat horrendous evil, Adams employs intimate relationship with the infinitely good God—a beatific vision in classical terms—as the element that defeats horrendous evils, even if this relationship must be fully realized in the life to come.

ISLAM: SCRIPTURAL ROOTS OF THE PROBLEM

Although the Qur'an claims repeatedly to be the same revelation that God, or Allah, entrusted to such servants as Abraham, Moses, and Jesus, the messages differ—something Muslims take as evidence that Jews and Christians have corrupted the original revelation. Certainly, the problem of evil is dealt with differently. The primary problem for Judaism is distribution, while for Christianity, it is vindication, with answers in both religions largely concerned to square suffering with the moral attributes of God (goodness, love, mercy, justice). However, in Islam, suffering seems most poignantly to be in conflict with God's power: the problem is the apparent absence of God's control over events in the world. The Qur'an puts the problem straightforwardly: "Did you suppose that you would go to Paradise untouched by the suffering which was endured by those before you? Affliction and adversity befell them; and so battered were they that each apostle, and those who shared his faith, cried out: 'When will the help of Allah come?' His help is ever near" (Qur'an 2.214). The strong emphasis throughout the Qur'an on God's omnipotence is the basis for various interpretations. Extreme renditions of this idea almost lead to an antitheodicy position: "The Almighty God is in total control and is not to be questioned." However, another strand of interpretation factors in God's compassion and thereby opens up avenues for creative analysis in relation to omnipotence.

On the theoretical level, then, the general direction for an answer must run along the lines of explicating what it means for God to have complete power. A fair interpretation of the Qur'an is that the concept of omnipotence must be taken seriously: if our imagination of God is not too small, then suffering cannot be a problem, because the facts of suffering must necessarily be contained within the omnipotence of God (see Qur'an 35.1). And the Qur'an contains abundant material substantiating the assertion that God is in control. Coupled with the assertion that God is also compassionate, the scripture, including its interpretation by teachers and commentators, explores ways in which suffering must in some sense be purposeful, intended, and used by God. Even the misuse of free will by creatures, human or angelic, is understood as within God's control.

Classical explorations of this theme include al-Ghazālī, Ibn Taymiyya, and Ibn 'Arabī. Al-Ghazālī is known for the dictum "There is nothing in possibility more wonderful than what is" (Hoover 2006, 75). This optimistic theodicy provides a rough analogue to the Leibnizian (and purportedly Christian) explanation of why the world contains the evil it does.[2] Of course, these historic explorations inevitably lead to discussions of whether a divine-command approach makes whatever God wills de facto good or whether the divine power must be viewed as guided by divine wisdom regarding the choice of what to create. In any event, a further challenge arises in giving evil real existence, since what God creates is good from God's perspective.

Over the centuries, two important ideas about suffering arise from the Qur'an and commentaries on it. First, much suffering is seen a punishment for sin, whether it comes in the form of natural disasters or defeat in battle. The Qur'an cites many examples, such as Moses and the killing of Pharaoh's army in the Red Sea. But there is also the ancient battle in which Meccans defeated the Muslims at Uhud, while surely not all of the Muslims who were killed and defeated were equally culpable. Implicitly, this raises the question of distribution of indiscriminate suffering and therefore questions the justice of the punishment. The Qur'an warns believers not to make the mistake of Job's friends and assume that suffering is a clear sign of sin, thus opening up logical space for a second idea about the meaning of suffering: that suffering is a trial or test. Again, since omnipotence is above question, suffering as test becomes a necessary part of the purposes of God, a way to create faithfulness and to distinguish the sincere from the insincere. Indeed, patience, servitude, and gratitude just begin the list of valuable traits that can be linked to suffering. So, suffering not only forms character, but it also exposes it, as indicated in the frequent and quite familiar statement of the scholars: "O my son! Gold and silver are to be examined by fire and the believer is to be examined by affliction."

ISLAM: PRACTICAL APPLICATIONS

Clearly, then, at the theoretical level, Islam holds an instrumental view of suffering. We might therefore expect that the natural and recommended practical response to suffering—based on the strong view of omnipotence, as well as the explorations of how God uses it—would be that the faithful should exhibit passive acceptance of what must be the will of God, almost a kind of fatalism. However, the Qur'an repeatedly demands that suffering should be contested and alleviated to the fullest possible extent. This is the foundation for the detailed requirements in scripture for a truly Muslim society that removes particular instances of injustice and suffering and thus displays the justice and compassion of God. Mohammed Ghaly provides a rich, comprehensive study of the literature in Islam dealing with theological interpretations of disability broadly conceived, as well as relevant jurisprudential considerations, ranging over such matters as the dignity, social treatment, medical treatment, employability, and charitable treatment of those with disabilities (Ghaly 2009).

The eschatological dimension of Islamic thought completes the main shape of its approach to evil and suffering. Since God is in control, the ultimate victory is his. There is no opposing principle, although there are conflicts and inequalities within his creation. Even the different schools of thought on the question of omnipotence in relation to free will agree that God is in some sense in control. The *hadith*, which are the traditions of Muhammad's life and teaching, are more deterministic, seeing omnipotence as directly creating the actions of human persons, as well the events of their lives, including suffering. The dissenting school—known as Qadariyya—maintains that God remains in control but delegates to persons responsibility for their actions and thus allows them to determine their own destinies.

HINDUISM: NEW CATEGORIES FOR THE PROBLEM

For Hinduism, there are many ways of looking at a single object, none of which provides the whole view but each of which represents a perspective. Diversity within Hinduism is even evident in the various efforts, often contradictory, in wrestling with the problem of evil and suffering. Yet in spite of the perspectives on evil that are detectable across a variety of scriptural sources and commentaries, many thinkers maintain that at the theoretical level, the doctrines of karma and rebirth are the heart of the Hindu explanation of evil. On the practical level, Hinduism advocates right perception and right action as the key to living in a world that contains suffering. This comprehensive approach, when explicated more fully, represents the striking differences between Western religious thought generally and the great Indian religious traditions.

The underlying metaphysical vision of Hinduism, often characterized as panentheism or a particular kind of monism, holds the conviction that ultimate reality is the Divine Ground of Being (Brahman) of which the individual self (*atman*) is an expression. The basic Hindu approach to suffering and evil, then, rests on other doctrines that are interwoven with this view. Karma is the universal law of moral cause-and-effect. Whereas Western religions involve a retributive element in some approaches to suffering, Indian thought makes the retribution perfect and exact, so that all suffering in each person's life can be explained by that individual's wrongdoing, whether in this or a prior life. Samsara is the cycle of rebirth into other forms of existence, the level of which depends, by the working of karma, on the quality of the individual's previous existence. Thus, it is possible to rise or fall in subsequent existences according to the integrity with which one has previously lived. Traditionally, the caste system was interpreted as an expression of this law.

Since what is normally taken to be the individual self is actually a manifestation of the one true reality, Brahman, individual personhood is an illusion (maya). Indeed, objects of all kinds in human experience that are taken to be distinct and separate only amount to "appearance" but are not "reality." Broadly speaking, then, suffering belongs to the world of maya and samsara. The foundational scriptures of Hinduism—the Vedas, the Brahmanas, and the Upanishads—progressively reveal a further insight: that suffering is the essence of the universe. The universe is the unending process of killing and being killed, devouring and being devoured, such that sacrifice developed in Hinduism as a form of identification with the process and a way of trying to bring it into some sort of control. "Cosmic process," as S. Radhakrishnan describes it, "is one of universal and unceasing change and is patterned on a duality which is perpetually in conflict" (Radhakrishnan 1953, 59). The duality (not dualism) is in reality aspects of a single entity seen from different sides of what is essentially a unity. So, ultimately, gaining the right perspective and right attitude toward suffering rests on seeing it in relation to the whole, as only relative. To designate the unpleasant experience of suffering as evil still would be to see it as particular and out of context. Furthermore, suffering can even be beneficial if it serves to cut us off from unworthy objects of our affection. So, true perception is to see the unity behind the variety of manifest forms. While the experience of suffering is real enough, seen in relation to the whole, it cannot be an ultimate reality.

Hinduism: Life in Relation
to Ultimate Reality

This is the point at which the theoretical understanding of evil and suffering provides guidance to practical response. *Moksha*, which is liberation from the cycle of birth-death-rebirth, is only possible when parts are seen to be parts, and Brahman is realized as the sole truth—and this realization might take a long time and many existences to attain. Suffering is only a problem as long as it appears to be a final and inescapable truth, a mistaken perception that causes the individual self to spend itself seeking a solid and secure home in objects that are ephemeral and transitory, still in the realm of maya. But when one realizes the famous goal of the Upanishads—"Atman is Brahman"—one sees that the self is not bound forever to the transient world of suffering, and suffering can no longer occur. Consider how Indra comes to understand that the body might suffer while the self that pervades it is not affected: "[T]his Self . . . will be blind when the body is blind, lame when the body is lame, deformed when the body is deformed. When the body dies, this same Self will also die! In such knowledge I can see no good" (Chandogya Upanishad 8.7–15). Prajapati, who is instructing Indra, explains that the realization of the true self is like being in a state of dreamless sleep, but it is surely possible that many "as it were" experiences will occur before that state is reached. To be born is to come into contact with evil and suffering, since the material body is full of corruption and potential conflict, a potentiality that is realized if the self gives way to its desires and passions that attach it to the world process.

Achieving *moksha* involves more than achieving right perception; it requires a certain way of living. "The acts done in former births never leave any creature. In determining the working out of karma the Lord of Creation saw them all. Man, since he is under the control of karma, must always have in mind how he can restore the balance and rescue himself from evil consequences" (Mahabharata Vanaparva 207.19). Dharma is doing whatever is appropriate in the circumstances in which one finds oneself, including one's station in society, without attachment to the results. It is easy to understand why classical Hinduism places considerable emphasis on asceticism (self-denial, privation) as a practical route to getting suffering in its right perspective and moving one toward final release. Of course, not just undergoing but also inflicting suffering is addressed in the Bhagavad-Gita, where as long as causing suffering is part of one's legitimate role or duty, it is in accord with dharma, although generally, Hinduism recommends ahimsa, nonviolence.

Interpreters of Hinduism argue that it is not an escapist attempt to avoid the miseries of the present world. The realization that "Atman is Brahman" cannot be attained by pretending that the world does not exist but only by seeing the world for what it is, in the right perspective, and by acting appropriately in the world. The foundational concept is that suffering is a direct result of karma, such that an individual self reaps the fruits of its own deeds and thoughts, in future existences if not in this life. This means that morality is strongly connected with suffering, but it is a quite different connection. The problem of Job as the paradigmatic case of the genuinely innocent sufferer cannot arise, because it is always the case that occurrences of suffering are a consequence of activities, not simply in this existence but also in previous ones. Thus, the question posed to Jesus—"Who sinned, this man or his parents?"—is readily answered, "This man."

RETROSPECTIVE ON EVIL IN WORLD RELIGIONS

The theodicies above, in both their theoretical and practical aspects, provide case studies, so to speak, that help us see how evil becomes problematical in somewhat different ways in various religions and how their responses differ accordingly. Over time, each tradition must reassert its relevance as new circumstances and fresh reflections stimulate new explorations of both the questions and the answers regarding evil and suffering. Yet amid the flavorful differences in theological formulations of the problem and responses to it, there is the undeniable common human experience of evil as a concrete reality. There is also the universal human question, expressed variously as: Why do the innocent suffer and the wicked flourish? Why is the world not better ordered and more just? Why is there suffering and death at all in the universe? It is important that studying the problems of evil and a variety of theodicies across cultures and around the globe puts us in touch with our shared humanity. Appreciation for this shared humanity is a strong basis for appreciating the serious and sustained attempts of the world's great religions to grapple with the deepest of human perplexities.

NOTES

1. The created end or purpose of humanity for classical Christianity is participation in the divine trinitarian life. The prologue of *The Catechism of the Catholic Church* articulates this theme: "God, infinitely perfect and blessed in himself, in a plan of sheer goodness freely created man to make him share in his own blessed life" (2002, 1.1). I develop the point that the essential nature of God would be revealed to humanity regardless of the fall in Peterson 2008.

2. Of course, a best-of-all-possible-worlds approach raises a number of subordinate questions. For example, does this mean that the actual world contains less evil than any other possible world or that this world contains the least amount of evil that is commensurate with this world being the best overall? And if God in his wisdom knows which world is the best, is it within his power to create that world? Alvin Plantinga, of course, contends

that if free will is included in a possible world, then it is not within God's power to strongly actualize it, a point that turns on the kind of free will (incompatibilist or compatibilist) that a world contains. See Plantinga 1974, chap 9.

REFERENCES

Adams, Marilyn. 1999. *Horrendous Evils and the Goodness of God*. Ithaca, N.Y.: Cornell University Press.

Augustine, Saint. 1887. *Enchridion* 22. J. F. Shaw, trans. In Philip Schaff, ed., *From Nicene and Post-Nicene Fathers*, first series, vol. 3. Buffalo, N.Y.: Christian Literature.

Babylonian Talmud. n.d. Available online at www.come-and-hear.com/berakoth/berakoth_5.html.

Berger, Peter. 1967. *The Sacred Canopy*. New York: Doubleday.

The Catechism of the Catholic Church, rev. ed. 2002. London: Burns and Oates. Available online at www.vatican.va/archive/catechism/prologue.html.

Ghaly, Mohammed. 2009. *Islam and Disability: Perspectives in Theology and Jurisprudence*. New York: Routledge.

Hick, John. 1978. *Evil and the God of Love*, rev. ed. San Francisco: Harper and Row.

Hoover, Jon. 2006. "The Justice of God and the Best of All Possible Worlds: The Theodicy of Ibn Taymiyya." *Theological Review* 28/2: 53–75.

The Koran. 1974. N. J. Dawood, trans. New York: Penguin.

Kushner, Harold. 1981. *Why Bad Things Happen to Good People*. New York: Avon.

Mahabharata Vanaparva. 1896. Kisari Mohan Ganguli, trans. New Delhi: Munshiram Manoharlal. The complete text is available online at www.mahabharataonline.com.

Peterson, Michael L. 2008. "C. S. Lewis on the Necessity of Gratuitous Evil." In David Baggett et al., eds., *C. S. Lewis as Philosopher: Truth, Goodness and Beauty*. Downers Grove, Ill.: InterVarsity, 175–192.

Plantinga, Alvin. 1974. *The Nature of Necessity*. Oxford: Clarendon.

———. 2004. "Supralapsarianism, or 'O Felix Culpa.'" In Peter van Inwagen, ed., *Christian Faith and the Problem of Evil*. Grand Rapids, Mich.: Eerdmans, 1-25.

Radhakrishnan, S. 1953. *The Principal Upanishad*. London: George Allen and Unwin.

Schwartz, Matthew B. 1983. "The Meaning of Suffering: A Talmudic Response to Theodicy." *Judaism* 32 (Fall): 444–451.

The Upanishads. 1957. Swami Prabhavananda and Frederick Manchester, trans. New York: New American Library.

FOR FURTHER READING

Glatzer, Nahum. 2002. *Dimensions of Job*. Eugene, Ore.: Wipf and Stock.

Herman, A. L. 2000. *The Problem of Evil and Indian Thought*, 2nd ed. Delhi: Motilal Banarsidass.

Hick, John. 1978. *Evil and the God of Love*, rev. ed. San Francisco: Harper and Row.

Kushner, Harold. 1981. *Why Bad Things Happen to Good People*. New York: Avon.

Neusner, Jacob. 2006. "Theodicy in Classical Judaism." In Jacob Neusner, Alan J. Avery-Peck, and William Scott Green, eds., *Encyclopaedia of Judaism*. New York: Brill, Leiden & Continuum.

O'Flaherty, Wendy Donager. 1976. *The Origins of Evil in Hindu Mythology*. Berkeley: University of California Press.

Ormsby, Eric. 1984. *Theodicy in Islamic Thought: The Dispute over al-Ghazālī's "Best of All Possible Worlds."* Princeton, N.J.: Princeton University Press.

Peterson, Michael L. 1998. *God and Evil: An Introduction to the Issues*. Boulder, Co.: Westview.

———, ed. 1992. *The Problem of Evil: Selected Readings*. South Bend, Ind.: University of Notre Dame Press.

Reichenbach, Bruce. 1991. *Karma: A Philosophical Assessment*. Honolulu: University of Hawaii Press.

Shams, C. Inati. 2000. *The Problem of Evil: Ibn Sînâ's Theodicy*. Newport Pagnell, U.K.: Global.

CHAPTER 13

RELIGION AND REVELATION

KEITH WARD

In most religions, the idea of revelation has a central role. Revelation is most widely regarded as knowledge provided by the action of a god or supernatural being. It contrasts with knowledge attained by human research and observation.

In some tribal societies, there is a special class of holy men or women who have access to a world of spirits; who can receive information from the spirits in dreams, visions, or trances; and who can mediate the healing power of the spirits to their clients. Insofar as these spirits are thought of as active and powerful agents, we could regard the information provided by them as revelations, given to shamans, seers, or specially gifted intermediaries between this world and the spirit world.

Where divination is practiced, as in the ancient Roman practice of divining the future from animal entrails, information is allegedly obtained from marks that can only be interpreted by specially gifted seers. Divination is an intermediate case between revelation by the action of a spiritual agent and a sort of human observation that requires the use of special techniques or rituals.

It is presupposed in all such processes that there exists a spiritual or nonmaterial reality, that it can have causal effects in our everyday physical reality, that it is hidden from ordinary human knowledge, but that some humans possess a special ability to access it and perhaps to use its powers, either for good or for evil.

Spiritual reality can be considered impersonal, to the extent that it can be observed and mediated by the actions of the human observer alone. It can be considered personal, to the extent that what is known and mediated depends either partly or wholly on the intentional acts of some spiritual being. One way of marking a difference between magic and religion is that in magic, no acts of a spiritual being are involved, or such acts can be compelled by humans, whereas in religion, a spiritual being plays an active role and can give or withhold information or causal power, either partly or wholly by its own decision.

Clearly, there can be a wide spectrum of possibilities, ranging from the total manipulation of spirit power by an adept to the passive human reception of information from a controlling spirit. There can be different senses of revelation, depending on how much of this spectrum the word is allowed to refer to. Usually, the term *revelation* is applied only when there is an active spiritual component thought to be at work. But one could speak of revelation in a broader sense, as information only accessible to humans with special, extraordinary, or even superhuman capacities for accessing a spiritual reality. Such persons reveal a normally hidden spiritual reality to others, and they can come to have great authority in matters of spiritual truth.

Revelation in Judaism

Most anthropologists think that the great religious traditions now existing in the world developed from earlier tribal notions of a spirit world accessed by broadly shamanic seers. The earliest virtually continuous written record of such a development is found in the Hebrew Bible, where those formerly known as "seers" became known as "prophets" (1 Samuel 9:9) and where early notions of many tribal gods and spirits were succeeded by the belief that there is just one creator and sovereign ruler of the world.

In this tradition, revelation is the active communication of information from God to prophets whom God raises up or who belong to partly institutionalized groups of religious visionaries. Thus, the people asked, "Is Saul also among the prophets?" (1 Samuel 10, 11) when he joined a band of prophets accompanied by musical instruments, fell into a prophetic frenzy, was possessed by the spirit of the Lord, and "turned into a different person."

This gives a fascinating glimpse into what prophecy was in ancient Hebrew religion, although other prophets were more like court functionaries whose job it was to advise kings on political outcomes. In one text, God says, "If Moses were your prophet and nothing more I would make myself known to him in a vision, I would speak with him in a dream" (Numbers 12, 5–8).

In these texts, the spirit is said to "possess" prophets; God appears in visions and speaks in dreams and riddles. This sort of revelation is not a matter of the provision of clear and intelligible information. It is a matter of visionary experiences, cryptic dreams, and partly unintelligible and frenzied utterances. Moreover, prophets often gave contradictory or false advice—four hundred prophets gave false or even lying advice to King Jehoshaphat of Judah (1 Kings 22). The Hebrew Bible is fully aware of the fact that there are many unintelligible and false prophecies and that it is not easy to distinguish reliable from unreliable revelations. It looks as if such prophetic experiences are clearly influenced by social context and personal psychology. There might be some form of causal and cognitive relationship to God, but it is from a very limited perspective, and it tells as much about the minds that claim to apprehend God as it does about any sort of information that God may be providing.

Nevertheless, Numbers 12 insists that Moses is not just like other prophets. He sees "the very form of the Lord," and God speaks to him "face to face, openly and not in riddles." So, one way or another, Moses and the major prophets whose words were edited into the canon of the Hebrew Bible were selected as reliable discerners of God's nature and interpreters of God's will.

The Orthodox Tradition

As Orthodox Judaism later developed, a hierarchy of types of revelation was put in place. At the bottom is inspiration by the spirit, by which human minds are brought to new heights of creativity and insight. The early judges of Israel, the architect of the First Temple, and the compilers of Psalms and Proverbs, were perhaps inspired in this rather general sense. God did not provide them with clear information or specific words. But God gave them extraordinary courage, wisdom, and artistic ability. This perhaps should not be called revelation, since it is seen as a form of the causal influence of God on human minds more than the provision of specific information. Yet insofar as it involves some form of claimed apprehension of God and dependence on God, it has a cognitive aspect. So it may provide some information about God that is not accessible to everyone, however obscure or limited that information is.

On a slightly higher level is a form of inspiration that puts specific ideas into the minds of the prophets. This is not verbal inspiration but very general ideas that might be conceptually expressed in many different ways. One example might be the idea that God is the one and only creator of the world. The words and images in which this idea is expressed might be those of the prophet, but what seeks expression might be said to be implanted in the mind by God.

Then there is the occurrence of dreams, visions, and oracular utterance. Such things are very important at times in the Hebrew Bible, although, as in the case of Joseph in Egypt, dreams need interpretation, and visions require explanation. God communicates in very cryptic ways, and this sort of revelation might be caused by the impact of the divine on a sensitive human mind, producing specific changes in that human consciousness without those changes being fully intelligible or comprehensible to the subject in whom they occur.

Revelation can thus exist as awareness of divine presence, as the prompting of ideas by God, and as divinely caused visions or utterances. But for many people, revelation is primarily recitation in words. The Hebrew prophets say, "Thus says the Lord," and then utter or write the words that the Lord gives. Some think that every word is placed in the prophet's mind by God, but others think that the words the prophet "hears" are generated in the mind by God out of data that are already present there, so that they still carry the imprint of their time and culture. The words might express limitations and even errors that exist in the beliefs of the prophet or culture, although they will overall convey what God wants them to convey. Or they might be protected from error by God while still conveying truths only in forms that are comprehensible for that time and culture.

The highest view of revelation is that the revealed words are the actual words of God, perhaps even miraculously "written with the finger of God" on stone tablets (Exodus 31:18), expressed just as God wishes to express them, using some human mind as a more or less passive instrument. They are thus true for all time, unrevisable, and not limited by the contents of any human mind or the beliefs of any human culture.

It should be noted that revealed words still need to be interpreted in changing circumstances and for difficult cases that might arise. The rabbinic tradition of interpretation in the light of precedents and judicious weighing of the text is of the greatest importance, and it would be quite wrong to think that rules should just be read off from the written text without a great deal of scholarly training. The legal tradition of interpretation is very important for Orthodox Judaism, and this introduces a human and fallible element even into a divinely written law.

Orthodox Jews accept all of these types of revelation. The Torah, the law of Moses, found in the written text from Genesis to Deuteronomy and preserved in oral form until written down as the major part (the *Mishnah*) of the Babylonian Talmud, is the dictated words of God. The Torah is sometimes said to be a copy of the eternal Torah that exists in the heavenly realm, or the eternal word of God, which is a pattern for the creation of the world. It is changeless and irrevocable and forms the basis of the covenant between God and the Jewish people.

The books of the major prophets (Isaiah, Jeremiah, etc.) are not written directly by God. They contain oracular utterances that were "heard" by the prophets but are expressed in distinctive and different ways by prophets of very different personalities, living in diverse historical situations.

The "writings" of the Hebrew Bible, such as the Psalms, the Proverbs, the Book of Ruth, and so on, do not on the whole record the words of God. They are human creations, but they arise out of and often record visions, ideas, histories, or stories that are inspired by God. Their inclusion in the canon of the Hebrew Bible gives them the authority of divine revelation. But they express many diverse viewpoints, often in tension with one another, and they have to be carefully interpreted by being taken in the context of the Bible as a whole and in the light of the definitive teaching of the Torah.

Finally, rabbinical pronouncements such as those found in the Talmud can be taken as binding on particular Jewish communities, but they are inspired or spirit-guided rather than revealed, and they do not, strictly speaking, have divine authority.

Non-Orthodox Jewish Traditions

Not all Jews are Orthodox. But most religious Jews accept that God is revealed to the Hebrew prophets in a special way and that this is an important fact about world history. A major issue in the non-Orthodox traditions is whether the Torah was dictated or written by God. The literal text of the Bible says that it was, but perhaps one should not take the Bible literally. Many Jewish biblical scholars see the final Torah as a collection of different law codes, histories (containing much legendary material), and priestly regulations that were built up over centuries and edited, probably after the Babylonian exile, into one dramatic narrative of Moses' encounter with God on Mount Sinai. When these various strands are disentangled, we are left with a fascinating story of a developing Jewish apprehension of God. In this story, the prophets played a major part, but there were also priests, historians, jurists, poets, and politicians, all of whom contributed to what is now called the Torah. It was not dictated by God. It was a cultural product built out of many diverse elements yet expressing in a highly imaginative form the history of a people's relationships with God.

In such accounts, Moses becomes an idealized figure whose connection with any historical prophet is obscure and remote. The specific statutes and ordinances of the Torah are not binding, and most of them are in any case obsolete—such as all of the rules for temple worship and for the conquest of Canaan. The Torah is seen as a progressive and developing tradition of human attempts to set out a code of justice and morality. But those attempts are made in response to belief in and apprehension of a God who is the source of the moral demand for justice, of the calling of Israel to pursue justice, of a power raising human minds to new perceptions of justice and heroic moral commitments, and of a promise that justice will triumph over oppression and evil.

The Torah is not just a set of *mitzvot*, of statutes and ordinances. Those commands are set in the context of the history of the patriarchs, a history in which God calls individuals into a special covenant of moral obedience and faithful hope, delivers Israel from Egypt, guides Israel through the wilderness, and promises Israel a future of shalom, of peace and human fulfillment.

So the heart of revelation, in Judaism, is the self-disclosure of God as the source and ground of morality and goodness and as the Lord of history, who calls Israel to pursue the divine purpose of human fulfillment in fellowship with the personal ground of all being. The prophets are those who, beginning as seers and oracle readers, become discerners of the absolute demand for goodness in an estranged and corrupted world and who see, in all of the ambiguities of history, the possibility and promise of a kingdom where love, justice, mercy, and peace rule.

For Liberal, Progressive and Reform Jews, revelation is not primarily in words, least of all in divinely dictated words. It is God's unveiling of the demand and promise of righteousness and the setting apart of Israel as a people devoted to the rule of righteousness in the human world. The prophets are those who can read the signs of the times, who condemn injustice and look for the advent of true justice: "What does the Lord require of you but to do justice, and to love kindness, and to walk humbly with your God?" (Micah 6:8).

Such revelation is God appearing as the morally sovereign Lord of history in specific historical events to persons whose minds and hearts are inspired by awareness of that appearing, of its specific demands, and of the promise of its fuller disclosure at some future time.

Verbal inspiration is less important for this view of revelation. It tends to be seen as the influence of the spirit on minds that use the concepts and images available to them in their culture to interpret and express their apprehensions of the God who discloses the divine being to them in the moral demands and exigencies of their history. As seers developed into prophets, so prophets faded away, to be succeeded by rabbinic scholars who seek to discern God's present will for goodness and for the specific vocation of Israel, in the light of the developing tradition of moral discernment and historical interpretation that is their heritage. Such a view of revelation is experiential, historical, and developing. Yet Moses and the Torah can stand as normative symbols of the apprehension of God as the ground of the absolute demands of morality, obedience to which is the way to the promised kingdom of divine justice and mercy. And they stand as symbols of the special vocation of Israel to be the vanguard of that kingdom.

REVELATION IN CHRISTIANITY

Christianity developed out of Judaism as the belief that Jesus of Nazareth was the Messiah, the one who would rule in God's kingdom. Since the ruler of the kingdom is God, this led, in orthodox Christianity, to Jesus being seen as the incarnation in human form of God. The church is the "new Israel," partner in a new covenant with God into which all humans are invited. This entails that God's act of self-revelation not only takes place in a written law (which Christians came to reject) but that it primarily takes place in the person of Jesus, who is God's self-expression in human history.

A specific human life now becomes revelation, as it discloses the character of God as loving, healing, forgiving, and caring for the poor and as it manifests God acting in history in such ways. This is a development of the Jewish view of God as acting in and through historical events to liberate and guide Israel. The moral demand of God is focused on the self-sacrificial love that is manifest in the crucifixion of Jesus. The liberating acts of God in history are focused on the new life of the spirit that Jesus evokes. And the final promise of fulfillment is focused on the resurrection of Jesus, his triumph over death, in which all are called to share. Thus, for Christians, Jesus is more than a prophet who hears and passes on the words of God. Jesus becomes the word of God in his own person. His life shows definitively what God is, and his death and resurrection show the ultimate goal for human life and how it is to be attained.

Such a personal revelation must be recorded if it is to be made available to the whole world. The church is a continuing society in which the main events of Jesus's life and the main tenets of his teaching are continually recalled and made present through sacraments and teaching. The New Testament is a set of recollections of Jesus, in the gospels, letters to early Christian churches, a short history of the apostolic church, and a set of visions and oracular messages experienced by an early Christian believer. This set of diverse documents arose out of the early church and was formed into the New Testament, becoming a normative standard against which subsequent teachings could be measured.

There is thus little room in orthodox Christianity for seeing the New Testament as the dictated words of God. The four gospels are written from different viewpoints, they emphasize different aspects of Jesus's life, and they place events in slightly different orders. The letters reflect the views of their writers; they are often written in a rather crude form of Greek, and while containing invaluable insights into the life of the early church, they also contain remarks that can seem very culturally conditioned or even unintelligible.

Nevertheless, Christian tradition has sought to give the New Testament an authority as great as it can bear. Many Christians believe that, while not actually being dictated by God, the New Testament, like the whole Bible, is "God-breathed" (*theopneustos*; 2 Timothy 3:16). They take this to mean that it is free from error and verbally inspired by God, in that the words were generated in human minds by God.

There are problems with such an inerrancy view, arising from the fact that some parts of the Old Testament, such as its calls for vengeance and even genocide, are very problematic for Christians, that the New Testament seems to modify Old Testament teachings rather radically—as in the Sermon on the Mount of Matthew 5–7 or Paul's rejection of the Torah as binding—and that there are disagreements, though small ones, about the exact form and sequence of the recorded events of Jesus's life. So the inerrancy view can be stated very subtly, as in the Roman Catholic *Dogmatic Constitution on Divine Revelation*, from Vatican II, which states, "The books of Scripture firmly, faithfully and without error, teach that truth which God, for the sake of our salvation, wished to see confided to the sacred Scriptures" (chap. 3, paragraph 11). Reading this sentence carefully, one can see that what is said to be inerrant is not every statement in the New Testament but those truths that God wished to see in scripture. We are not told which truths those are, but it seems they are those that exist "for the sake of our salvation." They are not truths about, for example, the date of the Last Supper, but they are truths that are important for salvation, such as the fact that Jesus proclaimed the kingdom, died for our sins, and rose again.

Such a sophisticated view of inerrancy—what we might call a "cooperative verbal inspiration" view—is compatible with seeing God's inspiration not as directing every word of the text but as influencing the choice of ideas and images, prompting the selection of memories, and ensuring that no errors about the goal of salvation and the way to attain it are found in the text. This can cover an "inspiration of ideas" view, as well as a sort of "verbal inspiration" view for which God influences rather than specifically generates human writings. God plays a causal role in the operations of human minds, but the thoughts and words that are written are genuinely products of those minds, "breathed upon," enlivened, and guided by the spirit.

This view stands between a strong verbal inerrancy view and a view that the New Testament texts are nothing but human responses to the life of Jesus. It enables one to say, for example, that the Sermon on the Mount does not record, word for word, an actual sermon preached by Jesus (he would probably have taught in Aramaic, in which case we do not have his actual words but a Greek translation). It is a collection of sayings, preserved in oral traditions, collected, and put together by the writer of Matthew's gospel, and it accurately conveys the substance of Jesus's teaching and probably some of the startling images and thoughts that he used. This would be a view very widely held by New Testament scholars, and that is a strong argument in its favor.

Of course, there remain problems about whether Jesus himself was verbally inspired, and his life specifically directed, by the will of God. As with questions of revelation in general, these questions are about how the divine will is related to human minds, as they receive and interpret their spiritual (nonsensory), visual, or verbal apprehensions of God. Some Christians hold that the whole life and thought of Jesus were directed entirely by the eternal word of God, his human mind and will being passively obedient. But it is within the bounds of orthodoxy to maintain a "cooperation" view of human and divine mind and will, which would reflect the weaker "cooperative verbal inspiration" view just outlined. This would reflect a general belief that the unity of humanity and divinity in Jesus must have been such as to fulfill, not negate, a full human autonomous creativity of will. Revelation in the person of Jesus could then be seen as the fulfillment of a properly human capacity for a unity of mind and will with God that would not obliterate human individuality but would allow the divine nature to be fully manifested in a human life. In that case, Christian revelation would provide, in a quite distinctive way, a disclosure of the potential of human nature for unity with the divine. It would radically modify the Jewish view of revelation as God's action in historical events that always remain distinct from God. The universe would be not the instrument of God but a means of generating persons who could participate in the divine nature (2 Peter 1:4). Revelation as a uniting of the finite and human to the infinite and divine is not just a communication of information from God. It would be a transformation of the physical to reveal its true goal as unity with the divine, when all things will be gathered up "in Christ" (Ephesians 1:10).

The major facts of Jesus's life and teaching are recorded in the New Testament. For that reason, Catholic and Orthodox Christians regard the New Testament as a normative authority for faith. But they give the church an important role in safeguarding and interpreting divine revelation in Jesus. Since 1870, the Roman Catholic Church has held that the pope is infallible when defining a doctrine of faith or morals as part of the deposit of divine revelation handed down from apostolic tradition. This is a very limited infallibility, which has rarely been exercised. But it means that the pope has authority not to invent new doctrines but to interpret the revelation in Christ in a definitive way.

Other Christians reject this claim, but Eastern Orthodox Christians hold that the fully ecumenical councils of the church (usually the first seven councils, ending in 787 CE) had a similar role of infallibly defining what belongs to authentic Christian faith. Protestants do not accept that any human institution has such authority. But it must be noted that these conciliar definitions are not new revelations. It is a matter of defining what belongs to or is implied in the original revelation in the person of Jesus. The point is that someone must interpret and apply that revelation in very different times and places. The church, the community of disciples in the widest sense, preserves and interprets the revelation and continues the process of uniting humanity to divinity through grace, which was inaugurated by Jesus. The New Testament provides the authoritative witness to the normative locus of revelation, the life and teachings of Jesus. Thus, Christian views of revelation stand in continuity with Jewish views yet introduce the radically new idea of revelation as a disclosure of the unity of human and divine, into which it invites the whole human world.

Revelation in Islam

Islam can be seen as a return to something more like a traditional Jewish position, for which human and divine are quite distinct and for which revelation is primarily an inerrant and irrevocable verbal communication from God. The Arabic word for "prophetic revelation" is *wahy*, which covers the inspiration of ideas, dreams and visions, and verbal utterances. Such revelation is said to come to prophets of every nation. But the supreme form of revelation is *tanzil*, the verbal dictation of a message from God. It is embodied only in the Qur'an, which was recited by Muhammad section by section at different times but is traditionally said to have been "received" by him from the archangel Gabriel in a single night. The present text was first written down in the reign of the third caliph Uthman, about twenty years after the death of the Prophet, but tradition maintains that it has remained unchanged since it was heard, remembered, and recited by the disciples of Muhammad.

The Qur'an is the supreme and final revelation, which corrects both the Torah and the Christian gospel where necessary. It is a copy of the eternal Qur'an, which exists before all worlds, and it contains *Shari'a*, the law of God for all peoples (not just for one ethnic group), as well as beautiful poetry expressing teaching on God, judgment, and resurrection. Since the text is given by God in Arabic, translations are not permitted in public use of the Qur'an in worship, it does not depend upon the human knowledge or experience of the Prophet, and its recitation does more than provide information; it makes present the direct address of God to its hearers, calling for a response of submission to God in faith.

The Qur'an, however, needs to be interpreted and applied. There are many schools of interpretation in Islam, ranging from the literalist and rigorist interpretations of the Wahhabis to the symbolic interpretations of some Sufi movements, which seek underlying principles that can apply in modern situations behind some of the specific rules of the Qur'an. In Sunni Islam, the democratic consensus of the community, informed by the *hadith*, or traditions of the Prophet's life and teachings, is held to be authoritative. In Shia Islam, the supreme imam is held to be an infallible interpreter, although most Shiites await the appearance of the Hidden Imam, who does not yet exist on earth.

The need to interpret revelation allows for and invites some sort of development and diversity, even in a religion that affirms one divinely given text. And the fact that the text is sometimes mysterious or obscure, and that it is a divine address in a highly poetic and rhetorical form rather than a textbook of information, heavily qualifies the view that the verbal revelation of the Qur'an is simply information given by God. It might primarily be seen as a form of divine speech that raises the heart to worship a reality that the words evoke and express but that remains hidden and mysterious even in the poetic imagery of its self-disclosure. That is perhaps why the Qur'an is said to be the final revelation—because it is the supreme and definitive temporal vehicle of the self-communicative speech of God, which can be responded to in different ways in every time and culture.

REVELATION IN INDIAN AND EAST ASIAN TRADITIONS

The word *revelation* is most at home in the Semitic religions, which think of one God actively disclosing his nature and purpose to humans. But in the Indian religious traditions, a distinction is made between writings that are heard (*sruti*) and writings that are memorized traditions (*smriti*). The Veda, Brahamanas, Aranyakas, and Upanishads are held to be heard by ancient *rishis*, sages or poets to whom the gods speak, whereas much religious literature, including, for example, the Bhagavad Gita, although it might have great spiritual influence, is not part of *sruti*.

Thus, Hinduism has a doctrine of divinely dictated speech. But this occurs in a set of very different and poetically expressed texts, which can be and are interpreted in widely different ways. This reflects the polyvalent nature of Indian religion, where many gods and goddesses can be worshipped in many different ways, and all are, broadly speaking, ways to truth, adapted to the needs of the devotee.

Most sophisticated Hindus hold that there is one supreme spiritual reality, Brahman, which may take many personal forms and can be approached through knowledge and meditation (*jnana*), through ritual ceremonial (karma), or through devotion (*bhakti*). But the variety of theological systems said to be derived from the revealed texts, ranging from impersonal nondualism to personal theism and even including an almost purely ritualistic materialism, is bewildering. Most devotees regard one of these traditions as the ultimately genuine one, while the others are often said to be suited to those at inferior states of spiritual development.

In practice, most Hindu movements follow the teachings of a guru, who is often said to be an avatar or embodiment of a god, or at least to be in a teaching lineage deriving from such an avatar. The most generally accepted Hindu doctrine is that all things are parts of the one self, Brahman, so that it is not impossible for that self, in one of its forms, to be fully present in a human life. Such humans will have divine knowledge and powers and be strictly superhuman. So their teachings, and the spiritual practices of yoga or meditation that they inaugurate, can be said to be of divine origin.

In modern movements, great emphasis is often placed on the personal experience of liberation from ego and apprehension of the unity of all things in the Supreme Self. This is the experience and knowledge possessed by the guru, and it can be passed on by practices of meditation and devotion that he (usually he) teaches. The line between knowledge given by God and knowledge attained by personal discipline, meditation, and insight is blurred, precisely because persons are parts of God anyway, and a perfectly enlightened human person will, in a real sense, be identical with God. What such persons teach will be divine revelation to humans at lower levels of spiritual development, although it will still not be *sruti*, the dictated words of the gods, existing as an eternal pattern for all worlds and passively heard and recited by ancient poets.

Some traditions originating in India, such as Buddhism, drop the idea of *sruti* and of a personal Lord (*Isvara*) while retaining the idea of personal liberation and unity with a higher spiritual reality of intelligence and bliss (Nirvana). The Buddha teaches the causes of suffering and the way to liberation from suffering. He has authority because he achieved enlightenment, and so he knows what it is and the way to it. This is not usually termed "revelation" in Buddhism, since no God speaks or acts.

Some Buddhists say that we should not accept any teaching simply on authority but should test the teaching by our own experience. But few have experience of Nirvana, and the way to it took many lifetimes even for Gautama. The great Buddhist teacher Buddhaghosa writes that personal opinion is outweighed by the commentarial tradition; that is outweighed by what is in conformity with scripture; and scripture (the monastic rule) "is incontrovertible. It is equal to the First Council in authority and is just as if the Buddha himself were alive today" (Vinaya i, 231).

This suggests that the words of the Buddha have supreme authority, and that might be called "revelation" from an enlightened person (who has attained supreme wisdom and knowledge of all things conducive to liberation, compassion, and mindfulness) to those who are still partly subject to the "three fires" of greed, hatred, and ignorance. The Buddha's teaching should be tested by personal experience of a gradual perfecting of mind, but it remains authoritative, since it is based on the experience of one who has passed beyond suffering and ignorance and achieved union with a supreme spiritual reality.

This reality is not conceived as personal or active, although in Mahayana Buddhism, there exist Bodhisattvas who are compassionate, who hear and respond to prayers, who reveal scriptures such as the Lotus Sutra by dictation, and who might even originate Buddha worlds (e.g., the Pure Land or Western Paradise) in which devotees can live in purified enjoyment. The boundary between personal gods and an impersonal spiritual realm of bliss and between active revelation and personal apprehension of a changeless liberated state of intelligence and bliss (as Nirvana is often described) is not clear and absolute. We might say that one form of revelation is based on the normative experience of spiritual reality attained by a person of exceptional spiritual knowledge, understanding, moral insight, and compassion. Those who interpret such a revelation accept the authenticity of that normative experience and seek to draw out its implications for the contemporary life of their religious community.

In East Asian religious traditions such as Confucianism and Daoism, there also tends to be a stress on the wisdom and insight of particular sages, since the supreme spiritual reality is conceived as a relatively impersonal moral order or balance in nature, to be accessed by persons of wisdom. Revelation, inspiration, and personal insight overlap, but the emphasis is much more on extraordinary personal wisdom than is the case in the Abrahamic traditions. Yet this coexists with beliefs in spirits, ancestors, astrology, and magical practices, which show the continuance of ancient local beliefs in a diverse and polyvalent spirit world. The emphasis on a normative wisdom, like that of K'ung Fu Tzu (Confucius), places moral and rational restraints on the wide diversity of alleged human interactions with the spirit world and provides a paradigm for interpreting personal experience and social principles within a specific culture or community.

CONCLUSIONS

In summary, there is a wide spectrum of ideas of revelation. At one end, humans are passive, and God dictates words (as in the Torah or the Qur'an). Those words do not just convey information; they convey the divine presence and power by their poetic and evocative form.

God can also reveal the divine purpose in actions in history, which nonverbally convey divine demands and judgments, as well as divine forgiveness and promise (as in the patriarchal narratives of the Hebrew Bible). Such acts are recorded in scripture, and many Jews and Christians accept the verbal inerrancy of scripture, where words are not dictated but are selected by God from various human minds.

Many theistic believers, however, favor a more "cooperative" form of verbal inspiration, where God influences but does not directly select the thoughts of human minds, perhaps preserving them from error, at least in truths concerning salvation, in guiding the development of a tradition of thinking about God. Christians think of God as primarily revealed in the life of a person, Jesus, who has such a close awareness of God and capacity to mediate divine love and power that he can be called the human image or incarnation of God, and his life becomes an authoritative revelation of God's nature and purpose.

For many, God or, more broadly, many gods and spirits can also be revealed in dreams, visions, and cryptic oracles. These are forms of prophetic or shamanistic possession. They are very diverse and unreliable, unless they are controlled by some normative concept of supreme spiritual reality and its nature. Divine revelatory action can also be conceived as the inspiration of ideas or symbols in human minds, which exerts some causal influence but leaves the formation of exact words and phrases to the creativity of the prophet and leaves open the possibility of limitations and errors in teaching. This is typical of more "liberal" forms of Judaism and Christianity. A weaker form of divine causality, which many religions acknowledge but to which they usually give only subsidiary authority, is the general heightening of mental and moral powers by God to extraordinary levels of wisdom and insight.

These are all forms of revelation in which God, or spiritual beings, contributes an active element. But one might speak of a liberated or enlightened sage, such as the Buddha, as revealing truths that are based on their own experience of liberation from ego and awareness of a supreme spiritual reality—an experience only rarely available to humans.

Finally, sages of extraordinary insight, such as Confucius, might integrate many spiritual intuitions and practices into one normative model of human existence (that one should follow "the Way of Heaven," in the Confucian case), and this can be taken as a revelation of spiritual truth obtained by human wisdom and not from any God. That is the other end of the spectrum of revelation.

If there is a supreme spiritual reality and if it is knowable by humans, one would expect there to be revelations of its nature. If there is a God, it is probable that God would actively reveal the divine nature and purpose to humans. Alleged revelations differ greatly, and the best explanation of this is that God acts within the linguistic and cognitive constraints that are characteristic of different cultures and histories. This is compatible with believing that one such time and culture is best placed to receive a revelation that will in principle be normative for all humans. But no neutral account can be provided of what that time and culture is, and one must allow that there is no neutral way of deciding whether there is one final and normative revelation. Decisions and commitments have to be made where so many differences exist. A wise decision takes the widest set of data into account, is concerned to state the most reasonable description of spiritual reality, given the state of general knowledge of the world, and is concerned to incorporate the highest moral insights of which one is aware.

In that case, revelation will not be self-validating. But one can see how the idea of knowledge of a spiritual reality, accessed by persons of extraordinary powers of discernment, develops into different normative models of spirit-human communication. The models of prophet, word, avatar and enlightened sage form templates that direct and set boundaries to subsequent disclosures of spiritual reality. They form final revelations, not in the sense that there is no further new understanding of the spiritual to be had but in that they define the basic truths that must underlie any genuine understanding of the spiritual (for Christians, e.g., that "God is love").

Thus, the idea of revelation is rightly central to religious belief. But there is a range of understandings of what revelation is, and part of any consideration of religious belief should be an assessment of what forms of revelation seem most internally coherent and most plausibly to be instantiated in the light of our general beliefs about the universe.

FOR FURTHER READING

Abraham, William. 2006. *Crossing the Threshold of Divine Revelation*. Grand Rapids, Mich.: Eerdmans.

Dulles, Avery. 1992. *Models of Revelation*. Dublin: Gill and Macmillan.

Farmer, H. H. 1999. *Revelation and Religion*. Lewiston, N.Y.: Edwin Mellen.

Menssen, Sandra, and Thomas Sullivan. 2007. *The Agnostic Inquirer*. Grand Rapids, Mich.: Eerdmans.

Smith, W. C. 1981. *Towards a World Theology*. Maryknoll, N.Y.: Orbis.

Ward, Keith. 1994. *Religion and Revelation*. Oxford: Clarendon.

B

SOCIOLOGICAL AND PUBLIC-POLICY ISSUES

CHAPTER 14

RELIGIOUS DIVERSITY AND GLOBALIZATION

PETER BEYER

GLOBALIZATION: IDENTITY AND DIFFERENCE

THE last decades of the twentieth century witnessed the birth, and then the wide-spread usage in public and scholarly discourse, of a number of new terms that sought to capture what was either a new world-historical context or at least a new perception of a situation that had perhaps existed for some time already. One of these terms, which by now has versions in most of the world's major languages, is *globalization*. In the early twenty-first century, the precise meaning of this idea has become as diverse as the concept has become widespread. For most under-standings, however, globalization is about the world becoming increasingly tied together and integrated through such features as capitalist economic structures and communication technologies such as satellites, cell phones, and the Internet. So far has this integrative trend gone that, in Roland Robertson's phrase, we now see the world as having become a single place, even a single world society (Robertson 1989, 8). The differences in conceptions of this globalization have to do with the details and the consequences of this process. While some consider *globalization* to be merely another word for the spread of a neoliberal capitalist ideology, most insist that while the rise of this ideology in the late twentieth century might be an important component and has contributed significantly to the popularity of the term, a fuller understanding includes a multiplicity of factors that have been pulling the world together, as well as the great diversity through which people all over the world have put globalization into effect. Within that context, a constant question is whether the process is leading to the different parts of the world becoming increasingly alike or whether, in fact, it is also bringing out a renewed emphasis on how we are all different (see Robertson 1995). This chapter very much favors the latter view of globalization, not least because it allows one to understand the role of religion and religious diversity in this process—how religion contributes to it, how it transforms within it, and how religious diversity reflects it.

As indicators of how the place of religion appears differently depending on one's understanding of globalization, one can look at three popular works that are frequently cited in discussions about the current world situation: *The End of History* by Francis Fukuyama, *The Clash of Civilizations* by Samuel Huntington, and *Jihad vs. McWorld* by Benjamin Barber, all dating from the period around the collapse of the Soviet Union in 1989–90.[1] This post–Cold War context is important. For all three authors, the old geopolitical division between the capitalist and socialist worlds, with its derivative and residual category of the "Third World," was no longer available for ordering one's conception about the world as a whole.[2] Therefore, the question became: How was one to conceive this world now? What fundamental ordering principle could represent the "new world order" as it was taking shape? Fukuyama posited the uncontested victory of a single world model, (economic and political) liberalism, which, he claimed, had been gaining ascendancy for some time. Effectively, not only had the capitalist world "won," but the existence of socialism and fascism during the preceding century had even turned out to be but a temporary detour. Notably, Fukuyama's expressly Hegelian and homogenizing vision held no important place for religion. In his book, Fukuyama discusses religion hardly at all, except to dismiss Islamic "fundamentalist" movements—still the most common moniker through which religion appears in most of the literature about globalization—as nonviable, not globalizable, and thus not the sort of challenge to liberalism that socialism and fascism seemed to have represented. Barber and Huntington disagreed; Western liberalism did not stand uncontested. For them, the world was not heading inexorably for a single globalized model; there was a new multiplicity, which was succeeding the now-defunct capitalist/socialist ordering to redefine the fundamental lines of global order and conflict. Barber opted for a new bipartite division, Huntington for a multipolar one. For both of them, the alternatives were defined in terms of religious categories: jihad, holy war; and a plurality of clashing "civilizations," distinguished predominantly in terms of religious differences. From this, we can provisionally conclude that, to the extent that these popular works are at all indicative of the wider debate, religion seems to enter globalization discussions in terms of difference, how the world as a single place is nonetheless fundamentally divided and how that difference manifests itself through conflict and resistance on the basis of religious identities.

Religious Diversity as Global Context

As in the broader literature on globalization and the current global situation, Fuku-yama, Barber, and Huntington were responding to specific historical events or developments that they felt called for a rethinking of how we understand the world in which we all live. All three of them clearly assumed that world to be global in both a social and a geographical sense. They also took as a given that the underlying driving force for this unification was what Fukuyama called (capitalist) liberalism but that whatever it was, these forces all tended toward the creation of a new and "modern" world. It is on the relation between globalization and this modernization that they differed. If for Fukuyama they were destined to be the same thing, for the other two authors they were not; and what prevents globalization from being simply the ongoing story of modernization for the latter two has a lot to do with religion, for Huntington with a diversity of religions. From that perspective, modernization and religion appear to be at odds. More pointedly, to the extent that globalization and modernization are the same, then globalization implies secularization, the absence of religion as a meaningful or universal force. If they are not the same, then globalization subsumes liberal modernization—McWorld for Barber, the "West" for Huntington—and its opposite or opponents, jihad and the "rest" of the religiously defined civilizations.

This contradiction between the modern and the religious is, of course, not new with the advent of the debate about globalization. Quite to the contrary, it has been a constant of Western thought since the eighteenth-century Enlightenment thinkers and the social sciences since their founding in the nineteenth century. From Voltaire and Hegel to Durkheim and Weber, the universalizing modern spelled the demise or marginalization of religion. This assumption carried through to Western thinking and much of that in the non-West through most of the twentieth century. It maintained itself through most of the Cold War era, the capitalist and socialist worlds (now including Japan and China, respectively) both being secularizing in their own way. It was only at the end of that era that widespread—but by no means unanimous—doubt asserted itself, in strict parallel with the rise of the idea of globalization. The parallelism is therefore not coincidental.

Isolated references to the idea of globalization date at earliest to the 1960s; its real arrival as a more common term did not occur before the 1980s; and its popularization had to await the 1990s. There are quite a number of events and developments that make sense of this periodization, but for the question at hand, three can be seen as either representative or seminal, each with consequences for the perception and understanding of religion, including the understanding of religion as inherently, and often problematically, diverse. These are the opening during the 1960s of Western countries to permanent migration from all over the world, facilitating and accelerating a "reverse flow" of people, ideas, and a multiplicity of religions that had been more restricted before; the rise of powerful political movements, inspired by various religions in various quarters of the world during the late 1970s and 1980s; and the definitive end of the Cold War era, including the collapse of the Soviet Union and the victory of the "capitalist roaders" in post-Mao China, in the early 1990s. It is arguable that these events contributed to increasing religious diversity in the world, but even if one does not accept that observation, they certainly had the effect of rendering this diversity more visible and geographically more widespread than it had been before and of making that religious diversity seem critically important, often even problematic.

If we turn now to the scholarly literature on religion during this era, we see a clear reflection of these events. Included is, first, a strong focus on "new religions"; then, as of 1979, on religiopolitical movements, often dubbed "fundamentalisms." The same period saw ever-increasing attention to noninstitutionalized religious expressions, this under various headings such as spirituality, popular religion, and, more recently, lived religion. Then, since roughly the late 1980s, the religions of immigrant and other minority groups, especially in Western countries, began to increase. And finally, contextualizing all of these empirical foci, one witnesses a serious reconsideration of the very idea of religion, including questioning and rejecting the notion that modern societies are necessarily secularizing societies, unpacking the concept of religion and of "world religions" in particular and searching for alternative conceptualizations that better capture the exceedingly diverse phenomena that seem to fall under the heading of "religious." Religious diversity in various dimensions—empirically, conceptually, geographically, and politically—is at the heart of each of these developments. A brief look at these several dimensions of religious plurality, and indeed religious pluralism, will serve to clarify how the global context is in all cases very much at issue and thereby how religious diversity as an issue and reality is closely connected to the idea of globalization.

Manifestations of Religious Diversity in Global Context

New Religious Movements

In the immediate postwar decades after 1945, religion did receive a certain amount of scholarly attention, but it was a comparatively low-key affair operating under a double assumption: that religion was either of marginal importance or important mostly for the marginalized of society and that religious diversity was relatively unproblematic (see, e.g. Herberg 1960) or actually contributed to the decreasing importance of religion (see, e.g., Berger 1967). Toward the end of the 1960s, that situation began to change with the advent of what came to be known as "new religious movements," often popularly known under the pejorative title of "cults." The earlier attention was actually focused not on Western countries—where most (social) scientific scholars were based—but on Japan. Here, the postwar era had seen both the revival of prewar religious movements and also the rise of an increasing number of new ones. From Soka Gakkai and Rissho Koseikai to Kofuku no Kagaku and Aum Shinrikyo, new religions grew in number, visibility, and variety, and they continued to do so; the sheer diversity and the fact of religious revival were what seemed so noteworthy, a combination nicely reflected by McFarland (1967). More critically for the topic at hand, this was not a temporary phenomenon. Since the 1960s, the category of "new religions" (*shinshukyo*) has in a real sense become the category of choice for scholarly attention to religion in Japan; the inherently diverse and constantly renewing character of religious groups is at the core of what religion is all about in Japan (see, e.g., Reader 1991; Inoue 2000; Shimazono 2004).

In Western countries, the concerted attention to what was in those regions the seemingly sudden popularity of new religious movements began slightly later and has abated somewhat since the late 1980s, but its preoccupations have been similar: surprise that this should be happening at all, that there should be signs of religious revival in modern, industrialized, and presumably secularizing societies; and fascination with the sheer "strangeness" and variety of these movements (see, from a vast earlier literature, Glock and Bellah 1976; Needleman and Baker 1978). Many, if not most, of these new manifestations were, in fact, the product of "non-Western" religious figures, founders, and leaders who migrated to the West under new, more open immigration policies and attracted local followers, predominantly from among the youth of the dominant classes and far less from among the marginalized. Among the more prominent were, for instance, Swami Prabhupada of ISKCON, Sun Myung Moon of the Unification Church, Guru Maharaj Ji of the Divine Light Mission, and Maharishi Mahesh Yogi of Transcendental Meditation. In that context, the new religious movements also became highly controversial. To many observers, they seemed positively dangerous; as a category of phenomena, they were not only unexpected but an aberration. Hence the pejorative term *cult*, with its parallel in other world languages, to describe them (Robbins 1988). The most visible factor in this negative assessment has been that some of these movements, such as the Peoples Temple of Jonestown, the Order of the Solar Temple, and Aum Shinrikyo, did turn out to be violent and deadly. Yet the controversy began well before these developments, showing that the larger and more subtle issue has been, for the observer, the problematic nature of their existence, that they were new, different, and multiplying. Symptomatic of this assessment is that for a great many of those outside the narrow confines of the subgroup of scholars studying them (and even some of these), these movements should not even count as religions; as "dangerous cults," they were illegitimate to the point of requiring suppression. This negative attitude and even fear of new religious movements continues into the twenty-first century and is moreover not confined to Japan and Western countries. Rather, it appears to have become worldwide. Irrespective of the fact that almost all of these movements actually attract very few followers, many people and governments continue to see this manifestation of religious diversity as highly problematic (see Richardson 2004).

Religiopolitical "Fundamentalisms"

If the new religious movements were one development of the postwar era to make religious diversity more visible and thereby more controversial, even more important was what followed from about the late 1970s. Beginning with the rise of what was then called the "New" Christian Right in the United States and the Islamic revolution in Iran, both in 1979, a series of highly visible, sometimes violent, and often successful religiopolitical movements arose, not just in the United States and Iran but also in a variety of countries as diverse as Nicaragua, Poland, India, Israel, and Sri Lanka. Many of these were cases of longer-standing movements or trends rising to renewed or unprecedented prominence, not entirely new movements. What attracted so much attention was the combination of their seemingly sudden success, the fact that most observers, just as in the case of the new religious movements, had not expected them, and that they arose in various corners of the world and from different religions. At play was the assumption, shared by most scholars and other elite observers, that in a modern secularizing world, such an assertion of religious power should at best be an exception, and where it occurred, it had to be a protest of the marginalized, a reactionary response to the encroachment of modern structures such as the secular nation-state, capitalist economy, and modern science (see Juergensmeyer 1993). Accordingly, parallel to the term *cult* referring to the similarly unexpected new religious movements, the word *fundamentalism* became the label of choice to describe these religiopolitical movements. Its dominant meaning is instructive. Rather than referring simply to religious movements that enter the political arena, *fundamentalism* denotes something both militant and defensive, harking to the past, in that sense "traditional" in its outlook, concerned with reinforcing threatened boundaries and above all combating secular institutions (see Almond, Appleby, and Sivan 2000, 17). The presumed opposition is to supposedly secular modernity, not to a different way of doing modernity. Accordingly, religiopolitical movements that take, for instance, a "socialist" option (see the discussion of Fukuyama's analysis above), such as the liberation-theological directions manifest during the same decades across the globe from Nicaragua to Korea, are not deemed to be fundamentalist. Yet the Iranian revolution and India's Hindu nationalism are lumped with the Lubavitcher Hassidim and Italy's Communione e Liberazione, the latter two not in any sense political movements like the former (Kepel 1994). Clearly, for many scholarly observers, manifestations of "strong" religion (Almond, Appleby, and Sivan 2000), as contrasted with presumably "weak" religion that accords with secular modernity, needed special explanation. In that context, a large part of the question requiring answers was that virtually every "world religion"—from Christianity, Islam, and Judaism to Hinduism, Sikhism, and Buddhism—was producing these fundamentalisms in every corner of the world (see Marty and Appleby 1991–1995). As with the new religious movements, religious strength and global diversity are as much at issue when discussing these religiopolitical movements as their unprecedented nature during the postwar period.

Transnational Migration and Global Religions

The migration of peoples more or less permanently from one part of the world to another is, of course, not new to the modern centuries; the late twentieth century has not been unprecedented in this regard. The specific character of post–World War II migration, in particular that which occurred after about the mid-1960s, is, however, highly significant in the present context. The relation between this migration and the flowering of new religious movements in the West has already been noted. More broadly, the opening up of the most powerful Western countries to migration from virtually all around the world has greatly enhanced the presence of religions that had hitherto had but a tiny presence in these regions. It also increased the awareness of this new diversity among both scholarly and non-scholarly observers.

Initially, it was western European countries that experienced an influx of new residents from their erstwhile colonial territories or that solved the labor shortages of a booming economy by allowing in non-European guest workers. Until the 1980s, the elites and dominant populations in most of these countries managed to ignore the implications of these developments, often by continuing to believe that the situation was temporary and that most of these people would eventually "go home." The European colonization states of North America and Australasia opened their doors to truly global migration only beginning in the 1960s; but then the influx of non-Europeans, complete with their often very different religions and different versions of the historically dominant Christianity, took on increasingly serious proportions. Although correspondingly serious attention to the religious implications of this new diversity was already notice-able in the 1980s (see, e.g., Waugh, Abu-Laban, and Qureshi 1983; Bhachu 1985; Burghart 1987), as with the idea of globalization itself, the takeoff period dates only from the later 1990s. Since then, the religion of immigrants, in all its diversity, has become a major scholarly preoccupation in Western countries, just as the migration patterns that brought this about continue virtually unabated into the twenty-first century. Unlike the case of new religious movements and religiopolitical movements, however, most of the literature on this kind of new religious diversity has not seen it to be nearly as problematic, symptomatic of which is the absence in this case of a new term, such as *cult* or *fundamentalism*, to speak about it. Much of the literature is even celebratory of the new diversity. Nonetheless, to the extent that this migration is seen in conjunction with the religiopolitical movements—especially the Islamic ones and these particularly in the wake of the events of September 11, 2001—there is a certain amount of concern that the migration will help establish those movements in the Western countries. And observers in Europe especially have been absorbed with the question of how the marginalization of many of these immigrant populations and their succeeding generations has created a persistent social and economic problem. Overall, however, the main questions that scholars have asked of the religious diversity thus introduced or enhanced are about how the religions of the migrants will change and adapt in the new "diaspora" environments, how they will add to the internal diversity of the religions in question as well as the religious diversity of the recipient countries (from a vast literature, see Deen 1995; Haddad and Esposito 1998; Vertovec and Rogers 1998; Baumann 2000; Nayar 2004; Kurien 2007), and how the already dominant religion, almost always Christianity, is changing as migrants bring with them their own variants and become increasingly important in the demographic makeup of the religion (see, e.g., Ter Haar 1995; Yang 1999; Adogame 2000). It is the transformation of religion through the spread and pluralization of its existing forms that is most at issue, less so how that new diversification represents a radically new, let alone threatening, global social reality. That theme of sheer plurality is especially evident in another growing focus of the last few decades, the possible transformations in the form of religion and religiousness itself.

Spirituality and Lived Religion

New religious movements, religiopolitical movements, and the religion of global migrants have captured attention to a large extent because they represent historically new, if not unprecedented, developments. Their effect has also, however, been to help change how scholars and others look at religion more generally in the current globalizing context. A prime example of this shift in observation concerns what can generally be called "noninstitutionalized" religious expression, or what Meredith McGuire has called "non-official" religion (McGuire 2002). Already in such designations, one can see that a key identifying feature of this sort of religiousness is that it contrasts with something else, whether institutional or official religion. The positive terms used to talk about it carry the same, but implicit, difference. Two such terms are increasingly common. *Spirituality* now generally refers to a highly variable sort of religious belief and practice characterized by its great stress on individual experience and individual construction and authenticity. It contrasts consistently and often explicitly with religion, by which is meant collectively authoritative, institutionalized religion (Heelas et al. 2005; Bouma 2007). The much greater diversity or variability of spirituality versus the relative concentration into a few religions is evident in this opposition. The second term, *lived religion*, follows suit: it is the religion actually practiced on a daily basis in the lives of usually nonelite individuals, which is not necessarily the religion that is ideally set forth in the dictates and institutional prescriptions of religious authorities (see Hall 1997; McGuire 2008). In this context, the idea has resonances with a third, much older term, *popular religion*, which contrasts even more clearly with "elite" religion, the latter referring not just or even primarily to the religion of elites but, again, to the religion controlled and set forth by religious elites. In the absence of that authoritative control, lived religion and popular religion are automatically variable, even fluid and unpredictable, in their directions and developments.

The concrete reference of these terms is correspondingly highly diverse. So-called New Age religion, with *New Age* itself a rather imprecise term with indeterminate range and variation, falls under the heading of spirituality especially, as arguably do the "new new religions" in Japan, cyberspace religion more generally, the religious expressions and traditions of indigenous peoples, certain developments in Sufi Islam, and quite often religious movements such as neo-Paganism/ Wicca that eschew or attempt to avoid clear institutionalization (see, e.g., Lewis 1996; Inoue 2000; Højsgaard and Warburg 2005; Howell 2007). Lived religion, like its older parallel, popular religion, more often than not focuses on the religion of the marginalized and powerless in society, although now very frequently urban as opposed to rural people. More ambiguously included appears to be a range of more clearly institutionalized religious movements such as the New World African religions Candomblé, Voudon, Santería, or even Rastafarianism and, above all, Christian Pentecostalism, especially the non–North American versions (Cox 1995; Corten and Marshall-Fratani 2001). The diversity of phenomena included is characteristic.

The key question in the present context is what the reasons are for the rise of these terms and their greatly varied referents. To what extent is this attention a reflection of the fact that the religious manifestations in question are new, growing, and thereby difficult to ignore? To what extent is this more a matter of increased observation, a new appreciation, of what was already there? While clearly the answer will always be that both are true, in this case, it is at least arguable that the balance favors the latter. Most of the movements and trends in question have indeed been growing, especially Pentecostalism in regions such as Africa and Latin America. Yet in most cases, we are also dealing with religious phenomena that are not particularly new—the main exceptions are those forms that involve cyberspace—or in many cases not all that widespread. The presence of those things designated as spirituality might be growing but not to the extent that one can really talk about a "spiritual revolution" (see Heelas et al. 2005). The categories of spirituality and lived religion are much more clearly a reflection of shifting attention, declarations on the part of the observers that we ought to revise our way of looking at religion and religious phenomena (see, e.g., Parker 1996). It is therefore arguable that the difference in the case of these categories is that, in contrast to those of new religious movements and "diaspora" religions, where it is usually the rest of the world that has arrived to impinge on the view of the (often Western) observer in his or her own backyard, spirituality and lived religion, like the religiopolitical movements, involve the globalization of the observer's attention to the rest of the world, taking seriously what so many people both "here" and in the rest of the world are doing. The simultaneous arising of all of these conceptual developments, in fact, points to more general transformations in the observation of religion, and religious diversity in particular, especially in the scientific disciplines most concerned with this observation.

The Observation of Religious Diversity in Global Context

Secularization and the "Return of the Sacred" in the Social Sciences

The two social-scientific disciplines that have historically paid the most attention to religion are sociology and anthropology. Until recently, these closely related disciplines have worked very much in the shadow of the secularization assumptions discussed above, though in somewhat different ways. For anthropology until about the 1970s and 1980s, the analysis of religion as an integral aspect of societies presented no difficulty, but the societies that dominated anthropologists' attention were small-scale, so-called tribal societies in the marginalized regions of the world system. These, according to the prevailing conception, were not "modern" but rather "traditional," and therefore, religion logically informed them because religion was something unmodern, belonging more to traditional societies. Sociology, the discipline primarily concerned with modern societies, again until relatively recently, isolated its study of religion into a rather marginal subdiscipline of the sociology of religion, reflecting the presumed marginal status of religion in modern societies; and even the sociology of religion was preoccupied with issues of religious decline and the "exceptional" cases of nondecline (Beckford 1989). In both cases, the latter decades of the twentieth century ushered in significant changes in this regard. Anthropologists abandoned their implicit distinction between modern and traditional societies, focusing on religious phenomena in virtually all areas of the world, including in the backyards of the anthropologists, who are still mostly people working in "developed," usually Western countries. In sociology, the subdiscipline has begun to move much more into the mainstream of the larger discipline, and within the subdiscipline itself, the secularization thesis has been not so much abandoned as removed from its formerly central position as the dominant assumption; now, secularized cases, rather than cases of religious strength or resurgence, call for special explanation and are treated increasingly as the exception (see, e.g., Davie 2003).

Looking at the case of the sociology of religion more closely, the recent transformations in theories, concepts, and orientations reflect and parallel rather precisely the empirical developments just discussed. The prominent focus on new religious movements during the 1970s and early 1980s already resulted in speculation that we were witnessing a "return of the sacred" (Bell 1977), but this did not bring about a change in orientation. The secularization assumption still prevailed; new religious movements were minor enough that they could still be considered aberrations. On first flush, it also seemed that the rise of religiopolitical movements, so-called fundamentalisms, could also be digested as protest and reaction to prevailing modern and secularizing trends, not as cause to rethink the sociology of religion. With hindsight, however, we can see that the situation was changing specifically with the rise of globalization theories, such as that of Roland Robertson, to a certain degree formed in the context of these movements (Robertson and Chirico 1985), and with the rise of religious economy theories, prominently those of Rodney Stark and his close collaborators (see Stark and Finke 2000). The former had the effect of insisting that the primary unit of sociological analysis had to be the entire world, with all of its religious diversity along several dimensions, including internal variety, variation in form, content, strength, and degree of institutionalization. As an indicator of paradigm change, the second encouraged the negation of the secularization thesis but, more important, sought to reverse the value polarity of two central and inherited concepts with respect to religion. Both the differentiation of religion as a separate social sphere and religious diversity, rather than being seen as prime symptoms or causes of the marginalization of religion in modern society, were henceforth to be regarded as prime conditions for the strength and "vitality" of religion. It is in the context of these and other parallel theoretical and conceptual changes that one must understand the current dominance in the contemporary subdiscipline of the great amount of attention that is being paid to religion precisely in its diversity: diversity through transnational migration; diversity in form as lived religion, spirituality, or institutionalized religion; diversity in strength of religion; diversity in relations between religion and the nonreligious domains of modern societies (Beyer 2007).

Religious Studies and World Religions

The study of religion as a distinct enterprise, more or less distinct from Christian theology, had its origins in the nineteenth century in the context of both Christian missionary and European imperial expansion all around the world. It was during that era that both the idea and the names of the non-Western religions were invented, first by Westerners but then increasingly taken up and developed by non-Westerners (see Smith 1991; Beyer 2006). The academic discipline that developed out of this crucible, going by various names, came to structure itself around the study of these "world religions" (Masuzawa 2005) and therefore, in one sense, had a global orientation from its beginnings. Yet, in parallel with the social sciences, this globalism was in subtle ways muted by the implicit assumption that the most authentic manifestations of religion and the world religions lay mostly in the past. Peculiarly modern developments in religion were correspondingly suspect, as was the discipline most concerned with modern society, sociology (see Sharpe 1986). This mirror image of the secularization thesis also reflected itself in dominance within this scholarly domain of historical methods, most notably the analysis of "core" religious texts as the privileged location and standard for genuine religion. The attempt in the mid-twentieth century to develop phenomenological method as one peculiar to religious studies went in the same direction, eschewing or at least underplaying the value of studying religion in the present. To the extent that such study occurred, it was largely "anthropological," focusing on the small-scale and traditional setting deemed relatively untouched by the corrosive influence of the modern.

As in the social-scientific disciplines, these prevailing orientations in religious studies began to change during the 1980s. One sign of a fundamental rethinking has been an increasingly serious questioning of the idea of religion as such and the "world religions" especially. Another is a greater emphasis on religion in the contemporary world, on present religion and religion around the globe, including in regard to the relation between religion and other, "secular" domains of society. Regarding the first, there has been an increasing preoccupation with the degree to which the idea of religion as a distinct domain of endeavor, as a reality sui generis (McCutcheon 1997), is not only a recently invented notion but one that uses Christianity as the standard by which to judge all religion (Masuzawa 2005). Thus, according to this critical trend, religion is a Western invention, an ideology whose function is as part of an imperialist strategy to impose Western ways on the rest of the world. Therefore, not only is the idea of the world religions a prime example of such illegitimate invention, but religious studies as a whole has been an ideological enterprise more than it has been a scientific one (Smith 1988; Fitzgerald 2000). The second development is far less concentrated in a specific literature, but strong indicators are the reassessment of sociology—the discipline of the modern—as an appropriate discipline for understanding religious phenomena (see Sharpe 1986; Crossley 2006) and a sharp increase in the sheer number of studies of contemporary religion, including especially the religion of transnational migrants and the "lived" religion of nonelites all around the world (see, e.g., Kumar 2000; Orsi 2005). In both cases, the critical reassessment of religion and the focus on religion in the modern present, the prime criteria are what is actually happening in the world, here including the entire world, and the great diversity of phenomena that such a study must then include. Above all, it is precisely the singularity of religion that has been put in question and, as in the social sciences, the diversity of (contemporary) religion that is becoming the increasingly dominant focus.

Conclusions

The advent and popularity of the idea of globalization have been accompanied in many quarters by what amounts to a global reassessment of religion. For those who understand globalization simply in terms of the homogenization of the entire world in terms of a Western (neo-)liberal model, religion might still seem at best a site of reaction and resistance. For those who see in globalization a trend toward homogenization but also the conditions for the renewed importance of differences, religion now appears as one of those factors through which the most important differences come to be identified. In light of this latter view, the story of religion in modern and global society no longer appears to be one of secularization—how religion, for better or worse, becomes increasingly marginalized as a potent force within society—but rather one of renewed importance. Today, there is far less talk of religious irrelevance and far more of resurgence. To what extent religion is really stronger in global society or to what extent the change is mostly in the eyes of the observer can remain an open question. What does seem to be certain is that the most outstanding feature of this resurgent or reconsidered religion is its diversity, along several dimensions.

Religion is, first of all, diverse in its strength. Religion is not equally powerful and equally present in all regions of the world. There is secularized Europe and theocratic Iran; there is China and Japan, where most people still do not consider themselves to be religious; and there are the countries of sub-Saharan Africa, where just about the opposite is the case. Religion is diverse in its forms, whether institutional or noninstitutional, whether highly organized and authoritative or more a matter of broadly based "lived" religion. Religion reacts against the homogenizing forces of globalization, as in so-called fundamentalist movements, or it resonates with them, as in "liberal" religion or "consumer" religion, and every possibility in between. The views of some religious scholars notwithstanding, religion manifests itself as diverse religions—and not just so-called world religions—and diverse versions of those religions, including diverse schools, denominations, and subdivisions, diaspora versions, and the versions of the historic heartlands. And finally, in all of this, there is definitely a diversity in the understanding of religion, in what counts as religion and what ought to count as religion.

In the context of these multiple religious diversities, the dominant issue seems to be less one of secularization, which, as just noted, is now just another axis of variation. The new self-evidence—that whatever religion is, it is in principle and reality diverse— poses a different set of abiding questions. Is that diversity a source of perpetual and severe problems, as in Huntington's idea of the clash of civilizations, the worry about "fundamentalisms," and the fear of "cults"? Is it a source of difficulty or a cause for celebration in the increasingly multicultural national societies around the world, especially in Europe and North America? Or is it simply the case that the situation of an increasingly integrated global society provides very fertile ground for the renewed importance of religious identities and, in close relation to this, the further diversification of religion? These are the sorts of questions with which scholars of religion and nonscholars alike are now preoccupied. Unlike the idea of modernization, which posited a fundamental problem for religion, globalization is bringing about a transformed perspective, from which the fact of religious diversity no longer lends itself to any clear and uniform prognostication. Depending on the circumstances, this new situation can continue to be a problem for religion, a problem with religion, or perhaps no problem at all.

NOTES

1. Fukuyama 1993; Barber 1996; Huntington 1996. Each book was preceded by an original, shorter, popular-magazine article version under the same title, Fukuyama's in the *National Interest* (1989), Barber's in the *Atlantic Monthly* (1992), and Huntington's in *Foreign Affairs* (1993).

2. Of some significance in this context is that probably the earliest technical use of the term *globalization* appears to be that of George Modelski in a 1968 article, "Communism and the Globalization of Politics" (Modelski 1968). Here, the realization was that "global communism" could not be identified with the "socialist states" and that therefore the globally political had to be conceived as something more than international relations or the actions of the world's states.

REFERENCES

Adogame, Afe. 2000. "The Quest for Space in the Global Spiritual Marketplace: African Religions in Europe." *International Review of Mission* 89: 409.

Almond, Gabriel A., R. Scott Appleby, and Emmanuel Sivan, eds. 2000. *Strong Religion: The Rise of Fundamentalisms around the World*. Chicago: University of Chicago Press.

Barber, Benjamin R. 1996. *Jihad vs. McWorld*. New York: Ballantine.

Baumann, Martin. 2000. *Migration—Religion—Integration: Buddhistische Vietnamesen und Hinduistische Tamilen in Deutschland*. Marburg, Germany: Diagonal Verlag.

Beckford, James A. 1989. *Religion and Advanced Industrial Society*. London: Unwin Hyman.

Bell, Daniel. 1977. "The Return of the Sacred?" *British Journal of Sociology* 28: 4.

Berger, Peter. 1967. *The Sacred Canopy: Elements of a Sociological Theory of Religion*. New York: Doubleday Anchor.

Beyer, Peter. 2006. *Religions in Global Society*. London: Routledge.

———. 2007. "Globalization and Glocalization." In James A. Beckford and N. J. Demerath III, eds., *The Sage Handbook of the Sociology of Religion*. London: Sage, 98–117.

Bhachu, Parminder. 1985. *Twice Migrants: East African Sikh Settlers in Britain*. London: Tavistock.

Bouma, Gary D. 2007. *Australian Soul: Religion and Spirituality in the 21st Century*. New York: Cambridge University Press.

Burghart, Richard, ed. 1987. *Hinduism in Great Britain: The Perpetuation of Religion in an Alien Cultural Milieu*. London: Tavistock.

Corten, André, and Ruth Marshall-Fratani, eds. 2001. *Between Babel and Pentecost: Transnational Pentecostalism in Africa and Latin America*. Bloomington: Indiana University Press.

Cox, Harvey. 1995. *Fire from Heaven: The Rise of Pentecostal Spirituality and the Reshaping of Religion in the Twenty-first Century*. Reading, Mass.: Perseus.

Crossley, James G. 2006. *Why Christianity Happened: A Socio-historical Account of Christian Origins (26–50 CE)*. Louisville, Ky.: Westminster John Knox.

Davie, Grace. 2003. *Europe: The Exceptional Case: Parameters of Faith in the Modern World*. London: Darton, Longman and Todd.

Deen, Hanifa. 1995. *Caravanserai: Journey among Australian Muslims*. St. Leonards, Australia: Allen and Unwin.

Fitzgerald, Timothy. 2000. *The Ideology of Religious Studies*. New York: Oxford University Press.

Fukuyama, Francis. 1993. *The End of History and the Last Man*. New York: Avon.

Glock, Charles Y., and Robert N. Bellah, eds. 1976. *The New Religious Consciousness*. Berkeley: University of California Press.

Haddad, Yvonne Yazbeck, and John L. Esposito, eds. 1998. *Muslims on the Americanization Path?* Atlanta: Scholars.

Hall, David D., ed. 1997. *Lived Religion in America: Toward a History of Practice*. Princeton, N.J.: Princeton University Press.

Heelas, Paul, Linda Woodhead, Benjamin Seel, Bronislaw Szerszyinski, and Karin Tusting. 2005. *The Spiritual Revolution: Why Religion Is Giving Way to Spirituality*. Oxford: Blackwell.

Herberg, Will. 1960. *Protestant, Catholic, Jew: An Essay in American Religious Sociology*. Garden City, N.Y.: Anchor.

Højsgaard, Morten T., and Margit Warburg, eds. 2005. *Religion and Cyberspace*. New York: Routledge.

Howell, Julia Day. 2007. "Modernity and the Borderlands of Islamic Spirituality in Indonesia's New Sufi Networks." In Martin van Bruinessen and Julia Day Howell, eds., *Sufism and the "Modern" in Indonesian Islam*. London: I. B. Tauris, 217-240.

Huntington, Samuel P. 1996. *The Clash of Civilizations and the Remaking of World Order*. New Delhi: Viking Penguin.

Inoue, Nobutaka. 2000. *Contemporary Japanese Religion* 25. Tokyo: Foreign Press Center.

Juergensmeyer, Mark. 1993. *The New Cold War? Religious Nationalism Confronts the Secular State*. Berkeley: University of California Press.

Kepel, Gilles. 1994. *The Revenge of God*. Oxford: Blackwell.

Kumar, Pratap. 2000. *Hindus in South Africa: Their Traditions and Beliefs*. Durban, South Africa: University of Durban-Westville.

Kurien, Prema A. 2007. *A Place at the Multicultural Table: The Development of an American Hinduism*. New Brunswick, N.J.: Rutgers University Press.

Lewis, James R., ed. 1996. *Magical Religion and Modern Witchcraft*. Albany: State University of New York Press.

Marty, Martin E., and R. Scott Appleby, eds. 1991–1995. *The Fundamentalism Project*. Chicago: University of Chicago Press.

Masuzawa, Tomoko. 2005. *The Invention of World Religions*. Chicago: University of Chicago Press.

McCutcheon, Russell T. 1997. *Manufacturing Religion: The Discourse on Sui Generis Religion and the Politics of Nostalgia*. Oxford: Oxford University Press.

McFarland, H. Neill. 1967. *The Rush Hour of the Gods: A Study of New Religious Movements in Japan*. New York: Macmillan.

McGuire, Meredith. 2002. *Religion: The Social Context*, 5th ed. Belmont, Calif.: Wadsworth.

———. 2008. *Lived Religion: Faith and Practice in Everyday Life*. New York: Oxford University Press.

Modelski, George. 1968. "Communism and the Globalization of Politics." *International Studies Quarterly* 12: 380–393.

Nayar, Kamala Elizabeth. 2004. *The Sikh Diaspora in Vancouver: Three Generations amid Tradition, Modernity, and Multiculturalism*. Toronto: University of Toronto Press.

Needleman, Jacob, and George Baker, eds. 1978. *Understanding the New Religions*. New York: Seabury.

Orsi, Robert A. 2005. *Between Heaven and Earth: The Religious Worlds People Make and the Scholars Who Study Them*. Princeton, N.J.: Princeton University Press.

Parker, Cristian. 1996. *Popular Religion and Modernization in Latin America: A Different Logic*. Robert R. Barr, trans. Maryknoll, N.Y.: Orbis.

Reader, Ian. 1991. *Religion in Contemporary Japan*. Honolulu: University of Hawaii Press.

Richardson, James T., ed. 2004. *Regulating Religion: Case Studies from around the Globe*. New York: Kluwer Academic/Penum.

Robbins, Thomas. 1988. *Cults, Converts, and Charisma: The Sociology of New Religious Movements*. London: Sage.

Robertson, Roland. 1989. "Internationalization and Globalization." *University Center for International Studies Newsletter*, University of Pittsburgh (Spring): 8–9.

———. 1995. "Glocalization: Time-Space and Homogeneity-Heterogeneity." In Mike Featherstone, Scott Lash, and Roland Robertson, eds., *Global Modernities*. London: Sage.

Robertson, Roland, and JoAnn Chirico. 1985. "Humanity, Globalization, Worldwide Religious Resurgence: A Theoretical Exploration." *Sociological Analysis* 46: 219–242.

Sharpe, Eric J. 1986. *Comparative Religion: A History*, 2nd ed. LaSalle, Ill.: Open Court.

Shimazono, Susumu. 2004. *From Salvation to Spirituality: Popular Religious Movements in Japan*. Melbourne, Australia: Trans Pacific Press.

Smith, Jonathan Z. 1988. "'Religion' and 'Religious Studies': No Difference at All." *Soundings* 71: 231–244.

Smith, Wilfred Cantwell. 1991. *The Meaning and End of Religion*. Minneapolis: Fortress Press.

Stark, Rodney, and Roger Finke. 2000. *Acts of Faith: Explaining the Human Side of Religion*. Berkeley: University of California Press.

Ter Haar, Gerrie. 1995. "Ritual as Communication: A Study of African Christian Communities in the Bijlmer District of Amsterdam." In Jan Platvoet and Karel van der Toorn, eds., *Pluralism and Identity: Studies in Ritual Behaviour*. Leiden, Neth.: Brill.

Vertovec, Steven, and Alisdair Rogers, eds. 1998. *Muslim European Youth: Reproducing Ethnicity, Religion, Culture*. Aldershot, U.K.: Ashgate.

Waugh, Earle H., S. M. Abu-Laban, and R. B. Qureshi. 1983. *The Muslim Community in North America*. Edmonton: University of Alberta Press.

Yang, Fenggang. 1999. *Chinese Christians in America: Conversion, Assimilation, and Adhesive Identities*. University Park: University of Pennsylvania Press.

FOR FURTHER READING

Almond, Gabriel A., R. Scott Appleby, and Emmanuel Sivan, eds. 2000. *Strong Religion: The Rise of Fundamentalisms around the World*. Chicago: University of Chicago Press.

Beyer, Peter. 2007. "Globalization and Glocalization." In James A. Beckford and N. J. Demerath III, eds., *The Sage Handbook of the Sociology of Religion*. London: Sage, 98–117.

Corten, André, and Ruth Marshall-Fratani, eds. 2001. *Between Babel and Pentecost: Transnational Pentecostalism in Africa and Latin America*. Bloomington: Indiana University Press.

Davie, Grace. 2003. *Europe: The Exceptional Case: Parameters of Faith in the Modern World*. London: Darton, Longman and Todd.

McGuire, Meredith. 2008. *Lived Religion: Faith and Practice in Everyday Life*. New York: Oxford University Press.

....

CHAPTER 15

RELIGIOUS DEMOGRAPHICS AND THE NEW DIVERSITY

....

FREDERICK W. NORRIS

THE changes in religious circles within the West have been rather dramatic in the last hundred years. Since World War I, European citizens have turned away from Christendom in droves, and many have joined the ranks of the nonreligious, whether agnostic or atheist. They represent a jagged break from the long reign of Western Christendom.

EUROPE

....

The heavy loss of life in Europe during World War I, which would be larger in World War II, made people uncertain that any deity provided assistance when they faced massive death in armed conflict. Having served as a nurse in England and on Malta during World War I, author Vera Brittain became keenly aware of the carnage. Among the many slain were almost all of the men in her family's circle of friends, including her brother and her fiancé. Brittain's struggle with faith was excruciating.[1]

The Western Christian confidence before World War I, however, stands out in the 1910 Edinburgh World Missionary Conference. It was inspirational and looked forward to winning all earth dwellers to Christ by 2000. Serious flaws, however, appeared. Too few of its representatives were indigenous people from other lands. There were no Africans. China and India, considered the most educated audiences, received attention, even some specific plans for evangelizing their peoples. A small minority at the conference did report significant problems with the goal, yet their voices, not shrill but clear and insistent, went mostly unheeded. Surely, the most remarkable blindness of the 1910 meeting was the total lack of any insight into what would soon become a world war. The European treaties looked as if they served as strong guarantors of peace, rather than chains that would pull all of Europe into the strife.[2] Unlike the case of World War II, when Christian missionaries in Asia warned of Japanese expansion, these conferees saw nothing warlike coming. And armed conflict among Europeans, partially to hold on to their African colonies, made numerous African converts queasy. That "Christian" nations could fight to the death in order to keep their political and economic advantages was senseless. Those countries should at least establish peace within the world Christian community.

World War II, which involved so much of the globe, ate a large part of the 1910 mission objective. The inability of First World countries to keep their national interests and Christian mission balanced brought serious questions. Before the twentieth century, several missionaries to China had sailed with clear consciences on European ships that served the opium trade. Indeed, missionaries to China eventually took full advantage of the European trading centers that were ceded to those powers in the Opium Wars. They tended to depend on European troops to keep the peace with the Chinese. "Progress" was made, but missions requiring overseas soldiers had a ticking time bomb in their midst. Only if they purposefully had moved toward being at the mercy of the local population could they have been taken as anything but agents of far-off cultures, most likely political intruders.

WESTERN WORLD CHRISTIAN MISSION

Christian soldiers of World War II, significantly many from the United States who had been on the winning side against both Germany and Japan, looked at the conditions they found in various countries, including those of the defeated enemies. When they sought to take them the gospel and what they saw as the clear advantages of their cultures, they often created better conditions. In the early years after the war, many from First World nations had food, clothing, and medical supplies sent to assist the indigenous people among whom they worked. One mission from my tradition had been sent to concentrate on influencing German theological faculty members yet spent much of its early years distributing necessities and forming a small free-church congregation in Tübingen, West Germany. When those missionaries planned to return to the United States decades later, the mayor gave them a key to the city, a surprising honor that recognized the aid they had supplied.

The twentieth century was marked both in the United States and in Europe by many mission efforts, but they began to decline in the last third of the century. That early Western confidence took another hit when Christians in Africa, Asia, and

South America became steadily growing communities while mainline Western churches wilted to a degree seldom seen before. The Western mission societies continued their work with some effectiveness, but their previous strength was fading. Korea became a powerhouse in Christian mission. Its efforts have not outdistanced the Western labors, but Korean Christianity has had a remarkable expansion, including its mission outreach. Mark Noll notes that mission from the United States has continued unabated during the weakening of the churches themselves. It has grown larger among free-church and Evangelical groups.[3] But the decline of Western Christianity has been rather remarkable.

African, Asian, and South American Christians

The shock received through this decline, and the growth of Christianity in Africa, Asia, and South America, calculated by extrapolations from previous statistics, shows that at least 65 percent of world Christians are now located on those three continents as the new heartlands of the faith.[4] Christians in the First World are a 35-percent minority. At the midpoint of the twentieth century, students of religion in Africa suggested that the success of Islam in the Sahara and elsewhere might mean that most of Africa would soon be Muslim. In recent years, however, the growth of churches started by Western missionaries and those that emerged from within indigenous African Christian communities has exploded. Of course, there have been failures, but now there are more African Christians than there are people in the United States and Canada, probably about 330 million.[5] Their vibrant communities have not only continued to increase, but they have sent their own missionaries to the United States and Europe. Seminaries in the United States assist a number of black students to return to the homelands, but across the United States, Africans are taking positions in college and seminary faculties, as well as in American churches.[6] The number is not large, but their presence is already felt.

Part of the reason is that their indigenous African congregations have a different sense of what "church" should be. Their stories indicate that their doctrines and practices are centered on Christ and the Trinity. Worship and service work together in helping those communities and each individual member to be in but not of the world. Kwame Bediako, one of the most gifted black theologians, who taught in Ghana and Scotland, recently passed away. He insisted that black theology had stunning leaders, some of whom emerged from African churches without foreign theological education. A Catholic Ghanaian woman belonged to a community that carefully listened to her astonishing prayers. She could neither read nor write. But the priest began to record her words, transcribe and print them in her native tongue, and then translate them into English. They are beautifully contextualized

hymns that for Bediako were examples of the best theology Africans have produced.[7] The strong spirituality, the African worldview, and the solidly based Christian life expressed in an African mode are stunning. Afua Kuma reaches her people
and does not concentrate on theological categories emanating from elsewhere.[8]
Western Christians can gain much from her insights.

A bright generation of African theologians is aging. Another generation,
however, is coming behind them, set to fulfill the promise that they will project
different worldviews and theological understanding into the First World's projects.
One after another of their predecessors has strengthened the roots and blossomed
with new flowers. Their lives in Africa included other religions as contemporary
opponents in some things and allies in others, discussion partners in villages and on
buses. They do not need to be made aware of numerous non-Christian religions;
strong Islam and indigenous religions exist in nearly every part of Africa. These
Christian leaders always have much to say to the 35-percent minority world Christians in the West.

Believers in Christ throughout Asia do not have the overwhelming numbers of
those in Africa, but they have provided vital churches, almost all of which exist as
religious minorities. Their doctrines and practices are useful for the West because
they come from minority communities. Too much of even recent Western theology
has tended to rely on the former majority status of Christendom. Thinking from
the majority has allowed a number of assumptions to pass as strong and convincing
primarily because they have not been seen as failing. Significant debaters have
attacked Christianity, but their arguments have not penetrated Western Christendom believers' circles.[9]

In Asia, no such conditions occur. Indeed, a seventh-century Christian author
in China wrote a tract entitled "The Jesus Messiah Sutra." He employed the Buddhist word for holy writings, *Sutra*, in order for a Christian tract to enter inspired
Chinese literature. He was successful in that this tract and others he composed seem
to have been considered as another type of Buddhism that should be kept in a Buddhist monastery. During the late nineteenth century they were found there sealed in
a library when Muslim strength had led to the destruction of Buddhist texts.[10]

We do not know how many Christians there are in China. Some are above-
ground and sanctioned by the government. Others keep their existence secret by
meeting in small underground groups away from the attention of ruling powers.
Estimates range from 10 million to 40 million, none of which can be given convincing weight.[11] Although Christians are a minority, small changes are taking
place without wholly dislodging the culture of persecution. Some state universities are developing departments of religion; professing Christians are banned
from holding positions there, but the government and the educated elite want to
write histories of Christianity in China and to study the lives of contemporary
believers.

South America has the largest number of Roman Catholics of any of the world's
continents. Battles within the Roman Catholic Church have seen the development
of educationally rigorous "liberation theologies" that were developed by Roman

Catholic priests who worked with the poor, the homeless, and the hungry in the slums of various metropolises of South America. These liberation leaders' hopes to free the church from its prison within the powerful upper classes met many obstacles, not the least Pope John Paul II's eventual insistence that priests should not work so much on political questions. Liberationists had always been strong pastors, but in his view, their writings weakened their liturgical responsibilities and created strife in the church. They raised sharp, compelling questions among the rich and have moved many South American Catholic leaders to take the plight of their slums with seriousness. When John Paul II came to São Paulo, he even gave his ring to a poor dweller in a slum. In Brazil, I saw one of the *favelas* in which citizens used cardboard in the neighborhoods because every rain of any strength soaked their paper "homes." Drug use was rampant, and drug lords ruled the area.

Liberation theology was not originally a set of positions primarily influenced by Marxists and thus against any sense of proper democratic traditions. It has always been a view of Jesus that sees him among the poor, the diseased, and the outcast as he is in the New Testament. For liberation theologians, Christian diversity must reflect the lower castes in every society, as well as the middle- and upper-class citizens.

Religions in Europe

The secularism and atheism/agnosticism that grew influential in Europe after the two world wars have continued to strengthen. Most statistics estimate that the world has 2.5 billion Christians and 1.5 billion Muslims. The third-largest religion is often considered to be Hinduism. But it is not inconceivable that secularism and atheism/agnosticism might displace or have displaced Hinduism as the third-largest "nonreligion" in the world. Secularists battle in the European Union with Islam, which might well ultimately win, Christianity possibly being the major loser.[12]

Surely because of Russian occupation and communism's influence in the schools, more than 50 percent of the citizens of the Czech Republic have no interest in religion of any kind, the highest percentage of any world nation. Eastern Europe as a whole has a high rejection of religion, and countries such as France, Germany, and Great Britain have many people who are not engaged in "religious faith commitments." Visits to Europe's great cathedrals, even as a tourist, will give anyone a sense of how many state-registered "believers" are not actively involved. Statistical surveys often employ numbers for state-supported religions that do not tell the full story. Christian are often minorities in some areas of Europe, while occasionally the statistics include anyone christened as an infant rather than only those who take part in catechesis, worship, and service. At the same time, however, some have insisted that Christianity in Europe is much healthier now than it was just a few decades ago. It is in no way the overpowering Christendom of the Middle Ages, but it does make attractive appeals to various citizens. Penelope Hall, executive director of Bibliothèque Européennes Théologie, who knows the condition of many congregations, insists that there is much more activity within and among congregations than some statistical reports observe.[13]

In France, the percentage of participating Roman Catholics has dwindled. Those people showing less interest in Catholicism have not regularly joined Protestant, Pentecostal, or Eastern Orthodox communities. In spite of Roman Catholic strength, the subculture of secularism or atheism/agnosticism has continued to grow, increasing through its power in education, publishing, television, and movies, where it tends to have enormous power.

For the French, such non-Christian strength is supplemented by religious immigration, particularly from Africa, both by Saharan Arab Muslims and by black Muslims from the sub-Saharan region. Various statistical surveys suggest that the number of Muslims in France ranges from 3.7 million to 4.1 million. Using a total number of 4 million, it is possible that among them, about 1.5 million are involved in the religion, another 1.5 million associate in Islam at the time of Ramadan, and yet another 1 million have a Muslim lineage but are not committed to the faith or practices of Islam. As a percentage of the French population, Muslims range from 3 percent to a high of 10 percent and thus might not appear to be of much consequence. Yet French news media attention to Muslims over the last decades indicates that there have been problems: rules about clothing in public schools and riots fueled by few jobs and poor housing. Muslims have claimed that they have been tied to a lower-class designation. The nearly 3 million immigrants from Algeria, Morocco, and Tunisia particularly have expected better treatment because they were part of the French colonies. Much of French society welcomed them in the late 1940s as guest workers in ill-thought-out programs that now seem disastrous to many.[14]

The story of religion in Germany is very similar. Protestants are especially strong in the north, Roman Catholics in the south. At present, the land of the Reformation has a Catholic majority not much larger than the Protestant population. Secularism and atheism/agnosticism had been vital in western Germany, but with the inclusion of eastern Germany, that percentage has grown substantially. The strict communism of the east had made inroads into the region that had been part of Luther's life and previously the home of strong Christian populations.

The German guest-worker programs brought people from many countries to fill the obvious need. Visiting immigrants from southern and eastern Europe came, many bringing their Christian traditions, including Eastern Orthodoxy. But the influx of Turks, not the least because Germany had been Turkey's ally in both world wars, has brought many Muslims into the land. By the 1960s, various inner-city sections of low-income housing were filling up with Turks. For decades, they worked and sent money back to their homeland. Now, many children of those families have German passports because they were born in the country.

Muslims have most often been treated as less than guests, let alone citizens—which they officially are not. When the German economy prospered, national needs to fill the dirtiest and hardest jobs in industry, street sweeping, garbage collecting, and so on, were obvious. All sorts of necessary employment were avoided by average Germans. As manufacturing slowed, many citizens wanted the guest workers removed. As the conditions of the families diminish, the growing children citizens of Turkish background become more disgruntled than the parents.

Religious conditions in Great Britain show likenesses to those in France and Germany. The state religion is Anglicanism, but its numbers have also dwindled. Christianity exists and at times thrives among Anglicans, mainline Protestants, and Pentecostals. When the York Minster, the largest cathedral in England (perhaps in northern Europe), was struck by lightning in 1984, however, Britons supported the use of nonchurch funds to pay its repair costs. It is an ancient part of British heritage and should be saved. But on Sundays, it is largely empty. Free churches struggle to keep the properties they formerly had. Many of their members who were soldiers in World War II have died. Again, the type of Christendom that had flourished since the Middle Ages now needs to make other claims than that most British citizens are christened Anglicans. A recent newspaper article indicated that one hundred thousand Anglicans in the last five years have asked for a certificate of debaptism even though no such official Anglican document exists. For Christianity to flourish again in Great Britain, it cannot depend on its deep and abiding cultural heritage.

Immigration of those belonging to other religions has been complicated in Great Britain. The bulk of its Muslims have come from Islamic countries in the former British Empire. They also are not a large minority in the country. Yet their numbers, half a million in 2004, rose to 2.4 million in 2008. In that period, they increased ten times as much as the rest of the population. Of religious significance, those older than seventy make up the largest number of people among the 42.6 million Anglicans. Children younger than four make up the largest number of the 2.4 million Muslims. No one can predict whether this four-year surge will continue, but it does suggest that percentages of Muslims in Great Britain might well be much higher at the end of the twenty-first century.[15]

Their influence can be seen everywhere. Many are shop owners. Their centers are found not only in formerly empty buildings but also in large mosques that they have built in various cities. One of the largest stands in Birmingham. Indeed, after years of discussion, the Oxford Muslim Study Center's (mosque's) minaret has a prominent place on the Oxford skyline.[16]

One unanticipated hope for European Christians is African Christian immigration. The two largest Christian congregations in Europe, one in London and the other in Kiev, are led by Nigerian Christian immigrant pastors. The Kiev church has a Ukrainian majority; the London church has an African majority. Jehu Hanciles's rigorously researched argument stands against any theory that Europe will eventually become either an Islamic or a secular region of the world.[17] So many Africans leave their economically wounded continent and immigrate to Europe that their numbers are being felt.

RELIGIONS IN THE UNITED STATES

The state of the Christian religion in the United States has begun to look more like northern Europe. The American Religious Identification Survey (ARIS) project, conducted through faculty research at the City University of New York and focused on religious affiliations in the United States, has some surprises. As expected, in 2004, Christianity had the highest numbers in the United States, more than 200 million. The ARIS report released in March 2009 tells a different story.[18] Nonreligious and secularists number almost 39 million. Adding agnostics and atheists, brings the figure to almost 42 million.[19] Although 73 percent of residents in the United States indicate that they believe in God or some manner of deity, there are no numbers for how many of these people are primarily part of U.S. civil religion. One of the statistics from the survey is that 15 percent of the U.S. populace have no interest in religion, whether traditional or contemporary. That figure, however, is surpassed by the revealing 27 percent who plan to refuse any kind of religious burial and thus are not even a part of civil religion. This has been a steadily increasing group. On top of that, fewer than 25 percent of Americans between ages eighteen and fifty-four attend church regularly. That is a smaller number than at any time since the Great Awakening. The claims of some growing Christian congregations to have reached nonbelievers should be questioned. Any occasional inroad into the nonreligious sector seems to dampen success with discouraged Roman Catholics and mainline Protestants. Services and preaching for the nonreligious fail to draw crowds of previously converted Christians.[20] Even the colorful attacks of fundamentalists on those they see as secularists have not transformed any sizable number of agnostics or atheists. Their archconservative doctrines and practices have drawn displeased Christians from elsewhere, particularly Catholics upset with the changes of Vatican II,[21] but they have not slowed the growth of those who prefer to be known as non- or irreligious.

Other studies show that the various religious subcultures within the United States are vibrant and influential. Evangelical Protestants and conservative Roman Catholics have spoken out about drugs, alcoholism, adultery, teen pregnancy, prostitution, gambling, and so on, but have too often failed to provide effective alternative communities that can care for those entrapped—as they see them—in such behavior. Christian groups in the United States are still active in world mission to the point where they have the largest missionary corps.[22]

Although nonreligious groups make up only 15 percent of the population, they have wide influence. Not all of them are based on a far different set of moral values; a number of well-educated people with scientific backgrounds believe that all religions are based on ill-formed assumptions and argued through faulty logic. They sense that they would have to abandon their whole form of life to become religious believers.

TRI-CITIES, TENNESSEE

A close look at the Tri-Cities area of northeastern Tennessee—Johnson City (population 62,000), Bristol (43,000), and Kingsport (45,000), as well as the town nearest the Tri-Cities Regional Airport, Blountville (3,000)—can provide a more nuanced depiction of religious changes in the United States.[23] Along with the airport, which has international import/export privileges, two large businesses draw professional workers from world locations: the Eastman Chemical plant in Kingsport and East Tennessee State University in Johnson City, with medical and pharmacy schools and nearly thirteen thousand students. In the early 1960s, when my wife and I met at Milligan College just outside Johnson City, the region was solidly a part of the Southern Bible Belt. A small Jewish group offered the most diversity, but it had neither synagogue nor rabbi. Christian denominations such as Assemblies of God, Baptists, Christian Churches, Churches of Christ, Churches of God, Episcopalians, Lutherans, Methodists, Presbyterians, and Roman Catholics, as well as Unitarian Universalists, were doing well. One of the more influential religious festivals of that decade was the Preaching Mission, supported by most of the cities' denominations. It was held in one of the largest auditoriums in the area. Nationally known ministers flew in for three nights of rousing singing and moving preaching. Smaller congregations, including snake handlers living primarily in the mountain valleys, did not participate, but they were part of the interesting diversity within the region's Christian community. White and black Pentecostals also had their separate services with music and manifestations of the spirit.

My wife and I returned in 1970 when I joined the Bible faculty of Milligan College. During two years of teaching, we noticed that the Preaching Mission had foundered. In another change, the Roman Catholic community, St. Mary's, had grown, partly because computer technicians who had lost their jobs in the Northeast had found work at a Texas Instruments plant in Johnson City and the large Eastman Chemical plant in Kingsport. During the summer, South American immigrants, who first arrived to pick melons and strawberries, were regularly seen. We had no idea how many of them were beginning to stay in the area and labor within various businesses.

We went back to Johnson City after five years (1972 to 1977) in West Germany. I became a professor at Emmanuel School of Religion, a graduate theological seminary.

Religious groups were following rather surprising paths. American mainline churches were in steep decline nationally, but here they had experienced only stagnation and some loss. A number of church buildings in the larger region, how-ever, had become restaurants or housed other businesses. Yet small conservative congregations kept themselves alive and grew.

The remarkable change in Christianity since 1977 has been in both the Roman Catholic and Pentecostal communities. The new influx of South American immi-grants has brought many more Catholics. They have helped the community build a new sanctuary and school.[24] South American and Mexican Pentecostal immigrants have access to one Assembly of God building; hand-lettered signs indicate that the community is Spanish-speaking. Indeed, at least one Christian Church and one Baptist Church offer their buildings for Spanish-language services in the afternoons. The Eastern Orthodox group is a small congregation downtown. Their nearest community formerly was in Knoxville, more than one hundred miles away.[25]

The full trappings of Bible Belt society are still a robust part of the local culture. An archconservative minister writes a column for the *Johnson City Press Chronicle* entitled "It is Written." The quotations come from the Christian Bible, "the one true scripture." It has not occurred to him, or probably to most of his congregation and readers, that there are several authoritative scriptures in the world. Lectures and sermons on the problems of evolution and secular moral values, fitted to conserva-tive Christian culture, are publicly advertised. Gospel singing takes place in local churches, but country music is also a vibrant part of the region's gift to wider Amer-ican culture.

Bible Belt culture has not been uprooted, but the old blue laws have almost disappeared. Several businesses are open on Sundays; alcohol can be purchased any day. Indeed Johnson City used to be called Little Chicago because in the 1920s, Al Capone stayed in the best hotel on his travels from Chicago to Miami and back. Local bootleggers had contracts with Capone and shipped moonshine in either direction through the railroad depot. For years, police were also corrupt. The Feb-ruary 28, 1952, issue of *Look* magazine listed Johnson City as one of the twenty-five most vice-ridden cities in the United States. For decades, the nonreligious had been quite strong in this apparently Bible-centered city.[26]

For me, the totally unforeseen development has been the growth and influence of various non-Christian religions. The small Jewish assembly, made up of Ameri-can Jews with some immigrants, now has both a synagogue outside Blountville and a rabbi.[27] One group of heart specialists and one of internal medicine specialists primarily connected to East Tennessee State University and the Medical Center Hospital are almost entirely staffed by Asians, particularly Indian Hindu and Paki-stani Muslim immigrants. The Hindus in Kingsport have erected a building that has a Hall of Worship and the Amy Community Center; Hindus in Bristol claim two centers from different Hindu traditions. The Islamic believers in Johnson City recently completed a new mosque, which depends primarily on immigrants, with their professional standings and wealth. There are, however, some indigenous con-verts. Bristol also has an Islamic Center.

Baha'i believers meet in a Unitarian Universalist church in Gray. Indigenous U.S. citizens participate in their programs from time to time. The Johnson City

Public Library served as a meeting place for a Baha'i group from 1999 to 2005, and there is also a Baha'i community at Bristol.

Before September 11, 2001, a group of Hindu and Muslim doctors from the Johnson City Medical Center Hospital, along with philosophers and historians in the various departments of East Tennessee State University, sponsored programs discussing whether any one religion could command the faith of all humanity. They specifically looked at the spirituality of Hinduism, Islam, and Christianity. Their open public meetings have been less frequent, but the discussions continue.

CONCLUSIONS

Many Western Christians seek to become more aware of secularism, atheism, or agnosticism, either to join or to resist. Although the influx of immigrants from other world religions has been small in size, evidence of their success—not anticipated by Christians—has caused various nations to awaken. Even in a small provincial area in northeastern Tennessee, U.S.A., Buddhist, Hindu, Islamic, and Baha'i communities are making their presence felt. Interpreters of statistics argue whether nonreligion or Islam will reshape Europe. The appeal of nonreligion is stronger in the United States than it has been in more than two hundred fifty years. Yet Christian renewal, now in relatively small numbers, might occur in both the United States and Europe. One African theorist insists that African Christian immigration into Europe will shift the struggle toward Christianity without the return of Christendom and might well change religion in the United States.

NOTES

1. Vera Brittain, *Chronicle of Youth: The War Diary, 1912–1917* (New York: Morrow, 1982); *Testament of Youth: An Autobiographical Study of the Years 1900–1925* (New York: Penguin, 2004). See also Hillary Bailey, *Vera Brittain* (New York: Viking Penguin, 1987), 11–46.

2. Brian Stanley, ed., *The World Missionary Conference 1910, Edinburgh* (Grand Rapids, Mich.: Eerdmans, 2009).

3. Mark Noll, *The New Shape of World Christianity* (Downers Grove, Ill.: InterVarsity, 2009). Noll sees the conditions in which U.S. Christianity grew as similar to those of world Christianity.

4. Not as yet another Christendom, as Philip Jenkins suggests in *The Next Christendom: The Coming of Global Christianity* (Oxford: Oxford University Press, 2002).

5. Lamin Sanneh, *Whose Religion Is Christianity? The Gospel beyond the West* (Grand Rapids, Mich.: Eerdmans, 2003); *Disciples of All Nations:Pillars of World Christianity* (Oxford: Oxford University Press, 2008).

6. For instance, Lamin Sanneh at Yale, Jakob Olupona at Harvard, and Emmanuel Larty at Emory. Ogbu Kalu at McCormick Theological Seminary died early this year. International students make up 15 percent of the student body at Emmanuel School of Religion, mostly from Africa and Brazil. We have a Kenyan mission-theology professor, Kiptolai Eloloia, the first Christian in his family.

7. Kwame Bediako, course on World Christianity, Divinity Faculty, University of Edinburgh, October 1981. Bediako had doctorates from France and Scotland but did not become strongly European in his thought.

8. Afua Kuma, *Jesus of the Deep Forest: Prayers and Praises of Afua Kuma* (Accra, Ghana: Asempa, 1981/1999).

9. For instance, see Richard Dawkins, *The God Delusion* (Boston: Houghton Mifflin, 2006); and Christopher Hitchens, *God Is Not Great: How Religion Poisons Everything* (New York: Twelve, 2007). Christian authors, such as Nobel laureate John F. Haight, in *God and the New Atheism: A Critical Response to Dawkins, Harris & Hitchens* (Louisville, Ky.: Westminster John Knox, 2007), have offered solid rejoinders, but nonreligion, secularism, agnosticism, and atheism continue to grow.

10. Li Tang, trans., "The Book of Jesus, the Messiah," in Li Tang, *A Study of the History of Nestorian Christianity in China and Its Literature in Chinese* (Frankfurt am Main: Peter Lang, 2001/2003/2004), introduction and 45–56.

11. The estimate of 40 million comes from an insightful and well-informed Korean PhD theologian, who has traveled widely in China to support congregations and clandestine schools. I withhold his name for obvious reasons.

12. Christopher Caldwell, *Reflections on the Revolution in Europe: Immigration, Islam and the West* (New York: Doubleday, 2009), esp. 349.

13. Conversations with Hall for nearly a decade have indicated that vital Christian congregations are either growing or are being planted successfully in Europe.

14. Caldwell's *Reflections on the Revolution in Europe* carefully deals with the data suggesting that most Muslims do not seek to assimilate. Europe had insufficient plans for absorbing so many guest workers, and now, although they are a minority, thousands of them prefer to stay. In Caldwell's view, European culture is relativistic and weak and will not easily resist Islam.

From news.bahai.org/story/390.

15. See www.baptism.org.uk/debaptism09.htm.

16. See www.timesonline.co.uk/tol/life_and_style/article56221482.ece.

17. The first proposed plan for the center pictured a minaret that dwarfed any other spire in Oxford.

18. Jehu J. Hanciles, *Beyond Christendom: Globalization, African Migration, and the Transformation of the West* (Maryknoll, N.Y.: Orbis, 2008). This brilliant thesis concerning African Christian migration to Europe is based on sociological research of different communities formed from those who have left African countries and immigrated to European ones. These churches might prove to be one of the largest growth factors in European Christianity.

19. Barry A. Kosmin and Ariela Keysar, American Religious Identification Survey (ARIS 2008), Trinity College, Hartford, Conn., 2009.

20. See www.gc.cuny.edu/faculty/research_briefs/aris/aris_index.htm.

21. In an anecdotal example, a church plant, Crosspoint, in Albuquerque, New Mexico has more than 80 percent of its members who have had no previous Christian experience. But those with such experience are uncomfortable with the people and the worship designed to reach them.

22. When I taught a course on TV evangelists as a visiting professor at John Carroll University in Cleveland in 1981, both professors and priests said that the largest loss of the city's Catholics was to fundamentalist and evangelical churches.

23. The estimated figures (from www.city-data.com) are adjusted from those used for 2007.

24. St. Mary's had originally been a Dominican mission effort. By the 1960s, it had a beautiful small sanctuary and a small school.

25. Holy Resurrection Antioch Orthodox Christian Church.

26. See www.johnsdepot.com/chicago/chicago.htm. In 2006, a new business in North Johnson City was built on the site of a much older structure. Excavations uncovered a speakeasy with multiple underground exits. Capone seems to have had a similar arrangement in Hot Springs, Arkansas.

27. B'nai Shalom Congregation.

FOR FURTHER READING

Barrett, David B., George Thomas Kurian, and Todd M. Johnson, eds. 2001. *World Christian Encyclopedia: A Comparative Survey of Churches and Religions in the Modern World*. New York: Oxford University Press.

Berger, Peter, Grace Davie, and Effie Fokos. *Religious America, Secular America? A Theme and Variations*. Aldershot, U.K.: Ashgate.

Caldwell, Christopher. 2009. *Reflections on the Revolution in Europe: Immigration, Islam, and the West*. New York: Doubleday.

Hanciles, Jehu J. 2008. *Beyond Christendom: Globalization, African Immigration, and the Transformation of the West*. Maryknoll, N.Y.: Orbis.

Noll, Mark. 2009. *The New Shape of World Christianity*. Downers Grove, Ill.: InterVarsity.

Norris, Frederick W. 2002. *Christianity: A Short Global History*. Oxford: Oneworld.

Sanneh, Lamin. 2008. *Disciples of All Nations: Pillars of World Christianity*. Oxford: Oxford University Press.

CHAPTER 16

....

NEW RELIGIOUS MOVEMENTS IN GLOBAL PERSPECTIVE

....

PETER B. CLARKE

SEVERAL of the new religious movements (NRMs) of modern times have become global movements, at least in terms of their wide international outreach and geographical spread and even in some cases in terms of the diverse nature of their ethnic composition (Machacek and Wilson 2000). Among these are the Japanese NRM Soka Gakkai ("Value Creation Society"); the Indian Brahma Kumaris ("Daughters of Brahma"), Sathya Sai Baba, and Hare Krishna; the Taiwanese Tzu Chi Buddhist Compassion and Relief Society; and Scientology, which began in the United States in the early 1950s. There are many other examples (Clarke 2006a).

Not all NRMs, it should be pointed out, in becoming global in their outreach or in a geographical sense have managed to diversify significantly in terms of their ethnic composition. Some continue to be composed largely of one ethnic group even outside their original heartland, at least in certain parts of the world. Present in Brazil for almost one hundred years, the membership of the Japanese NRM Tenrikyo ("Heavenly Wisdom") continues to be for the most part people of Japanese origin. Likewise in North America and Europe, the membership of the Taiwanese Tzu Chi movement is mainly people of Chinese descent. This is something that these movements would like to change.

Building an ethnically diverse membership is a demanding and difficult task. In order to become global movements, NRMs must often depend heavily on one particular ethnic group as they expand beyond their home base. On arrival in new cultural contexts, movements are most likely to appeal to first- or second-generation economic migrants from the same ethnic background as the missionaries who brought the movement to the region in the first place. As the spread of Japanese NRMs abroad shows (Clarke 2000), the new missionaries, in turn, are likely to have to depend on these migrants for support, at least in the early stages of their missionary work. In giving this support, the migrants—for whom the new religion is an important means of sustaining and maintaining their cultural identity—tend to want to make the movement a home for themselves abroad, rather than to see it diversify ethnically. For this reason, among others, the NRM becomes associated by the host community with a particular ethnic group, and this makes large-scale ethnic diversification extremely problematic. When pursued without regard for such issues as identity, both personal and cultural, it can lead to serious fragmentation (Clarke 2000).

Why a Global Perspective?

A full understanding of the impact and significance of the NRM phenomenon can only be had by considering it from a global standpoint. Movements that have attracted millions of followers globally are often dismissed as irrelevant in particular contexts where their membership is relatively small. Taiwanese Tzu Chi has only a handful of members in the United Kingdom, but worldwide it has millions, and the same applies in other cases.

A study of NRMs from a global vantage point also offers valuable insights into the kinds of religious changes that are taking place worldwide, including those occurring in standard or mainstream religion. It could be argued that the rise of NRMs has acted as a catalyst for change in the major religions of the world, including Buddhism, which has been profoundly influenced by the rise of Engaged Buddhism, beginning in the 1960s. Tzu Chi provides one of the most striking examples of this "new" kind of Buddhism (Clarke 2006a).

A global perspective further helps us to move beyond the thinking that sees NRMs as a mainly Western phenomenon, with its strongest appeal in North America, an appeal closely linked to the so-called counterculture of the 1960s. In reality, however, what was happening was global in scope. NRMs were emerging everywhere—Japan produced literally hundreds (McFarland 1967)—and this strongly suggests that religion as a phenomenon in itself was undergoing profound change on a worldwide scale as a result of the revolution in communications and transport, massive waves of economic migrants crisscrossing the globe, the emergence of the consumer-driven global economy, ever-increasing urbanization and related demographic changes, and, consequent upon these developments, the awakening of a clearer understanding of the self as a global citizen. With these changes, religions ceased to be less regionally based. In keeping with the postmodern relativism that fit well with greater religious and cultural pluralism, nondogmatic, nondoctrinal religion and new subjective forms of spirituality—the vehicles for which were often NRMs—began to appeal much more widely.

With these changes in communications and demographics, religions could no longer be defined by geography. Islam was much more than a Middle Eastern phenomenon, and Buddhism and Hinduism were much more than Asian phenomena. Every religion belonged everywhere, to a much greater extent than ever before, and provided people everywhere with alternative theories and methods of becoming spiritual. NRMs derived much of their appeal from this new situation. A world undergoing profound transformation required radically new forms of religion. It is worth mentioning briefly at this point, at the risk of some repetition, some of the principal ways in which new religion differs from standard or traditional religion.

Identifying "New" Religion Globally

Although clear similarities exist, "new" religion—I will speak of "new" spirituality below—seen globally is not all of a kind. Different, though converging, criteria are used to identify and evaluate the phenomenon in different cultural and even political contexts. Furthermore, the terms *sect* or *cult* or, as in China, *evil sect or religion* (*xiejiao*) (Chang 2004, 7) are used to describe what are here being referred to as NRMs. I use the term *new* in preference to such terms as *cult* or *sect*, both of which have not only a descriptive but also a normative use in the sense that they not only refer to empirical phenomena but also have acquired a negative value connotation. The term *NRMs* is not, of course, free of negative connotations, as it is sometimes used comparatively with older traditions to mean superficial or insignificant. It is also synonymous in the minds of many with such tragedies as Jonestown Guyana, where in 1978, more than nine hundred members of the People's Temple under the leadership of Jim Jones committed mass suicide (Hall 1987), and the Aum Shinrikyo event in March 1975, when the NRM spread sarin gas on the Tokyo underground, killing twelve commuters and injuring many others, some seriously (Shimazono 1995).

Focusing on the NRMs active in Europe and North America, Wilson (1993) identified a number of characteristics that, he believed, set them apart from the older religions, and some of these characteristics are also evident elsewhere in the world in other religions, including Buddhism. Among the more striking features of modern NRMs highlighted by Wilson was the stress they place on the central role of laypeople in managing their own spiritual advancement and the consequent deemphasis on the significance of the role of the clergy. Although there are countless gurus, they are generally perceived less as intermediaries whose role is essential to the spiritual advancement of their followers and more as context setters. It does happen, of course, that some claim indispensability, and in other cases, disciples endow them with authority and power that they do not seek. This growing "protes-tantization" of religion, described and analyzed by Gombrich and Obeyesekere (1988) in the case of Buddhism in Sri Lanka and by Martin (1990) in the case of Latin America, is occurring on a global scale.

Without going as far as Campbell (1999), who speaks of the Easternization of the Western mind, there is also a process of Orientalization occurring in the West, where people are becoming more Buddhist or Hindu, in the sense of taking on many of the religious assumptions and spiritual techniques of these religions. I will return to this point below when I discuss "glocalization."

Differences also exist between old and new religion over religious membership or belonging. Most NRMs resemble one or another form of client cult (Stark and Bainbridge 1985) and accept multiple membership. It is not only possible to be a member of several NRMs simultaneously, but it is also possible to remain at the same time a member of the religion of one's birth. This gives rise to a whole new under-standing of the meaning of conversion and is also of direct relevance to discussions of brainwashing as a means of conversion and the question of religious syncretism.

Modern NRMs are also organizationally different from those of the past, making greater use of more secular forms of management, administration, and as-sembly and of modern means of communication, architecture, music, and notions of sacred space. Networking, rather than a focus on religion as community, also characterizes much modern religion. Indeed, many NRMs, including Scientology, mirror in so much of their style, ethos, organization, orientation, and goals the wider society that Wilson (1990) describes them as modern "secularized religions."

With few exceptions—the majority of which are fundamentalist movements that incidentally are not as immune from mixing and managing beliefs and prac-tices as is sometimes suggested—hybridity is rife in contemporary religions, and some observers, including Robertson (1991, 217–218; 1992, 171), have suggested that the future of religion is with those movements that seek to integrate different aspects of different traditions, as well as the sacred and the secular. This "harmoni-zation" of faiths, and faiths and secularity, has already produced much innovation, and this is nowhere more evident than in the New Age movement (NAM), which Hanegraaff (1999) describes as a "secularist" movement, much in the same way as Wilson (1990) speaks of Scientology.

Claims to newness are often paradoxical, based as they can be on having discov-ered the "complete past," of having uncovered some ancient and foundational sacred text that enables for the first time a full understanding of how a religion began, what it taught, and how it was practiced. These discoveries allow the movement in ques-tion to contend that it is providing the first ever authentic interpretation of the teachings of a particular religion. An example is the Falun Gong movement, which, while acknowledging its debt to Buddhism, claims to be the most complete version of this religion. While Falun Gong maintains that standard Buddhism teaches only two of the universe's fundamental moral principles—benevolence and compassion—it claims to teach all three: benevolence, compassion, and forbearance (Chang 2004, 73–74).

Several Japanese movements explain their originality in a similar way, among them Agonshu, whose founder, Kiriyama Seiyu, professed to have discovered new, hidden truths by reading early Buddhist texts known as the Agama Sutras, which had previously been given no attention by Buddhism in Japan. Able to discern the hidden, inner meaning of these texts, Kiriyama claimed to have uncovered a direct and rapid road to Buddhahood (*jobutsu*) for the living and, even more important, for the dead, for it is believed that as long as the latters' spirits remain without *jobutsu*, the living are unable to enjoy peace or secure well-being and prosperity (Reader 1991, 211).

PATHWAYS OF GLOBAL EXPANSION

There are few societies that have not witnessed the rise of NRMs in recent times, and few NRMs have remained confined to the societies that gave birth to them. All have traveled using a variety of different routes across the world, some of these indirect and unexpected. Several Japanese NRMs, including Sekaikyusei Kyo ("Church of World Messianity"), have reached parts of Africa, including Angola, Mozambique, South Africa, and the Democratic Republic of the Congo, via the farthest point west of Japan, Brazil. The Brazilian NRM Santo Daime has traveled with Brazilian-Japanese migrant workers to Japan. Movements such as Subud have spread from Indonesia to Australia to Europe, others from Tibet to South Africa, while others have followed the path from India to Mauritius and the West Indies and still others from West Africa to Europe and the United States. Not unexpectedly, Taiwanese Tzu Chi is active in China and throughout Southeast Asia. It has also followed the Taiwanese diaspora to North America.

NRMs AND "GLOCALIZATION"

While being themselves part of the process of ever-increasing globalization, NRMs also throw light on the dynamics and mechanics of this process, on how it plays itself out. The transfer of religious culture from one part of the world to another is never a uniform process or one that leads to the extinction of the host culture and religion, as Mullins, among others, illustrates in his book *Christianity Made in Japan* (1998). Considered from a global standpoint, NRMs enable us to see something of the numerous forms of what Robertson (1992) called "glocalization" and/or domestication that have and are taking place as these movements attempt to embed themselves in different cultures. I have written elsewhere on this topic, for example, in relation to variety of forms of syncretism developed by the Japanese NRMs in Brazil (Clarke 2006b).

Other examples include yoga, particularly in the form of modern yoga, which has undergone a process of secularization in Britain and elsewhere in the West (De Michaelis 2003). Not all of the yoga performed in the West is secular modern yoga. What some in the West, and doubtless elsewhere, intend by taking up yoga as a spiritual discipline is to become divine or God, but that has not been historically the goal. On the contrary, traditionally the aim has been to become like God, not to participate in God. Furthermore, even those Westerners who retain this classical understanding of God are liable to introduce an element of worship into their practice, forgetting that there is no devotion to God in the classical Christian sense of the term, the reason being that God is seen as the divine exemplar of all human souls, and this makes contemplation of God useful rather than an act of worship.

The process of "glocalization" extends much wider than a few concepts or practices usually associated with yoga and includes radical reinterpretations of core notions of Eastern systems of thought. As Anthony and Ecker (1987, 35) point out: "Since Eastern systems tend to see collective social reality as an illusion . . . salvation therefore involves the transcendence of society's moral rules, the socially conditioned notions of good and evil. But this Eastern idea of salvation tends to be interpreted from the standpoint of an 'American-utilitarian-individualist mentality.'"

From a global perspective, thus, the picture is one of how various religious traditions are shaping, rather than displacing, one another's understanding of notions, such as transcendence and faith, good and evil, of the meaning, purpose, and functions of religion; of religious belonging; and of attitudes toward and methods of disseminating religious beliefs. This perspective also sheds light on the different criteria of religious innovation that exist from one culture and religious tradition to another, although globalization is making for greater uniformity of outlook on this and related questions.

NRMs as Vehicles of a New Spirituality

Here, I wish to say a little about the other side of the coin of new religion: new spirituality. The option for spirituality over religion and the stress on the need for a spirituality that pulls together, as it were, the world of the human and that of the divine and that is relevant and self-empowering are, clearly, developments promoted by many in the New Age movement (NAM) and many NRMs, including the Indian-derived NRMs, the self-religions, and the religions of the true self.

Such spirituality, which turns doctrinal tenets into matters of personal opinion, is seen by some of the older, mainstream denominations—such as the Catholic church, some of the more theologically conservative Protestant churches, Islam, and some branches of Buddhism—to constitute a serious threat to "authentic" religion. Official Catholicism and certain Buddhist communities have been particularly critical of the

form and content of the new spirituality as it is found in the NAM. This official criticism notwithstanding, the influence of the NAM has penetrated most mainstream
religions, and several of the so-called traditional religions, including Australian Aborig-
inal religion, for whom it has become one of the principal means of its globalization.

Looking again briefly at the situation from West to East, one kind of spirituality
that is increasingly sought after in the former context is the previously mentioned
inner-directed or internally focused spirituality, which gives rise to what Heelas
(1991) calls self-religion and to what I prefer to describe as religions of the true self.
The latter makes it clearer, I feel, that the essence of this type of spiritual quest is to
arrive at the deepest possible understanding and awareness of the authentic or real
self, which, it should be stressed, is not necessarily regarded as God in the sense of
the unique source of everything.

The new spirituality creates a new understanding of the historical space
between the actual and potential state of an individual, in that it brings the possibility of full self-realization within reach in the present. It makes it constantly available, the only hurdle to be overcome being that of ignorance about the nature of
one's true self. The distinction between earth and heaven is in this sense annulled.
The former is no longer seen as a place of limitations and the latter as one of unlimited potential.

This spirituality does not of necessity entail a denial of the existence of spiritual beings, powers, or forces or of an original energy beyond the self—that deep
inner, divine reality as opposed to the ego—nor is it necessarily so inwardly
focused as to be indifferent to and unconcerned with the social condition of the
wider society.

The new spirituality found in NRMs and the NAM is practice- rather than
reason- or faith-based. It is characterized by its experiential approach to spiritual
understanding and ultimate truth, and this sets it apart from creedal-based religion.

According to Ouspensky's recollections (1987, 228), Gurdjieff—on whose teachings the association known as the Work is based—was emphatic in his rejection of the
traditional idea of faith. Ouspensky quotes him as saying: "In properly organised
groups no faith is required; what is required is simply a little trust and even that only
for a little while, for the sooner a man begins to verify all he hears the better it is for
him."

ACCOUNTING FOR NRMs: RAPID CHANGE OR STAGNATION?

Even a short presentation like this should illustrate how difficult it is to reach anything other than very broad and general conclusions about the causes of the NRM
phenomenon, a point made by Wilson, who reminded students of NRMs that with
globalization, in both its subjective and material or objective senses notwith-

standing, the researcher continues to remain the captive of "the empirical circumstances of given cultures, of geography and history" (Wilson 1982, 17).

I have pointed to the revolution in communications and transport and to the emergence of a consumer-driven economy as part of a broad general explanation for the rise of NRMs, while other observers have highlighted other developments—some, it has to be said, with reference to one or another particular part of the world, which they have taken for the whole.

I also suggest that attention to the aims and objectives of NRMs can shed light on why they arose. For example, one cannot but be struck by the fact that virtually all NRMs, regardless of time, place, or religious and cultural origins—from Tenrikyo, which was founded in Japan in 1838, to the Ikhwan or Muslim Brotherhood, founded in Egypt in 1928, to Scientology, which formally began as a church in 1952 with its headquarters in the United Kingdom, and every movement founded since then—share a common belief in the millennium, in the coming of a new world order or earthly paradise. All are concerned with world transformation, which clearly indicates a strong dissatisfaction with the way things are compared with what they could and should be like.

Reasons for this widespread desire for world transformation can include existential longing, which many believe cannot be attained in the world as it is and which may consist of improved self-understanding and understanding of others, and freedom from every form of limitation and fragmentation. Following this line of thinking, NRMs can best be understood if seen as world-transforming movements that express the human desire to flourish in every aspect of life.

Rapid social change leading to anxiety, stress, and anomy is perhaps the most common explanation given for modern NRMs. This is not a very convincing way to explain the phenomenon, because rapid social change is a highly subjective notion and one that is difficult to measure. Moreover, it is not always in circumstances of rapid social change that NRMs arise but sometimes during periods of relative stagnation. Change or innovation can be seen as a way out of such stagnation, which can be as threatening to the foundations of society as revolution. Wuthnow (1982) asks why rapid industrialization in the United States in the 1880s and 1890s failed to produce relatively fewer NRMs than during the more turbulent period of the 1840s and why the disruption of the two world wars in the twentieth century failed to produce more NRMs than the 1960s. Theories of rapid social change also fail to explain the variability in the types, in terms of form, content, and radical emphasis, of new religions of different periods.

The "age of crisis" or "age of anxiety" kinds of explanations of the rise of NRMs suffer from weaknesses similar to those associated with the rapid social change type. The term *crisis*, for example, can mean so many different things to so many different people: unemployment, the scale of environmental pollution, the failure to attain a goal. As for the anxiety hypothesis, stress and strain conditions are ever present, and there is no way of knowing whether the modern period under review here has experienced more stress and strain than others.

SOME REGIONAL EXPLANATIONS

Limiting their observations to the United States and Europe, a number of sociologists have followed Robbins (1988, 60) in referring to an acute and distinctively modern form of dislocation conducive to anomy, alienation, and deprivation. This, it has been suggested, led a minority of young Americans and Europeans to look for new structures, new meaning systems, and new forms of community. NRMs moved in to meet these demands, which, as was pointed out above, often expressed themselves as demands for the total transformation of society. However, as Tipton's account (1982) of est (Erhard Seminar Training) illustrates, compromises had to be made in which the goal of total transformation was commuted to that of reform.

Dislocation occurred in different spheres, including in the area of moral certainty. Bellah (1976) and Tipton (1982) are among those who have argued that the failure of political protest movements and of movements of cultural experimentation in the 1960s and 1970s led to disillusionment and disorientation. Tipton speaks of the "ideological wreckage" that prevailed among those involved in many of these movements and in the counterculture generally. In search of guidance and rules for living while continuing to be committed to the ideals of self-expression, many of the disillusioned turned to NRMs, which did not just happen to be there but reflexively sought to meet this demand. A similar situation emerged in postindependence Africa, where the failure of politics often leading to military rule resulted in total disillusionment and a vast movement toward new forms of religion and spirituality.

As for the rise of NRMs in Africa under colonial rule and in other colonized societies, including those of South and Southeast Asia, the Middle East, and Melanesia, explanation is usually in terms of external impact/internal response theory. I suggest that we question seriously this impact/response schema of analysis. Such a framework fails to do justice to the dynamics of religious innovation in these contexts and overconcentrates on external factors at the expense of internal ones. As Gibb (1978) stresses, the rise of modern reform-minded Islam in North Africa and the Middle East cannot be explained according to impact/response theory. Nor can neo-Hinduism in Asia (Sen 2003) or neo-Pentecostalism in Latin America (Martin 1990).

To return to the United States and Europe, other accounts of religious innovation tend to give more emphasis to structural factors rather than dislocation (Robbins 1988). These include the search by the young for "surrogate families" as society's traditional mediating structures, particularly those institutions that bolstered the private sphere, such as the family, decline in strength. This had the effect of turning everything in the private sphere into a matter of choice, while the public sphere became increasingly institutionalized, bureaucratic, and uniform. It was in these circumstances, it is suggested, that those NRMs that offered a more holistic sense of self, including the spiritualities or religions of the true self and the NAM, found their appeal.

At the core of other explanations of the rise of NRMs in the United States and Europe are the interconnected processes of secularization, pluralism, and privatization

(Wilson 1982; Berger 1967). The argument developed to account for the rise of NRMs based on these processes takes different forms. One contends that the ever-increasing rationalization of society and the consequent institutional differentiation that follows have consigned religion to the private sphere, leaving religious institutions with little social influence and even less social purpose. In this situation, as Berger points out (1967), the more public religion seeks to be, the more it lacks substance, and the more substance it seeks to retain in terms of its truth claims, the less communal it is. Free enterprise reigns as beliefs, which can no longer be imposed, must instead be offered to potential clients, no longer obliged to purchase them, in a competitive religious marketplace. It was in this context of religious variety and competition that many NRMs were born.

Stark and Bainbridge (1985) see secularization not as a modern phenomenon but as a feature of all societies, whether modern or traditional, and go on to argue that where mainstream religions decline, there is usually revival and innovation in the form of NRMs, which can result in the reversal of the secularization process. Wilson (1991), by contrast, contends that the secularization process has now gone so far as to be virtually unstoppable. Moreover, NRMs would hardly be likely to stage a revival of religion as traditionally understood, since they are in themselves no more than secular versions of religion, particularly in the way they seek to use instrumental rational techniques to advance nonempirical goals. Wilson writes:

> New religious movements, whether in the Christian, Buddhist or any other tradition, are not in the strict sense revivals of tradition: they are more accurately regarded as adaptations of religion to new social circumstances. . . . In their style and in their specific appeal they represent an accommodation to new conditions and they incorporate many of the assumptions and facilities encouraged in the increasingly rationalised secular sphere. *Thus it is that many new movements are themselves testimonies to secularisation*: they often use highly secular methods in evangelism, financing, publicity and mobilisation of adherents. (1991, 204; emphasis added)

Conclusions

Whatever the difficulties associated with providing a general explanation of the emergence of NRMs, when seen from a global perspective, this phenomenon provides a clear indication that the potential for innovation both in ritual and in beliefs has grown exponentially in the modern world. Migration on a massive scale, increasing globalization, and the revolution in communications, including the development of cyberspace as a place of encounter and discovery, have all contributed to increased pluralism and religious interaction and, thus, to the build-up of a vast and deep pool of philosophies, notions, and techniques for religious and spiritual innovation.

This resource not only provides the raw materials of religious innovation that takes shape in the form of NRMs and the new types of spirituality but also has consequences for every religion—whether from the so-called traditional religions or world religions category—in terms of their functions and goals. What Gregory (2000) has said of Buddhism—that the changes that have taken place in doctrine and in institutions since the onset of colonialism are likely to be as significant in the longer term as such past developments as the Mahayana tradition—could also be said of Christianity, Islam, Hinduism, and all major religions.

REFERENCES

Anthony, Dick, and Bruce Ecker. 1987. "The Anthony Typology: A Framework for Assessing Spiritual and Consciousness Groups." In Dick Anthony, Bruce Ecker, and Ken Wilber, eds., *Spiritual Choices: The Problem of Recognizing Authentic Paths to Inner Transformation*. New York: Paragon, 35–106.

Bellah, Robert. 1976. "New Religious Consciousness and the Crisis of Modernity." In Charles Glock and Robert Bellah, eds., *The New Religious Consciousness*. Berkeley: University of California Press, 333–352.

Berger, Peter. 1967. *The Sacred Canopy*. New York: Doubleday.

Campbell, Colin. 1999. "The Easternisation of the West." In Bryan R. Wilson and Jamie Cresswell, eds., *New Religious Movements: Challenge and Response*. London: Routledge, 35–49.

Chang, Maria Hesia. 2004. *Falun Gong*. New Haven: Yale University Press.

Clarke, Peter B., ed. 2000. *Japanese New Religions: In Global Perspective*. Richmond, U.K.: Curzon.

———. 2006a. *New Religions in Global Perspective*. London: Routledge.

———. 2006b. "Religious Syncretism Japanese Style in Brazil." In Andre Droogers et al., eds., *Playful Religion*. Amsterdam: Eburon, 123–137.

De Michaelis, Elizabeth. 2003. *A History of Modern Yoga*. London: Cassell Continuum.

Gibb, H. A. R. 1978. *Islam*. Oxford: Oxford University Press.

Gombrich, Richard, and Gananath Obeyesekere. 1988. *Buddhism Transformed: Religious Change in Sri Lanka*. Princeton, N.J.: Princeton University Press.

Gregory, Peter. 2000. "Describing the Elephant: Buddhism in America." *Religion and American Culture: A Journal of Interpretation* 11/2: 233–263.

Hall, John H. 1987. *Gone from the Promised Land: Jonestown in American Cultural History*. New Brunswick, N.J.: Transaction.

Hanegraaff, Wouter J. 1999. "New Age Spiritualities as Secular Religion: A Historian's Perspective." *Social Compass* 46/2: 145–160.

Heelas, Paul. 1991. "Western Europe: Self-religions." In S. Sutherland and Peter B. Clarke, eds., *The Study of Religion: Traditional and New Religion*. London: Routledge, 167–173.

Heelas, Paul, et al. 2005. *The Spiritual Revolution: From "Religion" to "Spirituality" in Religion in the Modern World*. Oxford: Basil Blackwell.

Machacek, David, and Bryan R. Wilson. 2000. *Global Citizens*. Oxford: Oxford University Press.

Martin, David. 1990. *Tongues of Fire*. Oxford: Basil Blackwell.

McFarland, H. Neill. 1967. *The Rush Hour of the Gods.* New York: Macmillan.

Mullins, Mark. 1998. *Christianity Made in Japan: A Study of Indigenous Movements.* Honolulu: University of Hawaii Press.

Ouspensky, P. D. 1987. *In Search of the Miraculous: Fragments of an Unknown Teaching.* London: Arkana.

Reader, Ian. 1991. *Religion in Contemporary Japan.* Basingstoke, U.K.: Macmillan.

Robbins, Thomas. 1988. *Cults, Converts and Charisma.* London: Sage.

Robertson, Roland. 1991. "Social Theory, Cultural Relativity and the Problem of Global-ity." In Anthony D. King. ed., *Culture, Globalization and the World System.* New York: Macmillan.

———. 1992. *Globalization: Social Theory and Global Culture.* London: Sage.

Sen, Amiya P., ed. 2003. *Social and Religious Reform: The Hindus of British India.* Oxford: Oxford University Press.

Shimazono, Susumu. 1995. "In the Wake of Aum: The Formation and Transformation of a Universe of Belief." *Japanese Journal of Religious Studies* 22/3–4: 381–415.

Stark, Rodney, and William Sims Bainbridge. 1985. *The Future of Religion.* Berkeley: University of California Press.

Tipton, Steven M. 1982. *Getting Saved from the Sixties.* Berkeley: University of California Press.

Wilson, Bryan R. 1982. "The New Religions: Some Preliminary Considerations." In Eileen Barker, ed., *New Religious Movements: A Perspective for Understanding Society.* Lewiston, N.Y.: Edwin Mellen, 16–32.

———. 1990. *The Social Dimensions of Sectarianism.* Oxford: Clarendon.

———. 1991. "Secularization: Religion in the Modern World." In Stewart R Sutherland and Peter B. Clarke, eds., *The Study of Religion: Traditional and New Religion.* London: Routledge, 195–208.

———. 1993. "Historical Lessons in the Study of Cults and Sects." In David G. Bromley and Jeffrey K. Hadden, eds., *Religion and the Social Order*, vol. 3. West Yorkshire: Emerald Group Publishing 53–85.

Wuthnow, Robert. 1982. "World Order and Religious Movements." In Eileen Barker, ed., *New Religious Movements: A Perspective for Understanding Society.* Lewiston, N.Y.: Edwin Mellen, 47–69.

FOR FURTHER READING

Bellah, Robert. 1976. "New Religious Consciousness and the Crisis of Modernity." In Charles Glock and Robert Bellah, eds., *The New Religious Consciousness.* Berkeley: University of California Press, 333–352.

Clarke, Peter B., ed. 2000. *Japanese New Religions: In Global Perspective.* Richmond, U.K.: Curzon.

———. 2005. *Encyclopaedia of New Religious Movements.* London: Routledge.

———. 2006. *New Religions in Global Perspective.* London: Routledge.

Heelas, Paul, et al. 2005. *The Spiritual Revolution: From "Religion" to "Spirituality" in Religion in the Modern World.* Oxford: Basil Blackwell.

Machacek, David, and Bryan R. Wilson. 2000. *Global Citizens.* Oxford: Oxford University Press.

Wilson, Bryan R., and Jamie Cresswell, eds. 1999. *New Religious Movements: Challenge and Response.* London: Routledge, 35–49.

CHAPTER 17

RACE, ETHNICITY, AND RELIGION

GEORGE YANCEY

WHAT was the role of religion in the origin and perpetuation of slavery in the United States? How did religion affect the cruel treatment of Native Americans? Has religion had an impact on the fate of immigrants of color as they entered the nation? In short, did religious ideology in general, and Christianity in particular, challenge or support the historically overt racist social structure of the United States? The answer heavily depends on one's perspective on the role of religion. Some might argue that religion is a detriment to U.S. society.[1] For example, there is sufficient evidence that Christianity was one of the social-ideological constructs buttressing the white-supremacy ideology connected to chattel slavery (Swartley 1983; Wood 1991). However, those who argue for the benefits gained from religion can point out the presence of groups such as the Quakers, who were among the first to challenge slavery. Both groups are factually correct; thus, the answer to whether religion supported or challenged racist social structure is not an either/or but a both/and.

Looking at the past is not just an interesting exercise. Patterns picked up from historical encounters provide insight, allowing us to understand the contemporary relationship between race and religion. The exercise allows us to ask about the role of religious ideology in the more subtle contemporary racist social structures. Religious ideology plays the same role it has always played in the past: reinforcing the social and economic interest of the racial or ethnic group in which it originated.

I will explore more fully the idea that a particular religion has been generally used to promote the interests of the racial/ethnic group that promotes it.

Given this reality, religion can be perceived as beneficial if it satisfies the needs of a valued group or detrimental if it is used by a group that is hostile to a valued group. While religious ideology might develop outside the interest of a particular social group, this is the exception and not the rule. For the most part, religious belief has been used to promote the desires and needs of a particular group. This chapter is not just an exploration of the relationship of religion and race/ethnic groups but also an exploration of the nature of religion itself.

Religion as a System of Justification

To understand the potential role of religion in meeting the needs of racial groups, it is vital to comprehend the general purpose of religion. While a variety of definitions of religion are available, I have always tended to favor the ones that focused on religion as a way of answering questions of meaning (Niebuhr 1960; Tillich 1957; Yinger 1970). Questions of meaning deal with issues such as purpose and direction, making sense of tragedy, the meaning of good and evil, and so on. The drive to deal with such questions is overwhelming, and different religious systems enable individuals to find answers that comfort and sustain them in an uncertain social world.

It is not just that individuals need such answers. Societies and communities must provide answers about the purpose of their group, what is desirable about the group's culture, how to handle the unique challenges of the group, and so on. The religious beliefs within a group help to provide such answers. Rituals embed those answers among the group members and remind them of how questions of meaning should be addressed.[2] Clearly, certain members of the group deviate from the general meanings provided by that group's religious ideology; however, this does not eliminate the need for subcultures to provide these answers.

Racial groups are important subcultures for the development of answers to questions of meaning. One of the criteria for being a subculture that creates answers for questions of meaning is the sharing of similar social and cultural interests with the other members of one's group. One of the definitions of belonging to a minority group is the sharing of common burdens (Wagley and Harris 1958). Research in whiteness studies has demonstrated that majority group members tend to share similar social and cultural concerns (Dalton 2002; Dyer 1997; Twine 1997; Wildman and Davis 2002). These social concerns can be buttressed or opposed by a given religious belief system, and whether that system is adopted by minority or majority group members depends on its support, or nonsupport, of those social interests.

EARLY CHRISTIANITY AND WHITE SUPREMACY

Racism is a relatively new system of oppression in human history (Jordan 1968; Mosse 1985). Before its development, oppression had been based on cultural, regional, and/or religious differences but not on the idea of biological superiority. However, the development of the slave trade produced a need to justify notions of the innate inferiority of Africans. Quite simply, it was economically profitable to use the labor of the Africans without having to pay the true costs of that labor. This led to the development of the ideology of white supremacy (Jordan 1968; Wilson 1973). Soon this ideology was applied in relation not only to Africans but to all groups that were not considered part of the superior race, even southern and western European ethnic groups.

Materialist considerations were unlikely to provide sufficient justification for this status system. There was a powerful need to develop a moral system that allowed majority group members to turn blind eyes toward racial inequality. The dominant way that questions of meaning were addressed by the early Europeans and European-Americans was through Christian expressions. Teachings within Christian traditions also developed to legitimize racial oppression. Such teachings allowed majority group members to perceive the mistreatment of people of color as aligned with the will of God, rather than as an expression of their own economic greed and social arrogance.

For example, in the nineteenth century, a good deal of Christian literature was written to provide a systematic defense of slavery (Genovese 1998; Tise 1987; Wood 1991). This literature argued that the Bible does not overtly oppose slavery and thus indirectly supports the practice. Evangelists were allowed to convert slaves to Christianity if they also taught that obedience to their masters was an important part of their faith (Lincoln 1999). Native Americans suffered from a teaching called British Israelism (Barkun 1994; Callahan 2006), which perceived Europeans and European-Americans as the new chosen people and Indians as the enemies to be eliminated. This philosophy led to the ideology of the Manifest Destiny, which helped to enrich majority group members at the expense of the land and resources that indigenous peoples once controlled. Likewise, Hispanic and Asian immigrants encountered a Christian philosophy among majority group members that denigrated elements of their own culture and elevated the perceived value of European and European-American cultures. The Christianity practiced by majority group members in the early history of the United States served the interests of that majority group quite well.

However, it is a mistake to perceive Christianity merely as the promoter of white supremacy, since Christian expressions have also been used to resist racism. The Quakers provided the first organizational opposition to the institution of slavery. Christians such as the Grimke sisters and Catharine Beecher also made their opposition to racial brutality well known. Such moral challenges helped eventually to set up the Civil War, which ended the practice of slavery, although it did not impede the spread of white supremacy. As economic and ideological alterations created new racial understandings that moved away from a complete acceptance of majority group dominance, new religious structures also developed to justify those alterations.

The Emergence of White Racial Identity and Modern Racism

Since the emergence of the modern civil rights movement, there has been a sharp decline in the level of acceptance of white-supremacy ideology (Kluegel 1990; Schuman et al. 1997). Recent research in race and ethnicity illustrates the modern forms of racism that still fuel contemporary racial conflict (Bobo, Kluegel, and Smith 1997; Bonilla-Silva 1999; McConahay 1986; Sears 1988). These forms of modern racism condemn overt actions of racial bias but still work to support a status quo that maintains the advantages of majority group members. Majority group members base much of their rejection of governmental efforts to deal with racial inequality on a modern racism philosophy that minimizes the existence and damage done by institutional racism. In this way, they can deny that overt racism is their motivation for rejecting such policies.

In conjunction with this new philosophy has been the development of white racial identity. The theory of white racial identity asserts that majority group members develop values that aid them in the maintenance of their racial privileges. Some of these values include color-blindness, cultural Eurocentrism, individualism, and comfortableness in American society (Dyer 1997; Twine 1997; Wildman and Davis 2002; Yancey 2003b). By holding on to these values, majority group members can avoid the charge of racism while they still justify resisting overt efforts to deal with institutional racism (affirmative action, anti-racial-profiling legislation).

Emerson and Smith (2000) provide evidence that contemporary white evangelicals support at least one critical element of white racial identity, which is a strong adherence to free-will individualism. White evangelicals have a higher degree of adherence to individualism than whites in general. This individualism links the misfortune of the marginalized to their individual shortcomings, a philosophy that dismisses problems created by institutional racism. So white evangelicals are less open to structural alterations that promote racial justice than other majority group members. They have an expression of Christianity that condemns overt racism but supports the maintenance of a racial system that provides them with racially based social benefits. Future research might be able to document other elements of white racial identity, such as cultural Eurocentrism and color-blindness, disproportionately supported by white Christians. Yet even without such research, it can be asserted that contemporary Christianity among majority group members is used to support white racial identity and majority groups' social interest.

CHRISTIANITY OF COLOR

But Christianity is not merely a vehicle for majority group members. It has also been used to meet the needs of people of color. For example, the black church was the first institution that Africans and African-Americans were able to control. As such, early community leaders in the African-American communities were also church leaders. The Christian religion of slaves taught blacks to relate to the children of Israel as slaves whom God would eventually free (Raboteau 2004; Wilmore 1998). After the Civil War, an activist propensity continued to flourish in the African-American community and led to the development of a "black theology," an Afro-centric version of Christianity that envisions a Jesus sympathetic to the oppressed rather than the oppressors (Cone 1990). Black theology became a Christian expression justifying the resistance of African-Americans against institutional racism.

Christian ideology that supports people of color is not limited to African-Americans. Modern Native American Christians have promoted the concept of contextualization (Nicholls 2003; Woodley 2004), which is based on the notion that Christianity has to be contextualized to each unique culture. More than any other racial group in the United States, Native Americans are threatened with a loss of their cultural identity as a result of the intrusion of European-Americans. While many Native American Christians also discuss the need to deal with institutional racism (Kidwell, Noley, and Tinker 2001; Treat 1996; Woodley 2004), their emphasis on cultural maintenance somewhat separates them from other people of color and enables them to have a Christianity that meets their own unique cultural and historical needs.

There is also evidence that the Christianity practiced among Hispanic-Americans is reflective of the unique needs of their communities. Hispanic-American Christians have immigrated to the United States from several developing countries. Given the poverty in these societies, Marxian ideals are naturally attractive. This has allowed for the development of liberation theology among Hispanic Christians (Boff and Boff 1987; Espin 1995; Gutierrez 2001), which is a Marxian expression of Christian faith. In addition to the poverty Hispanics experience, they also have emerged from a society in which racial and cultural mixing is commonplace. This has produced a type of "mestizo Christianity," which emphasizes symbols and practices not limited to a single ethnic group (Aquino 1993; Banuelas 1995; Elizondo 1988; Goizueta 1989).

Finally, the unique experience of Asian-American Christians is also reflected in their version of Christianity. For example, Yang (1999) illustrates how Chinese Christians maintain elements of their native culture and values that help their transition into their new American culture. Thus, they develop a Christianity that helps them to meet their social needs of becoming "Americans" even while they maintain enough of their original culture to remain comfortable. Research into second-generation Koreans has suggested that those in ethnic-specific churches still utilize their churches as a way to enter the mainstream of the general society (Ecklund

2006). As a result, it is fair to assert that Asian-American Christianity has been used to help Asian-Americans make the transition from an immigrant group to a core constituency within modern society.

Christianity is a religion that can serve the needs of the dominant group, or it can buttress the interests of marginalized groups. Particular interpretations of Christian tenets can provide support for a given racial or ethnic group. Thus, how racialized Christians understand their faith is funneled through the perceived needs of their racial group.

Non-Christian Expressions
of Racial Protests

Given the above assertions, there is a temptation to conclude that unique qualities found within Christianity might account for how it developed in ways that meet the needs of particular racial groups. Yet it is only because of the predominance of Christianity in the United States that such examples are so easy to illustrate. Certainly, other religions can be utilized in such a manner.

The clearest example of this phenomenon in a non-Christian setting in the United States is the emergence of black Muslims, who would later become the Nation of Islam. This religious tradition contains racial elements rejected by traditional Islamic groups. Those racial elements postulate African-Americans as victims of the evil actions of majority group members. African-Americans are exhorted to be suspicious of majority group individuals and institutions. At the same time, they are encouraged to live moral lives and personally to overcome barriers they face in the United States. Such a religious ideology supported the efforts of African-Americans to deal with the oppressive racism they faced in the 1960s. The continuing existence of the Nation of Islam is a reflection of the indirect institutional racism that African-Americans still face. The lessons of mistrusting majority group members and of personal self-responsibility provide methods by which African-Americans can participate in their own liberation in a racialized society.

This pattern can be seen in some of the adaptations of the Eastern religions of many Asian-Americans. Gudykunst (2001) finds that the Buddhism of many Japanese was useful for helping them to maintain their ethnic heritage. However, these institutions also became somewhat Americanized in that they moved from Japanese to English in language and began to hold Sunday services. The Eastern religious tradition of the Japanese-Americans worked both to reaffirm their own cultural traditions and to help accommodate their transition into the dominant culture. A similar conclusion was drawn by Yang and Ebaugh (2001), who examined a Chinese Buddhist church that allowed its members to retain a secure Chinese identity even as the temple strove to develop an American identity. Jo (1999) documents how Korean-Americans utilized their Confucian beliefs to maintain their traditional family systems and their culture-normative structure in a non-Asian society. And Yang (1999) illustrates how Confucian beliefs can be used to buttress the economic success of Asian-Americans. Asian non-Christian religious institutions face the tasks of providing cultural support for Asian-Americans who are adjusting to the United States and helping those individuals become more acculturated. This is not much different from the way Christian churches in Yang's research aided both ethnic cultural maintenance and acculturation.

Sometimes ethnic groups create a religious expression that is a mixture of the dominant religion and their own non-Christian faith. This is seen in the emergence of the Ghost Dance among Native Americans in the 1890s (Brown 1971). This religious expression combined elements of Catholicism with the magical beliefs many Native Americans maintained from their own religion. It was believed that the performance of this dance would bring about spiritual powers that would reverse their losses in land, materials, and lives at the hands of the majority group. This expression was a reaction to the oppression and deprivation that the Native Americans suffered and the current social status quo (Jorgensen 1985).

These examples illustrate that the tendency to use religion to promote the interest of a racial/ethnic group is not limited to Christianity. Rather, racial/ethnic groups tend to adjust whatever religious belief system they currently have to create an ideology that serves their own group interest. Rather than being limited to Christian ideology specifically, it is the purpose of religion, generally, to promote systems of meaning that lend religion its power to support the interests of racial groups. The power to shape perspectives on issues of meaning is an important one that racial/ethnic groups are naturally eager to use.

New Horizons: Multiracial Churches and Racial Identity

According to Dougherty (2003), 42.9 percent of all religious congregations contain members of only a single racial group. The powerful tendency of individuals to worship with only members of their own race makes sense if religious institutions are used to promote the interest of the racial groups. But what happens when there is no dominant racial group? While the vast majority of religious institutions in the United States are racially homogeneous, there is a small group of religious institutions that are racially diverse. Religious organizations that are racially mixed have to meet the needs of more than one racial group and cannot easily sustain theologies and practices that work to the advantage of certain racial groups at the expense of other ones. It is important to understand what religion might look like when multiple racial-group interests shape them.

There is evidence that churches in which the numerical majority racial group accounts for less than 80 percent of the population have distinct racial dynamics that others lack (Emerson 2006; Yancey 2001; Yancey 2007). It is unclear whether such differences are related to the theology taught in such institutions. However, the institutional practices of these congregations are different from those of other congregations. Elsewhere (Yancey 2003a), I documented that multiracial churches are likely to create a racially diverse leadership structure, to have a worship style inclusive of different racial groups, and to have organizational flexibility that helps the members of these churches to deal with the cultural challenges that the different groups bring.

There is evidence that these differences are related to very real outcomes for those who attend these institutions. Previous work of mine (Yancey 1999; Yancey 2001) indicates that majority group members in such churches are more likely to have progressive racial attitudes than other majority group members, and people of color who attend these churches are more likely to enjoy economic and educational success than other people of color.[3] Those who attend multiracial churches have a different lifestyle or racial perspective from other individuals, and these churches likely help to shape such differences. These churches can provide racial information for majority group members and educational/economic social capital for people of color. In this sense, such religious institutions do not follow the similar pattern noted in other religious institutions by which they merely reinforce the social desires of a particular racial group. If the racial information and the economic/educational social capital that the majority and minority group members respectively receive from these churches are of value, then multiracial churches have evolved to answer the social needs of both majority and minority group members.

In addition, multiracial churches might serve group interests just as much as racially homogeneous churches. They might do this by serving the interest of a group that is not based on racial categories. For example, Marti (2005) documents a multiracial church concentrating on serving the entertainment community in Southern California. Such a church has become racially diverse in large part because of the fact that this entertainment community is also multiracial. Race no longer becomes the dividing factor; rather, whether a person has an identity as an "innovator" is what differentiates members of this church. In this way, this church can be inclusive of different racial groups and seeks to meet the needs of those of different races but can disregard the concerns of those who do not fit the social identity of innovators.

Whether a religious organization can be inclusive of social groups to such a degree that there is no significant out group rejected by the members of that organization is a question that has not yet been fully answered. It is possible that no religious institutions can be attractive to members of all social groups. Religious institutions that are racially inclusive are not necessarily inclusive across other social groups. If this is true, then all religious institutions might have a tendency to regard their own social group as important and disregard the needs of those in other social groups. Religious institutions are not unique in this propensity, but because it is within religious institutions that we deal with issues of meaning, we should be mindful of the power of this propensity. It allows groups to justify their existences as morally superior to all other groups. For this reason, it is vital to examine religious organizations as a potential source of ethnocentrism in society.

Conclusions

This chapter has focused on patterns of race and religion as they play themselves out in the United States. The concentration on the United States might bias arguments toward the type of religious and racial needs linkages made in this chapter, but these sorts of linkages should be found outside the United States as well. For example, there is no reason Islamic theology has to have the degree of anti-Semitism it currently has in many Middle Eastern countries. In fact, it has been pointed out that at certain points in world history, Jews were better served living in Muslim rather than Christian societies (Cohen 1995; Gil 2004; Lewis 1987). Yet contemporary Christian cultures exist a sizable geographical distance away from Israel, while some Muslim cultures have Israel in their own backyard. Because of this distance, the potential for a global Jewish/Muslim conflict over resources is much more plausible than conflict along Jewish/Christian lines. Thus, it is not surprising that contemporary Muslim theology is generally more overtly anti-Semitic than modern Christian theology.

Other examples would undoubtedly spring up with a careful analysis of other religious conflicts in the world. It is beyond the scope of this chapter to investigate such instances fully. However, linkage of religions and racial-group interests does not uniquely trouble the United States. It is more likely that the reaction of religious ideology and racial position is merely reflective of the general tendencies of religions to be used by social groups for their own ends. These groups do not have to be based on racial distinctions. In fact, racial differences, as they are understood in the United States, are not the most important social dimensions in many other countries. However, the social dimensions that serve to segment the citizens of a particular society or nation can also serve to create different religious expressions and ideologies that promote the social and economic interests of those particular groups.

Because of the power of religion to shape the legitimization forces of a society, it is quite useful for the promotion of these social groups. However, I am not so deterministic as to state that this is the fate of all expressions of faith. There are those, such as the early white abolitionists, who express their faith in such a way that it operates against their own group interest. In doing so, they exhibit the possibility that religion offers an overarching legitimization construct that can guide individuals into making decisions that are for the betterment of the entire society and not just their own racial or social group.

The work done to date suggests that religion generally does not enable individuals to rise above their own group interests, but there are exceptions to even this powerful sociological rule. My interviews with pastors of multiracial churches have indicated several instances of individuals creating churches that do not always support their own group interest. Several white pastors were quite willing to accommodate the needs of people of color through community activism, cultural adjustments within their churches, and incorporation of antiracism or multicultural programs. Some of the pastors of color I interviewed also showed sensitivity to concerns of majority group members in their formation of ministries and public expressions. My interviews confirmed that these efforts were intentional in nature (Yancey 2003a). Religion can be used to overcome some of the ethnocentric racial tendencies in our society if members of religious faiths are encouraged to interact with racial out groups.

NOTES

1. A recent group of atheist books have made this argument (Dawkins 2006; Harris 2005; Hitchens 2007). They contend that religion is a major factor behind many of the dysfunctions in U.S. society. As this chapter will show, some expressions of faith do exploit others, but religion can also be used to meet important sociopsychological needs.

2. Religious answers do not have to be based on supernaturalist expressions of faith. Certain social groups might address questions of meaning without reliance on the supernatural. For example, it is well established that belief in traditional religious expressions is low within the humanities and among social scientists (Ladd and Lipset 1975). Supernatural expressions might be a competitor for expression of morality to the scientific assertions of such individuals (Dynes 1974; Glock and Stark 1965; Waldo 1961), and more secular ideologies such as Marxism or feminism might replace supernatural religion as answers to questions of meaning among academics.

3. Some of these results may be the result of a self-selection effect in which racially progressive whites and economically, educationally successful people of color are more likely to attend multiracial congregations. But a significant amount of research debunks the notion that all of the effects can be explained by self-selection (Dixon and Rosenbaum 2004; Ellison and Powers 1994; Pettigrew and Tropp 2000).

REFERENCES

Aquino, M. P. 1993. "Directions and Foundations of Hispanic/Latino Theology: Toward a Mestiza Theology of Liberation." *Journal of Hispanic/Latino Theology* 1: 5–21.

Banuelas, A. J., ed. 1995. *Mestizo Christianity: Theology from the Latino Perspective.* Maryknoll, N.Y.: Orbis.

Barkun, M. 1994. *Religion and the Racist Right: The Origins of the Christian Identity Movement.* Chapel Hill: University of North Carolina Press.

Bobo, L., J. R. Kluegel, and R. A. Smith. 1997. "Laissez-Faire Racism: The Crystallization of a Kinder, Gentler, Antiblack Ideology." In S. A. Tuch and J. K. Martin, eds., *Racial Attitudes in the 1990s: Continuity and Change.* Westport, Conn.: Praeger.

Boff, L., and C. Boff. 1987. *Introducing Liberation Theology.* Maryknoll, N.Y.: Orbis.

Bonilla-Silva, E. 1999. "The 'New Racism': Toward an Analysis of the U.S. Racial Structure, 1960s–1990s. In P. Wong, ed., *Race, Ethnicity, and Nationality in the United States: Toward the Twenty-First Century.* Boulder, Colo.: Westview, 55–101.

Brown, D. 1971. *Bury My Heart at Wounded Knee: An Indian History of the American West.* New York: Holt, Rinehart and Winston.

Callahan, L. D. 2006. "Redeemed or Destroyed: Re-evaluating the Social Dimensions of Bodily Destiny in the Thoughts of Charles Parham." *Pneuma* 28/2: 203–227.

Cohen, M. R. 1995. *Under Crescent and Cross: The Jews in the Middle Ages.* Princeton, N.J.: Princeton University Press.

Cone, J. H. 1990. *A Black Theology of Liberation.* Maryknoll, N.Y.: Orbis.

Dalton, H. 2002. "Failing to See." In P. S. Rothenberg, ed., *White Privilege: Essential Readings on the Other Side of Racism.* New York: Worth, 15–18.

Dawkins, R. 2006. *The God Delusion.* Boston: Houghton Mifflin.

Dixon, J. C., and M. S. Rosenbaum. 2004. "Nice to Know You? Testing Contact, Cultural and Group Threat Theories of Anti-Black and Anti-Hispanic Stereotypes." *Social Science Quarterly* 85/2: 257–280.

Dougherty, K. D. 2003. "How Monochromatic Is Church Membership? Racial-Ethnic Diversity in Religious Community." *Sociology of Religion* 64/1: 65–85.

Dyer, R. 1997. *White.* New York: Routledge.

Dynes, R. R. 1974. "Sociology as a Religious Movement." *American Sociologist* 9/4: 169–176.

Ecklund, E. H. 2006. *Korean American Evangelicals: New Models for Civic Life.* New York: Oxford University Press.

Elizondo, V. P. 1988. *The Future Is Mestizo: Life Where Cultures Meet.* New York: Meyer-Stone.

Ellison, C., and D. Powers. 1994. "The Contact Hypothesis and Racial Attitudes among Black Americans." *Social Science Quarterly* 75/2: 385–400.

Emerson, M. 2006. *People of the Dream: Multiracial Congregations in the United States.* Princeton, N.J.: Princeton University Press.

Emerson, Michael O., and Christian Smith. 2000. *Divided by Faith: Evangelical Religion and the Problem of Race in America.* Oxford: Oxford University Press.

Espin, O. 1995. "Tradition and Popular Religion: An Understanding of the Sensus Fidelium." In A. J. Banuelas, ed., *Mestizo Christianity: Theology from the Latino Perspective.* Maryknoll, N.Y.: Orbis.

Genovese, E. D. 1998. *A Consuming Fire: The Fall of the Confederacy in the Mind of the White Christian South.* Athens: University of Georgia Press.

Gil, M. 2004. *Jews in Islamic Countries in the Middle Ages.* Boston: Brill.

Glock, C. Y., and R. Stark, R. 1965. *Religion and Society in Tension.* Chicago: Rand McNally.

Goizueta, R. S. 1989. "U.S. Hispanic Mestizaje and Theological Method." *Concilium* 4: 21–30.

Gudykunst, W. B. 2001. *Asian American Ethnicity and Communication.* Thousand Oaks, Calif.: Sage.

Gutierrez, G. 2001. *A Theology of Liberation.* Norwich, U.K.: SCM.

Harris, S. 2005. *The End of Faith: Religion, Terror, and the Future of Reason.* New York: Norton.

Hitchens, C. 2007. *God Is Not Great: How Religion Poisons Everything.* New York: Twelve.

Jo, M. H. 1999. *Korean Immigrants and the Challenge of Adjustment.* Westport, Conn.: Greenwood.

Jordan, W. D. 1968. *White over Black.* Baltimore: Penguin.

Jorgensen, J. G. 1985. "Religious Solutions and Native American Struggles." In B. Lincoln, ed., *Religion, Rebellion, Revolution.* London: Macmillan, 101–25.

Kidwell, C. S., H. Noley, and G. E. Tinker. 2001. *A Native American Theology.* Maryknoll, N.Y.: Orbis.

Kluegel, J. R. 1990. "Trends in Whites' Explanation of the Black-White Gap in Socioeconomic Status, 1977–1989." *American Sociological Review* 55: 512–525.

Ladd, E. C., and S. M. Lipset. 1975. *The Divided Academy: Professors and Politics.* New York: McGraw-Hill.

Lewis, B. 1987. *The Jews of Islam.* Princeton, N.J.: Princeton University Press.

Lincoln, C. E. 1999. *Race, Religion, and the Continuing American Dilemma.* New York: Hill and Wang.

Marti, G. 2005. *A Mosaic of Believers: Diversity and Innovation in a Multiethnic Church.* Bloomington: Indiana University Press.

McConahay, J. B. 1986. "Modern Racism, Ambivalence, and the Modern Racism Scale." In J. Dovidio and S. L. Gaertner, eds., *Prejudice, Discrimination, and Racism: Theory and Research.* New York: Academic.

Mosse, G. L. 1985. *Toward the Final Solution: A History of European Racism.* Madison: University of Wisconsin Press.

Nicholls, B. 2003. *Contextualization: A Theology of Gospel and Culture.* Vancouver, B.C.: Regent College.

Niebuhr, H. R. 1960. "Faith in God and in Gods." In H. R. Neibuhr, ed., *Radical Monotheism and Western Culture.* New York: Harper and Row.

Pettigrew, T. F., and L. R. Tropp. 2000. "Does Intergroup Contact Reduce Prejudice? Recent Meta-Analytic Findings." In S. Oskamp, ed., *Reducing Prejudice and Discrimination.* Mahwah, N.J.: Lawrence Erlbaum.

Raboteau, A. J. 2004. *Slave Religion: The "Invisible Institution" in the Antebellum South.* New York: Oxford University Press.

Schuman, H., C. Steeh, L. Bobo, and M. Krysan. 1997. *Racial Attitudes in America: Trends and Interpretations.* Cambridge, Mass.: Harvard University Press.

Sears, D. O. 1988. "Symbolic Racism." In P. A. Katz and D. A. Taylor, eds., *Eliminating Racism: Profiles in Controversy.* New York: Plenum, 53–84.

Swartley, W. M. 1983. *Slavery, Sabbath, War, and Women.* Scottsdale, Pa.: Herald.

Tillich, P. 1957. *Dynamics of Faith.* New York: Harper and Row.

Tise, L. E. 1987. *Proslavery: A History of the Defense of Slavery in America, 1701–1840.* Athens: University of Georgia Press.

Treat, J. 1996. *Native and Christian: Indigenous Voices on Religious Identity in the United States and Canada.* New York: Routledge.

Twine, F. W. 1997. "Brown-Skinned White Girls: Class, Culture, and the Construction of White Identity in Suburban Communities." In R. Frankenberg, ed., *Displacing Whiteness: Essays in Social and Cultural Criticism.* Durham, N.C.: Duke University Press.

Wagley, C., and M. Harris, M. 1958. *Minorities in the New World: Six Case Studies.* New York: Columbia University Press.

Waldo, D. 1961. "Panel Comments." *Research for Public Policy.* Washington, D.C.: Brookings Institute, 21–29.

Wildman, S. M., and A. D. Davis. 2002. "Making Systems of Privilege Visible." In P. S. Rothenberg, ed., *White Privilege: Essential Readings on the Other Side of Racism*. New York: Worth, 89–95.

Wilmore, G. S. 1998. *Black Religion and Black Radicalism: An Interpretation of the Religious History of the African Americans*. Maryknoll, N.Y.: Orbis.

Wilson, W. J. 1973. *Power, Racism and Privilege*. New York: Free Press.

Wood, F. 1991. *Arrogance of Faith*. New York: Knopf.

Woodley, R. 2004. *Living in Color: Embracing God's Passion for Diversity*. Downers Grove, Ill.: InterVarsity.

Yancey, G. 1999. "An Examination of Effects of Residential and Church Integration upon Racial Attitudes of Whites." *Sociological Perspectives* 42/2: 279–304.

———. 2001. "Racial Attitudes: Differences in Racial Attitudes of People Attending Multiracial and Uniracial Congregations." *Research in the Social Scientific Study of Religion* 12: 185–206.

———. 2003a. *One Body, One Spirit: Principles of Successful Multiracial Churches*. Downers Grove, Ill.: InterVarsity.

———. 2003b. *Who Is White? Latinos, Asians, and the New Black/Nonblack Divide*. Boulder, Colo.: Lynne Rienner.

———. 2007. *Interracial Contact and Social Change*. Boulder, Colo.: Lynne Rienner.

Yang, F. 1999. *Chinese Christians in America: Conversion, Assimilation, and Adhesive Identities*. University Park: Pennsylvania State University Press.

Yang, F., and H. R. Ebaugh. 2001. "Religion and Ethnicity among New Immigrants: The Impact of Majority/Minority Status in Home and Host Countries." *Journal for the Scientific Study of Religion* 40/3: 367–378.

Yinger, J. M. 1970. *The Scientific Study of Religion*. New York: Macmillan.

FOR FURTHER READING

Emerson, Michael O., and Christian Smith. 2000. *Divided by Faith: Evangelical Religion and the Problem of Race in America*. Oxford: Oxford University Press.

Lincoln, C. Eric, and Lawrence H. Mamiya. 1990. *The Black Church in the African American Experience*. Durham, N.C.: Duke University Press

Smith, Christian. 1998. *American Evangelicalism: Embattled and Thriving*. Chicago: University of Chicago Press.

Villafane, Eldin. 1992. *The Liberating Spirit: Toward an Hispanic American Pentecostal Social Ethic*. Lanham, Md.: University Press of America.

Weaver, Jace. 1998. "From I-Hermeneutics to We-Hermeneutics." In Jace Weaver. ed., *Native American Religious Identity: Unforgotten Gods*. Maryknoll, N.Y.: Orbis.

Yang, F. 1999. *Chinese Christians in America: Conversion, Assimilation, and Adhesive Identities*. University Park: Pennsylvania State University Press.

CHAPTER 18

RELIGIOUS DIVERSITY, SECULARIZATION, AND POSTMODERNITY

JOHN G. STACKHOUSE, JR.

"A religion is a very good thing to have—in moderation." This line is a staple of drawing-room comedy, but it's not funny when one considers the fate of religions in modernity. Indeed, religions have been moderated or otherwise manipulated by modern powers in various respects to suit various agendas. In what follows, we shall see how modernity—and particularly its offspring secularization and postmodernism—have attempted to domesticate religion and to manage religious diversity.

According to the so-called secularization thesis, preeminent in sociological theory by the middle of the twentieth century, the process of modernization included several subprocesses, each of which was understood to be a "carrier" of secularization. As societies became more modern, so the theory went, they would inexorably become more secular. Religions, that is, were understood as part of the premodern world and would inevitably decay and disappear in the light of modern progress.

As the modern world has turned out to be not nearly as secular as theorists had expected, however, this thesis has come under serious scrutiny, even certain forms of retraction. It is difficult to maintain that religion is ebbing in the face of resurgent Islamic and Hindu movements, floods of converts to Christianity and Islam in Africa and Asia, evangelical revivals in Latin America and Southeast Asia, and a burgeoning church in China as that country modernizes, not to mention the "Great Exception" already noticed a half-century ago, namely, the United States, arguably the most modern nation on earth and still one of the most religious, by at least most sociological measures of religious observance and influence.

The secularization thesis wasn't entirely wrong, however. Indeed, it simply needs modifying in terms of contingency and probability and away from the determinism of its first articulation. That is, it would be better to say that several processes of modernization act not as *carriers* of secularization (too strong a term, implying inevitability) but as *facilitators* of it. Secularization is not a *necessary* result of modernization, but the record shows that modernization certainly has seemed to help it along.

Secular, Secularity, Secularism, and Secularization

The word *secular* refers simply to "the world" and has no immediately antireligious connotation. Indeed, in the history of the Christian church, some clergy, such as the local priest, were called secular because they served parishioners out in the world while others remained cloistered.

Secularization in its earliest and most fundamental sense, however, is the process by which something that was previously sacred, or held to be sacred, is rendered profane or "worldly" or merely ordinary. It first applied to the seizure of properties belonging to religious orders by monarchs such as Henry VIII of England in the early modern period. The monasteries and their estates were *secularized*. The word now applies to any process by which something once seen in religious terms is reconstrued, reconfigured, or redeployed in secular terms. In this sort of conversation, it is almost always a social process, and on the largest level, it means the process by which a society becomes decreasingly influenced by the institutions, values, and symbols of religion—usually, a particular religion. Where once the Christian church, for example, played a central role in Europe, it now is reduced to mostly ceremonial and charitable functions on the edges of contemporary life.

Secularization, furthermore, must be distinguished from two other closely related terms. The first of these, *secularism*, is not a process but an ideology. More particularly, it is what we might call a genus of ideology. *Secularism* denotes any ideology that is opposed to religion, particularly religion as understood in the everyday sense of "dealing with the supernatural, with God or the gods." Marxism, social Darwinism, secular humanism, and sociobiology thus are all secularist ideologies. The enduring resistance to "organized religion" in France since the Revolution is secularism on a national scale.

The second term *secularity* is neither a process nor an ideology but a situation. It is the social situation in which religion plays no (important) part. Everything that matters in public life is transacted on a horizontal plane, with no reference to the supernatural or spiritual. Secularity, therefore, is the situation in Britain and Scandinavia today and increasingly also in Canada, Australia, New Zealand, the Netherlands, and other countries once much more observantly Christian.

Secularization can result in a condition of secularity, and it can be promoted by, and encourage in turn, secularism. But it need not result, and it has not always resulted, in one or the other of these. Indeed, secularization has often been a process that has emerged from one or another hegemony that so imposes its way of belief and practice on all of its subjects that it implicitly and sometimes drastically secularizes the religions of those subjects. The United States has been such a society, as it has forced non-Christian religions to jettison previous practices (such as the potlatch among West Coast Native Americans or polygamy among early Mormons) in order to conform with its dominant, and dominating, outlook of Protestant Christianity.

Let us return, then, to the plot line of modernization to see how it has facilitated secularization. We will then see how secularization appears to be a kind of social strategy to manage the challenges of religious diversity. And finally, we will see how late modernity—particularly in the ideological form of postmodernism—both confirms and complicates this narrative.

MODERNIZATION AND SECULARIZATION

Modernity is characterized particularly by *differentiation*, the process by which the various modes of life draw apart from one another into discrete social sectors. In order to make this process clear, let's begin with what happens before that process starts.

In a premodern society, such as a medieval village, every social activity is deeply and intrinsically connected with every other. Consider the village blacksmith. He provides a necessary service to the community via his trade. He also serves as a husband to a wife and the father of children, each of whom also functions in the community. He tends the grounds of the local church graveyard. He sits on the village council. He is a fixture at the local tavern. In short, he participates in all of the sectors of village life with the unconscious sense of always being part of village life. His values are the same in each place, as his sense of identity remains the same no matter where he is or what he is doing.

Consider now the modern auto mechanic. During the day, his world is one of technical efficiency. At the end of the workday, he hangs up his tools and stops by the health club, where the emphasis is entirely on the optimization of his physical body. From there, he heads home, where the values shift to the well-being of each member of his family and of the family unit as a whole. After supper, he goes out to attend a religious meeting of some sort, in which the focus is on personal spiritual and moral development.

In modernity, society evolves into a range of social sectors: education, health care, business, entertainment, politics, leisure, and so on. Moreover, each sector increasingly absolutizes its values on its own turf. Thus, at the auto shop, the mechanic's physical or spiritual well-being is completely unimportant. What matters is his technical and economic productivity. That productivity, so important at work, is literally useless—if not, in fact, counterproductive—when he attends his spiritual meeting. Each sector, that is, constitutes a kind of thought-world, and each claims absolute, if temporary, loyalty from those who occupy its space. In religious terms, each of these sectors fosters an idolatry. The modern person, then, proceeds from one temple to another, paying respect to this or that idol in turn, as he makes his way through his day, week, and year.

The differentiation of these various social sectors, furthermore, is facilitated by the suppression at least and eradication at best of all intermediate social structures that would interfere with the smooth passage of individuals from one sector to another. Religions in particular, in their historical and social givenness, in their bloc-ish solidity, are unhelpfully "lumpy" in the eyes of modernity. Religions bind individuals together into communities and ideologies that extend over the boundaries of social sectors and, indeed, make global demands on their adherents that thus interfere with the absolute focus required in each social sector on the values of that sector. Indeed, religious values frequently compete with the orthodoxies of various sectors: "Discipline the body in order to progress up the mystical ladder" versus "Get in shape to attract more bedmates"; "Give your money away to the poor" versus "Maximize your retirement savings." Religions, therefore, like any other mediating social structures, must be brought to heel, if they cannot be made to disappear entirely.

Thus, modernity tends toward *individualization* and particularly toward producing individuals as consumers. All human beings, of course, are consumers. We need to consume to live, taking in air, water, food, and so on. What modernity fosters, however, is an outlook of consumer*ism*. In such an outlook, an individual approaches the world as a sovereign self who is free to prefer just what he likes, to choose just what he likes, and therefore to buy and sell just what he likes. Consumerism results in the commodification of everything, the drastic disintegration of every ethnic tradition or aesthetic style or personal relationship into small, fungible units. (Now one can adopt dreadlocks without any association with Rastafarianism. One can stick Colonial columns on the front of a Bauhaus mansion. One can just "have sex" without "making love.") Life is a mall—or, at least, it must appear that way, however much our choices are indeed circumscribed by the market or the state.

Religions, which demand loyalty and issue commands for all aspects of life that they expect their adherents to obey, clearly get in the way. So if they cannot be eliminated entirely, religions must be commodified in turn. They must be seen to offer certain select "goods" among which individuals are sovereignly free to select just what suits them.

Thus, along with differentiation and individualization comes a *privatization*: the process by which choices that used to be made by societies—whether we shall

all be Christian or Muslim, Catholic or Protestant, Anglican or Puritan—are made by individuals. Further down the highway of modernization, these choices among religious options are expanded into choices among components of those religions, such that they can fit nicely into one's private life and do not interfere with one's enjoyment of other sectors of contemporary society.

In the modern world, then, one is free—nay, encouraged—to start the day with tai chi exercises, relieve the day's stresses with Transcendental Meditation, pursue a Tantric sex workshop on the weekend, and then, if that leads to unpleasantness, console oneself with the Twenty-third Psalm. Each and all of these can be perfectly fine as so many self-selected elements of one's lifestyle, as fragments with which one is assembling a happy private life—as one sovereignly construes "happiness" for oneself.

SECULARIZATION AND SOCIAL COHERENCE

With all of this emphasis on the individual making choices, however, we must recall that societies require coherence. In particular, societies require a certain kind and degree of loyalty to the common good. In the premodern era, societies organized themselves into one or another pyramid of sacred power, with the sovereign at the apex—whether chief, king, or emperor—and everyone participated in the rites of the religion of that society. In the modern era, various ideologies play the role of religion—communism, nationalism, imperialism, and so on. It seems that there is always sacred space to be filled in human life, whether it is in the idolatries of each social sector of a society or as an overarching framework for society as a whole. Scholars have remarked on the "resacralization" of modern life, as something must be found to fill the niche vacated by Christianity—or, in the case of other countries, whatever religion or ideology previously served to bind the individuals of a society together into an economy.

Yet here is where neither the secularization thesis nor the mere negation of that thesis will suffice. For under whatever ideology binds a society into a functioning unit, secularity continues as the everyday attitude of most people in that society. That is to say, in modern societies, the dominant ideology of the hegemonic power is paid lip service when the occasion calls for it, but otherwise, individuals get on with their lives, smoothly moving from one sector to another, enjoying life as best they can according to the shifting values of each successive sector they inhabit. Thus, in truth, has it ever been. The Roman Empire, for example, did not expect its subjects to think of the glory of Rome in everything they did all day. Rome required allegiance when it mattered according to Rome's agenda, namely, when peace or prosperity was threatened. Otherwise, Rome was content for people to believe whatever they wanted to believe and to undertake their choice of spiritual exercises as individuals, religious groups, or nations, with the expectation that they would go about their affairs in a deeply secular way. In this key respect, then, secularization is not a new thing. But modernization has helped it along, particularly in societies where the state's ideology is mild and makes few explicit demands on its citizens.

Modern life is characterized now by religious diversity among other forms of social diversity. There are very few urban societies in the world in which there is not a significant range of religious allegiances to be found. The combined forces of differentiation, individualization, and privatization drastically reconfigure religious societies into affinity groups functioning only in the "leisure" sector of society. Public life, when it is not focused on the ideology of the state, is transacted on an entirely horizontal plane. In one sense, of course, this arrangement is just common sense. People of various viewpoints still have to live together. They have to do business together, they have to make laws together, and so on. So, of course, they will meet and work where their interests coincide—regarding the quotidian.

Yet the marginalization of religions in modern public life amounts to an implicit devaluing of religions and the questions they raise and answer. Modern societies expend great attention on issues judged to be important: economic issues, political issues, moral issues, and more. Where, then, is the attention paid to the diverse and contradictory teachings of religion about whatever lies beyond the grave? Or about which deity deserves our allegiance, if any? Or about what is the highest good to which we can aspire? Or about the nature of humanity, such that we then can think properly about issues of human rights, care for the poor, promote justice, and so on?

The strongly implied judgment of modern societies around the world—whatever their official ideologies—is that the religions have nothing important to say, and therefore they do not deserve public attention. Indeed, the privileges enjoyed by religious institutions under previous regimes that were much more sympathetic to this or that religion or to "religion in general" are ebbing fast in modernity. Religions increasingly have to justify themselves on terms foreign to their own values. A Buddhist, for example, would say that his local temple is valuable particularly as his main access point to the teaching of the Buddha and to the community of Buddhists. But when society doesn't care about Buddhist teachings or communities per se, then the Buddhist temple has to make its case in terms of charity, education, and other secular values. And as it does so, furthermore, it will then be shaped at least to some extent by the social pressure to understand itself increasingly in those terms.

It needs to be made more clear than it sometimes is that modern societies do not have to become secularized. A society could enjoy all of the benefits of science and technology, democracy, free markets, and other indicators of modernity and still be thoroughly suffused with an Islamic or Confucianist religious consensus. But there are few of those, and the common experience of contemporary life is that of religious diversity. Much more common is the secularization of public life, and thus of the whole pattern of life, public and private, such that religion is relegated to the individual, private sphere of personal fulfillment.

SECULARIZATION AND POSTMODERNISM

Postmodernism is an outlook, and especially an epistemology, that is prompted by politics. Postmodernism is deeply concerned about oppression and violence and is deeply impressed by how violent oppressors characteristically justify themselves by way of a legitimizing ideology. Thus, it is "incredulous toward such meta-narratives," to paraphrase Jean-François Lyotard. Postmodernism attacks oppressive power by undermining its self-serving story at the root—that is, by undermining the validity of *any* such story. Postmodernism's skeptical epistemology is unleashed in the service of justice to the marginalized.

In its mild form, postmodernism is simply epistemological humility. It is the recognition that each of us and all of us are limited by our current place and time and by the effects of all of the places and times we have experienced heretofore. As such, this mild form of postmodernism is quite amenable to various religious out-looks, such as Judaism or Christianity, which also speak of the finitude and, indeed, the fallenness of human knowing.

In what we might call its medium form, however, postmodernism tries to mod-erate religion in the public sphere by undermining its epistemic claims. The hope here is that religious people will not kill one another or the rest of us if they can be convinced that they should not be as certain of their religious doctrines as they currently are. And the best way to do that, it is supposed, is to undermine every-body's certainty. Therefore, no one should be so confident of his or her values that he or she would forcibly impose them on others or live in any other way that would coerce other people according to those values.

Whether this approach should truly be called postmodern is an interesting question. It is the position of John Locke, who sought to preserve England from any more of the religious strife that had wracked it for almost two centuries. Locke taught that we can be certain of precious little, and so it would behoove all of us to practice more epistemic, which was to say religious, humility. Public life should be conducted according to commonly accepted principles, worked up from empirical evidence and universal reason. Religion was fine, as long as it was moderated in this way. And by that, Locke meant as long as religion stayed out of public view (except on ceremonial occasions, which in the nature of the case didn't really count) and remained a matter of private reflection and ritual. This was also the view of Imman-uel Kant, Thomas Jefferson, and many other influential modern thinkers, and it continues to be the view of many modern people today. It results in public secu-larity and the concomitant implicit devaluing of religion as worthy of only private pursuit by those citizens who happen to be disposed toward it.

Strong postmodernism, finally, amounts to an antireligious secularism. Since it is resistant to all metanarratives, to all claims to have "the Big Story" that explains all other stories, then it is resistant to religions, most of which claim to offer exactly such narratives. Some religious believers—notably, Christians in Europe and North America—have hailed the rise of postmodernism as a tide sweeping away the ideological dominance of scientism, materialism, nationalism, and other foes of religious belief. But they have often failed to realize that this tide sweeps *everyone* out to sea, to an ocean without shores or stars.

This form of postmodernism, however, is admirably suited to modern society and in this sense is really hypermodern, rather than something quite different from modernity, as might be understood by the word *postmodern*. A postmodernist of this sort can flit from one social sector to another as moderns do, but the postmodernist does so without the slightest sense of strain—even between social sectors with radically opposed values. Since everything is simply a shifting kaleidoscope of fragmented surfaces, one simply composes one's life as an ever-changing mosaic out of attractive bits that come one's way. (Postmodernists delight in the metaphor of the *bricoleur*, the rag picker who makes what he can out of the detritus he happens upon.) Postmodernism of this sort, therefore, might well undercut ideologies that legitimize power. But it has nothing to offer as an alternative to sheer consumerism and the powers that foster it. Instead, it nicely confirms the sense of the self as the center of choice—indeed, the center of authority. (The most radical postmodernists, it might be noted, question whether there is any self there at all to do the choosing or whether, instead, what we take to be selves are merely loci of various dynamic social forces. But that outlook isn't a happy one and doesn't serve marketing and political campaigns well at all, so it is discussed and believed only in select circles.)

The strong form of postmodernism is the one that gets the most attention and provokes the most fear among religious believers—as well it should. But it is not (yet) the view of most modern elites or of the rank and file. True, an informal, implicit version of it has been showing up more and more in opinion polls that demonstrate that no matter what people call themselves, increasingly they are practicing a sort of do-it-yourself religion—or, better, "spirituality." Such people are among the most interesting instances of religious diversity in our time, as they call themselves Christians or Jews, for example, while also asserting belief in reincarnation or astrology. Nonetheless, in its full-blown form, such strong postmodernism continues to be an exotic outlier in contemporary life, found mostly in university classrooms and bookstores. The main cultural struggle instead continues to be among devotees of various competing Big Stories: evolutionary naturalism, Christianity, Islam, native religions, nationalism, hedonism, and more.

THE SOCIAL CHALLENGE

What can and should be the destiny of all of those who strongly believe in this or that Big Story in religiously diverse societies?

The first fact to face is that some religions or philosophies simply cannot accommodate religious diversity. Such traditions teach that they alone have the truth or at least an adequate supply and interpretation of it. They assert that only their way will do in the structuring of human life, and so they are necessarily totalitarian. Some of us naturally think of Islamists, Christian fundamentalists, or members of the Indian Hindutva movement in this category. But let us be careful to include secularist ideologies as well. Nazis talked this way, as have Communists, with disastrous results. And we should recall that there are popular evolutionary naturalists, such as Richard Dawkins, who manifest similar disgust for ideological diversity and clearly prefer society to include as members only those who think as they do.

In the societies that pride themselves on tolerance of diversity and welcoming people from around the world, it is an unpleasant fact indeed to recognize that some people's most heartfelt convictions militate precisely against such a hospitable stance. But we must recognize that fact. And it is one that we have hardly yet begun to wrestle with seriously in our immigration policies, citizenship procedures, and public education. Many of us continue to believe that it should not matter what people think in the privacy of their own minds, as long as they behave themselves "properly" in public. But such a belief depends on Lockean divisions between belief and practice and between private and public that are completely impossible for serious believers in Big Stories. No, we have to see that people act according to their beliefs, and some beliefs are simply inimical to any society that wishes to protect, let alone promote, religious diversity.

Other strong believers, however, hold to religions or philosophies that can make room for and even endorse religious diversity in a society. It is true that most of the examples of religious diversity in a culture that we can find in the past are examples of cultures dominated by a single outlook that was tolerant and even welcoming of at least some other outlooks. (One thinks of Moghul India or Moorish Spain.) Still, those positive precedents of religious toleration do remain instructive for us. The present generation and those that follow will face the novel and more challenging task of constructing a genuine multiculturalism that welcomes all who will contribute to the common project out of their different fundamental commitments.

Multiculturalism, that is, can no longer be a sort of hobby for a white Christian—or white post-Christian—majority to enjoy as they patronize the foods and folkways of small minorities among them. Instead, we must recognize that formerly small minorities have risen to a sort of political and social critical mass in many countries. They are now significant players in our societies, with financial, political, and cultural power. And we need to find a way within our strong religious and philosophical commitments not only to endure but also to enjoy such important differences.

Jewish theologians have long reconciled the special status of the Jewish people under God with their varying social positions in a wide range of cultures over two millennia. Christian theologians have been working for more than a generation to develop a genuinely Christian embrace of cultural pluralism whereby Christians seek neither to dominate nor to withdraw from the tensions and compromises of religiously diverse public life. Today it is encouraging to see Islamic theologians engaging in the same work of exploring their religious traditions and scriptures for resources to equip and inspire Muslims to participate fully in cultures they do not dominate now or seek to dominate in the future—and even to make room, as Islamic regimes have in the past, in Muslim-majority countries for those of different views.

I emphasize theologians in this context not to deprecate the work of philosophers, political scientists, sociologists, and others within the ranks of the strong believers. These other experts have much to offer communities of strong belief as they analyze the nature of religiously diverse societies and offer counsel that emerges from such analysis. Nonetheless, it is the theologians who will be able to encourage their fellow believers with the crucial religious legitimization for participating in a society that is not fully, or even mostly, governed according to the values of that religion. It will be the theologians who will assure the nervous or the zealous among their ranks that it is all right—and, in fact, it might be best—for there to be multiple religious and philosophical options available to one's fellow citizens.

What, then, about social coherence? Each country and, indeed, each region will have to sort out the grounds upon which citizens of different ultimate commitments can make penultimate commitments to each other and to that society as a whole. Commitment to the rule of law, commitment to private property, commitment to compassion for one's fellow human being, commitment to justice and the human rights of everyone, commitment to democracy—these are the practical, procedural commitments that can frame a common life of mutual benefit among people of varying ultimate commitments.

Despite the long history of religious diversity in cultures around the world, therefore, it remains an urgent task for religions—and their secular philosophical counterparts—to work out a legitimate theoretical structure within which people can conceptualize and then enjoy genuine multiculturalism, including genuine religious diversity. This is, therefore, no time for such religions to allow themselves to be moderated by hegemonic powers that seek to keep them nicely out of public view and cultural influence.

FOR FURTHER READING

Berger, Peter L., ed. 1999. *The Desecularization of the World: Resurgent Religion and World Politics*. Washington, D.C.: Grand Rapids, Mich.: Eerdmans.

Casanova, José. 1994. *Public Religions in the Modern World*. Chicago: University of Chicago Press.

Gay, Craig M. 1998. *The Way of the (Modern) World: Or, Why It's Tempting to Live as if God Doesn't Exist*. Grand Rapids, Mich.: Eerdmans.

Griffiths, Paul J. 2001. *Problems of Religious Diversity*. Oxford: Blackwell.

Martin, David. 2005. *On Secularization: Towards a Revised General Theory*. Aldershot, U.K.: Ashgate.

Stackhouse, John G., Jr. 2002. *Humble Apologetics: Defending the Faith Today*. New York: Oxford University Press.

Taylor, Charles. 2007. *A Secular Age*. Cambridge, Mass.: Belknap.

Taylor, Charles, et al. 1994. *Multiculturalism: Examining the Politics of Recognition*. Princeton, N.J.: Princeton University Press.

CHAPTER 19

....

MULTIPLE MODERNITIES AND RELIGION

....

CHRISTIAN SMITH AND BRANDON VAIDYANATHAN

MODERNIZATION THEORY TO MULTIPLE MODERNITIES

....

ONE master theoretical concept in the social sciences that has for many decades organized focuses, problems, explanations, and interpretations in the study of religion has been that of "modernity." Social-scientific theories have long been organized around the premodern/modern conceptual divide, seeking to understand the institutional and cultural transformations from the one to the other. In sociology, Marx, Tönnies, Weber, Durkheim, Simmel, Parsons, and many others explored processes of economic growth, differentiation, rationalization, individualization, urbanization, and so on, as central dynamics of a theorized process of modernization. Until the end of the 1900s, anthropology likewise was defined as a discipline per se by the very constitutive idea of the existence and interest of "traditional" premodern tribes, societies, and cultures—in contrast to the societies of modernity. Particularly important is the fact that all such social-science theorists and theories consistently believed that modernity was unavoidably destructive of religion, belief in spiritual realities and objective universals, nonnaturalistic metaphysics, and "traditional" cultures and perspectives generally (see Birnbaum and Lenzer 1969). By theoretical definition, religious faith and belief in such things as gods and natural laws, for example, became cognitively deviant and were expected certainly to fade away with the progress of time and the advance of modernity (see, e.g., Wallace 1966, 265; Wilson 1982, 19).

This inherited central focus on modernity in the social sciences took a particularly sharp and systematized form after World War II. The second half of the twentieth century saw the development of theories that posited modernity and modernization as largely universal, uniform, predictable, and entailing inevitable dynamics inexorably transforming the world. As Weinberg noted, these convergence theorists, like the Enlightenment *philosophes*, assumed an evolutionary notion of human perfectibility—indeed, in this era, there seemed little reason to assume diversity when taking into consideration the notion of progress—and essentially posited that modern societies would have "common destinations, despite their origins" (1969, 1–2). In sociology, Talcott Parsons (1951) theorized universal "pattern variables"[1] and processes of evolutionary development of differentiation organizing the process of modernization. Along similar lines, economist Walt Rostow (1960) theorized the "Five Stages of Economic Growth" through which all societies would pass in order to develop and modernize. An entire "economic and social development" industry worked for decades under such theoretical notions.

Thus, until as late as the 1970s, a very particular theoretical model for understanding modernity and modernization dominated much of the social sciences. This model continues to exert powerful effects in the social sciences through its residual background assumptions and models of thought—even when individual social scientists were or are not "modernization" scholars. In addition to supposing that modernity and modernization are inevitable and inexorable, this model assumes that modernity produces predictable patters of uniformity and standardization (see, e.g., Theodorson 1953), which, it turns out, resembles the particular experience of western Europe. A key element of the uniformity that modernity was believed to engender was the necessary and inevitable decline or even abandonment of religion. Although many scholars have rejected such an approach, it is by no means entirely disbelieved even today, as the writings of scholars from Ronald Inglehart (1997) to Steve Bruce (2002) attest. The shared account, in C. Wright Mills's paraphrase of Parsons, was: "Once the world was filled with the sacred—in thought, practice, and institutional form. After the Reformation and the Renaissance, the forces of modernization swept across the globe and secularization, a corollary historical process, loosened the dominance of the sacred. In due course, the sacred shall disappear altogether except, possibly, in the private realm" (Mills 1959, 32–33).

Numerous developments in recent decades, however, have opened up an important theoretical space for the reconsideration of modernity in more empirically realistic and metaphysically open terms. Among the most promising of these is the multiple modernities thesis, which proposes that modernity and its features and forces can actually be received, developed, and expressed in significantly different ways in different parts of the world and—by extension, I suggest (Smith et al. 1998)—by different communities living in single societies. Thus, while the long-observed forces of modernization still operate through powerful historical changes around the globe, the original thesis of uniformity and standardization, including the related inevitable-secularization thesis, are suspended, if not rejected. This simple yet fundamental, even radical, change in the old assumptions, images, and expectations about modernity and modernization opens up at this moment an opportunity for rethinking, retheorizing, and reframing our empirical analyses in the social sciences, particularly with regard to religion. This new perspective allows us to recognize the significant diversity and pluralism of religious forms—within single societies as well as on a global level—which engage with different aspects of modernity in a variety of ways. This opportunity creates the conditions for a potential paradigm shift in social-science (and, in due time, popular) understandings of the actual nature of the world in which we live.

Several developments in recent decades have brought us to this moment. First, by the 1970s, scholars started to recognize and point out problems with the dominant theory of modernization. Gusfield (1967) argued that religious traditions and modern developments have a dynamic and at times mutually reinforcing relationship and exposed several false assumptions in modernization theory about the tradition-modernity relationship.[2] The assumption of industrialization as a necessary threat to tradition turned out to be false, with scholars putting forth evidence suggesting that "a considerable amount of traditional life can flourish at a higher level in the process of industrialization" (Lauer 1971, 885; see also Gusfield 1967). Indeed, as Casanova noted, even viewing secularization as a key process of modernity should have led us to expect a variety of historical patterns, pathways, and outcomes across societies in the first place (1994, 24–25).

Second, enthusiastic attempts in development economics to replace traditional forms with structures imported from the West led in many cases to embarrassing, if not disastrous, failures. As a result, development economists have recently begun to take much more seriously the importance of traditional communities and institutions, as well as religious and ethnic factors (Piasecki and Wolnicki 2004). Scholars began to argue that modernization at the social or political level could happen independently of industrialization, which opened the possibility of conceptualizing modernity without a conventionally understood "modernization" (Lauer 1971, 886; see also Anderson 1974; Wrigley 1972). This presented the possibility of a variety of pathways of "development" and, hence, forms of modernity.

Third, a growing disenchantment with modernity emerged in many sectors—particularly as expressed in "postmodernism"—in the later twentieth century, which focused on useful reconsiderations of the particular historical and cultural situatedness of the modern project (see Murphy 1988; Rosenau 1992), although not all aspects were particularly smart or salutary (such as postmodernist antihumanism and relativism).[3] Reflecting the "cultural turn" in the social sciences, various scholars have proposed a "cultural theory" of modernity (e.g., Taylor 1995; Friese and Wagner 2000), which allows us to recognize modernity itself as a specific "cultural program" and to understand its history as a "continual constitution and reconstitution of a multiplicity of cultural programs" (Eisenstadt 2000, 2).

Fourth, the emergence of various forms of ethnic and religious nationalism in the twentieth century served as a further affront to the standard received theoretical frame of modernization theory, which expected the predominance of a civic/secular nationalism and the extinction of the ethnic/religious variety (Spohn 2003). As Harle notes, theorists such as Parsons (1951) and Deutsch (1953) had assumed that modernization would produce individuals who would simply be unaffected by racial, traditional, or ethnic concerns and that such primitive institutional forms would disappear in modern society (2000, 2). In light of the new developments, some theorists saw the development of ethnic/religious nationalism and religious fundamentalism "as a defensive reaction against the forces of globalization or the emerging world system" (Spohn 2003, 266; see also Beyer 1994; Chase-Dunn 1989; Luhmann 1984; Wallerstein 1999). Another account that arose along similar lines was that of the "clash of civilizations" (Huntington 1996), which argued that the future of global politics would entail cultural and religious conflicts along the fault lines between various civilizations. In addition, "postcolonial" and "subaltern" studies have driven home a similar point about the capacities for resistance and alteration by local and subjugated cultures (Chakrabarty 2002). While recognizing these realms of conflict, the thesis of multiple modernities holds that neither the convergence nor the clash account can serve as "the one dominant narrative" each purports to be (Katzenstein 2006, 4). Rather, the evidence of diverse forms of secularization, as well as religious resurgence, forces us to consider how the cultural program of modernity is undergoing continual reinterpretations and reappropriations, thus generating new forms, dimensions, and processes of modernity (Eisenstadt 2000, 24; Spohn 2003, 268–269).

Analyzing Multiple Modernities

In light of the shortcomings of dominant understandings of modernity, the thesis of multiple modernities has been articulated by scholars from a variety of nationalities and disciplines (see Arnason 1989 and 1991; Arnason, Eisenstadt, and Wittrock 2004; Berger and Huntington 2003; Casanova 2008; Delanty 1999; Eisenstadt 2000 and 2003; Friese and Wagner 2000; Hefner 1998; Kamali 2006; Katzenstein 2006; Kaya 2003 and 2004; Lau 2003; Lee 2008; Martin 2005; Roniger and Waisman 2002; Spohn 2003; Taylor 2000, 2004, 2005, and 2007; Therborn 2003; Wagner 1993, 2000, 2001a, 2001b, and 2001c; Wittrock 2000; Yack 1997). The handful of scholars currently thinking about the idea of multiple modernities have not formulated a coherent and well-developed theory, but their statements are highly suggestive. Political theorist and philosopher Charles Taylor, for example, observes that a cultural approach to modernity appreciates that

> transitions to what we might recognize as modernity, taking place in different civilizations, will produce different results, reflecting the civilizations' divergent starting points. Their understandings of the person, social relations, states of mind, goods and bads, virtues and vices, sacred and profane, are likely to be distinct. The future of the world will be one in which all societies will undergo

change, in institutions and outlook, and for some these changes may be parallel. But it will not converge, because new differences will emerge from the old. Thus, instead of speaking of "modernity" in the singular, we should better speak of "multiple modernities" (2000, 367)

Similarly, sociologist Ibrahim Kaya argues that modernity should be treated as "an open-ended horizon in which there are spaces for multiple interpretations," which "implies a critique of totalizing theories of modernity" and opens the door to an understanding of "the plurality of modernities" (2004, 37–39; see also Kolakowski 1997). Although not shared by all of its proponents, the dominant approach in this paradigm—as well as the focus of the recent criticism it has begun to receive (e.g., Knöbl 2006a and 2006b; Schmidt 2006)—is comparative civilizational analysis (Arnason, Eisenstadt, and Wittrock 2004; Eisenstadt 2000 and 2003; Spohn 2003). One advantage of this approach is that it provides a broad enough comparative framework within which to study, on a global level, the diversity of ways in which the "distinct civilizational premises of modernity" unfold (Eisenstadt 2004, 49). A few key examples should serve to illustrate this:

1. *European modernities.* As the birthplace of the Enlightenment and hence of the project of modernity, Europe—western Europe in particular—has been considered by many sociologists of religion as the one place where the old secularization thesis of religious decline unambiguously holds true (Bruce 2002; Casanova 1994). However, several recent developments have brought questions of the role and importance of religion back to the fore: the fall of communism and the reunification of Europe, the growing ethnic and religious diversity as a result of immigration, and the intensification of cooperative and competitive interactions among various forms of secularism, Christianity, and Islam (Casanova 2008; Spohn 2007). In this light, the multiple modernities thesis serves as a more adequate theoretical approach than the prevailing modernization/secularization perspective to understand the continued importance of religion, both at the level of individuals and in its engagement with culture, politics, nation-states, and especially in the question of European identity (Byrnes and Katzenstein 2006; Davie 2000; Spohn 2007). The dominant model is unable to account, for example, for the diversity in forms of church-state relations and patterns of secularization across Europe (Martin 2005; Robbers 1995), the considerable ethnic and religious diversity resulting from immigration (Esposito and Burgat 2003; Spohn and Triandafyllidou 2003), new resurgent forms of Christianity in Europe (Catholic, Protestant, and Orthodox) (Kepel 1994; Madeley and Enyedi 2003; Shadid and Koningsveld 2002; Stoelting 1991), and the diverse paths that postcommunist societies appear to be forging with regard to their religious futures (Froese 2004a and 2004b; Ramet 1998).

Some scholars have argued that the present condition of European modernity needs to be understood as a "second modernity," characterized by globalization and a heightened unpredictability and "reflexivity" (Beck, Bonss, and Lau 2003). While this seems to denote a distinctly Eurocentric phenomenon—the concept aims to signify a development quite distinct from the first modernity, which arose in Europe during the Enlightenment—"it is possible to imagine 'other modernities' from which one could study the *'non-European routes to and through second modernity'*" (Beck, Bonss, and Lau 2003, 7; emphasis in original). However, scholars have argued that recent developments in several countries, especially in the Asian Pacific, cannot be considered as mirroring either first or second modernity. Differences in paths and outcomes across such cases suggest a model in which such second modernity can be seen as "only a particular expression rather than a template," that is, as one type within a broader conception of multiple modernities (Lee 2008, 63–64).

2. *Asian modernities.* Japan emerged in the 1980s as a global economic powerhouse, which did not simply come to conform culturally or socially to the western European model and serves as another case that defies the assumption of a single, secularizing pathway to modernity. As Bellah notes, while being influenced for several centuries by Buddhism, Confucianism, and Christianity, as well as Indian and Chinese civilizations, Japan has constantly adapted and reformulated these influences in light of its own traditions and heritage (2003). Such hybridization, along with its structure of a relatively autonomous and homogeneous state, enabled the importance of religion to persist even within a secular-democratic state, with the nation only selectively adopting elements of Western modernization (Spohn 2003, 280–281; see also Eisenstadt 1996; Eisenstadt 2003, 723–758; Gusfield 1967). In addition, studies of Japanese modernities have now begun to consider modern Japanese influences on other cultures (Befu and Guichard-Anguis 2001; Lau 2003).

China, while clearly economically modernizing at an impressive rate, again does not seem to be simply evolving inexorably toward conformity to a western European model. As Zhang argues, China's unique path to modernity suggests the possibility of modernity emerging without the conventional pathway of industrialization (2000; see also Lauer 1971; Anderson 1974; Wrigley 1972). Religion continues to remain an important concern in contemporary Chinese society, and studies have examined the relationship between Christianity and the communist state, Buddhist and Daoist revivals, and debates on the significance of Confucianism (Yang and Tamney 2005; Weiming 1999).

India serves as yet another case in which the developments of modernity are characterized by peculiar hybridizations. In particular, the meaning of secularism in India is markedly different from conventional Western understandings, such as the French ideal of *laïcité*. Understanding how the multiple meanings of this concept are anchored in diverse forms of Hinduism sheds light on why the question of secularism in contemporary Indian politics has become polarized between Hindu-accommodationist and Hindu-exclusivist perspectives (Rao 2006, 63, 77). Another complication in the Indian case is that the Western/Christian understanding of secular as implying a church-state separation makes little sense when analyzing religious traditions that lack a centralized authority. (Casanova makes a similar observation about the case of Confucianism in China [2008].) In India, this situation has further given rise to the thorny questions of Hindu identity and what counts as Hinduism (Rao 2006, 48–49, 66–68), matters that scholars argue have been significantly influenced by Westernized/Orientalist constructions of the Indian other (Sontheimer and Kulke 1991; Thapar 1993; van der Veer 1994). In such light, not surprisingly, prominent Indian scholars have argued for the need to reject conventional understandings of modernity in favor of something along the lines of a multiple-modernities approach (Chatterjee 1997; Gidwani 2002; Oommen 2004; Prakash 1999; Sivaramakrishnan and Agrawal 2000).

The analysis of religion in modern India is not restricted to the diverse forms of Hinduism but also examines the importance of Islam, Christianity, and Buddhism, as well as the interactions between these various traditions and secular institutions (Robinson 2004; see also Fazalbhoy 1997; Monius 2001; van der Veer 1994). Hinduism, furthermore, is not confined to India but plays an important role in other countries in Southeast Asia (Bakker 1993, Hefner 1985; Hefner and Horvatich 1997; Lee and Ackerman 1997) and in its global diaspora (Vertovec 2000).

3. *Islamic modernities.* The horizon of modernity is also characterized by the numerous modern Islamic and quasi-Islamic states and societies, such as Saudi Arabia, Iran, Oman, and others, which appear to be appropriating modernity selectively and applying it in more customized fashion than traditional modernization theory would have expected. While some scholars have held to the secularization perspective that modernization in Islamic countries will lead to privatization (Tibi 1990), others have argued that Islamic tradition, because of its unique historical and theological resources, is exceptionally suited to supporting both modernization and religious traditionalism (Gellner 1981). Still others take issue with both such perspectives, pointing out, for example, the significant divisions among Muslims regarding whether or not Islam should be understood as a "complete social order" (Hefner 1998, 91; see also Eickelman and Piscatori 1996, 159; Moussalli 1995, 69–70). Tensions among the variety of traditionalist, populist, neotraditionalist, and intellectualist groups in some cases have fostered democratization and in others have provoked antimodern and neofundamentalist reactions (Hefner 1998, 91). These factors are further complicated in regions that were under colonial rule, such as various African nations. As a result, monolithic categorizations of "the Muslim world" are simply untenable; in fact, even within a single society such as Iran, it is possible to recognize several distinct modernization programs undertaken by the state, with significantly different goals and ideological motivations (Kamali 2006). Turkey is yet another case with a unique trajectory, from its central position in the Islamic tradition, to adopting a state-imposed secularization and modernization program that entailed a privatization of religion, to the recent forms of resurgence of Islam in the public sphere (Mutlu 1996; Spohn 2003, 277). Studies have also shown that the rise of fundamentalism is not merely a reactionary movement against globalization emerging from people living in poverty but is in many cases a middle-class phenomenon (Moaddel 2002; Mutlu 1996; Tamney 1979). Additionally, there is the experience of the many traditional Muslims living in urban centers of western Europe who, by all accounts, are very selectively adopting "Western" ways, even if they seek to be and understand themselves to be entirely "modern" (Allievi and Nielsen 2003; Modood, Triandafyllidou, and Zapata-Barrero 2006;

Samad and Sen 2007), as disruptive events in Paris in 2005 demonstrated (Brown 2007; Haddad and Balz 2006).

What was once taken to be a straightforward secularization theory has been further complicated by the empirical fact of the widespread continuation of "traditional" religion both in the United States (Casanova 1994; Davidman 1991; Neitz 1987; Smith 1996; Smith et al. 1998; Stark and Finke 2000; Warner 1993) and in much of the global South (e.g., Berger 1996; Jenkins 2006). Particularly important is the recent growth of Pentecostalism in Latin America, Africa, and, indeed, throughout the world (Anderson 1992; Casanova 2001 and 2008; Freston 1997; Gifford 2004; Robbins 2004).

The point here is not that these facts and events are to be praised or that they decisively refute the standard model of modernization that posited inexorable movement to uniformity but rather that these real-world facts and events have forced a reconsideration of the received model of modernity and, instead, call for an account that is more capable of recognizing the significant pluralism and diversity across modern societies.

CRITICISMS AND FUTURE DIRECTIONS

The thesis of multiple modernities is not without its critics. Knöbl contends that "civilization" is a problematic unit of analysis that suffers from definitional imprecision and assumes an unwarranted endogenous homogeneity (2006a and 2006b). Another limitation it suffers from is the "small-N problem" of too many variables and too few cases; attributing (or rejecting) causal factors becomes problematic in the absence of sufficient cases. The empirical problem is only exacerbated when theorists try to incorporate the role of religious factors from the distant past— Eisenstadt goes as far back as the origin of the Axial Age—in order to explain different development paths of civilizations (Knöbl 2006b).

One solution might be to use *region* rather than *civilization* as the unit of analysis, as Knöbl does in his study examining how the contingencies that shaped the history of the American South are neglected by the civilizational model which can impose a false unity (2006a). Region can serve as a "more open and multidimensional" concept than civilization and would allow us to include geographical areas not restrained by present nation-state boundaries (Knöbl 2006a, 129). Knöbl also counsels that we restrict ourselves to more recent history, for example, within the last two centuries, instead of looking for empirically untenable explanatory factors in the remote past (2006b).

A stronger criticism is launched by Schmidt, who complains that the multiple modernities thesis overstates the claim of diversity, offers no new insights compared with modernization theory, and itself provides only a rather poor account of modernity (2006). Its theorists, he claims, have not provided a coherent alternative definition of the concept of modernity to justify speaking of the term in plural form. Furthermore, he argues that the multiple modernities thesis prematurely rejects the homogenization claims of modernization theory; its excessive focus on culture, religion, and diversity neglects the homogeneity of institutional forms across cultures and civilizations. Jameson has argued similarly that theorists of multiple modernities or "alternative modernities" have simply ignored the fact of hegemonic global capitalism (2002, 13). As important as these criticisms are, Schmidt's suggestion simply to adopt a version of the old modernization theory and continue to assume stages of modernization or the inevitability of convergence are untenable (2006, 83, 86–87).

Such critics do establish that more work needs to be done to explore, refine, and develop the thesis of multiple modernities. In the absence of a shared cohesive framework, this calls for future collaboration among its many proponents. We can, for present purposes, name a few of the key ideas underlying the multiple modernities thesis, to give at least a preliminary sense of its central assumptions and approach. First, from the multiple-modernities perspective, a sound understanding of modernity must reject older social-evolutionary and functionalist assumptions about social change that cast certain processes as universal and inevitable. In their stead, assumptions about the centrality of contingency, complexity, timing, and context—which themselves reflect deeper assumptions about human agency and freedom—are adopted. While this does not rule out the possibility of various forms of institutional convergence, it eliminates the component of inevitability from the account.

Second, modernity needs to be seen not simply as a series of institutional changes, which positive science can somehow track and predict, but as a cultural project of purposive human agents operating from the start with different categories and beliefs about humanity, society, morality, purpose of life, and so on. This cultural dimension of modernity opens up possibilities for dramatic differences that the older institutionally focused theories of modernity could not appreciate. Modernity needs to be understood as a *cultural* entity every bit as much as it is a *structural* fact. By reflecting social science's "cultural turn" in this way, the multiple modernities thesis opens up new possibilities for considering ranges of options that modern people and societies might take when it comes to matters of religion, science, and morality. At the same time, critics of the civilizational approach have pointed out problems with essentializing notions of "culture" or "civilization" that assume an internal homogeneity that is not always tenable. In this regard, smaller units of analysis such as regions or subcultures, as well as the importance of exogenous and contingent factors shaping cultural trajectories, should prove helpful.

Third, the multiple modernities thesis recognizes that modernity itself is not a simple coherent unity but is in certain key ways an internally conflicted conglomeration of movements (see Himmelfarb 2004; Eisenstadt 2004, 53–54). For example, contained within the single project of modernity are strong tendencies toward both autonomy and control—concepts that have their own internal ambiguities (Friese and Wagner 2000, 33). On the one hand, modernity liberates individuals from the constraining bonds of tradition, generating a multiplicity of options that give rise to choice and pluralism. At the same time, modernity imposes certain forms of discipline, uniformity, rationalization, and social control that counter individual liberation. Most early sociological theorists were aware, at least in some ways, of such complexities, contradictions, and unintended consequences involved in the processes of modern social change. What remains to be developed, however, is a fuller understanding about the implications of how this internally contradictory and "unstable compound" of modernity shapes prospects for multiplicity and diverse outcomes. This also calls for work toward improved definitional and conceptual clarity on the concept of modernity itself, in order to make meaningful comparisons across its multiplicity of forms.

Fourth, rather than working with an underlying positivist-empiricist model of social science, theorists might adopt an approach such as critical realism, which conceives of societies as open systems in which multiple and complex real (though perhaps directly unobservable) causal forces operate interactively to produce distinct outcomes (see, e.g., Archer 1995 and 2000; Bhaskar 1997 and 1998; Collier 1994; Smith 2008).

Fifth, much of what has been promoted by the received modernization model is actually less a scientific description of actual processes of social change and more a particular normative (antireligious, skeptical Enlightenment) ideology of "progress" and the good society (secular) masquerading as objective social science. Having unmasked the normative and ideological biases baked into standard theories of modernity, we will stand in a much better position to conduct open, relatively objective, empirical and analytical social science that better interprets the operations of the real social world.

Debates and limitations notwithstanding, the multiple modernities thesis provides a promising and helpful theoretical approach to frame and interpretively explain the vast body of empirical knowledge that has accumulated in recent decades about the failure of the "inevitable and homogenizing" version of modernization theory. Particularly for scholars trying to understand religious pluralism and diversity in the modern world, it should serve as a more adequate and compelling alternative.

NOTES

1. Parsons is credited with having famously set up the antithesis between tradition and modernity as two distinct and opposed sets of pattern variables, which are fundamental relational choices. Here, tradition is characterized by "ascribed" status, "collective" orientation, "particularist" action (emphasizing special relationships such as family), and "affective" and "diffuse" relationships (which fulfill a large range of needs, e.g., parent). Conversely, modern social orders value "achieved" status, "individual" orientation,

"universal" norms, relationships that cater to only "specific" needs and that are "affective-neutral" or impersonal.

2. Conventional accounts of tradition and modernity, Gusfield argued, seemed to make several false assumptions: (1) that traditional societies are static over time, (2) that norms and values in traditional culture are consistent, (3) that traditions are homogeneous, (4) that traditions are displaced by modernity, (5) that tradition and modernity are essentially conflicting, (6) that tradition and modernity are mutually exclusive, and (7) that modernity always weakens tradition.

3. The thesis of multiple modernities can enable us to move beyond the false strictures of modernity without having to fall into the serious problems of postmodernism, not to mention an unhelpful nostalgia for premodern times and conditions.

REFERENCES

Allievi, Stefano, and Jørgen S. Nielsen, eds. 2003. *Muslim Networks and Transnational Communities in and across Europe*. Leiden, Neth.: Brill.

Anderson, A. 1992. *Bazalwane: African Pentecostals in South Africa*. Pretoria: University of South Africa Press.

Anderson, P. 1974. *Lineages of the Absolutist State*. London: NLB.

Archer, Margaret. 1995. *Realist Social Theory: The Morphogenetic Approach*. Cambridge, U.K.: Cambridge University Press.

———. 2000. *Being Human: The Problem of Agency*. Cambridge, U.K.: Cambridge University Press.

Arnason, Johann. 1989. "The Imaginary Constitution of Modernity." *Revue Européenne des Sciences Sociales* 86: 323–337.

———. 1991. "Modernity as a Project and as a Field of Tension." In Axel Honneth and Hans Joas, eds., *Communicative Action: Essays on Jürgen Habermas's The Theory of Communicative Action*. Cambridge, U.K.: Polity.

Arnason, Johann, S. N. Eisenstadt, and Bjoern Wittrock, eds. 2004. *Axial Civilizations and World History*. Leiden, Neth.: Brill.

Bakker, F. L. 1993. *The Struggle of the Hindu Balinese Intellectuals: Developments in Modern Hindu Thinking in Independent Indonesia*. Amsterdam: VU University Press.

Beck, Ulrich, Wolfgang Bonss, and Christoph Lau. 2003. "The Theory of Reflexive Modernization." *Theory, Culture and Society* 20/2: 1–33.

Befu, Harumi, and Sylvie Guichard-Anguis, eds. 2001. *Globalizing Japan: Ethnography of the Japanese Presence in Asia, Europe, and America*. London: Routledge.

Bellah, Robert N. 2003. *Imagining Japan: The Japanese Tradition and Its Modern Interpretation*. Berkeley: University of California Press.

Berger, Peter. 1996. "Secularism in Retreat." *National Interest* 46 (Winter): 3–12.

Berger, Peter, and Samuel P. Huntington, eds. 2003. *Many Globalizations: Cultural Diversity in the Contemporary World*. New York: Oxford University Press.

Beyer, Peter. 1994. *Religion and Globalization*. London: Sage.

Bhaskar, Roy. 1997. *A Realist Concept of Science*. London: Verso.

———. 1998. *Critical Realism*. London: Routledge.

Birnbaum, Norman, and Gertrude Lenzer, eds. 1969. *Sociology and Religion: A Book of Readings*. Englewood Cliffs, N.J.: Prentice-Hall.

Brown, Bernard E. 2007. "God and Man in the French Riots." *American Foreign Policy Interests* 29/3): 183–199.

Bruce, Steve. 2002 *God is Dead: Secularization in the West*. Oxford: Blackwell.

Byrnes, Timothy, and Peter Katzenstein, eds. 2006. *Religion in an Expanding Europe*. New York: Cambridge University Press.

Casanova, José. 1994. *Public Religions in the Modern World*. Chicago: University of Chicago Press.

———. 2001. "Religion, the New Millennium and Globalization." *Sociology of Religion* 62/4: 415–441.

———. 2008. "Public Religion Revisited." In Hent de Vries, ed., *Religion: Beyond a Concept*. New York: Fordham University Press, 101–109.

Chakrabarty, Dipesh. 2002. *Habitations of Modernity: Essays in the Wake of Subaltern Studies*. Chicago: University of Chicago Press.

Chase-Dunn, Christopher. 1989. *Global Formation*. Oxford: Oxford University Press.

Chatterjee, Partha. 1997. *The Present History of West Bengal: Essays in Political Criticism*. New Delhi: Oxford University Press.

Collier, Andrew. 1994. *Critical Realism: An Introduction to Roy Bhaskar's Philosophy*. London: Verso.

Davidman, Lynn. 1991. *Tradition in a Rootless World: Women Turn to Orthodox Judaism*. Berkeley: University of California Press.

Davie, Grace. 2000. *Religion in Modern Europe: A Memory Mutates*. New York: Oxford University Press.

Delanty, Gerard. 1999. *Social Theory in a Changing World: Conceptions of Modernity*. Cambridge, U.K.: Polity.

Deutsch, Karl. 1953. *Nationalism and Social Communication*. New York: Free Press.

Eickelman, D. F., and J. Piscatori. 1996. *Muslim Politics*. Princeton, N.J.: Princeton University Press.

Eisenstadt, S. N. 1996. *Japanese Civilization: A Comparative View*. Chicago: University of Chicago Press.

———. 2000. "Multiple Modernities." *Daedalus* 129/1: 1–29.

———. 2003. *Comparative Civilizations and Multiple Modernities*. Leiden, Neth.: Brill.

———. 2004 [2001]. "The Civilizational Dimension of Modernity: Modernity as a Distinct Civilization." In S. A. Arjomand and E. A. Tiryakian, eds., *Rethinking Civilizational Analysis*. Thousand Oaks, Calif.: Sage, 48–66.

Esposito, John, and Francois Burgat. 2003. *Modernization of Islam: Religion and the Public Sphere in Europe and the Middle East*. New Brunswick, N.J.: Rutgers University Press.

Fazalbhoy, Nasreen. 1997. "Sociology of Muslims in India: A Review." *Economic and Political Weekly* 32/26: 1547–1551.

Freston, Paul. 1997. "Charismatic Evangelicals in Latin America: Mission and Politics on the Frontiers of Protestant Growth." In Stephen Hunt, Malcolm Hamilton, and Tony Walker, eds., *Charismatic Christianity. Sociological Perspectives*. New York: St. Martin's, 184–205.

Friese, Heidrun, and Peter Wagner. 2000. "When 'The Light of the Great Cultural Problems Moves On': On the Possibility of a Cultural Theory of Modernity." *Thesis Eleven* 61 (May): 25–40.

Froese, Paul. 2004a. "After Atheism: An Analysis of Religious Monopolies in the Post-Communist World." *Sociology of Religion* 65/1: 57–75.

———. 2004b. "Forced Secularization in Soviet Russia: Why an Atheistic Monopoly Failed." *Journal for the Scientific Study of Religion* 43/1: 35–50.

Gellner, E., ed. 1981. *Muslim Society*. Cambridge, U.K.: Cambridge University Press.

Gidwani, Vinay. 2002. "The Unbearable Modernity of 'Development'? Canal Irrigation and Development Planning in Western India." *Progress in Planning* 58/1: 1–80.

Gifford, Paul. 2004. *Ghana's New Christianity: Pentecostalism in a Globalizing African Economy*. Bloomington: Indiana University Press.

Gusfield, Joseph. 1967. "Tradition and Modernity: Misplaced Polarities in the Study of Social Change." *American Journal of Sociology* 72/4: 351–362.

Haddad, Yvonne Y., and Michael J. Balz. 2006. "The October Riots in France: A Failed Immigration Policy or the Empire Strikes Back?" *International Migration* 44/2: 23–34.

Harle, Vilho. 2000. *The Enemy with a Thousand Faces: The Tradition of the Other in Western Political Thought and History*. Westport, Conn.: Praeger/Greenwood.

Hefner, R. W. 1985. *Hindu Javanese: Tengger Tradition and Islam*. Princeton, N.J.: Princeton University Press.

———. 1998. "Multiple Modernities: Christianity, Islam, and Hinduism in a Globalizing Age." *Annual Review of Anthropology* 27: 83–104.

Hefner R. W., and P. Horvatich, eds. 1997. *Islam in an Era of Nation States: Politics and Religious Renewal in Muslim Southeast Asia*. Honolulu: University of Hawaii Press.

Himmelfarb, Gertrude. 2004. *The Roads to Modernity: The British, French, and American Enlightenments*. New York: Knopf.

Huntington, Samuel P. 1996. *The Clash of Civilizations and the Remaking of World Order*. New York: Simon and Schuster.

Inglehart, Ronald. 1997. *Modernization and Postmodernization: Cultural, Economic, and Political Change in 43 Societies*. Princeton, N.J.: Princeton University Press.

Jameson, Fredric. 2002. *A Singular Modernity*. London: Verso.

Jenkins, Philip. 2006. *The New Faces of Christianity: Believing the Bible in the Global South*. New York: Oxford University Press.

Kamali, Masoud. 2006. *Multiple Modernities, Civil Society, and Islam: The Case of Iran and Turkey*. Liverpool: Liverpool University Press.

Katzenstein, Peter J. 2006. "Multiple Modernities as Limits to Secular Europeanization?" In Timothy A. Byrnes and Peter J. Katzenstein, eds., *Religion in an Expanding Europe*. New York: Cambridge University Press, 1–33.

Kaya, Ibrahim. 2003. *Social Theory and Later Modernities*. Liverpool: Liverpool University Press.

———. 2004. "Modernity, Openness, Interpretation: A Perspective on Multiple Modernities." *Social Science Information* 43/1: 35–57.

Kepel, Gilles. 1994 [1991]. *The Revenge of God: The Resurgence of Islam, Christianity and Judaism in the Modern World*. Alan Braley, trans. University Park, Pa.: Pennsylvania State University Press.

Knöbl, Wolfgang. 2006a. "Of Contingencies and Breaks: The US American South as an Anomaly in the Debate on Multiple Modernities." *Archives Européennes de Sociologie* 47/1: 125–157.

———. 2006b. "Max Weber, Multiple Modernities and the Re-orientation of Social Theory." *Dados* 49/3: 483–509.

Kolakowski, Leszek. 1997. *Modernity on Endless Trial*. Chicago: University of Chicago Press.

Lau, Jenny Kwon Wah, ed. 2003. *Multiple Modernities: Cinemas and Popular Media in Transcultural East Asia*. Philadelphia: Temple University Press.

Lauer, Robert H. 1971. "The Scientific Legitimation of Fallacy: Neutralizing Social Change Theory." *American Sociological Review* 36/5: 881–889.

Lee, Raymond. 2008. "In Search of Second Modernity: Reinterpreting Reflexive Modernization in the Context of Multiple Modernities." *Social Science Information* 47/1: 55–69.

Lee, Raymond L. M., and Susan E. Ackerman. 1997. *Sacred Tensions: Modernity and Religious Transformation in Malaysia*. Columbia: University of South Carolina Press.

Luhmann, Niklas. 1984. *Religion und Gesellschaft*. Frankfurt am Main: Suhrkamp.

Madeley, John, and Zsolt Enyedi, eds. Editors. 2003. *Church and State in Contemporary Europe: The Chimera of Neutrality*. London: Frank Cass.

Martin, David. 2005. *On Secularization: Toward a Revised General Theory*. London: Ashgate.

Mills, C. Wright. 1959. *The Sociological Imagination*. New York: Oxford University Press.

Moaddel, M. 2002. *Jordanian Exceptionalism: An Analysis of State-Religion Relationship in Egypt, Iran, Jordan, and Syria*. New York: Palgrave.

Modood, Tariq, Anna Triandafyllidou, and Ricard Zapata-Barrero, eds. 2006. *Multiculturalism, Muslims and Citizenship: A European Approach*. London: Routledge.

Monius, Anne E. 2001. *Imagining a Place for Buddhism: Literary Culture and Religious Community in Tamil-speaking South India*. New York: Oxford University Press.

Moussalli, A. S. 1995. "Modern Islamic Fundamentalist Discourses on Civil Society, Pluralism and Democracy." In A. R. Norton, ed., *Civil Society in the Middle East*. Leiden, Neth.: Brill, 79–119.

Murphy, John W. 1988. "Making Sense of Postmodern Sociology." *British Journal of Sociology* 39/4: 600–614.

Mutlu, K. 1996. "Examining Religious Beliefs among University Students in Ankara." *British Journal of Sociology* 47: 353–59.

Neitz, Mary Jo. 1987. *Charisma and Community: A Study of Religious Commitment within the Charismatic Renewal*. New Brunswick, N.J.: Transaction.

Oommen, T. K. 2004. *Nation, Civil Society and Social Movements: Essays in Political Sociology*. New Delhi: Sage.

Parsons, Talcott. 1951. *The Social System*. New York: Free Press.

Piasecki, Ryszard, and Miron Wolnicki. 2004. "The Evolution of Development Economics and Globalization." *International Journal of Social Economics* 31/3: 300–314.

Prakash, G. 1999. *Another Reason: Science and the Imagination of Modern India*. Princeton, N.J.: Princeton University Press.

Ramet, Sabrina. 1998. *Nihil Obstat*. Boulder, Colo.: Westview.

Rao, Badrinath. 2006. "Variant Meanings of Secularism in India." *Journal of Church and State* 48/1: 47–81.

Robbers, Gerhard, ed. 1995. *Staat und Kirche in der Europäischen Union*. Baden-Baden, Ger.: Nomos.

Robbins, Joel. 2004. "The Globalization of Pentecostal and Charismatic Christianity." *Annual Review of Anthropology* 33: 117–143.

Robinson, Rowena, ed. 2004. *The Sociology of Religion in India*. New Delhi: Sage.

Roniger, Luis, and Carlos Waisman, eds. 2002. *Globality and Multiple Modernities: Comparative North American and Latin American Perspectives*. Brighton, U.K.: Sussex Academic.

Rosenau, Pauline. 1992. *Post-modernism and the Social Sciences*. Princeton, N.J.: Princeton University Press.

Rostow, W. W. 1960. *The Stages of Economic Growth: A Non-Communist Manifesto*. Cambridge, U.K.: Cambridge University Press.

Samad, Y., and K. Sen, eds. 2007. *Islam in the European Union: Transnationalism, Youth and the War on Terror*. New York: Oxford University Press.

Schmidt, Volker H. 2006. "Multiple Modernities or Varieties of Modernity?" *Current Sociology* 54/2: 77–97.

Shadid, W. A. R., and P. S. van Koningsveld, eds. 2002. *Intercultural Relations and Religious Authorities: Muslims in the European Union*. Leuven, Belgium: Peters.

Sivaramakrishnan, K., and A. Agrawal, eds. 2000. *Regional Modernities: The Cultural Politics of Development in India*. Stanford, Calif.: Stanford University Press.

Smith, Christian, ed. 1996. *Disruptive Religion: The Force of Faith in Social Movement Activism*. New York: Routledge.

———. 2008. "Future Directions in the Sociology of Religion." *Social Forces* 86/4: 1561–1589.

Smith, Christian, Michael Emerson, Sally Gallagher, Paul Kennedy, and David Sikkink. 1998. *American Evangelicalism: Embattled and Thriving*. Chicago: University of Chicago Press.

Sontheimer, G., and H. Kulke, eds. 1991. *Hinduism Reconsidered*. New Delhi: Manohar.

Spohn, Willfried. 2003. "Multiple Modernity, Nationalism and Religion: A Global Perspective." *Current Sociology* 51/3–4: 265–286.

———. 2007. "Europeanization, Religion and Collective Identities in an Enlarged Europe: A Multiple Modernities Perspective." Paper presented at American Sociological Association annual meeting, New York, August 11.

Spohn, Willfried, and Anna Triandafyllidou, eds. 2003. *Europeanization, National Identities and Migration: Changes in Boundary Construction between Western and Eastern Europe*. London: Routledge.

Stark, Rodney, and Roger Finke. 2000. *Acts of Faith: Explaining the Human Side of Religion*. Berkeley: University of California Press.

Stoelting, Erhard. 1991. *Nationalitäten und Religionen in der UdSSR*. Berlin: Elefant.

Tamney, J. B. 1979. "Established Religiosity in Modern Society: Islam in Indonesia." *Sociological Annals* 40: 125–135.

Taylor, Charles. 1995. "Two Theories of Modernity". The Hastings Center Report 25(2): 24–33.

———. 2000. "Modernity and Difference." In Paul Gilroy, Lawrence Grossberg, and Angela McRobbie, eds., *Without Guarantees: In Honour of Stuart Hall*. London: Verso, 364–374.

———. 2004. *Modern Social Imaginaries*. Durham, N.C.: Duke University Press.

———. 2005. "A Catholic Modernity?" In James Heft, ed., *A Catholic Modernity?* New York: Oxford University Press, 13–37.

———. 2007. *A Secular Age*. Cambridge, Mass.: Harvard University Press.

Thapar, Romila. 1993. *Interpreting Early India*. New Delhi: Oxford University Press.

Theodorson, George A. 1953. "Acceptance of Industrialization and Its Attendant Consequences for the Social Patterns of Non-Western Societies." *American Sociological Review* 18/5: 477–484.

Therborn, Goeran. 2003. "Entangled Modernities." *European Journal of Social Theory* 6/3: 293–305.

Tibi, B. 1990. *Islam and the Cultural Accommodation of Social Change*. Boulder, Colo.: Westview.

Van der Veer, P. 1994. *Religious Nationalism: Hindus and Muslims in India*. Berkeley: University of California Press.

Vertovec, Steven. 2000. *The Hindu Diaspora: Comparative Patterns*. New York: Routledge.

Wagner, Peter 1993. *A Sociology of Modernity: Liberty and Discipline*. London: Routledge.

———. 2000. "Modernity—One or Many?" In Judith Blau, ed., *The Blackwell Companion to Sociology*. Malden, Mass.: Blackwell.

———. 2001a. *A History and Theory of the Social Sciences: Not All That Is Solid Melts into Air*. London: Sage.

———. 2001b. "Modernity: History of the Concept." In Neil Smelser and Paul Baltes, eds., *International Encyclopedia of the Social and Behavioral Sciences*. Amsterdam: Elsevier, 9949–9954.

———. 2001c. *Theorizing Modernity: Inescapability and Attainability in Social Theory*. London: Sage.

Wallace, Anthony. 1966. *Religion: An Anthropological View*. New York: Random House.

Wallerstein, Immanuel. 1999. *The Essential Wallerstein*. Washington, D.C.: American.

Warner, R. Stephen. 1993. "Work in Progress toward a New Paradigm for the Sociological Study of Religion in the United States." *American Journal of Sociology* 98/5: 1044–1093.

Weiming, Tu. 1999. "The Quest for Meaning: Religion in the People's Republic of China." In Peter Berger, ed., *The Desecularization of the World*. Grand Rapids, Mich.: Eerdmans, 85–102.

Weinberg, Ian. 1969. "The Problem of the Convergence of Industrial Societies: A Critical Look at the State of a Theory." *Comparative Studies in Society and History* 11/1: 1–15.

Wilson, Bryan. 1982. *Religion in Sociological Perspective*. Oxford: Oxford University Press.

Wittrock, Björn. 2000. "Modernity: One, None, or Many? European Origins and Modernity as a Global Condition." *Daedalus* 129/1: 31–60.

Wrigley, E. A. 1972. "The Process of Modernization and the Industrial Revolution in England." *Journal of Interdisciplinary History* 3: 225–259.

Yack, Bernard. 1997. *The Fetishism of Modernities: Epochal Self-Consciousness in Contemporary Social and Political Thought*. Notre Dame, Ind.: University of Notre Dame Press.

Yang, Fenggang, and Joseph Tamney, eds. 2005. *State, Market, and Religions in Chinese Societies*. Leiden, Neth.: Brill.

Zhang, Xin. 2000. *Social Transformation in Modern China*. New York: Cambridge University Press.

FOR FURTHER READING

Eisenstadt, S. N. 2000. "Multiple Modernities." *Daedalus* 129/1: 1–29.

Friese, Heidrun, and Peter Wagner. 2000. "When 'The Light of the Great Cultural Problems Moves On': On the Possibility of a Cultural Theory of Modernity." *Thesis Eleven* 61 (May): 25–40.

Kaya, Ibrahim. 2004. "Modernity, Openness, Interpretation: A Perspective on Multiple Modernities." *Social Science Information* 43/1: 35–57.

Martin, David. 2005. *On Secularization: Toward a Revised General Theory*. London: Ashgate.

———. 2000. "Modernity—One or Many?" In Judith Blau, ed., *The Blackwell Companion to Sociology*. Malden, Mass.: Blackwell

CHAPTER 20

RELIGIOUS VIOLENCE AND PEACE

DALIA MOGAHED, TOM PYSZCZYNSKI, AND JESSICA STERN

Is God Dead?

IT is currently in fashion to confess one's atheism in print. Religion poisons everything, Christopher Hitchens insists in *God Is Not Great*. Richard Dawkins, Sam Harris, Daniel C. Dennett, Victor J. Stenger, David Mills, and Susan Jacoby have all made similar arguments in recent books.[1] Until recently, scholars of religion predicted that as societies modernized, God would become obsolete. In 1966, *Time* magazine ran a cover story entitled "Is God Dead?" Peter Berger famously predicted that by "the 21st century, religious believers are likely to be found only in small sects, huddled together to resist a worldwide secular culture."[2] But Berger's prediction did not come to pass; religion is now enjoying a global resurgence. Except in Europe, people the world over attend religious services more regularly and claim to believe more fervently, according to a wide variety of polls.[3] Berger, Rodney Stark, and many other scholars of religion now argue that the earlier claim that secularization and modernity go hand-in-hand was wrong—that it was, again in Berger's words, "a mistake."[4] Those predicting the downfall of religion missed the crucial point that religious faith meets some extremely important psychological needs that have existed since the emergence of humankind: it provides a sense of security, safety, meaning, and comfort in a threatening world in which the only real certainty is that someday we will die. Whether God exists or is merely a fanciful human invention—as a multitude of literary confessions insist—faith in God is playing a large and increasing role in people's individual lives, as well as in politics, that is unlikely to fade away anytime soon.

More troubling is that ideologically inspired violence—both terrorism and war—is also on the rise. Some, such as Blaise Pascal, have argued that faith-motivated aggression is unbounded: "Men never do evil so completely and cheerfully as when they do it from religious conviction."[5] When one or both sides of a conflict view the dispute in ideological terms, the conflict becomes more difficult to resolve. When belligerents fight over sacred territory, beliefs, or values, wars last longer and are less likely to be resolved through negotiation. According to research by Monica Toft, religious wars are more common than secular ones, and they are more brutal. They are also more likely to recur.[6] Similarly, terrorists who claim to kill in the name of God are more common than secular ones today. Their numbers are increasing, and they kill more innocent civilians than their secular counterparts. The years 2004 through 2006 saw more than three times as many attacks by radical Islamist terrorist groups than the two previous years.[7]

How can it be that the same force—faith—that inspired Mahatma Gandhi and Martin Luther King Jr. also inspires religious killers? This question has haunted us for years, leading us to work on interviews, large-scale surveys, and psychological experiments that explore the links among religion, radicalism, and violence. We have asked radicals and extremists to explain in their own words why they think what they think and do what they do. Is faith in God a driver, an impediment, or a catalyst to hatred and violence? One terrorist, who had by then retired, insisted that God was key to every action he had ever taken in his life, including one he now regretted, joining an Identity Christian cult dedicated to bringing down the American government and killing homosexuals, Jews, blacks, and "mud people." Asked to explain how a Christian ethic could be used to justify violence against innocents, the retired terrorist conceded that most Christians think of God as a source of "light" and "love" and that many try to manifest those qualities in their own lives. But, he said, "the scriptures describe another aspect of God: 'The Lord God is a man of War' (Exodus 15:3). And in Deuteronomy, the Lord proclaims, 'If I wet my glittering sword, and my hand take hold of judgment: I will render vengeance to my enemies, and will reward them that hate me. I will make my arrows drunk with blood and my sword shall devour flesh' (Deuteronomy 32:39, 41, 42). We wanted to mimic this more violent aspect of God," a practice common to terrorist groups coming from all three monotheistic religions.

Jewish terrorists similarly focus on passages in Genesis and Deuteronomy for evidence that Israel was given to the Jews in a sacred contract and that killing those who would take it away from the Jews is morally sanctioned. When asked for a reading list, Jewish terrorists point to passages such as "In that day the Lord made a covenant with Abram, saying: Unto thy seed have I given this land, from the river of Egypt unto the great river, the river Euphrates" (Genesis 15:18) and "Every place whereon the sole of your foot shall tread shall be yours: from the wilderness, and Lebanon, from the river, the river Euphrates, even unto the hinder sea shall be your border. There shall no man be able to stand against you: the Lord your God shall lay the fear of you and the dread of you upon all the land that ye shall tread upon, as He hath spoken unto you" (Deuteronomy 11:24–25).[8]

Islamist terrorists also focus on particular aspects of their religion to justify killing innocents. The Arabic word *jihad*, which means "to strive, to exert oneself, to struggle," is never far from any discussion of Muslim militants. However, if we listen to the terrorists, jihad, even if understood as a military struggle, might be much less the ideological driver for terror than is commonly assumed. In a religious context, it can be used to express the idea of struggling with oneself to do the right thing or exertion on behalf of the Muslim community. Mainstream Islamic schools of thought teach that the meaning of jihad includes the struggle of the soul as well as the sword but detail strict regulations for the latter. These include a prohibition on targeting civilians, cutting down trees, poisoning wells, and surprise attacks. Sometimes "the jihad of the sword" is called "the smaller jihad," in opposition to the peaceful forms named "the greater jihad." Not only do extremists reject the notion that the moral and spiritual jihad is the greater jihad, focusing instead on passages on combat, but they also ignore the religious restrictions on military jihad altogether. While sometimes citing verses such as "Fight them until there is no persecution and the religion is God's [entirely]" (Qur'an 2:193, 8:39) or "When the sacred months have passed, slay the idolaters wherever you find them, and take them, and confine them, and lie in wait for them at every place of ambush" (9:5),[9] modern terrorists, such as Al Qaeda, rely heavily on arguments of "reciprocity."

To get around the traditional restrictions regulating military jihad, especially those prohibiting accidentally hurting, let alone targeting, civilians, terrorists use what can be characterized as "secular" logic. For example, when Osama bin Laden was asked to defend in light of Islamic teachings the satisfaction he expressed about the attacks of September 11, 2001, he conceded that Islam generally prohibits hurting civilians in war: "The Holy Prophet (peace be upon him) was against killing women and children. When he saw a dead woman during a war, he asked why was she killed?"[10] But he still justified the attacks, by citing not the Qur'an but instead his geopolitical perceptions: "In my view, if an enemy occupies a Muslim territory and uses common people as human shield, then it is permitted to attack that enemy. America and its allies are massacring us in Palestine, Chechenya, Kashmir and Iraq. The Muslims have the right to attack America in reprisal."[11]

To give this line of argument religious validity, Al Qaeda's leadership relies on the principle of proportional retaliation, a concept shared by the three Abrahamic faiths,[12] as well as the secular world.[13] "A Treatise on the Legal Status of Using Weapons of Mass Destruction against Infidels," which Al Qaeda leadership issued in May 2003, states: "Anyone who considers America's aggressions against Muslims and their lands during the past decades will conclude that striking her is permissible on the basis of the rule of treating one as one has been treated. No other argument need be mentioned."[14] It is interesting to note that the Qur'anic "eye for an eye" verse that the statement refers to continues with "But if any one remits the retaliation by way of charity, it is an act of atonement for himself" (Qur'an 5:45).

Not surprisingly, despite their talk of fulfilling God's will, terrorists suggest in interviews that the perception that their group or people have been humiliated and mistreated is never far from their thinking. The word *humiliation*, or a synonym, came up in almost every conversation we had with terrorists who claimed to be inspired by religious teachings, regardless of which religion they turned to for justification of their actions. Islamist terrorists commonly focus wistfully on Islam's golden age and the extent to which Islamic civilization has fallen behind the West. Globalization itself is a source of humiliation, according to Ayman Zawahiri, in that it implicitly denies the unique values of traditional cultures. In all of these cases, it appears that aggrieved people are picking and choosing religious teachings that justify the violent actions that they believe will restore their sense of dignity, pride, and righteous order, which has been lost to outsiders.

THE FUNCTION OF RELIGION

Might it make sense to see religion as a kind of technology that can be employed to mobilize either violence *or* peace? Max Weber saw religion as a force that is often used to promote social change, for example, to inculcate and strengthen a work ethic.[15] But if religion can be used to make people work harder, could it not also be used to make them fight harder, sowing discord and violence or, instead, compassion and peace? Some new experimental results suggest that this might be true. New studies by Brad Bushman and colleagues suggest that when people are exposed to violent passages in the Bible, they become more aggressive, especially if they are believers.[16] Would exposing people to compassionate passages lead them to become less aggressive?

Terror management theory (TMT), a social-psychological approach to understanding the relationship among cultural beliefs, self-esteem, intergroup conflict, and deeply rooted fears about life and death, might shed light on these issues.[17] TMT posits that human awareness of the inevitability and potential finality of death creates the potential for existential terror. This terror is mitigated by faith in an internalized cultural worldview, such as religious faith or patriotism, and self-esteem, which is attained by living up to the standards of value prescribed by one's worldview. Because people are aware that there are many different ways of construing reality, confidence in one's worldview and the protection from anxiety that it provides depend on consensual validation from others. Those who share one's worldview increase one's faith in it and its effectiveness as a shield against anxiety. Unfortunately, the mere existence of others with divergent worldviews undermines this consensus, threatens faith in the absolute validity of one's worldview, and reduces its anxiety-buffering effectiveness. People defend against threats posed by alternative worldviews by disparaging them and those who subscribe to them, attempting to convert their adherents to their own worldview, or simply killing them, which neatly eliminates the threatened consensus and asserts the superiority of their own system of beliefs and values.

To date, more than three hundred experiments conducted in sixteen different countries have provided support for TMT hypotheses.[18] Research has shown that increasing people's self-esteem makes them less prone to anxiety in response to threats and that subtle reminders of mortality increase positive reactions to those who support their worldview and negative reactions to those who threaten it. Experiments also show that threats to self-esteem or worldview bring death-related thoughts closer to consciousness and that, in contrast, boosts to self-esteem or faith in worldview push them away. Of particular relevance to present concerns, research has shown that reminders of death lead people to conform more closely to the norms of their culture, punish violators of those norms more severely, show greater reverence for symbols of their culture, such as flags and crucifixes, and react with greater hostility and aggression toward those whose worldviews conflict with their own. Especially relevant to present concerns, studies have shown that reminders of death increase Americans' support for the use of extreme military might, Israelis' belief in the justness of harsh counterterrorist tactics, and Iranians' support for suicide bombings. Control conditions—in which participants are induced to think about other aversive topics, such as failure, embarrassment, physical pain, uncertainty, social exclusion, paralysis, or meaninglessness—do not produce these results. Taken together, this body of research provides converging evidence for the TMT proposition that cultural worldviews and self-esteem provide protection against the problem of death by reducing the potential for anxiety engendered by the heightened accessibility of death-related thoughts.

Among Americans and Europeans, reminders of September 11, 2001, have similar results to reminders of death. Mark Landau and colleagues[19] performed a series of experiments in which American college students were randomly assigned to be reminded of either September 11, their own mortality, or aversive control topics (e.g., pain, uncertainty) before assessing their evaluations of and intention to vote for President George W. Bush. An initial study showed that reminders of death increased agreement with an essay praising Bush and his policies in Iraq. This finding was replicated in another study that showed that reminders of the events of September 11 produced the same increase in support for Bush and his policies that were produced by thoughts of one's own death. Another study showed that reminders of death increased support for Bush and decreased support for Senator John Kerry in the then-upcoming 2004 election and that this effect occurred across the political spectrum, for conservatives and liberals alike. Yet another study showed that when asked whom they intended to vote for, a sample of predominantly liberal college students chose Kerry over Bush by a four-to-one margin under neutral conditions, but when reminded of death, they exhibited better than a two-to-one preference for Bush over Kerry.

One study reported by Landau showed that presentations of the numbers 911 or the letters WTC (for World Trade Center) at speeds too rapid for conscious recognition produced an increase in the speed with which death-related thoughts came to mind; specifically, after such subliminal priming of 911 or WTC, participants were more likely to complete word stems such as COFF__ with the word COFFIN than with COFFEE or SK__L with SKULL than with SKILL. Similar results have been reported regarding the effects of media publicity about September 11 or the

London subway bombing. This shows that reminders of terrorism quite clearly do bring death-related thoughts closer to consciousness. The fact that thoughts of September 11 and one's own death produced equivalent effects on support for Bush suggests that a substantial part of the reason reminders of September 11 increased his support was the reminder of death that this topic provided and the clinging to sources of security that reminders of this core fear produced.

But what is it about Bush and his policies that provided this much-needed security to those seeking respite from the horrors of the terrorist attack? Of course, Bush was a complex and multifaceted leader, with many policies that might provide comfort to those facing existential anxiety. TMT, following from the work of Ernest Becker, Erich Fromm, and Otto Rank, suggests that leaders who help their followers view themselves as part of a special, superior, and unique group are especially valuable for managing deeply rooted fears. Bush clearly portrayed the American people as a special breed, virtuously working to bring freedom and democracy to the world and rid the planet of "evil-doers." He argued that those responsible for the terrorist attacks "hate us because of our freedom," and he promised to wage war against the "axis of evil" that put the entire planet in jeopardy. This research suggests that at least part of the reason reminders of death or terrorism increased the appeal of the Bush presidency is the patriotic vision he portrayed of the United States as pursuing a grand mission to vanquish evil.

Terrorist leaders also describe themselves as vanquishing evil, often by referring to the enemy as subhuman and to the terrorist recruits as chosen by God for their mission. This language would seem to serve several goals consistent with TMT. It helps bolster the self-esteem of recruits, validates a worldview that gives moral superiority to us over them, and justifies violent action to restore the justice that was subjugated by the evil ones. Radical Islamists refer to their enemies as "infidels," "crusaders," and "enemies of God." Claiming that God is on "our" side helps mobilize recruits, especially if recruits can be made to see themselves as specially chosen to follow their calling.

When the experimentalist and the terrorism researcher joined with Gallup to study these issues in a third way—through large-scale surveys—we were astonished to discover the similarity of our findings. In recent surveys of ten major Muslim-majority countries,[20] representing more than half of Islam's followers worldwide, Gallup found that the vast majority of Muslims opposed terrorist strikes against American civilians. The 7 percent of respondents who thought that the September 11 strikes were completely justified felt most strongly that America aimed to dominate the Islamic world militarily and politically and that Americans disrespected Islam. Members of this "high-conflict group" were no more religious than moderates, nor were they more likely to be unemployed. In fact, those who approved of the September 11 strikes were slightly more likely to be affluent and educated than the general population and were more likely to be supervisors at work. While the high-conflict group shared the sense that the West deeply disrespected Islam and Muslims with the moderate majority, what defined those with extremist views from the rest was not poverty, illiteracy, or religious fanaticism but the perception of being threatened and controlled by the West, the United States in particular.

Both groups' number one response to what the West could do to improve relations with the Muslim world was for Western societies to stop looking at Muslims as inferior and disrespecting Islam. However, the second most frequent response among the general population was a call for greater investments and job creation, while the high-conflict group called on the West simply to stop interfering in the internal policies of their countries. When asked to describe in their own words their greatest fear, the general population's most frequent response dealt with issues of personal safety, crime, and economic insecurity. In contrast, the high-conflict group's greatest worry was "foreign domination and U.S. occupation." In addition, members of this group disproportionately believed that the invasion of Iraq did "more harm than good." The high-conflict group was also more likely to say that the United States would not allow people in their region to fashion their own political future and to express skepticism that the United States was serious about supporting democracy in their part of the world. While as likely to express personal concern for better relations with the West, those with extremist views were less likely to believe the West showed the same concern. Rather than being motivated by piety or poverty, those who condoned terror in the Muslim world were found to be differentiated by a sense of being threatened and dominated and a lack of faith in the goodwill of the West. These triggers combined with the fuel of feeling deeply disrespected to create a justification for violent revenge.

Another study, from the University of Michigan, found similar trends: "Findings from representative national surveys in Algeria and Jordan show that neither religious orientations, judgment about Western culture, nor economic circumstances account for variance in approval of terrorists acts against U.S. targets. Alternatively, in both countries, approval of terrorism against the United States is disproportionately likely among men and women with negative judgments about their own government and about U.S. foreign policy."[21]

The latest results from TMT experiments prompted Zachary Rothschild, Abdolhossein Abdollahi, and Tom Pyszczynski to write an essay titled "Does Peace Have a Prayer?"[22] An initial study conducted in the United States revealed that religious fundamentalism was associated with stronger support for the use of extreme military tactics except under one condition: when participants were reminded of both the compassionate teachings of Jesus and their own mortality (e.g., "So in everything, do to others what you would have them do to you, for this sums up the Law and the Prophets"). Unlike previous studies in which reminders of death led to increased support for the use of extreme military might, in this one, when participants were reminded of compassionate Christian values, fundamentalist Christians became *less* supportive of such tactics; reminders of other aspects of Christian teaching did not produce the same effects. Our colleague Abdollahi, in Iran, recently found parallel effects among young Muslims. Although reminders of death increased anti-American attitudes, under neutral conditions or when ideas about compassion were raised, these same frightening thoughts led to *less* anti-American attitudes when the Qur'anic origin of these values was made clear.

Similar results were obtained by Gallup when respondents were asked to defend their assessment of the moral justifiability of the September 11 attacks. For example, in Indonesia, the largest Muslim-majority country in the world, many of those who condemned terrorism cited humanitarian or religious justifications to support their response. One woman in an Indonesian city said, "It was similar with a murder, an act forbidden in our religion." Another said, "Killing one's life is as sinful as killing the whole world," paraphrasing verse 5:32 in the Qur'an.

On the other hand, not a single respondent in Indonesia who condoned the attacks of September 11 cited the Qur'an for justification. Instead, this group's responses were markedly secular and worldly. One Indonesian respondent said, "The U.S. government is too controlling toward other countries, seems like colonizing." Another said, "The U.S. has helped the Zionist country, Israel, to attack Palestine."

Other studies conducted by our group in the United States have shown that activating a sense of shared or common humanity—by simply viewing pictures of families or reading recollections of cherished childhood memories from diverse countries—can have a similar effect of eliminating or redirecting the usual hostility-enhancing effects of existential fear. Of course, the idea that all humans are part of the same family is a theme echoed by most of the major religions of the world—and it is one that follows well from modern scientific explanations of the origins of our species and nonreligious value systems such as secular humanism.

Yes, religion has indeed been used by many over the course of history to fan the flames of hatred and violence. Yes, religion is being used today to justify unspeakable acts of cruelty that feed a seemingly unending cycle of killing. But it is not religious belief per se that is responsible for this travesty. Humans' inhumanity to fellow humans is driven by desperate clinging to beliefs, values, and self-esteem as protective shields against the rumble of panic that results from our awareness of the fragile, vulnerable, and temporary nature of human existence. Humankind stubbornly insists that out of the many possible ways of understanding the reality in which we live, our own understanding must be the only one that is true and correct. This makes people who see the world differently from how we do, or who don't value us as much as we think we deserve, inherently threatening. Rather than face the uncertainty introduced into our lives by a complex and diverse world, we declare the others evil incarnate and struggle to stamp them out. This would be the case—and has been the case—regardless of whether the beliefs and values that divide peoples are sacred or secular, religious or scientific. The genocides committed in the last century by Nazis, Stalinists, Maoists, Khmer Rouge, Serbians, and many other secular groups with grand visions of a new world order make this abundantly clear.

The question of whether any one set of religious beliefs and values is literally true and correct is moot. Religion exists and persists because it meets very basic human needs. Humankind has used religion to provide comfort and solace in the face of despair ever since human abilities to think abstractly had matured to a point where conceiving of a world beyond the present was possible. Perhaps systems of religious thought came to include values of compassion, tolerance, and nonviolence as an antidote to the pervasive human tendency to lash out against those who are different. But just as those who are angry and aggrieved often use certain aspects of religious teachings to promote violence, so, too, can those who can no longer tolerate the wanton destruction of human life use the compassionate aspects of religious doctrine—which we suspect are central to the messages of most faiths—to promulgate an end to the ongoing cycle of violence. Our research suggests that people clearly do respond to compassionate religious values with reduced hostility toward perceived enemies. Perhaps it is time for new prophets of peace to spread this more hopeful message to the faithful in the hopes of moving beyond the conflicts that are extracting such intolerable costs from all of us.

NOTES

1. Richard Dawkins, *The God Delusion* (London: Bantam Press, 2006). See also Daniel Clement Dennett, *Breaking the Spell: Religion as a Natural Phenomenon* (New York: Viking, 2006); Sam Harris, *Letter to a Christian Nation* (New York: Knopf, 2006); Christopher Hitchens, *God Is Not Great: How Religion Poisons Everything* (New York: Twelve, 2007); Susan Jacoby, *The Age of American Unreason* (New York: Pantheon Books, 2008); Alister E. McGrath, Daniel Clement Dennett, and Robert B. Stewart, *The Future of Atheism: Alister McGrath & Daniel Dennett in Dialogue* (Minneapolis: Fortress, 2008); David Mills and Dorion Sagan, *Atheist Universe: The Thinking Person's Answer to Christian Fundamentalism* (Berkeley: Ulysses, 2006); Victor J. Stenger, *God: The Failed Hypothesis: How Science Shows That God Does Not Exist* (Amherst, N.Y.: Prometheus, 2007).

2. Cited in "A Bleak Outlook Is Seen for Religion," *New York Times*, April 3, 1968. See also Peter L. Berger, *The Sacred Canopy* (Garden City, N.Y.: Anchor, 1967, 1990), cited in Rodney Stark, "Secularization, R.I.P. (Rest in Peace)," *Sociology of Religion* 60/3 (Fall 1999).

3. Data on and analysis of global trends in religious worship and belief can be found in Assaf Moghadam, "A Global Resurgence of Religion?" Working Paper 03–03, Weatherhead Center for International Affairs, Harvard University, August 2003. For an account of heightened enthusiasm among religious believers and the link between such sentiments and recent conflict, see, e.g., Marc Gopin, *Between Eden and Armageddon: The Future of World Religions, Violence, and Peacemaking*, new ed. (New York: Oxford University Press, 2004). Further readings on the political consequences of increased religiosity include Scott M. Thomas, *The Global Resurgence of Religion and the Transformation of International Relations: The Struggle for the Soul of the Twenty-first Century* (New York: Palgrave Macmillan, 2005); and Timothy Samuel Shah and Monica Duffy Toft, "Why God Is Winning," in *Foreign Policy* (July/August 2006): 38–46.

4. Cited in "Epistemological Modesty: An Interview with Peter Berger," *Christian Century* 114/114 (October 1997): 972–975, 978. See also Stark, "Secularization, R.I.P."; Shah and Toft, "Why God Is Winning"; Pippa Norris and Ronald Inglehart, *Sacred and Secular: Religion and Politics Worldwide* (New York: Cambridge University Press, 2004).

5. Blaise Pascal, *Pensées*, multiple versions.

6. Monica Toft, "Getting Religion?" *International Security* 31/4 (Spring 2007): 97–131. For more on the role of religion in warfare and terrorism, see Ron E. Hassner, "Fighting Insurgency on Sacred Ground," *Washington Quarterly* 29/2 (Spring 2006): 149–166; Mark Juergensmeyer, *Terror in the Mind of God: The Global Rise of Religious Violence*, 3rd ed. (Berkeley: University of California Press, 2003); and Jessica Stern, *Terror in the Name of God: Why Religious Militants Kill* (New York: HarperCollins, 2003).

7. Although religion and secularism are at times understood as competing ideologies, sociologist Bryan Wilson argued in *Religion in Secular Society: A Sociological Comment* (London: C. A. Watts, 1966) that secularism does not necessarily disregard religion completely; rather, he held that a secular worldview would deny religion a meaningful place in the social sphere.

8. Other passages that could be read to support terrorism include "When the Lord your God brings you into the land you are entering to possess and drives out before you may nations . . . then you must destroy them totally. Make no treaty with them and show them no mercy" (Deuteronomy 7:1–2). Other passages from the Old Testament that are frequently cited to show the Jewish connection to the land of Israel include Genesis 13:14–15: "God said to Abram: 'Lift up now thine eyes, and look from the place where thou art, northward and southward and eastward and westward; for all the land which thou seest, to thee will I give it, and to thy seed for ever.'" In Genesis 26:3, God confirms to Abraham's son Jacob: "Sojourn in this land, and I will be with thee, and will bless thee; for unto thee, and unto thy seed, I will give all these lands, and I will establish the oath which I swore unto Abraham thy father."

9. Rudolph Peters, *Jihad in Classical and Modern Islam* (Princeton, N.J.: Markus Weiner, 1996), 118. For an extended commentary by Hasan al-Banna, founder of the Muslim Brotherhood, see "Risalat al-Jihad" ("Letter on Jihad") in his collected writings, *Majmu'at Rasa'il al-Banna* (Cairo: Dar al-Da'wa, 1990). Frequently, those advocating the lesser jihad will look to verse 9:5 of the Qur'an, the "Verse of the Sword," which commands Muslims to defend Islam by punishing unbelievers with death. See, e.g., David Cook, *Understanding Jihad* (Berkeley: University of California Press, 2005). Figures such as Sayyid Qutb and Abul Ala Mawdudi considered an external and universal jihad to be necessary in protecting against modern *jahiliyyah*, or ignorance, which could be found in the West as well as among Muslims. To them, a successful and authentic Islamic renewal required the practice of *takfir*, or the declaration that someone is an unbeliever (*kafir*). *Takfir* has been a subject of debate in Islamic law, with other leaders such as Yusuf al-Qaradawi disallowing the concept as contrary to Islam. In modern times, *takfir* has also been invoked to justify the use of violence against political leaders in the Muslim world who allegedly did not live up to the principles of Islam. Muhammad Abd al-Salam Faraj, for example, published and distributed *The Neglected Duty* throughout Cairo in the early 1980s. Typically, it is thought that the support for jihad included in that publication was influential in bringing about the 1982 assassination of Egyptian president Anwar Sadat. For more on jihad and the views of Islamic thinkers on the matter, see, e.g., Sayyid Qutb, *Milestones along the Way* (Damascus: Dar al-Ilm, 1993); Karen Armstrong, *The Battle for God: A History of Fundamentalism* (New York: Ballantine, 2001); and Gilles Kepel, *Jihad: The Trail of Political Islam* (Cambridge, Mass.: Harvard University Press, 2002).

10. Hamid Mir, "Osama Claims He Has Nukes," *Dawn*, November 10, 2001.

11. Ibid.

12. Exodus 21:23–27; Qur'an 5:45.

13. The doctrine of proportionality originated with the 1907 Hague Conventions, which govern the laws of war, and was later codified in Article 49 of the International Law

Commission's 1980 Draft Articles on State Responsibility. The doctrine is also referred to indirectly in the 1977 Additional Protocols of the Geneva Conventions.

14. "A Treatise on the Legal Status of Using Weapons of Mass Destruction against Infidels," Nasir bin Hamd Al-Fahd, May 2003. Online at www.carnegieendowment.org/static/npp/fatwa.pdf.

15. The idea of religion as a form of technology was introduced by German philosopher Max Weber with his 1905 publication of *The Protestant Work Ethic and the Spirit of Capitalism* (*Die Protestantische Ethik und der Geist des Kapitalismus*). Although that text focuses on Protestantism as a driving force behind the rise of capitalism, Weber's work demonstrates that religious belief in general can be employed strategically to control and influence social change. For a study on this topic outside the context of Christianity, see Max Weber, *The Religion of India: The Sociology of Hinduism and Buddhism*, Hans H. Gerth and Don Martindale, trans. (Glencoe, Ill.: Free Press, 1958).

16. Brad J. Bushman, Robert D. Ridge, Enny Das, Colin W. Key, and Gregory L. Busath, "When God Sanctions Killing: Effect of Scriptural Violence on Aggression," *Psychological Science* 18/3 (2007).

17. See Sheldon Solomon, Jeff Greenberg, and Tom Pyszczynski, "A Terror-Management Theory of Self-esteem and Its Role in Social Behavior," in M. Zanna, ed., *Advances in Experimental Social Psychology*, vol. 24 (New York: Academic, 1991); Tom Pyszczynski, Sheldon Solomon, and Jeff Greenberg, *In the Wake of 9/11: The Psychology of Terrorism* (Washington, D.C.: American Psychological Association, 2003).

18. For a recent review, see J. Greenberg, S. Solomon, and J. A. Arndt, "A Uniquely Human Motivation: Terror Management," in J. Shah and W. Gardner, eds., *Handbook of Motivation Science* (New York: Guilford, 2008).

19. Mark Landau and colleagues.

20. Bangladesh, Egypt, Indonesia, Iran, Jordan, Lebanon, Morocco, Pakistan, Saudi Arabia, Turkey.

21. Mark Tessler and Michael D. H. Robbins, "What Leads Some Ordinary Men and Women in Arab Countries to Approve of Terrorist Acts against the West: Evidence from Survey Research in Algeria and Jordan," *Journal of Conflict Resolution* (April 2007): 305–328.

22. Zachary Rothschild, Abdolhossein Abdollahi, and Tom Pyszczynski, "Does Peace Have a Prayer? The Effects of Mortality Salience, Compassionate Values, and Religious Fundamentalism on Hostility toward Outgroups," *Journal of Experimental Social Psychology* 45/4 (2009).

FOR FURTHER READING

Esposito, John, and Dalia Mogahed. 2008. *Who Speaks for Islam? What a Billion Muslims Really Think*. New York: Gallup.

Pyszczynski, T., Z. Rothschild, and A. Abdollahi. 2008. "Terrorism, Violence, and Hope for Peace: A Terror Management Perspective." *Current Directions in Psychological Science* 17: 318–322.

Zachary Rothschild, Abdolhossein Abdollahi, and Tom Pyszczynski, "Does Peace Have a Prayer? The Effects of Mortality Salience, Compassionate Values, and Religious Fundamentalism on Hostility toward Outgroups." *Journal of Experimental Social Psychology* 45/4 (2009).

CHAPTER 21

....

RELIGIOUS DIVERSITY IN PUBLIC EDUCATION

....

DAVID BASINGER

"Congress shall make no law respecting an establishment of
religion, or prohibiting the free exercise thereof."
    —First Amendment to the United States Constitution

PUBLIC *education* is in one sense an appropriate descriptor for any government-
funded and/or government-regulated educational activity in any country or distinct
social/political territory in the world. However, the types of government-supported
educational activity worldwide are so diverse, the demographics of those allowed to
access these educational systems so varied, and the stated or actual goals and objectives of these educational activities so different that I see limited value in attempting
to discuss religious diversity in public education from a comparative global perspective. In fact, such diversity in educational activity and purpose makes it difficult
to engage in fruitful comparative discussion of this issue if we focus only on the
industrialized nations or even just industrialized nations with predominantly Western cultures. And even within the United States, there are significant distinctions in
scope and purpose between those educational institutions that are fully funded by
tax dollars and those that receive some government support and/or are government-regulated to some extent. So, although I believe that the issues I address might
well be of relevance and significance in many educational settings, I focus my
discussion on what I see as the most significant and pervasive form of public education in the United States today: kindergarten through twelfth grade (K-12) public
education.

THE BASIC TENSION OUTLINED

K-12 public schools in the United States have always been to some extent a "melting pot" where children from diverse populations, including children with diverse religious backgrounds, meet and assimilate. But while such assimilation traditionally involved children from groups with Western cultural values and religious commitments—such as Irish, Italian, Polish, or Hispanic immigrants— there are today an increasing number of public school students with non-Western cultural values and religious traditions. For example, while there are currently only about 5 million Muslims in the United States (a little less than 2 percent of the population), 14 percent of all newcomers, many of whom are school-age children, are Muslim (Lessow-Hurley 1999). There are also increasing numbers of students who are at least nominally Hindus, Buddhists, Zoroastrians, Sikhs, or adherents to other non-Western religions, with no end to this trend in sight. And technology, especially growing Internet access, is exposing students to diverse cultural and religious perspectives in ways unimaginable a generation ago.

On the other hand, although the United States has a Constitution that ensures, in principle, free exercise of religion, "we continue to speak," Robert Wuthnow correctly points out, "as if our nation is (or should be) a Christian nation, founded on Christian principles, and characterized by public references to the trappings of this tradition" (2005, 6–7). Moreover, as Wuthnow also correctly notes, while "diversity is always challenging, whether it is manifest in language differences or in modes of dress, eating, and socializing . . . when religion is involved, these challenges are multiplied" (3).

So it should not be surprising that public school educators are finding themselves grappling in new and often uncomfortable ways with the question of how our public schools should respond to the increasing religious diversity to which students are exposed. Given that these educators can no longer assume that the vast majority of students are from homes with Western religious traditions, given that the non-Western cultures and religious traditions out of which an increasing number of students come implicitly or explicitly challenge the traditional Western (Christian) cultural and religious values so embedded in our public education system, and given that our public schools continue to be the setting in which diverse religious perspectives are most likely to be encountered, the increasingly complicated question of how our public schools ought to respond to this religious diversity simply can no longer be avoided.

The purpose of this chapter is to assess current responses to this question and offer reasonable ways forward. While I note and briefly comment on two common challenges that increasing religious diversity poses for administrators and school boards, I focus primarily on the pedagogical question of how the public school classroom teacher ought to respond to the increasing religious diversity to which the children in her or his class are exposed.

FUNCTIONAL TENSIONS FACING ADMINISTRATORS

Probably the most publicized challenge religious diversity poses for public school administrators and school boards centers on the question of whether religious exemptions or modifications should be granted to students from non-Western religious traditions when the religious norms of these traditions conflict with standard school policy. For example, schools with Muslim students often find themselves faced with the question of whether students can wear head coverings inside the school building or can refuse to uncover certain parts of their bodies for swimming or can refuse to change clothes in the presence of those of the same gender. And as more and more students in a given school district are from non-Christian religious cultures, the question of how Christian holidays—such as Christmas and Good Friday—can be designated as school holidays while non-Christian holy days—such as Eid-Ul-Fitr (the end of Ramadan for Muslims)—are not so designated, will only become more pronounced.

These are not easy questions, as they not only raise consistency issues but also challenge us to rethink the extent to which we can justifiably continue to give preference to the religious traditions of our still predominantly Judeo-Christian culture without violating the constitutional mandate that the state not promote a given religion. I will, though, share a few general thoughts on what I see as the best way forward.

The operative principle in this context, as I see it, should be the "rule of reasonable accommodation," the obligation of a school to allow a student to be excused from an activity or to participate with modification when the basic educational goals in question can be met in other ways without placing an undue burden on the school or other students. This appears to be the rule that rightly governs school response to conflicts between school policy and Judeo-Christian religious beliefs. For example, most public schools have for years routinely granted students exemptions or modifications when what is being taught (e.g., sex education) or common student activities (e.g., holiday celebrations and birthday parties) are incompatible with the Judeo-Christian beliefs of a student's family, because it has been determined (I think properly) that doing so does not significantly inhibit an exempted student's learning or place prohibitive burdens on teachers or other students. And I see no reason that applying this rule would not quite reasonably allow for exemptions or modifications in relation to the types of non-Western conflicts noted above. For instance, it is difficult to see how allowing a Muslim girl to wear a head covering will inhibit her learning or cause undue hardship for others. Nor is it easy to see how allowing a Muslim boy to wear a shirt while swimming will put him or others at risk.

Why, then, are such exemptions or modifications not granted in some cases? The hesitance of some schools to institute "reasonable accommodations" often has little to do with educational concerns and/or practical problems. The real (primary) reason administrators and school boards sometimes enforce the "letter of the law" is often the manifestation of their conscious or subconscious desire to increase student assimilation into the dominant (Western) culture and/or their uneasiness with cultural manifestations that differ significantly from the school norm. But these are the exact sorts of beliefs and attitudes that need to be challenged by parents, educators, and the community at large.

The other challenge that increasing religious diversity poses for some school administrators and school boards centers on a potential fiscal implication of increasing student exposure to religious diversity. Almost all administrators will acknowledge that the Constitution itself does not require or even encourage "freedom from" religion. That is, they understand that while the Constitution does not allow the government (and thus public education) to promote any specific religion, it clearly does not forbid public schools from exposing students to diverse religious perspectives. Accordingly, the vast majority of administrators will publicly state that they support such exposure.

It is also true, though, that many public school administrators are forced daily to consider the fact that their schools' ability to educate children is tied in a very real sense to the funding (school budgets) approved by the taxpayers living in their school districts. But controversy breeds discontent, which can and often does influence how taxpayers respond to new funding requests. And given the deep-seated ambivalence or negative attitudes toward non-Christian religions often held by some vocal taxpayers within a district, any attempt by a school to expose students (or increase student exposure) to diverse religious perspectives carries with it the very real potential of creating controversy within the district. So it is understandable that some administrators are tempted at times to encourage in actual practice "freedom from" religion—for example, to discourage religious music of any type at holiday concerts, to prohibit any group of students from using rooms for voluntary religious meetings, and/or to minimize curricula or activities intended to expose students to diverse religious perspectives.

I don't want to diminish the importance of this practical, utilitarian concern for any given administrator or school board. However, I agree with the majority of public school educators that while the minimization of controversy within a district is a valid goal, it is more important to give students a holistic exposure to all aspects of our world, both past and present, and this requires that the public school not, in the words of Jeffrey Milligan, bracket "religion out of history, culture, and human experience" (2003, 415). That is, I assume, along with most public school administrators and teachers, that it is important to increase student exposure to diverse religious perspectives, even given the practical fiscal difficulties that doing so might generate.

Exactly what, though, is the supposed value of increasing student exposure to religious aspects of our world? For some educators, the main reason (or perhaps at least a primary reason) might well be tied to the inherent value of education. That is, some believe that we ought to increase students' exposure to diverse religions not because (or primarily because) doing so will benefit the student or society but, rather, because gaining knowledge of any sort is good for its own sake.

However, while few public school educators deny the inherent value of increased knowledge, including increased knowledge of religious diversity, few want to stop there. Most also want to increase student exposure to diverse religious perspectives because they believe this will increase understanding and that the increased understanding will have positive social outcomes. One popular outcome of this sort is succinctly stated by Robert Kunzman. Public schools, he tells us, should equip students to participate effectively in our democratic society. However, our democratic society is made up of an increasingly diverse population (both nationally and locally), and our democratic society functions in a very diverse world. Accordingly, Kunzman concludes, to equip our students to participate effectively in our society, public schools must help them understand such diversity, including religious diversity (2006).

Not all educators, of course, phrase this desired outcome in exactly this way. But most are in agreement with Kunzman's general point: that it is important to increase student understanding of diverse religious perspectives because doing so will better prepare students to live in a peaceful, productive manner in social contexts that will increasingly be characterized by diversity of this sort.

However, whether the basis for attempting to increase student understanding of diverse religious perspectives is tied to inherent value or desired social outcomes or both, if we assume, as most public school educators do, that increasing such understanding is a worthy goal, the key pedagogical question becomes how this is best accomplished. Or, to be more specific, given that increased student understanding of diverse religious perspectives (traditions) is an acknowledged goal, the most important basic pedagogical task facing teachers and administrators is to determine the most appropriate ways to increase such understanding in our public schools.

PEDAGOGICAL TENSIONS FACING TEACHERS

The most common and least controversial way of increasing student understanding of diverse religions is simply to disseminate accurate information. While most students are aware of the multiplicity of religions in the world, most also have very limited knowledge of such religions. And what they do claim to know is often inaccurate. For many students, for instance, the totality of their understanding of Buddhism is captured by the image of monks with shaved heads burning incense, while their understanding of Islam centers around the concept of exclusivistic world domination at any cost. Accordingly, since most educators agree that an accurate factual understanding of religions is a necessary condition for effective communication and peaceful interaction among those with diverse perspectives, few educators deny that helping students gain a more accurate factual understanding of diverse religions is of vital importance.

However, even this seemingly unobjectionable way of increasing student understanding has not gone completely unchallenged. As Lorraine Kasprisin points out, while students can be taught words, the meanings given to these words will always to some extent "require that students understand the social construction of knowledge itself and the ways conceptual paradigms frame" our understanding of what is being said. Or, to state this important point differently, language is never neutral. Rather, Kasprisin argues, it is based on "assumptions about human nature, society, and values . . . that privilege one perspective over another" (2003, 421), which means that even the seemingly objective task of disseminating factual information about other religions is fraught with a form of subjectivity that always biases to some extent the information being received.

In one sense, this is surely correct. Both the meaning intended and the meaning understood in any attempt to communicate seemingly neutral "factual" information of any sort, including information about diverse religions, will inevitably be shaped by the embedded cultural coding and life experiences of all parties. I don't see, however, that this makes such attempts so ineffective or inappropriate that they serve no useful purpose. All human discourse, including discourse about religions, is fraught with this form of subjectivity. However, it has been my experience that if those involved in discussions of diverse religions recognize this fact—that is, as long as all parties acknowledge that their understanding of the "facts" about other religions will always to some extent be shaped by the preconceptions embedded in their view of the world—the dissemination of such information can still foster better understanding of other religious perspectives and at times even foster useful reflection about the preconceptions in question. So, as long as teachers explicitly note that the "factual" information shared is not fully free of bias (and why), I favor sharing such information with students.

Many educators, however, want to go further. It is not adequate, they believe, for students to increase only their cognitive, propositional understanding of diverse religious perspectives. It is also important for students to clarify *their feelings* about other religions and their followers. The desired goal here is not simply to increase tolerance of other religions—to strengthen the belief that adherents of these religions have the right to believe and act as they do. Nor is the goal to persuade students to agree with everything that adherents to other religions think and do. The goal is to foster a more empathetic understanding of other religious perspectives, an understanding that encourages students to *appreciate* the other religions from the point of view of an adherent of that religion (Kunzman 2006). Or, as Warren Nord states, the goal of this empathetic approach is to help students "look at the world and human experience and feel it from the point of view of the categories of that religion" (1995, 8).

If the intent here is not to encourage students to accept all religious perspectives as equally valid (an issue that will be discussed later) but rather simply to help students "feel" what it would be like to be an adherent of diverse religions, I see no legal or ethical difficulty. Students in public schools are routinely encouraged to attempt to appreciate ("feel") what it would be like to be a member of an ethnic minority, or to have been a woman in our culture one hundred years ago, or to have been a Jew in Germany in 1940, or to be a citizen in China today. And I see no reason for this not to be the same with respect to diverse religions. In all such cases, to encourage this type of empathetic understanding can contribute significantly to the types of respectful interaction among proponents of various religions that is rightly a goal of public education.

There is, though, continuing controversy over some of the *methods* by which educators attempt to engender this type of empathy in students. As long as the relevant curricula are made up of in-class activities such as assigned readings, video, and classroom discussion, there is little concern. However, not all educators believe that this is sufficient. As some see it, while having students *think about* diverse religions is an important step past the mere dissemination of factual information toward empathetic understanding, having students *directly experience* these religions in some way is also necessary (or at least very desirable). Paul Hurst has argued, for instance, that "schools should teach 'about' religion, provided that is interpreted to include a direct study of religions, which means entering as fully as possible into an understanding of what they claim to be true, [an understanding that] will demand a great deal of imaginative involvement in expressions of religious life and even a form of engagement in these activities themselves" (1974, 187–188).

Such involvement might include, for instance, having an adherent to a non-Western religious perspective—a representative from a local mosque or Buddhist center—discuss the religion in question with students. Or it might involve asking middle school and high school students individually or as a group to attend a non-Western religious service. It might even involve having students role-play religious practices—for instance, look toward Mecca at the appropriate times each day.

While no one denies that these forms of direct experience might broaden a student's empathetic understanding of a religion, concerns have been raised. First, I personally believe that having students experience a religion, even as "observers," can test the limits of the separation of church and state. While the intent of having students attend a mosque or a synagogue or having a Buddhist talk with students is seldom to promote a religion, the line between exposure and intended or unintended promotion (and even proselytization) is a fine one, especially given the widely varying communication skills and deeply embedded values and preconceptions of the teacher and/or the representatives of a given religion to whom students might be exposed.

Second, there is growing ethical concern that to experience a religion as an observer might in some cases trivialize or demean the religion in question. Some Native Americans, for instance, are becoming increasingly concerned with the growing desire of "outsiders" to seek understanding of their religion(s) by watching or experiencing sacred ceremonies, since such observation, they believe, can trivialize these ceremonies (Kasprisin 2003, 422).

This also seems a valid point. The fact that the majority of us from Western cultures view with great interest the religious artifacts from the Egyptian pyramids or Mayan ruins with little knowledge of or seeming interest in the religious signifi-cance of such items illustrates just how easy it is to disassociate our interest in and appreciation of finely crafted, rare, unusual, and/or ancient religious artifacts from the sacred contexts in which they were originally embedded. I can understand the concerns of those who fear that exposing students to the practices of other religions, especially if these religions are quite different from those with which the students are familiar, can devolve into "religious safaris" or visits to "religious museums."

However, it seems that as long as schools recognize this potential difficulty, work with both parents and the representatives of the religions in question to de-velop acceptable policies and procedures, and then work with teachers to ensure that they understand and adhere to these policies and procedures, the benefits of directly experiencing diverse religions outweigh the potential problems.

Is it justifiable, though, for the public school teacher to go even further than the dissemination of accurate information and the attempted engendering of empa-thetic understanding? Specifically, is it justifiable for the public school teacher to attempt to bring it about that all students affirm a core set of "appropriate" beliefs about other religions and their adherents?

Since any attempt by a teacher to bring it about that all students hold certain beliefs will quite likely require the teacher to encourage some students to retain their current beliefs while at the same time encouraging other students to modify their current beliefs, I want briefly to outline some recent scientific findings on the nature of belief modification and retention and note the relevance of these findings to the question at hand.

Recent studies in brain function have confirmed just how difficult belief mod-ification can be. This is true in part because we appear to be wired in such a way that our preconceptions or expectations significantly affect how we interpret and respond to new information presented to us. In fact, this effect is so dramatic that new information or counterarguments to what we currently believe seem to have little or no effect in many cases, which might in part explain why it is so easy for people, even educated people aware of diverse perspectives, to retain "their core beliefs over the course of their lifetime" (Goldman 2000, 236–237).

Of equal significance is the fact that our emotive attachment to beliefs strongly influences belief retention. Specifically, current studies seem to indicate that the more strongly we feel that our beliefs are correct, the less predisposed we are to examine the evidential basis for these beliefs and the less likely we are to modify these beliefs, even when we acknowledge relevant counterevidence (Goldman 2000, 236–241).

If we were to stop here, it might appear that while attempts to encourage stu-dents to retain deeply engrained beliefs about religion in any context, including a public school classroom, would be relatively easy, to encourage students to modify such beliefs would be relatively fruitless. But there is an additional finding of sig-nificance. While the normal functioning of the brain strongly favors belief reten-tion, conscious reflection on beliefs can result in belief modification. Specifically, it has been demonstrated that when individuals are made consciously aware of inconsistencies among their beliefs and/or counterevidence to these beliefs in a context where there is strong reinforcement of new or modified beliefs, we can "get a shift in emphasis from one [belief] to the other" (Taylor 2005). And the public school classroom is, of course, an ideal setting to help students reflect on their beliefs in just this way. Thus, the question of whether a public school teacher should attempt to bring it about that students affirm certain appropriate beliefs about religions and their adherents is valid and significant.

It should first be noted that almost all public school teachers currently do attempt to bring it about that students hold certain beliefs related to pervasive human characteristics such as race, gender, and disabling conditions. Specifically, students are encouraged to continue to believe, or come to believe, that engaging in intolerant or discriminatory behavior is wrong. And students are encouraged to continue to affirm, or come to affirm, the inherent worth and rights of the disabled, those of other racial/ethnic backgrounds, and the opposite gender.

Moreover, few teachers, parents, or community members question attempted belief indoctrination of this sort. Curricular and co-curricular activity in public schools has never been value-neutral. Such activity has always had embedded within it numerous normative (value) judgments about acceptable social responses to diverse groups and perspectives, judgments that are for the most part noncontroversial when they reflect the dominant values in society at a given point in time. Hence, since currently dominant societal norms include not only the belief that it is wrong to discriminate against persons with respect to characteristics over which they have no control—for instance, to discriminate against someone because of her or his race, gender, or physical/mental condition—but also the belief that these persons have equal inherent worth and are deserving of equal rights, it should not be surprising that public school teachers feel justified (I believe rightly) in attempting to bring it about that students hold these beliefs.

Would a similar line of reasoning justify attempts by public school teachers to bring it about that students hold certain beliefs about religions and their adherents? If the question is whether teachers can justifiably encourage all students to hold certain beliefs about how followers of diverse religions should be treated and how they should be viewed as persons, I think the answer is yes. While some in the United States have wanted to claim, especially since September 11, 2001, that certain non-Western religions—such as Islam—have anti-American agendas and, thus, that these religions should not be "tolerated," most Americans at present favor (at least in principle) "the free exercise of religion." I see no reason why teachers in public schools cannot justifiably attempt to bring it about that students believe it is wrong to treat those of other religions in intolerant or discriminatory ways and believe it is right to accept those of other religions as persons with equal inherent value.

But need teachers stop there? Might there not be other beliefs about religions and their adherents that public school teachers can justifiably attempt to bring it about that all students affirm? I want to extrapolate from some recent work on religious diversity by Wuthnow to introduce two beliefs that might be proposed to fit into this category. As Wuthnow sees it, the most appropriate response to the increasing religious diversity in the United States is what he labels "reflective pluralism" (2005, 286–307). To engage in this sort of reflection, he tells us, is not simply to become better informed or to strive to "live peacefully with those with whom one disagrees" (be tolerant) or even to attempt to develop an empathetic understanding of diverse religions. It is to engage intentionally and purposefully with "people and groups whose religious practices are fundamentally different from one's own" (289). And such engagement, as Wuthnow understands it, includes both (1) the recognition that since all of our beliefs, including our religious beliefs, depend on a point of view "shaped by the culture in which we live," we should not regard our "own position[s] as inherently superior" and (2) "a principled willingness to compromise" in the sense that we must be willing to move out of our social and emotional comfort levels "in order to arrive at a workable relationship with another person" (292).

The benefit of this form of engagement, we are told, is not only that it can minimize the likelihood of the sorts of "religious tensions, conflicts, and violence [that] have been so much a part of human history" (293). Such reflective engagement also allows us to focus on "the shared concerns for basic human dignity" found in the teachings of many of the world's religions, which can furnish a basis for interreligious cooperation to combat social ills and meet basic social needs (294).

It is important to note that Wuthnow does not explicitly claim or deny that encouraging students in a public school setting to become reflective pluralists would be appropriate. But not only does he highlight two increasingly popular pluralistic claims about religions—(1) that the beliefs of many religions are equally valid expressions of faith, expressions that adherents of these religions should be allowed or even encouraged to maintain, and (2) that religious believers of all faiths should identify and focus on what these religions have in common—he also highlights what such pluralists often note as the main benefits of widespread affirmation of these beliefs: a reduction in violent religious conflicts and an increase in socially beneficial interreligious cooperation. These outcomes are clearly quite compatible with what we have seen to be a key reason public school educators want to increase students' understanding of other religions—namely, their desire to better prepare students to live in a peaceful, productive manner in social contexts that will increasingly be characterized by religious diversity. Accordingly, since it seems reasonable to believe that widespread acceptance of the validity of diverse religious perspectives and increased focus on the commonalities in diverse religions might well result in more peaceful, mutually beneficial interaction among followers of diverse religions, the question of whether public school teachers can justifiably attempt to bring it about that students affirm the beliefs in question is worthy of exploration.

Let's first consider the contention that many religions contain equally valid expressions of faith. Even if we make the debatable assumption that this is true, it isn't at all clear that a public school teacher could justifiably attempt to bring it about that students believe this to be so.

The problem here, of course, is that various religions affirm conflicting doctrinal beliefs on significant issues. For example, while conservative Christians maintain that one must affirm certain beliefs about the saving power of Christ in order to spend eternity in God's presence, conservative Muslims strongly deny this. Orthodox Christians and Muslims are not only taught that the sacred scriptures of other religions contain false beliefs, but they are also encouraged to try to convert those of other religions to their religious perspective. And while many Muslims and Christians believe in a personal supernatural creator and personal immortality, some Buddhists deny both.

This means that a teacher can justifiably attempt to convince students that all religions are equally valid expressions of faith only if he or she can justifiably attempt to convince conservative proponents of some of these religions that some of their core doctrinal beliefs need to be modified or rejected. But to attempt to do this in a public school setting could reasonably be seen as violating the constitutional prohibition against both restricting the free exercise of religion and promoting a given religion.

Might it not at least be justifiable, though, for a public school teacher to encourage students to respect the right of adherents to other religions to retain their current religious beliefs? If we interpret this as asking whether a teacher can justifiably encourage students not to attempt to prohibit adherents to other religions from expressing and acting in accordance with their beliefs, the answer is yes, as this is only to say once again that teachers should encourage students to be tolerant. However, to encourage respect for the religious beliefs of others often carries with it the explicit or implicit assumption that it is inappropriate, if not unethical, to attempt to convince adherents of one religion that they should convert to another. For a public school teacher to attempt to convince all students that it is wrong to proselytize might once again place the teacher in the legally and morally questionable position of attempting to convince some students that their fundamental belief that they should try to convert others should be rejected.

There is, however, yet another option. In an attempt to do more than simply encourage tolerance of expression and empathetic understanding, is it not at least justifiable for the public school teacher to attempt to point out the important common values affirmed by most of the world's major religions—values that we can all accept and should all desire to see lived out? Is it not justifiable for the teacher to point out, for instance, that most of the world's major religions prohibit such things as killing, lying, stealing, and sexual exploitation and that these same religions encourage such things as helping those in need and treating adherents of other religions with respect? To do so, it has been argued, would not simply be of value within the classroom or the community. Since religious convictions clearly influence social, political, and economic activity on a global scale, emphasizing the shared common values of religions has the potential to facilitate better global relationships. And to encourage such relationships is surely an appropriate goal of public education (Shingleton 2008).

Not all agree that highlighting "positive commonalities" is an appropriate way to approach diversity, including religious diversity, in the classroom. Pedro Noguera maintains, for instance, that schools should move away from attempts to focus on the shared beliefs and values of culturally distinct groups, as this tends to render them "largely invisible." We are better served, he maintains, by teaching students "to respect differences and develop curricula aimed at helping them to understand more about themselves and others" (1999). But I am not convinced. While I agree that encouraging understanding of and respect for diverse religions is important, it seems that to claim that this should be the focus instead of "positive commonalities" creates a false dilemma. I see no reason that a teacher could not justifiably and fruitfully focus on both.

Others will see any focus on "positive commonalities" as yet another thinly veiled attempt to encourage students to modify their current religious beliefs in ways that make them more accommodating of other religious perspectives. This is, I agree, a danger. The country was founded on a form of "civil religion"—a Judeo-Christian value system—that is with us still. So it is always possible that a teacher focusing on commonalties in diverse religions will actually end up implicitly or explicitly encouraging students to adopt a more inclusive religious perspective. This, however, need not be the case. And we do live in a world that would benefit from an increase in shared values. So I see no legal or ethical reason that a teacher should not, given the potential difficulties noted, expose students to the "positive commonalities" in diverse religious perspectives.

CONCLUSIONS

I have outlined and assessed the most significant responses to the general question of how public school educators should respond to the religious diversity to which students are increasingly exposed, with a focus on the specific pedagogical question of the ways in which public school teachers can justifiably respond to the increasing religious diversity facing students in the classroom.

We have seen that there are few easy, noncontroversial answers. In fact, some of the most fundamental issues—for example, the extent to which we can continue to base our public education primarily on Western cultural/religious values and the extent to which we can encourage religious belief reflection without favoring one religion—are just beginning to receive the attention they deserve.

Regardless of the complexities, however, discussions about the appropriate extent and nature of the public school response to diverse religious perspectives must continue. Religious belief increasingly motivates impassioned behavior that affects the lives of an expanding number of individuals worldwide. And the public school is the ideal setting to start the sort of dialogue that can help students prepare to live in such a world in a more peaceful, productive manner.

REFERENCES

Goldman, Ronald. 2000. "Is There a Cognitive Basis for Religious Belief." *Journal of Psychology and Judaism* 24: 234–241.

Hurst, Paul. 1974. *Knowledge and the Curriculum*, London: Routledge and Kegan Paul.

Kasprisin, Lorraine. 2003. "Religious Diversity, Education, and the Concept of Separation: Some Further Questions." In Kal Alston, ed., *Philosophy of Education 2003*. Urbana, Ill.: Philosophy of Education Society/University of Illinois, 420–422.

Kunzman, Robert. 2006. "Imaginative Engagement with Religious Diversity in the Public School Classrooms." *Religious Education* (Fall): 101(4): 516-531

Lessow-Hurley, Judith. 1999. "Religious Diversity in the Public Schools: Multicultural Perspectives." *Multicultural Perspectives* 1: 8-12

Milligan, Jeffrey Ayala. 2003. "Religious Diversity, Education, and the Concept of Separation: Do Good Fences Make Good Neighbors?" In Kal Alston, ed., *Philosophy of Education 2003*. Urbana, Ill.: Philosophy of Education Society/University of Illinois, 411–419.

Noguera, Pedro. 1999. "Confronting the Challenge of Diversity in Education." *In Motion Magazine*, April 10.

Nord, Warren. 1995. *Religion and American Education: Rethinking a National Dilemma*. Chapel Hill: University of North Carolina Press.

Shingleton, Bradley. 2008. "In Search of Common Ground: The Role of a Global Ethic in Inter-Religious Dialogue." *Carnegie Ethics Online*, Carnegie Council www.cceia.org/resources/ethics_online/0023.html.

Taylor, Kathleen. 2005. Quoted in Alok Jha, "Where Belief Is Born." *Guardian*, June 30.

Wuthnow, Robert. 2005. *America and the Challenge of Religious Diversity*. Princeton, N.J.: Princeton University Press.

FOR FURTHER READING

Bellah, Robert. 1975. *The Broken Covenant: American Civil Religion in Time of Trail*. New York: Seabury.

Eck, Diana. 2001. *How a "Christian Country" Has Become the World's Most Religiously Diverse Nation*. New York: Harper.

Kunzman, Robert. 2006. *Grappling with the Good: Talking about Religion and Morality in Public Schools*. Albany: State University of New York Press.

Meacham, John. 2006. *American Gospel: God, the Founding Fathers, and the Making of a Nation*. New York, Random House.

Nash, Robert. 2001. *Religious Pluralism in the Academy: Opening the Dialogue*. New York: P. Lang.

Nord, Warren. 1995. *Religion and American Education: Rethinking a National Dilemma*. Chapel Hill: University of North Carolina Press.

Wuthnow, Robert. 2005. *America and the Challenge of Religious Diversity*. Princeton, N.J.: Princeton University Press.

CHAPTER 22

RELIGIOUS DIVERSITY AND RELIGIOUS ENVIRONMENTALISM

ROGER S. GOTTLIEB

"There's a song that they sing of their home in the sky,
maybe you can believe it if it helps you to sleep, but singing
works just fine for me."

—James Taylor, "Sweet Baby James"

IN some perspectives, religious diversity is a regrettable problem. According to this view, truth and error are clear-cut categories. Here, diversity is to be stamped out or, if that is impossible, to be lamented. Here, we can speak of the "one true faith" (1TF) and the need to spread or at least teach this faith to the nonbelievers. Given the premises of this view, such proselytizing would seem to be completely justified, at least if we take for granted that religion is about something important. If we possess the truth about what God wants, the afterlife, moral values, and the meaning of life, we'd be selfish and derelict if we didn't try to spread it around. Here, diversity in religion makes about as much sense as diversity in science. And while there are areas of scientific controversy and countless unsettled questions, we tend to believe that we can identify what we actually do know. We don't usually tolerate diversity regarding what we take to have been settled.

A rather different view proposes that *religious diversity* and the related term *pluralism* are conditions to be acknowledged, accepted, and perhaps even celebrated, for two reasons. First, the presence of a multitude of religious traditions is an ineluctable fact of modern life. In a globalized world, rife with the legacies of imperialism and rising rates of emigration, we simply will have a variety of religions in many nations. And even nations that are religiously homogeneous will still be forced to deal with people of other faiths in international affairs. If we cannot muster a little acceptance, a little tolerance, for the other, then our social life and international affairs will be an endless cycle of conflict and bloodshed. If, as some say, diversity is the fact and pluralism is the acceptance and/or celebration of the fact,[1] we have a choice between pluralism and war. Given that we can't wipe the other out, we'd better learn to get along.

Second, however, is a position that goes one very large step further. Rather than offering mere acceptance, we should value diversity. Learning to coexist happily with other religions actually teaches us something we need to know about religious life. Exactly what that something is will vary, but some of the candidates are as follows:

- *Noncoercion* (NC). We will learn that religious faith by its nature must be freely given, and therefore any attempt to force a person to believe something fundamentally mistakes the nature of faith (Locke 1689).
- *Learning from the other* (LO). We will see that even if other people's core religious beliefs are different from ours, we can still learn something from them that will help us in our own spiritual life. In recent years, American Christians, for example, have been utilizing Buddhist meditation techniques and yoga.
- *From many to one* (FM1). We will shift our understanding of our own faith, realizing that what is essential to it is something that is common to other faiths. Whatever the differences in scripture, God language, or rituals, the core values of love and respect for others unite us. In this sense, an appreciation of religious diversity turns, ironically, into the end of diversity. This perspective devalues a faith's traditional metaphysics in favor of its more philosophical ethics, spiritual yearnings, or "life cycle" (birth, death, marriage, etc.) concerns. Or at least it interprets those metaphysics metaphorically and in motivational terms rather than literally. Exactly what God is, what he or she is called, and what books appear on the cosmic CV diminish in significance compared with general imperatives to love one another; lessen our attachment to desire; develop humility, kindness, and compassion; and nurture our children.

As a religious liberal of the first order, whose attitude toward faith in general is tolerant, if not politically and psychologically opportunistic, I am mainly concerned with how religious environmentalism serves as a negation of 1TF and moves faiths, like it or not, toward LO and FM1. Precisely because the environmental crisis, if honestly and openly faced, shows us a degree of commonality perhaps never before faced, other aspects of what we share become clearer, and our differences diminish.

WHAT DOES THE ENVIRONMENTAL CRISIS HAVE TO DO WITH RELIGION?

The environmental crisis negates many central principles of traditional religion, for it is first of all a crisis of our biological, and thus essentially our physical, reality. To take but one telling example, a random study of twelve newborns in 2004 revealed a horrific average of 197 toxic chemicals in their placental blood. These included known carcinogens, endocrine disrupters, and neurological threats (Environmental Working Group 2005). As a process that inscribes itself on the very inside of our bodies as well as on the landscape and other species, the environmental crisis assaults us at the very lowest common denominator of our existence, our existence as bodies. But much of world religion has denied the importance or reality of that dimension of our existence, at best emphasizing the need to regulate, restrict, and transcend it.

The environmental crisis undercuts this devaluation and dismissal of the body. For while religions were teaching that an immortal soul existed outside the body or that our bodily impulses had to be controlled by our higher selves, they were simultaneously trying to ensure the generational continuity of believers. Such continuity required great attention to sexual reproduction, food supply, buildings in which the bodies of believers could gather, economies to support physical needs, and so forth. Bodies were taken for granted theologically but given a tremendous amount of attention practically.

The environmental crisis makes this posture, if not impossible, at least a good deal harder. For now, the future of the earth as a habitable planet for our species is in doubt. This is a global threat that dwarfs any war, famine, flood, or drought of the past.[2] Once we see that there might not be future generations or that instead of hope, we face the prospect of a slow but irrevocable decline in which apocalypse is a "way of life" (Buell 2003), the denigration of the body becomes that much harder to maintain.

To put it another way, all of our children are being born with toxins in their bloodstreams. In just this fact, we now have a common problem with people of all other faiths and nonfaiths. The enormous emphasis we place on differences in beliefs and practices might remain, but alongside it is the new reality that the cancer ward or special needs school of ill, defective children will be defined not by beliefs but by malformed and damaged physical structures.

It can be argued that this sense of commonality is not different from, say, people of different faiths realizing that they share a threat of any natural disaster or invading army. I believe, first, that the very magnitude of the threat means that even if it resembles the past in conceptual structure, it has a different impact. Other issues make the environmental threat distinct as well.

For one thing, the environmental crisis is something we are bringing on ourselves. The Protestants, Jews, and Catholics of 1940s England might have shared a sense of threat from Hitler's military aggression, but they were not the cause of that aggression. To the extent that ordinary people of faith, as well as the leaders of their religions, support the current environmental regime by their participation and complicity, they share not only a common threat but also a common (failure to take) responsibility. As a Jew, I am, just like my Catholic and Methodist friends (and like my atheist, secularist ones as well), poisoning my own children. Guilt and shame about our past blindness and present moral laziness give me something in common with people whose theology is alien to me. Like people of wildly different classes, ethnicities, and personal beliefs who meet at a twelve-step meeting to confess the many harms they have done as addicts, religious people who gather to focus on environmental issues will spend less time agreeing or disagreeing about "religion" and more time about admitting and commiserating about their own and one another's moral failings.

This is especially significant for people of faith, for yet another thing that people of faith have in common historically is precisely the attitudes that attend 1TF: the idea that religious people, institutions, texts, and so on, have a special moral insight, cosmic knowledge, and ethical value. Religions are forever telling everyone else what to think and what to believe. The basis for this presumption supposedly is the idea that religious people act more rightly and know more than others. The Bible, the Qur'an, and the meditation cushion give us special insights before which, in some fashion or another (as a traditional Jewish prayer would have it), "every knee must bend."

The dawning awareness of the environmental crisis undercuts this self-evaluation. What a surprise to find that religions have done no better than anyone else. The world's religious communities were almost without exception supporters of modern industrialization, blind to the effects on humans and other species and dependent on secular forces for understanding what was going on. It was free-lance spiritual types, some single individuals with religious values, rather than recognized theologians or faith leaders, German existential phenomenologists, anticommunist Western Marxists, postbeatnik hippie types, and disgruntled social critics, who sounded the alarm. If this is no longer the case, if religions are now among world leaders in environmental awareness, that is both a big and a recent change.

Facing the magnitude of this change is extremely important, in part because the most important people to whom we endlessly proclaim our wisdom and virtue are our own children. Every religion that instructs its young, which means every religion whatsoever, now faces a situation in which any student at any Sunday school can say, with no small justification, "Who are you to teach me anything? Look what you've done, or allowed to be done, to the earth." If all religions don't acknowledge their past failings, they will, however subliminally, be perceived by many of their own young as hypocrites and moral failures.

The environmental crisis also threatens some of the basic physical practices of religious life. Again, while the more philosophically oriented theology of our traditions tends almost exclusively to privilege the mental or spiritual aspects of religious life—experiences of God, beliefs about God, the mental transformations involved in enlightenment—the actual practice of religion typically involves a great deal of physicality.[3] What does it mean, then, to take communion when the wafer contains pesticide residue, or to sanctify Sabbath wine made with genetically engineered grapes, or to focus one's attention on the breath (as a basic Buddhist meditation technique) when the air is so unhealthy that people are cautioned not to go outside and exercise, in a sense, that is, not to breathe?

Thus, to the extent that the environmental crisis is a crisis of our past and our future, of our moral status and our ability to instruct our children, of our basic theological self-conception and our essential rituals, the environmental crisis is indeed a crisis for religion as a whole. In that sense, it is a crisis that turns religion outside itself to the wider world of politics, economics, and culture. For if religions had a serious part in creating the crisis, they certainly did not do it all by themselves. Therefore, if the crisis is to be met, religions need to involve themselves in the wider worlds of legal structures, government economic policy, public control of corporations, and cultural meanings. Religions necessarily will see that the point is not just to lament what we've done to the earth (and one another) but to change what we are doing. Whatever their theologies, they now must become agents of political and social change. They are catapulted (if they are not there already) into difficult political strategic questions of how to balance tolerance and principles, reform and revolution, coalition building with different groups and the need to publicly witness the truth regardless of the strategic benefits.

Since this reality implicates all organized world religions, they are all in the same boat. Their theologies might be no more similar than they were, say, forty years ago, but they won't be thinking about theology quite so much just because they have to think about these other issues as well.

How Do We Know It's possible?
Because It Is Real

There are theoretical criticisms that can be made of the above statement. All of these things might be what religions *should* do, but that doesn't mean that they *will* do them. Clearly, a lot of religious leaders and (often self-appointed) spokespeople are still spending a great deal of time distinguishing between their (true) faith and everyone else's. 1TF might be getting a lot of bad press in some circles, but it is alive and well in others.

However, the simplest way to establish that a historical development is possible is to point out that it is actual. Let us, therefore, examine some interesting examples of religious cooperation and spiritual solidarity in response to the environmental crisis, cooperation that unfolds in the face of a still highly diverse religious world. These examples come from the global movement of religious environmentalism, which involves deep theological change, profound institutional commitment, and thousands of examples of real-world political action.[4]

In southern Zimbabwe, a remarkable coalition of independent African Christian churches and indigenous spirit-worshiping groups worked in response to a ravaged landscape. Erosion, damaged stream banks, and deforestation had left the region's agriculture in a perilous condition. Formed by the initiative of a South African professor of theology who had studied the role of Zimbabwe's churches in the struggle for independence, the organization (ZIRRCON) eventually involved more than thirty paid employees, more than a hundred local churches with more than a million members, and women's and youth clubs. In less than a decade, it planted more than 8 million trees, altered local attitudes toward political activism and soil control, and provided countless contexts in which otherwise very different groups could interact productively (see Daneel 2001 and 2005).[5]

The most instructive fact about ZIRRCON is the theological distance between the participants, which was far larger and more serious than among participants in ecumenical efforts in varieties of Christian or even interfaith connections among different kinds of monotheists. In the context of the ecological struggle, profound religious differences were put aside. As the president of the African Association of Earthkeeping Churches, Bishop Machokoto, put it: "We must be fully prepared to recognize the authority of our krallheads [local chiefs] and chiefs. For if we show contempt for them, where will we plant our trees? . . . Let our bishops in their eagerness to fight the war of the trees not antagonize the keepers of the land. . . . Let us fully support our tribal elders in this struggle of afforestation" (Daneel 2001, 155).

Given what was accomplished by the disparate elements in ZIRRCON, it is not surprising that for umbrella organizations such as the National Council of Churches (NCC) and the World Council of Churches (WCC), collective action on behalf of environmental causes has now become commonplace. These actions range over educational and liturgical innovation, well-publicized proclamations concerning important environmental problems, and local efforts. Since these are the flagship organizations of world Protestant Christianity and since many of the coalitions in which they work involve non-Christians as well, this is no small matter.

While the generally liberal Protestants of the NCC and the WCC might be expected to engage in common environmental action, a more surprising development is the emergence of a profoundly different attitude toward alien religious traditions by the Catholic church. In a range of pronouncements by important Catholic leaders, we have the example of at least some of the essential attitudes of ZIRRCON writ much larger. The change of which I am speaking is a newfound respect for indigenous traditions. Bearing out some of what I have described above as some of the implications of the environmental crisis for religious self-examination and transformation, we find examples of Catholic leadership speaking respectfully and even favorably of indigenous peoples' ability to understand and interact with the natural world in a sustainable way. These statements suggest that this ability is seen as more than simply a technical competence. (Catholic leaders would, for example, be highly respectful of the people who fix their computers, but respect in such an instance is not religiously significant.) Rather, indigenous environmental wisdom is viewed as a kind of spiritual and/or moral gift from which the Catholic world has something to learn.

For example, in 1988, the bishops of the Philippines—the religious leaders of a country with 70 million Catholics—uttered a heartfelt plea: "What is happening to our beautiful land?" Their document described the wide range of disastrous environmental and human consequences of unplanned and reckless development and called for a profound rethinking and change of direction. So far, so good. But remarkably, the bishops defined themselves in solidarity with

> [t]ribal people all over the Philippines, who have seen the destruction of their world at close range [and] have cried out in anguish. Also men and women who attempt to live harmoniously with nature and those who study ecology have tried to alert people to the magnitude of the destruction taking place in our time. The latter are in a good position to tell us what is happening since they study the web of dynamic relationships which support and sustains all life within the earthly household. This includes human life. (Bishops of the Philippines 1988)

But it is not just that Catholics should have compassion for the suffering of indigenous people; it is also that for generations, "the hunting and food gathering techniques of our tribal forefathers showed a sensitivity and respect for the rhythms of nature." And "Our forefathers and tribal brothers and sisters today still attempt to live in harmony with nature. They see the Divine Spirit in the living world and show their respect through prayers and offerings. Tribal Filipinos remind us that the exploitative approach to the natural world is foreign to our Filipino culture."

For example: after an extensive process of reflection and consultation, the bishops from the Columbia River watershed (Washington, Oregon, Idaho, British Columbia) published a lavishly illustrated booklet entitled *The Columbia River Watershed: Caring for Creation and the Common Good*. Like "What Is Happening?" the document included a wide-ranging concern for the ecology of the region and called on all responsible parties to take in the negative consequences of destructive practices and cooperate in finding ways toward ecological sanity. In a section on regional traditions, the bishops observed:

> Native religions taught respect for the ways of nature, personified as a nurturing mother for all creatures. They saw the salmon as food from this mother, and the river as the source of their life and the life of the fish. They adapted themselves to the river and to the cycles of the seasons. Among the Wanapum, the River People, some elders were set apart as dreamers and healers, respected for their visions and healing powers. (Columbia River Bishops 2005)

What does it mean that the Catholic church, which for centuries held native traditions in contempt and persecuted them, can now speak of them with respect? The simple answer can only be that great change is often possible in the face of great threat and that honest Catholics cannot help but notice that their own teachings simply had not prepared them to understand the dangers of the forms of life they unwittingly endorsed. Something was missing, and in their honest appraisal of their predicament, they came upon spiritually oriented practical attitudes that contain something they had missed.

This is not to say that Western religion is necessarily hostile to ecological sanity. As the work of a broad range of ecotheologians has shown, many (if, in all probability, not all) of the needed metaphysical and moral resources are there already. From the stewardship reading of Genesis to the teachings of Saint Francis, from the widespread idea that God speaks to us in two books—that of nature as well as scripture—to the kind of spiritual subjectivity attributed to nature in Psalms, the Judeo-Christian tradition has a plethora of ecological themes and resources.[6]

Yet it was not these motifs that Christianity lived by for centuries. And as far as we can tell, in recent centuries, native peoples did. This difference is the basis for an openness to and appreciation of (to put it mildly) diverse spiritual traditions.

JUST HOW DIVERSE IS DIVERSITY?

We can only speak of religious diversity if we know what religions are and can count them. To count them, we must be able to distinguish them from one another. While this might seem obvious, in contemporary religious life, it is important to keep in mind. To take a simple example, is Judaism a religion, or is it a collection of different religions with certain historical sources and common practices but encompassing such radically different beliefs and practices (in, say, modern Chasidism and Jewish Renewal) that it makes little sense to count it as a unitary tradition? The answer, surely, is that it depends on the purpose for which we are counting. To a Nazi, a Jew of any kind is a Jew; to an Evangelical who is sure that only belief in Jesus gets you into heaven, the distinctions between those who keep kosher and have only male rabbis and those who welcome female rabbis and drive on the Sabbath are insignificant. Yet to my brother, who is an ultra-Orthodox rabbi, my own Reform synagogue is so far from being "really Jewish" that he would not set foot in it (for fear that anyone seeing him enter might get the wrong impression and think that it was really a place for Jews).

In a broader context, we might wonder what distinguishes a religion from other worldviews or forms of life. The religious right in the United States has argued that secularism is just another religious viewpoint—and they have a point. To the extent that religions are identified not by sacred texts or belief in the supernatural but by adherence to certain foundational values and assertions about the meaning of life, this position has some validity. What John Rawls called "comprehensive doctrines" can be based on the Bible or the Communist Manifesto, the Buddha or Ayn Rand. In this sense, we face a bewildering variety not just of religions conceived of in the traditional sense of alternative teaching about God or spiritual truth but also of worldviews that range over a plethora of moral and metaphysical questions, from the privileged or limited nature of science to the spiritual meaning of sexuality. All of these worldviews share a common inability to justify their essential premises, whether those premises involve, for example, metaphysical claims about God or moral ones about human rights.[7]

What effect does the environmental crisis have on this kind of religious diversity?

In precisely the same way that it has led some Catholic bishops to appreciate native wisdom, it has led in at least some cases to a powerful rapprochement of religion and science and religious and secular environmental activists.

The example of science, coming after centuries of distrust, hostility, and at times direct conflict on both sides, is perhaps the most remarkable. For one thing, virtually every serious ecotheologian and countless pronouncements by religious leadership contain detailed accounts of the environmental crisis derived from . . . scientific ecology! To take just one example, the United Methodist Church includes in its comparatively brief statement on environmental issues the following:

> Economic, political, social, and technological developments have increased our
> human numbers, and lengthened and enriched our lives. However, these
> developments have led to regional defoliation, dramatic extinction of species,
> massive human suffering, overpopulation, and misuse and overconsumption of
> natural and nonrenewable resources, particularly by industrialized societies.
> (United Methodist Church n.d.)

That is, familiar uses of scripture or deep moral pieties are not enough but must be joined with facts and figures about global warming, toxic rivers, and desertification. There is a widespread if tacit acknowledgment that the practice of religion now requires ideas (e.g., sustainability) and information (e.g., asthma rates in polluted areas, global climate feedback loops) that it cannot generate on its own. The closed world of religion, in which tradition, authority, and abstract theology were supposed to provide the basis for a religious life, has opened up to something else.

Second, and even more impressive, there are examples of practical cooperation between religious leaders and leading scientists over environmental issues. In 1992, for instance, a joint statement signed by one hundred fifty scientists and religious leaders in a shared "Mission to Washington" proclaimed:

> We are people of faith and of science who, for centuries, often have traveled
> different roads. In a time of environmental crisis, we find these roads
> converging . . . our two ancient, sometimes antagonistic, traditions now reach out
> to one another in a common endeavor to preserve the home we share. . . . We
> believe that science and religion, working together, have an essential contribution
> to make toward any significant mitigation and resolution of the world
> environmental crisis. What good are the most fervent moral imperatives if we do
> not understand the dangers and how to avoid them? What good is all the data in
> the world without a steadfast moral compass? (Joint Appeal 1992, 735)

More recently, in January 2007, at a press conference at the Harvard Club in Cambridge, Massachusetts, a group of Evangelical Christian leaders and leading scientists addressed the president, Congress, and other leading political figures, calling for serious action on global warming. Asserting that defense of life on earth is a "profound moral imperative," the group cautioned that "reckless human activity has imperiled the Earth—especially the unsustainable and short-sighted lifestyles and public policies of our own nation [and] we share a profound moral obligation to work together to call our nation, and other nations, to the kind of dramatic change urgently required in our day." The group effort had been initiated by Rich Cizik, head of the enormous National Association of Evangelicals, a religious grouping not typically aligned with tolerant, ecumenical Protestantism, progressive Catholicism, or Reform Judaism. Cizik was joined by Eric Chivian of Harvard Medical School, who said, in a statement that crystallizes all of these remarkable religious (in the broad sense) changes: "There is no such thing as a Republican or Democrat, a liberal or conservative, a religious or secular environment" (Zaberenko 2007).

This is as remarkable a move for a scientist as it is for a religious leader, for while scientists have not had the social power to oppress religion, the culture of science has often understood itself as being in profound opposition to the irrational, faith-not-reason-based, superstitious, irredeemably old-school style of religion. Yet where in scientific theory was Chivian to turn when he wanted to express the shared "profound moral obligation" that he felt so strongly? Is there a scientific way to prove moral obligation? Actually, no. There is only a multifaceted—religious and secular—tradition of trying to support it, explaining what it means, and arguing over tough cases. In other words, there are only a wide range of comprehensive doctrines, and in this way, the barriers between science and religion, in the face of the environmental crisis considered as moral as well as instrumental, begin to shatter.

After the watershed of cooperation with science, it is perhaps less impressive but certainly still significant to cite an example of a religious group engaging in direct cooperation with a secular political organization. As the Philippines bishops observed, those who "study ecology" and seek to live "in harmony with nature" are a religious environmentalist's natural allies. In January 2002, the Sierra Club and the National Council of Churches cooperated on a television advertisement to resist drilling in the Arctic National Wildlife Sanctuary. The groups had compromised on the language used—leaving out "God" but including "creation"—and the heads of both groups reported nearly unanimous positive response. In July 2008, the Sierra Club helped recruit for an initiative that took as its goal the training of hundreds of Christian clergy as presenters of the slide show made famous in Al Gore's film *An Inconvenient Truth*. The goal of the training, wrote Sierra Club staffer Lyndsey Moselely, was "to equip faith leaders with the best science available so that [they] can help educate and inform [their] communities" (Moselely 2008).[8]

How Is This Possible? FM1

The irony of the liberal, tolerant, modern response to religious diversity, the one that celebrates diversity by embracing pluralism, is that differences among religions become minimized, and by an ironic turning of concepts, diversity, if not completely eliminated, starts to fade out.

For example, Margaret Bullitt-Jonas is an Episcopal priest and a colleague of mine on the Leadership Council of Religious Witness for the Earth, a national, independent, interfaith network dedicated to creating a society in which human beings live in loving, just relationships with one another and with all of creation.[9] As a religious environmentalist, Bullitt-Jonas has spoken out and demonstrated, and in 2001, she was arrested for nonviolent civil disobedience protesting President George W. Bush's energy policy. Bullitt-Jonas has a defined theology. She is a very specific kind of Protestant Christian, and she believes, as Jesus says in the New Testament, that "No one comes to the Father except through [him]." In her interfaith work, however, that belief, while not being negated, simply recedes in importance. As she looks around the room at members of the Council—which include other kinds of Christians, Unitarians, Jews, and eclectic spiritual types— another of her beliefs rises in importance: that there are "different ways of imaging the divine and structuring our path to it." This is not anything-goes relativism, she is clear, for all these different ways can be subjected to the same test: Do they lead their respective followers to greater compassion? On this basis, Bullitt-Jonas feels that a liberal Jew (with overtones of paganism and Buddhism) like myself is in a sense closer to her religiously than a doctrinaire, intolerant, rigid Christian (Bullitt-Jonas 2008).

In a sense, then, calculations of diversity are subject to (at least) two different conceptions of religious identity. For one, religions are distinguished by their formal creed, particular holy books, institutions, and rituals. For a second—the one in terms of which Gottlieb and Bullitt-Jonas are more religiously alike than Bullitt-Jonas and, say, Jerry Falwell—vague but real values such as compassion (and typically some kind of ecological consciousness and an acceptance of gender equality) are the key.[10] This sense of religious commonality permeates a good deal of the world's religious culture now and is dramatically furthered by participation in religious environmentalism. For while the struggles of religious environmentalism are clearly practically oriented—cleaning up a river, protecting infants' bloodstreams, and so on—they are not *simply* practical. Whether one thinks of the natural world as a place where divinity resides or simply the divinity's miraculous gift to humans, there is a sense among the vast majority of religious environmentalists that action on behalf of "all of life" involves an expression of specifically religious values and has as its object the care of something that itself possesses at least a modicum of holiness. When we all work together on this holy task, then, there is a sense in which we are all part of the same religion. We are engaged in a fellowship. We practice together. We support each other's calling. We celebrate life—and defend it—arm-in-arm. Are there differences? Of course, but as I have observed already, the world's identified religions are filled with differences in any case, and even in the most homogeneous religious community, there will be wide variations in the ways people imagine or experience the holy.

This result might not please everyone, to say the least. It is not hard to imagine hearing a traditionalist argue, "Either Jesus is the Son of God, or he is not. If he is and was indeed sent to us to teach us how to get to the Father, then we had better acknowledge him, or we simply won't make real religious progress. The most pedestrian logic tells us that either this kind of claim is true, or it is not. No fancy footwork about compassion or ecological concern will change that."

There is much to admire in this position, not the least of which is the idea that religion has boundaries, rules, constraints, and truths. Without those, it would seem to fall back into a mish-mash of emotional responses, aesthetic enjoyments, and mildly pleasing socializing.

But while I am aware of that danger and think that, for example, Bullitt-Jonas's test of religious adequacy would do a good deal to remove its sting, I am more concerned with another religious problem: that the Orthodox believer, the one who is so eager to present me with a clear either/or of true belief or false error, has actually mistaken the nature of religious life. That is because we cannot ever unproblematically know what "acknowledging Jesus" consists in. Does it mean simply saying over and over, "I acknowledge (believe, have faith, etc.) that Jesus is the Son of God," as if true faith consists in nothing more than verbal repetition? Does it mean quoting scripture, as if we can know what scripture means simply by saying it often enough? Can one perhaps show more love of Jesus by caring for one's (disagreeable, foreign-looking) neighbor than by going to church, or repeating Jesus's name over and over, or even knowing who Jesus is? Is it a matter of internal, experiential feeling that guarantees the truth of our love of God? Perhaps, but can't we be mistaken about the power of our feelings or about how important they are for the way we will live in the future? The deep religious problem is that there is no objective way to know who has religious faith, because faith cannot be measured.

In short, whether or not one believes in any religion is to some extent a subjective question, based on the degree of internal commitment and subject to a variety of not easily applied interpretative criteria of authenticity. As Kierkegaard puts it, "All paganism consists in this, that God is related to man directly" (1941, 219)[11] For just that reason, in a sense, Bullitt-Jonas cannot really be sure whether I, who would never say that I believe Jesus to be the Messiah, am as much a follower of Jesus as any of her fellow Episcopal priests. Even if we have to love Jesus to get into heaven, there might be a whole host of ways to do that, some of which might include not knowing that he ever existed. And then the difference between those who embrace diversity and those who reject it would be that the former, unlike the latter, are not at all sure what that love consists in, outside of the chancy, all-encompassing, always questionable practice of something like compassion.

Now that this compassion extends to all of life, its power for effecting a specifically religious transformation of the social world has radically deepened. Since we are beset with a threat to us all, we have the chance to manifest love for us all. If we are all in the same boat, sailing on or going down together, at least we do not have to face the terrors of the storm by ourselves.

NOTES

1. The official account of Harvard's well-funded "Pluralism Project." See Eck 2006.

2. Nuclear war can be seen as the ultimate environmental catastrophe.

3. A great deal could be made of this contradiction, as, indeed, theologies influenced by feminism's critique of patriarchy have done.

4. My own account, as well as that of other scholars, can be found in Gottlieb 2006a, 2006b, and 2003.

5. By comparison, the Kenyan Green Belt movement, the leader of which received the Nobel Peace Prize, planted about 30 million trees.

6. The same can be said of Buddhism, Hinduism, Islam, and others. The passages from key scriptures and theologians are not hard to find, if one really wants to find them. Taking them seriously, of course, is another matter entirely.

7. It could certainly be argued that there are, to the contrary, lots of solid justifications for comprehensive views. Yet the fact that there are so many justifications for so many different views and that both the justifications and the views keep on coming actually reinforces rather than contradicts my point.

8. The Sierra Club has a permanent and significantly funded office to reach out to faith communities. For an account of their work and wide-ranging information on recent faith-based environmental initiatives, see Sierra Club 2008.

9. For further information, see the group's Web site: www.religiouswitness.org.

10. None of this is meant to suggest that there couldn't be a vast amount of real debate on what "compassion" means in any given context.

11. This entire critical line originated with Kierkegaard. See Kierkegaard 1941.

REFERENCES

Bishops of the Philippines. 1988. "What Is Happening to Our Beautiful Land?" Marquette University Web site, www.marquette.edu/theology/interfacing/ChurchonEcological-Degradation/documents/WhatisHappeningtoOurBeautifulLand_000.pdf.

Buell, Frederic. 2003. *From Apocalypse to Way of Life: Environmental Crisis in the American Century.* New York: Routledge.

Bullitt-Jonas, Margaret. 2008. Phone interview with author, July 8.

Columbia River Bishops. 2005. "The Columbia River Watershed: Caring for Creation and the Common Good." Columbia River Project Web site, www.columbiariver.org.

Daneel, Marthinus L. 2001. *African Earthkeepers: Wholistic Interfaith Mission.* Maryknoll, N.Y.: Orbis, 2001.

———. 2005. "African Earthkeeping Churches." In Bron Taylor, ed., *Encyclopedia of Religion and Nature*. London: Continuum.

Eck, Diana. 2006. "What Is Pluralism." Pluralism Project Web site, www.pluralism.org/pluralism/what_is_pluralism.php.

Environmental Working Group. 2005. "Body Burden—The Pollution in Newborns." Body Burden Web site, www.ewg.org/reports/bodyburden2/execsumm.php.

Gottlieb, Roger S. 2003. *This Sacred Earth: Religion, Nature, Environment*, 2nd ed. New York: Routledge.

———. 2006a. *A Greener Faith: Religious Environmentalism and Our Planet's Future*. New York: Oxford University Press.

———. 2006b. *The Oxford Handbook of Religion and Ecology*. New York: Oxford University Press.

Joint Appeal by Religion and Science for the Environment. 1992. "Declaration of the Mission to Washington." In Roger S. Gottlieb, *This Sacred Earth: Religion, Nature, Environment*, 2nd ed. New York: Routledge, 2003.

Kierkegaard, Søren. 1941. *Concluding Unscientific Postscript*. David Swenson and Walter Lowrie, trans. Princeton, N.J.: Princeton University Press.

Locke, John. 1689. *A Letter Concerning Toleration*. Constitution Web site, www.constitution.org/jl/tolerati.htm.

Moselely, Lyndsey. 2008. E-mail to religious leaders.

Sierra Club. 2008. *Faith in Action: Communities of Faith Bring Hope to the Planet*. Sierra Club Web site, www.sierraclub.org/partnerships/faith/report2008/report2008.pdf.

United Methodist Church General Board. n.d. "Statement on Environmental Racism." United Methodist Church Web site, www.umc-gbcs.org/site/apps/nl/content3.asp?c=frLJK2PKLqF&b=3631781&ct=3986175.

Zabarenko, Deborah. 2007. "US Scientists, Evangelicals Join Global Warming Fight." Reuters Web site, www.alertnet.org/thenews/newsdesk/N17341633.htm.

FOR FURTHER READING

Berry, Thomas. 1988. *Dream of the Earth*. San Francisco: Sierra Club.

Gottlieb, Roger S. 2006a. *A Greener Faith: Religious Environmentalism and Our Planet's Future*. New York: Oxford University Press.

———. 2006b. *The Oxford Handbook of Religion and Ecology*. New York: Oxford University Press.

Palmer, Martin. 2003. *Faith in Conservation: New Approaches to Religion and the Environment*. Washington, D.C.: World Bank.

Taylor, Bron, ed. 2005. *Encyclopedia of Religion and Nature*. London: Continuum.

PART III

DIFFERING PERSPECTIVES ON RELIGIOUS DIVERSITY

A

MULTIFAITH PERSPECTIVES

CHAPTER 23

A HINDU PERSPECTIVE

ARVIND SHARMA

I

RELIGIOUS diversity is a central issue in the study of religion. To begin with, there are the diverse religions that are conventionally listed minimally as Judaism, Christianity, Islam, Hinduism, Buddhism, Confucianism, and Daoism. These were the original world religions, three from the West, two from India, and two from China. There is now a tendency to enlarge the term *world religions* to include Bahā'ī as a Western religion, Jainism and Sikhism as the two other religions from India, and Shinto from the Far East. Moreover, there is also a tendency now, released by the movement of the indigenous peoples for political and cultural recognition, to include primal religions within this category. If we change the locution to *world's religions*, then semantic room is created to include a host of other religions, such as Zoroastrianism, Mandeanism, Wicca, and, of course, the various new religious movements (NRMs). In other words, the more we extend the scope of the term *religions*, the greater the diversity.

But this is only part of the picture, for each of these religions is often internally differentiated. At least four major forms of Judaism—Orthodox, Conservative, Reform, and Reconstructionist—can be identified. At least three major forms of Christianity are known—Roman Catholicism, Protestantism, and Eastern Orthodoxy—while Protestantism itself embraces quite a number of denominations. Islam divides into the two major streams of Sunni and Shī'ī Islam, and by another reckoning, Islam is said to possess more than seventy sects. The point is that religious diversity possesses both an external and an internal dimension, and religions are both externally and internally differentiated.

The ball could be unwound even further from a Weberian perspective, if the distinctions in the perspectives of the various social classes that make up a religion or a denomination are taken into account. Finally, each individual within the major traditions and denominations also has a unique personal version of the religion or denomination the individual belongs to. In other words, not only are the religions externally and internally differentiated, but they can also be said to be perspectivally differentiated, although such diversity could be considered a subset of internal diversity.

All that has been said about how a religion might be externally, internally and perspectivally differentiated also applies to Hinduism. Hinduism can be externally differentiated from other religions such as Islam or Christianity; it is also internally differentiated in various ways, varying according to sects, philosophical schools, and so on, as well as perspectivally varied in terms of gender or caste. It was necessary to offer this general introduction in order to appreciate fully the Hindu view of religious diversity, because although other religions of the world, along with Hinduism, share this fact of religious diversity, their attitudes toward such diversity are radically different. In other religions, such diversity arises *despite* the unitary assumptions of their traditions; in Hinduism, it flows *from* its plural assumptions. It is critical to appreciate this fact in order to comprehend the true nature of the Hindu attitude toward religious diversity, because other religions are also characterized by religious diversity. But whereas in the other traditions, this has happened in spite of their centralizing beliefs and practices and is historical in nature, within Hinduism, it is theological and philosophical in nature, a nature that finds expression in its history. For example, while Christianity first had the Roman Catholic Church, then the Eastern Orthodox Church emerged, and later the Protestant movement broke away from Catholicism, diversifying Christianity, Hinduism accepted diversity as its initial principle and has always been aware of itself as a plural and diverse tradition from the very beginning. Just as the Abrahamic traditions take their cue from the principle of the Decalogue—"Thou shall have no other gods to set against me" (Exodus 20:2–17)—Hinduism takes its cue from the scriptural injunction that "the truth is one, sages call it variously" (ṚgVeda I.164.46). Thus, Hinduism possesses religious variety not out of historical or geographical necessity, although its religious variety possesses these dimensions, but as a matter of first principles. It is because of this fact that it is easier to identify a Hindu than to define Hinduism and that when Hinduism is defined as "the religion of the Hindus," the definition is analytical rather than tautological.

How the religious variety of Hinduism frustrates efforts to define it might be one thing that highlights the scope and range of the religious variety that characterizes Hinduism. Historian Percival Spear, after devoting two and a half pages to an attempt to define Hinduism, remarks: "Thus we arrive at a definition which, through its very imprecision, seeks to convey the indefiniteness and infinite variety of Hinduism itself. Hinduism, one may say, is a body of customs and a body of ideas, the two having such persuasive power and defensive force as to absorb or resist passively for centuries any system which comes into contact with it" (1961, 41). That is to say, the immense variety of Hinduism need not drive one to despair, as seems to be the case in the following lines: "There is no end to the study of

Hinduism and to statements about it which cannot be contradicted. No one can be sure that he has fully penetrated its mystery. Veil screens veil, and when, drawing all aside, we believe that we have penetrated to the innermost sanctuary, we are uncertain whether we have reached the All, or nothing" (50).

A. C. Bouquet attributes the description of Hinduism that "so long as one keeps out the idea that the historical process as such has any value in religion, one can pack anything into Hinduism" to its rampant variety, when he remarks:

> Within Hinduism, as within Catholicism, there is almost incredible variety. Heiler once declared that Catholicism included and tolerated at least seven distinct kinds of religion within a single institutional framework, and something of the same sort can be said of Hinduism. It is thus possible to find within its range philosophic mystics who disclaim belief in a personal Deity; fervent monotheists who direct their devotions towards a single personal God, of Whom and to Whom they speak in terms resembling those used by many Christians; and at the other extreme, crude animists whose main concern is with some local godling, generally a female tutelary divinity of the village, and polytheists of a type familiar to readers of Greek and Roman literature, closely resembling the scrupulously superstitious character outlined by Theophrastus. (1969, 15)

II

This variety of Hinduism can be demonstrated at various levels. One major dimension of it is regional:

> Stand by a street in an Indian city and watch the endless variety of people who pass: men in slacks and sport shirts or Western suits; men in loosely wrapped dhotis with a cloth draped over bare shoulders; women in saris, some of rough peasant cloth and some silk, in constantly changing colors and styles; a few boys, some in blue jeans, with a Beatles record; a holy man in loincloth and sandals and long tangled hair; a Sikh, with turban and beard; a group coming from a nearby temple, with flowers in hand and fresh spots of red powder on their foreheads; priests from the Rāmakrishna Mission in long saffron robes; a funeral party, led by drummers, carrying a corpse on a palanquin; a beggar. Go to another city nearby and the pattern is the same, but subtly different. Go to another part of the country and the variety is still there but the styles and types of people have changed; what you were learning to identify is no longer seen, and there is much that is new and never seen before. (Hopkins 1971, 1)

Such variety exists not only at the regional level but also at the level of the family:

> If you know a family, there are more questions. The mother, a widow, is a devout worshiper of Śiva; her sister-in-law, equally devout, follows the teachings of Rāmakrishna; the eldest son is an engineer trained in England, a worshiper of

Śiva but not as knowledgeable or dedicated—at least not yet—as his mother and younger brother; his wife's father worships Krishna, as does all her family. (1)

Moreover:

The family worships Śiva in the home; they go to a temple of the Goddess Cāmuṇḍā or Durgā for special occasions; they visit a temple and teaching center dedicated to Vishnu; they sing devotional songs to Krishna. There are ties to all these, family traditions that connect them and personal preferences that make each family member unique. Another family would have a different pattern; a third would have yet another. (1–2)

There is then the scriptural level. As David Smith notes:

Other great religions have extensive literatures but tend to rejoice in a single sacred text. Hinduism has many sacred texts. The four Vedas are the holiest text for most Hindus, but few can read them. The "Great Epic of India," the *Mahabharata*, is called the Fifth Veda, and has been vividly alive for Hindus for more than two millennia. It contains the *Bhagavad Gita*, which in the twentieth century was elevated to the status of a kind of New Testament of Hinduism. Then there is the *Ramayana*, whose god, Rama, has risen to new heights of popularity among Hindu fundamentalists in the last two decades. There is the *Bhagavata Purana*, the gospel of Krishna worship, written around 800, and the central text for followers of the Hare Krishna movement, as for many others. But just as there are nominally 330 million gods in India, there are many sacred texts. There are Sanskrit texts—all those mentioned above were written in Sanskrit; there are versions of these texts in modern Indian languages, from the tenth century onwards; there are new texts in the modern languages; and there are visual texts. A key aspect of the divine in Hinduism is that, apart from the ineffable absolute, it is fully visible. Each deity has one or more well-known forms, and can be present in accurate representations in temples and in home shrines. This detailed imagery can be a powerful theological statement, as in the iconographic programme of the huge temple gateways of Chidambaram. (2003, 33–34)

In the rest of this chapter, the self-consciousness of Hinduism as a plural religious tradition will be documented, some major dimensions of its religious variety explored, and the limitations of its self-understanding identified.

III

The statement "The truth is one, sages call it variously" occurs in the oldest accessible text of the tradition, the ṚgVeda, although not in its earliest portions. Similar sentiments, however, both precede and follow this statement, while some are coeval with it. The Atharvaveda (which along with the ṚgVeda, Sāmaveda, and Yajurveda constitutes the tetrad of revealed books in Hinduism collectively known as the Vedas) contains a hymn to Goddess Earth, tentatively dated to around 1000 BCE.

It describes the earth as inhabited by people with diverse practices. The expression used is *nānā-dharmāṇam* (*janam*) (Atharvaveda [Śaunaka] XII.1.45). Both words are still in use in Sanskrit: *nānā* as a synonym for "many" or "varied" and *dharma* for traditional usages and customs. It is also the word used to translate the English word *religion* into most of the Indian languages, which is semantically stultifying because of the limiting assumptions associated with the Western concept of religion (see Smith 1963, 59). Although the exact connotation of *dharma* at this stage in its lexical history might not be entirely clear, few doubt that it corresponds broadly to what we regard as the cultural and religious dimension of life. Subsequently, in a text tentatively dated to the fourth century CE, one encounters the remarkable statement in which the author reckons, much as we do now, with the striking fact that "men and women dwelling in India belonged to different communities, worshipped different Gods, and practiced different rites" (Radhakrishnan 1993, 12). It is significant that although one traditionally speaks of the four *varṇas* or classes (*cāturvarṇya*) in Hinduism, this verse speaks of various classes (*nānāvarṇas*), thereby insinuating the Weberian perspective of religious variety that almost outdoes Weber.

By the early medieval period, the Mahānāṭaka of Hanumān (eleventh century) could open with a stanza that to this day is recited at functions to celebrate India's religious diversity. By this time, the two religions of Buddhism and Jainism have also found a place in a varied panorama of Hinduism, for the verse clearly alludes to them alongside various "Hindu" philosophical schools. The benedictory opening verse runs as follows: "He whom the Śaivas worship as Śiva; the Vedantins as the Absolute; the Buddhists as the Buddha; the Logicians, great demonstrators, as the Creator; those attached to the teaching of Jina as the Arhat and the ritualists as Sacrifice—may that Hari, the Lord of the three worlds, give us the desired fruit" (Raghavan 1938, 322).[1]

Just as Hindu religious pluralism had to come face-to-face with Buddhism and Jainism earlier, it had to come face-to-face with Islam during the periods of Muslim (c. 1000–1800) and Christian rule over India (c. 1800–1947). It is significant that these two traditions were approached in the same spirit, and a fifth verse was added, in certain circles, to the above-mentioned stanza, which includes a reference to "socially active" Christians and the Muslims who revere Allah.[2]

In our own times, Mahatma Gandhi (1869–1948) remains one of the major exemplars and propagators of this Hindu attitude toward religious variety (Gandhi 1950, 229).

IV

Thus, the tolerant and even welcoming attitude toward religious diversity is evidenced in Hinduism at several levels: deities, scriptures, scriptural interpretation, sects, and so on. It would be tedious to document it in full detail, but some illustrations might amplify the point further.

At the level of the gods, the *Bṛhadāraṇya Upaniṣad*, usually dated to the eighth century BCE, contains a famous passage (III.9.1) that begins by stating that the number of gods is more than three thousand, before they are reduced to one. In our own times, Klaus K. Klostermaier has noted:

> Many Hindu homes are lavishly decorated with color prints of a great many
> Hindu gods and goddesses, often joined by the gods and goddesses of other
> religions and the pictures of contemporary heroes. Thus side by side with Śiva
> and Viṣṇu and Devī one can see Jesus and Zoroaster, Gautama Buddha and Jina
> Mahāvīra, Mahātmā Gandhi and Jawaharlal Nehru, and many others. But if
> questioned about the many gods even the illiterate villager will answer: *bhagvān
> ek hai*—the Lord is One. He may not be able to figure out in theological terms
> how many gods and the one god hang together and he may not be sure about the
> hierarchy obtaining among many manifestations, but he does know that
> ultimately there is only One and that many somehow merge into the One.
> (1994, 149)

At the level of the sacred literature, to begin with, the Vedas are already four, which constitute the *śruti* or revelation. If we add to this the secondary scriptures called *smṛti*, which include "books which are specifically called Smrti, . . . the *Itihāsa*, *Purāṇas*, *Āgamas*, the *Darśana* literature and the treatises and poems in the popular languages," then the sacred literature threatens to become infinite, which the Vedas are claimed to be (Mahadevan 1971, 31, 39).

At the level of the sects, one could begin with the six established cults of the worship of the two sons of Śiva and Pārvatī: (1) Gaṇeśa and (2) Skanda, then list the worship of (3) Śiva and (4) Pārvatī (especially as Śakti), and then include worship of (5) Viṣṇu and (6) Sūrya (the sun). But this is only the beginning, because Hinduism is a religion of many paths, as enshrined in the saying "There are as many paths as there are minds," as the Bengali jingle runs (Lipner 1994, 188).

These examples could be multiplied in virtually any context of Hinduism, ranging from mysticism to religious practices (Chaudhuri 1978, 156–163) and music to art.

V

....

Thus, Hinduism as a religion is characterized by variety at virtually all levels— regional, linguistic, iconographic, scriptural, and so on—and this variety makes a deep impression on the observers of the tradition, whether insiders or outsiders. However, what has impressed such observers most is what can be called its soteri- ological variety, or the fact that it allows for multiple paths in approaching the ultimate reality, whatever it might be. This soteriological variety of Hinduism, therefore, deserves to be explored in greater detail as perhaps the most striking demonstration of the religious variety that characterizes it. For no matter how varied a religious tradition might be, it often reserves for itself the right to be the ultimately valid source of approaching the ultimate. Judaism and Hinduism provide two striking exceptions in this regard. One does not need to belong to these two traditions even to be saved, so deep-rooted is the conviction of these religions in religious variety. The most persuasive and at times eloquent articulation of the soteriological variety of Hinduism has been offered in our times by Rāmakṛṣṇa Paramahaṁsa (1836–1886). He states forthrightly: "God can be realized through all paths. All religions are true. The important thing is to reach the roof. You can reach it by stone stairs or by wooden stairs or by bamboo steps or by a rope. You can also climb up by a bamboo pole" (Nikhilananda 1952, 111).

The roots of this soteriological variety of Hinduism are both divine and human. They are divine in the sense that the real nature of God defies description and hence precludes dogmatism. Therefore:

> dogmatism is not good. You have no doubt heard the story of the chameleon. A man entered a wood and saw a chameleon on a tree. He reported to his friends, "I have seen a red lizard." He was firmly convinced that it was nothing but red. Another person, after visiting the tree, said, "I have seen a green lizard." He was firmly convinced that it was nothing but green. But the man who lived under the tree said: "What both of you have said is true. But the fact is that the creature is sometimes red, sometimes green, sometimes yellow, and sometimes has no colour at all."
>
> God has been described in the Vedas as both with attributes and without. You describe Him as without form only. This is one-sided. But never mind. If you know one of His aspects truly, you will be able to know His other aspects too. God Himself will tell you all about them. (Nikhilananda 1952, 559)

The roots of soteriological variety are also divine in the sense that one cannot fathom the saving activity of the divine in all its variety:

> The Saviour is the messenger of God. He is like the viceroy of a mighty monarch. As when there is some disturbance in a far-off province, the king sends his viceroy to quell it, so wherever there is a decline of religion in any part of the world, God sends his Saviour there. It is one and the same Saviour that, having plunged into the ocean of life, rises up in one place and is known as Krishna, and diving down again rises in another place and is known as Christ. (cited in Smith 1991, 74)

This soteriological variety carries an important implication with it at the human level. It means once again that dogmatism should be avoided:

> What I mean is that dogmatism is not good. It is not good to feel that my religion alone is true and other religions are false. The correct attitude is this: My religion is right, but I do not know whether other religions are right or wrong, true or false. I say this because one cannot know the true nature of God unless one realizes Him. Kabir used to say: "God with Form is my Mother, the Formless is my Father. Which shall I blame? Which shall I praise? The two pans of the scales are equally heavy."
>
> Hindus, Mussalmas, Christians, Śāktas, Śaivas, Vaishnavas, the Brahmajnānis of the time of the rishis, and you, the Brahmajnānis of modern times, all seek the same object. A mother prepares dishes to suit the stomachs of her children.

Suppose a mother has five children and a fish is bought for the family. She doesn't cook pilau or kāliā for all of them. All have not the same power of digestion; so she prepares a simple stew for some. But she loves all her children equally. (Nikhilananda 1952, 558–559)

And now that we have descended to the human level, one can examine the human (as distinguished from the divine) roots of such soteriological variety. Rāmakṛṣṇa Paramahaṁsa again explains:

Do you know what the truth is? God has made different religions to suit different aspirants, times, and countries. All doctrines are only so many paths; but a path is by no means God Himself. Indeed, one can reach God if one follows any of the paths with whole hearted devotion. Suppose there are errors in the religion that one has accepted; if one is sincere and earnest, then God Himself will correct those errors. Suppose a man has set put with a sincere desire to visit Jagannāth at Puri and by mistake has gone north instead of south; then certainly someone meeting him on the way will tell him: "My good fellow, don't go that way. Go to the south." And the man will reach Jagannāth sooner or later.

If there are errors in other religions, that is none of our business. God, to whom the world belongs, takes care of that. Our duty is somehow to visit Jagannāth. (Nikhilananda 1952, 559)

Thus, from a human perspective, soteriological variety is to be explained in terms of differences in human temperament. There are many ways to God, because persons differ; strictly speaking, there are as many ways to God as there are individuals. Hinduism tries to anchor soteriological variety in good measure in the human personality, and this enables us to identify a firm compass that can be consulted as one floats on the uncharted waters of the sea of spiritual possibilities. A pattern is provided at one level by the fact that the human person can easily be construed as consisting of a body and a mind—given that a human being is quite obviously a psychophysical organism. If one takes the body as the starting point, then Hinduism offers *haṭha-yoga* as a starting point. This yoga uses the human body as its basis and creates soteriological possibilities by manipulating it in various ways. If one takes the mind as the starting point, then one is led to *rāja yoga*. This form of yoga uses the mind stuff as its basis and manipulates it for its salvific potential.

One can, of course, look at the mind in general, but one can also focus on the distinct aspects of the psyche, which, in a human being, often takes the form of knowing, feeling, and willing. If one chooses knowing as the starting point on account of it constituting the primary orientation of one's psyche, then Hinduism provides for *jñāna yoga*, or the path of knowledge that is said to lead to the supreme. However, should one choose feeling as the starting point, one is led to *bhakti yoga*, or the path of devotion to God. This is the path that plays so prominent a role in Judaism, Christianity, and Islam. Should one select willing as the starting point, one is led to *karma yoga*, or the path of action. This path has an interesting parallel in the way Martin Luther tried to sanctify daily life as opposed to monastic life.[3]

Thus, the soteriological variety of Hinduism is firmly anchored in the divine and human person.

VI

A question naturally arises at this point: How does Hinduism manage its diversity? It does not possess a central ecclesiastical structure as with Roman Catholicism, it does not possess a central creed statement as with Christianity and Islam, nor is it allied to the state the way Confucianism was. How, then, does Hinduism avoid collapsing into chaos?

Scholars once identified the caste system as the stabilizing structure in Hinduism, but caste also participates in the same variety of Hinduism that it is said to stabilize, anthropologists at times identifying no fewer than four thousand *jātis*, or castes. An Indian thinker at around 1000 CE, Udayana, identified this common element in the domestic rituals of Hinduism (Joshi, 1967, 408), and so the search goes on.

One could propose that, although Hinduism does possess a bewildering variety, it does provide certain anchors to keep the ship in port. True to its acceptance of variety, perhaps it offers several common threads whose overlapping tapestry keeps Hinduism from getting frayed. Hinduism worships numerous gods, but it anchors them in monotheism; reveres numerous scriptures, but they are directly or indirectly anchored in the Vedas; possesses many schools of thought, but they tend to accept Vedic authority in one sense or another; allows for many interpretations of its scriptures, but it also contains the institution of *śāstrārtha*, or debates on the true meaning of the scripture, which prevents verbal authority from dissolving into verbal mist; consists of numerous social groups, but they are ultimately anchored in the overarching concepts of the *varṇa* (or four classes) and *āśrama* (or the four stages of life); does not distinguish, in a modern Western way, between religion and culture or secular and religious domains, but it encompasses them all in its concept of *puruṣārthas* (or the four goals of life, which are sacred as well as secular). What makes this approach intriguing is that it seems to explain conceptually Hinduism's one great failure after the seventh century: its inability to provide a political anchor in the face of the historical vicissitudes it had to face. It did develop the concept of the *cakravartī*, or the world conqueror, but it never quite got anchored, as with the other concepts, for various reasons, giving Hinduism the dubious distinction of having its followers be ruled over by rulers of different religious persuasions for a longer period than probably any other religious tradition in history.

VII

The religious variety within Hinduism has had profound implications for the way it looks at other religious traditions. It tends to view these traditions as a further extension of its own variety and, therefore, in principle capable of being assimilated within it. This has major implications for Hindu identity. A good indication of this is provided by Alex Michael on the basis of his experiences in Nepal: "A Nepali, asked if he was a Hindu or a Buddhist, answered, 'Yes.' All these answers may be imagined with a typical India gesture: the head slightly bent and softly tilted, the eyelids shut, the mouth smiling" (Michael 2004, 6).

Apparently, he was quite impressed by this phenomenon, for he refers to it again in the book:

> Therefore, the views of "there is only one god" and "all gods are one" are not so far from one another in the Hindu religions as has often been held. "Thou shalt not make unto thee any graven image" (Exodus 20:4) can also lead to the conclusion: Thou shalt not make only a single graven image. Hence, there is not *one* single word for god in Sanskrit, but many: *īsa/īśvara* ("ruler"), *bhagavat* ("elevated"), *prabhu* ("mighty"), *deva* ("god"), among others; the poet-saint Kabīr uses eighty-six terms for "god." . . .
>
> The consequences of this notion of god are tangible in popular religiosity all over. To use an example I have already cited (chapter 1), if a Newar in Nepal is asked if he is a Hindu or a Buddhist, he might simply answer "yes." To restrict oneself to one position, one god, would be a stingy perspective of divinity for him: He can worship both Buddha and Śiva without getting into a conflict of belief. (211)

Nor is this attitude necessarily limited to religions of Indian origin, which possess family resemblances: "It is related of an Indian Christian convert who attended the church on Sunday and the Kali Temple on Friday, that when the missionary gentleman asked him whether he was not a Christian, he replied: 'yes, I am, but does it mean that I have changed my religion?'" (Radhakrishnan 1993, 53–54)

VIII

The Hindu attitude toward religious variety faces a major problem when Hinduism is forced to come to terms with a tradition that rejects its attitude toward religious variety and refuses to be part of it, spurning its tolerance. It has quite a difficult time conceptually coming to terms with what appear to be Islamic and Christian prose-lytization. Considering itself as the "original" revelation and an ongoing one, Hinduism has trouble dealing with a final revelation in the form of Islam; and believing in the view that all religions are valid, as an external application of its internal acceptance of religious variety, it has trouble accepting Christian evangelism, involving as it does conversion from one religion to another. If both religions lead to salvation, what is the point?

Religious variety within Hinduism also creates a problem within the tradition, that of managing this diversity. We considered some of the ways in which it tries to do so. One can conclude by pointing out that the goal of such diversity is to maximize religious choice for the members of the tradition, and lest the members of the tradition be overwhelmed by the range of the choice, there are also suggested criteria for making such a choice, in terms of what one might consider true and what one might consider wholesome. The terms used for these two criteria, one theoretical and ontological and the other pragmatic and therapeutic, are, respectively, *param* and *pathyam* in a famous verse from the *Śivamahimnastotra* often ascribed to Push-padanta, which must have been composed before the eleventh century, as it has been found inscribed on a temple dated to that period. This verse was paraphrased by Swami Vivekananda in the very first address he delivered at the Parliament of World Religions in Chicago in 1893, as follows: "As the different streams having their sources in different places all mingle their water in the sea, so, O Lord, the different paths which men take through different tendencies, various though they appear, crooked or straight, all lead to Thee."[4]

NOTES

1. For other translations, see Mahadevan 1971, 198; Radhakrishnan 1993, 46–47.
2. Radhakrishnan 1948, 159: *kraistvāḥ krīstur iti kriyāpararatāḥ alleti māhammadāḥ.*
3. For a brief description of these three yogas, see Sharma 2000, chaps. 16–18.
4. The Sanskrit text is as follows:

trayī sāṅkhyaṁ yogaḥ paśupatimataṁ vaiṣṇavamiti
   prabhinne prasthāne paramidamadaḥ pathyamiti ca
   rucīnāṁ vaicitryādṛjukuṭilanānāpathajuṣām
   nṛṇāmeko gamyastvamasi payasāmar ṇava iva. (Vivekananda 1986, I, 4)

Its translation by Radhakrishnan:

The Vedas, the Sāmkhya, the Yoga, the Pāśupata and the Vaiṣṇava creeds, each of them is encouraged in some place or another. Some think that this is better, or that is better owing to differences of taste, but all men reach you, the Supreme, even as all rivers, however zigzag their courses may be, reach the sea. (1948, 20)1948.

REFERENCES

Bouquet, A. C. 1969 [1949]. *Hinduism*. London: Hutchinson University Library.
Chaudhuri, Nirad C. 1978. *Hinduism: A Religion to Live By*. London: Chatto and Windus.
Gandhi, Mahatma.1950. *Hindu Dharma*. Ahmedabad, India: Navajivan.
Hopkins, Thomas J. 1971. *The Hindu Religious Tradition*. Encino, Calif.: Dickenson.
Joshi, Lalmani. 1967. *Studies in the Buddhistic Culture of India*. Delhi: Motilal Banarsidass.
Klostermaier, Klaus K. 1994. *A Survey of Hinduism*, 2nd ed. Albany: State University of New York Press.

Lipner, Julius. 1994. *Hindus: Their Religious Beliefs and Practices*. London and New York: Routledge.

Mahadevan, T. M. P. 1971 [1956]. *Outlines of Hinduism*. Bombay: Chetana.

Michael, Alex. 2004. *Hinduism: Past and Present*. Barbara Harshav, trans. Princeton, N.J.: Princeton University Press.

Nikhilananda, Swami, trans. 1952. *The Gospel of Sri Ramakrishna*. New York: Ramakrishna-Vivekanand Center.

Radhakrishnan, S. 1948. *The Bhagavadgītā*. London: George Allen and Unwin.

———. 1993 [1927]. *The Hindu View of Life*. New Delhi: Indus.

Raghavan, V., trans. 1938. *Prayers, Praises and Psalms*. Madras: G. A. Natesan.

Sharma, Arvind. 2000. *Classical Hindu Thought: An Introduction*. New Delhi: Oxford University Press.

Smith, David. 2003. *Hinduism and Modernity*. Oxford: Blackwell.

Smith, Huston. 1991. *The World's Religions*. San Francisco: Harper.

Smith, Wilfred Cantwell. 1963. *The Meaning and End of Religion*. New York: Macmillan.

Spear, Percival. 1961. *India: A Modern History*. Ann Arbor: University of Michigan Press.

Vivekananda, Swami. 1986. *The Complete Works of Swami Vivekananda*, Mayavati memorial ed. Calcutta: Advaita Ashrama.

FOR FURTHER READING

Klostermaier, Klaus K. 1994. *A Survey of Hinduism*, 2nd ed. Albany: State University of New York Press.

Michael, Alex. 2004. *Hinduism: Past and Present*. Barbara Harshav, trans. Princeton, N.J.: Princeton University Press.

Radhakrishnan, S.1993 [1927]. *The Hindu View of Life*. New Delhi: Indus.

Murty, K. Satchidananda. 1993. *Vedic Hermeneutics*. Delhi: Motilal Banarsidass.

Smith, David. 2003. *Hinduism and Modernity*. Oxford: Blackwell.

CHAPTER 24

....

A BUDDHIST PERSPECTIVE

....

DAVID BURTON

THIS chapter examines Buddhist views about intrareligious and interreligious diversity. For a Buddhist, religious others can be Buddhists of other sects and schools, as well as those aligned to religions external to Buddhism. What are Buddhist attitudes to Buddhist teachings and practices from outside their respective traditions and to the religious beliefs of those who are not Buddhist? There is a common view of Buddhism as tolerant, nondogmatic, and willing to embrace religious diversity. This interpretation is simplistic although not entirely wrong; Buddhism has supported a range of attitudes toward religious others. There are Buddhist examples of religious exclusivism and inclusivism. Largely in recent times, there have also been tendencies toward pluralism.

INTRARELIGIOUS DIVERSITY

....

Buddhism is extremely varied and encompasses numerous traditions that developed in many cultures and historical periods, each with distinctive beliefs, practices, and scriptures. Consequently, for many Buddhists, an important issue has been whether, or to what extent, the teachings of other Buddhist groups are true and can lead to liberation. Indeed, there is a rich and venerable history of vigorous Buddhist intrareligious polemics in which competing interpretations of the Buddhist teaching (the Dharma) vie for the position of ultimate truth.

A popular Buddhist strategy has been hierarchical inclusivism, which acknowledges the validity of the teachings and practices of other Buddhist groups while ranking them as less valuable than those of one's own tradition. Buddhists have often combined tolerance of sectarian diversity with an assertion of the superiority of their own school. A widespread Buddhist hermeneutical technique is to categorize one's own scriptures as having definitive and precise meaning, whereas those of other groups are relegated to provisional or interpretable status (Lamotte 1992, 16–23). Other forms of Buddhism are the lower steps on a path to liberation that are preparatory to the final and complete teaching of one's own tradition.

There are numerous Buddhist scholastic classification systems that involve such hierarchical ordering. For example, the Yogacara form of Mahayana Buddhism claims that there have been three turnings of "the wheel of the Dharma": the non-Mahayana teachings are the first and lowest Buddhist teaching, supplanted by the Madhyamika doctrine of universal emptiness, which itself is superseded by the Yogacara mind-only teaching. Unsurprisingly, the Madhyamikas reverse the second and third turnings, so that the teaching of universal emptiness becomes the supreme teaching, and the mind-only view is provisional (Lopez 1992). In Chinese Buddhism, Zhiyi (538–597) of the Tiantai school ranks the Buddhist scriptures based on the content of the teachings, the disposition of the student, and the period of the Buddha's teaching career; he places the Lotus Sutra at the pinnacle. By contrast, the Huayan school identifies ten levels of Buddhist teachings, with the vast Avatamsaka Sutra expressing the highest standpoint (Habito 2003, 364). Another classification system was developed by Zongmi (780–841), according to whom the supreme teaching is contained in the Awakening of Faith. And the Japanese Buddhist Kukai (774–835) arranges Buddhist schools hierarchically, with the Shingon esoteric teaching at the apex and other forms of Buddhism as lower, preparatory stages (Kiblinger 2005, 58–59).

This inclusivism is frequently employed by Mahayana Buddhists to subordinate other Mahayana sects and also non-Mahayana Buddhist traditions. The Mahayana Buddhists refer to the latter pejoratively as the Hinayana, literally translated as "the lesser vehicle." Some Mahayana sources—such as the Vimalakirti Sutra—appear to be largely hostile to the Hinayana, stressing the foolishness of the Hinayana saints and their incorrect understanding of the Buddha's teaching (Robinson and Johnson 1997, 85). However, other Mahayana texts are more conciliatory; they regard the Hinayana dispensation as a pragmatic concession. The Hinayana goal of a personal Nirvana for oneself alone was taught for those who were not spiritually developed enough for the more exalted Mahayana goal of becoming an omniscient Buddha who is compassionately devoted to helping others achieve enlightenment. The Mahayansutralamkara regards the Hinayana Nirvana as a permanent soteriological end that is inferior to that of the Mahayana but still admirable. Thus, there is a genuine plurality of final goals in Buddhism. The Lotus Sutra disagrees, claiming that the Hinayana goal of Nirvana is merely a temporary stage, inevitably to be supplanted by the Mahayana, so that all Hinayana Buddhists— indeed, all sentient beings who are capable of enlightenment—must eventually adopt Mahayana teachings and aim for the only true goal: the full and complete Nirvana of a perfect Buddha (Kiblinger 2005, 44–48).

A key concept in the Mahayana discourse about intrareligious diversity is skillful means (*upaya kausalya*). Just as a kindly and experienced doctor prescribes medicines in accordance with the malady, so the Buddha has the skill and compassion to adapt his teachings to the capacity of those he teaches. The methods employed to advance people on the path to enlightenment will vary depending on their needs and ability to understand. So the views of other Buddhist sects can be accommodated as appropriate for those who are not yet ready for or do not have access to the highest teaching as expressed by one's own group.

It is arguable that the notion of skillful means suggests the more radical message—often forgotten by Buddhists themselves—that *all* Buddhist teachings and practices are skillful means because the experience of the ultimate truth is linguistically transcendent. The goal of Buddhism is enlightenment, an immediate, nonconceptual experience of "things as they really are." In this case, the teachings of no Buddhist sect can have absolute status, as they are all simply proverbial fingers pointing toward the moon (Pye 1978, 1990). This raises the possibility that the teachings of various Buddhist sects can be equally effective methods to achieve the same ineffable end. Diverse Buddhist teachings are employed because of differing psychological temperaments and individual needs, as well as differing cultural and historical circumstances. So it is possible to interpret the doctrine of skillful means as compatible with a nonhierarchical intrareligious pluralism, which acknowledges that the teachings of a range of (perhaps all) Buddhist groups might be equally efficacious at bringing about the ultimate goal of enlightenment. This pluralistic position is appealing to some contemporary Buddhists because it transcends sectarianism by acknowledging that the Buddhist path to enlightenment can take a variety of equally valid forms.

However, the historical evidence suggests that Buddhists in many cases have not advocated such an egalitarian view. On the contrary, Buddhist sects and textual sources, including the Lotus Sutra as the locus classicus of the concept of skillful means, have used the notion of skillful means to justify the elevation of their own doctrines to a superior position while accommodating the doctrines of other Buddhists at a lower level. It is the teachings of other Buddhists that tend to be labeled as skillful means, while those of one's preferred Buddhist group are given a higher epistemic and soteriological status (Hubbard 1995). Alternatively, if the teachings of one's own school are themselves skillful means, then they are considered to be superior skillful means to those of other sects. The various teachings of other Buddhist traditions might point toward the same enlightened experience of the ultimate truth and might be useful for practitioners at certain stages in their training and given their individual propensities and needs, but the teachings of one's own sect have often been thought to point most effectively and accurately.

In addition, Buddhists have sometimes exhibited an exclusivist attitude toward the beliefs of some other Buddhist traditions, which are accused of advocating views that are simply false and of no soteriological benefit. For example, many ancient Indian Buddhists dismissed the rival Pudgalavada sect, which advocated the existence of an enduring person, as a harmful deviation from the genuine Buddhist teaching that there is no self (Williams and Tribe 2000, 124–128). And the Dge-lugs-pa school of Tibetan Buddhism frequently accused the rival Jo-nang-pa school of reifying emptiness (*sunyata*) into a substantial, independently existing reality. The Dge-lugs-pa considered this to be a misguided and dangerous departure from the authentic Buddhist teaching of emptiness—that is, the nonsubstantial and de-pendently originating nature of all things (Ruegg 1963). A more sweeping example of an exclusivist attitude toward other Buddhists is that of Japanese thinker Nichi-ren (1222–1282), who maintained an uncompromising approach to the truth, con-demning other Buddhist teachings prevalent in his day. He accused the Pure Land, Zen, Vinaya, and Shingon sects of disseminating erroneous and slanderous views that contradict the true teaching of the Buddha as stated in the Lotus Sutra. Nichi-ren contended that these false Buddhist teachings, far from bringing about libera-tion, will lead their practitioners to rebirth in hell (Habito 2003, 372–375).

In contemporary Japanese Buddhist studies, Hakamaya Noriaki and Matsu-moto Shiro, the principal proponents of the Critical Buddhist movement, have argued against syncretic tendencies in East Asian Buddhism, which they claim have conflated Buddhism with non-Buddhist traditions such as Daoism. For example, they argue that the popular East Asian Buddhist belief in the Buddha nature, under-stood as a static, ineffable absolute or essence, distorts the authentic Buddhist teachings of no self, impermanence, dependent origination, and so forth. Thus, many forms of East Asian Buddhism are not truly Buddhist. Opponents have replied that Critical Buddhism assumes a very narrow definition of Buddhism and, ironically, that genuine Buddhism has an unchanging core or pure essence (Hub-bard and Swanson 1997).

INTERRELIGIOUS DIVERSITY

Buddhism arose in the late Vedic period in northern India, an environment in which there were many competing and conflicting religious beliefs about the nature of the universe and the place of human beings within it (Jayatilleke 1975, 3–9). Thus, the encounter with other religions has been a significant issue in Buddhism from its inception. Furthermore, once Buddhism was transplanted into other cultures, it came into contact with traditions such as Daoism, Confucianism, and Shinto. So it is unsurprising that throughout Buddhist history, there are many examples of Bud-dhists who have addressed explicitly the relationship between Buddhism and other religions.

On the whole, Buddhism has been less brutal and dismissive in its reaction to other religions than has Christianity. This is partly because Buddhism has been ac-customed to operating in religiously diverse cultures in which it has often not been dominant. Consequently, Buddhism has in many cases sought for peaceful coexis-tence rather than resorting to persecution of other religions. Moreover, there is a nondogmatic current evident in some Buddhist texts, which warn against the spiritual dangers of partisan and disputatious clinging to any religious and philosophical views, including those of Buddhism itself (Jayatilleke 1975, 9–10; Fuller 2005). This accommodating attitude is exemplified by the Buddhist convert emperor Asoka (304–232 BCE), who expressed, in his rock edicts, the desire that members of all religious traditions should live together harmoniously in his kingdom. He praised religion generally and not simply Buddhism (Kiblinger 2005, 38–40).

Nevertheless, one would be hard pressed to find many examples in traditional Buddhism of interreligious pluralism, in the sense of an outlook that would grant that the teachings of other religions are as able as Buddhism to communicate truth and bring about salvation. Richard Hayes claims that this is not surprising, given that religious pluralism in this egalitarian sense is "a distinctly modern ideology" that has developed in reaction to older triumphalist and supremacist ideologies by which most religions, including Buddhism, have been influenced (1991, 93–94). Consequently, he contends that to seek genuinely pluralist messages in traditional Buddhism would be "anachronistic" and "intellectually dishonest." David Chappell observes that traditional Buddhism did not usually assent to the pluralist view that other religions are equal to it (1999, 4–5). Nevertheless, he notes that some Buddhists claimed that Buddhism, Confucianism, and Daoism have the same essence or substance. For instance, Ch'ongho Hyujong (1520–1604) believed that "the ways to enlightenment of the three religions resonated with each other." Their use of many different words and names should not be a distraction from "the universal One" beyond concepts toward which their teachings are directed (Chappell 1999, 9). A precedent for this attitude is found in the writings of Ta-hui Tsung-kao (1089–1163), who declared that although Daoism, Confucianism, and Buddhism are different in their conceptual expressions, they "see with one eye, they hear with one ear, they smell with one nose, they taste with one tongue, they touch with one body, they think with one mind" (Chappell 1999, 8–9). However, this syncretic tendency was criticized by Dogen (1200–1253) as a departure from genuine Buddhism (Habito 2003, 370). Moreover, it has been objected that Ta-hui Tsung-kao interpreted the common core of the three religions in Buddhist terms, thereby overlooking the possibility that the religious experiences of Daoism and Confucianism might not be consonant with his own (Chappell 1991, 363).

If there are some examples of interreligious pluralism in traditional Buddhism, they appear to be the exceptions that prove the rule. Indeed, the Buddha is often represented in the scriptures as adopting a critical outlook toward other religions, rather than regarding them as equals. For instance, the Buddha attacks the epistemological foundation of the Vedic religion, with its dependence on inherited and unexamined traditions passed down over many generations. He likens the Brahmins to a file of blind men, each holding on to the one in front of him and led by a man who is also blind (Hayes 1991, 84). And the Buddha rejects Vedic animal sacrifice as contrary to the ethical principle of nonviolence (Bailey and Mabbett 2003, 22–23). Moreover, common religious views such as the belief in God and an eternal, unchanging soul are frequently subjected to muscular and sustained refutations.

The Buddhists often contend that these religious doctrines arise out of ignorance, an unwillingness to face unpalatable truths, and wishful thinking. The soul is rejected as contrary to the Buddhist teaching that the individual is simply a complex process of impermanent mental and physical events (Siderits 2003). The nature of the Buddhist critique of God is often misunderstood to be an assertion of atheism. However, the Buddhist cosmology accepts the existence of various deities that populate the universe. Buddhism preserves reference to the gods esteemed by other religions such as Hinduism and Shinto and often grants them an exalted status; nevertheless, Buddhists describe these deities as inferior to the Buddha, because they are unenlightened and remain subject to karma and rebirth.

In Mahayana Buddhism, in addition to these unenlightened gods, the Buddhas and Bodhisattvas are commonly regarded as enlightened deities with extraordinary powers. What most Buddhists reject is the notion of a creator God, since they do not assert that the universe has an ultimate beginning. Indian Buddhist philosophers argued for many centuries against the Hindu belief in a divine creator. Moreover, many Buddhists repudiate the view that there is a savior deity; a prevalent Buddhist view is that individuals are ultimately responsible for their own liberation, and no divine being is capable of bestowing liberation upon anyone (Cabezon 2003, 24–28). However, this is not the only attitude expressed by Buddhists; most notably, Pure Land Buddhists rely on the grace of Amida Buddha for their salvation (Robinson and Johnson 1997, 253–5).

The Buddhist scriptures represent the Buddha as advocating that a person should employ his or her personal experience in order to test religious beliefs and practices, accepting them only if they are found to be justified and lead to the cessation of suffering (Jayatilleke 1975, 17–19). On the one hand, this can be construed as exhibiting openness to the possible value of other religions; on the other hand, the Buddha is represented as confident that Buddhism in the end will pass this experiential test more successfully than any other religion. Indeed, there are various stories in the Buddhist scriptures of followers of other religious traditions converting to Buddhism when convinced of its superiority (Schumann 1989, 226–229).

Buddhists have commonly related to other religious traditions as inferior. If there is truth communicated by other religions, it is at a lower, more fragmentary level than the truth expressed by Buddhism. In some cases, the Buddhist texts claim that these religions distort the truth so much that they do not lead toward liberation. This is the message of the often misconstrued Buddhist parable of the elephant and the blind men. Each blind man is instructed by a king to use his hands to grasp a different part of an elephant in order to get some understanding of its nature. Religious pluralists have employed this parable to explain their view that all (or many) religions are equally valid and complementary insofar as they each understand some aspect of the sacred reality, just as each blind man grasps one part of the elephant. It is striking that the Buddhist rendition of this parable does not support this pluralist interpretation. On the contrary, the Buddha is compared to the sighted king who is far superior, in that he can see the elephant in its entirety, whereas other religious teachers are compared to the blind men, who are inferior in that they have only a limited understanding of the truth. Furthermore, the text comments that, unlike the Buddha, these non-Buddhist religious teachers engage in dogmatic bickering based on their attachment to their partial perspectives, and they do not have enough insight to attain liberation (Ireland 1997, 81–6; Schmidt-Leukel 2005, 19).

However, the Buddhist scriptures express a different view when they accept the notion of the lone Buddha (*pratyekabuddha*), a category of saints that achieved enlightenment independently of the Buddha's teaching. This concept allowed Buddhists to acknowledge that although Buddhism is superior to other traditions, spiritual insight has been possible outside the Buddhist community (Kloppenborg 1974). Furthermore, the Pali scriptures record the Buddha as saying that he does not deny that some non-Buddhist sages achieved enlightenment (Norman 1985, 172–173). Moreover, although Buddhist texts contain warnings against associating with and consulting non-Buddhists, they also give occasional examples of Buddhist practitioners who are said to have learned from non-Buddhist teachers (Chappell 1999, 5–6).

We have seen that hierarchical inclusivism is a frequent Buddhist strategy when dealing with intrareligious diversity. It is also a popular Buddhist way of relating to non-Buddhist traditions. Many Buddhists have regarded their tradition as not having a monopoly on the truth. This attitude is both accommodating and subordinating, because it leaves open the possibility for others to discover aspects of the truth for themselves while asserting the superiority of Buddhism. A partial grasp of the truth is arguably better than no understanding at all. Thus, it is not surprising that Buddhists frequently have been open to the soteriological value of at least some other religious traditions.

For example, the Pali scriptures exhibit a degree of inclusivism when they divide non-Buddhist religions into two categories. While one group is constituted by false or pseudo-religions that advocate teachings such as immorality, fatalism, and nonsurvival after death, the other group is made up of religions that are unsatisfactory though not completely false. The former are of no value, whereas the latter have a limited value, insofar as they encourage moral values, some kind of survival after death, and the need for one to take responsibility for one's progress toward salvation (Jayatilleke 1975, 23). Some religions are considered to be simply wrong and entirely deleterious, whereas others contain some truth and are of some efficacy, though inferior to Buddhism itself. In the Pali scriptures, the Buddha indicates that any religion is spiritually efficacious only insofar as it incorporates renunciation of possessions and the domestic life, strict rules of ethical conduct as set out by the Buddha, and the practice of forms of meditation that overcome both attachment to sense objects and the tendency to regard the body and mind as one's self (Hayes 1991, 83). The extent to which the teachings and practices of other religions overlap with the Noble Eightfold Path is the criterion by which their soteriological worth is to be measured, and no other religion has taught the Noble Eightfold Path as completely as Buddhism (Chappell 1991, 358).

Chinese Buddhists often recognized Confucianism and Daoism as having relative value as preliminary stages to Buddhism. This is evident in some of the aforementioned scholastic classification systems. For instance, both Kukai and Zongmi ranked Confucianism and Daoism below all forms of Buddhism but accepted that their beliefs and practices overlapped with those of Buddhism and were of some worth (Kiblinger 2005, 58–60). An interesting case is that of Nichiren. He condemned rival Buddhist groups, regarding their views and practices as completely erroneous and without merit. However, he was more charitable toward non-Buddhist traditions such as Confucianism and Hinduism, declaring them to teach people about moral values and thus preparing the way for the arrival of the genuine Buddhist teaching as contained in the Lotus Sutra. Nichiren combined intrareligious exclusivism with a degree of interreligious inclusivism. By contrast, Dogen displayed an exclusivist attitude toward Confucianism and Daoism; he dismissed them as unworthy of consideration because of their inability to produce an authentic experience of enlightenment (Habito 2003, 370–375).

Buddhist interreligious inclusivism can sometimes involve attributing different functions to Buddhism and its competitors. Buddhism has the supreme role of bringing about final liberation, but this is seen to be compatible with the more mundane, worldly purposes of other religions. For instance, Confucianism is often valued as giving ethical instructions and governing human interactions, whereas Daoism provides good health and guidance about living in harmony with nature (Chappell 1991, 359). And the deities of other religions can be consulted and propitiated in order to ensure a good harvest, cure an illness, or achieve success in business. For example, rather than denying the existence and usefulness of the Japanese Shinto deities, Buddhism frequently construes them as "worldly assistants" of the Buddha, who are "still of legitimate use in *this* world, while the Buddha held the key to the *eternal* world of full salvation" (King 1999, 37) Only Buddhism is capable of guiding people to enlightenment. In Japan, this view that different religions have different functions means that many people have multiple religious identities simultaneously; one need not be exclusively Buddhist (Reader 1994, 169).

Another approach is evident in the early Indian Buddhist attitude toward some Vedic beliefs and practices. The Buddha is said to have reinterpreted rather than simply dismissed them. For example, Vedic religion sought concord and harmony with the god Brahma through the performance of Vedic sacrifices. The Buddha proposed that the genuine way to gain the fellowship of Brahma was by developing the same admirable ethical qualities that he possessed (Jayatilleke 1975, 28–30). Moreover, the notion of a Brahmin is not refuted but ethicized: the Buddha claimed that a true Brahmin was not a person born into a superior social class; on the contrary, he was someone who had developed moral virtues and had achieved enlightenment (Kiblinger 2005, 43). In such cases, the Buddha redefined rather than rejected the inherited Indian beliefs and practices, although the redefinitions were sometimes so radical that they were arguably tantamount to refutations.

There are also examples of Buddhists seeking to turn devotees of other religious traditions into "anonymous Buddhists" who worship Buddhist deities without realizing that this is the case. For instance, in Japanese Buddhism, the indigenous Shinto god Amaterasu was sometimes understood to be Buddha, while Hachiman, a Shinto war god, was promoted to the role of a Bodhisattva (King 1999, 37; Kiblinger 2005, 54). They manifest in a non-Buddhist guise motivated by compassion and as an example of skillful means. Non-Buddhist traditions can be used with the ultimate intention of promoting Buddhist goals.

RECENT DEVELOPMENTS

A significant number of Buddhist thinkers have been active in the interreligious dialogue that has become common in the contemporary world. Increased awareness of and interactions with a wider variety of religious traditions have led many Buddhists to reexamine the issue of interreligious diversity, sometimes reaffirming old attitudes toward non-Buddhist religions and in other cases developing new views. What follows is a selective survey of some prominent contributions.

There has been a particularly strong inter religious dialogue between Buddhists and Christians. One Buddhist strand of this dialogue has been predominantly exclusivist in tone, stressing that core Christian beliefs are irreconcilable with Buddhism and harmful to Buddhist goals. For example, Sangharakshita maintains that the acceptance of Buddhism entails a rejection of the conventional Christian God, whom he construes as an oppressive, coercive and authoritarian deity (1978). Sangharakshita claims that belief in the Christian God results in irrational and harmful feelings of guilt and fear, which can be expunged by means of therapeutic blasphemy. Another example is Dharmasiri, who presents a rigorous and detailed critique of the Christian concept of God. For instance, he finds Christian theodicies unconvincing, contending that the undeniable suffering of innocents is incompatible with the existence of a benevolent, omniscient, and omnipotent God (1988, 41–51). Although Dharmasiri occasionally makes the inclusivist move of conceding that Christianity can have pragmatic value by encouraging moral development, his usual emphasis is on the "extremely dangerous" and "morally disastrous" implications of the belief in God (260). He sees dependence on God viewed as the ultimate moral arbiter as compromising one's moral autonomy. Despite the efforts of Christian theologians, belief in an omniscient God cannot be successfully reconciled with free will, leading to a morally stultifying determinism (51–57). Dharmasiri blames the Christian belief in a patriarchal, intolerant God for manifold ills such as religious persecution, holy wars, and the subjugation of women (259–271). Moreover, he claims that the Christian belief in the soul is rooted in the misguided attachment to one's individual life and the futile desire for immortality (7–8). According to Dharmasiri, Buddhists view the soul as "an essentially evil idea that leads to spiritually harmful results," such as conceit and the illusion of separateness from others that undermines community (22–23). For Dharmasiri, the differences between Buddhism and Christianity are much more important than any superficial similarities.

Buddhist attitudes toward Christianity have often been affected by the experience of colonialism and Christian missionary zeal. This is one reason Buddhists
have sometimes focused on Christianity in a critical manner. There has also been
some caution about the enthusiasm among some Christians for interreligious
dialogue: "The suspicion is still rife that the new Christian enthusiasm for open
dialogue and exchange might simply be yet another strategy in the unaltered goal
of religious conquest" (Schmidt-Leukel 2005, 13). However, there are also numerous recent cases of Buddhists who have been very engaged in discussions with
those from other religions and have identified what they see to be significant
common ground with Christianity in particular.

For example, the fourteenth Dalai Lama is very active in interreligious dialogue. He likens the world's religions to different types of medicine required for
diverse ailments; the various religious traditions are necessary in order to meet the
various needs of people with many different mental dispositions (Dalai Lama
1998, 15–18). He also claims that excessive attachment to one's own religion or
philosophy leads to intolerance and conflict, as one seeks to impose one's ideas on
others (Chappell 1999, 22–23). He warns converts to Buddhism against criticism of
their former religion, because "we can be certain that it has been an inspiration to
millions of people in the past, that it inspires millions today, and that it will inspire
millions in the path of love and compassion in the future" (cited in Kiblinger
2005, 35).

The Dalai Lama contends that despite their philosophical and doctrinal differences, the world's religions serve a broadly similar purpose of cultivating a "good
heart"—that is, ethical virtues such as love, compassion, and tolerance (Dalai Lama
1996, 6, 81). Moreover, he emphasizes that Buddhism can learn from other religions
in certain respects. For example, he has expressed the view that the Jewish diaspora
experience might provide some practical lessons for modern Tibetan exiles who
have experienced a similar loss of their homeland (Kiblinger 2005, 66–67). And he
sees Jesus as an inspiring exemplar of love and compassion akin to a fully enlightened being or a very spiritually advanced Bodhisattva (Dalai Lama 1996, 83).

While acknowledging the worth of non-Buddhist religions—particularly at the
level of ethical values—the Dalai Lama also contends that religions such as Buddhism and Christianity have genuinely different philosophical and metaphysical
perspectives, salvific goals, and means of attaining them (Dalai Lama 1996, 81–82;
Makransky 2003, 355). However, it is not clear whether the Dalai Lama's position is
best understood as a form of hierarchical inclusivism, which acknowledges the
shared values and usefulness of non-Buddhist religions at lower levels of spiritual
development, while still asserting the ultimate superiority of Buddhist philosophy
and its soteriological goals. Alternatively, he might be privatizing religions and rel-
ativizing their truth claims to such an extent that Buddhist philosophy and goals are
simply different but not superior. This would mean that "different religions are best
for different people, period" (Kiblinger 2005, 61–62). It is also possible that in stressing the common moral outlook of the world's religions, the Dalai Lama has not
given sufficient weight to the serious disagreements in ethical perspective that occur

between and within religious traditions—for example, different moral views about sexual behavior, animal welfare, capital punishment, war and violence, abortion, euthanasia, and so forth. Nor is it obvious, given the many cases of hatred and intolerance that are given religious justifications, that the Dalai Lama is correct to assert that religions are united by the common aim to develop compassion and tolerance.

Another recent Buddhist who has been active in interreligious dialogue is Bhikkhu Buddhadasa. He claims that the differences among religions occur at the level of conventional language, causing conflicts and egoistic assertions of beliefs. By contrast, at the level of what he calls "dhamma language," or ultimate truth, these differences are transcended, because the religions are alike in promoting nonattachment and the overcoming of selfishness (Buddhadasa 1989, 147–155; Kiblinger 2005, 50–51). He contends that at the outer and most superficial level, religions appear dissimilar. At a deeper level, all religions share a common nature. At the very deepest level, religion itself disappears, because one "cannot particularize that dhamma or truth as Buddhism, Christianity, or Islam, for whatever it is, you cannot define it by giving it labels." (Buddhadasa 1989, 147). Buddhadasa uses an analogy with water to clarify his point. The conventional level of religious discourse corresponds to the many different types of water that exist, such as sewer water, rain water, and ditch water. At a deeper level, religions share a common, unpolluted essence, as the varieties of water all have pure water as their underlying nature. At the deepest level, the various religions are understood to be empty and void. There is no such thing as religion, just as water is seen not to exist when analyzed into hydrogen and oxygen (Buddhadasa 1989, 146–147; Chappell 1991, 363–364).

Buddhadasa uses the Buddhist notion that reality ultimately transcends all dualities in order to assert that one should relinquish attachment to any and all religions. The common reality to which religions refer is beyond conceptualization and all labels. The irony is that Buddhadasa's apparently egalitarian analysis remains hierarchical and contains a Buddhist bias. He implies that Buddhism is superior to other religions because it recognizes the ultimate truth of emptiness and thus speaks the dhamma language most fluently. By contrast, religions such as Christianity are inferior and do not penetrate as successfully into the ultimate truth. Their preoccupation with immature beliefs such as the personal nature of God means that theistic theology often remains at the level of dualisms and conventional discourse (Kiblinger 2005, 50–51).

In agreement with Buddhadasa and the Dalai Lama, Masao Abe claims that religions such as Buddhism and Christianity have their own distinctive and unique beliefs and practices but "typically share a common message of peace, harmony and salvation to be gained by overcoming self-centredness in its various forms" (1995, 71). Moreover, he thinks that they have a common interest in repelling the common enemy of contemporary antireligious ideologies such as Marxism, scientism, and nihilism (19–20). And he contends that Buddhism can be transformed by its encounter with Christianity. For example, Abe is impressed by the Christian emphasis on social justice, from which he thinks Buddhism can learn (56–59). This is a point echoed by many recent Buddhists, although Cabezon also comments that from a Buddhist perspective, Jesus's apparent lack of concern for the welfare of nonhuman sentient beings is an ethical shortcoming (2003, 23).

While Abe admires Christianity, he judges Christian monotheism to be dualistic and therefore superseded by the Mahayana Buddhist nondualistic ontology of emptiness (Kiblinger 2005, 106–107). He describes the latter as a "positionless position," which recognizes the relativity of all religious traditions and is the remedy for all one-sided, dogmatic, and prejudiced views (Abe 1995, 23, 47). However, this claim appears naive given his evident commitment to the superiority of the nondualistic emptiness philosophy; irrespective of his protestations of neutrality, his own view contains a Buddhist bias (Kiblinger 2005, 104–106).

Despite Abe's critique of monotheism, he sees a parallel between the Mahayana notion of emptiness and the biblical reference to the self-emptying (*kenosis*) nature of Christ (Abe 1990). However, a number of Christian theologians have been unconvinced by this comparison (Kiblinger 2005, 108–109). For example, Hans Küng objects that the biblical meaning of *kenosis* refers to Jesus's act of self-denial, that is, the self-emptying of Jesus's will in his "ethical, exemplary humiliation" during his short and self-sacrificial life. Abe distorts the biblical meaning by interpreting it, in accordance with his Buddhist preconceptions, as "an ontological emptying, and emptying of God himself," akin to emptiness understood as the impersonal, ineffable, and dynamic ultimate ground of all phenomena. Küng comments that "as a Buddhist, [Abe] discovers his own world—even on foreign Christian soil," but does so by interpreting selective passages in a way that changes the meaning they have in their biblical context (Küng 1990, 32–35).

Like Abe, Thich Nhat Hanh focuses on the relationship between Buddhism and Christianity. He is impressed by the example of Jesus, whom he declares to be one of his "spiritual ancestors" (1995, 4). In common with many recent "socially engaged" Buddhists, Nhat Hanh praises Jesus for his compassionate involvement with the oppressed and disadvantaged. Jesus was an exemplary activist against social injustices (Muck 2003, 146–147). Nhat Hanh also stresses that despite their different "roots, traditions and ways of seeing," Christianity and Buddhism "share the common qualities of love, understanding, and acceptance" (1995, 11).

Nhat Hanh contends that religious concepts such as God and Nirvana are inexact attempts to express a reality that is the common core of religions and can only be fully "touched" in an experiential, nonconceptual manner (139–150). Thus, he warns against dogmatic attachment to one's own religion, which he sees as a cause of violence and suffering, and encourages receptivity to non-Buddhist religions: "To me, religious life is life. I do not see any reason to spend one's whole life tasting just one kind of fruit. We human beings can be nourished by the best values of many traditions" (2). He maintains that differences among religions are largely a matter of emphasis rather than points of fundamental disagreement (154, 193–195). And he claims that a genuine interreligious dialogue must involve being aware of the strengths and weaknesses of one's own tradition, as well as a willingness on both sides to be changed by the encounter and to accept that people from outside one's own religion might have valuable insights into the truth (8–9). He sees receptivity to other religions as a practical implication of the Buddhist teachings of no self and interconnectedness (10–12). Rather than establishing barriers between themselves and others, Buddhists should recognize the reality of interdependence by engaging in a mutually transformative dialogue with non-Buddhist religions. Nhat Hanh sometimes goes so far as to claim that there is no real distinction between Buddhism and Christianity and asserts, along with recent Buddhist Christians or Christian Buddhists, a dual religious allegiance: "Buddhism has no separate self. When you are a truly happy Christian, you are also a Buddhist. And vice versa" (197).

A notable feature of Nhat Hanh's position is that while he emphasizes the need to be open to and learn from other religions, he tends to interpret those religions in explicitly Buddhist terms. His understanding of Christian beliefs and rituals is selective and appears contrived to cohere with his view of Buddhism. The stress on similarities among religions leads Nhat Hanh to impose Buddhist readings on Christianity that do not necessarily accord with the understanding that Christians themselves would have of their own faith. Nhat Hanh appropriates Jesus for his own purposes and "doesn't hesitate to tell Christians what the true core of Jesus' teachings is. He explains Christianity to Christians" (Muck 2003, 147). The essence of Jesus's teaching turns out to be remarkably similar to Nhat Hanh's interpretation of Buddhism.

The difficulty here is that Nhat Hanh effectively turns Christians into anonymous Buddhists. For instance, he construes the Christian communion ritual as simply a practice of mindfulness, thereby stripping it of much of its theological significance in a way that would be unacceptable to many Christians (Nhat Hanh 1995, 30–32; Kiblinger 2005, 98). Furthermore, he sees the exemplary life of Jesus as the most important Christian teaching, rather than faith in the resurrection and an eternal afterlife (Nhat Hanh 1995, 36). A fundamental belief of many Christians is that Jesus Christ is the unique Son of God, whose self-sacrifice on the cross should be the focus of redemptive faith. By contrast, Nhat Hanh presents Jesus as an enlightened teacher like the Buddha who teaches the Dharma and whom we can emulate. He claims that the belief in Jesus as the unique incarnation of a monotheistic deity "excludes dialogue and fosters religious discrimination and intolerance" (192–193). A similar difficulty confronts Mahayana Buddhists who view Jesus as one of many earthly manifestations of a celestial Buddha or Bodhisattva; although this approach accommodates Jesus, it does so on Buddhist terms and in a way that compromises central features of orthodox Christology (Cabezon 2003, 26–27).

Nhat Hanh is a prominent example of a tendency among some recent Buddhists to assert the rhetoric of religious pluralism, in which religions are regarded as equal, while interpreting non-Buddhist religions in a manner that imposes Buddhist concepts on them. Significant and possibly fundamental differences between these religions and Buddhism are thus deemphasized or overlooked. A promising way forward is offered by Kristen Kiblinger, who argues for "alternative-ends-recognizing inclusivism." This position recognizes that there can be common ground between Buddhism and other religions, while also acknowledging significant differences, particularly with regard to ultimate goals. The aims of other religions will sometimes be incompatible with those of Buddhism. In other cases, these aims might overlap with Buddhism. On other occasions, the aims might be different from Buddhism without causing conflict (Kiblinger 2005, 69–89). Kiblinger accepts that there can be significant areas of agreement between Buddhism and other religions. However, she seeks to avoid the superficial and inaccurate assimilation of other religions into Buddhism. Interreligious dialogue is not simply about finding similarities; it also has the important function of clarifying genuine diversity and disagreements.

REFERENCES

Abe, M. 1990. "Kenotic God and Dynamic Sunyata." In J. B. Cobb and C. Ives, eds., *The Emptying God: A Buddhist-Jewish-Christian Conversation*. Maryknoll, N.Y,: Orbis, 3–65.

———. 1995. *Buddhism and Interfaith Dialogue*. Honolulu: University of Hawaii Press.

Bailey, G., and I. W. Mabbett. 2003. *The Sociology of Early Buddhism*. Cambridge, U.K.: Cambridge University Press.

Buddhadasa, B. 1989. "No Religion!" In D. K. Swearer, ed., *Me and Mine: Selected Essays of Bhikkhu Buddhadasa*. Albany: State University of New York Press, 146–57.

Cabezon, J. 2003. "A God, but Not a Savior." In R. M Gross and T. C. Muck, eds., *Buddhists Talk about Jesus, Christians Talk about the Buddha*. New York: Continuum, 17–31.

Chappell, D. W. 1991. "Buddhist Responses to Religious Pluralism: What Are the Ethical Issues?" In C. Wei-hsun Fu and S. A. Wawrytko, eds., *Buddhist Ethics and Modern Society: An International Symposium*. New York: Greenwood, 355–370.

———. 1999. "Buddhist Interreligious Dialogue: To Build a Global Community." In S. B. King and P. O. Ingam, eds., *The Sound of Liberating Truth: Buddhist-Christian Dialogues in Honor of Frederick J. Streng*. Richmond, U.K.: Curzon, 3–35.

Dalai Lama. 1996. *The Good Heart: A Buddhist Perspective on the Teachings of Jesus*. Boston: Wisdom.

———. 1998. *Spiritual Advice for Buddhists and Christians*. New York: Continuum.

Dharmasiri, G. 1988. *A Buddhist Critique of the Christian Concept of God*. Antioch, Calif.: Golden Leaves.

Fuller, P. 2005. *The Notion of Ditthi in Theravada Buddhism: The Point of View*. London: Routledge Curzon.

Habito, Ruben L. F. 2003. "Japanese Buddhist Perspectives and Comparative Theology: Supreme Ways in Intersection." *Theological Studies* 64/2: 362–387.

Hayes, R. P. 1991. "Gotama Buddhism and Religious Pluralism." *Journal of Religious Pluralism* 1: 65–96.

Hubbard, J. 1995. "Buddhist-Buddhist Dialogue? The 'Lotus Sutra' and the Polemic of Accommodation." *Buddhist-Christian Studies* 15: 119–136.

Hubbard, J., and P. L. Swanson, eds. 1997. *Pruning the Bodhi Tree: The Storm over Critical Buddhism*. Honolulu: University of Hawaii Press.

Ireland, J. D. 1997. *"Udana" and the "Itivuttaka": Two Classics from the Pali Canon*. Kandy, Sri Lanka: Buddhist Publication Society.

Jayatilleke, K. N. 1975. "The Buddhist Attitude to Other Religions." Kandy, Sri Lanka: Buddhist Publication Society.

Kiblinger, K. B. 2005. *Buddhist Inclusivism: Attitudes towards Religious Others*. Aldershot, U.K.: Ashgate.

King, W. 1999. "Response to David Chappell." In S. B. King and P. O. Ingam, eds., *The Sound of Liberating Truth: Buddhist-Christian Dialogues in Honor of Frederick J. Streng*. Richmond, U.K.: Curzon, 36–40.

Kloppenborg, R. 1974. *The Paccekabuddha: A Buddhist Ascetic: A Study of the Concept of the Paccekabuddha in Pali Canonical and Commentarial Literature*. Leiden, Neth.: Brill.

Küng, H. 1990. "God's Self-renunciation and Buddhist Emptiness: A Christian Response to Masao Abe." In R. Corless and P. F. Knitter, eds., *Buddhist Emptiness and Christian Trinity: Essays and Explorations*. Mahwah, N.J.: Paulist, 26–43.

Lamotte, É. 1992. "The Assessment of Textual Interpretation in Buddhism." In D. S. Lopez, ed., *Buddhist Hermeneutics*. Honolulu: University of Hawaii Press, 11–28.

Lopez, D. S. 1992. "On the Interpretation of the Mahayana Sutras." In D. S. Lopez, ed., *Buddhist Hermeneutics*. Honolulu: University of Hawaii Press, 47–70.

Makransky, J. 2003. "Buddhist Perspectives on Truth in Other Religions." *Theological Studies* 64/2: 334–361.

Muck, T. C. 2003. "Buddhist Books on Jesus." In R. M. Gross and T. C. Muck, eds., *Buddhists Talk about Jesus, Christians Talk about the Buddha*. New York: Continuum, 143–153.

Nhat Hanh, T. 1995. *Living Buddha, Living Christ*. New York: Riverhead.

Norman, K. R. 1985. *The Rhinoceros Horn and Other Early Buddhist Poems (Sutta Nipata)*. London: Pali Text Society.

Pye, M. 1978. *Skilful Means: A Concept in Mahayana Buddhism*. London: Duckworth.

———. 1990. "Skillful Means and the Interpretation of Christianity." *Buddhist-Christian Studies* 10: 17–22.

Reader, I. 1994. "Japanese Religions." In J. Holm and J. Bowker, eds., *Rites of Passage*. London: Pinter, 169–183.

Robinson, R. H., and W. L. Johnson. 1997. *The Buddhist Religion: A Historical Introduction*, 4th ed. Belmont, Calif.: Wadsworth.

Ruegg, D. S. 1963. "The Jo Nan Pas: A School of Buddhist Ontologists according to the Grub Mtha' Sel Gyi Me Lon." *Journal of the American Oriental Society* 83/1: 73–91.

Sangharakshita, V. M. S. 1978. *Buddhism and Blasphemy*. London: Windhorse.

Schmidt-Leukel, P. 2005. "Intimate Strangers: An Introduction." In P. Schmidt-Leukel, ed., *Buddhism and Christianity in Dialogue: The Gerald Weisfeld Lectures 2004*. Norwich, U.K.: SCM, 1–28.

Schumann, H. W. 1989. *The Historical Buddha: The Times, Life and Teachings of the Founder of Buddhism*. Harmondsworth, U.K.: Penguin.

Siderits, M. 2003. *Empty Persons: Personal Identity and Buddhist Philosophy*. Aldershot, U.K.: Ashgate.

Williams, P., and A. Tribe. 2000. *Buddhist Thought: A Complete Introduction to the Indian Tradition*. London: Routledge.

FOR FURTHER READING

Dharmasiri, G. 1988. *A Buddhist Critique of the Christian Concept of God*. Antioch, Calif.: Golden Leaves.

Gross, R. M., and T. C. Muck, eds. 2003. *Buddhists Talk about Jesus, Christians Talk about the Buddha*. New York: Continuum.

Kiblinger, K. B. 2005. *Buddhist Inclusivism: Attitudes towards Religious Others*. Aldershot, U.K.: Ashgate.

King, S. B., and P. O. Ingam, eds. 1999. *The Sound of Liberating Truth: Buddhist-Christian Dialogues in Honor of Frederick J. Streng*. Richmond, U.K.: Curzon.

Schmidt-Leukel, P., ed. 2005. *Buddhism and Christianity in Dialogue: The Gerald Weisfeld Lectures 2004*. Norwich, U.K.: SCM.

CHAPTER 25

AN AFRICAN RELIGIONS PERSPECTIVE

KWASI WIREDU

A very fundamental fact about African religions is that they are not institutional religions. They do not have an organization that one becomes a member of upon converting or being converted to the religion. Such an organization has a hierarchy of officials in charge of the propagation of a certain metaphysic and the promotion of virtue. One has to accept certain doctrines before qualifying to be a member of such a religion. If the religion is a God-oriented one, then a most important duty of the officialdom will be to arrange regular sessions of God worship. A considerable amount of infrastructure, such as chapel buildings, needs to be taken care of. In sophisticated instances, the maintenance of the officers alone calls for the command of good economic resources. None of these things is pertinent to traditional African religions. In the this discussion, I will first, as an Akan,[1] frequently call upon my direct knowledge of Akan traditional religion to illustrate generalities. Second, I will offer a basic description of African traditional religion. I will then reflect on specific issues of religious diversity with respect to this traditional religion.

SOME CONSEQUENCES OF THE NONINSTITUTIONAL CHARACTER OF TRADITIONAL AFRICAN RELIGION

Many consequences follow from the noninstitutional character of traditional African religion. Because there is no such thing as a membership doctrine, there is not a tendency to develop a dogmatic attitude. In institutional religions, such an attitude comes quite easily, for the articles of faith are usually claimed to be the word of God or of some adequately infallible being. A reluctance to accept propositions of such origins has been known to be met sometimes with severe punishment.

A consequence of the nondogmatic attitude in African traditional religion is that there is not the slightest tendency among Africans to try to proselytize other people. African missionaries are not known anywhere, or if they are, then they must be extraordinarily rare. This is not because Africans don't believe in the existence of a supreme being. Many, though not all of them, do. But they think that everybody should be left to determine the issue for himself or herself. The Akans, for example, say, "*Obi nkyere akwadaa Nyame,*" that is, "Nobody teaches a child God." To the average Akan, it is obvious that God exists. But if somebody does not believe so, then that is his or her own business. The idea of trying to force somebody to believe that God exists would be unintelligible. Let us also quickly note that this belief in God is not a "faith" in the sense in which faith is a mental condition that thrives in the absence of reason. To declare faith in this sense would merely promote derision. People consider that there are good reasons to believe. I will come back to this below.

Another important difference between African religions and institutional ones is that there is no such thing as a worship of God in the former. Worshipping is usually a formalized group activity that takes place at a designated area or facility. No such activity is found in Akan society. Nor is there a practice of individualized personal worship. The problem is conceptual. The word *worship* does not correspond to anything in the Akan language. The nearest thing to worship in Akan is the word *Som*. But this means "to serve," and it is not apparent how any being can serve the supreme being. What can he possibly need? What difference can such "service" possibly make to him? So, even though in Christian missionary translations in Ghana, *Som* is used to mean "worship," that practice is open to question.

The difference between an institutional and a noninstitutional religion has an important implication for the place of morality in religion. In an institutional religion, one of the duties of the officers of the institution is to promote good morals, as noted above. To the extent to which their efforts are successful—although we know that the success is not uniform—we can speak of the dependency of morality on religion in institutional religion. It hardly needs to be pointed out that one cannot speak of any such dependency in a noninstitutional religion.

There is another and more subtle sense in which one might speak of the dependency of morality on religion. One might define morality itself in terms of the will and commandments of God, an expedient that has come to be known as the divine command theory of ethics in Western philosophy. This does not need to be done, even in an institutional religion. But the tendency therein is great. Institutional authorities are apt to feel the need for divine (and therefore infallible) authorization behind their moral teachings for the effective guidance of the flock. Identifying moral rightness with the will of God is expected to give maximum authority. However, this can only be done at a high logical price. If to say that something is morally right is equivalent to saying that God approves of it and to say that it is morally wrong is equivalent to saying that God disapproves of it, then to say that God disapproves of what is morally wrong is equivalent to saying that God disapproves of what he disapproves. A tautology can be a prized possession of a logician, but this one is surely maximally unhelpful.

In Western philosophy, Socrates gave what amounts to an early refutation of the divine command theory in the dialogue *Euthyphro*. However, in various shapes and forms, it has remained tempting to this day. In Akan ethical thinking, no such temptation exists. Morality is explicitly humanistic. What is morally right in the strictest sense is what conduces to the well-being of human individuals when that is in harmony with the well-being of society. Conversely, we can phrase the humanistic idea by saying that what is morally right is what conduces to the well-being of human society when that is in harmony with the well-being of human individuals. The principle of this harmonization is what in Christian terminology is called the Golden Rule. The Akans are, of course, not beholden to Christianity for this principle, which is, not surprisingly, known to all tribes of humankind in one form or another.

While the Golden Rule is necessary for the determination of the morality of any action, it is not sufficient in all cases. In the sphere of custom, for example, many things that are not contrary to the Golden Rule are done or eschewed because they are or are not the things done in the given culture. Frequently, the reflective inquirer will find that there are commonsensical reasons for them based on utility. Note, though, that this is utility chastened by the Golden Rule. Thus, for example, in Akan society, there is a rule against sex in the bush. The Earth Goddess is supposed to dislike it. One need not be excessively reflective, however, in order to see that the motive of the prohibition is the protection of lone females in the bush.

For now, the point to be grasped is that Akan morality is founded not on the will of God but on the well-being of human society, as adjusted to the well-being of human individuals, and on utility, as chastened by the Golden Rule. Let us note some analogy with John Stuart Mill (1806–1873).[2] Mill usually stated his principle of utility in a form such as "The creed which accepts as the foundation of morals 'utility' or the 'greatest happiness principle' holds that actions are right in proportion as they tend to promote; wrong as they tend to produce the reverse of, happiness." However, when defending his theory against attacks, he could be moved to say something like "In the golden rule of Jesus of Nazareth we read the complete spirit of the ethics of utility. 'To do as you would be done by' and 'to love your neighbor as yourself' constitute the ideal perfection of utilitarian morality." If he had toned down his rhetoric here and incorporated this ethical principle into his official statement of what utilitarianism means, he would have forestalled certain very popular criticisms of his theory. Suppose, for example, that framing up an innocent loiterer as responsible for a mysterious murder would bring more happiness to a greater number of people than having the crime remain unsolved despite the best effort. The criticism is that Mill's principle of utility would find the frame-up to be the morally right thing to do, which is absurd beyond description. If moral rightness per utilitarianism presupposes satisfying the Golden Rule, then whatever else it might require, the criticism is disabled.

On the Akan front, chastened utility might be formulated in some such manner as "If an action that has passed the test of the Golden Rule—as any permissible action should—remains indeterminate regarding its moral status, then it is to be judged right as it tends to promote, and wrong as it tends to produce, the reverse of human well-being." This, in part, follows Mill's style. There is also obviously some similarity in thought. But it must be noted that the Akans entertained these ideas centuries before Mill.

Nature and Character of African Religions

To return to the question of the noninstitutional character of African religions, one might ask what that kind of religion amounts to. The answer is that it consists of one's belief in the reality of the object of one's unconditional veneration, as distinct from worship, and one's sense of trust and dependence on him (certainly, in the Akan case). It is a personal religion, although the conception of the divine being itself is basically communal. This is because such concepts emerge out of the common concerns and conversations that go on among people regarding concrete as well as abstract issues.

The average Akan believes that there is a supreme being who is responsible for the cosmos. This being hates evil and will punish people who wrong others and evade human justice. That will occur in this world, not the afterworld. There is a great number of names by which the supreme being is described. I will note only a few here.[3] We have *Onyankopon*. This must make Anselm smile in his grave, for it means literally "he who is alone great," which, idiomatically, means the greatest possible being. Then we have *Oboadee*, the maker of things, the creator, and also *Borebore*, which J. B. Danquah (1895–1965)—the most famous Ghanaian philosopher—translates lavishly as "Creator, Excavator, Hewer, Carver, Architect, Originator, Inventor" (1968). There are also phrases that seem to indicate belief in the omniscience, omnibenevolence, and omnipotence of God.

Problems of interpretation arise with almost any of the attributes listed. These result not from the noninstitutional character of the religion but from its being African and, more specifically, Ghanaian. Take the notion of creation. In orthodox Christianity, it is the bringing into existence of the universe out of nothing. The problem is that this requires a notion of absolute nothingness that is not intelligible in Akan. The fundamental reason for this is that in Akan, to exist is to be at some place.[4] For there to be nothing, properly speaking, means the absence, at a given place, of objects of a particular universe of discourse. Furthermore, on this showing, if God exists, he exists in space.[5]

The spatial conception of existence has a further metaphysical consequence. It implies that there cannot be spiritual entities, if to be spiritual is to be nonextended, as Descartes stipulated. There is another sense of *spirit*, however, in which spirits are partially physical. Consider the idea of a ghost. It can sometimes be seen, supposedly. But it cannot be pinned down, because it is not fully constrained by the laws of dynamics, and it will disappear into thin air on any attempt at contact. In stories of ghost sightings in Africa and, for example, in the United States, ghosts are unanimously alleged to dress in white. I call any such entities, that is, entities that appear to have spatial properties in some respects but not in others, quasi-physical. There is supposed to be a great diversity of them, such as poltergeists, witches (when in full demonic activism), angels, ancestor spirits, and so on.

Here, then, is an ontological difference between African and Western discourse. In the Western context, it is possible to speak, with an appearance of coherence, of physical entities, quasi-physical entities, and spiritual entities in the Cartesian sense. But in the African context, one can, with a similar appearance, speak only of the physical and the quasi-physical. As we will see, for many, the world of African religions is the world of a certain class of quasi-physical beings. We will come back to this view of African religions. However, for the present, let us continue trying to confront the problems that arise when one tries to interpret the terms used above to render Akan conceptions of divinity into English.

GOD AS CREATOR AND THE PROBLEM OF EVIL

Take the notion that God is the creator of the universe. We have suggested that within the Akan conception, the creation involved here cannot be ex nihilo creation. It must be something more like building a house than anything else. Danquah's translation of the Akan word *Borebore*, which is used to refer to God, as "Creator, Excavator, Hewer, Carver, Architect, Originator, Inventor," begins to make sense here. In fact, all of these terms, except the first, are unambiguously demiurgic. According to Danquah, the Akan God "does not stand over against his own creation. He is, if we may be frank, 'of it'" (1968, 88). In any case, as we have already seen, for conceptual reasons, the Akan God cannot be an ex nihilo creator. But can he be omnibenevolent and omnipotent? For Danquah, he can be omnibenevolent but not omnipotent. And Danquah's claim is that this is how the traditional Akan saw the matter.

Danquah argued that the problem of how an omnibenevolent and omnipotent God could allow evil is insoluble. "It is quite otherwise," he continues, "if we deny that the principle (God) is omnipotent, but is itself a 'spirit striving in the world of experience with the inherent conditions of its own growth and mastering them' at the cost of all the physical pain and evil as well as the moral pain or disharmony that stain the pages of human effort" (1968, 88).

Danquah might be right in sensing this attempted solution of the problem of evil among the Akans. But it is not the only attempt. K. A. Busia (1913–1978), sociologist and philosopher, once prime minister of Ghana, maintains that the problem of evil does not arise in the African conception of God. He says, as does Danquah, that it is only when you hold that God is an omniscient, omnibenevolent, and omnipotent being that you get into the problem of evil. In Africa, however, even though the supreme being is the creator and the source of life, "between him and man lie many powers and principalities good and bad, gods, spirits, magical forces, witches to account for the strange happening in the world" (Busia 1965).

K. Gyekye, a currently active Akan philosopher, has argued that the Akan concept of God still generates the problem of evil, because one could still ask why God does not "intervene in the evil operations of the independent free wills of the lesser spirits in order to eliminate evil." His answer is, "But if he had done so, would he not have disrupted the free wills with which he endowed them?" One can imagine an interlocutor asking why God should have endowed such beings with free will at all or why he should have created them in the first place. But still, Gyekye's point holds that we have the problem of why God does not create humans such that they always choose the good. The answer Gyekye mentions is that if God had done that, human beings "would have been nonrational and thus less human, wholly without the ability to choose." He continues, "The Akan thinkers, like thinkers in most other cultures, would rather have humankind endowed with rationality and conscience than to have them fashioned to behave like a beast. Hence, God's provision of rationality and freedom of the will and of choice is justified" (1995, 127–128).

This answer to the problem of evil is quite like what has come in Anglo-American philosophy to be known as the free-will defense. It has similar difficulties. For example, it might be noted that those among human parents who are wise and skillful can bring up their children to be generally good and virtuous without compromising their free will. Why can't the supreme being do even better? And is he not actually supposed, by those who believe in heaven, to do better there where resurrected persons, with improved bodies, will live a spotlessly clean life eternally, without, presumably, losing their free will? In any case, granting the soundness of the free-will defense, it still pertains only to moral evil. Natural evil still awaits a plausible theodicy. The challenge is receiving the attention of a good number of philosophers in the currently exciting field of the philosophy of religion in both Africa and the West.

Contemporary African philosophers do have at their disposal not only formulations of the free-will defense in their tradition but also a variety of other reactions to the problem of evil. The Akans, for instance, have a huge repertoire of proverbs,[6] and a great number of them are philosophical. With an obvious reference to the problem of evil, one proverb has it that if God gives the disease, he also gives the remedy. Another says that if something does not go wrong, something does not go right, either. And a third, using the hawk as a metaphorical spokes agent, states: "The hawk says that all that God created is good." (The Akans have the habit of crediting their aphorisms to selected animals.) It can be seen from all of this that the Akans in both their oral and literary traditions had varying attempts at the solution to the problem of evil. This, by the way, is contrary to the tendency to attribute unanimity freely in some anthropological accounts of African thought. Of course, there can sometimes be unanimity on some specific issues.

It is apparent that the Akans were deeply engaged with the problem of evil in their traditional thought. The same is true of the problem of divine predestination and human responsibility. It is believed that before an individual comes to the world to be born of man and woman, his life principle, in the form of a replica of himself, meets God to take leave of him. At this meeting, God apportions to the individual the destiny that he will live out in his earthly career. The Yoruba account is even more memorable. An individual kneels before God to propose or receive his destiny. In either case, the destiny, once apportioned, is unalterable.

Idowu gives a Yoruba example of what a destiny investiture might be like. A man receives his destiny and sets out to the world to live it. On his way, he encounters God's gate keeper, who asks him where he is going and what he is going to do there. He replies:

> I am going to be born to a man named X, of a woman named Y, in the town of Z.
> I shall be an only son. I shall grow up to be handsome and in favour with
> everybody; everything I touch will prosper; when I am twenty five, my father will
> die and when I am fifty, my mother will die. I shall build a large house and
> possess a large prosperous farm, and be the father of a large family through my
> twenty wives. When I am sixty years old two of my children will have a quarrel
> and one will be killed. At the age of ninety, I shall be ill for a short while and then
> die peacefully in my house, to be mourned by all and be accorded a grand burial.
> (1962, 174)

This narrative of a meeting of a yet unborn individual with God is most likely an extended metaphor, although there are those who seem to take it literally. As a metaphor, it simply affirms that every individual has a unique destiny that he or she owes to God. In whichever way it is taken, it raises two questions. First, do human beings have free will or responsibility in the face of this divine predestination; second, are the things that happen to people always inevitable? In the example above of an assigned destiny, there are kinds of activities that involve choice, such as marrying twenty women. The question is, if the individual's choices are all antecedently determined by God, then how can he be said to have free choice?

Contained in that same sketch of a destiny are the statements that at twenty-five, the subject's father will die, and so, too, will his mother when he reaches fifty. Again, when he is sixty, one of his children will kill another in an argument. Even though it is included in the destiny that everything the man touches will "prosper," this is still a rather mixed destiny. In fact, much worse destinies have been spoken of in common discourse, and attempts at improvements have been known. The problem is that any such improvement will seem to constitute an attempt to change divine dispensation, which, by an emphatic declaration earlier on, cannot be done.

What is happening here is perhaps an apparent contradiction riding on an ambiguity. There is here—and I suspect in the thought of many other peoples of the world—the interplay of two levels of conceptualization in the African notion of God. There is a personalized level at which God is thought of on the model of Nana, grandfather. And there is a more cosmological conception in which God is conceived of as the force responsible for the cosmic order. These are not mutually exclusive conceptions, but the one that is uppermost in mind on a given occasion of discourse might incline one to suppositions that are implausible in terms of the other one that is shelved for the time being.

Take now, again, the question of the changeability of destiny. The idea is that what God has determined no human can change. But if God is a grandfatherly figure, perhaps he might listen kindly to the prayers and appeals of his beleaguered grandchildren and grant them respite from the continual reverses that seem to be scheduled in their destiny. A noted Akan lyric calls on God to come down from on high to help his children. What emerges then is that although what God has ordained no human can change, God himself can change it.

Yet if the more cosmological concept of God is what is predominant in one's mind, one might assert that not even God can change what he has ordained. And this would be a way of emphasizing the indefeasibility of ("natural") law in the cosmic order. Thus, in a drum text famous among the Akans, an unnamed metaphysician says, "The creator created death, and death killed him." Danquah calls this "the hardest of Akan sayings" (1968, 75). Busia considers sayings of this kind as "riddles that conceal reflective thought and philosophy" (1962, 11). At all events, the saying in question is not intended literally. The thought seems to be that death and renewal are regular features of phenomena, and this regularity is just an instance of the higher-order regularity that defines the universe as a cosmos.

It is sometimes suggested that African explanations of natural phenomena tend to be framed in terms of personalized entities, such as spirits, because African perceptions of order come primarily from the sphere of human behavior (see Horton 1967). In fact, the extreme opposite is the truth. Cosmic order was seen, by Akan traditional metaphysicians at least, to be presupposed by the natural order of things, which, in turn, is presupposed by order or disorder in behavior. Not even behavioral disorder is conceivable without natural order. The thought of this cosmological priority of order is expressed in another drum text. The drummer-metaphysician makes a reference to Odomankoma, the Creator, and continues:

> "Hewer out" creator
> He created the thing
> What did He create?
> He created Order
> He created Knowledge
> He created Death.
>   (Danquah 1968, 70; his translation
>   from the Akan)

The priority of order also has implications for the problem of free will. If God is thought of as a kind of grandfather, his dispensation will not be seen as a debilitating constraint on one's ability to make free choices. On the other hand, if the divine being is viewed principally as the force behind cosmological order, predestination begins to seem like an inexorable foreclosure of any possibility of free will. Consciousness of this disjunction can be seen as the cause of the earnest questionings of the implications of destiny that one, for example, hears in the lyrics of some Akan popular music.

But of course, the disjunction is not exclusive, and a solution to the problem of free will and divine predetermination can be reached if close attention is paid to Akan ways of evaluating conduct. Any system of causes and effects that enables an individual to think rationally and act with (basic) moral maturity is conducive to free will. That, in fact, is the essence of free will. Therefore, it is not the sheer fact of causal determination, whatever the agent of the process might be, that determines whether a piece of conduct instantiates free will; it is what kind of causal pattern is at issue. Thus, if an individual's action is caused by an addiction to alcohol, his action lacks free will, not because it is caused but because it is the result of a socially pernicious cause (see Wiredu 1996, 130).

Among the causes that can, in the minds of most Akans, interfere with the moral and mental competence of an individual and thus put his or her ability to make free choices at risk are the activities of hostile quasi-physical agents, such as witches. For this reason, an average Akan would seek the protection of sufficiently capable counterspirits. Such agents are thought to enjoy flattery and an occasional sprinkling of schnapps, although in dire circumstances, they might demand animal sacrifice. The flattery comes in the form of singing, drumming, and dancing.[7] These sessions, while supposedly pleasing to the spirits, also bring considerable satisfaction to the participants.

These observances—or, if you like, diversions—will continue, given a reasonable calendar, as long as the spirit in question seems to the folks in question to provide the protection sought after. However, if the group develops the impression that the spirit is not effective, there are ways to dispose of it, which include "killing" it, and move on to a more competent one. Occasionally, a skeptic would emerge out of frustration with the incapacities of consecutive spirits, but that was rare.

AFRICAN RELIGION AND CHRISTIANITY

According to the Christian missionaries, I have just described the essence of African traditional religion. Traditional Africans did not worship God; they worshipped stones or, a little more charitably, various spirits, including ancestor spirits. Salvation will elude them unless they can be made to abandon their pagan superstitions and join the church of Christ, the Son of God.

The missionaries were correct in thinking that the traditional Akans did not worship God. But they seem to have assumed that if a people do not worship God, there surely must be something that they worship. Given such an assumption, it was easy to be overimpressed with superficial analogies between worship—or, let us be more explicit, religious worship—and the procedures by which the traditional

Akans sought to establish good relations with the spirits to whom they entrusted their salvation from evil spirits.

The crucial consideration is that the traditional attitude toward the spirits was a purely utilitarian one. Listen to three famous Akan thinkers:

1. Danquah, speaking of Akan society: "the general tendency is to sneer at and ridicule the fetish and its priest" (1952, 6).
2. Busia: "The Gods are treated with respect if they deliver the goods, and with contempt if they fail. . . . Attitudes to [the gods] depend upon their success, and vary from healthy respect to sneering contempt" (1954, 205).
3. Abraham: "The proliferation of gods that one finds among the Akans is in fact among the Akans themselves superstitious. Minor gods are artificial means to the bounty of *Onyame* [God]" (1962, 56).

On all of this showing, it is not plausible to regard the practices revolving around the so-called minor gods—that is, the spirits—as an integral part of Akan traditional religion, let alone to make them the essence of traditional African religion.

In fact, belief in various kinds of spirits is more entrenched in Christianity than it is in traditional African religion. Christianity believes in the existence of those spirits spoken of in African culture, plus extra ones, such as angels. The difference is only that whereas Christianity holds great reservations about African spirits as a group, traditional Africans believe that not all of them are bad. Good, bad, or indifferent, spirits are important in African traditional *culture*, if for no other reason than their perceived ability to help or hinder human enterprises. But we must be careful not to conclude from this that they are particularly important in traditional *religion*. We are here discounting the suggestion, sometimes heard, that every aspect of African traditional culture is religious (see, e.g., Mbiti 1989, 2).

As suggested earlier, Akan religion is totally focused on the supreme being as the demiurgic creator of the world. Recall that one of his descriptions is (in literal translation) "he who is alone great." All the rest of the universe is viewed as dependent on him and therefore incapable of being the object of religious feelings. The Akan sense of human dependence on God is hard to miss. If you ask an Akan whether he is going to, say, travel tomorrow, the chances are that he would, all being well, reply, "*Se Onyame pe a*" ("If God permits"). Or suppose you ask, "Did you go?" The reply might be, "*Onyame dom, me koe*" ("Yes, by the grace of God, I did"). And if some good thing happens, the reaction is to say, before anything else, "We thank God" (see Gyekye 1995, 71, for a collection of such sayings). Such is the Akan manifestation of piety. It is evident that the Akans do not think that you need a structured routine for that purpose. It should therefore not be surprising that Akan religion excludes a system of worship. The noninstitutional character of the religion is, of course, of the same tendency.

It might be thought that this discussion gives too abridged a scope to African traditional religion. Specifically, it might look as if we have given short shrift to the role therein of the ancestors. Indeed, some have actually spoken of ancestor worship and have seemed to think that it constitutes the principal part of African traditional religion. (Against this idea, see Mbiti 1989, 8–9.) In fact, the status of the ancestors is that of revered elders. They are conceived to be in constant quasi-physical interaction with their living relatives, bringing help when needed and punishment when necessary. They themselves are supposed, at least among the Akans, to live in an abode contiguous to our own and to have a political life continuous with our own. Thus, kings in this life are supposed to remain kings hereafter.

Notice that this afterlife is very different from, say, the Christian afterlife of beatitude for the blessed. The whole point of the Akan afterlife, as far as the ancestors are concerned, is to work for the well-being of the living. We might therefore say that the Akan afterlife is a this-worldly one (see, further, Wiredu and Gyekye 1992). This should discourage the notion of the religious significance of the ancestors. They do not need any special divine dispensation in order to carry out their worldly duties. The nature of the world is already attuned to both physical and quasi-physical processes and interactions. So the activities of the ancestors do not smack of the miraculous. And, actually, any atheistic ancestor would have no problem going about his or her duties.

Religious Pluralism and Exclusivism

We have noted some differences between Akan traditional religion and the Christian religion. Think of the differences in the conceptions of the afterlife that we have just explained. In colonial times, this was not a problem. The established policy of church authorities, who were usually Europeans, was that the African ideas were unsound, and the right thing to do was to replace them with Christian ones, which constituted the truth. Since the African attainment of independence, however, the authorities have become more tolerant of the idea of introducing some African cultural elements into church practices. Thus, African drumming, which used to be viewed almost as a symbol of paganism, can now be heard in chapels. Moreover, the senior personnel, such as high priests and archbishops, have increasingly become Africans, often very proud of their culture, including its religious parts.

Nevertheless, the problem of pluralism can hardly be said to have become even mitigated. It is a problem not of practice but of doctrine. Given, as the traditional Akans say, that "truths don't conflict" (*abra nni nokware mu*), how can an African be a Christian? From the side of the Africans, at least two approaches have been perceivable. On the part of the illiterate African churchgoers—illiterate, by the way, not necessarily in terms of their own culture but rather in terms of Western culture—the personal policy has been one of pragmatic selection. If, for example, an illness proves resistant to all of the best in Western and indigenous herbal medicine, the time is assumed to be at hand when one should consult an indigenous "specialist," capable of communicating with the ancestors. Perhaps the patient has offended the ancestors with some unacknowledged act of vice that is harmful to the lineage. Any such consultation would have to be done with the utmost secrecy, for it is still, after independence, contrary to Christian teaching to have any sort of trafficking with such beings as the African ancestors. This problem is still resisting solution.

The second approach, which is favored by many Western-educated African Christians, who yield ground to none in their love of their indigenous culture, is to suggest that there is no real difference between Christianity and indigenous religion. Both believe in the same God. This position was most forcefully stated by Bolaji Idowu, who was for many years professor of the study of religions at the University of Ibadan, Nigeria: "There is no being like 'the African God' except in the imagination of those who use the term, be they Africans or Europeans. . . . [T]here is only one God, and whilst there may be various concepts of God, according to each people's spiritual perception, it is wrong to limit God with an adjective formed from the name of any race" (1973). Unfortunately, even if this were an adequate characterization of the situation regarding the concept of God, it would still offer no guidance about how to deal with other disparities of belief, such as varying conceptions of the afterlife. But in fact, the differences in the concepts of God that philosophers, theologians, and others have offered from time to time cannot be dissolved in the manner of Idowu. Spinoza believed that God and the universe are one. Dewey believed that God is the "unity of all ideal ends arousing us to desire and action." The slightest attention reveals that Spinoza and Dewey are not talking of the same being as between each other or as between both of them and, say, an orthodox Christian. Note that, in truth, Dewey is not talking of a being at all.

Religious pluralism holds that there are many different ways of seeking (and, perhaps, gaining) salvation. No one way is to be privileged over others as the only right way. Religious exclusivism maintains that some ways (ours) might be right and other ways wrong. Pluralism is a noble idea with a shaky logic. The logic of exclusivism is inexorable, but its sensitivity is limited. A follower of African traditional religion might declare himself or herself exempt from these dilemmas, since there is no such thing as a search for salvation in that person's religion. However, African traditional religion, as with any other kind of religion or system of beliefs or disbeliefs, has specific doctrines that are true or false when they are fact stating or right or wrong when they are normative. It cannot, therefore, escape the problem completely. For example, if God created the universe out of some preexisting indeterminate stuff, as I think some African peoples believe, then it is false that God created the world out of nothing, as some Christians think. If there is not, or has never been, a God at all, then, of course, both groups are mistaken, and some atheist type is right. What to do? Well, if they have time, they should enter into dialogue.

Advocates of both pluralism, as spearheaded by John Hick, and exclusivism, as led by Alvin Plantinga, are aware of the importance of dialogue. But the process should be on the basis of respect of all parties for all parties concerned. And this respect should consist in the acknowledgment that each party to the dialogue is a possible source of insight. This implies that I might turn out to be wrong on a given issue, and my partner (or partners) might be right, and vice versa. Furthermore, dialogue should not be among the religious alone; it should sometimes also be between the religious and the irreligious. If dialogue follows this principle, it will become possible to imagine something that is now nonexistent, namely, genuine dialogue between African traditional religion and the "world" religions.

NOTES

1. The Akans live in southern, middle, and central parts of Ghana. They are also found in parts of the Ivory Coast. They account for just less than half the population of Ghana, which is upward of 20 million. I am a Ghanaian Akan.

2. See page 114 of the selection from Mill's *Utilitarianism* in Curd 1992. See also page 119.

3. But see Gyekye 1995, chap. 5, section 1; and Oguah 1984.

4. Alexis Kagame, the great Rwandan poet, linguist, and philosopher, did an empirical and analytic survey of the numerous Bantu languages. One of his conclusions was that to be is to be at some place. See, for example, Kagame 1976.

5. I might point out that the fact, if it is a fact, that absolute nothingness is unintelligible in Akan does not prove that it is so objectively. It just means that there is an issue here that cannot be taken for granted by anybody, Akan or not. If our aim here were to prove the soundness of the Akan idea, as distinct from just explaining what it is, it would be necessary to adduce considerations that are independent of any peculiarities of the Akan language or, for that matter, any other relevant language. In that process, we would inevitably have had to deal with the question of relativism. We must forgo that enterprise here.

6. A collection edited by Kwame Anthony Appiah and his mother, Peggy Appiah, numbers 7,015 proverbs. See Appiah and Appiah 2000.

7. Note that drumming in African society is not always for dancing. It sometimes conveys information and at other times, as on previous occasions in this discussion, communicates abstract reflection.

REFERENCES

Abraham, W. E. 1962. *The Mind of Africa*. Chicago: University of Chicago Press.

Appiah, Peggy, and Kwame Anthony Appiah, with Agyeman-Dua. 2000. *Bu me Be: Akan Proverb*. Accra, Ghana: Center for Intellectual Renewal.

Busia, K. A. 1954. "The Ashanti." In Daryll Forde, ed., *African Worlds: Studies in the Cosmological Ideas and Social Values of African Peoples*. New York: Oxford University Press, 190–209.

———. 1962. *The Challenge of Africa*. New York: Frederick A. Prager.

———. 1965. "The African World View." *Presence Africaine* 4: 16–23.

Curd, Martin, ed. 1992. *Argument and Analysis: An Introduction to Philosophy*. New York: West.

Danquah, J. B. 1952. "Obligation in Akan Society" In *West African Affairs*. London: Department of Extra Mural Studies, University College of the Gold Coast, 3–21.

———. 1968. *The Akan Doctrine of God: A Fragment of Gold Coast Ethics and Religion*, 2nd ed. London: Frank Cass.

Gyekye, Kwame. 1995. *An Essay on African Philosophical Thought: The Akan Conceptual Scheme*, rev. ed. Philadelphia: Temple University Press.

Horton, Robin. 1967. "African Traditional Thought and Western Science." *Africa* 37/1–2: 50–71. Also in Robin Horton, *Patterns of Thought in Africa and the West: Essays on Magic, Religion and Science*. Cambridge, U.K.: Cambridge University Press, 1993.

Idowu, E. Bolaji. 1962. *Olodumare: God in Yoruba Belief*. London: Longman.

———. 1973. *African Traditional Religion: A Definition*. Maryknoll, N.Y.: Orbis.

Kagame, Alexis. 1976. "The Empirical Acceptation of Time and the Conception of History in Bantu Thought." In Louis Gardet et al., eds., *Cutures and Time*. Paris: UNESCO, 89–116.

Mbiti, John S. 1989. *African Religions and Philosophy*, 2nd ed. London: Heinemann.

Oguah, B. E. 1984. "African and Western Philosophy: A Comparative Study." In Richard A. Wright, ed., *African Philosophy: An Introduction*, 3rd ed. Lanham, Md.: University Press of America, 213–25.

Plato. 1988. *Euthyphro*. Benjamin Jowett, trans. Buffalo: Prometheus.

Wiredu, Kwasi. 1996. *Cultural Universals and Particulars: An African Perspective*. Bloomington: Indiana University Press.

Wiredu, Kwasi, and Kwame Gyekye. 1992. *Person and Community: Ghanaian Philosophical Studies 1*. Washington, D.C.: Council for Research in Values and Philosophy.

FOR FURTHER READING

Hick, John. 2003. "Religious Pluralism and Ultimate Reality." In Louis P. Pojman, ed., *Philosophy of Religion: An Anthology*, 4th ed. Belmont, Calif.: Wadsworth, 499–507.

Olupona, Jacob K., and Sulayman S. Nyang, eds. 1993. *Religious Plurality in Africa: Essays in Honour of John S. Mbiti*. Berlin: Gruyter.

Plantinga, Alvin. 2003. "A Defense of Religious Exclusivism in Pojman." In Louis P. Pojman, ed., *Philosophy of Religion: An Anthology*, 4th ed. Belmont, Calif.: Wadsworth, 507–20.

Sharma, Arvind. 2006. *A Primal Perspective on the Philosophy of Religion*. Dordrecht, Neth.: Springer.

Shaw, Rosalind. 1990. "The Invention of 'African Traditional Religion.'" *Religion* 20: 339–353.

CHAPTER 26

A CHINESE RELIGIONS PERSPECTIVE

CHUNG-YING CHENG

DIVERSITY AS A PRINCIPLE OF RELIGIOUS DEVELOPMENT

IF we take religion to be the ultimate belief concerning truth of human life and its value, religion has to be diverse and as diverse as there are diverse communities of peoples—or, for that matter, as diverse as there are diverse individuals. One must see that our beliefs can relate to many things, particularly matters of life, death, and postdeath or prelife. It is up to individual persons to decide which belief is worthy of being believed. This inevitably leads to considerations of questions about what the beliefs are about and what they might tell us. It might also bear on what urgent needs a person or a people might have under their life circumstances. There seem to be two opposite ways to go against each other. The first is to make religion as objective as science so that we can all share the religious knowledge as we share scientific knowledge. But the problem is that there is no such objective religious knowledge. Second, we could make our beliefs extremely private and subjective, and in this case, nobody can dictate what you should believe by way of religion. You have to decide what you do believe or what you wish to believe.

With these two views, we have a conflict of absolute objectivism against absolute subjectivism. We need a balancing power that will mediate between these two extremes so that we can claim some objective validity for our religious beliefs and at the same time allow our conscience to work out its best judgments. Since we are exposed to many vicissitudes of life, insofar as we are capable of learning from experience, we might even have to examine our beliefs and make adjustments in time in our own understanding. A given religious tradition might serve as a framework or reference for us to think over our beliefs and assess our new judgments.

Zhu Xi has compiled a book, titled *Reflections on Things at Hand*, from thoughts of his predecessors in Neo-Confucianism precisely for this purpose of reference and providing such a framework.[1] But given this process, religion is obviously subject to philosophical inquiry, which could theoretically be used to defend a belief or even critically upset a belief. In this light, there cannot be absolute tight systems of religious beliefs without consideration of how changes are possible for such a system, for if it is such a tight system, it would smother life and distance it from real life. If we speak of a religion that is truly rooted in life, not just based on history or theory, it has to sustain its beliefs in different times, under different circumstances, with regard to different peoples. This means that it must provide a sophisticated system of acceptable interpretations of changes and differences whereby individual differentiation of doctrine by individual understanding is always possible. In this sense, we must see diversity and differentiation as natural ingredients of any religious belief or belief system.

In connection with the contrast between objectivism and subjectivism, we can take note of two kinds of diversity resulting from each position. From the side of objectivism, we come to diversity of opinions from possibilities of interpretation of the objective truth. This cannot be avoided even in the case of scientific inquiry. This is because many equally legitimate theories could be compatible with the same set of evidences, even though they themselves are not compatible with one another. From the side of subjectivism, we come to the diversity of opinions from our own unique ways of seeing things differently. We might represent different perspectives, and we have different goals and different needs. The diversity of interpretations or understandings would have to come from our conditions as existing human beings. While there could be strong incompatible differences among various subjective views, there could still be possible compatible opinions about the similarly intended object, or even possibly differently intended objects.

Thus, not only will we have a case of how blind people have touched different parts of the same elephant, but we might have a case of how blind people have touched on different parts of two or more different animals or refer to two or more different mountains. We can therefore speak of different things even though we might appear to speak of the same thing. In either case, we might be able to clarify and recognize the differences and appreciate that they are different and yet compatible, because they could represent two new discoveries, each of which is useful to the human species. This type of diversity will enrich our experiences and will not put us on the path of conflict and contradiction. Instead, we might come to enjoy the harmony of differences. This is how Confucius came to speak of "harmony without being the same" (*he er butong*) (Analects 13–23). This need not be the end of the story, for we can go one step further in trying to identify the deeper source of different perceptions or appearances and reach for a transcendental or transcendent integrative unity by integrating them into a meaningful unity through inquiry and reflection.

To contrast with this case of "harmony with difference," the first case could be labeled "difference without harmony," whereby incompatible views and interpretations of the same object produce different predictions with regard to the same object. The crucial difficulty of this lies in speaking of the same object, such as the same god or the same real world. The diversity resulting from dealing with the same object therefore has to be incompatible, particularly when each could claim that it is directed to the same aspect of the same object, such as arising from the famous conflict of interpretations in solar-centric theory versus geocentric theory of the earth-sun relationship. The different and incompatible interpretations of scientific hypotheses have to be tested as either true or false. There cannot be a case of both being true, as in the second case noted: among two or more hypotheses, one has to be true, or all could be false. Such is the purpose of scientific confirmation. The result of such confirmation is that we have a clearer identification of what we refer to in our understanding and that we will eliminate diversities in light of a unified theory of truth.

Clearly, it is not so with regard to the first kind of compatible hypotheses. We might reach the conclusion that two or more views could be true or more or less true, or we might see them as equally false but not necessarily one being true and the other being false. The reason is that it depends on what we are talking about and whether we know what we are talking about with respect to the object. It is possible that we do not know the object or that the object is a changeable or indeterminate one and has to be defined by our own ways of thinking or our own ways of action and practice. Then, insofar as we are to reach a consensus of our talk or a consensus on the differences among our forms of life, we have to recognize the truth of the diversity and its beneficial values resulting from it. We need not impose on others what we personally believe and have experienced in our different lives.

It is interesting to note that the first kind of diversity is what has taken place in the Western tradition of religious diversity, which involves incompatible difference and which is addressed to the same object (or so we think), such as God. On the other hand, the second kind of diversity is what has been experienced in the Chinese (and even possibly the Indian) tradition of religious diversity. This second kind of diversity involves essentially no incompatible differences and hence differences that can be resolved as different forms of practices or forms of life, which are then harmonized in a state of living harmony. The large question for the globalized world and the whole of humankind is whether we can transform the first kind of incompatible diversity into the second kind of compatible diversity, so that a global harmony and peace can result and prevail. Or do we have to push to extend the first kind to the second kind or transform the second kind into the first kind and thus increase the quantity and quality of conflict and contradiction in this world from which we will all suffer because we will fight all against all.

Since diversification appears to be the way a world religion develops, it is interesting to see how the process of globalization of economy and politics in the world can affect our diversity of religions in the world. But the facts tend to show that various globalization processes bring in various processes of localization, and no doubt diversification of religion will have to be sustained, while dialogues and alliances among religions will be intensified so that no religion can claim absolute dominance even in one locality without serious critique from other religious groups (which might be minorities). We see that while diversification accelerates, mutual acceptance and friendly cooperation also become necessary and desirable. These two forces seem to bring an equilibrium and balance between diversification and integration that could assure us of a robust outburst of the vitality in religious activities in the world.

In examining the development of religion in world cultures, we can easily see how diversity and diversification are always a force for the spreading of religion. If there is no diversification, there could not be a spreading of the religion. It is equally true that diversification and diversity are natural forces always at work in religions. Even highly rationally organized religion cannot escape from the force of diversity and diversification. This, no doubt, is true of the development of both Christianity and Buddhism, the two most rationally organized religions of the world. It is interesting to note that in the case of Chinese religions, there is a strong underlying philosophy that explicitly recognizes diversity and diversification as a way of extension and duration, even though diversity can be seen as a manifestation of the same principle or truth of the original and hence to contain ultimate principles of unity. The unity in diversity is what actually gives itself the momentum toward diversification as a way of realizing the unity. This can be seen in the first development of the philosophy of the Yi (change) in the Yijing (also called the I Ching, one of the oldest extant Chinese texts), which transforms the ancient religion of *tian* (heaven) into a moral consciousness of self-discipline and cultivation of moral reason in individual human beings (or at the very beginning, in the rulers of people), which makes it necessary for the person or the ruler to act out one's virtue in a process of self-realization that embodies a diversity of virtues.

Two Characteristics of Chinese Religious Diversity

In light of Chinese history, it is important to realize first that unlike in the West, religion—or, for that matter, belief in God—is not the dominating factor or the driving force for cultural and historical development of Chinese society or Chinese government. If a religion has to do with the dao, namely, the way of realization of life or anything significant, it is necessary to see that the dao is embodied in life and things in the world and is never to be separated from them, even though it is not dominating or even self-presenting.[2] The core understanding is that dao is the comprehensive dynamic power of creation and transformation that pervades all things, the invisible and the visible, and we can learn and know the dao by observing changes in the world and reflecting on our own life activities.

We will come to see the dao at rest and in motion and thus the dao in vacuity of mind and natural spontaneity of feeling and response. In order to gain wisdom of the dao, we must always do self-cultivation and prepare ourselves for ever-refreshing changes of things in the world. Eventually, we will come to see the creativity of the dao and how it allows all possible things to happen without dominating, possessing, and controlling. This is clearly said in Laozi: "Dao is such that it creates without possession, doing things without claiming authority, growing things without dominating [*shengbuyou, weierbuchi, changerbuzai*]."[3] But we have to experience this powerful action of the dao deeply in our open observations of nature and our reflections on life in order truly to learn from it and benefit from it.

The question is how the vision of dao as the ultimate natural force of creation and transformation is first developed. For this, we will bring in the formation of the ideas of change in the texts of the Yijing. We will see that it is the Yijing that gives rise to the idea of the dao as a creativity force and the idea of humanity as a co-creative force that leads to the establishment of Confucianism. But before this development, the most important thing to know is that it is through Yijing that the idea of heaven as an external authority of creation becomes internalized and eventualized as the dao, first described as *tiandao* by the Confucians and then described as the dao by the Daoists.

Since no dominating religion has been established in the ancient period, it is to be assumed that from the very early stages, Chinese religion and Chinese polities were separated, and no religious beliefs have developed as simple dogmas in China. On the other hand, the development of religious beliefs in Chinese history (or, for that matter, in Chinese society) was subject to many forces (social, political, and even economic), and among them the political force is often most important. But the ultimate force in the development of a religion is its commitment to question and answer human identity and human destiny in regard to forces external to human beings. We can look into the belief in heaven, for example, and see how it was transformed into belief in the mandate of heaven for the purpose of ruling and taking care of the people.

In the West, the history of Christianity is revealing in that it is rooted in the idea of a transcendent God. For the followers of Christianity, God cannot be seen or fully known but can only be believed. In fact, it is required that one should believe in God in order to know God. Given this theology, we also see how a religion of a single transcendent God can be differentiated into sectarian denominations that include opposite and conflicting elements of beliefs. In the first place, one sees that the Jewish religion of Jehovah (Yahweh) led to the rise of Catholic Christianity, which, in turn, led to the Protestant religions in Europe and England. This process of diversification reflects claims and movements and dialogues for reconciliation and possible unification, which are intended to eliminate wars and clashes, for the purpose of peaceful coexistence but not for the achievement of any unity—whether in theory or in practice. The rise of Islam from the Abrahamic sources, however, does not make it in any way an ally to already existing Jewish or Christian religion. In fact, because of political conflicts, they became enemies in the time of crusaders.

Nowadays, it is difficult to see how Judaism and Islam could be related to each other as brotherly allies. Here, we have diversity from one source, and yet the diversity is a source of conflict and war. This is in strict contrast with the Chinese diversity of religions in Confucianism, Daoism, and Buddhism, which are largely conceived in harmony, or at least are capable of harmonization.

In China, even though there are various forms of competition and currying favor between Daoism and Buddhism on the political level, there were no large-scale clashes between Daoism and Buddhism until they were manipulated by the imperial power of the court. History has witnessed three imperial campaigns for extinguishing Buddhism, two times favoring Daoism and once hurting both Buddhism and Daoism.[4] But in actual practice, the two religions tended to learn from each other as two schools of philosophy. One can note how Buddhist texts have been translated into Chinese with the help of scholars of Daoist philosophy. In latter-day developments, when Buddhism became established as a court religion, Daoist religionists wanted to do the same and made successful efforts in establishing Daoism in the ruler's court. For religious teachings, many Daoist materials are written as inspired by or in imitation of the Buddhist texts. Because of the negative lessons learned from political disasters, both Daoists and Buddhists tended to shy away from the ruler and slowly established better and even harmonious relationships with one another.

We can say that the spirit of religion in China is basically the spirit of unity in variety and variety in unity with religion understood in both the narrow sense of explicit commitments and the broad sense of implicit beliefs. Specifically, I refer here to the traditional religions in the Chinese context, not the newer religions such as Christianity. This spirit is informed by three kinds of understanding and beliefs: the spirit of the dao (the way), the spirit of the de (the virtues), and the spirit of wu (the awakening), which respectively stand for Daoism, Confucianism, and Chinese Buddhism. When I use these terms, I have in mind the origins of these religious spirits in the heart and mind of Chinese culture, which is characterized by the spirit of creative transformation in *hua* from the texts of the Yijing. In essence, I want to say that these three religions are themselves diverse expressions of the creativity in the mode of thinking in the Yijing, which crystallizes the deep experiences and reflections in the Chinese mind.

It is not accidental that this takes place, for it does take a long time to shape this scenario of diversity in unity and unity of diversity in a dynamic way. For this phenomenon, it does take the dao, the de, and the wu as contents of development that are both empirical and reflective. In an even more general sense, we can characterize the Chinese religious and philosophical consciousness overall as rooted in the concepts of dao and de and their transcendence in the concept of wu. Hence, any Chinese religion, including Chinese Buddhism, could fall into the spirit of dao and thus can be labeled a religion of the dao. It is equally true of the idea of de. As for the spirit of wu, which I use to characterize Chinese Buddhism, it is also a common quality in the understanding of Confucianism and Daoism. But that is not to say that there are no differences among these different religious schools. On the contrary, there are as many differences between any two of them as differences are allowed and promoted.

The point here is to indicate that diversity becomes a native and natural feature of Chinese religion, and it goes together with unity, intermediation, and interrelations as we find in the unity of the way (dao), the virtue (de), and the awakening (wu). We have said that the interaction between unity and diversity is possible because of the philosophy of change embodied in the texts of the Yijing, which has transcendentally integrated the three and provides the source of inspiration and foundation of development for each of them. In light of this, we can make a second point about the diversity of the three Chinese religions, namely, that diverse religions in China remain more interconnected and even interpenetrated than the three Abrahamic religions of Judaism, Christianity, and Islam in the West.

The three religions in China deal with different aspects of the problem of humanity and thus form a functional complementation similar to what we find in a high-level organism whose main purpose is perceived to help society face different problems of life and different challenges of the engagement of life. In contrast, the three religions in the Abraham tradition that split into conflicting subtraditions are intended to deal with essentially the same issue in different ways but constitute a complex conflict. They are regarded more or less as dealing with problems of a transcendent God and the afterlife of human beings and therefore present directly conflicting views and approaches that also become a matter of competing for political power through their organizations.

I have spoken of Confucianism and Daoism as religions, but one must be warned that they are embodiments of philosophical worldviews, which become guiding principles of practical life. There is indeed a Daoist religion, which is organized in complex ways, has an origin in the Han period, and has lasted to the present day. But there is no organized Confucian religion that we can liken to either Daoist or Buddhist religion, because there are no Confucian priests or temples as religious shelters or places of concentrated cultivation; the Confucian temples are traditionally for performing Confucian religious rites only. It is true that Confucians are traditionally taught in Confucian academies on local levels for civic examination. There are indeed family temples for ancestral memorial rituals, but they are conducted or not conducted by families freely, and there is no requirement for such memorial rites in modern families. There is also no fixed object of worship, and while performing sacrificial rites to heaven is an ancient duty and right for the ruler, it is not for the common people. Yet we can perhaps speak of an informal Confucian religion that amounts to taking care of the normal business of cultivating our virtues as convention requires. The important thing here is that Confucianism deals with positive activities of the development of life of the individual and the community and hence is usually not regarded as a religion like Daoism and Buddhism.[5]

In present-day China, there is some appeal to make Confucianism a religion so that Chinese people can find a faith in life and a norm to follow in conducting their lives. But this is no doubt a naive and misguided move. Not only would it not succeed because no one has the authority to reintroduce an ideology that should come naturally from one's free choice and natural sentiment, but it would distort and misrepresent Confucianism as it was originally developed and practiced in the tradition. As such, Confucianism will not substitute for the role that Daoism and Buddhism have played in society. Unlike Daoism and Buddhism, Confucianism is devoted to achieving a good life, consisting in robust participation in society and government based on one's cultivation of a moral personality. Such a life is sufficient to give intrinsic justification to its completion and to offer a role model for descendants. Of course, it is important to have descendants so that one will be remembered and live on in the minds of those descendants, and the ancient doctrine of immortality by virtue, by deeds, and by words is all that Confucianism can offer here.

This understanding should provide a reason for requiring diversity of religions to be allowed, for there is no reason to consider human life other than in such a mode of social and moral cultivation and participation. Hence, a Confucian is considered to be one not to exclude but rather to include and to be open to all other forms of beliefs insofar as they are not interfering with the practice of Confucian duties at home and at work. There is no reason and there are no efforts to convert other believers on religious grounds. It is said in the Zhong Yong that "the different daos can proceed in parallel, and there is no contradiction between them"; it also says that "the great virtue transforms, the small one flows in parallel" (Zhong Yong 30). This is precisely the meaning of the statement by Confucius that "there is harmony in which there are differences" (Analects 13–23). The principle of diversity and its use are fully realized in the founding of Confucianism.

THREE FORMS OF RELIGIOUS CONSCIENCE IN CHINESE TRADITION

Whereas Chinese religion in some primitive sense has turned out to be more humanistic and naturalistic, Western religion has become even more antihumanistic and supernaturalistic.[6] For this reason, it might be appropriate to label Chinese religious consciousness as human-centered to contrast with the Western religious consciousness as God- or divine-centered.

One can easily appreciate how there is a natural and harmonious diversification of the religious consciousness in the Chinese tradition in contrast with a forced and often disharmonious diversification of the religious consciousness in the Western tradition. We have mentioned the split of the Abrahamic tradition into three religions—Jewish, Christian, and Muslim—in contrast with the natural division of the Yi tradition into the three schools of philosophical teachings: Confucianism, Daoism, and Chinese Buddhism. Without going into detail about how these schools developed, I will briefly mention their ideas of diversity and unity, which apparently can be said to be under the influence of the paradigm of the Yijing in both theoretical and practical perspectives.

First, we can introduce Confucianism as a religion of virtues (de) as a result of early influences of the doctrine of *tian-ming*. It is interesting to note that Confucius has taken seriously the concept of humanity, which he sees as an innate quality of human nature. When he says, "If I wish to have *ren* [a term used to describe the inward expression of Confucian ideals], this *ren* will arrive" (Analects 7–30), this could mean either that care for others is something I can decide to have or that *ren* can be readily recognized in life if I desire to have it. I believe that both meanings are relevant and should be included in the saying. For we could recognize that *ren* as *ren* is a quality that has deeply benefited human society in its growth. The question is whether we can keep our conscientious focus on *ren* and extend it for the benefit of developing the human self and the society at large. For Confucius, there is a purpose in developing the *ren* as a source of virtue for other virtues, for it would help to transform the whole society into a high state of moral order.

It is clear that Confucius is highly conscious of the importance of unity and diversity, for he sees them as two sides of the same entity of humanity. Humanity must be one so that we can share our common feelings and needs. Confucius says: "Human beings are born as straight, if one becomes crooked, it would be sheer luck that he will not remain unhurt" (Analects 6–19). He might not have come to the explicit notion of human nature (*xing*), but he does presuppose a common notion of human nature in order to talk about the diversity of human tempers and talents.

For this diversity of human tempers and talents, there is a long passage in the eleventh chapter of the Analects that describes how four different disciples of Confucius responded to Confucius's request to speak out their wishes and ambitions. First, Zilu describes how he would like to take care of a small state and train it in courage. Yan You, on the other hand, focuses on his ambition to govern a state at peace, so it can be ready for refinement in *li* (rites) and *yue* (music). The third disciple, Gong Xihua, confesses that he would be satisfied with being a petty minister in a state. Finally, Zeng Dian speaks of taking a swim in the River Yi, cooling out at the Wuyi woods, and singing on the road back. Confucius says that he prefers the way Zeng Dian chooses to describe his wish. This shows that as a teacher, Confucius is open to different ways of development on the part of his students. To become what you wish to become, yet within the limits of virtues, is to see diversity as a natural way of realizing yourself.

On this basis, Confucius describes his principle of teaching as teaching without making a distinction of classes (*youjiao wulei*). This lets his disciples reach for what they can reach and be themselves while they become virtuous and humane.

We have spoken of the notion of "having harmony without being the same" in Confucius. It is important to link this idea to his understanding of the philosophy of the Yijing as one in which a person recognizes the importance of "diverse ways for reaching the same end" and the importance of having "a deep sense of unity based on a hundred considerations for its realization."[7] These basic thoughts eventually inspired the Neo-Confucians to develop a doctrine of many manifestations and one principle (*liyifenshu*).

As we have seen, Confucian ethics is founded on the principle of diversity in unity and unity in diversity. Every virtue has a place in the system of virtues and specifically relates to our understanding of benevolence (*ren*) and human relationships. People can decide what to do under various social conditions, but one should not forget the request for *ren* as a basic virtue of human action. This deep sense of respect for diversity in human persons and in realization of the human self has made Confucian ethics an open and realistic way of consolidating the human community. As Confucius's Analects show, it is on the basis of knowing how to cultivate oneself in different stages and on different levels that one can become a truly self-ruling person (*junzi*) so as to bring peace and harmony to the world.[8] In both Mencius and Xunzi, the principle of *yi* (righteousness) and the principle of *li* (ritual propriety) are based on the idea of diversity, for it is because of different needs and diverse circumstances that we must come to see what is proper and what is improper. But again, diversity of *yi* and *li* cannot be separated from the unity of *ren*, which comprehends the whole of humanity.

As for Daoism, which I describe as the religion of the dao, it is a central tenet of the Daoist philosophy that all things must go back to the origin in the dao from which we become what we are. Following the model of ontocosmology of the Yijing, the Daodejing speaks of one giving rise to two and two giving rise to three. Diversity is a natural cosmic process that nevertheless would also go back to the beginning of the one. The Daodejing says, "Reversion is the movement of the dao, being weak is the function of the dao. All the things under heaven are born from being and Being is born from Non-Being" (40). We can see this as a statement about how unity gives rise to variety and diversity, whereas diversity and variety would return to the oneness in the beginning. In the case of Zhuangzi, a fourth-century BCE Daoist philosopher (who is also purported to have written the Daoist book that bears his name), we might well see in his essays a strong desire and ability to bring in a diversity of individual human lives and examples of living species exhibited in the world of nature. Nevertheless, Zhuangzi also takes the oneness of the dao very seriously and says, "It is in the dao that we reach the oneness" (Qiwulun essay on making all things equal). For Zhuangzi, diversity in dao is also a cosmological principle, not just a biodiversity principle that allows all things to be equal in regard to their common origin and their common end.

While Daoist philosophy in Laozi and Zhuangzi does not speak of special natural forces while concentrating on a naturalistic understanding of the dao, which is basically cosmological, when we come to the Daoist religion, we have a different scenario, whereby there is a strong push for cultivating a way of life in order to achieve longevity and immortality. This uses the Daoist philosophy for a positive mastery of life process in this world. In this sense, we have to understand it as derived not only from Daoist philosophy but also from the spirit of creative life in the Yijing. Its deep care for a comprehensive use of natural elements for elixir making also reveals how diversity of life is founded on the deep source of life in the unity in nature, and to find this unity of life for the individual is one of the most important tasks of the Daoist religious practice. The gradual diversification of

Daoist religion in latter times shows how different needs of life and society are a basis for such diversification.[9]

Now we come to the development of Chinese Buddhism. Again, we can see how a deepening understanding enables Chinese peoples to take interest in the Buddhist development into diverse schools. There is, first, the introduction of the Hinayana schools and the Dyana school of meditation. But Hinayana Buddhism has to give way to the Mahayana school in China, which allows more diverse ways of salvation and understanding as the cultural and philosophical tradition demands. It is therefore no surprise to see how the Madhyamika school, based on Nagarjuna, prepares a ground for the development of special insights into other sutras (Buddhist scriptures), which eventually gives rise to two major schools of original Chinese Buddhism: Tiantai and Huayan. The Tiantai school bases its development on the interpretation of the Lotus Sutra, whereas the Huayan school bases its development on the interpretation of the Huayan (Avamtasaka) Sutra. This diversification is, of course, natural for both schools and presents a highly dynamic and useful representation and understanding of the schools of Buddhism, as well as its own development. While both schools have shown a comprehensive scope of allowing all things and principles to be presented in harmony (Huayan) and/or allowing all people or even all forms of life to be enlightened to Buddhahood and saved on all expedient occasions (Tiantai), their prospectuses come to present the entire set of Buddhist schools and their developmental stages in their famous doctrines of critical distinction of Buddhist teachings (*panjiao*).

These teachings present a fresh way of understanding unity in variety and variety in unity by introducing a hierarchical system of both explanation and evaluation. Of course, both schools have presented a self-sufficient picture of the Buddhist schools, with their own respective teachings placed at the apex of the development. This idea of organic and dynamic diversity suggests how diversity can be an intrasystemic feature that is required if the system is to be perfected and reaches for a final stage of perfection. When we come to the development of Chan Buddhism (known in Japan as the Zen school of Buddhism), we see finally a practice and theory that would make all diversities ways for reaching awakening or enlightenment. In awakening or enlightenment of this nature, we would have arrived at the uniform goal of both achieving a vision and consummating a living state of Buddhahood, which would transcend all ways of diversity and diversification. The third patriarch of the Chan school, Seng Zhan, says: "One is all, all is one, if we can understand this, what is that which we do not understand?"[10] Following this, we can indeed also say that unity is diversity, diversity is unity, and once we understand this, we understand all. We must remark that after the development of the Chinese Chan, all diverse schools of Chinese Buddhism—or, for that matter, all known schools of Buddhism in Asia, come to have a meeting of minds in the meditation of the Chan. It is indeed surprising to see how diversity has urged unity and harmony in the case of the development of Chinese Buddhism.

Finally, we must note that as a result of social, economic, and political factors, the Buddhist schools not only converge toward interpenetration and integration (such as we see in the slogans of *jin-chan heyi* ("unity of pure land and Chan") and *jiao-chuan heyi* ("unity of teaching and meditation"), at the end of the Ming Dynasty, the Buddhist Chan masters also started to promote and argue for the unity of the three teachings, namely, the unity of Confucianism, Buddhism, and Daoism.[11] They wished to embody the Confucian philosophy and avoid conflict with the ethics of society. This was also promoted by the Daoist religionists such as Zhang Yuchu and Lu Xixing. This heralded a new age in which Chinese philosophy and various branches of Chinese religion became united under the fold of the dominating Confucianism of Li and Xin from the Song-Ming period, perhaps in readiness for confronting an onset of a Western religion (namely, Christianity). The unity and harmony of the three teachings do not really change the original contents of each teaching but only provide a canopy for which diversity can be recognized, enriched, or even supported by the totality.

CONCLUSIONS

I have discussed the basic concept of diversity as a natural element in the development of Chinese religious consciousness and philosophical-religious schools. Diversity becomes a necessity primarily because the creative development of a single source requires it. This is made known and justified on the ground of the ontocosmology of the Yijing, which becomes the precondition and foundation for all later forms of philosophical-religious schools in China. The Yijing philosophy, through its own creative transformation of identity and difference by way of divination (*pushi*), has given rise to the schools of Confucianism and Daoism, each of which represents a religious conscience in respective practices of de and dao, moralism and naturalism. For Confucianism, I have brought forward the underlying influence of the doctrine of *tian-ming* to give reasons for the articulation of innate virtues in human nature. Under the influence of Daoism and Confucianism, Buddhism becomes a religion of awakening (wu), which also draws its inspiration from the Confucian doctrine of humanity for the purpose of universal salvation.

We have thus seen how the three Chinese religions have worked basically under the paradigm of creative harmony of the Yijing, which stresses the importance of comprehensiveness, harmonization, interdependence, and unity in variety or variety in unity. The principles of one end with many roads (*tongguiyitu*) and one mind (*yizhi*) with many thoughts (*yizhibailue*) have a profound impact on all three religious-philosophical schools and their developments. It is important to see how all of this is possible: they basically all subscribe to an ontohermeneutical view of inner transcendence over external transcendence in which there is no domination of an invisible, separate, absolute one single personal God. It is because of the dissolution and deconstruction of an essential objective and transcendent God that human beings come to achieve autonomy of will and face the responsibility of self-cultivation in which salvation is found.

By the end of the Ming period, when the three teachings became promoted as a unity, the introduction of Christianity became a factor of change and a forceful challenge to the religious teachings of China. The consequent controversy (called the Rites Controversy) between two polar modes of thinking, one represented by the West and one represented by scholars of mainstream Neo-Confucianism in China, already had begun in the end of the Ming.[12] It led to sharp conflict, contradiction, and opposition between the doctrine of outer transcendence of a personal God and the philosophy of inner transcendence in the nonpersonal dao. This controversy has carried on over the last three hundred years, and whether and how the doctrine of unity in variety and variety in unity as based in the philosophy of Yijing harmonizes with the teachings of dualism, personalism, and the absolute transcendence of God for a globalized world is something to be further explored.

NOTES

1. Zhu Xi (1130–1200) is the Southern Song scholar and philosopher who has developed the Neo-Confucian philosophy of *li* (principles), *qi* (vital force), *xin* (mind), and *xing* (human nature) on the basis of his synthesis of the four important Neo-Confucian thinkers in the Northern Song.

2. This is because from the very early stage, religion as religious beliefs has to do with some external power that affects our life. But once Dao is seen as the power that creates and shapes our life and a way for attaining value and wisdom, what is believed to be external also becomes part of our experience of the power.

3. See Daodejing 10, 51. Laozi is also purported to have written the book titled the Laozi, also called the Tao Te Ching (or Daodejing).

4. It is called "Destruction of Buddhism by Three Wu's." The three emperors involved are Taiwu in northern Wei, Wudi in Bei Zhou, and Wuzong of the Tang; the first and the third have to do with the conspiracies of the Daoists.

5. To say the least, in Confucianism, there is no new answer about death and immortality beyond what is given by Daoism and Buddhism. In this sense, Confucianism cannot be a religion like them, for it does not offer a genuine account of afterlife.

6. Early Chinese religious consciousness of heaven as an external divinity has been transformed into a nonobjectual and nonstationary way of realization of life and the world. Although we can speak of the *shangdi* and *tian*, we have to understand them in terms of the activities and processes of eventuation of things in nature, even, furthermore, not to be separated from our experiences of these activities and processes. What makes this transformation possible is the use of divinations in the development of philosophy of the Yi in Yijing and the use of the doctrine of *tian-ming* in the Shujing. Both traditions were established very early, and their influences at the turn of the Zhou founding revolutionizes the ancient Chinese religion of ruler on high and heavenly will, which could be comparable to the theism or panentheism of the West in the ancient world.

7. See Yizhuan, Confucian Commentaries on the Yijing, part 2, section 5, paragraph 1.

8. For details on self-cultivation, see the Confucian Four Books, especially the book known as Daxue ("The Great Learning").

9. For example, we might see that a section of elixir (*danding*), charm graphs (*fulu*), and breath control (*qigong*) are reflections of the social needs for different functions of communal and individual life.

10. See this quotation in the famous anthology of Chan sayings *Zhi Yue Lu* ("Records of Pointing to the Moon").

11. See the writings of Chan masters in the period from the middle of the sixteenth century to the middle of the seventeenth century. Some Daoists have argued for the unity of three teachings even earlier, at the end of fifteenth century.

12. Mateo Ricci (1552–1610) came to China in 1581. His basic teachings and arguments with Neo-Confucian scholars are contained in his work, *Essential Teachings of the Lord in Heaven* (*Tianzhu Shiyi*).

FOR FURTHER READING

Cheng, Chung-ying. 1991. "Religious Reality and Religious Understanding in Confucianism and Neo-Confucianism." In Chung-ying Cheng, *New Dimensions of Confucian and Neo-Confucian Philosophy*. Albany: State University of New York Press, 451–480.

———. 2005. "Toward an Integrative Pluralism of Religions: Embodying *Yijing*, Whitehead, and Cobb." In David Griffin, ed., *Deep Religious Pluralism*. Louisville, Ky.: Westminster John Knox, 210–222.

———. 2007. "Chinese Religions." In Chad Meister and Paul Copan, eds., *The Routledge Companion to Philosophy of Religion*. London: Routledge, 37–53.

Overmyer, Daniel L., ed. *Religion in China Today*. Cambridge, U.K.: Cambridge University Press.

Thompson, Laurence G. 1995. *Chinese Religion: An Introduction*. Belmont, Calif.: Wadsworth.

CHAPTER 27

A JEWISH PERSPECTIVE

DAVID SHATZ

THE question "How does Judaism relate to other religions?" can be divided into five subquestions:

1. Does Judaism believe that adherents of other religions can achieve salvation in the hereafter—"the world to come"—without converting to Judaism?
2. Does Judaism aim at converting Gentiles?
3. What is Judaism's eschatological vision—specifically, what is the fate of non-Jews and adherents of other religions at the end of days?
4. Does Judaism believe that other religions are also true? If so, in what sense and to what degree? Does Judaism believe that they have value even if they are false in important respects?
5. Does Judaism believe that interfaith dialogue, in the sense of discussion and critical assessment of one's religious tenets, and possibly appropriation of teachings of other religions, is advisable and proper?

When we speak about what "Judaism" believes about these matters, we must not expect monolithic answers. Judaism values—in fact, celebrates—debate and disagreement; indeed, the very many Jewish theologians and *halakhic* (legal)[1] authorities who have addressed the topic at hand differ with one another, at times sharply. I therefore present differing approaches, even while accentuating certain strains more than others and aiming to construct a particular type of theory.

Specifically, this chapter seeks to demonstrate that resources are available to forge a Jewish perspective that is grounded in classical sources but accords to a significant degree with modern sensibilities. Indeed, it is striking that despite negative, often horrific experiences that Jews have endured as a minority interacting with other societies and religions, Jewish law and thought have displayed—through the centuries but especially in modern times—opinions that take a liberal and universalistic approach to the questions articulated above. I do not explore here discomfiting teachings of those Jewish authors who see innate differences between Jews and non-Jews with respect to spiritual capacities and holiness or that denigrate non-Jews and diminish their dignity. While I do not dismiss the influence of the doctrine of chosenness on such views, the teachings can be attributed in considerable measure to the history and circumstances of which I just spoke and sometimes to the natural effects of social separateness on one's perception of the other. The existence of such intensely particularist and binary perspectives and theories must be noted, but they are far from being the tradition's only voice.

The term *other religions* is coarse. We really ought to be asking how Judaism relates to Christianity, how Judaism relates to Islam, how Judaism relates to Buddhism, and so on. These questions, in turn, might be broken down into questions about specific denominations of these religions. Here, however, my focus (though not my exclusive concern) is Christianity, for the simple reason that the almost overwhelming majority of Jewish writings about other religions are directed toward it. Rather than discuss contemporary views straight off, I will grapple with the classical sources in which any Jewish perspective must be rooted. These include ancient texts—Bible, Talmud, Midrash—and writings of medieval and modern thinkers and legal authorities. Our evidence on many questions consists not of broad, systematically stated theories—few can be found until the modern period—but of fragmentary and often ambiguous statements, whose content and motivation we often can fathom only through educated conjecture.[2]

WILL ADHERENTS OF OTHER RELIGIONS ATTAIN SALVATION IN THE HEREAFTER?

A simple quotation would appear to settle this question: "Righteous [or pious] Gentiles have a portion in the world to come."[3] Even if a theologian rejects the possibility of a literal hereafter or finds the framework of reward and punishment grating and immature, understanding this passage sheds substantial light on the status of other religions.

The rabbis in the Talmud declare that Noahides (Gentiles) must observe seven commandments: the prohibitions against illicit sexual relations, murder, theft, blasphemy, *avodah zarah* (often translated as "idolatry" but best rendered literally as "foreign worship," that is, worship of a being other than God), and eating the limb of a living animal, along with the positive duty to establish a court system.[4] The most common way to understand the term *righteous Gentiles* in the statement quoted above is as referring to those who observe the Noahide laws, which are often taken to reflect a form of natural law theory.[5]

The simplest explanation of the Talmudic position that embracing Judaism is not necessary for a Gentile's entering the world to come is that God wants to give all people just rewards. He would not consign most of the world to hell or nihility without giving them opportunities for salvation. In fact, Rabbi Israel Lifshutz (1782–1860), a significant commentator on the major body of teaching known as the Mishnah (200 CE), goes further, asserting in his commentary to the tractates *Avot* 3:14 and *Sanhedrin* 10:1 that even non-Jews who are not *fully* righteous earn a portion. Moreover, according to some modern halakhic authorities, ethical behavior on the part of atheists—a phenomenon unknown to medieval interpreters—is sufficient grounds for admission. The Mishnah teaches that all human beings are precious because all are created in God's image (*Avot* 3:14). Based on this and a substantial number of other Jewish texts that cherish all of Adam's descendants—and not only the progeny of Abraham and Isaac—it stands to reason that God would afford Gentiles such opportunities for reward. Ironically, in one regard, it is easier for a righteous non-Jew to enter the next world than for a Jew: there is a larger list of heresies and sins that deprive Jews of shares in the hereafter.[6] (We must allow, though, for the fact that *mitzvot* [commandments] that bind Jews but not non-Jews would give Jews an advantage, according to most accounts of the reasons for the commandments, and greater opportunities to exhibit devotion, obedience, and sacrifice.)

For most medieval Jews, however, the liberal view of who will enter the hereafter was not applicable to Christians. Nearly all medieval Jewish legal authorities held that Christians violate the Noahide law that prohibits *avodah zarah* (worship of a being other than God), this by virtue of their belief in the divinity of Jesus and what Jews took to be worship of a human being. One might seek to explain this view psychologically by reference to the persecutions of the Crusades. It is therefore striking that a significant rabbinic authority, Menahem ha-Meiri (1249–1316), living in a Christian society, is cogently interpreted as regarding any believer in a cosmic deity who is ethically upright—decidedly including Christians—as entitled to full status, presumably including eternal felicity. In fact, ha-Meiri might have stressed adherence to religion only because he thought that ethics can flow only from religion, in which case, with the modern erosion of that assumption, his teaching might be applicable even to ethically upright atheists.[7] More to the point, by the modern period, many rabbinic authorities, based on a particular reading of a major medieval source, declared that what is *avodah zarah* for Jews is not necessarily *avodah zarah* for non-Jews. In contrast to worship modes of ancient pagans, non-Jews' worship of Jesus as part of a triune God is not, in the opinion of the modern authorities, a violation of Noahide law, even though such worship is forbidden to Jews. Mistaken conceptions of God held by Gentiles do not, in this approach, bar them from the world to come. In fact, Rabbi Jacob Emden, a leading rabbinic figure of the eighteenth century, declared that Christians (and Muslims) "act for the sake of Heaven, for their goal is to promote Godliness among the nations." Hence, "they will not be denied reward for their benevolent intentions" (Miller 2008, 130–131). "Judaism is for Jews, Christianity for non-Jews" aptly summarizes this frequently encountered view (see Greenberg 1978, 363; Miller 2008).[8]

Moses Mendelssohn (1729–1786), the most prominent figure in the Jewish Enlightenment (*Haskalah*), reveled in the egalitarianism implied by the Talmudic passage about non-Jews attaining the world to come. In correspondence with the millenarian cleric Johann Caspar Lavater, who had sought to convert him through rational argument, Mendelssohn emphasized with pride that whereas Christianity believes that salvation can come only through the church, Judaism believes that those who do not embrace Judaism can be saved if they act morally; and he argued that moral truth is accessible to everyone by reason. Correct theology is not necessary for salvation (Mendelssohn 1975).

One obstacle to Mendelssohn's view, however, was a qualification that was placed on the Talmudic statement about righteous Gentiles by the great jurist and philosopher Moses Maimonides (1138–1204). Maimonides wrote that a non-Jew who observes the Noahide laws because his reason induces him to do so will not attain the world to come. Instead, the Gentile must observe them because God conveyed those laws through Moses. In effect, the Gentile must accept the authority of Moses as a universal lawgiver (*Mishneh Torah*, Laws of Kings, 8:11).

Mendelssohn was deeply troubled. Could it be, he asked, that ethical paragons such as Confucius and Solon would be deprived of their share in the hereafter because they might never have heard of Moses? One wonders whether a medieval authority would even know about nontheistic religions, so the consequence is frustrating. Some have reinterpreted the Maimonidean passage (Kook 1985, 99–100; Korn 1994; Kellner 2006, 241–247), and in any event, other texts by Maimonides clearly exude a different spirit. For example, Maimonides declares that "anyone from among the world's inhabitants"—not necessarily a Jew and not necessarily a convert—whose intelligence and spirit move him to consecrate himself to God is regarded as holy, indeed, as the "holy of holies" (*Mishneh Torah*, Laws of Sabbatical and Jubilee Years, 13:13). Certainly, Maimonides' portrait of the founding patriarch, Abraham—as one who knew God through reason before the legislation at Sinai—suggests the possibility of reaching spiritual heights without revelation (and without practicing Judaism as it later crystallized).[9] Although even these other texts do not allay Mendelssohn's worries about Confucius and Solon—after all, Maimonides is speaking of monotheists—they do blunt much of the effect of Maimonides' proviso and suggest on his part an inclusive conception of who has genuine religion. In addition, some rabbinic figures, as we noted, regard moral observance as sufficient, maybe even when accompanied by *avodah zarah*.

So much for Christianity. The overwhelming consensus of Jewish authorities is that Islamic beliefs and practices do not constitute *avodah zarah*. Maimonides and other Jewish philosophers greatly admired Islamic thinkers and absorbed from them many ideas about God. Whether this translates into a portion in the world to come for Muslims is a separate question. (See Shapiro 1993.)

Does Judaism Aim at Converting Gentiles?

In his letter to Lavater, Mendelssohn exclaims: "Convert a Confucius or a Solon? What for? . . . It seems to me that anyone who leads men to virtue in this life cannot be damned in the next" (1975, 268–269). But the real picture of Judaism's attitude toward seeking converts is quite complex—both as regards the extent to which Jews have actively sought to convert Gentiles (there was such activity in ancient times) and as regards attitudes reflected in rabbinic texts. Robert Goldenberg presents an instructive summation: "Overall, the rabbinic corpus [i.e., the corpus dating from the centuries of the Talmud and Midrash] presents a wide variety of attitudes toward the value of proselytism. . . . These diverse opinions cannot be homogenized into a single 'normative' rabbinic view" (1997, 93). Goldenberg's statement can be extended to later periods.

Jewish tradition certainly ascribes great achievements to converts such as the biblical Ruth, ancestress of King David, and Onkelos, traditionally said to have translated the Bible into Aramaic during the Talmudic period. Still, according to Talmudic law, when individuals seek to convert, the court hearing the request (Jewish conversions take place before judges) probes their sincerity in a way that seems calculated to discourage: "Do you not know that the Jews at this time are persecuted and oppressed, despised, harassed, and overcome by afflictions?" If a prospective proselyte answers with a sufficiently vigorous affirmative, the court impresses upon that candidate that acts that are of no consequence for a non-Jew carry heavy punishments when done by a member of the Jewish faith (*Yevamot* 47a). This approach seems aimed at dissuading, or, better put, at accepting only those with the sincerest motives, a very low likelihood of backsliding, and a true willingness to take on the burdens of Jewish law and the existential risks of joining the Jewish people.

Jewish reluctance to proselytize might arise from a variety of considerations. As usefully outlined by David Berger (2008), these include the sheer danger of trying to do so (especially in the Middle Ages); the improbability of succeeding; a desire to retain the uniqueness of Jews as a people; wanting Gentiles to be damned, notwithstanding the texts considered above; and finally, of course, the belief that non-Jews have a path to salvation without joining the Jewish people, rendering conversion to some degree superfluous. One could also argue[10] that having seen humanity twice sin—first Adam and Eve, then the generation of the Flood—and having seen, in the story of the Tower of Babel, the bad consequences of leveling distinctions among people, God took a different route. He chose a particular people, Abraham and his descendants, who would be commanded to teach and inspire others to act ethically and follow the path commanded by God. Choosing this people with universalist goals in mind "is God's way of taking a longer, slower, surer path to the achievement of His universal objective" (Berger 2005b, 84). While this approach might be understood to call upon the Abrahamic people to attract proselytes, it can be argued, first of all, that the conversion would be only to monotheism and adherence to the Noahide laws and, second, that, to the contrary, the approach militates against homogenization and large-scale conversion. For the universal objective can be attained only by keeping the particular character of the people charged with actualizing that objective; and God is satisfied to wait till the end of days to be widely recognized.

What Is Judaism's Eschatological Vision, Specifically Regarding the Fate of Non-Jews and Adherents of Other Religions?

Jewish texts concerning eschatology sometimes stress retribution, sometimes acknowledgment by others of religious truths held by Judaism, and sometimes both: acknowledgment subsequent to punishment, or punishment subsequent to acknowledgment, or destruction following acknowledgment.[11] While views are often developed in a dispassionate way, in some or many cases, psychological motives might drive the views. Vindication is sweet, but so is vengeance.

Certainly, some Jews in the Middle Ages maintained that in messianic times, Gentiles (specifically, those who seek to eradicate Jews) will get their deserts in hell or be destroyed. But the prevalent model aspires to acknowledgment and vindication, along with a salutary change in belief and behavior on the part of others.

Precisely what will Gentiles admit to at the end of days? Will they embrace monotheism and (here projecting later rabbinic categories onto the Bible) the Noahide laws alone, or will they embrace Judaism? The liturgical text known as *Aleinu*, recited thrice daily and featured dramatically in the high holiday service, envisions God eradicating idolatry and the nations of the world one day prostrating themselves before the true God and affirming his sovereignty. The prayer concludes: "The Lord will be king over all the earth. On that day the Lord shall be one, and His name one" (Zechariah 14:9). Since there is no mention of the nations embracing Judaism but only of their accepting God's sovereignty, *Aleinu* suggests a universalistic vision in which multiple peoples remain—but united under the banner of monotheism and with a Jewish theology. This universalistic vision is most naturally taken as a sign of tolerance and of belief in the partial validity of other religions. In reality, though, there might be an interplay of forces here; the willingness to envision non-Jews continuing in their ways might be grounded, as well, in a desire to preserve the singularity of the Jewish people at the end of days (see Berger 2000).

Some biblical texts, such as Isaiah 2:3, Micah 4:2, and Zephaniah 3:9, could be read as saying that at the end of days, non-Jews will collectively accept Judaism. But the verses are logically compatible with the theory outlined earlier: practice of Noahide law combined with an embrace of Jewish theology. Maimonides' formulation—always important—is that at the end of days, "the earth will be filled with knowledge of the Lord" (quoting Isaiah 11:9), and all people "will accept the true religion." But what is "the true religion," monotheism or Judaism? This question has been vigorously disputed (see Kellner 2007, 2008; Rapoport 2008;). Perhaps it does not matter, for any and all abiding differences among the religions lose significance insofar as the whole world has reached the highest goal: knowledge of God. Put another way, conversion to a full Judaism would not be necessary, according to Maimonides, given his views that Judaism aims ultimately at knowledge of God, that anyone with the proper orientation can be among the "holy of holies," and that Abraham knew God even before the legislation at Sinai. The Abrahamic model might be a model for religion at the end of days as well—the end circles back to the beginning. On the other hand, the notion that differences will lose significance, so that in messianic times, it is of no importance for spirituality whether one observes the Jewish Sabbath or keeps laws of kosher consumption, would prima facie make observance of those laws pointless in that period. (There is a view that the commandments will not be in force in messianic times. In that text, however, the reason that observance would be pointless is not the one I mention.[12])

I stress that having a particularist eschatological vision does not entail actively proselytizing before the *eschaton*. Indeed, Jewish sources separate ultimate vision from practical premessianic policy.

DOES JUDAISM BELIEVE THAT OTHER RELIGIONS ARE TRUE?

Analytic philosophy of religion tends to cluster Judaism, Christianity, and Islam under a single rubric: theism. But obviously, terms such as *theistic tradition* and *Judeo-Christian tradition* homogenize distinct belief systems. Many Jews, Christians, and Muslims clearly agree on certain propositions: that God exists, that he is the creator, and that he exercises providence; and Jews and Christians alike accept the divinity of the Hebrew Bible. Equally clearly, theistic religions differ profoundly on many issues: Is Jesus the Messiah? Did Jesus rise from the dead? Is God a Trinity? Have the laws of the Hebrew Bible been abrogated? Who is God's elect? Is Muhammad a true prophet? Are the stories in the Bible (or the Qur'an) true? It is difficult to see how the various answers to these questions that have been proffered by the different religions—or, for that matter, the answers proffered by different denominations within a religion—can all be true (Margalit 1996). Furthermore, if they were all true, it would be a matter of indifference what belief system one adopts, making it difficult to fathom, for example, why, when a Jew is faced with a choice between dying at a coercer's hands and violating the prohibition of *avodah zarah*, Judaism demands martyrdom. In a nonexclusivist view, switching from one religion to another should make little difference.[13]

Important Jewish thinkers, however, insisted that although other religions are false by Judaism's lights with regard to fundamental matters of doctrine, they have value and play a critical, positive role in the dramatic unfolding of history. Using an analogy between Israel and a seed, Judah Halevi (1075–1141) portrayed Christianity and Islam as preparation for the fruit of the historical process—the Messiah's arrival—after which the tree will become one and others will esteem the root they formerly despised (Halevi, *Kuzari*, 4:23; see also 2:36). Likewise, Maimonides, although he had harsh, angry, stinging words about Jesus and Muhammad, asserted: "All those words of Jesus of Nazareth and of this Ishmaelite [Muhammad] who arose after him are only to clear the way for the messianic king and to prepare the whole world to serve the Lord together" (Laws of Kings, 12:4, in uncensored editions). One could even say that in some sense, God—allowing ourselves here a rather un-Maimonidean anthropomorphic expression—*wanted* Christianity and Islam to arise and spread, even if his reasons for doing things that way are hidden.[14]

Not only do Jewish thinkers assign positive value to other monotheistic religions with regard to the shaping of world history, but some also saw Christianity as a healthy moral and religious force and a vital influence on Jewish behavior and faith. Remarkably, even though he was exiled in the Spanish Expulsion, Rabbi Joseph Yaabez stated: "The Christians believe in Creation, the excellence of the Patriarchs, revelation, retribution and resurrection. Blessed is the Lord, God of Israel, who left this remnant after the destruction of the second Temple. But for these Christian nations we might ourselves become infirm in our faith" (cited by Heschel 1975, 346). The illustrious biblical exegete Isaac Abarbanel, another who left Spain, declared in the same spirit of gratitude that God exiled the Jews not among pagan societies but among nations who uphold the Torah, although these nations understand the Torah differently. In this way, the Torah endures (commentary to Deuteronomy 4:25; see also Isaac Arama, *Akedat Yitzhak*, *Va-Ethanan*, 88). The eighteenth-century rabbi Jacob Emden, mentioned earlier, saw great value in Jesus's ethical teachings. And despite their insistence on demarcating the religions, prominent Jewish theologians of recent vintage have integrated ideas from Christian thought (e.g., the centrality of dialectic in religious life).

These appreciative, at times deeply grateful, assertions of value in other religions do not establish pluralism, of course. Few Jewish thinkers embrace the well-known pluralistic view of religions championed by British philosopher John Hick, according to whom all religions are culturally conditioned manifestations of the one divine reality.[15] One who comes close to Hick's position is Rabbi Abraham Isaac Kook (1865–1935).[16]

Kook was a Kabbalist and accordingly believed that all existence emanates from a single divine source. All things are therefore holy, and every idea and movement has at least an element of spiritual worth. All world religions, therefore, are in some way manifestations of the divine. Kook found values to extract even from idolatrous religions, such as those whose adherents passed their children through fires. Those religions are morally and intellectually odious, but they exhibit some worthy characteristics from which other religions could learn—most important, infinite, intensely passionate commitment to the divine. Kook further believes—reminiscent of Hick—that the supernal infinite cannot be captured in our categories. Different religions exemplify different efforts to represent the same transcendent reality. But in terms of metaphysical truth, all are inadequate. The notion we encountered earlier that heathen nations might, within limits, persist in worshipping God in their own way, can readily be understood within a perspective that takes different religions as differing responses to one reality.

It has been argued that pluralism leads to relativism, that is, to the assertion that all religions are true.[17] Kook, however, is not truly pluralist. He believes that other religions contain areas of validity and value, but there is a particular religion that takes a comprehensive, inclusivist approach to religious diversity and thus "gets it right"—namely, Judaism. (He is speaking here about an ideal Judaism inspired by the Kabbalistic vision of unity, not what he regarded as impoverished and narrow Jewish outlooks that arose through the centuries as a result of circumstance.) In addition, although Kook believes that in absolute terms, all formulated religions are off the mark, "religious claims are not a total free-for-all" (Ross 1997, 493). Choices can be made among religions, based on criteria besides, or in addition to, evidence in the normal sense, such as comprehensiveness, psychological impact (Kook valued optimism and growth), moral influence, and effect on human welfare (Ross 1997). These values might be tied to ontological truth. Thus, Kook's view is not through and through pluralistic,[18] and in fact, he critiques specific religions: Christianity for fleeing the physical world, Buddhism for breeding despair (see Rappaport 2005). Judaism will purify and elevate other religions. Hick, too, ends up conceding that some religions "mediate God to mankind better than others" and are "more adequate than others." Thus, for both Hick and Kook, there is a hierarchy of religions (Hick 2002, 530).

Recently, Jewish theologians have put forth pluralistic theologies that posit multiple covenants with humanity and at the least flirt with the idea of plural truths (e.g., Greenberg 2004). This view has been contested, in large part because, notwithstanding its advocates' strong efforts to argue otherwise, critics remain firm that pluralism entails relativism (see Berger 2005a; Kimelman 2007).

DOES JUDAISM BELIEVE THAT INTERFAITH DIALOGUE IS ADVISABLE AND PROPER?

The materials considered so far have been drawn largely from classical (biblical, Talmudic, Midrashic, medieval, and early modern) sources. Our final subject, interfaith dialogue, involves a question that essentially did not arise for Jews until the past half-century.

In the early to mid-1960s—some believe because of the Holocaust—Vatican II articulated a rethinking of certain Catholic teachings, including some about

Judaism and the Jewish people. Over time, Catholics have officially abandoned anti-Semitism and modified their teachings that Jews were guilty of deicide and that they deserved the ill fate they suffered throughout history. Many have abandoned the ideal of mission with respect to the Jews; and the church has legitimized the state of Israel. For many centuries, the typical mode of interfaith communication between Jews and Christians had been public oral "disputation" and written polemics. In medieval times, each side tried to prove it was the true religion, wielding primarily biblical texts and logic to establish correctness. Responding to what many saw as a new environment created by Vatican II, Jewish theologians, along with lay professionals involved in communal relations, debated both the theological propriety of interfaith dialogue and its pragmatic benefits and risks.

Dialogues can assume different forms.

1. One type of dialogue aims at the participants understanding each other's doctrines and practices, without subjecting the latter to critical scrutiny. The motive for achieving this mutual understanding might be political (to achieve social harmony) or purely educational.

2. In a second type of dialogue, each participant is expected to be genuinely open to appropriating theological ideas from adherents of other religions, "even to be transformed through internalization of the values imparted by the other" (Blidstein 2009).

3. In a third type, not only are participants open to accepting the perspectives of the others, but they are also permitted to seek to persuade others. They can ask their interlocutors to give up certain beliefs, practices, and policies and/or accept additional ones. (Such activity might not generally be the stated purpose.)

4. The purpose of the dialogue might be for participants to use the insights of thinkers from another religion to deepen their understanding of their own religion—without entertaining abandonment of the tenets of their religion. For example, a Jewish theologian's appreciation of the theme of suffering, which is found in Judaism, might benefit from hearing what Christians have to say, with no attempt to substitute Christian belief for Jewish. "Each partner can recover main themes from the other, often by recognizing that this has been a minor theme in its own tradition" (Greenberg 2004, 212). On occasion, exposure also creates better appreciation of the contrast between one's own religion and others, thereby sharpening understanding of the former.

5. Although no participant in a dialogue is likely to take this as his or her aim—it might be regarded as a degenerating dialogue—a dialogue could be conducted like a barter, not an intellectual discussion of the merits of certain positions but what has been called "a trading of favors."

6. A quite different mode of dialogue is a joint venture by participants of different persuasions to address social issues such as civil rights, freedom, war and peace, poverty, and technology or to combat the challenge of secularism. "No religion is an island"; religions are no longer independent and self-sufficient (Heschel 1975). According to the eminent Talmudist-philosopher Rabbi Joseph B. Soloveitchik (1903–1993), who opposed dialogues of other types, rabbis and clergy of other

religions should band together to discuss and promote moral causes. Moreover, they "cannot discuss sociocultural and moral problems . . . in agnostic or secularist categories. . . . We define ideas in religious categories." They should operate with such shared ideas as that human beings are created in the image of God (Soloveitchik 2005, 261). Regarding Jews in particular, Soloveitchik states that participation with other religions in social causes had for centuries been precluded by historical factors—Jews were not allowed to be full participants—but today it is to be encouraged and lauded (Soloveitchik 1964, 20).

The arguments for holding dialogues of certain other types catalogued earlier—a course urged by, inter alia, Rabbi Abraham Joshua Heschel (1907–1972), a leading thinker of the Conservative movement (1975), Irving Greenberg (2004), and David Hartman (see Meir 2004)—generally involve a rejection of exclusivism, reference to common ground, and an allaying of Jewish fears by noting that church doctrines have changed. The Conservative and Reform movements in Judaism overwhelmingly embrace dialogue. Soloveitchik, however, a leader of Orthodoxy, argued that a (or the) crucial part of a faith commitment is incommunicable. Theological dialogue is therefore not only ill advised but in certain forms based on an impossible presupposition. To be sure, throughout their history, Jews have knowingly absorbed philosophical ideas from surrounding Muslim and Christian cultures—recall Maimonides' high regard for Muslim philosophers. More to the point, Soloveitchik himself, as already noted, read and drew on Christian theology. In fact, the incommunicability thesis itself is derived from Protestant theology. But for Soloveitchik, there is still a part of faith that cannot be communicated and cannot be assimilated to intellectual categories (Berger 2003).

While Soloveitchik's philosophy reflects very extensive "dialogue" of type 4 above, his did not take place in public forums and discussion groups. Soloveitchik also advances arguments that apply to dialogue of types 3 and 5: to ask another religious community to "shed its uniqueness" is "undemocratic" and contravenes religious freedom. This point holds symmetrically: a Jewish faith community must respect the integrity of other faith communities. Jews ought not to seek to persuade Christians to give up their views and practices, such as belief in the Trinity, their eschatological vision, or the Eucharist, let alone trade favors and barter fundamental beliefs. Missionizing would—by the very logic advanced—be an exception, because the doctrine of mission would violate freedom. Soloveitchik's ethical argument, like the one about incommunicability, would apply to all faith communities.

This approach coheres with the Jewish view cited earlier, namely, that religious diversity is for Judaism an acceptable and perhaps even desirable state of affairs. Ironically, Judaism's liberal live-and-let-live approach to our questions 1 through 3 can thus lead to a weakening of the case for dialogue, yet thinkers of a universalist outlook generally champion dialogue. Be that as it may, in nearly all views, ethical violations of Noahide law call for protest and persuasion. In practice, Orthodox Jews have participated in dialogue, but many or most attempt to adhere to Soloveitchik's guidelines.

CONCLUSIONS

Despite ambiguities in key Jewish sources, often profound disagreements, and the existence of insular and stingingly deprecatory attitudes toward other peoples and religions, we find Jewish texts that allow for multiple paths to salvation; texts that respect, within limits, the integrity of other religions; texts that find value in other religions, whether historical, social, or even ideological; and writings that support interfaith dialogue or alternatively reject certain forms of it, partly out of respect for the integrity of different faith communities. It is an exciting question how these approaches, which are generally in accord with certain twenty-first-century sensibilities, will function in today's—and tomorrow's—globalized world.

NOTES

I thank David Berger, Yitzchak Blau, Allen Friedman, Rachel Friedman, Dov Linzer, and Joel B. Wolowelsky for their comments on an earlier draft and Shnayer Z. Leiman and Marc Shapiro for help with certain references.

1. *Halakhah* means "Jewish law."

2. My focus on classical sources, combined with limitations of space, unfortunately precludes consideration of some important and stimulating thinkers of the past two centuries, such as Hermann Cohen and Franz Rosenzweig. Unfortunately, this chapter went to press before the appearance of Brill 2010, which presents many valuable sources and much valuable discussion. See also Brill 2004.

3. See Maimonides, *Mishneh Torah* (his legal code), Laws of Kings, 8:11, which is based on a passage in *Mishnat Rabbi Eliezer*. See also the view of R. Joshua in Tosefta *Sanhedrin* 13:2 and *Sanhedrin* 105a. The latter two passages cite a contrary view, but Maimonides' ruling is widely accepted. See also Hirsch 1997, 225–227. The term *world to come* is subject to differing interpretations. In the Talmud, it refers to a certain period in history, while Maimonides held that it refers to the continued existence of an individual's soul after the death of the body.

4. *Sanhedrin* 56a–b.

5. This last point is not certain, since Noahide laws are presented in the Talmud as commandments. At the same time, commandment is the major way in which Jews relate to God; the existence of commanded Noahide laws, therefore, as Dov Linzer pointed out to me, could suggest a concern on the part of the Talmudic rabbis to afford Gentiles an opportunity to achieve closeness in this way. In this regard, it is noteworthy that a view in the Talmud asserts that a non-Jew who studies the Torah (here generally taken to refer to study of Noahide laws) is like the high priest (*Avodah Zarah* 3a). This suggests further optional modes for non-Jews to relate to God. The view cited did not prevail, however. There was a period in which non-Jews adopted certain Jewish practices without converting; later, this was forcefully discouraged. See Hirschman 2000; Linzer 2005; Blidstein 1990.

6. On the Noahide laws, see Novak 1983.

7. See Halbertal 2000; Berger 2005b.

8. On the notion of "different religions for different peoples" in ancient times, see Goldenberg 1997; note, e.g., Deuteronomy 4:19, which implies that God has allocated the sun and moon for other nations to worship.

9. See *Mishneh Torah*, Laws of Idolatry, chap. 1. See also the letter to Ovadyah the Proselyte in Twersky 1972, esp. 466–468.

10. As in, for example, Berger 2005b, and as Allen Friedman urged in correspondence.

11. The retribution and acknowledgment models can be combined in a different way: conversion (to Judaism or to monotheism) will be followed by a tumultuous period of war, during which most of the converts will return to their wayward conduct. This is not a mainstream conception.

12. See Babylonian Talmud, *Niddah* 61b.

13. See also Soloveichik 2007.

14. On Halevi and Maimonides, see Lasker 2008. The view of Christianity and Islam as preparation for the Messiah is, whether or not so intended by Halevi and Maimonides, a foil to the Christian view that Judaism was a preparation for Christianity, though with the qualification noted earlier that in some Jewish schools of thought, non-Jews will not convert to Judaism at the end of days.

15. This is different from the thesis that God actively reveals himself differently to different peoples, held by the early medieval thinker Netanel ibn al-Fayumi (see Jospe 2007), since Hick stresses the human role in creating religions.

16. See also Sacks 2003, 196–205; Shapiro 2003.

17. See, however, Jospe 2007.

18. See also Carmy 1994.

REFERENCES

Berger, David. 2000. "On the Image and Destiny of Gentiles in Ashkenaz in Polemical Literature" [in Hebrew]. In Yom Tov Assis et al., eds., *Facing the Cross: The Persecutions of 1096 in History and Historiography*. Jerusalem: Magnes Press, 74–91.

———. 2003. "Revisiting 'Confrontation' Forty Years Later: A Response to Rabbi Eugene Korn." See www.bc.edu/research/cjl/meta-elements/texts/center/conferences/soloveitchik/Berger_23Nov03.htm.

———. 2005a. "Covenants, Messiahs and Religious Boundaries." *Tradition* 39/2 (Summer): 66–78.

———. 2005b. "Jews, Gentiles, and the Modern Egalitarian Ethic: Some Tentative Thoughts." In Marc Stern, ed., *Formulating Responses in an Egalitarian Age*. Lanham, Md.: Rowman and Littlefield, 83–108.

———. 2008. "Reflections on Conversion and Proselytizing in Judaism and Christianity." *Studies in Jewish-Christian Relations* 3: R1–R8

———. 2008. "Reflections on Conversion and Proselytizing in Judaism and Christianity," *Studies in Jewish-Christian Relations* 3: R1–R8, available at http://escholarship.bc.edu/cgi/viewcontent.cgi?article=1140&content=scjr.

Blidstein, Gerald J. 1990. "Maimonides and Mei'iri on the Legitimacy of Non-Judaic Religion." In Leo Landman, ed., *Scholars and Scholarship: The Interaction between Judaism and Other Cultures*. New York: Yeshiva University, 27–35.

———. 2009. "Rabbi Joseph B. Soloveitchik's Letters on Public Affairs." *Torah u-Madda Journal* 15, 1–23.

Brill, Alan. 2004. "Judaism and Other Religions: An Orthodox Perspective." www.bc.edu/research/cjl/meta-elements/texts/cjrelations/resources/articles/Brill.htm.

———. 2010. *Judaism and Other Religions: Models of Understanding.* New York: Palgrave Macmillan.

Carmy, Shalom. 1994. "Dialectic, Doubters, and a Self-Erasing Letter: Rav Kook on the Ethics of Belief." In Lawrence J. Kaplan and David Shatz, eds., *Rabbi Abraham Isaac Kook and Jewish Spirituality.* New York: New York University Press, 205–236.

Goldenberg, Robert. 1997. *The Nations That Know Thee Not: Ancient Jewish Attitudes toward Other Religions.* Sheffield, U.K.: Sheffield Academic.

Greenberg, Blu. 1978. "Rabbi Jacob Emden: The Views of an Enlightened Traditionalist on Christianity." *Judaism* 27: 351–363.

Greenberg, Irving. 2004. *For the Sake of Heaven and Earth: The New Encounter between Judaism and Christianity.* Philadelphia: Jewish Publication Society.

Halbertal, Moshe. 2000. *Between Torah and Wisdom: Rabbi Menahem ha-Meiri and Maimonidean Halakhists in Provence* [in Hebrew]. Jerusalem: Magnes.

Heschel, Abraham Joshua. 1975. "No Religion Is an Island." In Frank Talmage, ed., *Disputation and Dialogue: Readings in the Jewish-Christian Encounter.* New York: Ktav, 343–359.

Hick, John. 2002. "Towards a Philosophy of Religious Pluralism." In David Shatz, ed., *Philosophy and Faith.* New York: McGraw-Hill, 521–530.

Hirsch, Samson Raphael. 1997. "Talmudic Judaism and Society." *Collected Writings of Rabbi Samson Raphael Hirsch.* New York: Feldheim.

Hirschman, Marc. 2000. "Rabbinic Universalism in the Second and Third Centuries." *Harvard Theological Review* 93/2 (April): 101–115.

Jospe, Raphael. 2007. "Pluralism out of the Sources of Judaism: Religious Pluralism without Relativism." *Studies in Jewish-Christian Relations* 2/2: 92–113.

———. 2006. *Maimonides' Confrontation with Mysticism.* Portland, Ore.: Littman Library of Jewish Civilization.

Kellner, Menachem. 2007. "*Farteicht un Farbessert* (On "Correcting" Maimonides)," *Meorot* 6, 2. http:www.yctorah.org/content/view/330/10.

———. 2008. "Maimonides' 'True Religion': For Jews or for All Humanity? A Response to Chaim Rapoport." *Meorot* (September):. http://www.yctorah.org/content/view/436/10/.

———. 2007. Review of Irving Greenberg, *For the Sake of Heaven and Earth. Modern Judaism* 27/1: 103–125.

Kook, Abraham Isaac. 1985. *Letters of Rabbi Abraham Isaac Ha-Kohen Kook* [in Hebrew]. Jerusalem: Mossad Harav Kook.

Korn, Eugene. 1994. "Gentiles, the World to Come, and Judaism: The Odyssey of a Rabbinic Text." *Modern Judaism* 14/3: 265–287.

Lasker, Daniel. 2008. "Tradition and Innovation in Maimonides' Attitude to Other Religions." *Maimonides after 800 Years: Essays on Maimonides and His Influence.* Cambridge, Mass.: Harvard University Press.

Margalit, Avishai. 1996. "The Ring: On Religious Pluralism." In David Heyd. ed., *Toleration: An Elusive Virtue.* Princeton, N.J.: Princeton University Press, 147–157.

Meir, Ephraim. 2004. "David Hartman on the Attitudes of Soloveitchik and Heschel Towards Christianity." In Jonathan Malino, ed., *Judaism and Modernity: The Religious Philosophy of David Hartman*, Aldershot, U.K.: Ashgate, 262–273.

Miller, Moshe. 2008. "R. Jacob Emden's Attitude toward Christianity." In Michael A. Shmidman, ed., *Turim: Studies in Jewish History and Literature Presented to Dr. Bernard Lander.* New York: Touro College Press, 105–136.

Mendelssohn, Moses. 1975. "Letter to Johann Caspar Lavater [1769]." In Frank Talmage, ed., *Disputation and Dialogue: Readings in the Jewish-Christian Encounter*. New York: Ktav, 265–272.

Linzer, Dov. 2005. "On the *Mitzvot* of Non-Jews: An Analysis of *Avodah Zarah* 2b-3a." *Milin Havivin* 1: 25–37.

Novak, David. 1983. *The Image of the Non-Jew in Judaism*. Lewiston, N.Y.: Edwin Mellen.

Rapoport, Chaim. 2008. "'Dat Ha-Emet' in Maimonides's Mishneh Torah." *Meorot* (September). http://www.yctorah.org/content/view/436/10/.

Rappaport, Jason. 2005. "Rav Kook and Nietzsche: A Preliminary Comparison of Their Ideas on Religions, Christianity, Buddhism, and Atheism." *Torah u-Madda Journal* 12: 99–129.

Ross, Tamar. 1997. "The Cognitive Value of Religious Truth Statements: Rabbi A. I. Kook and Post-Modernism." In *Hazon Nahum: Studies in Jewish Law, Thought, and History Presented to Dr. Norman Lamm on the Occasion of his Seventieth Birthday*. New York: Yeshiva University Press, 479–528.

Sacks, Jonathan. 2003. *The Dignity of Difference*. London: Continuum.

Shapiro, Marc B. 1993. "Islam and the Halakhah." *Judaism* 42/3 (Summer): 332–343.

———. 2003. "Of Books and Bans." *Edah Journal* 3/2. http://www.edah.org/backend/JournalArticle/3_2_Shapiro.pdf.

Soloveichik, Meir. 2007. "Of (Religious) Fences and Neighbors." *Commentary* 123/3: 38–43.

Soloveitchik, Joseph B. 1964. "Confrontation." *Tradition* 6/2 (Spring–Summer): 5–29.

———. 2005. "On Interfaith Relationships." In Nathaniel Helfgot, ed., *Community, Covenant and Commitment*. New York: Toras HoRav Foundation, 259–265.

Twersky, Isadore. 1972. *A Maimonides Reader*. New York: Behrman.

FOR FURTHER READING

Boston College Center for Jewish-Christian Learning, www.bc.edu/research/cjl.

Brinner, William M., and Stephen D. Ricks, eds. 1986–1989. *Studies in Islam and Judaic Tradition*. Atlanta: Scholars.

Coppola, David, ed. 2006. *What Do We Want the Other to Teach about Us?* Fairfield, Conn.: Sacred Heart University Press.

Greenberg, Moshe. 1995. "Mankind, Israel and the Nations in the Hebraic Heritage." In *Studies in the Bible and Jewish Thought*. Philadelphia: Jewish Publication Society, 369–393.

Halbertal, Moshe, and Avishai Margalit. 1992. *Idolatry*. Naomi Goldblum, trans. Cambridge, Mass.: Harvard University Press, 1992.

Hartman, David. 1999. *A Heart of Many Rooms: Celebrating the Many Voices Within Judaism*. Woodstock: Jewish Lights.

Jacob, Walter. 1974. *Christianity through Jewish Eyes*. New York: Hebrew Union College Press.

Jospe, Raphael, Truman Madsen, and Seth Ward, eds. 2001. *Covenant and Chosenness in Judaism and Mormonism*. Teaneck, N.J.: Fairleigh Dickinson University Press.

Kaminsky, Alan. 2008. *Yet I Loved Jacob: Reclaiming the Biblical Concept of Election*. Nashville, Tenn.: Abingdon.

Kellner, Menachem. 1991. *Maimonides on Judaism and the Jewish People*. Albany: State University of New York Press.

Kimelman, Reuven. 2004. "Rabbis Joseph B. Soloveitchik and Abraham Joshua Heschel on Jewish-Christian Relations." *Modern Judaism* 24/3: 251–271.

Novak, David. 1989. *Jewish-Christian Dialogue: A Jewish Justification*. New York: Oxford University Press.

———. 1995. *The Election of Israel: The Idea of the Chosen People*. New York: Cambridge University Press.

Poorthuis, Marcel, Joshua Schwartz, and Joseph Turner, eds. 2008. *Interaction between Judaism and Christianity in History, Religion, Art and Literature*. Leiden, Neth.: Brill.

Wyschogrod, Michael. 2007. *Abraham's Promise: Judaism and Jewish-Christian Relations*. Grand Rapids, Mich.: Eerdmans.

CHAPTER 28

A CHRISTIAN PERSPECTIVE

CHARLES TALIAFERRO

TRADITIONAL Christianity makes some radical claims about God and creation. The God of Christianity is not a god of some finite region who has limited power and knowledge but the omnipotent, omniscient, omnipresent creator of all. Moreover, the redeemer in Christianity is not simply an inspired prophet or priest; rather, Jesus Christ is believed to be the unique incarnation of God. Persons are to find salvation by dying to selfish and sinful life and by being united with Jesus Christ, whose birth, life, suffering, death, and resurrection bring about an atonement (or at-onement) with God. In light of these extraordinary claims, is the existence of diverse, alternative religions, as well as the existence of diverse secular cultures, a problem?

SOME BACKGROUND

It might be thought that diversity is not at all surprising given the history of the Judaism from which Christianity emerged. Judaism often understood God's action to be manifest in ways that were at odds with worldly prestige and expectations. The tradition was thus fully aware of its being one tradition among a diversity of other traditions and cultures, some of which were of far greater prestige and power. The teaching that God works through means other than proud, worldly powers can be seen in the Hebrew Bible on various levels, including the biblical treatment of younger brothers and barren women. In both categories, the cultural assumption was that the elder brother was privileged in honor and heritance, and a woman with many children had God's blessing. But in the Hebrew Bible, it is the younger brother, Abel, whom God favors rather than Cain; Jacob is visited with a divine revelation rather than his older brother Esau; Joseph (the ultimate younger brother, who was betrayed by his older brothers) is blessed rather than his older brothers; and the two greatest kings of Israel were younger brothers: David and Solomon. Women who were for a time without child and thus deemed unblessed, such as Sarah, Rebecca, and Hannah all became the bearers of special divine blessing. Similarly, the people of Israel were not on the same world-historical stage in terms of prestige with the empires of Egypt, Assyria, and Babylon. The ancient image of God being revealed through a burning bush (Exodus 3:2–4) is fitting for its simplicity and the ostensible insignificance of a desert plant (perhaps a thorn bush), for it might symbolize the way God selected an insignificant people (from the standpoint of the great imperial powers) to be the recipient of God's revelation. This is not to say that Judaism did not come to see itself in increasingly important terms. According to Genesis and Exodus, Joseph achieved great fame and power in Egypt, and Moses led the people of Israel from captivity to settlement in the Promised Land, delivering a crushing blow to the Egyptian people. In 2 Kings, Israel stands up to a siege by the powerful Assyrians; in Jonah, a prophet goes to the capital of the Assyrian Empire and brings about a major religious penance instituted by its king; in the Book of Daniel, Daniel has direct exchanges with the king of Babylon, and the king of Persia, Cyrus (c. 600–530 BCE), takes a personal interest in the restoration of the Temple. I will not comment specifically on the historical credibility of these narratives, but my point is that while the Hebrew people did see themselves as interacting with imperial powers, they did not see themselves as one of the great, diverse, elite worldly powers; God had chosen a humble, virtually unknown people to manifest great divine glory.

The Christian tradition shared some of this insistence on humility among diverse, elite powers (elite from a worldly point of view): Jesus was born of a poor girl who was at risk of being considered an outcast (pregnant outside of marriage). Jesus's family might have had links to royal lineage, but his life was not made up of a royal court, a palace, and so on. The apostles are traditionally seen as "low-born": a tax collector, fishermen, and so on. Some of Jesus's most important dialogues are with the nonelite. As highly educated persons turned to the Christian faith, it was sometimes observed (as it was by Augustine) that the Christian New Testament did not have the aristocratic tone or courtly grace of classic pagan works such as Virgil's *Aeneid*.

Like some Jewish thinkers in antiquity, early Christians were not always content with this lack of worldly prestige. There is at least one incident of (probable) forgery in the first century, when someone produced a correspondence between Saint Paul and the prominent statesman-philosopher Lucius Seneca. And under Constantine and imperial sponsorship, Christianity evolved into a dominant force. But overall, early Christians (especially before the conversion of Emperor Constantine) were at home with insisting on God's nonaristocratic, nonprestigious ways among diverse, powerful forces. This is especially apparent in the debate between Origen of Alexandria (c. 185–254) and Celsus, a Roman Platonic philosopher who wrote around 177. Celsus was not attracted to a God who might be so profligate that God welcomed the uneducated and the undisciplined into a life of grace. Origin's defense of Christianity highlights God's working in humble terms that escape the notice of powerful representatives of imperial Roman culture.

I note by way of background that the existence of diverse cultures, civilizations of power, and the worship of other gods was not surprising or unrecognized by early Christians and Jews. Over the centuries, however, two matters emerged requiring substantial reflection. First, traditional Christianity involves an affirmation of a universal creator and redeemer. This belief has historically motivated great missionary work to convert people to the recognition and love of God and Christ the savior. But as Christians came to learn of other great cultures—in the Americas and Africa but especially in China—it became essential to consider whether God had been working through these other cultures and "scriptures" to offer illumination and union with God. Could it be that revelation and salvation were exclusively Judeo-Christian and that without missionary outreach and conversion, great numbers of people might never be saved? This question would have made sense from the very beginning of Christianity, but it came to have more significance the more Christians took seriously global world history.

A second challenge concerned matters of rationality. Arguably, people born in a different culture might appear to be just as reasonable in their belief and practice of a non-Christian religion as Christians are in accepting their religion. Can one recognize the equal reasonability of different religions from different vantage points?

Let us consider each of these areas, first filling out the challenge to traditional Christianity and then weighing the resources of Christianity in addressing religious diversity.

UNIVERSAL CREATION AND REDEMPTION

The bare existence of different accounts of reality and different religious views on how to address world problems does not itself seem to threaten the conviction that there is one creator of all and that salvation and atonement are through the particular work of God through Jesus Christ. There are abundant accounts of Jesus's saving work, some involving vicarious suffering, the paying of a debt for sin, the overcoming of sin and death through Jesus's life and resurrection, and so on. I favor the Christus Victor account of redemption, according to which the saving work of Jesus is carried out by Jesus's teaching and love, his taking on the full weight of the effects of sin (suffering injustice) and overcoming sin and death by his resurrection. The importance of the belief in the resurrection can be appreciated when one considers the respects in which none of us is able to make up fully for the evil we have done. If you harm or (to use an extreme example) kill someone, only a power that could raise the dead could begin to set up the conditions of full reconciliation. The resurrection of Christ is a sign of the irrepressible loving power of God as this bears on the incarnate Lord Christ, but it is also a sign that the restorative power of God is made available to all people. So far, no problem, in my view. Difficulties might emerge, however, when we ask about whether the benefits of Jesus's life, passion, death, and resurrection can only be gained by believers in Christ, those who trust in God's saving work. The worry is whether Christianity is committed to some kind of (to use a popular term) exclusivism or even elitism.

Terms such as *exclusivism* or *elitism* suggest a patronizing, clublike approach to faith and are completely at odds with Christian teachings about grace, love, generosity, the bounty of God, and so on. I suggest, instead, that we refer to the *particularity* of Christian claims. Is there something amiss (religiously, ethically, or philosophically) with the claim that God works in specific, particular ways, such as in the life, death, and resurrection of Jesus Christ?

There might be some merit in holding that the path of salvation and union with God should occur on an abstract, nonlocal level (perhaps by way of contemplating some moral and spiritual teaching accessible to any sensitive, inquiring mind), but in the traditional Christian framework, one has testimony that God's love of the creation is so great that he sought union with creation in human life. We might call the values involved incarnate goods, goods that are embodied, particular, and concrete as opposed to disembodied, general, and abstract. In many areas of life, the idea of incarnate goods seems evident: what is better, someone who proposes abstractly that loving kindness is good or someone who concretely and in bodily, particular ways lives out loving kindness? In traditional Christianity, the belief in the incarnation has been part and parcel of the belief in the hallowed, blessed goodness of human flesh and the natural world. God's incarnation as human is a sign of the goodness of creation and a blessing of that creation insofar as God then makes the human-divine life of Christ a means of redemption and atonement. The union of God and flesh was taken by early Christians as a key means by which creation is to be restored. In *De Resurrectione Carnis*, Tertullian claims:

> To such a degree is the flesh the pivot of salvation, that since by it the soul
> becomes linked with God, it is the flesh which makes possible the soul's election
> by God. For example, the flesh is washed that the soul may be made spotless: the
> flesh is anointed that the soul may be consecrated: the flesh is singed that the soul
> too may be protected: the flesh is overshadowed by the imposition of the hand
> that the soul may be illuminated by the Spirit: the flesh feeds on the body and
> blood of Christ so that the soul also may be replete with God. (8)

In these respects, traditional Christianity is radically opposed to forms of Manichaeism and Gnosticism that treat bodily life in derogatory, debased terms. Tertullian insisted that the affirmation and restoration of the body in Christian salvation ruled out denigrating the body. Against one Gnostic, Marcion, Tertullian wrote: "This sacred course of nature, you, O Marcion, spit upon; and yet, in what way were you born? You detest a human being at his birth; then after what fashion do you love anybody? . . . Well then, loving man, Christ loved his nativity also, and his flesh as well" (*De Carne Christi*, v). Tertulliian argued that it would be absurd for Christ to become incarnate if the goal was a disembodied salvation only involving the soul: "And since they assume it as a main tenet, that Christ came forth not to deliver the flesh, but only our soul, how absurd it is, in the first place, that he made it into just that sort of bodily substance which he had no intention of saving" (x).

Because salvation involves a restoration and healing of embodiment, the incarnation had to involve a hallowing of a particular, bodily kind. It is difficult to see how one could have incarnate goods without particularity. Perhaps one might envisage multiple incarnations in all regions of the world throughout history, but this would seem to have its own difficulties in terms of coherence, potential rivalry, and the loss of unity that is made possible if there is a unique incarnation that all persons are called to respond to (Hebblethwaite 2001).

As for the problem of assessing the plight of those who never hear of Christ or for whom the message of the incarnation and redemption is so contorted that persons are confronted more with a monstrosity than with incarnate love, Christians have various options. Some argue that there is a chance after death when all shall be made aware of the means of salvation offered through Christ, and so all will have the opportunity of salvation. Others have argued that even in this life, the choice for or against salvation can be made in terms other than with explicit reference to Christ. Imagine someone who does not know Christ but endeavors to practice a life of self-sacrificing love. Perhaps such a life can be deemed as amounting to a choice for what is ultimately Christlike.

Recently, there has been an objection to the idea that God would leave others in the dark about God's reality and ways of redemption. John Schellenberg presents two thought experiments designed to show that the God of Christianity would be more evident than God seems to be. This is called the Hiddenness of God objection. If Schellenberg is correct, God would not permit there to be diverse religions or secular cultures in which God is not manifested as one's loving creator and redeemer:

> Imagine yourself in the following situation. You're a child playing hide-and-seek with your mother in the woods back of your house. You've been crouching for some time now behind a large oak tree, quite a fine hiding place but not undiscoverable—certainly not for someone as clever as your mother. However, she does not appear. The sun is setting and it will soon be bedtime, but still no mother. Not only isn't she finding you, but, more disconcerting, you can't *hear* her anywhere: she's not beating the nearby bushes, making those exaggerated "looking for you" noises and talking to you meanwhile as mothers playing this game usually do.
>
> Now imagine that you start *calling* for your mother. Coming out from behind the tree, you yell out her name, over and over again. But no answer. Oh, there *is* a moment when suddenly you hear sounds you are sure must signal your mother looking for you, but they turn out to come from nothing more than leaves rolling in the wind. So you go back to calling and looking everywhere: through the woods, in the house, down to the road. Several hours pass and you

are growing hoarse from calling. Is she anywhere around? Would your mother—
loving and responsible parent that she is—fail to answer if she were around?
(2007, 228)

Schellenberg thinks that just as the mother would not leave her child bewildered
and bereft of knowledge and aid, the God of Christianity would not leave persons
without saving knowledge and aid. The existence of diverse, non-Christian cultures
bereft of God is therefore evidence against God's existence. Just to give Schellenberg
even more space to develop his position, consider this more extensive thought
experiment:

> Suppose that your daughter, whom you dearly love, is in the grip of an
> erroneous picture as to what sort of person you are and what you intend in
> relation to her. No matter what you do in seeking to facilitate real contact with
> the truth and choice in favor of a full and meaningful relationship with you, the
> response is only fresh resistance. And you correctly conclude that very likely
> nothing else of the same sort will work in the future. Now suppose that some
> way of instantaneously transforming her perspective is made available to you: if
> you press this button she will see you for who you really are and all the snagged
> and tangled and distorted beliefs will rearrange themselves into a clear
> perception of the truth. Surely you will use this means of cutting through that
> mess, for it represents only an abbreviated version of what you have already
> been seeking. But suppose also that in facilitating a correct picture of who you
> are and what you intend in this way, you will render it inevitable that your
> daughter make at least an initial choice in favor of meaningful relationship with
> you—that is, her choice to do so will not be free in the sense we have been
> emphasizing. (She will say, "Oh, what a fool I've been," and immediately be
> prompted to seek to make up for lost time.) Surely you will still do it, for you see
> that a free choice, yea or nay, in favor of meaningful relationship with you of the
> sort that would have *real* value and that you ought never to take lightly *isn't
> threatened thereby*: given the deficient information available to your daughter
> about who you are, even if you leave her alone she will not have been able to
> make such a choice. And you will also see that what you and your daughter
> would have to give up in order to keep in place the possibility of such limited
> free choices as *are* possible is far more valuable than they are. (Wouldn't any
> parent make the correct view available, even if the choice facing the child is then
> so obvious and attractive as not to be free, rather than have the child persist
> forever in her misunderstanding-based free choice? And what would be chosen
> by a perfectly loving God, the one who according to spiritual geniuses like Jesus
> of Nazareth never ceases to seek the lost sheep and to reveal to it a shepherd?)
> (224–225)

How might a traditional Christian reply? Consider two ways. The first is simply
to note the strong thesis that Schellenberg is advocating and to question the values
involved. He seems committed to the view that there can be no time at all when an
honest searcher for God is not given sufficient evidence that God exists and loves
him or her. It seems as though Schellenberg is picturing the God of Christianity as
a being who should make "looking for you" noises and be as evident as a human

mother's voice whenever one is in perplexity. Doesn't this overshadow the idea that there can be many goods that are and can be achieved by persons who do not have an explicit awareness of God? Working with the second parable, imagine that your child wrongly thinks of you as an alcoholic, kidnapping arms dealer, when you are nothing of the sort. But imagine that, partly in rebellion against you, she lives a life that involves alcohol awareness and works with addicts, and she also works tirelessly to release hostages and reduce or eliminate the evils in the arms trade. Imagine further that you are an overwhelming, charismatic person and that if you were to push the button or somehow be revealed to her, she would not have the strength or resources to engage in her good action. Would you push the button then? I suspect you would not, especially if we bring the parable in line with what is advocated by most Christians: that there will come a time when God as creator will be revealed to all.

A second point is that the parable of the button seems to involve a violation or manipulation of the child. What Schellenberg is picturing is a direct bypassing of the daughter's own thinking, feeling, and decision making. The idea that one should subvert her character by pressing a magic button might be tempting but is hardly something obvious that a good parent would do. Especially (again) in light of the Christian teaching that eventually all will come to know the truth about the "heavenly father" or parent.

RESPECTFUL RELIGIOUS DISAGREEMENTS?

Let us now take up the second worry: Does the existence of diverse non-Christian traditions and cultures with reasonable people challenge the reasonability of Christianity? I have argued elsewhere that there are good reasons for adopting Christian theism (e.g., Taliaferro 1994) rather than being agnostic or adopting naturalism or other non-Christian options. For present purposes, however, I will assume that the evidence for Christianity is good and seems to justify Christian belief; someone equally intelligent might rightly claim that he or she has good evidence for a non-Christian religion or secular naturalism.

Under these circumstances, consider an argument from John Schellenberg: Imagine a Christian who embraces her faith based on what she thinks is an authentic encounter with the living Christ. She feels, for example, Christ's love for her and creation. Now, imagine a Buddhist who has a no-self experience through mediation. Imagine that this gives him some reason to embrace a Buddhist belief that is incompatible with Christianity, namely, that there are substantial selves.

We might be tempted to think that each person is entitled to his or her own conclusion. Each might be said to have a kind of private, experiential disclosure. But Schellenberg thinks not, and he introduces the following thought experiment to secure his point:

Though privacy considerations are often taken to *strengthen* the claim of religious experience (when I experience something for myself in a way that is not accessible to you, I appear to have more *direct* access to it, and direct access certainly seems less liable to error), in fact they lead to the *downfall* of justifications grounded in religious experience, given religious diversity. For who *knows* what I would think if I could have *your* experience? A Christian might be inclined to say to members of other traditions: "You would understand my reticence to give up my belief if you could only see what I see." But a better thought here is this: "What if the Christian (or the Hindu or the Buddhist . . .) could see from the inside what *all* religious experients have seen, perhaps in sequence, with a clear memory afterward of what she had seen—would her belief be affected *then*?" Presumably the answer is "perhaps yes, perhaps no." But that is just the point. Who *knows* what would result if one could see from the inside what everyone else has seen? Perhaps one would conclude that one's own experience was the most illuminating and likely to be reliable, then again perhaps one would notice that the clouds were thicker on one's own side. Who could say? Certainly one's own experience can provide no grounds for going one way or the other on *this* matter. (That I have a powerful experience apparently of Christ may entail, at least for that moment, that I form a religious belief about Christ, and this belief may entail the falsity or incompatible beliefs from other traditions; but neither of these things entails that, *should I experience the world as does a Hindu or a Buddhist, I would not conclude that their experience was more illuminating and convincing than mine*.) But then it could well be that one would judge someone else's experience at least as epistemically impressive as one's own were one's evidential situation suitably enlarged, as in the imagined situation. (That it *cannot* be thus enlarged—at least as things stand at present—is irrelevant here . . . evidence unavailable to us may still have a bearing on the worthiness of belief.) Indeed, it could well be that one would think *all of a number of different experiences* to be equally convincing and apparently illuminating. (182–183)

There are several replies. First, one might question how different religious experiences and traditions actually are. Buddhism and Christianity share significant ground (both teach that egotism is a vice; both promote compassion), but for present purposes, I will assume that we share genuine cases of different experiences that give rise to conflicting beliefs. The second approach is to consider the framework in which the experiences occur. This strategy has been effectively explored by Keith Yandell. He takes seriously that Buddhist meditation can be an authentic state in which one does not have an explicit awareness of oneself. But he goes on to argue that this is because Buddhists, like David Hume, are looking for the self in the wrong place. The self is not akin to some patch of color in one's visual field. We do, however, experience the self all the time, and we can be reflexively aware of this when we realize that when you feel pain, you are feeling a state of your*self* (*you* feel pained); when you see something, you are experiencing *yourself* seeing; and so on (see Yandell 1993 and 2009; Chisholm 1979). Yandell argues further for the incoherence of the Buddhist/ Humean view of the self. Without going into details, I submit that this kind of reasoning can break the epistemic deadlock and provide a Christian with evidential backing without denying the authenticity and honesty of his or her Buddhist friend.

Consider another argument that diversity should undermine Christian convictions. Richard Feldman claims that in the case of conflicting, seemingly equally reasonable beliefs about some phenomenon, the best decision is to suspend judgment concerning it without thinking one's own or the other's belief unreasonable:

> Suppose you and I are standing by the window looking out on the quad. We think we have comparable vision and we know each other to be honest. I seem to see what looks to me like the dean standing out in the middle of the quad. (Assume that this is not something odd. He's out there a fair amount.) I believe that the dean is standing on the quad. Meanwhile, you seem to see nothing of the kind there. You think that no one, and thus not the dean, is standing in the middle of the quad. We disagree. Prior to our saying anything, each of us believes reasonably. Then I say something about the dean's being on the quad, and we find out about our situation. In my view, once that happens, each of us should suspend judgment. We each know that something weird is going on, but we have no idea which of us has the problem. Either I am "seeing things," or you are missing something. I would not be reasonable in thinking that the problem is mine. (2007, 207–208)

Feldman believes that cases such as the above support the following principle:

> After examining this evidence, I find in myself an inclination, perhaps a strong inclination, to think that this evidence supports P. It may even be that I can't help but believe P. But I see that another person, every bit as sensible and serious as I, has an opposing reaction. Perhaps this person has some bit of evidence that cannot be shared, or perhaps he takes the evidence differently than I do. It's difficult to know everything about his mental life and thus difficult to tell exactly why he believes as he does. One of us must be making some kind of mistake or failing to see some truth. But I have no basis for thinking that the one making the mistake is him rather than me. And the same is true of him. And in that case, the right thing for both of us to do is to suspend judgment on P. (212)

There are several problems with Feldman's position. First, it is self-refuting. There are persons (e.g., Roderick Chisholm) who are as sensible and serious as Feldman who think (and have a strong inclination to believe) that Feldman's principle is false. Under these conditions, it seems that if Feldman adheres to his principle, he should reject the principle itself. Second, the example of whether one sees a dean in a quad is light-years away from the context of religious belief and practice. There is not space to explore this in detail here, but locating an academic on a campus is profoundly different from someone believing they have had a living encounter with Christ and comparing notes with a friend who has not had such an experience. Perhaps related to this is a third point: there is a slight edge to be given to experiences that appear to justify a positive claim as opposed to the failure to experience some presence, be it God, the self, or a dean. Adopting Feldman's example, if you seem to see the dean waving at you (her wild hair and academic robes seem just as you would expect if she were in the quad), why would my failing to see this give you reason to suspend judgment? You might have reason to call out to the dean to get some confirmation (however elusive) of her presence, but suspending judgment does not seem at all a requirement. Suspension seems especially inappropriate if you do have some evidence for your belief and yet you realize that "perhaps [a person not sharing your belief] has some bit of evidence that cannot be shared." If the mere *possibility* of counterevidence undermines belief, would any belief be reasonable?

Diversity should, however, give one reason to reflect on the goods that might be in play in other religions, and it is also a reason to explore whether or not one's own faith is indeed the true faith or the one that is most reasonable. I will develop this point by distinguishing four types of faith: *tmimut* faith, absolute faith, academic faith, and Platonic faith.

Jerome Gellman is a representative advocate of the first. Gellman gives a certain epistemic advantage to someone who has *tmimut* (a Hebrew word concerned with personal relationships, including concepts of being loyal, faithful, simple, innocent, etc.) in a situation of conflicting beliefs about something or someone:

> Consider this analogy: the police present a mother with evidence that her son has committed a serious crime. She is certain he did not do it. She displays *tmimut* with regard to her son's innocence. Granted, this can be an irrational attitude for her to take with regard to her son's guilt. However, there will be cases where she will be perfectly rational in her belief that her son did not commit the crime, in spite of the contrary evidence. These will be cases where she is rationally convinced that her loving relationship with her son gives an advantage over others in knowing deeply what he is like, and knowing, therefore, that it is extremely unlikely that he could ever find the power within him to do such a heinous act. Her sensitivity to his soul gives her a privileged understanding of what her son could and could not do. For this reason, she alone may possess a plausible way of interpreting the evidence so that it no longer points to his guilt. This, of course, will not always be the case, but it can be the case sometimes. In such cases, the mother's *tmimut* can grant her an epistemic advantage over others. My point is that *tmimut* can be an epistemic virtue in that it affords an insight into the truth of the matter lacking to those devoid of *tmimut*. (2008, 377)

This form of faith can certainly be defended in some cases. It might be that some relationships allow for evidence not available to external observers. My only qualification would be that in the thought experiment, one would hope that *tmimut* faith would not preclude the mother attending to and weighing the disinterested information.

Absolute faith is not subject at all to counterevidence. Presumably, someone embracing *tmimut* faith would gradually give way, given insurmountable evidence.

Academic faith might stand for the kind of belief in Feldman's parable about two scholars speculating about the location of a dean. The beliefs at issue seem not to be related to matters of deep passion or value.

My own preferred option is Platonic faith. Christian Platonists such as Augustine and the Cambridge Platonists did not embrace academic or absolute faith. While they did not rule out *tmimut* faith, they believed that faith in God did involve values and that the pursuit and maintenance of faith involved wisdom, patience, self-questioning, and so on. In the face of diversity of beliefs, the Cambridge Platonists in the seventeenth century followed the practice suggested above. They sought to consider carefully the non-Christian, diverse alternatives and yet concluded that these did not undermine but indirectly strengthened their Christian faith, insofar as other traditions often shared with Christianity some profound truths.

OTHER CHRISTIAN ALTERNATIVES TO DIVERSITY

In closing, it should be noted that I have been working with the traditional Christian outlook, which I share, about the uniqueness of the incarnation and the reality of God as creator. Some self-identified Christians have proposed alternative positions worthy of exploration. At the extreme, one can deny that Christianity is committed to truth claims about a God who creates and redeems us. Some philosophers adopt a form of nonrealism according to which Christianity is more a matter of moral, compassionate living than beliefs about reality. Less extreme is that a Christian might be a realist about God and yet hold that Christ is a saving figure for Christians but not necessarily for others. For a Hindu or a Buddhist, there are other figures who are saving or enlightening or liberating. Some self-identified Christians might even deny the classic, canonical teaching about the incarnation and instead claim that what it means to think of Christ as incarnate is for us to find Christ as an inspiring, profound force in our lives or as a model for spiritual growth and maturity. The most well-known religious pluralist working today, John Hick, proposes that Christians see classical Christian teaching as a "true myth," something not true literally but expressive of important truths. What is sometimes underappreciated is that a more traditional Christian can accept some of the positive content of these alternatives. So while a traditional Christian will have to not accept nonrealism insofar as it claims that there is no God (as the nonrealist Christian atheist Gordan Kaufman does), he or she can claim that Christianity is about moral, compassionate living and not simply abstract belief.

REFERENCES AND FOR FURTHER READING

Chisholm, Roderick. 1979. *Person and Object: A Metaphysical Study*. Chicago: Open Court.

Feldman, Richard. 2007. "Reasonable Religious Disagreements." In Louise M. Antony, ed., *Philosophers without Gods*. New York: Oxford University Press, 194–215.

Gellman, Jerome. 2008. "In Defense of a Contented Religious Exclusivism." In Andrew Eshleman, ed., *Readings in Philosophy of Religion*. Malden, Mass.: Blackwell 374–382.

Hebblethwaite, B. 2001. "The Impossibility of Multiple Incarnations." *Theology* 104: 323–34.

Schellenberg, J. 2007. *The Wisdom to Doubt: A Justification of Religious Skepticism.* New York: Cornell University Press.

Taliaferro, Charles. 1994. *Consciousness and the Mind of God.* Cambridge, U.K.: Cambridge University Press.

Yandell, Keith. 1993. *The Epistemology of Religious Experience.* Cambridge, U.K.: Cambridge University Press.

———. 2009. *Philosophy of Religion: A Contemporary Introduction.* London: Routledge.

CHAPTER 29

AN ISLAMIC PERSPECTIVE

MAJID FAKHRY

I. INTRODUCTION

ISLAM, the third of the three Semitic, monotheistic religions, appeared on the world scene in the seventh century. The official date marking that event corresponds to Prophet Muhammad's migration to the northern city of Yathrib (Medina) in Arabia from his birthplace of Mecca in 622 CE, known as the Hijra.

Both in the Qur'an and in the Traditions of the Prophet, known as Hadith, it is proclaimed that the Prophet is not out to preach a new religion but rather to "confirm" the true Hanif or pure religion of Abraham, Moses, Jesus, and the other prophets without discrimination (Qur'an 2:135). Although religion was corrupted over the years, Islam is further described as the true "guidance" addressed to the whole of mankind, whereby God "brings them out of the darkness into the light by His leave and guides them into a straight path" (5:12–16).

As for other religions, only the Sabeans, followers of an unknown Middle Eastern religion, are mentioned as worthy of receiving "their reward from God and having nothing to fear" (2:62, 5:69). To this unknown religious group can be added the Magians (Majus), corresponding probably to the Zoroastrian and mentioned only once in the Qur'an, in an all-inclusive verse that refers to "the believers [i.e., Muslims], the Jews, the Sabeans, the Christians, the Magians [Majus] and the polytheists," who will all be judged by God on the Day of the Resurrection.

II. CHRISTIANITY, ISLAM, AND JUDAISM

Historically speaking, the relations between Islam and Christianity, whether during the period of Conquest in the seventh century or the late-medieval period, tended to vacillate between open warfare and active cultural contact. Thus, following the conquest of Byzantium, which put an end to Byzantine rule of the Near East, the Muslim world—especially during the Abbasid period (750–1258)—entered an age of cultural assimilation of Greek and Hellenistic culture, without parallel in medieval history, as we will see in greater detail below. It was during that period that the great monuments of Greek culture in science, medicine, and philosophy were rendered into Arabic by a host of brilliant Syriac and Arab translators, expounded or commented on by the great philosopher-physicians of the tenth, eleventh, and twelfth centuries, such as al-Razi (d. c. 925), Avicenna (d. 1037), and Averroes (d. 1198).

By the middle of the twelfth century, the process was reversed, and the great philosophical, scientific, and medical monuments of Islamic learning were now rendered into Latin, with the decisive consequence that the ancient Greek legacy was recovered by western Europe after centuries of almost total oblivion. This recovery led in due course to the great philosophical and theological upsurge known as Latin Scholasticism and subsequently the Italian Renaissance of the fifteenth century.

Regarding the relations of Muslims and Christians from the seventh century on, it is not sufficiently appreciated—especially by ill-informed or biased publicists—that these relations were characterized by far greater tolerance than western Europe had known during the Middle Ages.

Contrasting the attitudes of Christians in medieval times toward Muslims and Jews, Bernard Lewis has argued that whereas Christianity accorded some measure of tolerance to the Jews in the Middle Ages, such tolerance was not extended to Muslims. "For the Muslims on the other hand," he writes, "Christianity, like Judaism, was a predecessor religion and deserving the same degree of tolerance." But in general, "Muslim theologians were willing to concede the tolerance to the earlier religions enjoined by the Qur'anic law," despite their objections to the Christian doctrines of the Trinity and the divinity of Christ (Lewis 1993, 6). The Qur'an actually distinguishes clearly among the three aforementioned groups—assigning the first group, according to the Islamic tradition, to the "Abode of Peace," the second to the "Abode of War," and the third to an intermediate region, to which the People of the Book, namely, the Christians and the Jews, are consigned. The term *infidels*, or, rather, its Arabic equivalent, *kafirun*, originally meant unbelievers and is applied in the Qur'an primarily to the polytheists, except in those qualified instances where it may be construed to mean "renegades" or "apostates."

It is those infidels who are the subject of the Qur'an's harshest denunciations, which exclude decidedly Jews and Christians, as we will see shortly. Thus, Qur'an 47:4 reads: "So, when you meet the unbelievers, strike their necks till you have bloodied them," whereas Qur'an 2:190 calls upon the believers, that is, the Muslims, to "fight in the Cause of God those who fight you," without any specific reference to their religious or legal status. However, in both cases, the order to fight the unbelievers, or plain antagonists, is qualified in a variety of ways. In the first case, the verse goes on to stipulate that once "the shackles [of the infidels] are removed," the

Muslims are ordered to "release them freely or for a ransom, till the war is over." In the second case, the order to fight in the cause of God is qualified by the proviso: "But do not be aggressive. Surely God does not like the aggressors." More significantly, the order in the second instance is historically circumscribed. For the verse goes on to state: "Kill them wherever you find them and drive them wherever they drove you out," which the traditional commentators interpreted to refer to Mecca, where the fighting had taken place, as the sequel clearly implies. The verse adds: "Do not fight at the sacred mosque [of the Ka'ba in Mecca], until they fight you at it" (2:191).

In these circumstances, even the order to fight the infidels embodied in 47:7 can be interpreted today as equally historically circumscribed and applying exclusively to the Muslim period of Conquest, when Islam was pitted against its enemies throughout the Near East and Persia.

It should be noted in this context that Islam, which divided the world into the Abode of Peace and the Abode of War, recognized a third region, the Abode of the People of the Book, or those religious groups, including Jews, Christians, and Sabeans, who had received a "divine" revelation, as Qur'an 2:62 and 5:69 stipulate. To these groups, the "Magians" or "Zoroastrians" were later added. Generally speaking, the Qur'an had condemned recourse to aggression in a number of verses, such as 2:190, quoted above. The most general stipulation in dealing with the three above-mentioned non-Muslim groups is contained in verse 5:69: "Surely the believers [i.e., Muslims], the Jews, the Sabeans and the Christians, whoever believes in God and the Last Day and performs good deeds shall have no cause to fear and they shall not grieve." Equally general is this statement in 3:199: "Truly, of the People of the Book, there are some who indeed believe in God and what had been revealed to you, or has been revealed to them, humbling themselves before God and not selling God's revelation for a small price. Those will have their reward with their Lord; indeed God's reckoning is swift." Although this verse appears to be selective in scope, since it seems to limit God's reward and his reckoning to some of them, it is nonetheless obvious that the criteria of religious piety and the preconditions of salvation are belief in God and his revelations to mankind, to which belief in the Last Day and the performance of good deeds are added here and elsewhere. In some verses, such as 5:82, a sharp distinction is made between Jews and Christians, the Jews and pagans being declared to be the Muslims' worst enemies, whereas the Christians are declared to be "the closest in friendship to the believers [or Muslims]. For they say: 'We are Christians' and among them are priests and monks and they are not arrogant."

In practice, Muhammad's relations with the Jews passed through two distinct stages. Following the migration of Muslims to the city of Yathrib—later designated the Madinah (Medina) or City of the Prophet, which had a large Jewish population—the Muslims signed in 624 the Madinah Treaty, which stipulated, among other things, that "the Jews of Banu' Awf shall form one community with the believers [or Muslims]. The Jews shall have their own religion and the Muslims their religion" (see Watt 1999, 132). The same provision is then applied to the remaining Jewish tribes, listed by name. The only exclusion made in that treaty was the stipulation that the Jews not be allowed to join the ranks of the Muslims in fighting without the authorization of the Prophet himself, and when they did, they would be required to contribute to the expenses of the battle, although no mention of a tribute, later exacted from Jews and Christians, is made at this stage.

However, following the battles of Uhud and al-Khandaq (the Ditch) in 625 and 627—against the marauding forces of Quraysh, the Prophet's own Meccan tribesmen, in which the Muslims were beaten and the Prophet's arm was injured—the picture changed radically. A large number of the Jewish tribes of Banu al-Nadir and Banu Qurayzah were put to the sword and the rest driven out of the city of Medina, which had become by this time the capital of the nascent Muslim commonwealth.

With respect to the Muslims' relation to the Christians, the earliest document defining the manner of dealing with them by the Muslims is Muhammad's letter to the Christian people of Najran in Yemen. After detailing the material and financial obligations, including a certain amount of silken clothing, coats of arms, camels, and so on, incumbent on the people of Najran as part of the tribute, the letter declares:

> The people of Najran shall have the protection of God and the pledge of
> Muhammad regarding their monies, persons, lands and kinsmen; as well as their
> rite of worship, their churches and whatever else they possess, be it small or large.
> No bishop shall be removed from his bishopric or a monk from his monastery or
> a priest from his parish. They are not required to pay blood or pagan ransom.
> They shall not be subjected to extortion or required to pay the tithe and no army
> shall set foot on their territory. (see Khadduri 1960, 179)

Other documents are mentioned in the ancient sources, such as the covenant of the Muslim general Khalid Ibn al-Walid with the Christians of Hira in southern Iraq and the covenant of the second caliph 'Umar with the Christians of Syria (Khadduri 1960, 183). However, the document that defined the relations of Muslims and Christians in a definitive way is the treaty concluded in 638 between the caliph 'Umar and the patriarch of Jerusalem, Sophrosynos. This treaty stipulated that the caliph "guarantees the lives, properties, churches and crosses" of the people of Jerusalem. It added that the Christians "shall not be persecuted for their religion, nor will they be molested. . . . Those who prefer to leave with the Rum [or Byzantine] inhabitants of Jerusalem shall be secured in their lives and properties, provided they leave their churches and crosses behind" (214).

Significantly, even the Arab occupation of territories under Byzantine rule was welcomed at first by the native Christian inhabitants of those territories, as a form of liberation from foreign Byzantine rule, complicated by the Christological squabbles of Melchites (Greek Orthodox), Jacobites, and Nestorians. The native population actually resented the imposition of the Melchite dogma of the dual nature of Christ or the status of the Virgin Mary as *Theotokos*, or "Mother of God." The Nestorians and Jacobites preferred their Christology, declared by the Nicene Council in 325 as heretical.

As an instance of this resentment or general disaffection, we might mention the role that Christian leaders played in the capture of Damascus, capital of Syria, by the Arab general Khalid Ibn al-Walid in 636, after the siege of six months. Historians tell us that the capture was made possible by the collusion of the Christian community of that ancient city, led by Mansur Ibn-Sarjun, grandfather of the great theologian of the Eastern Church, Saint John of Damascus (d. 748). This Mansur is reported to have opened the eastern gate of Damascus to the invading Arab armies. Both Mansur and his son, Sarjun, we are further told, served the Umayyad caliphs as financial advisors. John himself was, in his youth, a boon companion of the Umayyad prince and successor to the caliphate, Yazid, before his ordination as a monk and may have served the Umayyads in an administrative capacity, as did his father and grandfather (Hitti 1953, 195).

Although the Qur'an refers to the Christians as "the closest in friendship to the Believers [Muslims]" (5:82), it was exactly the Crusades (1099–1291) that brought the Muslim and Christian worlds into direct confrontation for the first time, with such adverse consequences. The historical context in which this confrontation took place was, in a sense, purely political and military in nature. The advance of the Seljuk Turks northward was perceived by the Byzantine emperor, Alexius Comnenus, as a threat to his imperial domain. He appealed in 1094 to Pope Urban II to urge the European princes to come to the rescue of their "Christian brethren" in the East. Urban called upon the Christian princes at the Council of Clermont to "march to the rescue of their brethren in the East" and to "wrest the Holy Land from the wicked race" (Runciman 1951, 1071).

It is important to understand that the motives of the Crusaders, whether princes, knights, or laymen, who had undertaken this bloody and perilous expedition, were not entirely spiritual or pious. It is reported by both Latin and Arab historians that when the Crusaders captured Jerusalem on July 15, 1099, they put to the sword no fewer than fifty thousand Muslims and Jews. Those Jews who managed to escape and sought refuge in the synagogue met with a terrible fate as the synagogue was burned over their heads.

Moreover, the Crusaders, who were, on the whole, moved by worldly ambition, greed, or adventurism, were met by a weakened and disunited Muslim world. This was the time when two rival caliphates governed the eastern parts of the empire, namely, the Shiite Fatimids in Cairo and the Sunnite Abbasids in Baghdad. Arab historians, such as Ibn al-Athir (d. 1233) and Abu'l-Fida (d. 1331), comment with a sense of melancholy on the collusion of the Fatimids with the Franks, as the Crusaders are generally called in the Arabic sources, and the open jubilation with which the news of the Crusaders' successes against the Seljuks in Asia Minor were received by the Fatimids. In fact, the Fatimid visier, al-Malik al-Afdal, we are told, sent a delegation bearing his felicitations to the Byzantine emperor, Alexius. He is also reported to have appealed to the Crusaders to march on Syria, which could then serve as a buffer against the Sunnite Seljuks (al-Athir, 1965, 332).

III. Modernists, Liberals, and Fundamentalists

By the sixteenth century, the Muslim world was dominated by the Ottomans, who were in almost constant warfare with their Christian or European neighbors, including the Russians, the Austrians, the Hungarians, and the Greeks. This warfare continued to the end of World War I, which saw the collapse of the Ottoman Empire and the dismemberment of its former dependencies in the Near East.

However, by the end of the eighteenth century and, more specifically, in the sequel of the Napoleonic expedition to Egypt in 1798, the Muslim world was beginning to fall under the domination of Western powers, starting with France. But it is significant, from a cultural perspective, that the first contacts with Europe were not exclusively military or political. Instead, they heralded a period of active cultural interaction, which reached its zenith in the so-called Arab Renaissance (*al-Nahdah*) and which flourished concurrently with Islamic modernism in India. Muslims were thus exposed, during the nineteenth century, to the great strides that modern Europe had made in the fields of philosophy, science, and technology. This exposure to Western culture had the unexpected effect of splitting the Muslim world into two opposing groups, the "liberal" or pro-Western and the "radical" or anti-Western.

At the religious level, the so-called secularist-fundamentalist controversy, which started in the nineteenth century, has continued ever since to be one of the most violent controversies pitting Islam against the West. This controversy, which turned in the last analysis on the right of reason to resolve theological disputes, can be described as the continuation of the age-old controversy that pitted the rationalist Mu'tazilite theologians against their traditionalist Hanbalite rivals during the classical period. Consequently, the modern and contemporary fundamentalists were committed to the literal interpretation of the Qur'anic text and to accusing their rivals of blind adherence to Western rationalism and its alleged repudiation of the spiritual component of religious faith. In this respect, it can be noted that the relations of Islam and the West have passed through two principal stages. During the nineteenth century, intellectuals who came under the influence of Western thought—such as Ahmed Khan of Bahadur (d. 1898) and Muhammad Iqbal (d. 1938) in India, as well as Muhammad 'Abdu (d. 905) in Egypt—exhibited a distinct sympathy with Western thought, which they believed was perfectly reconcilable with Islam, and called upon their fellow Muslims or Arabs to emulate it with certain reservations.

It must be stated that the modern or contemporary intellectual impact of the West has been potent and many-faceted, as illustrated by the valiant effort of some contemporary liberal intellectuals to highlight the areas of agreement between Islamic and Western thought and their willingness to espouse the cause of Western thought without reservation. Those intellectuals include a number of leading Arab or Muslim authors or scholars—such as Farah Antun (d. 1922), Taha Husayn (d. 1973), Ibrahim Madkur (d. 1988), and 'Abd al-Rahman Badawi (d. 1975)—who have contributed significantly to the interpretation of Arab-Islamic heritage and its affinity to Western thought.

How that heritage was viewed by the first generation of Arab-Islamic intellectuals and philosophers is of great historical interest. There was first a certain hankering after the past and a profound loyalty to its literary and cultural achievements, which the great linguists of the period—such as Nasif al-Yazigi (d. 1871) and Faris al-Shidiaq (d. 1887)—exhibited in a very impressive manner and tried to emulate almost slavishly, illustrating thereby the profound spell Arabic literature and the Arabic language exercised on their minds. Historically speaking, the so-called period of Decadence (*Inhitat*), stretched from the sixteenth to the beginning of the nineteenth century, had virtually severed the links of those *litterateurs* and intellectuals with their past, and accordingly a general theme that dominated their speculation was the call to renew or revive the classic Arab-Islamic literary and cultural heritage (*Turath*).

Second, the spectacle of European culture, set against the background of that heritage, appeared to some to be challenging and therefore worthy of emulation and to others threatening and calling for repudiation. Here, the religious sentiment played a decisive role, as far as pious Muslims and conservative Eastern Christians were concerned, for whom European culture appeared by reason of its materialism and this-worldliness to be irreconcilable with the spirituality and otherworldliness of the East.

This sense of polarity generated at the turn of the century that acrimonious controversy between the secularists and the fundamentalists, which figures so prominently in the ideological debates of the modern and contemporary periods and continues to be a burning cultural, religious, and political issue today.

Third, the European revolt against medieval authoritarianism—whether political or ecclesiastical, giving rise in due course to the Renaissance of the fifteenth century and the Enlightenment of the eighteenth—did not fail to resound loudly in those cultural circles that were in close interaction with the West in Lebanon and Egypt. Confronted with the rationalist and secularist challenges that European culture presented, Arab and Muslim intellectuals have been forced to define their attitude to it, without appearing to forgo their own heritage. In its most articulate form, this form of European thought, designated as positivism, has exercised a certain spell on the minds of a group of Arab intellectuals who were dedicated to what Zaki Najib Mahmud has termed the drive "toward a scientific philosophy."

The most radical champion of the new scientific spirit, which positivism consecrated as an organic characteristic of European culture during the nineteenth century, was Lebanese physician and philosopher Shibli Shumayil, who studied at the American University of Beirut and subsequently in France but lived and wrote for the most part in Egypt until his death in 1917. Other intellectuals, including Mahmud and Fu'ad Zakariayah, have defended recently the scientific or positivist methodology or spirit associated with the names of Auguste Comte, Bertrand

Russell, and other European philosophers. A basic feature of this positivism is the violent onslaught of its champions on traditional Arab-Islamic culture, its unscientific character, and its verbalism or cult of language, as those contended and continue to contend.

In short, the modern intellectual impact of the West has been widespread. A pro-Western group of Arab and Muslim intellectuals has tried valiantly to highlight the agreement between Islamic and Western thought without any attempt at reconciliation. Others have not hesitated to espouse the cause of Western culture without reservation. Still others have been calling recently for conciliation and dialogue with the West and for moderation and rational discourse in dealing with the problems that divide the Muslim community itself. Those scholars or intellectuals include Muhammad al-Ghazālī, Fahmi Huwaydi, and Yusuf al-Qaradawi, who belong to a liberal group in Egypt today, referred to as advocates of centrism (*Wasatiyah*).

The struggle between those conflicting groups continues today and is a feature of the current cultural discourse in the Arab-Muslim world. The liberal group, which includes political activists as well, denies that Islamic and Western cultures are irreconcilable.

Some, such as Ahmed Khan (d. 1898) in India and Muhammad 'Abdu (d. 1905) in Egypt, had nothing but praise for the rationalist and progressive aspects of Western civilization but remained committed to the unalterable truth of Islam and its validity at all times. Still others, such as Ali Abd al-Raziq (d. 1965) and Khalid Muhammad-Khalid (d. 1996), have gone so far as to defend the revolutionary thesis of the separation of the spiritual and the temporal. Still others were willing to abandon the basic tenets of Islam and supernaturalism in general, as Marxists such as Sadiq al-'Azim of Syria and Abdallah Laraoui in Morocco have recently done. On the other hand, the anti-Western group, referred to sometimes as "fundamentalists," such as Pakistani Abul'-A'la Maududi (d. 1979) and the Egyptian Sayyid Qutb (d. 1966), have resisted any attempts at bringing Islam and Western culture together and have remained committed to the doctrine of the superiority of Islam as the only hope for liberating humankind from the shackles of Western materialism. Maududi goes so far as to declare secularism, nationalism, and democracy the major banes of Western civilization today (1976, 45).

IV. Conclusions

Relations between Islam and the West have exhibited, from the earliest times, a characteristic pattern of confrontation, followed by interaction or clash, followed by dialogue. The conquest of the Byzantines and their eventual expulsion from the Near East in the seventh century was followed, in the eighth and ninth centuries, by a period of intense cultural interaction and exchange, leading to the assimilation of the Greek legacy in science, medicine, and philosophy, to which Byzantium and Alexandria had fallen heir. This legacy was fully developed and expanded by the great philosophers, physicians, and scientists of Islam, during a period of five centuries at Baghdad, Córdoba, and elsewhere. During that period, the Muslims were the only custodians of Greek culture, which the western Europeans had almost completely forgotten from the time of Boethius (d. 525), the Roman consul, who was the first to translate the Aristotelian logical corpus into Latin. Apart from Boethius's translations of Aristotle and Chalcidius's translations of parts of Plato's *Timaeus*, much of the Middle Ages had virtually no knowledge of that vast Greek and Hellenistic legacy.

It was in Muslim Spain that Arab-Muslim culture reached its apogee and was transmitted to western Europe across the Pyrenees. Starting in the twelfth century, the process of translating Arabic scientific and philosophical works at Toledo, Córdoba, and Sicily into Latin culminated in the thirteenth century in the translation of Averroes's commentaries on Aristotle, at the hands of brilliant scholars hailing from all parts of western Europe, such as Michael the Scot (d. 1236) and Herman the German (d. 1272). The impact of these translations was immense. They led to (1) the rediscovery of Aristotle and the Greek philosophical and scientific legacy by the western Europeans, (2) the rise and development of Latin Scholasticism, one of the glories of medieval thought, as Etienne Gilson has put it, and (3) the spread of rationalism and humanism, which became the hallmark of the Italian Renaissance in the fifteenth century.

Even the Crusades were instrumental in bringing the Muslims and the Europeans into close cultural contact, and despite intermittent warfare, these contacts exposed the Europeans to the much more advanced civilization of the Near East, from which they were eventually driven in the thirteenth century. In fact, the Crusaders learned a great deal from their Muslim counterparts in the Near East in the military, social, and agricultural fields. This is reflected, among other things, in the large number of Arabic loan words, which found their way into most European languages. Examples include *sugar, orange, alcohol, safron, arsenal, algebra, caliber, cipher*, and *zero* (see Watt 1972, 107–125). In a more specific way, it was particularly in the field of medicine that the Crusaders learned a great deal from the peoples of the Near East. The art of chivalry, one of the boasts of medieval knights, also owes much to those Near Eastern peoples.

From this brief introductory sketch, it should appear that far from being in a state of constant clash or confrontation—as Samuel P. Huntington claims in *Clash of Civilizations* (1996)—Islam and the West have been engaged in a process of active cultural exchange or dialogue that has had a lasting impact on the cultural growth of Europe and Asia, extending well into the New World. In fact, some American scholars agree with Richard Bulliet, who has gone so far as to argue that Islam and Christianity are siblings bound together by a long history of active and peaceful relationships: "Despite the enmity that has often divided them, Islam and the West have common roots and share much of their history" (Bulliet 2004, vii).

In his book *Crossing the Threshold of Hope*, Pope John Paul II has written:

Yes, certainly, it is a different case when we come to these three monotheistic religions, beginning with Islam. In the Declaration *Nostra Aetate*, we read: "The Church has a high regard for Muslims, who worship one God, living and subsistent, merciful and omnipotent, the Creator of heaven and earth. As a result of their monotheism, believers in Allah are particularly close to us." (1994, 91)

He then refers to the call of the Council to have a dialogue with followers of the Prophet and, despite centuries of dissentions and quarrels, "to forget the past and to work toward mutual understanding, as well as toward the preservation and promotion of social justice, moral welfare, peace and freedom, for the benefit of all mankind" (94).

REFERENCES

Al-Athir, Ibn. 1965. *Al-Kamil fi al-Tarikh*, vol. 10. Beirut: Dar Sadir.

Bulliett, R. W. 2004. *The Case for an Islamo-Christian Civilization*. New York: Columbia University Press.

Hitti, P. 1953. *History of the Arabs*. London: Macmillan.

Huntington, Samuel P. 1996. *The Clash of Civilizations and the Remaking of World Order*. New York: Simon and Schuster.

John Paul II. 1994. *Crossing the Threshold of Hope*. New York: Knopf.

Khadduri, M. 1960. *War and Peace in the Law of Islam*. Baltimore: Johns Hopkins University Press.

Lewis, Bernard. 1993. *Islam and the West*. New York: Oxford University Press.

Maududi, A. 1976. *Moral Foundations of the Islamic Movement*. Lahore: Islamic Publications.

Runciman, S. 1951. *History of the Crusades*, vol. 1. Cambridge, U.K.: Cambridge University Press.

Watt, W. Montgomery. 1972. *The Influence of Islam on Medieval Europe*. Edinburgh: Edinburgh University Press.

———. 1999. *Islamic Political Thought*. Edinburgh: Edinburgh University Press.

FOR FURTHER READING

Fakhry, M. 1997. *Islamic Philosophy, Theology and Mysticism*. Oxford: Oneworld.

———, trans. 2004. *Interpretation of the Qur'an*. New York: New York University Press.

Gibb, H. A. R. 1945. *Modern Trends in Islam*, Chicago: Chicago University Press.

Goldziher, I. 1981. *Introduction to Islamic Theology and Law*. Andras Hamari and Ruth Hamari, trans. Princeton, N.J.: Princeton University Press.

Lewis, Bernard. 1993. *Islam and the West*. New York: Oxford University Press.

Rahman, F. 1966. *Islam*. London: Weidenfeld and Nicholson.

Watt, W. Montgomery. 1999. *Islamic Political Thought*. Edinburgh: Edinburgh University Press.

Wensinck, A. J. 1932. *The Muslim Creed*. Cambridge, U.K.: Cambridge University Press.

B

GENDER AND WORLD PERSPECTIVES

CHAPTER 30

A FEMINIST PERSPECTIVE

PAMELA SUE ANDERSON

"Humanity's face has been the face of man. Feminist humanity must have another shape, other gestures; but, I believe, we must have feminist figures of humanity. They cannot be man or woman; they cannot be the human as historical narrative has staged that generic universal."

—Donna Haraway (1992)

INTRODUCTION: ON "FEMINIST" AND "DIVERSITY"

A feminist perspective on religious diversity goes to the very heart of the movement and waves of feminism(s), and it faces an inherent paradox of identity and diversity. A feminist must claim an identity; at the same time, diversity is the reality generated from the differences among individual women and among groups of women. The questions of identity and of diversity feed the ongoing debates about women and their relations to, or differences from, men but also about relations of women to women and of men to men. Ongoing disagreement about the nature of gender is found in and between religions as a result of diverse beliefs about human beings.

A complex dimension of religious diversity is constituted by the various assumptions about women and men inherent within a religion and among religions. These assumptions vary partly because differences of race, ethnicity, sexual orientation, class, and material and social conditioning render gender a cultural variable. But even when a religion has assumed that gender is based on a shared, universal (human) nature, it can conceal essentially contested claims about women; the latter claims are inherent in the former, unquestioned assumptions about the human situation, or humanity.

When it comes to debates about religious diversity, a significant common issue for our global world is the question of the salvation, liberation, or fulfillment of human beings. Religious diversity raises a question that religions share but that each gives conflicting answers to: What is wrong with humanity, and how can we solve the problem? A feminist perspective raises a similar but gender-critical question, exposing the gender bias in the humanity problem of religions. This bias emerges in the exclusion, in some form or another, of women as the obstacle to "human" (i.e., man's) salvation, liberation, or other ultimate fulfillment. A religion's solution to the human problem has (often) required the separation of man from woman insofar as woman has been variously construed as the source of sin, bodily defilement, inordinate desire, or worse.

So a feminist perspective, its paradox of identity and diversity, is interlinked with the ways in which our religiously diverse world conceives the human situation, its problem, and the solution. The question of religious diversity raises a matter of truth. This is the truth on which a religion establishes its practices and beliefs. But this is also the truth that will be essentially contested by a feminist perspective.

A Feminist Perspective and the Problem of Religious Diversity: A Matter of Truth

A "feminist" perspective is not the same as a "feminine" perspective; the latter might or might not be feminist, depending on who (i.e., which subject) or which religion defines "the feminine." Femininity could be determined by nature and/or by culture. Religions differ on this question of nature or culture as much as, if not more than, feminists who have different perspectives on the matter. The fact that our conception of femininity is a question of gender and/or sex tends to obscure the truth.

For purposes of clarity, it will be stipulated here that what distinguishes a feminist perspective is its political focus and aim: to expose the falsehoods about women and those relations that denigrate and/or oppress humanity. For example, a feminist might seek to eliminate the false beliefs about gender in the Christian religion; the oppressive structure of male privilege—known as Christian patriarchy—extends its gender deception to racism, homophobia, ethnocentrism, and so on. A paradox of identity and diversity renders any feminist perspective on religious diversity a matter of truth, but in this context, truth is complex and requires teasing out. As will become more apparent, the crucial epistemic norm in debates about feminisms and religions cannot be simplicity. Instead, if truth is to be sought for a feminist perspective on religious diversity, then the epistemic norms must be flexible enough to include the complexity of the diverse relations of men to women but also of men to men and of women to women. Truth is necessary anytime a feminist asks whether human relations are inhuman; this includes relations of privileged men to women and to less privileged men, of patriarchal women to nonprivileged men and other women, and so on.

Epistemic issues are at the cutting edge of feminist debates today (Assiter 2003, chaps. 6–8; Fricker 2007, 147), and they are integral to the present paradox. On the one hand, a feminist perspective is not able to avoid—at least, not for long—confronting diversity. Arguably, religious diversity is one of the most significant reasons for a large and diverse range of assumptions about women and gender, and this diversity inevitably feeds into the complexity of a feminist perspective. So religions have had a great role to play in constituting our gender relations, knowledge, and understanding. On the other hand, a feminist perspective has to assume an identity that will ensure its own coherence as a politics *for women*. So questions of truth about gender, like religious truth claims about the human situation, cannot avoid epistemic issues of simplicity and complexity, universality and individuality, particular and general, equality and difference. If false beliefs of a certain kind are endemic in a society as a result of its systems of religious belief, the epistemic inertia—the resistance to recognizing and giving up false beliefs—will be very powerful indeed (Manson 2009, 294–298).

In a book on religious diversity, it is essential to include a feminist perspective, if truth matters. Even though diversity renders impossible one and only one feminist perspective, it can still be argued that a feminist makes universal claims about women (e.g., their needs), transcending the gender relations of different religions. The epigraph of this chapter captures a widely embraced feminist view that (1) in the past, "humanity" has not been gender-neutral but has been "the face of man" and that (2) "feminist figures of humanity" cannot be a woman or a man (Haraway 1992, 86). Instead, these figures can be read to indicate the problem of the truth for religious diversity.

The philosophical question is whether truth can be plural. Can truth inhabit the different figures of humanity constituting the diversity of religions? It could be argued that the truth of humanity's situation is independent of the contingent truths about gender within diverse religions. Yet (how) can the truth of a feminist perspective on religious diversity be independent of our figures of the human? It would be simple if we could choose one configuration of humanity, but at least for a feminist, it is an urgent concern of truth and justice that the gender of the human differs, often unwittingly, according to religion and the gender differentials of race, class, ethnicity, sexual orientation, and social and material conditioning.

It is not unproblematic to make a descriptive claim about the complexity of gender as a result of the embedded nature of systems of religious beliefs, including diverse beliefs about women, in our different social worlds. These cultural configurations of humanity and the human are necessarily plural. Donna Haraway's account could be unproblematic, if merely descriptive of human diversity. It could also suggest that we cannot capture the complete truth of humanity. Her point, then, would be that as soon as we equate humanity with man or woman, we reduce and distort the truth. Haraway's claims are both epistemological and ethical and, as such, grounding for a feminist politics:

> My focus is the figure of a broken and suffering humanity, signifying—in ambiguity, contradiction, stolen symbolism, and unending chains of non-innocent translation—a possible hope. But also signifying an unending series of mimetic and counterfeit events implicated in the great genocides and holocausts of ancient and modern history. But, it is the very non-originality, mimesis, mockery, and brokenness that draw me to this figure and its mutants. (1992, 87; see also Anderson 2002, 112–118)

This feminist picture of "non-originality" in the changing figures of "a broken and suffering humanity" poses a serious challenge to those philosophers of religious diversity who, on the basis of their rationally justified or warranted religious beliefs, insist on an objective and exclusive view of what it is to be human (and to believe in God). Feminist philosophers such as Haraway and those who agree with her would not only question the gender-neutrality that has been assumed in some of the strongest claims of contemporary religious philosophers to truth but also point to the suffering—such as "the genocides and holocausts"—that indicates the brokenness of human reality. This is not a picture of a certain truth or of a confident hope in the salvation of humanity. Instead, Haraway's reconfiguration(s) of hope in a broken and suffering humanity could not be more different from the confident assurance of human salvation in the Christian theism of a religious exclusivist such as Alvin Plantinga. And yet both Plantinga and Haraway raise a serious matter of truth.

Religious Exclusivism: The Dangerous Truth of Gender-Blindness

Plantinga presents the problem of religious diversity in terms of truth without any comment on the gender of the human being. But he clearly assumes something about the nature of the human in the second of his two major claims for the exclusivity of religious belief (see Plantinga 1995, in Meister 2008, 41–42). His gender assumption about the divine is clear: God must be a father, since Plantinga refers to "his" divine son. Philosopher of religion John Hick similarly does not question the gender-neutrality of the human in his discussion of religious diversity. Although Hick supports a plurality of religions, rather than the exclusivist position of Plantinga on religious truth, he agrees that "in contemporary philosophy of religion it is customary to use the tripartite distinction between exclusivism, inclusivism, and pluralism. . . . [N]ote that the entire discussion [of

religious diversity] can be conducted in terms of truth claims or salvation claims
or both" (Hick 2007, 216; for an account of different forms of religious inclusivism, see Runzo 2008, 51–66).

In light of the strength and popularity of Plantinga's philosophical defense of
one religion and truth, let us consider his account of exclusivism:[1]

> There are several possible reactions to awareness of religious diversity. One is to
> continue to believe what you have all along believed; you learn about this
> diversity but continue to believe, that is, take to be true, such propositions as (1)
> [The world was created by God, an almighty, all-knowing, and perfectly good
> personal being (one that holds beliefs; has aims, plans, and intentions; and can
> act to accomplish these aims).] and (2) [Human beings require salvation, and
> God has provided a unique way of salvation through the incarnation, life,
> sacrificial death, and resurrection of his divine son.] consequently taking to be
> false any beliefs, religious or otherwise, that are incompatible with (1) and (2).
> Following current practice, I call this *exclusivism*; the exclusivist holds that the
> tenets or some of the tenets of one religion—Christianity, let's say—are in fact
> true; he adds, naturally enough, that any propositions, including other religious
> beliefs, that are incompatible with those tenets are false. (Plantinga 1995 in
> Meister 2008, 42)

Even without any discussion of the unquestioned gender assumptions in the
two propositions above, the epistemic structure that remains in place for Plantinga's system of properly basic Christian beliefs can be questioned on the grounds of
the truth of religious exclusion. What are the epistemic pathways for the formation
of these beliefs about "God" and "the unique way of salvation" for (some) human
beings? Also, without a detailed answer to this question, an implicit problem is that
a Christian theist will place great weight on "faith" in insisting that certain kinds of
beliefs—or belieflike attitudes toward Plantinga's two propositions—must be
maintained. The point is that fundamental questions of truth are blocked by the
epistemic structure of this debate. For instance, contrary to otherwise good evidence
such as that found in the conflicting truth claims of other religions, the Christian
exclusivist renders core beliefs, in its structure of religious beliefs, exempt from
revision or question.

Moreover, Plantinga's religious exclusivist must assume that people with, or
without, Christian faith are separated from one another by a moral partition; those
with faith know the truth and are saved. But this underpins an arguably pernicious
assumption about the variation of moral status within the human species. In turn,
this assumption of moral status creates an epistemic inertia to prevent the
questioning of basic religious beliefs. For instance, this epistemic situation would
reinforce teaching (a child) that there are serious penalties—horrific and eternal—
for a lack of faith. Paradoxically, the obstacles to truth in a position of religious
exclusivism not only are serious ethically but are also at the level of epistemic concerns that otherwise would be a preoccupation of such philosophers of religion as
Plantinga. The question is why this epistemic blindness is not recognized in its full
extent, including the distinctive implications of certain core beliefs for women.

A strange sort of epistemic blindness allows a serious variability in the moral status of humans who differ according to faith, or lack of faith. And this blindness is extended to gender, especially to the gender-blindness perpetuated by a religious upbringing that protects certain sources of pernicious epistemic inertia. The problem for the religious exclusivist is that this inertia—along with a range of false beliefs— might only be recognized by learning to see from the point of view of the excluded.

For instance, Fatima Mernissi illustrates how conservative religious men either force or allow women in Islamic societies with serious economic and gender inequalities to maintain deceptively strange practices—on the basis of false religious beliefs about gender and relevant biological facts—in order to secure the male status required by the norms of their patriarchal society. In her example, a man must control, or think that he controls, "the movements of women related to him by blood or by marriage, and by forbidding them any contact with male strangers" (1996, 34). The contentious religious norm is a bride's virginity in Islam (but the same norm, though in a different religious context, might be upheld by a Roman Catholic or other conservative Christians). To maintain a religious belief about the rightness of this norm, the contemporary (Islamic) woman might go to great lengths to deceive, with the help of modern technology, her future husband. As Mernissi explains, to uphold the role of virginity in patriarchal societies where some forms of modernization are completely acceptable, the "artifices of the most up-to-date medical technology are placed at the service of the age-old imperatives of the patriarchal family" (35). The deception is telling:

> It is no secret that when some marriages are consummated, the virginity of the bride is artificial. . . . [Y]oung women . . . resort to a minor operation on the eve of their wedding in order to erase the traces of pre-marital experience. Before embarking on the traditional ceremonies of virginal modesty and patriarchal innocence, the young woman has to get a sympathetic doctor to wreak a magical transformation. (34)

A combination of outdated religious beliefs about female sexuality and no understanding between the sexes not only undermines religious claims to truth but also perpetuates violence and often tragic outcomes of a failure of contemporary religions to counteract the epistemic inertia posed by religious assumptions concerning women, men, and the human situation.

Myth and Imagination in Pursuit of Truth

To tackle these false beliefs and contradictory practices, a feminist argument has been put forward for employing myth and imaginative variations in the miming of traditional myths, that is, mythical configurations of women's relations to men, family, and private and public social norms. The point is to expose sexism (but including racism and other forms of gender bias) by coming to recognize, by contrast with what has been assumed, the truth that has been hidden (Anderson 1998, 78–83, 128–129, 135; Assiter 2003, 93–96, 102–108). This feminist argument for introducing myth and mimesis into contemporary philosophy of religion has been met by a lack of understanding on behalf of those analytic philosophers of religion who find truth only in the rigor, clarity and gender-neutrality of their arguments rather than in being able to imagine the reality of a broken and suffering humanity (Coakley 2005, 512–516). Nevertheless, the social-moral epistemology deriving from engagement with recent philosophical debates about feminist-standpoint epistemology continues to give support to the idea that myth can have a productive role (Anderson 2002, 112–122; Benhabib 2002, 97, 100–104; Assiter 2003, 93, 109–110, 114–125, 128–145; Fricker 2007, 131–151). Miming myths can help both in coming to see the problems of gender injustice in the context of religious diversity and in imagining new possibilities for perennial myths of gender. Arguably, the most sexist of myths can be exposed and reconfigured in order to tackle the gender-blindness most resistant to change in debates about religious exclusivism, inclusivism, and pluralism.

Let us consider how the myths of gender (e.g., the role of sexuality in human sin and redemption) have, wittingly or not, accompanied the Christian system of religious beliefs, even as this system varies from a fundamentalist to a more liberal construal of Christianity. bell hooks's landmark text for twentieth-century feminists, *Ain't I a Woman?* (1981),[2] draws on good evidence but also powerfully draws on her readers' imagination, in order to expose the horrific violence suffered by black women at the hands of not only white slave owners but also other black men and the white women who preserved their sexual innocence by projecting the Christian belief in the absolute evil of female sexuality onto the enslaved black woman.

hooks's text bristles with pain, insight, and irony, exposing the truth of Christian misogyny and its historical embeddedness in the American institution of slavery. hooks captures the horrific projection of sin and inordinate desire onto women, culminating in the projection of hatred (of all sexuality) onto the enslaved black woman. The epitome of brokenness and suffering becomes the heart of the sexist-racist myth about the human problem of sin; the myth's solution is salvation for those men who punish and destroy the dangerous object of their desires: the female temptress. The figure in the misogynous myth without any moral status is ultimately the enslaved black woman.

To capture fully the damage of this human situation, it is worthwhile to quote from *Ain't I a Woman?*:

> In fundamentalist Christian teaching woman was portrayed as an evil sexual temptress, the bringer of sin into the world. Sexual lust originated with her and men were merely the victims of her wanton power. Socialization of white men to regard women as their moral downfall led to the development of anti-woman sentiment. . . . Appointing themselves as the personal agents of God, [white male religious teachers] became the judges and overseers of women's virtue. . . . Severe punishments were meted out to those women who overstepped the boundaries white men defined as woman's place. (hooks 1981, 29–30)

hooks's distinctive historical account of this Christian myth continues:

> In the 19th century, the growing economic prosperity of white Americans caused them to stray from the stern religious teachings that had shaped the life of the first colonizers. With the shift away from fundamentalist Christian doctrine came a change in male perceptions of women. 19th century white women were no longer portrayed as sexual temptresses; they were extolled as the "nobler half of humanity" whose duty was to elevate men's sentiments and inspire their higher impulses. . . . She was depicted as goddess rather than sinner; she was virtuous, pure, innocent, not sexual and worldly. . . . White male idealization of white women as innocent and virtuous served as an act of exorcism, which had as its purpose transforming her image and ridding her of the curse of sexuality. . . . [As] long as white women possessed sexual feelings they would be seen as degraded immoral creatures; remove these sexual feelings and they become beings worthy of love, consideration, and respect. Once the white female was mythologized as pure and virtuous, a symbolic Virgin Mary, white men could see her as exempt from negative sexist stereotypes of the female. . . . Given the strains of endless pregnancies and the hardships of childbirth, it is understandable that 19th century white women felt no great attachment to their sexuality and gladly accepted the new, glorified de-sexualized identity white men imposed upon them. . . .
>
> The shift away from the image of white woman as sinful and sexual to that of white woman as virtuous lady occurred at the same time as mass sexual exploitation of enslaved black women. . . . As American white men idealized white womanhood, they sexually assaulted and brutalized black women. . . . The deep hatred of woman that had been embedded in the white colonizer's psyche by patriarchal ideology and anti-woman religious teachings both motivated and sanctioned white male brutality against black women. . . . As white colonizers adopted a self-righteous sexual morality for themselves, they even more eagerly labeled black people sexual heathens. Since woman was designated as the originator of sexual sin, black women were naturally seen as the embodiment of female evil and sexual lust. They were labeled jezebels and sexual temptresses and accused of leading white men away from spiritual purity into sin. (31–33)

The shift in economic conditions and the changing configurations of the myth of female sinfulness had a deep impact on relations between white and black women, too. The white woman exhibited not only racism but also sexism in relegating the moral status of the enslaved black woman to a figure of original sin that had formerly been her own state:

> The use of the word prostitution to describe mass sexual exploitation of enslaved black women by white men not only deflected attention away from the prevalence of forced sexual assault, it lent further credibility to the myth that black females were inherently wanton and therefore responsible for rape.
>
> Rape was not the only method used to terrorize and de-humanize black women. Sadistic floggings of naked black women were another method employed to strip the female slave of dignity. In the Victorian world, where white women were religiously covering every body part, black women were daily stripped of their clothing and publicly whipped. . . .

It takes little imagination to comprehend the significance of one oppressed
black woman being brutally tortured while the more privileged white women
look passively at her plight. . . . Surely, it must have occurred to white women
that were enslaved black women not available to bear the brunt of such intense
anti-women male aggression, they themselves might have been the victims. . . .
While white women rarely physically assaulted black male slaves, they tortured
and persecuted females. Their alliance with white men on the common ground of
racism enabled them to ignore the anti-woman impulse that also motivated
attacks on black women (34, 37–39).

The process of reconfiguring the antiwoman myth is the flip side to the supposed solution to the problem of humanity: men are saved from sin by punishing
the figure of a sinner and so protecting themselves from evil and damnation.
Clearly, if truth matters, then what is assumed to be the nature of the human
requires scrutiny of gender, especially the violent and abusive nature of sexual
relations. Truth in this context is an outcome not only of rigorous argument but
also of understanding the gender bias of blind men (and sexist-racist women) to
their own sexual violence and injustice. It is not clear why religious smugness, as in
(over)confidence in one's personal salvation, has stood for truth.

DIVERSITY OF RELIGIONS AND
A PROPHETIC VOICE

The feminist message in Western debates about religions has often been prophetic.
In the spirit of biblical prophets, a voice calls for justice and righteousness,
condemning those men and "their white women" who fail to recognize and atone
for their evil acts and shocking misogyny. Unsurprisingly, feminists from various
religious perspectives, whether Hindu, Buddhist, Jewish, Muslim, or Christian (in
its various forms), have voiced their concerns about gender injustice on issues of
diversity within and outside a religion (see, e.g., hooks 1981, 108–113; Mernissi 1996,
92–108; Nussbaum 1999, 82–84; Mahmood 2005, 104–117; Filipczak 2007, 349–381).
But consider Rita Gross's telling reflection on Western feminism's legacy in the
appropriation of diverse religions:

> Western feminism clearly was in continuity with the prophetic stream found in
> the Hebrew Bible, and, to a lesser extent in my view, in the New Testament.
> There is no similar stream in Buddhist thought. . . . [I]ts social ethic takes a form
> different from active confrontation with injustice and calls for reform of the
> social-political order. . . . I am especially interested in what might result from a
> serious conversation between the Buddhist emphasis on compassion and the
> Christian prophetic emphasis on justice and righteousness. . . .
>   [But] Buddhists' reactions to [this] caught me by surprise . . . [their] distaste
> for the prophetic voice itself, claims that it is strident and oppressive, that it

promotes intolerance, self-righteousness, and sometimes violence. (Gross and
Ruether 2001, 164–165)

Clearly, personal appropriations of the "emphasis" of different religions do not
lessen the conflict of diverse religious truth claims. But when Rosemary Radford
Ruether responds to Gross (as above), she proposes a different conceptualization of
relations among diverse religions:

> Unlike Rita, who was first a Christian who then converted to Judaism before
> finding her primary identity in Buddhism, I have not journeyed through
> affiliation with several religions. But I have explored a number of religions,
> starting with the ancient Near Eastern and Greek religious worlds, and then
> Judaism, Buddhism and Islam. . . .
>
>   In my explorations of religious world views, I have come to think of three
> major paradigms of religion: first, sacralization of nature, seen in seasonal and life
> cycles; second, prophetic, historical religions; and third, contemplative religions
> of inward transformation. There may be more paradigms than these, or other
> ways of naming them, but these are what I have identified. . . .
>
>   With new challenges, people may desire to renew one of the paradigms that
> has faded from the tradition of their upbringing. (Gross and Ruether 2001, 183)

From the above, it is clear that Ruether and Gross approach religious diversity
from a woman's perspective that is highly personal and seriously committed to the
truth found by and for herself in a particular religion that is seen as modifiable with
insights from other religions. Each woman's autobiography is shaped in large part
by her own distinctive reflections on different religions. However, the philosophical
problem with this is that the personal nature of these reflections can avoid the more
difficult, ethical and epistemological questions of truth; these questions, however
unanswerable, are necessary for a feminist politics—at least as conceived so
far here.

Saba Mahmood is equally eager to voice her feminist concern for contemporary women's personal and social commitments to a traditional religion. The focus
of Mahmood's concern is on the Islamic practice of piety. However, she is keenly
attentive to and highly critical of the politics of the contemporary liberal feminist.
Mahmood argues against the dominant Western, liberal feminist interpretations of
women's relation to diverse religious practices, insisting that not all women are
motivated by a desire for freedom or by the subversion of traditional religious
norms. Another example of the diverse motivations on a religious matter for
women in Islam is *l'affaire du foulard* in France, which reflects the complexity of
truth in an ongoing political situation of conflicting cultural, personal, and religious norms (for details, in terms of diversity in our global era, see Benhabib 2002,
94–104).

It needs to be stressed that Mahmood's original reading of Islamic women's
politics is contentious for contemporary feminism and for liberal political theory
generally. She illustrates brilliantly how a specific women's religious movement in
Cairo significantly reconfigures the gendered practice of Islamic pedagogy and

the social institution of mosques, and crucially, she demonstrates that this particular women's movement cannot be based on the liberal woman's freedom of
choice. Instead, she reveals how these particular Egyptian women desire submission to certain religious norms. To make sense of this desire as something different
from a "deplorable passivity and docility," Mahmood attends to "the specific
logic of the discourse of piety," insisting that "an appeal to understanding the
coherence of a discursive tradition is neither to justify that tradition, nor to argue
for some irreducible essentialism or cultural relativism" (2005, 15, 17). In other
words, Mahmood's account of the ways in which women "inhabit" the norms of
a religion assumes a critique (which she finds in the feminist-queer theory of
Judith Butler) of human agency understood in terms of a liberal political subject.
The significant point is that Mahmood exposes the conflicting range of feminist
perspectives on religions and gender justice. Unlike Martha Nussbaum, Mahmood does not draw on the well-known liberal feminist politics of religion and
women's human rights (Nussbaum 1999, 81–87); and unlike Mernissi, Mahmood
does not uncover the ways in which Islamic women have subverted patriarchal
norms in rebelling against oppressive gender practices. These different liberal,
socialist, and cultural (embodied and embedded) feminist politics generate a
diverse range of feminist relations to religions. Nevertheless, a common concern
for the actual needs and practices of women in the context of their religious traditions might be enough to give a feminist perspective an identity, while still
allowing for religious diversity.

A Feminist Perspective and the Epistemic Norms of Truth

Women who have actually struggled for their own bodily integrity, their human
dignity, their cognitive ability, their rational capabilities, their equal moral status,
and/or their sexual difference might understand the seriousness of the personal and
political debates about religious diversity better than those nonfeminist philosophers of religion who offer an "objective" account of diversity—whether in exclusive, inclusive, or pluralist terms. Nevertheless, it is undeniable that truth matters to
a feminist perspective; it matters just as much as, and at times more than, the truth
claims of a religious exclusivist. Critical assessment of a religious commitment
confronts a similar paradox of identity and diversity in aiming to bind diverse individuals and communities together. Religion binds individuals into communities
both in shared ritual practices and in belief-motivated thinking and acting, while
the relation of individual and community informs "understanding feminism":
"The problem of differences among and within women provides a rich understanding of the complexity of individual identities and the complexity of group

interactions. . . . [I]t is emblematic of the necessity for feminist theory and practice to build complexity and the salience of intersecting oppressions into its core" (Bowden and Mummery 2009, 121).

At this point, it is possible to answer some questions. How do the categories developed in discussions of religious diversity, notably those of religious exclusivism, inclusivism, and pluralism, inform a feminist perspective on religious diversity?[3] Can a feminist perspective be inclusivist, exclusivist, pluralist, or something else? A feminist perspective could force a defender of the truth of religious diversity to consider a different set of epistemic norms, that is, to make sense of the diversity of religions, while also uncovering a politics that is both for women and against the degrading myths of gender embedded in the systems of religious belief most resistant to change and self-criticism.

In the history of twentieth-century feminism alone, women's recognition of the interlinking of gender oppression with that of other differences has forced some feminists to include in their projects resistance to all forms of social marginalization and exclusion. The result is that "a feminist perspective" must include the how and why of feminist resistance to religious forms of gender exclusion, whether these are on the grounds of race, sexuality, ethnicity, class, or other material and social differences. However, Mahmood offers a highly significant critical, dissenting voice in her exception to sweeping forms of resistance (by feminists) that fail to understand certain forms of women's religious practice.

Generally, without critical-imaginative exposure (e.g., by hooks) of the mythology of Christian misogyny and its destructive focus on enslaved black women, a feminist perspective on religions could have remained misguided and exclusionary. Without struggling constantly to distinguish and see reality from a feminist perspective, sexism could be easily shifted from one woman or a group of women to another. Before the generation of feminists enlightened by hooks, Mernissi, and Mahmood, a feminist perspective could largely have neglected the challenge of race, class, sexual orientation, and ethnicity to the white-privileged beliefs about women but also the beliefs of women who simply accept the myths and the configurations of sin and salvation built on the exclusion of (some) women for the sake of (privileged) men.

Before the 1980s and still today, much feminist attention focuses on the problems of oppression and embodiment, but this attention could also be revolutionized by use of the imagination to expose the myths and truth hidden by historical narratives that have excluded the distinctive reality of women's sexually or racially specific lives. hooks, Mernissi, Mahmood, and other so-called third-wave feminists, who are not merely concerned with liberal forms of equality and free choice (the first-wave feminist concerns) or the sexual difference between women and men (the second-wave feminist concern), have transformed accounts of gender roles, knowledge, and understanding (Anderson 2007, 816–817, n. 6). This transformation includes confronting the diversity within a religion (e.g., Christianity, Islam) and among religions (e.g., Christianity-Judaism-Islam, Buddhism-Daoism-Confucian).

Conclusions

....

This chapter aimed to capture the highly significant, critical, and imaginative challenge of third-wave feminism for a feminist perspective. A prophetic voice speaks through and is modified by the repetition of a critical feminist figure. As Haraway says, "The title of bell hooks's provocative 1981 book, echoing Sojourner Truth, *Ain't I a Woman?* bristles with irony as the identity of 'woman' is both claimed and deconstructed simultaneously" (1992, 93; see hooks 1981, 3, 159–160; Anderson 2002, 115–116). Personified in bell hooks's figure of a "woman" is the question of truth and diversity. A black woman dares to raise this question (as above) in a historical context of a women's rights movement where she was forbidden to speak; thus, she forces the other (white) women present to see and to hear the truth spoken; the renaming of this black woman as Sojourner Truth takes on the status of myth.[4] In this manner, historical-mythical imagination produces the critical ground for a feminist perspective. If we assume that religions themselves are structures of both gender oppression and gender liberation, then whatever the different religions claim about (the reality of) gender, of who we are as humans, as men and as women, must be both variable and critical. The critical point is that religions make claims about our situation, our problem and its solution, and they make implicit claims about gender, that is, whether this means that humanity is gender-neutral, is exclusive for men as essentially a different sex from women, includes both men and women, or is the inclusive figure that we still need to imagine and embrace.

Thus, the question of religious diversity raises a feminist issue. Its unwitting gender claims, especially those embedded in myths of religious belief, continue to shape gender relations, knowledge, and understanding. The dangers of falsehoods about gender are the exclusion, degradation, and horrific treatment of individual women or specific groups of women in the name of religious truth. Insofar as "to accept a religion" is to embrace some particular and connected account of the human situation, its problem and solution, it is a feminist perspective that makes explicit the gendering of what has been accepted. A range of feminists writing on religions provides access to the myths about women and/or their sexuality—in Christian, Jewish, Muslim, Buddhist, and Hindu contexts.

A crucial feature of feminism is the struggle both against reductively sexist accounts of women's religious practices and for personal-social transformation of reality and its depiction insofar as false beliefs have obscured the truth about our lives as women and men. Too often, religions have implicitly or explicitly justified the inordinate suffering of women as a result of sexist violence in this life with the hope for salvation in the next life. In contrast with the religious exclusivist, inclusivist, and pluralist who, in their own different ways, claim a soteriological truth about an afterlife, a feminist perspective more often than not allows for religiously diverse solutions to the human problem in order to expose obstacles to truth in this life. These obstacles include the epistemic norms that obscure the ways in which false beliefs and practices continue to denigrate women with violence and abuse.

Ultimately, a feminist perspective would embrace a common humanity that cuts across religious diversity just enough to give women their bodily integrity, their dignity as religiously conservative or not, and their hope for a life in which the natural needs of those they love, including themselves, can be met.

NOTES

1. Another label for a position similar to religious exclusivism in its rejection of any liberal politic view of universally shared norms, even universals that transcend the particularities of diverse forms of religious traditions, is "particularism," a position that is addressed by feminists in debates about feminist ethics and epistemology (see Assiter 2003, 4–5, 109–110).

2. The title is a quotation from Isabella Baumfree, who, in 1856, spoke to the second annual convention of the women's rights movement in Akron, Ohio, where it was deemed inappropriate for a black woman to say anything. But in asking the question "Ain't I a woman?" Baumfree, a black woman, demonstrated the epistemological power of renaming; she answered her own question by calling herself Sojourner Truth, and so she names truth as situated and moving, in a manner that is not contradictory (see hooks 1981, 159–160). This figure of Sojourner Truth takes on the significance of a new, founding myth in generating a narrative that represents the difference between what a particular concept signifies within a system of meanings and practices and what it ought to represent. One interpretation is that feminist philosophers must be constantly prepared to reconfigure false concepts and arbitrarily fixed myths of humanity (Anderson 2002, 115–118).

3. For a current argument on religious diversity against religious pluralism as opposed to either exclusivism or inclusivism, see Kvanvig 2009, 1–26. Also see Meister 2009, chap. 2.

4. See note 2 above.

REFERENCES

Anderson, Pamela Sue. 1998. *A Feminist Philosophy of Religion: The Rationality and Myths of Religious Belief.* Oxford: Blackwell.

———. 2002. "Myth and Feminist Philosophy." In Kevin Schilbrack, ed., *Thinking through Myths: Philosophical Perspectives.* New York: Routledge, 101–122.

———. 2007. "Feminism and Patriarchy." In Andrew W. Hass, David Jasper, and Elisabeth Jay, eds., *The Oxford Handbook of English Literature and Theology.* Oxford: Oxford University Press, 810–828.

Assiter, Alison. 2003. *Revisiting Universalism.* New York: Palgrave.

Benhabib, Seyla. 2002. *The Claims of Culture: Equality and Diversity in the Global Era.* Princeton, N.J.: Princeton University Press.

Bowden, Peta, and Jane Mummery. 2009. *Understanding Feminism.* Stocksfield, U.K.: Acumen.

Coakley, Sarah. 2005. "Feminism and Analytic Philosophy of Religion." In William
   Wainwright, ed., *The Oxford Handbook of Philosophy of Religion*. Oxford: Oxford
   University Press, 494–526.

Filipczak, Dorota. 2007. *Unheroic Heroines: The Portrayal of Women in the Writings of
   Margaret Laurence*. Lodz, Poland: Wydawnictwo Uniwersytetu Lodzkiego.

Fricker, Miranda. 2007. *Epistemic Injustice: Power and the Ethics of Knowing*. Oxford:
   Oxford University Press.

Gross, Rita M., and Rosemary Radford Ruether. 2001. *Religious Feminism and the Future of
   the Planet: A Buddhist-Christian Conversation*. New York: Continuum.

Haraway, Donna. 1992. "Ecce Homo, Ain't (Ar'n't) I a Woman, and Inappropriate/d
   Others: The Human in a Post-Humanist Landscape." In Judith Butler and Joan Scott,
   eds., *Feminists Theorize the Political*. New York: Routledge, 86–100.

Hick, John. 2007. "Religious Pluralism." In Chad Meister and Paul Copan, eds., *The
   Routledge Companion to Philosophy of Religion*. New York: Routledge, 216–225.

hooks, bell. 1981. *Ain't I a Woman? BlackWwomen and Feminism*. Boston: South End.

Kvanvig, Jonathan L. 2009. "Religious Pluralism and the Buridan's Ass Paradox." *European
   Journal for Philosophy of Religion* 1/1 (Spring): 1–26.

Mahmood, Saba. 2005. *Politics of Piety: The Islamic Revival and the Feminist Subject*.
   Princeton, N.J.: Princeton University Press.

Manson, Neil C. 2009. "Epistemic Inertia and Epistemic Isolationism." *Journal of Applied
   Philosophy* 26/3: 291–298.

Meister, Chad, ed. 2008. *The Philosophy of Religion Reader*. New York: Routledge.

———. 2009. *Introducing Philosophy of Religion*. New York: Routledge.

Mernissi, Fatima. 1996. *Women's Rebellion and Islamic Memory*. London: Zed.

Nussbaum, Martha. 1999. "Religion and Women's Human Rights." *Sex and Social Justice*.
   Oxford: Oxford University Press, 81–117.

Plantinga, Alvin. 1995. "Pluralism: A Defense of Religious Exclusivism." In Thomas Senor,
   ed., *The Rationality of Belief and the Plurality of Faith*. Ithaca, N.Y.: Cornell University
   Press. Reprinted 2008 in Chad Meister, ed., *The Philosophy of Religion Reader*. New
   York: Routledge, 40–59.

Runzo, Joseph. 2008. "Religious Pluralism." In Paul Copan and Chad Meister, eds.,
   Philosophy of Religion: Classic and Contemporary Issues. Oxford: Blackwell, 51–66.

FOR FURTHER READING

Anderson, Pamela Sue, ed. 2010. *New Topics in Feminist Philosophy of Religion:
   Contestations and Transcendence Incarnate*. Dordrecht, Neth.: Springer.

Butler, Judith. 2006. *Precarious Life: The Powers of Mourning and Violence*. London:
   Verso.

Clément, Catherine, and Julia Kristeva. 2001. *The Feminine and the Sacred*. Jane Marie
   Todd. trans. New York: Columbia University Press.

Doniger, Wendy. 1998 "Medical and Mythical Constructions of the Body in Hindu Texts."
   In Sarah Coakley, ed., *Religion and the Body*. Cambridge, U.K.: Cambridge University
   Press, 167–184.

Grace, Daphne. 2004. *The Woman in the Muslim Mask: Veiling and Identity in Postcolonial
   Literature*. London: Pluto.

Howie, Gillian. 2008. "Feminist Generations: The Maternal Order and Mythic Time." In
    Luce Irigaray with Mary Green, eds., *Luce Irigaray: Teaching*. New York: Continuum,
    103–112.
Joy, Morny, and Eva K. Neumaier-Dargyay, eds. 1995. *Gender, Genre and Religion: Feminist
    Reflections*. Waterloo, Ont.: Wilfrid Laurier University Press.
Mukta, Parita. 2002. *Shard of Memory: Woven Lives in Four Generations*. London:
    Weidenfeld and Nicolson.
Weil, Simone. 2002. *Letter to a Priest*. A. F. Wills, trans. London: Routledge.
Zack, Naomi. 2007. "Can Third Wave Feminism Be Inclusive? Intersectionality, Its
    Problems and New Directions." In Linda Martin Alcoff and Eva Feder Kittay, eds.,
    The Blackwell Guide to Feminist Philosophy. Oxford: Blackwell, 193–207.

CHAPTER 31

A CONTINENTAL PERSPECTIVE

BRUCE ELLIS BENSON

THE very idea that there is something that one can term "Continental philosophy of religion" is remarkably recent. Certainly, the field is not nearly as coherent and self-contained as is "analytic philosophy of religion." Although religious concerns are undoubtedly present in many historical Continental figures (such as René Descartes, Immanuel Kant, G. W. F. Hegel, and Friedrich Nietzsche), only in the past few decades have religious questions become central to Continental philosophical discourse. And that centrality is signaled appropriately enough by the idea of a "return to religion" in European thought and, more specifically, a "theological turn" in French philosophy in the last two decades of the twentieth century that continues unabated (Janicaud 2000). It is instructive that this theological turn is particularly instigated by Jewish philosopher Emmanuel Levinas; continued by such Christian philosophers as Jean-Luc Marion, Jean-Louis Chrétien, Gianni Vattimo, John D. Caputo, and Richard Kearney; and then, in one way or another, appropriated by such decidedly secular philosophers as Jacques Derrida, Alain Badiou, and Slavoj Žižek for their own respective ends. In one way or another, all of them have appropriated certain themes found in Christianity.

PHENOMENOLOGY: EMMANUEL LEVINAS, JEAN-LUC MARION, AND JEAN-LOUIS CHRÉTIEN

With Levinas comes a particular attentiveness to the phenomenon of the other, a phenomenon so extraordinary in its infinity and alterity that it cannot be properly thematized phenomenologically. It is important to see exactly what Levinas is criticizing. While it might at first seem that he is giving us a particular sort of ethics, Levinas's point goes much deeper than that. In effect, his criticism is that the Western philosophy—from its origins—has been an attempt to "master" our experience (and thus other people). It might seem that phenomenologist Edmund Husserl, with his "principle of principles," which demands that all phenomena be accepted as they are presented, had finally allowed for phenomena to appear as they truly are. Yet when he adds (in the same principle of principles) that the apprehension of phenomena is limited by the "horizon" on which they appear (in effect, the interpretive limits of the subject), the phenomena become "subject" to our interpretation. In contrast to Husserl, Levinas insists that with the appearance of the other, the horizon of the subject is burst open by the sheer uncontainable excess of the other. And such excess, or what Levinas calls "infinity," is particularly true of the human other. Although Levinas makes a point of keeping his explicitly religious writing—Talmudic commentary—separate from his philosophy (even having different publishers for each genre), even his philosophical writing follows the Hebrew scriptural and prophetic tradition of privileging the widow, orphan, and stranger as paradigmatic figures of otherness, as well as incorporating Christian ideas.

As becomes clear in Levinas's later philosophy, however, our encounter with the other is hardly ordinary; rather, it is "traumatic." The very face of the other calls out to be recognized and treated correctly, and our self-preoccupation is profoundly called into question. There is a deep reorientation of the self: instead of it being the "subject"—able to master the world—the subject now becomes "subject" to the other that appears. This remarkable change in orientation likewise means that neither metaphysics nor epistemology is "first philosophy" but ethics. It is not hard to see that Levinas is suggesting a reorientation of philosophy itself. For what underlies ethics is religious "metaphysics" of the ethical call, making that call prior to every other discourse.

This move has even more profound religious implications since we encounter God in the face of the other. Of course, this raises more than one question. On the one hand, if both the other and God are infinite, then what separates them? As Levinas puts it, "the God of the Bible signifies the beyond being, transcendence" (1996a, 130). To make this even stronger, he goes on to say: "God is not simply the 'first other [autrui],' the other [autrui] par excellence, or the 'absolutely other [autrui],' but other than the other [autre qu'autrui], other otherwise, other with an alterity prior to the alterity of the other [autrui] . . . transcendent to the point of absence, to a point of possible confusion with the stirring of the *there is*" (141).

So there is something even more significantly "other" about God than about the human other, for God is beyond all human categories. Levinas says that "the Infinite affects thought by devastating it and at the same time calls upon it; in a 'putting it back in its place' it puts thought in place. It awakens it" (138). On the other hand, Levinas wants to move beyond the logos of philosophy, to think of God as "otherwise than according to knowledge" (1996b: 154). Yet can Levinas escape from philosophy so easily? Derrida questions whether Levinas can leave the rationality of Greek thought behind. Quoting an ancient Greek philosopher, Derrida says, "If one does not have to philosophize, one still has to philosophize" (1978, 152). Levinas insists that he is unwilling to submit to the "vassalage" of philosophy and that his thinking about God is a kind of thought that is not contained by philosophical thought. As examples, Levinas points to Plato's concept of the "Good" that is beyond being (*epekeina tes ousias*) and Descartes's idea of an "infinite" God who surpasses all human consciousness. Yet the question remains: Has Levinas really escaped from classical philosophy?

Marion takes up the question of the conditions of appearance that Levinas never fully addresses, although they are certainly implicit in his account of the other. In Marion's view, religious discourse, specifically of a Christian sort (writing, as he is, from a Roman Catholic perspective), appears as a possible interpretive horizon that both discloses new phenomena and enables the proper reception of certain phenomena that exceed the limits of the horizon. Working with Husserl's conception of the principle of principles, Marion speaks of what he terms the "saturated phenomenon." By definition, a saturated phenomenon contains much more than any human interpretive framework could take in. It is a kind of "super" phenomenon, one that is very much like Levinas's infinite other. Further, this phenomenon does not appear against the backdrop of classical metaphysics—which is subjugated to "being"—but is beyond being. Thus, Marion postulates an alternative horizon to that of being.

The most obvious of these phenomena is God. Of course, this God is not the god of metaphysics, of which Marion sees Friedrich Nietzsche as rightly proclaiming the demise. Such a god, which is actually an idol, "does not have any right to claim, even when it is alive, to be 'God'" (Marion 2001, 1). Central to "God without Being" is the distinction between idols and icons. In that it is Christ who is taken by Saint Paul to be the "icon" of God (Colossians 1:15), Marion takes him to be the "norm" of all icons. Like the person who escapes from Plato's cave, the experience is one of "bedazzlement." Yet this experience is not painful but is one of "glory, joy, excess" (2000, 200). Since Marion thinks that God is "beyond" being, he suggests that we think of God in terms of love, since "love gives itself only in abandoning itself, ceaselessly transgressing the limits of its own gift" (1991, 48). In effect, this is Marion's version of thinking "otherwise." God comes to us as a gift, not as something or someone that we can control. What this means in practice is that God displaces the ego from the center of the world.

Thus, Marion takes Christianity—not some kind of "scientific" or "secular" background—to be the true horizon of interpretation, despite being soundly criticized by Dominique Janicaud for leaving "pure" phenomenology (Janicaud 2000). Phenomena disclosed in Christian discourse are not like other phenomena, even though Marion admits that such things as great historical events or art can be saturated phenomena. In this way, religious phenomena overturn the self-assured foundations of phenomenology by exceeding their conditions of appearance. Further, Marion argues that the fundamental call to us is not that of Heidegger's call of being but that of Deuteronomy 6:4: "Hear, O Israel: The Lord is our God, the Lord alone." Of course, Marion freely admits that "between these two interpretations of a single phenomenological situation . . . no reason could decide" (2002, 306).

Although Chrétien writes on such topics as the body, memory, the presence of the voice, and testimony, the theme of a call that "wounds" appears in various texts and could be taken as a dominant motif for his thought. Chrétien thinks that the call always already precedes us and comes to us with the effect of decentering and constituting us. Once again, the phenomenological paradigm set up by Husserl is radically reversed. "We speak only for having been called," and "we are entangled in speech as soon as we exist" (Chrétien 2004, 1, 28). Given that speech precedes us, it should be no surprise that the subject is intersubjectively constituted for Chrétien, which means that "my" voice is at once mine and that of others. We exist as part of an ongoing conversation, and so our existence is an ever-evolving hybridity.

When Chrétien says that "each new encounter shatters us and reconfigures us," it is significant that this statement is part of an essay on prayer (2000, 156). In quite remarkable ways, Chrétien uses the phenomenon of prayer to illuminate speech and conversation. In prayer and conversation, one touches and is touched in return. Yet this movement is not simply two-way: the response to a call goes out not merely to the sender but also to many others. It is as a gift that speech comes to us, and we give it back and also away. There is no sense of "reciprocity" of speech: "No response will ever correspond. The perfection of the answer will lie forever in its very deficiency, since what calls us in the call is from the start its very lack of measure, its incommensurability" (Chrétien 2004, 23). This exchange is profoundly connected to wounding, for the very "opening up" is like a wound. Prayer is particularly exemplary here, since it "exposes [the one praying] in every sense of the word *expose* and with nothing held back" (2000, 150). So we find the same kind of reversal that we found in Levinas and Marion. The subject is "intended" and so constituted by the call, rather than being self-constituting. The concrete form of the call comes in a plurality of prior voices, which oblige a response and constitute us anew.

DECONSTRUCTION: JACQUES DERRIDA

Although Derrida claimed that all of his thought had been motivated by religious and ethical themes, it is more toward the end of his career that he begins explicitly engaging such themes, having been increasingly influenced by Levinas. It came as a surprise to many when Derrida made the claim that "deconstruction is violence" (2002b, 243). Yet one way of defining *deconstruction* is as the questioning and modification of all beliefs, laws, or formulas. With this idea in mind, Derrida claims in "Force of Law" (2002b) that deconstruction promotes justice precisely by asking whether specific laws actually promote justice. Unlike laws, justice is an absolute regulative ideal that laws attempt to embody but never do so fully or adequately. Thus, true justice is always deferred and so has a messianic structure. In light of this, Derrida calls not for some kind of weak resignation but instead for hypervigilance and a strong sense of responsibility in order to avoid violence.

In the same way that laws only imperfectly implement justice, so Derrida sees all specific "messianisms" (whether Christian, Jewish, or Islamic) as too definitive and thus violent. In their place, he speaks of a faith that has no definite messiah and thus is "messianic," which is characterized by "the opening to the future or to the coming of the other" that comes as an "absolute surprise" (2002a, 56). Thus, Derrida speaks of a "nondogmatic doublet of dogma . . . a *thinking* that 'repeats' the possibility of a religion without religion" (1996, 49). This would be something quite different from what he terms a "dogmatic faith" which "claims to know" and so "ignores the difference between faith and knowledge" (2002a, 49). Despite saying that "I quite rightly pass for an atheist," Derrida refers to "my religion about which nobody understands anything" and maintains that "I pray, as I have never stopped doing all my life" (1993, 154–155, 156). Given what Derrida says, it is not surprising that he finds himself asking the question of Augustine: "What do I love when I love my God?" Yet one can ask whether there can be a radically "nondogmatic" religion that is always "to come" and thus never arrives. What is the content of such a religion, if it can even be called that? It is also worth questioning whether Derrida does a kind of "violence" to concrete messianisms by borrowing their structure for something quite different. Derrida says he attempts to "think the possibility of such an event, but not the event itself" (1996, 49). In effect, Derrida's "religion" is something like a completely radicalized Christianity in which responsibility to the other becomes the central element.

Hermeneutics: Gianni Vattimo, John D. Caputo, and Richard Kearney

Although he was raised as a Roman Catholic, Gianni Vattimo's Christianity is very much a return to belief. Or, more exactly, it is a return to a "believing that one believes" (the literal translation of the title of his book *Credere di Credere*, which has been translated to English simply as *Belief*). It is a "recovery" of faith but not of certainty or conviction. According to Vattimo's "hermeneutical nihilism," the end of modernity means that there are no longer any compelling reasons to exclude religion. Vattimo freely admits that his return to Christianity is very much a feature of his reading of Nietzsche and Heidegger. In Vattimo's view, both of them give us a nihilism in which being is continually weakened by hermeneutics. If there are (as Nietzsche would have it) only interpretations and no longer any facts, then nihilism is the logical result—and nihilism is even the very logic of modernity. But this is hardly something to be mourned. Rather, it is the very condition for the kind of Christianity that Vattimo wishes to embrace. Because objectivity is destroyed by way of hermeneutics, hermeneutics makes room for religious interpretation. "The incarnation, that is God's abasement to the level of humanity, what the New Testament calls God's kenosis, will be interpreted as the sign that the non-violent and non-absolute God of the post-metaphysical epoch has as its distinctive trait the very vocation for weakening" (Vattimo 1999, 39). Taking a cue from René Girard, Vattimo sees Jesus as undermining the "natural sacred" and its violence.

Once we get beyond the violence of metaphysics, we get a Christianity that distances itself from dogma and theological particularity. Christianity, in its law of freedom and charity, is the ethos of the hermeneutical age, which frees subjects and communities to give up authoritarian and ideological power plays in order to practice openness and understanding in human community. Every law, dogma, and authority is suspended for the sake of Christian charity. Instead of being about "an objective truth," revelation is about "an ongoing salvation" (Vattami 1999, 48). The God of Christianity is thus a kenotic God, who gives up sovereignty, power, and transcendence to reveal himself in weakness and death. In his own kenotic act, Christ has shown us that God is love and that the most important message of Christianity is that of love. For Vattimo, "the only truth revealed to us by Scripture, the one that can never be demythologized in the course of time . . . is the truth of love, charity" (Rorty and Vattimo 2005, 50–51). Of course, Vattimo realizes that this is a very weak form of Christianity, and so he speaks of himself as being a "half-believer." Those who see themselves as "serious Christians" will likely see Vattimo's version of Christianity as simply untenable, for it is a version so weak and so eviscerated that there would seem to be little left. However, it is this very weakness that allows Vattimo to return to Christianity.

Although John D. Caputo would term his view "radical hermeneutics" as opposed to Vattimo's "nihilist hermeneutics," they share an emphasis on the weakness of God. Caputo appropriates Derrida's idea of "a nondogmatic doublet of dogma" and speaks of "a 'theology without theology' that accompanies what Derrida calls a 'religion without religion'" (Caputo 2006, 7). Caputo recognizes his indebtedness to both Derrida and Vattimo, yet he also finds support in Saint Paul, who speaks of the "weakness of God" (1 Corinthians 1:25) and also proclaims that "God chose what is weak in the world to shame the strong" (1 Corinthians 1:27). Indeed, Caputo identifies this weakness with what Paul calls the "logos of the cross" (1 Corinthians 1:18). Thus, Caputo sees any rigid doctrinal formulas as being the very opposite of true religion, which is always about faith. He distances himself from any kind of rigid Christian dogma, viewing it in such a way that could be called deconstructive dogmatics (which would be the dynamics of the impossible). As should be clear, following Derrida, Caputo is also unwilling to adhere to any concrete messianisms. Of course, this raises the same kinds of questions for Caputo noted in regard to Derrida and his "appropriation" of the messianic structure from specific messianisms: Is such an appropriation possible, and does it, in some sense, show a disregard for such messianisms? Caputo would see himself as a Christian, but the "weakness" of Caputo's God will likely be too weak for many who would identify themselves as Christians.

In any case, in Caputo's radical hermeneutics "God" is the name that allows for the event, which is the unexpected happening: "The event jolts the world, disturbs, disrupts, and skews the sedimented course of things, exposing the alternate possibilities" (Caputo 2007, 59). Of course, the name of God can never *contain* such an event, for the event is the impossible. Again following Derrida, Caputo claims that it is "the impossible" that we most desire. As such, "the impossible" can never be brought into the conditions of experience, the development of history, and controlling and intelligible systems. Instead, Caputo construes his deconstructive desire evangelistically, such that individual traditions—Christianity in particular— become sites for the desire of impossibility. Indeed, the true vocation of religion is that of serving this impossibility. Yet Caputo also takes aim at any Enlightenment-inspired thinkers who believe that there is no room for religion. Caputo is all for the return of religion in postmodernity but in this weakened form: "Religion means to make God happen in the world and make ourselves worthy of what happens to us. We are functionaries of the event, sent into the world to serve it, to respond to it, to realize it and make it happen" (2007, 64).

In an attempt to recapitulate and revitalize the question of the divine in our age, Richard Kearney speaks of his "diacritical hermeneutics" and the interdisciplinary discernment of the intercommunications of the divine in various religious traditions. Precisely in order to open up a space in which the question of religion can be raised anew, Kearney wants to return to a place before the divine. He uses the notion of "anatheism" to speak about that which "operates *before* as well as *after* the division between theism and atheism; it makes them both possible." He goes on to say that it is "a primary scene of religion: the encounter with the radical Stranger who we choose or don't choose to call God" (Kearney 2009, 7). This is a move that Kearney first makes in *Strangers, Gods and Monsters*, where he critiques both Derrida and Caputo. Whereas Caputo sees the *khora* as a place of barrenness and meaninglessness, Kearney takes this barrenness and meaninglessness to be an essential moment of the religious life. For it is here that real faith and divine transcendence can come to be. In the space of anatheism, either atheism or theism can be chosen. It is here that both belief in the divine and forms of belief are always challenged and raised anew.

Here, the primordial emergence of the divine is to be found. In Judaism, it is Abraham's welcoming of the strangers. In Christianity, it is Mary's openness to the announcement of a divine child. In Islam, it is found in Muhammad's encounter of the divine proclamation. Each of these instances demands a kind of charity, humility, and hospitality. In each case, the strange character of the divine must be accepted—one says, "Here I am"—before the divine can be truly known. To be sure, Kearney calls for a moment of discernment: one can choose to accept or ignore the voice that calls. Strangers can be divine strangers or else monsters. For Kearney, it is these kinds of encounters with the divine—rather than in determined and systematized forms of religion—that are true encounters. The sacrament is central to Kearney's religious hermeneutics, for it marks the sacred from the profane.

In effect, Kearney proposes a "postreligious faith" in which we have gone through the hermeneutics of suspicion. It is what lies beyond the questioning of unbelief but also beyond the state of certainty and dogma. Specifically, Kearney says that anatheism "is not an end but a way . . . a third way that precedes and exceeds the extremes of dogmatic theism and militant atheism" (2009, 166). Although Kearney writes from the perspective of a Christian, his conception of religious life is one that attempts to be open to rich and profound discussion among religious traditions. True, one might criticize Kearney for being too open. Yet he at least attempts to allow for a religious dialogue that, following Karl Jaspers, is a "loving combat (*liebender Kampf*) between different faiths and nonfaiths," in which both faith and God are put into question (181).

Atheism Appropriating Christianity: Slavoj Žižek and Alain Badiou

As much as Slavoj Žižek makes clear that he is a Marxist, Leninist, atheist thinker, one can hardly read him apart from theology and religion. It is not merely that so much of Žižek's thought is driven quite explicitly by religion—and Christianity in particular—but that it is largely concerned with an analysis of Christianity, not to mention that Žižek describes himself as a "Paulinian materialist." It is for this reason that Žižek has been well received by Christian theologians such as John Milbank as a provocative and constructive dialogue partner. Unlike theorists such as Derrida, Vattimo, and Caputo, who are interested in the structure of Christianity stripped from its dogmatic and institutional elements, Žižek is interested precisely in these dogmatic and institutional elements. Indeed, when Žižek uses the term *postmodern*, it is always with scorn, and those postmodern philosophers whom he targets include such thinkers as Derrida and Levinas.

It is the central dogma of Christ's crucifixion—both its purpose and Christ's own cry of abandonment—that particularly interests Žižek. Of course, he reads the crucifixion in light of the idea that there is something "perverse" in the very logic of Christianity. For instance, Žižek asks why God put the Tree of Knowledge in Eden in the first place: "Is it not that this was a part of His perverse strategy first to seduce Adam and Eve into the fall, in order to save them?" (Žižek 2003, 15). Žižek then raises the further point made by Paul that it is the law that creates within him a desire to sin. Yet Christ's death proves equally problematic or perverse, for it raises the question of why the "atonement" was necessary. The "ransom theory" is problematic, for Žižek wonders "who demanded this price? To whom was the ransom paid?" (2001, 46) Such a theory provokes either the heretical explanation that it is Satan being paid or that, for some reason, God demands this payment. The "psychological account," in which we are reassured that God truly loves us, is undermined by the fact that such a view cannot be argued psychologically but only theologically. The "legalistic account," that God demands legal "satisfaction," is problematic, since it begs the question of "why does God not forgive us *directly*?" (2001, 48). The "edifying religious-moral effect account" fails because it is strange (and seemingly perverse) that God would do something so drastic as to sacrifice his own son.

Following René Girard, Žižek insists that something very different is going on here: Christ's statements, which disturb—or, rather, simply *suspend*—the circular logic of revenge or punishment . . . the logic of sin and punishment, of legal or ethical retribution, of 'settling accounts,' by bringing it to the point of self-relating. . . . [L]ove, at its most elementary, is nothing but such a paradoxical gesture of breaking the chain of retribution" (2001, 49–50). Christ breaks this logic or chain by sacrificing himself. Yet, says Žižek, there is an even more significant change that takes place: with Christ's death; the transcendent God is no more: "When Christ dies, what dies with him is the secret hope discernible in 'Father, why hast thou forsaken me?': the hope that there is a father who has abandoned me" (2003, 171). There is no more father and, now, no more son. Yet in the end, Christianity can only emerge at the moment that Christ dies. Žižek, however, insists that there *is* a Holy Spirit: it is the very Christian community itself that becomes the Holy Spirit. This new community is formed by way of Christian *agape*, which is the practice of love that upsets the very balance of the organic, cosmic totality. For Žižek, *agape* is the emergence of love in a form that disengages the self and others from symbolic organization, by regarding each and every other as a distinctive subjectivity. The crucifixion is the sacrifice of that value, which orders the subject and enables the Christian community to give up the spectral supplement to the symbolic order (such is the goal of Saint Paul's suspension of the law) that inspires and enlivens it. Further, a community is created that looks to an authentic future and opens the door to revolutionary activity. Such a Christian community—a collection of outcasts who are unified by their uncoupling from the normal social order—is the Holy Spirit at work. No doubt, this conception of Christianity is one that is very far from any kind of historic Christian orthodoxy. Yet Žižek is hardly seeking any kind of orthodoxy. Instead, he is seeking a way to appropriate Christianity for his own distinctive Marxist cause.

In the same way that Žižek freely appropriates from Christianity, so Alain Badiou freely appropriates from Saint Paul. Of course, there should be no expectation that Badiou's Paul will be much like the Paul of the New Testament. Badiou freely admits: "For me, truth be told, Paul is not an apostle or a saint. I care nothing for the Good News he declares, or the cult dedicated to him. But he is a subject of primary importance" (2003, 1). What makes Paul important for Badiou is that he is the thinker of "the event," which in Paul's case means a rupture and an overturning that open the door to a whole new era. Rather than Peter, it is Paul who founds the church for Badiou. He is the inventor not merely of a new society but also of a new identity. Paul inaugurates a new way of thinking that negates both Greek philosophy and Jewish law. As an event, Paul's move is irreducible to historical or cultural mediation. For it is the founding of truth and a new universality that itself has no further justification. In Badiou's account, truth is always "evental": "it is neither structural, nor axiomatic, nor legal" (2003, 14). Paul's declaration of such a universality is just such an event. When he writes that "there is neither Jew nor Greek, there is neither slave nor free, there is neither male nor female" (Galatians 3:28), this is the moment of an event of truth. In direct opposition to Levinas's otherness, Badiou proclaims—by way of Paul—a universality of all. Like Žižek, Badiou has no room for vague talk of "otherness"; instead, he sees such concerns as both misplaced and divisive. What he wants in place of otherness is the unconditioned Christian subject that is a "universal singularity." Precisely because of the singular character of the event, it is indifferent to differences.

Paul raises a community that, not being impressed by Greek philosophy or Jewish law, has its own values. When Paul mentions the Greeks and the Jews, he is not so much mentioning two distinct actual groups as two "regimes of discourse." Whereas Greek discourse is cosmic and constitutes a totality, Jewish discourse is about exceptionality and election. What Paul recognizes is that each discourse presupposes the other. Thus, what he needs is a discourse that is absolutely new, one that is not that of the philosopher or the prophet but that of the apostle. What the apostle announces is something unheard of: the resurrection. For this point, Badiou says, Paul has no need of proof, even of a miraculous sort; he simply announces this conviction, and it becomes truth. In place of works, Paul speaks of faith. In place of the law, Paul preaches the gospel of grace. But what, then, replaces the law? It is that which Paul says fulfills the law: love (Romans 13:10). Badiou interprets love as what finally "breaks" with the law. Yet what about faith and hope? Badiou says that "faith allows one to have hope in justice" and that "hope is the subjectivity of a victorious fidelity" (2003, 93, 95).

With Badiou, we have the militant Paul. No doubt, Badiou picks up on some very "Paulinian" elements. Yet Paul's achievement for Badiou is the development of a new conception of the subject that is as revolutionary today as it was two thousand years ago and that still has the potential to struggle for a new social order.

Conclusions

It should be clear that recent Continental philosophers have appropriated, critiqued, and investigated Christianity in quite a variety of ways. Some of these developments are more promising than others. Yet all deal with Christianity as a source of phenomena, a phenomenon itself, a form of political and religious collectivity, and an essential aspect of the development of the West.

REFERENCES

· ·

Badiou, A. 2003. *Saint Paul: The Foundation of Universalism* Ray Brassier, trans. Stanford, Calif.: Stanford University Press.

Caputo, J. 2006. *The Weakness of God: A Theology of the Event*. Bloomington: Indiana University Press.

———. 2007. "Spectral Hermeneutics: On the Weakness of God and the Theology of the Event." In J. Caputo and G. Vattimo, *After the Death of God*. J. Robbins, ed. New York: Columbia University Press, 47–88.

Chrétien, J.-L. 2000. "The Wounded Word." In *Phenomenology and the "Theological Turn": The French Debate*. New York: Fordham University Press.

———. 2004. *The Call and the Response*. A. Davenport, trans. New York: Fordham University Press.

Derrida, J. 1978. "Violence and Metaphysics: An Essay on the Thought of Emmanuel Levinas." In *Writing and Difference*. A. Bass, trans. Chicago: University of Chicago Press.

———. 1993. *Circumfession*. In G. Bennington and J. Derrida, *Jacques Derrida*. Chicago: University of Chicago Press.

———. 1996. *The Gift of Death*. Chicago: University of Chicago Press.

———. 2002a. "Faith and Knowledge: The Two Sources of 'Religion' at the Limits of Reason Alone." In G. Anidjar, ed., *Acts of Religion*. New York: Routledge.

———. 2002b. "Force of Law: The 'Mystical Foundation of Authority.'" In G Anidjar, ed., *Acts of Religion*. New York: Routledge.

Janicaud, D. 2000. "The Theological Turn of French Phenomenology." B. Prusak, trans. In *Phenomenology and the "Theological Turn": The French Debate*. New York: Fordham University Press, 16–103.

Levinas, E. 1996. "God and Philosophy" In A. Peperzek, S. Critchley, and R. Bernasconi, eds., *Basic Philosophical Writings*. Bloomington: Indiana University Press, 129–148.

———. 1996b. "Transcendence and Intelligibility." In A. Peperzek, S. Critchley, and R. Bernasconi, eds., *Basic Philosophical Writings*. Bloomington: Indiana University Press, 149–159.

Kearney, R. 2009. Anatheism: Returning to God after God. New York: Columbia University Press.

Marion, J-L. 1991. *God without Being*. T. Carlson, trans. Chicago: University of Chicago Press.

———. 2000. "The Saturated Phenomenon." T. Carlson, trans. In *Phenomenology and the "Theological Turn": The French Debate*. New York: Fordham University Press, 176–216.

———. 2001. *The Idol and Distance*. T. Carlson, trans. New York: Fordham University Press.

———. 2002. *Being Given: Toward a Phenomenology of Givenness*. J. Koskey, trans. Stanford, Calif.: Stanford University Press.

Rorty, R., and G. Vattimo. 2005. *The Future of Religion*. Santiago Zabala, ed. New York: Columbia University Press.

Vattimo, G. 1999. *Belief*. Luca D'Isanto and David Webb, trans. Stanford, Calif.: Stanford University Press.

Žižek, S. 2001. *Did Somebody Say Totalitarianism?* London: Verso.

———. 2003. *The Puppet and the Dwarf: The Perverse Core of Christianity*. Cambridge, Mass.: MIT Press.

FOR FURTHER READING

Benson, B. E. 2002. *Graven Ideologies: Nietzsche, Derrida and Marion on Modern Idolatry*. Downers Grove, Ill.: IVP.

Depoortere, F. 2008. *Christ in Postmodern Philosophy: Gianni Vattimo, René Girard and Slavoj Zizek*. New York: T. and T. Clark.

De Vries, Hent. 1999. *Philosophy and the Turn to Religion*. Baltimore: Johns Hopkins University Press.

Dooley, Mark, ed. 2004. *A Passion for the Impossible: John D. Caputo in Focus*. Albany: State University of New York Press.

Hallward, Peter, ed. 2004. *Think Again: Alain Badiou and the Future of Philosophy*. New York: Continuum.

Manoussakis, J. 2005. *After God: Richard Kearney and the Religious Turn in Continental Philosophy*. New York: Fordham University Press.

Pound, Marcus. 2008. *Zizek: A (Very) Critical Introduction*. Grand Rapids, Mich.: Eerdmans.

CHAPTER 32

A NATURALISTIC PERSPECTIVE

MICHAEL RUSE

RELIGIOUS diversity, I guess, is the easy one. We are talking about all of the different religions of the world, past and present, from the sorts of things that used to go on in ancient Egypt and Greece—and much earlier—to the sorts of things that go on in the Vatican City, in Saudi Arabia, in India, and in the American South. We are talking about the fact that these are not all the same religion, anything but. Some embrace a God, some do not. Some have a priesthood, some do not. Some are obsessed with the afterlife, some are not.

What about naturalism? This is a bit more tricky. I take it that it has something to do with laws, empirical or physical laws. A good first definition is that naturalism is trying to explain nature through laws. Some odd event occurs and the naturalist nevertheless says that there must be a law-governed explanation behind it. The naturalist eschews supernatural explanations, miracles, and that sort of thing. If someone turned water into wine, the naturalist would be looking for deception or for impurities in the water that could ferment.

Many people today distinguish between methodological naturalism, meaning the spirit of science—one insists on explanation through law—and metaphysical naturalism, the philosophy that there is nothing beyond science. The metaphysical naturalist is a materialist, an atheist, and so on. For the moment, at least, I am more interested in methodological naturalism. I distinguish all forms of naturalism from scientism, the belief that science can solve all of our problems. This seems to me a very dubious proposition.

A naturalistic approach to religious diversity, therefore, is one that attempts to explain such diversity naturally, that is, through unbroken law. Just as the modern linguist would explain language diversity through law, rather than through miracles such as that at the Tower of Babel, so the modern naturalist with respect to religion explains religious diversity through law, rather than through miracles and the like. Claims that Satan led us astray are ruled out. Whether this means that claims that Satan led us astray are meaningless or false is another matter.

My intuition is that most naturalistic approaches to religion are going to start with religion as such and then go on to corollaries about diversity. There are, of course, as many options as there are naturalists—biological, anthropological, economic, Freudian, and so forth. This said, my suspicion is that most naturalists are going to be evolutionists in some way or another. In other words, for whatever reasons, they are going to see today's religion grow out of a much more primitive form. It is going to be a matter not of religion arising overnight from nowhere but of it coming into being relatively slowly and gradually—and naturally.[1]

HUME AND DARWIN

Let us start there, and in particular, let us start with the fundamental naturalist attack on the problem, namely, that of the great Scottish philosopher David Hume in *A Natural History of Religion*, a work that was written around 1749–1751 and first appeared in print in 1757. Hume kicked off his discussion suggesting that the original belief state of humankind is polytheism, a function of a tendency to see life in all things, including the inanimate. Primitive man is worried about food and security and such, and a natural consequence of this is an interpretation of the world as though it were full of animate beings:

> There is a universal tendency among mankind to conceive all beings like
> themselves, and to transfer to every object, those qualities, with which they are
> familiarly acquainted, and of which they are intimately conscious. We find
> human faces in the moon, armies in the clouds; and by a natural propensity, if
> not corrected by experience and reflection, ascribe malice or good-will to
> everything, that hurts or pleases us. (Hume 1963 [1757], 40–41)

This is but a short step away from thinking that the whole world is filled with gods or deities of one sort or another. In a somewhat eighteenth-century fashion, Hume added that women are often thought to play a big role here. It is the softer sex that is most given to this sort of thing and to infecting men with their enthusiasms. Hume quotes Greek philosopher, historian, and geographer Strabo: "It is rare to meet with one that lives apart from the females, and yet is addicted to such practices" (44). One presumes that monastic institutions were not a commonplace in Enlightenment Scotland.

The god idea once under way, Hume then supposed that some divinities start to get pumped up in importance over all others, until we go all the way to monotheism. Hume noted how in the Middle Ages, the Virgin Mary was on the way to being pushed to the very top rank in people's minds—until the Protestant Reformation took the gloss off her glory. Not that Hume was that enthused by the end results, because he was inclined to think that the more a god gets in charge, the less tolerant are its supporters of rivals, and this leads to all kinds of tensions and frictions. Also, a more exalted god, taken away from the everyday nature of life, starts to take on attributes that reason suggests are absurd. Once a Calvinist, always a Calvinist. Hume was particularly scornful of the Catholic doctrine of transubstantiation, the very idea that we might be eating our god.

> Upon the whole, the greatest and most observable differences between a traditional, mythological religion, and a systematic, scholastic one are two: The former is often more reasonable, as consisting only of a multitude of stories, which, however groundless, imply no express absurdity and demonstrative contradiction; and sits also so easy and light on men's minds, that, though it may be as universally received, it happily makes no such deep impression on the affections and understanding. (85)

Now, there are lots of things that one can, and that people did, build on this sort of thing. For the sake of discussion, particularly since it has such a high profile today, let me focus more on the biological approach that follows on Hume. There is a nice historical reason for doing this, because although I think that often the influence of Hume on Charles Darwin is overstretched, in this particular case, there are good reasons to think that the great nineteenth-century naturalist drew heavily on the great eighteenth-century philosopher. The key discussion came in Darwin's work on our own species, *The Descent of Man*, published in 1871:

> There is no evidence that man was aboriginally endowed with the ennobling belief in the existence of an Omnipotent God. On the contrary there is ample evidence, derived not from hasty travellers, but from men who have long resided with savages, that numerous races have existed, and still exist, who have no idea of one or more gods, and who have no words in their languages to express such an idea. (1, 65)

Darwin added that if we are thinking in terms of vague spiritual sentiments, then obviously, savages and other primitive folks come under the religion blanket. "If, however, we include under the term 'religion' the belief in unseen or spiritual agencies the case is wholly different; for this belief seems to be universal with the less civilised races" (1, 65).

How, in Darwin's opinion, did this sentiment or belief about unseen forces arise? Here he started to sound very Humean—no great surprise, since he had read Hume's essay very carefully. Apparently, it is all a question of seeing spirits in inanimate objects, feeling or pretending or mistakenly believing that they are truly alive:

> The tendency in savages to imagine that natural objects and agencies are animated by spiritual or living essences, is perhaps illustrated by a little fact which I once noticed: my dog, a full-grown and very sensible animal, was lying on the lawn during a hot and still day; but at a little distance a slight breeze occasionally moved an open parasol, which would have been wholly disregarded by the dog, had any one stood near it. As it was, every time that the parasol slightly moved,

the dog growled fiercely and barked. He must, I think, have reasoned to himself in a rapid and unconscious manner, that movement without any apparent cause indicated the presence of some strange living agent, and that no stranger had a right to be on his territory. (1, 67)

From here, we are off and running toward a more sophisticated religious framework. Important is the notion of religious devotion—love of a god and so forth—and it is clearly animal in origin. Of course, you need to have developed a certain level of intellectual power and sophistication, but "we see some distant approach to this state of mind in the deep love of a dog for his master, associated with complete submission, some fear, and perhaps other feelings" (1, 68). Like Hume, Darwin saw a move from primitive religion, through polytheism, and thus on to monotheism. And completing the story, still in the vein of the Scottish philosopher, Darwin saw religion as connected with vile superstitions and practices, things that only the rise to reason could conquer and prevent:

> Many of these [superstitious practices] are terrible to think of—such as the sacrifice of human beings to a blood-loving god; the trial of innocent persons by the ordeal of poison or fire; witchcraft, &c.—yet it is well occasionally to reflect on these superstitions, for they shew us what an infinite debt of gratitude we owe to the improvement of our reason, to science, and to our accumulated knowledge. (1, 68–69)

To this day, one can hear the condescension of the Victorian English gentleman.

CONTEMPORARY THINKING

Let us fast-forward now so we can get to the main focus of our discussion. The social scientists took over, although some, Freud in particular, were never far from biology:

> Religion is an attempt to get control over the sensory world, in which we are placed, by means of the wish-world which we have developed inside us as a result of biological and psychological necessities. . . . If one attempts to assign to religion its place in man's evolution, it seems not so much to be a lasting acquisition, as a parallel to the neurosis which the civilized individual must pass through on his way from childhood to maturity. (Freud 1964 [1932–1936], 168)

In the 1970s, the biologists themselves picked up the torch again, with Harvard entomologist and sociobiologist E. O. Wilson, in his *On Human Nature* (1978), leading the way. Some, starting with Wilson, see religion as something straightforwardly adaptive in a biological sense. Religious humans have a better chance of surviving and reproducing than nonreligious humans. It is apparently all a matter of group identity and sticking together:

The highest form of religious practice, when examined more closely, can be seen to confer biological advantage. Above all, they congeal identity. In the midst of the chaotic and potentially disorienting experiences each person undergoes daily, religion classifies him, provides him with unquestioned membership in a group claiming great powers, and by this means gives him a driving purpose in life compatible with his self interest. (Wilson 1978, 188)

David Sloan Wilson, author of *Darwin's Cathedral* (2002), is another in this camp. Wilson analyzes the society that John Calvin founded in Geneva in the sixteenth century, listing the rules that governed this group: "Obey parents"; "Obey magistrates"; "Obey pastors"; and on down the list to "No lewdness and sex only in marriage"; "No theft, either by violence or cunning"; and so forth. Of this, he writes:

> To summarize, the God-people relationship can be interpreted as a belief system that is designed to motivate the behaviors [examples of which are listed just above]. Those who regard religious belief as senseless superstition may need to revise their own beliefs. Those who regard supernatural agents as imaginary providers of imaginary services may have under-estimated the functionality of the God-person relationship in generating real services that can be achieved only by communal effort. Those who already think about religion in functional terms may be on the right track, but they may have underestimated the sophistication of the "motivational physiology" that goes far beyond the use of kinship terms and fear of hell. Indeed, it is hard for me to imagine a belief system better designed to motivate group-adaptive behavior for those who accept it as true. When it comes to turning a group into a societal organism, scarcely a word of Calvin's catechism is out of place. (Wilson 2002, 105)

Others are not so sure. They (like Hume and Darwin) are inclined at most to see these sorts of things as byproducts. To student of culture Pascal Boyer, religion simply subverts or borrows features that our biology has put in place for good adaptive reasons. For whatever reason, it cannot be eradicated:

> The building of religious concepts requires mental systems and capacities that are there anyway, religious concepts or not. Religious morality uses moral intuitions, religious notions of supernatural agents recruit our intuitions about agency in general, and so on. This is why I said that religious concepts are parasitic upon other mental capacities. Our capacities to play music, paint pictures or even make sense of printed ink-patterns on a page are also parasitic in this sense. This means that we can explain how people play music, paint pictures and learn to read by examining how mental capacities are recruited by these activities. The same goes for religion. Because the concepts require all sorts of specific human capacities (an intuitive psychology, a tendency to attend to some counterintuitive concepts, as well as various social mind adaptations), we can explain religion by describing how these various mind capacities get recruited, how they contribute to the features of religion we find in so many different cultures. We do not need to assume that there is a *special* way of functioning that occurs only when processing religious thoughts. (Boyer 2002, 311)

But what is it that allows religion to get its hold in the first place? Anthropologist Scott Atran argues that religion grabs something adaptively useful and exploits it. For him, the big question facing organisms such as humans is other living beings—above all, other living beings as threats. In an argument reminiscent of Darwin and his dog—in fact, reminiscent of Hume's speculations—Atran suggests that what we have is a somewhat overeager projection of the living onto the inanimate. Cuckoos exploit the innate mechanisms that their host birds have for raising their young. Religion does much the same for humans:

> Supernatural agent concepts critically involve minimal triggering of evolved agency-detection schema, a part of folk psychology. Agency is a complex sort of "innate releasing mechanism." Natural selection designs the agency-detection system to deal rapidly and economically with stimulus situations involving people and animals as predators, protectors, and prey. This resulted in the system's being trip-wired to respond to fragmentary information under conditions of uncertainty, inciting perception of figures in the clouds, voices in the wind, lurking movements in the leaves, and emotions among interacting dots on a computer screen. This hair-triggering of the agency-detection mechanism readily lends itself to supernatural interpretation of uncertain or anxiety-provoking events.
>
> People interactively manipulate this universal cognitive susceptibility so as to scare or soothe themselves and others for varied ends. They do so consciously or unconsciously and in causally complex and distributed ways, in pursuit of war or love, to thwart calamity or renew serendipity, or to otherwise control or incite imagination. The result provides a united and ordered sense for cosmic, cultural, and personal existence. (Atran 2004, 78)

And then there are those who think that religion is a case of something going wrong. It might be something of adaptive significance but not necessarily to us. This is Dan Dennett's position. He begins his book *Breaking the Spell: Religion as a Natural Phenomenon* (2006) by introducing the reader to the lancet fluke (*Dicrocelium dendriticum*), a parasite that corrupts the brain of an ant, causing it to strive to climb blades of grass, so that it can get eaten by a sheep or cow, and thus the fluke can complete its life cycle before its offspring are excreted and take up again with ants:

> Does anything like this ever happen with human beings? Yes indeed. We often find human beings setting aside their personal interests, their health, their chances to have children, and devoting their entire lives to furthering the interests of an *idea* that has lodged in their brains. The Arabic word *islam* means "submission," and every good Muslim bears witness, prays five times a day, gives alms, fasts during Ramadan, and tries to make the pilgrimage, or *hajj*, to Mecca, all on behalf of the idea of Allah, and Muhammad, the messenger of Allah. Christians and Jews do likewise, of course, devoting their lives to spreading the Word, making huge sacrifices, suffering bravely, risking their lives for an idea. So do Hindus and Buddhists. (Dennett 2006, 4)

To be fair, Dennett adds that secular humanists are often not much better in this regard.

RELIGIOUS DIVERSITY

Now, what about the diversity issue? Jews, Christians, Muslims, and the others? Catholics, Anglicans, Quakers, and the others? Prima facie, one would think that diversity is going to be a piece of candy to all of our evolutionary naturalists. Darwin's great book was not called the *Origin of Species* for nothing. Evolution is about change, where one of the main forms of change is of groups splitting into different forms: speciation. It is the very fabric of evolution as we know it, the tree of life, with branches spreading out over the globe. So surely, whatever your particular take on the evolutionary forces being about religion, you are going to expect diversification. Anglicans are to Catholics as dogs are to cats. At a higher taxonomic level, Christians are to Muslims as mammals are to birds. Primitive religions are the bacteria of the business, and sophisticated religions are the higher apes.

Not so fast! At least some of your thinking about diversity is going to be a function of where you put the evolutionary action. If you are an old-fashioned evolutionist, thinking that ultimately everything comes down to the genes, the units of heredity, then you are probably going to stress the unity of humankind—we are one species, and we know that the diversity at the genetic level in humans is not that great (Ruse 2006). In fact, it is rather less than you might expect of a group of our size, because it is believed that about 140,000 years ago, humans leaving Africa might have gone through something of a bottleneck with very much reduced numbers and hence diversity. Of course, there are many different religions, just as there are many different languages. Presumably, this is a function of culture, but you should not read too much into this. The differences among religions are likely to be transitory. Especially anyone who tries to step out of line biologically, such as the Shakers with their beliefs about celibacy, is going to be short-lived. (Universal celibacy, that is. Celibates in religions such as Catholicism or Buddhism may be like worker ants, helpers of the group.)

Edward O. Wilson thinks this way. He does allow that there can be cultural selection among sects, but essentially, we start with the biology, and all else is on the surface:

> Because religious practices are remote from the genes during the development of individual human beings, they may vary widely during cultural development. It is even possible for groups, such as the Shakers, to adopt conventions that reduce genetic fitness for as long as one or a few generations. But over many generations, the underlying genes will pay for their permissiveness by declining in the population as a whole. Other genes governing mechanisms that resist decline of fitness produced by cultural evolution will prevail, and the deviant practices will disappear. Thus culture relentlessly tests the controlling genes, but the most it can do is replace one set of genes with another. (Wilson 1978, 178)

Other evolutionists have taken up an idea, first floated by Richard Dawkins in *The Selfish Gene* (1976), that units of culture are akin to units of biological heredity, memes to genes. This is the position of Dennett. For him, therefore, the real action is going to be at the cultural level. The memes are parasites that take over our minds, reproducing when they have adaptations that serve their ends and not necessarily ours. Either way, my sense is that both sides, gene supporters and meme supporters, are inclined to stress the transitory nature of culture, including religion. Here today, gone tomorrow.

Where I think you do find differences between the gene and the meme supporters is that the gene people tend to stress the need to stay in tune with biological realities, whereas meme people do not. One might expect, therefore, that gene people would be more likely to find underlying similarities among religions, at least reasonably successful ones, whereas meme people would not. Certainly, whereas Edward O. Wilson and David Sloan Wilson stress the biological virtues of morality, and hence the expectation that religions will likewise promote morality, Dennett does not feel this way at all: "I have uncovered no evidence to support the claim that people, religious or not, who *don't* believe in reward in heaven and/or punishment in hell are more likely to kill, rape, rob, or break their promises than people who do. The prison population in the United States shows Catholics, Protestants, Jews, Muslims, and others—including those with no religious affiliation—represented about as they are in the general population" (2006, 279).

This does not mean that those who think biology is important will never see biologically mediated differences among religions. There have been suggestions that there might be a "God gene" (Hamer 2004). Even if there is, I suspect that most regular biologists, even those who think that the genes play a major role in human thought and behavior, doubt that there is any simple one-on-one link between genes and thought and behavior. Moreover, I don't think anyone is seriously looking for different God genes for different religions. Even if there are genetic differences among races, and these races are marked by different religious beliefs and practices, I doubt that there are specific genetic differences making for different religious practices—a Methodist gene, for instance, as opposed to a Lutheran one. Henry IV of France did not a have a gene makeover when he decided that "Paris is worth a mass" and became a Catholic so that he could become king.

However, genes can have effects in more subtle ways than that, where we all have the same genes but they express themselves differently—for good biological reasons—when we are in different circumstances. For instance, physical anthropologist Vernon Reynolds and scholar of religion Ralph Tanner are quite accepting of hypotheses that the circumcision of males, something central to religious practices of Jews and others, is something that prevents disease. This is a practice that has direct adaptive benefit for individuals. They use this discussion, somewhat ingeniously, to launch off into a suggestion that religions tend to divide into those that promote high reproductive rates (many Semitic religions) and those that do not (northern European Calvinism, for instance) (Reynolds and Tanner 1983).

As it happens, this is something that echoes interests and concerns of Darwin in the *Descent*. In that work, the great evolutionist worried that the worthless Catholic Irish seemed to have lots of children, whereas the hardworking Presbyterian

Scots had but few. This was a horrific reflection, seemingly negating the upward, progressive nature of the evolutionary process, a picture so dear to the heart of Darwin and his fellow Victorians. However, Darwin consoled himself with the reflection that the Irish did not look after their kids, whereas the Scots did, and so, on balance, the Scots, if anything, did better than the Irish.

Reynolds and Tanner draw on something known as r and K selection theory, which claims that organisms (such as herrings) that live in variable conditions are selected for adaptations that produce lots of offspring. If conditions are good, then even though they put no effort (after birth) into their offspring, they will score well. Organisms such as elephants that live in stable conditions have few offspring but invest in a lot of parental care. Reynolds and Tanner refer to these two modes as r^c- and r^c+ selection, the superscript signifying that they think the selection has to work through culture, although it presumably filters down to the genes. In the case of male circumcision, acknowledging that there are questions about the evidence, Reynolds and Tanner nevertheless write:

> Despite the confused state of the data, it is not unreasonable to put the question: If circumcision does reduce the risk of penile or cervical carcinoma, what effects would this have on reproductive success? The answer is that such success should be increased (all other things being equal) in families or groups practising circumcision. Circumcision would thus be a pro-reproductive practice and should be favoured in situations in which r^c+ selection was operative. We know that it is a characteristic of long-standing in Judaism and Islam. In the case of Judaism it represents part of Abraham's Covenant with God, the covenant in which God called him to leave Ur and to found a new nation; also in the Covenant was the promise from God that his "seed" would inherit the land. A charter for r^c+ selection indeed! In the case of Islam, circumcision appears to have been simply continued without question from a prior Arabic tradition. The practice is not mentioned at all in the Koran and was adopted without question by Muhammad; it is regarded as an essential of the faith. (1983, 240)

Overall, apparently, religions such as Judaism that put a big emphasis on family are those that developed at times when the groups were under threat, from the environment or other humans. You cannot plan that far ahead. Religions such as (let us say) Anglicanism, in which having a very large family is not necessarily religiously mandated, are those that developed in more stable situations. Threats from the environment or from other humans were not as great. Darwin would obviously have welcomed this explanation for the Irish and the Scots.

Of course, it would be possible for someone into the science of memetics (the study of memes) to come up with a theory showing that certain cultural units are likely to be more successful than others—just as advertisers know that certain things trigger responses in ways that others do not—and so one might go on to have a theory of religion showing basic patterns or some such thing. No one has done so yet, and given the hostility that the leading meme folk—notably Dennett and Dawkins—have toward religion, I am not sure we are about to see one in the near future.

TRUTH AND FALSITY

Let us switch to a couple of epistemological issues. First, does the naturalistic approach (let us continue to restrict ourselves to the evolutionary approach) prove that religion is false? Edward O. Wilson thinks so. As it happens, Wilson thinks that the human psyche demands religion, and thus, he sees the place to move in with a kind of evolutionary humanism. But this is because Darwinism has already done its corrosive work:

> But make no mistake about the power of scientific materialism. It presents the human mind with an alternative mythology that until now has always, point for point in zones of conflict, defeated traditional religion. Its narrative form is the epic: the evolution of the universe from the big bang of fifteen billion years ago through the origin of the elements and celestial bodies to the beginnings of life on earth. The evolutionary epic is mythology in the sense that the laws it adduces here and now are believed but can never be definitively proved to form a cause-and-effect continuum from physics to the social sciences, from this world to all other worlds in the visible universe, and backward through time to the beginning of the universe. Every part of existence is considered to be obedient to physical laws requiring no external control. The scientist's devotion to parsimony in explanation excludes the divine spirit and other extraneous agents. Most importantly, we have come to the crucial stage in the history of biology when religion itself is subject to the explanations of the natural sciences. As I have tried to show, sociobiology can account for the very origin of mythology by the principle of natural selection acting on the genetically evolving material structure of the human brain.
>
> If this interpretation is correct, the final decisive edge enjoyed by scientific naturalism will come from its capacity to explain traditional religion, its chief competition, as a wholly material phenomenon. Theology is not likely to survive as an independent intellectual discipline. (1978, 192)

Hume and Darwin, to the contrary, disagree. I am not sure to what extent they really thought this, but they said so. First Hume:

> As every enquiry, which regards religion, is of the utmost importance, there are two questions in particular, which challenge our attention, to wit, that concerning its foundation in reason, and that concerning its origin in human nature. Happily, the first question, which is the most important, admits of the most obvious, at least, the clearest, solution. The whole frame of nature bespeaks an intelligent author; and no rational enquirer can, after serious reflection, suspend his belief in a moment with regard to the primary principles of genuine Theism and Religion. But the other question, concerning the origin of religion in human nature, is exposed to some more difficulty. (1758)

Then Darwin (which we have already quoted above):

> There is no evidence that man was aboriginally endowed with the ennobling belief in the existence of an Omnipotent God. On the contrary there is ample evidence, derived not from hasty travellers, but from men who have long resided

with savages, that numerous races have existed, and still exist, who have no idea
of one or more gods, and who have no words in their languages to express such
an idea. (1871, 1, 65)

To which sentiment, in Humean style, Darwin added immediately: "The question
is of course wholly distinct from that higher one, whether there exists a Creator and
Ruler of the universe; and this has been answered in the affirmative by some of the
highest intellects that have ever existed."

In the light of Hume's critique of the design argument, one can be forgiven for
wondering at his sincerity in the passage quoted above; but taking it at its face value,
the question is: Wilson or Hume and Darwin? And clearly, the answer is Hume and
Darwin. In itself, the fact that we can give a naturalistic explanation says nothing
about the truth of religion. I can give a naturalistic explanation of why I can see a
cabbage on my kitchen counter. It does not deny the existence of that cabbage. But
you might say that there are adaptive reasons for seeing the cabbage. (Or else I
starve to death.) If there are no adaptive reasons, then why truth? Two points. First,
as we have seen, some evolutionists—both Wilsons—think that there are adaptive
reasons for religion. Second, even if religion is a byproduct, even if it is a parasite, it
could still be true. If you take methodological naturalism seriously, and I would say
that you can and still be a good Christian (or whatever), then you expect some kind
of natural explanation. How God gets it done is his business. To deny that religion
could be true if it is a parasite is like those Victorians who could not believe that
God had set up so disgusting a mechanism for making babies. In any case, not all
parasites are bad. We would be in trouble without *E. coli* in our bowels.

But what about the diversity issue? We need to tread carefully here. Many
people—I am one—look upon religious diversity as one of the biggest arguments
against the truth of religion. How can it be true both that we are justified by faith
alone and yet that we get into the kingdom of heaven only by helping others? If the
pope is the successor of Peter, then what about the grand mufti of Jerusalem and
the head rabbi and so forth, let alone the archbishop of Canterbury? The question
here is whether the evolutionary explanations of diversity throw additional light on
the truth status of religion. And generally, it is hard to see that they do. If evolution
argued that there was no diversity, we wouldn't deny diversity, we would deny
religion.

But shouldn't evolution point to one religion only if there is a true one? The
fact that it does not suggests that there is no true one. This conclusion could follow
only if religion were like the cabbage. Evolution points to the cabbage and does not
kid you into thinking that it is (forgive me, but I need something really not in your
interests) a turd, or conversely. Those of our would-be ancestors who got the
answer right survived and reproduced, and those who did not did not. If religion
were a material object—or the beings of religion were material objects—then you
might expect some convergence. But religions don't work that way. They are not in
the empirical-world business quite like that—the Christian God is not a material
object like a cabbage—and so you simply would not expect the convergence that
you get in the cabbage case.

I speak of the lack of convergence, but note that it is not entirely true that anything goes in religion and that (because it talks about the nonmaterial) the defender of a particular religion cannot critique other religions. One can use reason and evidence to sift through religions, and some simply fail the test thus judged. Religions do make some empirical claims, and when they do, they are fair game. The Mormons just cannot be correct that the North American Indians are the lost tribes of Israel, any more than the creationists can be right about a six-thousand-year-old earth and a universal flood. Some would say that you can go even further than that, perhaps with proofs of God's existence. Like most sophisticated believers today, I don't accept them, but this would be one way to trim the number of true religion believers.

And note that today's evolutionists would argue strongly that the powers of reason and of sensation that you are using to do all of this did not just arrive from nowhere. We think and reason and sense as we do because of our evolutionary past. So, at least in this sense, you can say that evolution is not entirely irrelevant to issues of sifting through religious diversity to see if it can be brought under control somewhat.

CONCLUSIONS

Any naturalist, any methodological naturalist, is going to expect a naturalistic explanation of religion. Even the most devout believer is going to feel uncomfortable with claims that religions are the functions of divine intervention. It means not that God is not active but rather that he works through the medium of unbroken law instead of otherwise. This being so and given what we know about humankind, it is hard to imagine an explanation that is not going to be evolutionary in some sense. Even the weirdest of religions are found to have roots in their society in some sense. To what extent this evolution might be biological and to what extent cultural is the sixty-four-thousand-dollar question. At the moment, keen Darwinian that I am, I would hesitate to say where the balance will end. Contemplating today's hypotheses, even a friend must conclude that we have much imagination and too little rigorous empirical checking.

Religious diversity is right in the thick of all of this. It is a major—*the* major—characteristic of religious belief and practice. So many people want to do and believe so many different things. A naturalistic approach to religion cannot ignore this, nor would it want to. I think already that there are some interesting things that the naturalist can say on this topic, and I suspect that as the years go by and our naturalistic theories get more sophisticated, we will have more to say. What I don't think is that the naturalistic approach is quite the religion destroyer that some enthusiasts clearly think it is. I am not saying that religious diversity poses no challenges to the believer—I think it poses massive challenges—but I have yet to be shown that the naturalist looking at such diversity adds significantly to the challenge.

NOTE

1. For my discussion of evolutionary accounts of religion, I am relying heavily on my recent book *Charles Darwin* (Ruse 2008). For my assumption that one can be a methodological naturalist and be religious, I rely on conclusions in my *Can a Darwinian Be a Christian?* (Ruse 2001).

REFERENCES

Atran, S. 2004. *In Gods We Trust: The Evolutionary Landscape of Religion*. New York: Oxford University Press.

Boyer, P. 2002. *Religion Explained: The Evolutionary Origins of Religious Thought*. New York: Basic.

Darwin, C. 1859. *On the Origin of Species by Means of Natural Selection, or the Preservation of Favoured Races in the Struggle for Life*. London: John Murray.

———. 1871. *The Descent of Man, and Selection in Relation to Sex*. London: John Murray.

Dawkins, R. 1976. *The Selfish Gene*. Oxford: Oxford University Press.

Dennett, D. C. 2006. *Breaking the Spell: Religion as a Natural Phenomenon*. New York: Viking.

Freud, S. 1964 [1932–1936]. "The Question of a *Weltanschauung*." In *The Standard Edition of the Complete Psychological Works of Sigmund Freud* 22. *New Introductory Lectures on Psychoanalysis and Other Works*. J. Strachey, trans. London: Hogarth 158–184.

Hamer, D. H. 2004. *The God Gene: How Faith Is Hardwired into Our Genes*. New York: Doubleday.

Hume, D. 1963 [1757]. *A Natural History of Religion*: *Hume on Religion*. R. Wollheim, ed. London: Fontana.

Reynolds, V., and R. Tanner. 1983. *The Biology of Religion*. London: Longman.

Ruse, M. 2001. *Can a Darwinian Be a Christian? The Relationship between Science and Religion*. Cambridge, U.K.: Cambridge University Press.

———. 2006. *Darwinism and Its Discontents*. Cambridge, U.K.: Cambridge University Press.

———. 2008. *Charles Darwin*. Oxford: Blackwell.

Wilson, D. S. 2002. *Darwin's Cathedral*. Chicago: University of Chicago Press.

Wilson, E. O. 1978. *On Human Nature*. Cambridge, Mass.: Harvard University Press.

FOR FURTHER READING

Besides the references listed above, to get a handle on historical treatments of religion from a naturalistic perspective, one should read Hume's *A Natural History of Religion* and then go on to Darwin's *Descent of Man* (many editions), as well as Freud and other classics such as Sir James Frazer's *The Golden Bough* (many editions). Scottish Victorian Orientalist William Robertson Smith, author of *Religion of the Semites* (various editions), is very highly regarded in knowledgeable circles. Edward O. Wilson's *On Human Nature* (revised in 2004) is already a modern classic. I found Vernon Reynolds and Ralph Tanner's *The Social Ecology of Religion*, 2nd ed. (Oxford: Oxford University Press, 1995) very thought-provoking. As one can probably tell, I am not overwhelmed by the recent literature, but my top picks are Scott Atran's *In Gods We Trust* (2002) and Pascal Boyer's *Religion Explained* (2001).

Index